KT-416-320

ning
ial
e

Visit the *Prolog Programming for Artificial Intelligence,* 4th
edition Companion Website at **www.pearsoned.co.uk/bratko**
to find valuable **student** learning material including:

- PROLOG code available to download
- Additional problems and solutions

# Prolog Programming for Artificial Intelligence

Fourth edition

IVAN BRATKO

Faculty of Computer and Information Science
Ljubljana University
and
J. Stefan Institute

**Addison Wesley**
is an imprint of

Harlow, England • London • New York • Boston • San Francisco • Toronto
Sydney • Tokyo • Singapore • Hong Kong • Seoul • Taipei • New Delhi
Cape Town • Madrid • Mexico City • Amsterdam • Munich • Paris • Milan

**Pearson Education Limited**
Edinburgh Gate
Harlow
Essex CM20 2JE
England

and Associated Companies throughout the world

*Visit us on the World Wide Web at:*
www.pearson.com/uk

First published 1986
Second edition 1990
Third edition 2001
**Fourth edition 2012**

ISBN: 978-0-321-41746-6

**British Library Cataloguing-in-Publication Data**
A catalogue record for this book is available from the British Library

**Library of Congress Cataloging-in-Publication Data**
Bratko, Ivan, 1946–
   Prolog programming for artificial intelligence / Ivan Bratko. -- 4th ed.
      p. cm.
   ISBN 978-0-321-41746-6 (pbk.)
   1. Artificial intelligence--Data processing. 2. Prolog (Computer program language)
   I. Title.
   Q336.B74 2011
   006.30285'5133--dc23

                                             2011010795

ARP impression 98

Typeset in 9/12pt Stone Serif by 73
Printed and bound in Great Britain by Ashford Colour Press Ltd

# Contents

## Supporting resources

Visit **www.pearsoned.co.uk/bratko** to find valuable online resources:

### Companion Website for students
- PROLOG code available to download
- Additional problems and solutions

### For instructors
- PowerPoint slides
- Password-protected solutions for lecturers

**Also:** The Companion Website provides the following features:
- Online help and support to assist with website usage and troubleshooting

For more information please contact your local Pearson Education sales representative or visit **www.pearsoned.co.uk/bratko**

# From Patrick Winston's Foreword to the Second Edition

I can never forget my excitement when I saw my first Prolog-style program in action. It was part of Terry Winograd's famous Shrdlu system, whose blocks-world problem solver arranged for a simulated robot arm to move blocks around a screen, solving intricate problems in response to human-specified goals.

Winograd's blocks-world problem solver was written in Microplanner, a language which we now recognize as a sort of Prolog. Nevertheless, in spite of the defects of Microplanner, the blocks-world problem solver was organized explicitly around goals, because a Prolog-style language encourages programmers to think in terms of goals. The goal-oriented procedures for grasping, clearing, getting rid of, moving, and ungrasping made it possible for a clear, transparent, concise program to seem amazingly intelligent.

Winograd's blocks-world problem solver permanently changed the way I think about programs. I even rewrote the blocks-world problem solver in Lisp for my Lisp textbook because that program unalterably impressed me with the power of the goal-oriented philosophy of programming and the fun of writing goal-oriented programs.

But learning about goal-oriented programming through Lisp programs is like reading Shakespeare in a language other than English. Some of the beauty comes through, but not as powerfully as in the original. Similarly, the best way to learn about goal-oriented programming is to read and write goal-oriented programs in Prolog, for goal-oriented programming is what Prolog is all about.

In broader terms, the evolution of computer languages is an evolution away from low-level languages, in which the programmer specifies how something is to be done, toward high-level languages, in which the programmer specifies simply what is to be done. With the development of Fortran, for example, programmers were no longer forced to speak to the computer in the procrustian low-level language of addresses and registers. Instead, Fortran programmers could speak in their own language, or nearly so, using a notation that made only moderate concessions to the one-dimensional, 80-column world.

Fortran and nearly all other languages are still how-type languages, however. In my view, modern Lisp is the champion of these languages, for Lisp in its Common Lisp form is enormously expressive, but how to do something is still what the Lisp programmer is allowed to be expressive about. Prolog, on the other hand, is a language that clearly breaks away from the how-type languages, encouraging the programmer to describe situations and problems, not the detailed means by which the problems are to be solved.

Consequently, an introduction to Prolog is important for all students of Computer Science, for there is no better way to see what the notion of what-type programming is all about.

In particular, the chapters of this book clearly illustrate the difference between how-type and what-type thinking. In the first chapter, for example, the difference is illustrated through problems dealing with family relations. The Prolog programmer straightforwardly describes the grandfather concept in explicit, natural terms: a grandfather is a father of a parent. Here is the Prolog notation:

**grandfather( X, Z) :- father( X, Y), parent( Y, Z).**

Once Prolog knows what a grandfather is, it is easy to ask a question: who are Patrick's grandfathers, for example. Here again is the Prolog notation, along with a typical answer:

**?- grandfather( X, patrick).**
**X = james;**
**X = carl**

It is Prolog's job to figure out how to solve the problem by combing through a database of known father and parent relations. The programmer specifies only what is known and what question is to be solved. The programmer is more concerned with knowledge and less concerned with algorithms that exploit the knowledge.

Given that it is important to learn Prolog, the next question is how. I believe that learning a programming language is like learning a natural language in many ways. For example, a reference manual is helpful in learning a programming language, just as a dictionary is helpful in learning a natural language. But no one learns a natural language with only a dictionary, for the words are only part of what must be learned. The student of a natural language must learn the conventions that govern how the words are put legally together, and later, the student should learn the art of those who put the words together with style.

Similarly, no one learns a programming language from only a reference manual, for a reference manual says little or nothing about the way the primitives of the language are put to use by those who use the language well. For this, a textbook is required, and the best textbooks offer copious examples, for good examples are distilled experience, and it is principally through experience that we learn.

In this book, the first example is on the first page, and the remaining pages constitute an example cornucopia, pouring forth Prolog programs written by a passionate Prolog programmer who is dedicated to the Prolog point of view. By carefully studying these examples, the reader acquires not only the mechanics of the language, but also a personal collection of precedents, ready to be taken apart, adapted, and reassembled together into new programs. With this acquisition of precedent knowledge, the transition from novice to skilled programmer is already under way.

Of course, a beneficial side effect of good programming examples is that they expose a bit of interesting science as well as a lot about programming itself. The science behind the examples in this book is Artificial Intelligence. The reader learns about such problem-solving ideas as problem reduction, forward and backward chaining, 'how' and 'why' questioning, and various search techniques.

In fact, one of the great features of Prolog is that it is simple enough for students in introductory Artificial Intelligence subjects to learn to use immediately. I expect that many instructors will use this book as part of their Artificial

Intelligence subjects so that their students can see abstract ideas immediately reduced to concrete, motivating form.

Among Prolog texts, I expect this book to be particularly popular, not only because of its examples, but also because of a number of other features:

- Careful summaries appear throughout.

- Numerous exercises reinforce all concepts.

- Structure selectors introduce the notion of data abstraction.

- Explicit discussions of programming style and technique occupy an entire chapter.

- There is honest attention to the problems to be faced in Prolog programming, as well as the joys.

Features like this make this a well done, enjoyable, and instructive book.

I keep the first edition of this textbook in my library on the outstanding-textbooks shelf, programming languages section, for as a textbook it exhibited all the strengths that set the outstanding textbooks apart from the others, including clear and direct writing, copious examples, careful summaries, and numerous exercises. And as a programming language textbook, I especially liked its attention to data abstraction, emphasis on programming style, and honest treatment of Prolog's problems as well as Prolog's advantages.

I dedicate the fourth edition of this book
to my mother, the kindest person I know,
and to my father, who, during world war II
escaped from a concentration camp by
digging an underground tunnel, which he
described in his novel, *The Telescope*

# Preface

........................................................................................................................

## Prolog

Prolog is a programming language based on a small set of basic mechanisms, including pattern matching, tree-based data structuring and automatic back-tracking. This small set constitutes a surprisingly powerful and flexible programming framework. Prolog is especially well suited for problems that involve objects – in particular, structured objects – and relations between them. For example, it is an easy exercise in Prolog to express spatial relationships between objects, such as the blue sphere is behind the green one. It is also easy to state a more general rule: if object X is closer to the observer than object Y, and Y is closer than Z, then X must be closer than Z. Prolog can now reason about the spatial relationships and their consistency with respect to the general rule. Features like this make Prolog a powerful language for artificial intelligence (AI) and non-numerical programming in general.

There are well-known examples of symbolic computation whose implementation in other standard languages took tens of pages of indigestible code. When the same algorithms were implemented in Prolog, the result was a crystal-clear program easily fitting on one page. As an illustration of this fact, the famous WARPLAN planning program, written by David Warren, is often quoted. For example, Russell and Norvig[1] say 'WARPLAN is also notable in that it was the first planner to be written in a logic programming language (Prolog) and is one of the best examples of the economy that can sometimes be gained with logic programming: WARPLAN is only 100 lines of code, a small fraction of the size of comparable planners of the time'. Chapter 18 of this book contains much more complicated planning algorithms (partial-order planning and GRAPHPLAN) that still fit into fewer than 100 lines of Prolog code.

## Development of Prolog

Prolog stands for *programming in logic* – an idea that emerged in the early 1970s to use logic as a programming language. The early developers of this idea included Robert Kowalski at Edinburgh (on the theoretical side), Maarten van Emden at Edinburgh (experimental demonstration) and Alain Colmerauer at Marseilles (implementation). David D.H. Warren's efficient implementation at Edinburgh in the mid-1970s greatly contributed to the popularity of Prolog. A more recent development is *constraint logic programming* (CLP), usually implemented as part of a Prolog system. CLP extends Prolog with constraint processing, which has proved in practice to be an exceptionally flexible tool for

---

[1] S. Russell, P. Norvig, *Artificial Intelligence: A Modern Approach*, 3rd edn (Prentice-Hall, 2010).

problems like scheduling and logistic planning. In 1996 the official ISO standard for Prolog was published.

## Learning Prolog

Since Prolog has its roots in mathematical logic it is often introduced through logic. However, such a mathematically intensive introduction is not very useful if the aim is to teach Prolog as a practical programming tool. Therefore this book is not concerned with the mathematical aspects, but concentrates on the art of making the few basic mechanisms of Prolog solve interesting problems. Whereas conventional languages are procedurally oriented, Prolog introduces the descriptive, or *declarative*, view. This greatly alters the way of thinking about problems and makes learning to program in Prolog an exciting intellectual challenge. Many believe that every student of computer science should learn something about Prolog at some point because Prolog enforces a different problem-solving paradigm complementary to other programming languages.

## Contents of the book

Part I of the book introduces the Prolog language and shows how Prolog programs are developed. Programming with constraints in Prolog is also introduced. Techniques to handle important data structures, such as trees and graphs, are also included because of their general importance. In Part II, Prolog is applied to a number of areas of AI, including problem solving and heuristic search, programming with constraints, knowledge representation and expert systems, planning, machine learning, qualitative reasoning, language processing and game playing. AI techniques are introduced and developed in depth towards their implementation in Prolog, resulting in complete programs. These can be used as building blocks for sophisticated applications. The concluding chapter, on meta-programming, shows how Prolog can be used to implement other languages and programming paradigms, including pattern-directed programming, abductive reasoning, and writing interpreters for Prolog in Prolog. Throughout, the emphasis is on the clarity of programs; efficiency tricks that rely on implementation-dependent features are avoided.

## New to this edition

All the material has been revised and updated. The main new features of this edition include:

- Most of the existing material on AI techniques has been systematically updated.
- The coverage and use of constraint logic programming (CLP) has been strengthened. An introductory chapter on CLP appears in the first, Prolog language, part of the book, to make CLP more visible and available earlier as a

powerful programming tool independent of AI. The second part includes expanded coverage of specific techniques of CLP, and its application in advanced planning techniques.

- The coverage of planning methods has been deepened in a new chapter that includes implementations of partial order planning and the GRAHPLAN approach.

- The treatment of search methods now includes RTA* (real-time A* search).

- The chapter on meta-programming has been extended by *abductive* reasoning, query-the-user facility, and a sketch of CLP interpreter, all implemented as Prolog meta-interpreters.

- Programming examples have been refreshed throughout the book, making them more interesting and practical. One such example in Chapter 4 introduces the well-known lexical database WordNet, and its application to semantic reasoning for word sense disambiguation.

## Audience for the book

This book is for students of Prolog and AI. It can be used in a Prolog course or in an AI course in which the principles of AI are brought to life through Prolog. The reader is assumed to have a basic general knowledge of computers, but no knowledge of AI is necessary. No particular programming experience is required; in fact, plentiful experience and devotion to conventional procedural programming – for example in C or Java – might even be an impediment to the fresh way of thinking Prolog requires.

## The book uses standard syntax

Among several Prolog dialects, the Edinburgh syntax, also known as DEC-10 syntax, is the most widespread, and is the basis of the ISO standard for Prolog. It is also used in this book. For compatibility with the various Prolog implementations, this book only uses a relatively small subset of the built-in features that are shared by many Prologs.

## How to read the book

In Part I, the natural reading order corresponds to the order in the book. However, the part of Section 2.4 that describes the procedural meaning of Prolog in a more formalized way can be skipped. Chapter 4 presents programming examples that can be read (or skipped) selectively. Chapter 10 on advanced tree representations can be skipped.

Part II allows more flexible reading strategies as most of the chapters are intended to be mutually independent. However, some topics will still naturally be covered before others, such as basic search strategies (Chapter 11). Figure P.1 summarizes the natural precedence constraints among the chapters.

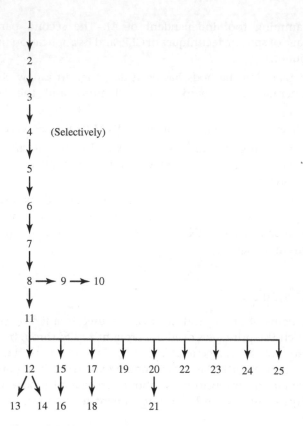

**Figure P.1** Precedence constraints among the chapters.

## Program code and course materials

Source code for all the programs in the book and relevant course materials are accessible from the companion website (www.pearsoned.co.uk/bratko).

## Acknowledgements

Donald Michie was responsible for first inducing my interest in Prolog. I am grateful to Lawrence Byrd, Fernando Pereira and David H.D. Warren, once members of the Prolog development team at Edinburgh, for their programming advice and numerous discussions. The book greatly benefited from comments and suggestions to the previous editions by Andrew McGettrick and Patrick H. Winston. Other people who read parts of the manuscript and contributed significant comments include: Damjan Bojadžiev, Rod Bristow, Peter Clark, Frans Coenen, David C. Dodson, Sašo Džeroski, Bogdan Filipič, Wan Fokkink, Matjaž Gams, Peter G. Greenfield, Marko Grobelnik, Chris Hinde, Tadej Janež, Igor Kononenko, Matevž Kovačič, Eduardo Morales, Igor Mozetič, Timothy B. Niblett, Dan Peterc, Uroš Pompe, Robert Rodošek, Aleksander Sadikov, Agata Saje, Claude Sammut, Cem Say, Áshwin Srinivasan, Dorian Šuc, Peter Tancig, Tanja Urbančič, Mark Wallace, William Walley, Simon Weilguny, Blaž Zupan and Darko Zupanič. Special thanks to Cem Say for testing many programs and his gift of finding hidden errors. Several readers helped by pointing out errors in the previous editions, most notably G. Oulsnam and Iztok Tvrdy. I would also like to thank Patrick Bond, Robert Chaundy, Rufus Curnow, Philippa Fiszzon and Simon Lake of Pearson Education for their work in the process of producing this book. Simon Plumtree, Debra Myson-Etherington, Karen Mosman, Julie Knight and Karen Sutherland provided support in the previous editions. Much of the artwork was done by Darko Simeršek. Finally, this book would not be possible without the stimulating creativity of the international logic programming community.

Ivan Bratko
January 2011

# PART I

# The Prolog Language

# Chapter 1

# Introduction to Prolog

This chapter reviews basic mechanisms of Prolog through example programs. Although the treatment is largely informal many important concepts are introduced, such as: Prolog clauses, facts, rules and procedures. Prolog's built-in backtracking mechanism and the distinction between declarative and procedural meanings of a program are discussed.

## 1.1 Defining relations by facts

Prolog is a programming language for symbolic, non-numeric computation. It is specially well suited for solving problems that involve objects and relations between objects. Figure 1.1 shows an example: a family relation. The fact that Tom is a parent of Bob can be written in Prolog as:

    parent( tom, bob).

Here we choose **parent** as the name of a relation; **tom** and **bob** are its arguments. For reasons that will become clear later we write names like **tom** with an initial lower-case letter. The whole family tree of Figure 1.1 is defined by the following Prolog program:

    parent( pam, bob).
    parent( tom, bob).
    parent( tom, liz).
    parent( bob, ann).
    parent( bob, pat).
    parent( pat, jim).

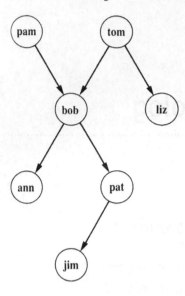

**Figure 1.1** A family tree.

This program consists of six *clauses*. Each of these clauses declares one fact about the **parent** relation. For example, **parent( tom, bob)** is a particular *instance* of the **parent** relation. In general, a relation is defined as the set of all its instances.

When this program has been communicated to the Prolog system, Prolog can be posed some questions about the **parent** relation. For example: Is Bob a parent of Pat? This question can be communicated to the Prolog system by typing:

   ?- **parent( bob, pat).**

Having found this as an asserted fact in the program, Prolog will answer:

   **yes**

A further query can be:

   ?- **parent( liz, pat).**

Prolog answers:

   **no**

because the program does not mention anything about Liz being a parent of Pat. It also answers 'no' to the question:

   ?- **parent( tom, ben).**

More interesting questions can also be asked. For example: Who is Liz's parent?

   ?- **parent( X, liz).**

Prolog will now tell us what is the value of X such that the above statement is true. So the answer is:

   **X = tom**

The question Who are Bob's children? can be communicated to Prolog as:

?- parent( bob, X).

This time there is more than just one possible answer. Prolog first answers with one solution:

X = ann

We may now request another solution (by typing a semicolon), and Prolog will find:

X = pat

If we request further solutions (semicolon again), Prolog will answer 'no' because all the solutions have been exhausted.

Our program can be asked an even broader question: Who is a parent of whom? That is:

Find X and Y such that X is a parent of Y.

This is expressed in Prolog by:

?- parent( X, Y).

Prolog now finds all the parent-child pairs one after another. The solutions will be displayed one at a time as long as we tell Prolog we want more solutions, until all the solutions have been found. The answers are output as:

X = pam
Y = bob;
X = tom
Y = bob;
X = tom
Y = liz;
. . .

We can always stop the stream of solutions by typing a return instead of a semicolon.

Our example program can be asked still more complicated questions like: Who is a grandparent of Jim? This query has to be broken down into two steps, as illustrated by Figure 1.2.

(1)  Who is a parent of Jim? Assume that this is some Y.

(2)  Who is a parent of Y? Assume that this is some X.

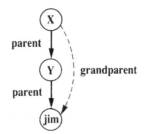

**Figure 1.2** The **grandparent** relation expressed as a composition of two **parent** relations.

Such a composed query is written in Prolog as a sequence of two simple ones:

?- parent( Y, jim), parent( X, Y).

The answer will be:

X = bob
Y = pat

Our composed query can be read: Find such X and Y that satisfy the following two requirements:

parent( Y, jim)   and   parent( X, Y)

If we change the order of the two requirements the logical meaning remains the same. We can indeed try this with the query:

?- parent( X, Y), parent( Y, jim).

which will produce the same result.
    In a similar way we can ask: Who are Tom's grandchildren?

?- parent( tom, X), parent( X, Y).

Prolog's answers are:

X = bob
Y = ann;
X = bob
Y = pat

Yet another question could be: Do Ann and Pat have a common parent? This can be expressed again in two steps:

(1)  Who is a parent, X, of Ann?

(2)  Is X also a parent of Pat?

The corresponding question to Prolog is:

?- parent( X, ann), parent( X, pat).

The answer is:

X = bob

Our example program has helped to illustrate some important points:

• It is easy in Prolog to define a relation, such as the **parent** relation, by stating the n-tuples of objects that satisfy the relation.

- The user can easily query the Prolog system about relations defined in the program.

- A Prolog program consists of *clauses*. Each clause terminates with a full stop.

- The arguments of relations can (among other things) be: concrete objects, or constants (such as **tom** and **ann**), or general objects such as X and Y. Objects of the first kind in our program are called *atoms*. Objects of the second kind are called *variables*. Atoms are distinguished from variables by syntax. Atoms are strings that start with a lower-case letter. The names of variables are strings that start with an upper-case letter or an underscore. Later we will see some other syntactic forms for atoms and variables.

- Questions to Prolog consist of one or more *goals*. A sequence of goals, such as:

    **parent( X, ann), parent( X, pat)**

  means the conjunction of the goals:

    X is a parent of Ann, *and*
    X is a parent of Pat.

  The word 'goals' is used because Prolog interprets questions as goals that are to be satisfied. To 'satisfy a goal' means to logically deduce the goal from the program.

- An answer to a question can be either positive or negative, depending on whether the corresponding goal can be satisfied or not. In the case of a positive answer we say that the corresponding goal was *satisfiable* and that the goal *succeeded*. Otherwise the goal was *unsatisfiable* and it *failed*.

- If several answers satisfy the question then Prolog will find as many of them as desired by the user.

## EXERCISES

**1.1** Assuming the **parent** relation as defined in this section (see Figure 1.1), what will be Prolog's answers to the following questions?

  (a)  ?- **parent( jim, X).**

  (b)  ?- **parent( X, jim).**

  (c)  ?- **parent( pam, X), parent( X, pat).**

  (d)  ?- **parent( pam, X), parent( X, Y), parent( Y, jim).**

**1.2** Formulate in Prolog the following questions about the **parent** relation:

  (a)  Who is Pat's parent?

  (b)  Does Liz have a child?

  (c)  Who is Pat's grandparent?

## 1.2 Defining relations by rules

Our example program can be easily extended in many interesting ways. Let us first add the information on the sex of the people that occur in the **parent** relation. This can be done by simply adding the following facts to our program:

    female( pam).
    male( tom).
    male( bob).
    female( liz).
    female( pat).
    female( ann).
    male( jim).

The relations introduced here are **male** and **female**. These relations are unary (or one-place) relations. A binary relation like **parent** defines a relation between *pairs* of objects; on the other hand, unary relations can be used to declare simple yes/no properties of objects. The first unary clause above can be read: Pam is a female. We could convey the same information declared in the two unary relations with one binary relation, sex, instead. An alternative piece of program would then be:

    sex( pam, feminine).
    sex( tom, masculine).
    sex( bob, masculine).
    . . .

As our next extension to the program, let us introduce the **mother** relation. We could define **mother** in a similar way as the **parent** relation; that is, by simply providing facts about the **mother** relation, each fact mentioning one pair of people such that one is the mother of the other:

    mother( pam, bob).
    mother( pat, jim).

However, imagine we had a large database of people. Then the **mother** relation can be defined much more elegantly by making use of the fact that it can be logically derived from the already known relations **parent** and **female**. This alternative way can be based on the following logical statement:

> For all X and Y,
>     X is the mother of Y if
>         X is a parent of Y, and X is female.

This formulation is already close to the formulation in Prolog. In Prolog this is written as:

    mother( X, Y) :- parent( X, Y), female(X).

The Prolog symbol ':-' is read as 'if'. This clause can also be read as:

> For all X and Y,
>     if X is a parent of Y and X is female then
>     X is the mother of Y.

Prolog clauses such as this are called *rules*. There is an important difference between facts and rules. A fact like:

   **parent( tom, liz).**

is something that is always, unconditionally, true. On the other hand, rules specify things that are true if some condition is satisfied. Therefore we say that rules have:

- a condition part (the right-hand side of the rule) and
- a conclusion part (the left-hand side of the rule).

The conclusion part is also called the *head* of a clause and the condition part the *body* of a clause. This terminology is illustrated by:

   mother( X, Y) :- parent( X, Y) , female( X).

   goal        goal

   head            body

If the condition part 'parent( X, Y), female( X)' is true then a logical consequence of this is **mother( X, Y)**. Note that the comma between the goals in the body means conjunction: for the body to be true, all the goals in the body have to be true.

   How are rules actually used by Prolog? Consider the following example. Let us ask our program whether Pam is the mother of Bob:

   **?- mother(pam, bob).**

There is no fact about **mother** in the program. The only way to consider this question is to apply the rule about **mother**. The rule is general in the sense that it is applicable to any objects X and Y; therefore it can also be applied to such particular objects as **pam** and **bob**. To apply the rule to **pam** and **bob**, X has to be substituted with **pam**, and Y with **bob**. We say that the variables X and Y become *instantiated* to:

   X = **pam**   and   Y = **bob**

After the instantiation we have obtained a special case of our general rule. The special case is:

   **mother( pam, bob) :- parent( pam, bob), female( pam).**

The condition part has become:

   **parent( pam, bob), female( pam)**

Now Prolog tries to find out whether the condition part is true. So the initial goal:

   **mother( pam, bob)**

has been replaced with the goals:

   **parent( pam, bob), female( pam)**

These two (new) goals happen to be trivial as they can be found as facts in the program. This means that the conclusion part of the rule is also true, and Prolog will answer the question with yes.

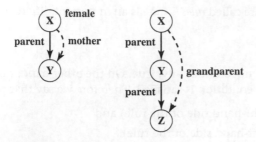

**Figure 1.3** Definition graphs for the relations **mother** and **grandparent** in terms of relations **parent** and female.

Relations such as **parent** and **mother** can be illustrated by diagrams such as those in Figure 1.3. These diagrams conform to the following conventions. Nodes in the graphs correspond to objects – that is, arguments of relations. Arcs between nodes correspond to binary relations. The arcs are oriented so as to point from the first argument of the relation to the second argument. Unary relations are indicated in the diagrams by simply labelling the corresponding objects with the name of the relation. The relations that are being defined are represented by dashed arcs. So each diagram should be understood as follows: if the relations shown by solid arcs hold, then the relation shown by a dashed arc also holds.

Such graphical illustrations may be very helpful when we think about how to define new relations. Consider the **grandparent** relation. It can be, according to Figure 1.3, immediately written in Prolog as:

    grandparent( X, Z) :- parent( X, Y), parent( Y, Z).

At this point it will be useful to make a comment on the layout of our programs. Prolog gives us almost full freedom in choosing the layout of the program. So we can insert spaces and new lines as it best suits our taste. In general we want to make our programs look nice and tidy, and easy to read. To this end we will often choose to write the head of a clause and each goal of the body on a separate line. When doing this, we will indent the goals in order to make the difference between the head and the goals more visible. For example, the **grandparent** rule would be, according to this convention, written as:

    grandparent( X, Z) :-
       parent( X, Y),
       parent( Y, Z).

Figure 1.4 illustrates the **sister** relation:

    For all X and Y,
       X is a sister of Y if
       (1)  both X and Y have the same parent, and
       (2)  X is a female.

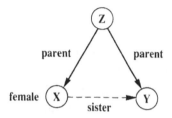

**Figure 1.4** Defining the **sister** relation.

The graph in Figure 1.4 can be translated into Prolog as:

```
sister( X, Y) :-
    parent( Z, X),
    parent( Z, Y),
    female( X).
```

Notice the way in which the requirement 'both X and Y have the same parent' has been expressed. The following logical formulation was used: some Z must be a parent of X, and this *same* Z must be a parent of Y. An alternative, but less elegant, way would be to say: Z1 is a parent of X, and Z2 is a parent of Y, and Z1 is equal to Z2. We can now ask:

```
?- sister( ann, pat).
```

The answer will be 'yes', as expected (see Figure 1.1). Therefore we might conclude that the **sister** relation, as defined, works correctly. There is, however, a rather subtle flaw in our program, which is revealed if we ask the question Who is Pat's sister?:

```
?- sister( X, pat).
```

Prolog will find two answers, one of which may come as a surprise:

```
X = ann;
X = pat
```

So, Pat is a sister to herself?! This is not what we had in mind when defining the **sister** relation. However, according to our rule about sisters, Prolog's answer is perfectly logical. Our rule about sisters does not mention that X and Y must be different if they are to be sisters. As this is not required Prolog (rightfully) assumes that X and Y can be the same, and will as a consequence find that any female who has a parent is a sister of herself.

To correct our rule about sisters we have to add that X and Y must be differ-ent. We can state this as X \= Y. An improved definition of the **sister** relation can then be:

```
sister( X, Y) :-
    parent( Z, X),
    parent( Z, Y),
    female( X),
    X \= Y.
```

Some important points of this section are:

- Prolog programs can be extended by simply adding new clauses.
- Prolog clauses are of three types: *facts*, *rules* and *questions*.
- *Facts* declare things that are always, unconditionally, true.
- *Rules* declare things that are true depending on a given condition.
- By means of *questions* the user can ask the program what things are true.
- A Prolog clause consists of the *head* and the *body*. The body is a list of *goals* separated by commas. Commas between goals are understood as conjunctions.
- A fact is a clause that just has the head and no body. Questions only have the body. Rules consist of the head and the (non-empty) body.
- In the course of computation, a variable can be substituted by another object. We say that a variable becomes *instantiated*.
- Variables are assumed to be *universally quantified* and are read as 'for all'. Alternative readings are, however, possible for variables that appear only in the body. For example:

      **hasachild( X)  :- parent( X, Y).**

  can be read in two ways:

  (a) *For all* X and Y,
        if X is a parent of Y then
        X has a child.

  (b) *For all* X,
        X has a child if
        there is *some* Y such that X is a parent of Y.

  Logically, both readings are equivalent.

## EXERCISES

**1.3** Translate the following statements into Prolog rules:

(a) Everybody who has a child is happy (introduce a one-argument relation **happy**).

(b) For all X, if X has a child who has a sister then X has two children (introduce new relation **hastwochildren**).

**1.4** Define the relation **grandchild** using the **parent** relation. Hint: It will be similar to the **grandparent** relation (see Figure 1.3).

**1.5** Define the relation **aunt( X, Y)** in terms of the relations **parent** and **sister**. As an aid you can first draw a diagram in the style of Figure 1.3 for the **aunt** relation.

# 1.3 Recursive rules

Let us add one more relation to our family program, the **ancestor** relation. This relation will be defined in terms of the **parent** relation. The whole definition can be expressed with two rules. The first rule will define the direct (immediate) ancestors and the second rule the indirect ancestors. We say that some X is an indirect ancestor of some Z if there is a chain of parents between X and Z, as illustrated in Figure 1.5. In our example of Figure 1.1, Tom is a direct ancestor of Liz and an indirect ancestor of Pat.

The first rule is simple and can be written in Prolog as:

```
ancestor( X, Z) :-
    parent( X, Z).
```

The second rule, on the other hand, is more complicated. The chain of parents may present some problems because the chain can be arbitrarily long. One attempt to define indirect ancestors could be as shown in Figure 1.6. According to this, the **ancestor** relation would be defined by a set of clauses as follows:

```
ancestor( X, Z) :-
    parent( X, Z).

ancestor( X, Z) :-
    parent( X, Y),
    parent( Y, Z).

ancestor( X, Z) :-
    parent( X, Y1),
    parent( Y1, Y2),
    parent( Y2, Z).

ancestor( X, Z) :-
    parent( X, Y1),
    parent( Y1, Y2),
    parent( Y2, Y3),
    parent( Y3, Z).
```
. . .

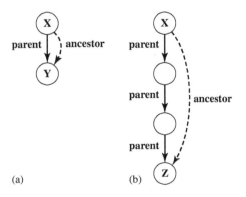

(a)  (b)

**Figure 1.5** Examples of the **ancestor** relation: (a) X is a direct ancestor of Z; (b) X is an indirect ancestor of Z.

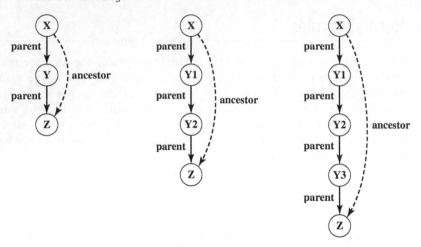

**Figure 1.6** Ancestor–successor pairs at various distances.

This program is lengthy and, more importantly, it only works to some extent. It would only discover ancestors to a certain depth in a family tree because the length of the chain of people between the ancestor and the successor would be limited by the length of our **ancestor** clauses.

There is, however, a much more elegant and correct formulation of the **ancestor** relation. It will work for ancestors at any depth. The key idea is to define the **ancestor** relation in terms of itself. Figure 1.7 illustrates the idea:

> For all X and Z,
>    X is an ancestor of Z if
>    there is a Y such that
>    (1) X is a parent of Y and
>    (2) Y is an ancestor of Z.

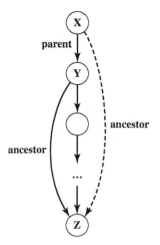

**Figure 1.7** Recursive formulation of the **ancestor** relation.

A Prolog clause with the above meaning is:

```
ancestor( X, Z) :-
    parent( X, Y),
    ancestor( Y, Z).
```

We have thus constructed a complete program for the **ancestor** relation, which consists of two rules: one for direct ancestors and one for indirect ancestors. Both rules are rewritten together as:

```
ancestor( X, Z) :-
    parent( X, Z).

ancestor( X, Z) :-
    parent( X, Y),
    ancestor( Y, Z).
```

The key to this formulation was the use of **ancestor** itself in its definition. Such a definition may look surprising in view of the question: When defining something, can we use this same thing that has not yet been completely defined? Such definitions are called *recursive* definitions. Logically, they are perfectly correct and understandable, which is also intuitively obvious if we look at Figure 1.7. But will the Prolog system be able to use recursive rules in computation? It turns out that Prolog can indeed easily use recursive definitions. Recursive programming is, in fact, one of the fundamental principles of programming in Prolog. It is not possible to solve tasks of any significant complexity in Prolog without the use of recursion.

Going back to our program, we can ask Prolog: Who are Pam's successors? That is: Who is a person that has Pam as his or her ancestor?

```
?- ancestor( pam, X).
X = bob;
X = ann;
X = pat;
X = jim
```

Prolog's answers are, of course, correct and they logically follow from our definition of the **ancestor** and the **parent** relation. There is, however, a rather important question: *How* did Prolog actually use the program to find these answers?

An informal explanation of how Prolog does this is given in the next section. But first let us put together all the pieces of our family program, which was extended gradually by adding new facts and rules. The final program is shown in Figure 1.8. Looking at Figure 1.8, two further points are in order here: the first will introduce the term 'procedure', the second will be about comments in programs.

The program in Figure 1.8 defines several relations – **parent**, **male**, **female**, **ancestor**, etc. The **ancestor** relation, for example, is defined by two clauses. We say that these two clauses are *about* the **ancestor** relation. Sometimes it is convenient to consider the whole set of clauses about the same relation. Such a set of clauses is called a *procedure*.

In Figure 1.8, *comments* like 'Pam is a parent of Bob' were added to the program. Comments are, in general, ignored by the Prolog system. They only serve as a further clarification to a person who reads the program. Comments are distinguished in Prolog from the rest of the program by being enclosed in special brackets '/*' and '*/'. Thus comments in Prolog look like this:

    /* This is a comment */

Another method, more practical for short comments, uses the percent character '%'. Everything between '%' and the end of the line is interpreted as a comment:

    % This is also a comment

```
parent( pam, bob).          % Pam is a parent of Bob
parent( tom, bob).
parent( tom, liz).
parent( bob, ann).
parent( bob, pat).
parent( pat, jim).

female( pam).               % Pam is female
male( tom).                 % Tom is male
male( bob).
female( liz).
female( ann).
female( pat).
male( jim).

mother( X, Y) :-            % X is the mother of Y if
    parent( X, Y),          % X is a parent of Y and
    female( X).             % X is female

grandparent( X, Z) :-       % X is a grandparent of Z if
    parent( X, Y),          % X is a parent of Y and
    parent( Y, Z).          % Y is a parent of Z

sister( X, Y) :-            % X is a sister of Y if
    parent( Z, X),
    parent( Z, Y),          % X and Y have the same parent and
    female( X),             % X is female and
    X\ = Y.                 % X and Y are different

ancestor( X, Z) :-          % Rule a1: X is ancestor of Z
    parent( X, Z).

ancestor( X, Z) :-          % Rule a2: X is ancestor of Z
    parent( X, Y),
    ancestor( Y, Z).
```

**Figure 1.8** The family program.

## EXERCISE

.....................................................................................................................................................

**1.6**  Consider the following alternative definition of the **ancestor** relation:

ancestor( X, Z) :-
  parent( X, Z).

ancestor( X, Z) :-
  parent( Y, Z),
  ancestor( X, Y).

Does this also seem to be a correct definition of ancestors? Can you modify the diagram of Figure 1.7 so that it would correspond to this new definition?

## 1.4  Running the program with a Prolog system

.....................................................................................................................................................

How can a program like our family program be run on the computer? Here is a simple and typical way.

There are several good quality and freely available Prologs, such as SWI Prolog, YAP Prolog and CIAO Prolog. Constraint programming system ECLiPSe also includes Prolog. Another well-known, well-maintained and inexpensive (for academic use) Prolog is SICStus Prolog. We will now assume that a Prolog system has already been downloaded and installed on your computer.

In the following we describe, as an example, roughly how the family program is run with the SICStus Prolog system. The procedure with other Prologs is essentially the same; only the interface details of interacting with Prolog may vary.

Suppose that our family program has already been typed into the computer using a plain text editor, such as Notepad. Suppose this file has been saved into a chosen directory, say 'prolog_progs', as a text file 'family.pl'. SICStus Prolog expects Prolog programs to be saved with name extension 'pl'.

Now you can start your Prolog system. When started, SICStus Prolog will open a window for interaction with the user. It will be displaying the prompt '?-', which means that Prolog is waiting for your questions or commands. First, you need to tell Prolog that the 'working directory' will be your chosen directory 'prolog_progs'. This can be done through the 'Working directory' entry in the 'File' menu. Prolog will now expect to read program files from the selected directory 'prolog_progs'. Then you tell Prolog to read in your program from file 'family.pl' by:

?- consult( family).

or equivalently:

?- [family].

Prolog will read the file family.pl and answer something to the effect 'File family.pl successfully consulted', and again display the prompt '?-'. Then your conversation with Prolog may proceed like this:

?- parent( tom, X).
X = bob;
X = liz;

```
no

?- ancestor( X, ann).
X = bob;
X = pam;
. . .
```

## How Prolog answers questions

This section explains informally *how* Prolog answers questions. A question to Prolog is always a sequence of one or more goals. To answer a question, Prolog tries to satisfy all the goals. What does it mean to *satisfy* a goal? To satisfy a goal means to demonstrate that the goal is true, assuming that the relations in the program are true. In other words, to satisfy a goal means to demonstrate that the goal *logically follows* from the facts and rules in the program. If the question contains variables, Prolog also has to find what are the particular objects (in place of variables) for which the goals are satisfied. The particular instantiation of variables to these objects is displayed to the user. If Prolog cannot demonstrate for any instantiation of variables that the goals logically follow from the program, then Prolog's answer to the question will be 'no'.

An appropriate view of the interpretation of a Prolog program in mathematical terms is then as follows: Prolog accepts facts and rules as a set of axioms, and the user's question as a *conjectured theorem*; then it tries to prove this theorem – that is, to demonstrate that it can be logically derived from the axioms.

We will illustrate this view by a classical example. Let the axioms be:

All men are fallible.
Socrates is a man.

A theorem that logically follows from these two axioms is:

Socrates is fallible.

The first axiom above can be rewritten as:

For all X, if X is a man then X is fallible.

Accordingly, the example can be translated into Prolog as follows:

```
fallible( X) :- man( X).        % All men are fallible

man( socrates).                 % Socrates is a man

?- fallible( socrates).         % Socrates is fallible?

yes
```

A more complicated example from the family program of Figure 1.8 is:

```
?- ancestor( tom, pat).
```

We know that **parent( bob, pat)** is a fact. Using this fact and rule *a1* we can conclude **ancestor( bob, pat)**. This is a *derived* fact: it cannot be found explicitly in our program, but it can be derived from the facts and rules in the program. An inference step, such as this, can be written as:

parent( bob, pat) $\Rightarrow$ ancestor( bob, pat)

This can be read: from **parent( bob, pat)** it follows that **ancestor( bob, pat)**, by rule *a1*. Further, we know that **parent( tom, bob)** is a fact. Using this fact and the derived fact **ancestor( bob, pat)** we can conclude **ancestor( tom, pat)**, by rule *a2*. We have thus shown that our goal statement **ancestor( tom, pat)** is true. This whole inference process of two steps can be written as:

parent( bob, pat)  $\Rightarrow$  ancestor( bob, pat)

parent( tom, bob) *and* ancestor( bob, pat)  $\Rightarrow$  ancestor( tom, pat)

We will now show how Prolog finds such a proof that the given goals follow from the given program. Prolog starts with the goals and, using rules in the program, substitutes the current goals with new goals, until new goals happen to be simple facts. Let us see how this works for the question:

?- mother( pam, bob).

Prolog tries to prove the goal **mother( pam, bob)**. To do this, Proog looks for clauses about the mother relation. So it finds the rule:

mother( X, Y) :- parent( X, Y), female( X).

This rule is true for all X and Y, so it must also be true for the special case when X = **pam**, and Y = **bob**. We say that variables X and Y get 'instantiated', and this results in the special case of the **mother** rule:

mother( pam, bob) :- parent( pam, bob), female( pam).

The head of this clause is the goal Prolog wants to prove. If Prolog manages to prove the body of the clause, then it will have proved **mother(pam,bob)**. Prolog therefore substitutes the original goal **mother(pam,bob)** with the goals in the body:

parent( pam, bob), female( pam)

These now become Prolog's next goals. Prolog tries to prove them in turn: first **parent(pam,bob)**, and then **female(pam)**. The first goal is easy because Prolog finds that **parent(pam,bob)** is given as a fact in the program. So it remains to prove **female(pam)**. Prolog finds that this is also given as a fact in the program, so it is also true. Thus the proof of **mother(pam,bob)** is completed and Prolog answers the question with 'yes'.

Now consider a more complicated question that involves recursion:

?- ancestor( tom, pat).

To satisfy this goal, Prolog will try to find a clause in the program about the **ancestor** relation. There are two clauses relevant to this end: the clauses labelled by *a1* and *a2*. We say that the heads of these rules *match* the goal.

The two clauses, *a1* and *a2*, represent two alternative ways for Prolog to proceed. This is graphically illustrated in Figure 1.9 which shows the complete execution trace. We now follow Figure 1.9. Prolog first tries the clause that appears first in the program, that is *a1*:

ancestor( X, Z) :- parent( X, Z).

Since the goal is **ancestor(tom,pat)**, the variables in the rule must be instantiated as follows:

X = tom, Z = pat

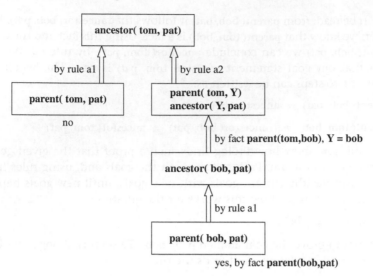

**Figure 1.9** The complete execution trace to satisfy the goal **ancestor( tom, pat)**. The left-hand branch fails, but the right-hand branch proves the goal is satisfiable.

The original goal **ancestor( tom, pat)** is then replaced by a new goal:

> **parent( tom, pat)**

There is no clause in the program whose head matches the goal **parent(tom,pat)**, therefore this goal fails. This means the first alternative with rule *a1* has failed. Now Prolog *backtracks* to the original goal in order to try the alternative way to derive the top goal **ancestor(tom,pat)**. The rule *a2* is thus tried:

> **ancestor( X, Z) :-**
> **parent( X, Y),**
> **ancestor( Y, Z).**

As before, the variables X and Z become instantiated as:

> **X = tom, Z = pat**

But Y is not instantiated yet. The top goal **ancestor( tom, pat)** is replaced by two goals:

> **parent( tom, Y),**
> **ancestor( Y, pat)**

Prolog tries to satisfy the two goals in the order in which they appear. The first goal matches two facts in the program: **parent(tom,bob)** and **parent(tom,liz)**. Prolog first tries to use the fact that appears first in the program. This forces Y to become instantiated to **bob**. Thus the first goal has been satisfied, and the remaining goal has become:

> **ancestor( bob, pat)**

To satisfy this goal the rule *a1* is used again. Note that this (second) application of the same rule has nothing to do with its previous application. Therefore, Prolog uses a new set of variables in the rule each time the rule is applied. To indicate this we shall rename the variables in rule *a1* for this application as follows:

> ancestor( X′, Z′) :-
>   parent( X′, Z′).

The head has to match our current goal **ancestor( bob, pat)**. Therefore:

> X′ = **bob**, Z′ = **pat**

The current goal is replaced by:

> parent( bob, pat)

This goal is immediately satisfied because it appears in the program as a fact. This completes the execution trace in Figure 1.9.

Here is a summary of the goal execution mechanism of Prolog, illustrated by the trace in Figure 1.9. An execution trace has the form of a tree. The nodes of the tree correspond to goals, or to lists of goals that are to be satisfied. The arcs between the nodes correspond to the application of (alternative) program clauses that transform the goals at one node into the goals at another node. The top goal is satisfied when a path is found from the root node (top goal) to a leaf node labelled 'yes'. A leaf is labelled 'yes' if it is a simple fact. The execution of Prolog programs is the searching for such paths. During the search Prolog may enter an unsuccessful branch. When Prolog discovers that a branch fails it automatically *backtracks* to the previous node and tries to apply an alternative clause at that node. *Automatic backtracking* is one of the distinguishing features of Prolog.

## EXERCISE

**1.7** Try to understand how Prolog derives answers to the following questions, using the program of Figure 1.8. Try to draw the corresponding derivation diagrams in the style of Figure 1.9. Will any backtracking occur at particular questions?

(a)  ?- parent( pam, bob).
(b)  ?- mother( pam, bob).
(c)  ?- grandparent( pam, ann).
(d)  ?- grandparent( bob, jim).

## 1.6 Declarative and procedural meaning of programs

In our examples so far it has always been possible to understand the results of the program without exactly knowing *how* the system actually found the results. It therefore makes sense to distinguish between two levels of meaning of Prolog programs; namely,

- the *declarative meaning* and
- the *procedural meaning*.

The declarative meaning is concerned only with the *relations* defined by the program. The declarative meaning thus determines *what* will be the output of the program. On the other hand, the procedural meaning also determines *how* this output is obtained; that is, how the relations are actually derived by the Prolog system.

The ability of Prolog to work out many procedural details on its own is considered to be one of its specific advantages. It encourages the programmer to consider the declarative meaning of programs relatively independently of their procedural meaning. Since the results of the program are, in principle, determined by its declarative meaning, this should be (in principle) sufficient for writing programs. This is of practical importance because the declarative aspects of programs are usually easier to understand than the procedural details. To take full advantage of this, the programmer should concentrate mainly on the declarative meaning and, whenever possible, avoid being distracted by the execution details. These should be left to the greatest possible extent to the Prolog system itself.

This declarative approach indeed often makes programming in Prolog easier than in typical procedurally oriented programming languages such as C or Java. Unfortunately, however, the declarative approach is not always sufficient. It will later become clear that, especially in large programs, the procedural aspects cannot be completely ignored by the programmer for practical reasons of execution efficiency. Nevertheless, the declarative style of thinking about Prolog programs should be encouraged and the procedural aspects ignored to the extent that is permitted by practical constraints.

## 1.7 A robot's world – preview of things to come

In this section we preview some other features of Prolog programming. The preview will be through an example, without in-depth explanation of the illustrated features. The details of their syntax and meaning will be covered in chapters that follow.

Consider a robot that can observe and manipulate simple objects on a table. Figure 1.10 shows a scene from the robot's world. For simplicity, all the objects are blocks of unit size. The coordinates on the table are just integers, so the robot can only distinguish between a finite number of positions of the objects. The robot can observe the objects with a camera that is mounted on the ceiling. The blocks **a**, **d** and **e** are visible by the camera, whereas blocks **b** and **c** are not. The robot's vision system can recognize the names of the visible blocks and the *x-y* positions

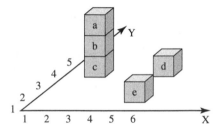

**Figure 1.10** A robot's world.

of the blocks. Now assume that the vision information is stored in a Prolog program as the three place relation **see**:

```
% see( Block, X, Y):  Block is observed by camera at coordinates X and Y
see( a, 2, 5).
see( d, 5, 5).
see( e, 5, 2).
```

Assume also that the robot keeps track of what each block is standing on, e.g. that block **a** is on block **b**. Let this information be stored as binary relation **on**:

```
% on( Block, Object):  Block is standing on Object
on( a, b).
on( b, c).
on( c, table).
on( d, table).
on( e, table).
```

The robot may be interested in some simple questions about its world. For example, what are all the blocks in this world? Each block has to be supported by something, so relation 'on' offers one way of finding all the blocks:

```
?- on( Block, _).
Block = a;
Block = b;
. . .
```

Note the underscore character in the question. We are only interested in Block, and not in what the block is standing on. The underscore indicates an 'anonymous' variable. It stands for anything, and we are not interested in its value.

The robot may ask about pairs of visible blocks that have the same $y$-coordinate. This is an attempt at asking about such pairs of blocks B1 and B2:

```
?- see( B1, _, Y), see( B2, _, Y).          % B1 and B2 both seen at the same Y
B1 = a, B2 = a;
B1 = a, B2 = d;
. . .
B1 = e,  B2 = e
```

Some answers are a surprise! The intention was that B1 and B2 are not the same, but we did not state this in the question. So Prolog quite logically also considers the cases when B1 = B2, and thus reports also the cases like B1 = B2 = a, B1 = B2 = e, etc. We can correct the question as:

```
?- see( B1, _, Y), see( B2, _, Y), B1 \= B2.      % B1 and B2 not equal
B1 = a,  B2 = d;
B1 = d,  B2 = a;
no
```

The robot may find non-visible blocks B by the question:

```
?- on( B, _),                    % B is on something, so B is a block
   on( _, B).                    % Something is on B, so B is not visible
B = b;
```

      B = c;

      no

Equivalently, we may ask:

    ?- on( B, _),                    % B is on something, so B is a block

       not see( B, _, _).         % B is not seen by the camera

    B = b;

    . . .

The condition  not see( B, _, _) is Prolog's negation of see( B, _, _). This is not exactly the same as negation in mathematics, which will be discussed in Chapter 5. To emphasize this difference with respect to mathematics, a more standard notation for negation in Prolog is '\+' instead of 'not'. So the negated condition is written as \+ see(B,_,_).

Now suppose the robot wants to find the left-most visible block(s). That is, find the block(s) with minimum $x$-coordinate. The usual algorithm for such a task is roughly: loop over all the blocks, whereby for each block check whether its $x$-coordinate is less than the minimum $x$-coordinate Xmin of the blocks considered so far. If yes, update Xmin (set Xmin to the $x$-coordinate of the current block). When the loop is over, Xmin is equal to the minimum $x$-coordinate. We may do the same in Prolog, but there is a simpler way, not possible in other programming languages. The question about the left-most block B can be stated as: B is seen at $x$-coordinate X, and there is no other block B2 whose $x$-coordinate is X2, such that X2 is less than X. A corresponding question to Prolog is:

    ?- see( B, X, _),

       not ( see( B2, X2, _), X2 < X).      % Not B2 seen at X2 and X2 < X

    B = a,  X = 2

To be able to manipulate the blocks, the robot has to reason about the relations between the blocks and to determine the exact blocks' positions. For example, to move block **b** on block **d**, the robot first has to know whether block **b** is free to grasp. This can be found by asking Prolog:

    ?- on( What, b).            % What is on block b?

    What = a

If Prolog would have answered 'no', then block **b** would have been directly accessible for grasping. But now the robot knows that **b** is not clear, so the robot first has to remove block **a** from the top of **b**, by, say, moving **a** from **b** to the table. To do that, the robot first has to check that block **a** is accessible, by asking Prolog:

    ?- on( What, a).

    no

OK, this means that block **a** can be grasped immediately as there is nothing on top of **a**. But to grasp **a**, the robot has to move the arm to the position of **a**. Therefore it has to work out the precise $x$-$y$-$z$ coordinates of block **a**. $x$-$y$ coordinates for block **a** are easy – they can simply be obtained by asking Prolog:

    ?- see( a, X, Y).

    X = 2,  Y = 5

It is harder to work out the $z$-coordinate of block **a**. The robot may now reason like this. First, find all the blocks between **a** and the table by the query:

```
?- on( a, B1), on( B1, B2), on( B2, B3).
B1 = b,   B2 = c,   B3 = table
```

This can be used to determine the z-coordinates of blocks a, b and c as follows. Since c is on the table, c's z-coordinate Zc is 0 (adopting the convention that for the blocks on the table, Z = 0). Since b is on c and all the blocks are of unit size 1, Zb = Zc + 1 = 0 + 1 = 1. Similarly, since a is on b, Za = Zb + 1 = 2.

We will now implement the idea above as the predicate z( B, Z) to compute for any given block B its z-coordinate Z. If B is on the table then Z = 0:

```
z( B, 0) :-
    on( B, table).
```

For the cases when B is not on the table, but on another block, B0, Figure 1.11 shows important relations between B and B0, and their z-coordinates. These relations translate into Prolog as the following recursive definition:

```
z( B, Z) :-
    on( B, B0),
    z( B0, Z0),
    Z is Z0 + 1.
```

The last line in this clause **Z is Z0 + 1** has a form we have not seen before. This makes Prolog carry out numerical computation. The expression to the right of 'is' is numerically evaluated, and the result is assigned to the variable on the left of 'is'. We will look into details of numeric operations in Chapter 3. We can ask Prolog:

```
?- z( a, Za).
Za = 2
```

There are interesting variations of the predicate z. Let us look into these, again without going into detailed explanation at this stage. One idea is to shorten the definition of z above by substituting Z in the head of the clause with Z0 + 1. To avoid confusion we will call this new predicate zz. The first clause about zz is analogous to that of z, and the second clause is:

```
zz( B, Z0 + 1) :-
    on( B, B0),
    zz( B0, Z0).
```

This looks equivalent and more elegant. It basically says: z-coordinate of B is Z0 + 1 where Z0 is the z-coordinate of the block underneath B. However, this definition does not make Prolog carry out numerical summation, and Prolog's answer will now be different:

```
?- zz( a, Za).
Za = 0 + 1 + 1
```

**Figure 1.11** Relations between blocks B and B0, and their z-coordinates.

This answer also makes sense, and it is in some respect more interesting than the answer **Za = 2**. This time, Prolog has actually constructed a formula for computing Za, but did not evaluate the formula. The resulting formula indicates how the result **Za = 2** comes about. But once the formula has been constructed, we can force Prolog to actually evaluate it, for example by extending the query with an 'is' goal:

```
?- zz( a, ZaFormula), Za is ZaFormula.
ZaFormula = 0 + 1 + 1,  Za = 2
```

Let us develop the idea in predicate **zz** a bit further. Suppose that the blocks are not of equal size. We can choose to denote the blocks' heights by symbolic expressions. For example, the height of a block B will be denoted in the program by the expression **height(B)**. Specifically, the heights of the blocks in our robot's world will be **height(a)**, **height(b)**, etc. We can then generalize the predicate **zz**, obtaining its variant **zzz**, by modifying the second clause of **zz** as follows:

```
zzz( B, Z0 + height(B0) ) :-
  on( B, B0),
  zzz( B0, Z0).
```

Our question about the z-coordinate of block **a** will now be answered as:

```
?- zzz( a, Za).
Za = 0 + height(c) + height(b)
```

This formula looks even more interesting because it explicitly tells how the z-coordinate of block **a** is determined. However, this time we cannot make Prolog evaluate the formula simply with 'is' because the formula contains non-numerical symbols, not just numbers.

We can complete our robot program with the predicate to determine the x and y coordinates of a block. First, for blocks that are visible by the camera, their x-y coordinates are simply retrieved from the see predicate. Second, for non-visible blocks we may use the fact that all the blocks in the same column have the same x-y coordinates. So, a block B that is under block B0 'inherits' x-y coordinates from block B0. This translates into Prolog as:

```
% xy( B, X, Y):  x-y coordinates of block B are X and Y
xy( B, X, Y) :-
  see( B, X, Y).

xy( B, X, Y) :-
  on( B0, B),
  xy( B0, X, Y).
```

The robot may find all three coordinates of block **a** with the question:

```
?- xy( a, X, Y), z( a, Z).
X = 2, Y = 5, Z = 2
```

This completes our robot example. We implemented the robot's reasoning to determine objects' coordinates from sensory information. The knowledge of these coordinates enables the robot to carry out actions to manipulate the objects. We did not implement the robot's planning procedure which would allow the robot to find *plans* – that is *sequences of actions* to achieve goals given to the robot. A task the user may give to the robot is to re-arrange the column of blocks **a**, **b** and **c** into a column in the reverse order of blocks from top to bottom. The user may state this by setting the goals for the robot: achieve **on(c,b)** and **on(b,a)**. After the next couple of chapters, we will be sufficiently equipped to program automatic search for such plans. We will look into more sophisticated AI methods for planning in Part II of this book.

## 1.8 Crosswords, maps and schedules

In this section we look at three additional example programs that show how we can sometimes use Prolog's built-in backtracking mechanism to solve, practically without effort, problems that appear a bit tricky otherwise. These examples are: solving a crossword puzzle, colouring a map and scheduling a meeting. All the three programs will be easy and straightforward, although they may seem a little longer than one would ideally expect. In later chapters we will soon learn data structures that will  enable the shortening of these programs.

### 1.8.1 Solving crossword puzzles

Figure 1.12 shows a small crossword puzzle and a program that solves the puzzle. The cells in the puzzle are to be filled with letters. The cells are labelled L1, L2, ..., L16. In the program, these labels will be the names of the variables whose values will be found by the program when solving the puzzle. The possible values of these variables are the letters from the given vocabulary. The vocabulary is given by the predicates **word** with 3 to 6 arguments. For example, the clause

    word( g,r,e,e,n).

says that 'green' is an allowed word to use in a solution. Note that each letter of the word is a separate argument of the predicate. The program in Figure 1.12 defines a

| L1 | L2 | L3 | L4 | L5 | |
|---|---|---|---|---|---|
| L6 | | L7 | | L8 | |
| L9 | L10 | L11 | L12 | L13 | L14 |
| L15 | | | | L16 | |

% Words that may be used in the solution

| | | | |
|---|---|---|---|
| word( d,o,g). | word( r,u,n). | word( t,o,p). | word( f,i,v,e). |
| word( f,o,u,r). | word( l,o,s,t). | word( m,e,s,s). | word( u,n,i,t). |
| word( b,a,k,e,r). | word( f,o,r,u,m). | word( g,r,e,e,n). | word( s,u,p,e,r). |
| word( p,r,o,l,o,g). | word( v,a,n,i,s,h). | word( w,o,n,d,e,r). | word( y,e,l,l,o,w). |

solution( L1,L2,L3,L4,L5,L6,L7,L8,L9,L10,L11,L12,L13,L14,L15,L16)  :-
    word( L1,L2,L3,L4,L5),          % Top horizontal word
    word( L9,L10,L11,L12,L13,L14),    % Second horizontal word
    word( L1,L6,L9,L15),           % First vertical word
    word( L3,L7,L11),             % Second vertical word
    word( L5,L8,L13,L16).        % Third vertical word

**Figure 1.12** A crossword puzzle and a program to solve it. All the cells labelled $L_i$ are to be filled with letters so that the horizontally or vertically adjacent letters form legal words from the given vocabulary.

vocabulary of 16 words. The predicate **solution**, whose arguments are all the 16 letters in the puzzle, states the constraints that have to be satisfied by these letters: (a) they must all belong to allowed words, and (b) they must satisfy the structure of the puzzle, that is the way the words are put into the puzzle. For example, the top horizontal word and the left-most vertical word both start with the same letter, **L1**. **L3** is both the third letter of the top horizontal word and the first letter of the second vertical word. To solve the puzzle, Prolog is asked:

?- **solution**( L1,L2,L3,L4,L5,L6,L7,L8,L9,L10,L11,L12,L13,L14,L15,L16).

The solution is conveyed by the values of variables **L1**, **L2**, . . . . The reader may try to find how many solutions the puzzle has.

## 1.8.2 Colouring a map

The problem of map colouring is: given a map with a number of countries, paint each country with one of the available colours, but avoid painting neighbouring countries with the same colour. It is known that four colours suffice to paint any map. Let these colours be red, blue, green and yellow. In the program in Figure 1.13, the problem is tackled as follows. The relation **n(Colour1,Colour2)** gives the possible pairs of colours of neighbouring countries. Any combination of two colours is fine as long the two colours are different, for example:

n( **red, green**).
n( **red, blue**).
n( **red, yellow**).
. . .

The program in Figure 1.13 can be used to colour the map of a part of Central Europe that covers ten countries (Italy, Slovenia, Austria, Croatia, etc.) and the

---

% Map colouring

% Possible pairs of colours of neighbour countries

| | | |
|---|---|---|
| n( red, green). | n( red, blue). | n( red, yellow). |
| n( green, red). | n( green, blue). | n( green, yellow). |
| n( blue, red). | n( blue, green). | n( blue, yellow). |
| n( yellow, red). | n( yellow, green). | n( yellow, blue). |

% Part of Europe (IT = Italy, SI = Slovenia, HR = Croatia,  CH = Switzerland, ...)

colours( IT, SI, HR, CH, AT, HU, DE, SK, CZ, PL, SEA) :-
    SEA = blue,                        % Adriatic Sea has to be coloured blue
    n( IT, CH), n( IT, AT), n( IT, SI), n( IT, SEA),   % Italy and Switzerland are neighbours, etc.
    n( SI, AT), n( SI, HR), n( SI, HU), n( SI, SEA),
    n( HR, HU), n( HR, SEA),
    n( AT, CH), n( AT, DE), n( AT, HU), n( AT, SK), n( AT, CZ),
    n( CH, DE),
    n( HU, SK),
    n( DE, SK), n( DE, CZ), n( DE, PL),
    n( SK, CZ), n( SK, PL),
    n( CZ, PL).

**Figure 1.13**  Colouring the map of part of Europe.

Adriatic Sea. In the program, for each country there is a variable which will be assigned a value – a suitable colour. For brevity, the names of these variables are chosen as the countries' e-mail codes. The program specifies the neighbouring relations among the countries and the sea in the map. This is done by requiring, for example, **n(IT,AT)**, which means that the neighbours Italy and Austria will be assigned different colours. The program will automatically, through Prolog's built-in backtracking, search among possible colourings of the countries and ensure to produce 'legal' colourings only. The program also states that the sea must always be blue. To colour this part of Europe, the question to Prolog is:

?- **colours( IT, SI, HR, CH, AT, HU, DE, SK, CZ, PL, SEA).**
**IT = red**
**SI = green**
. . .

This is, of course, just one possible solution, in which Italy is painted red, Slovenia green, etc.

## 1.8.3  Scheduling a meeting

Suppose we are in charge of organizing a large project meeting according to the following specifications. The meeting takes one day and is organized in three sessions, each of them devoted to a separate topic of the project: artificial intelligence, bioinformatics and databases. Each session takes half a day, the morning or the afternoon. Each session concerns a topic, and at least two participants of a session have to be experts in the session's topic. As long as we have ensured the participation of two experts on a session's topic, the other participants of the meeting are free to choose which sessions to attend. The problem is to assign times and experts to the three sessions. One question also is, would it be possible to shorten the duration of the whole meeting so that all three sessions are squeezed into the morning?

In the program shown in Figure 1.14, the predicate **schedule** generates schedules that satisfy the above constraints. The predicate has nine arguments that specify the complete schedule, that is for each of the three sessions: the time and the two experts on the session's topic. So, three arguments per each session which gives the total of nine arguments. Each triplet of these arguments has to satisfy the predicate **session** which relates the session's topic with the topic's experts. There must be no conflict between the sessions in terms of the experts: an expert cannot attend two sessions at the same time. A query to Prolog to produce a schedule is:

?- **schedule( Ta, A1, A2, Tb, B1, B2, Td, D1, D2).**

Is there an express meeting possible, lasting just half a day, with the same ambitions regarding the experts? In that case all the three sessions have to be at the same time T:

?- **schedule( T, A1, A2, T, B1, B2, T, D1, D2).**

Again, a comment on all the three programs of this section is in order. They were all rather easy exercises exploiting Prolog's automatic backtracking. On the other

```
% Scheduling a meeting

% schedule( TimeA, A1, A2, TimeB, B1, B2, TimeD, D1, D2):
%   TimeA and experts A1, A2 assigned to session on Artificial Intelligence,
%   TimeB, B1, B2 assigned to session on bioinformatics, and similar for databases

schedule( Ta, A1, A2, Tb, B1, B2, Td, D1, D2) :-
    session( Ta, artificial_intelligence, A1, A2),   % Session AI at time Ta, with experts A1 and A2
    session( Tb, bioinformatics, B1, B2),            % Bioinformatics at Tb, with experts B1, B2
    session( Td, databases, D1, D2),                 % Databases at Td, with experts D1 and D2
    no_conflict( Ta, A1, A2, Tb, B1, B2),            % No conflict between AI and Bioinfo
    no_conflict( Ta, A1, A2, Td, D1, D2),            % No conflict between Databases and AI
    no_conflict( Tb, B1, B2, Td, D1, D2).            % No conflict between Bioinfo and Databases

% session( Time, Topic, P1, P2):
%   session at Time on Topic attended by responsible experts P1, P2

session( Time, Topic, P1, P2) :-
    time( Time),                                     % Time is morning or afternoon
    expert( Topic, P1),                              % Person P1 is expert on Topic
    expert( Topic, P2),                              % P2 is also expert on Topic
    P1 \= P2.                                        % P1, P2 different persons

% no_conflict( Time1, P1, P2, Time2, Q1, Q2):
%   There is no time conflict between two sessions at Time1 and Time2
%   and experts P1, P2, and Q1, Q2, respectively

no_conflict( Time1, _, _, Time2, _, _) :-
    Time1 \= Time2.                                  % Two sessions at different times – not conflict

no_conflict( Time, P1, P2, Time, Q1, Q2) :-          % Two sessions at the same time
    P1 \= Q1,  P1 \= Q2,                             % No overlap between experts
    P2 \= Q1,  P2 \= Q2.

% Possible times of sessions

time( morning).        time( afternoon).

% Experts for topics

expert( bioinformatics, barbara).          expert( bioinformatics, ben).
expert( artificial_intelligence, adam).    expert( artificial_intelligence, ann).
expert( artificial_intelligence, barbara). expert( databases, adam).
expert( databases, danny).
```

**Figure 1.14** Scheduling a project meeting and assigning experts to sessions.

hand, they are rather wordy because at this time we are not yet able to use language constructs that will enable much shorter statements of the same ideas.

## Summary

- Prolog programming consists of defining relations and querying about relations.
- A program consists of *clauses*. These are of three types: *facts*, *rules* and *questions*.

- A relation can be specified by *facts*, simply stating the n-tuples of objects that satisfy the relation, or by stating *rules* about the relation.

- A *procedure* is a set of clauses about the same relation.

- Querying about relations, by means of *questions*, resembles querying a database. Prolog's answer to a question consists of a set of objects that satisfy the question.

- In Prolog, to establish whether an object satisfies a query is often a complicated process that involves logical inference, exploring among alternatives and possibly *backtracking*. All this is done automatically by the Prolog system and is, in principle, hidden from the user.

- Two types of meaning of Prolog programs are distinguished: declarative and procedural. The declarative view is advantageous from the programming point of view. Nevertheless, the procedural details often have to be considered by the programmer as well.

- The following concepts have been introduced in this chapter:

  clause, fact, rule, question
  the head of a clause, the body of a clause
  recursive rule, recursive definition
  procedure
  atom, variable
  instantiation of a variable
  goal
  goal is satisfiable, goal succeeds
  goal is unsatisfiable, goal fails
  backtracking
  declarative meaning, procedural meaning

# References

Various implementations of Prolog use different syntactic conventions. However, most of them follow the tradition of the so-called Edinburgh syntax (also called DEC-10 syntax, established by the historically influential implementation of Prolog for the DEC-10 computer; Pereira *et al.* 1978; Bowen 1981). The Edinburgh syntax also forms the basis of the ISO international standard for Prolog ISO/IEC 13211-1 (Deransart *et al.* 1996). Major Prolog implementations now largely comply with the standard. In this book we use a subset of the standard syntax, with some small and insignificant differences. In rare cases of such differences, there is a note to this effect at an appropriate place.

Bowen, D.L. (1981) *DECsystem-10 Prolog User's Manual*. University of Edinburgh: Department of Artificial Intelligence.

Deransart, P., Ed-Bdali, A. and Ceroni, L. (1996) *Prolog: The Standard*. Berlin: Springer-Verlag.

Pereira, L.M., Pereira, F. and Warren, D.H.D. (1978) *User's Guide to DECsystem-10 Prolog*. University of Edinburgh: Department of Artificial Intelligence.

# Chapter 2

# Syntax and Meaning of Prolog Programs

This chapter gives a systematic treatment of the syntax and semantics of basic concepts of Prolog, and introduces structured data objects. The topics included are:

- simple data objects (atoms, numbers, variables)
- structured objects
- matching – the fundamental operation on objects
- declarative (non-procedural) meaning of a program
- procedural meaning of a program
- relation between the declarative and procedural meanings of a program
- altering the procedural meaning by reordering clauses and goals.

Most of these topics have already been reviewed in Chapter 1. Here the treatment will become more detailed.

## 2.1 Data objects

Figure 2.1 shows the types of data objects in Prolog. The Prolog system recognizes the type of an object in the program by its syntactic form. This is possible because the syntax of Prolog specifies different forms for each type of data object. We have already seen a method for distinguishing between atoms and variables in Chapter 1: variables start with upper-case letters whereas atoms start with lower-case letters. No additional information (such as data-type declaration) has to be communicated to Prolog in order to recognize the type of an object.

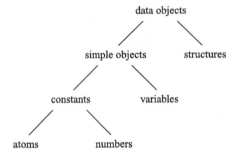

**Figure 2.1** Data objects in Prolog.

## 2.1.1 Atoms and numbers

In Chapter 1 we have seen some examples of atoms and variables. In general, however, atoms can take more complicated forms – that is, strings of the following characters:

- upper-case letters A, B, . . . , Z
- lower-case letters a, b, . . . , z
- digits 0, 1, 2, . . . , 9
- special characters such as $+ - * / < > = : . \& \_ \sim$

Atoms can be constructed in three ways:

(1) Strings of letters, digits and the underscore character, '_', starting with a lower-case letter:

> **anna**
> **nil**
> **x25**
> **x_25**
> **x_25AB**
> **x_**
> **x_ _ _y**
> **alpha_beta_procedure**
> **miss_Jones**

(2) Strings of special characters:

> **<- - ->**
> **= = = = = = >**
> **+**
> **. . .**
> **. : .**
> **: : =**

When using atoms of this form, some care is necessary because some strings of special characters already have a predefined meaning. An example is ':-'.

(3) Strings of characters enclosed in single quotes. This is useful if we want, for example, to have an atom that starts with a capital letter. By enclosing it in quotes we make it distinguishable from variables:

'Tom'
'South_America'
'Sarah Jones'

Numbers used in Prolog include integer numbers and real numbers. The syntax of integers is simple, as illustrated by the following examples:

1       1313      0      −97

Not all integer numbers can be represented in a computer, therefore the range of integers is limited to an interval between some smallest and some largest number permitted by a particular Prolog implementation.

The syntax of real numbers is as shown by the following examples:

3.14      −0.0035      100.2      7.15E-9

The last example uses the exponent notation and is equivalent to 0.00000000715. Some care is needed when using real numbers because of numerical errors that arise due to rounding when doing arithmetic. For example, the evaluation of the expression:

10000000000 + 0.0000001 − 10000000000

may result in 0 instead of the correct result 0.0000001.

## 2.1.2  Variables

Variables are strings of letters, digits and underscore characters. They start with an upper-case letter or an underscore character:

X
Result
Object2
Participant_list
ShoppingList
_A
_x23
_23

When a variable appears in a clause once only, we do not have to give it a name. We can use the so-called 'anonymous' variable, which is written as a single underscore character. For example, let us consider the following rule:

has_a_child( X) :- parent( X, Y).

This rule says: for all X, X has a child if X is a parent of some Y. We are defining the property **has_a_child** which does not depend on the name of the child. In such a case it is appropriate to use an anonymous variable. The clause above can thus be rewritten:

has_a_child( X) :- parent( X, _).

Each time a single underscore character occurs in a clause it represents a new anonymous variable. For example, we can define that an object is visible if it is seen by the camera at some *x-y* coordinates:

> visible( Object) :- see( Object,_, _).

This is equivalent to:

> visible( Object) :- see( Object, X, Y).

But this is, of course, quite different from:

> visible( Object) :- see( Object, X, X).

If an anonymous variable appears in a question then its value is not output when Prolog answers the question. If we are interested in people who have children, but not in the names of the children, then we can simply ask:

> ?- parent( X, _).

The *lexical scope* of variable names is one clause. This means that, for example, if the name X15 occurs in two clauses, then it signifies two different variables. But each occurrence of X15 within the same clause means the same variable. The situation is different for constants: the same atom always means the same object in any clause, throughout the whole program.

## 2.1.3  Structures

Structured objects (or simply *structures*) are objects that have several components. For example, the date can be viewed as a structure with three components: day, month, year. The components themselves can, in turn, be structures. Although composed of several components, structures are treated in the program as single objects. In order to combine the components into a single object we have to choose a *functor*. A suitable functor for our example is **date**. Then the date 1 May 2001 can be written as (see Figure 2.2):

> date( 1, may, 2001)

All the components in this example are constants (two integers and one atom).  Components can also be variables or other structures. Any day in May can be represented by the structure:

> date( Day, may, 2001)

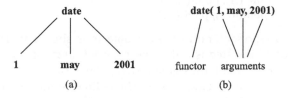

**Figure 2.2** Date is an example of a structured object: (a) as it is represented as a tree; (b) as it is written in Prolog.

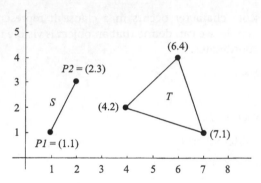

**Figure 2.3** Some simple geometric objects.

Note that **Day** is a variable and can be instantiated to any object at some later point in the execution.

This method for data structuring is simple and powerful. It is one of the reasons why Prolog is so naturally applied to problems that involve symbolic manipulation.

Syntactically, all data objects in Prolog are *terms*. For example,

  **may**

and

  **date( 1, may, 2001)**

are terms.

All structured objects can be pictured as trees (see Figure 2.2 for an example). The root of the tree is the functor, and the children of the root are the components. If a component is also a structure then it is a subtree of the tree that corresponds to the whole structured object. Our next example will show how structures can be used to represent some simple geometric objects (see Figure 2.3). A point in two-dimensional space is defined by its two coordinates; a line segment is defined by two points; and a triangle can be defined by three points. Let us choose the following functors:

|  |  |
|---|---|
| **point** | for points, |
| **seg** | for line segments, and |
| **triangle** | for triangles. |

Then the objects in Figure 2.3 can be represented as follows:

  P1 = **point(1,1)**
  P2 = **point(2,3)**
  S = **seg( P1, P2)** = **seg( point(1,1), point(2,3) )**
  T = **triangle( point(4,2), point(6,4), point(7,1) )**

The corresponding tree representation of these objects is shown in Figure 2.4. The functor at the root of the tree is called the *principal functor* of the term. So **seg** is the principal functor in the term **seg(point(1,1),point(2,3))**.

If in the same program we also had points in three-dimensional space then we could use another functor, **point3**, say, for their representation:

  **point3( X, Y, Z)**

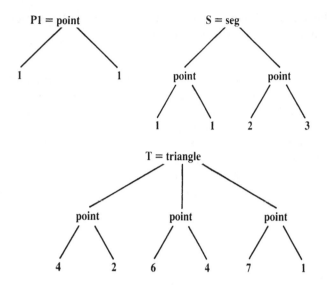

Figure 2.4 Tree representation of the objects in Figure 2.3.

We can, however, use the same name, **point**, for points in both two and three dimensions, and write for example:

  **point( X1, Y1)**    and    **point( X, Y, Z)**

If the same name appears in the program in two different roles, as is the case for point above, the Prolog system will recognize the difference by the number of arguments, and will interpret this name as two functors: one of them with two arguments and the other one with three arguments. This is so because each functor is defined by two things:

(1) the name, whose syntax is that of atoms;

(2) the *arity* – that is, the number of arguments.

    As already explained, all structured objects in Prolog are trees, represented in the program by terms. We will study two more examples to illustrate how naturally complicated data objects can be represented by Prolog terms. Figure 2.5 shows the tree structure that corresponds to the arithmetic expression:

  $(a + b) * (c - 5)$

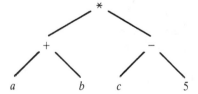

Figure 2.5 A tree structure that corresponds to the arithmetic expression $(a + b) *$ $(c - 5)$.

According to the syntax of terms introduced so far this can be written, using the symbols '*', '+' and '−' as functors, as follows:

    *( +(a, b), − ( c, 5) )

This is, of course, a legal Prolog term, but it is not in the form that we would normally use. We would normally prefer the usual infix notation as used in mathematics. In fact, Prolog also allows us to use the infix notation so that the symbols '*', '+' and '−' are written as infix operators. Details of how the programmer can define his or her own operators will be discussed in Chapter 3.

As the last example we consider some simple electric circuits shown in Figure 2.6. The right-hand side of the figure shows the tree representation of these circuits. The atoms **r1**, **r2**, **r3** and **r4** are the names of the resistors. The functors

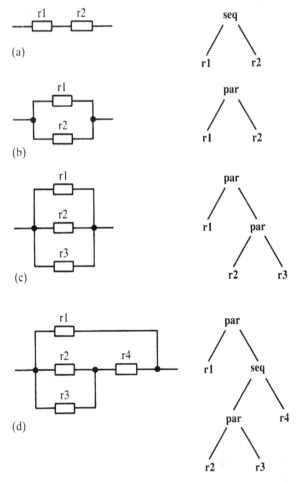

**Figure 2.6** Some simple electric circuits and their tree representations: (a) sequential composition of resistors r1 and r2; (b) parallel composition of two resistors; (c) parallel composition of three resistors; (d) parallel composition of r1 and another circuit.

**par** and **seq** denote the parallel and the sequential compositions of resistors respectively. The corresponding Prolog terms are:

seq( r1, r2)
par( r1, r2)
par( r1, par( r2, r3) )
par( r1, seq( par( r2, r3), r4) )

We can in principle construct a circuit of any complexity. For example, a sequential circuit consisting of 10 resistors is represented by:

seq( r1, seq( r2, seq( r3, seq( r4, seq( r5, seq( r6, seq( r7, seq( r8, seq( r9, r10)))))))))

## EXERCISES

**2.1** Which of the following are syntactically correct Prolog objects? What kinds of object are they (atom, number, variable, structure)?

(a)  Diana

(b)  diana

(c)  'Diana'

(d)  _diana

(e)  'Diana goes south'

(f)  goes( diana, south)

(g)  45

(h)  5( X, Y)

(i)  +( north, west)

(j)  three( Black( Cats) )

**2.2** Suggest a representation for rectangles, squares and circles as structured Prolog objects. Use an approach similar to that in Figure 2.4. For example, a rectangle can be represented by four points (or maybe three points only). Write some example terms that represent some concrete objects of these types using the suggested representation.

## 2.2 Matching

In the previous section we have seen how terms can be used to represent complex data objects. The most important operation on terms is *matching*. Matching alone can produce some interesting computation.

Given two terms, we say that they *match* if:

(1)  they are identical, or

(2)  the variables in both terms can be instantiated to objects in such a way that after the substitution of variables by these objects the terms become identical.

For example, the terms date( D, M, 2001) and date( D1, may, Y1) match. One instantiation that makes both terms identical is:

- D is instantiated to D1
- M is instantiated to may
- Y1 is instantiated to 2001

This instantiation is more compactly written in the familiar form in which Prolog outputs results:

D = D1
M = may
Y1 = 2001

On the other hand, the terms date( D, M, 2001) and date( D1, M1, 1444) do not match because the third arguments 2001 and 1444 do not match. The terms date( X, Y, Z) and point( X, Y, Z) do not match because their functors date and point are different.

   *Matching* is a process that takes as input two terms and checks whether they match. If the terms do not match we say that matching *fails*. If they do match then matching *succeeds* and it also instantiates the variables in both terms to such values that the terms become identical.

   Let us consider again the matching of the two dates. The request for this operation can be communicated to the Prolog system by the following question, using the operator '=':

   ?- date( D, M, 2001) = date( D1, may, Y1).

We have already mentioned the instantiation D = D1, M = may, Y1 = 2001, which achieves the match. There are, however, other instantiations that also make both terms identical. Two of them are as follows:

D = 1
D1 = 1
M = may
Y1 = 2001

D = third
D1 = third
M = may
Y1 = 2001

These two instantiations are said to be *less general* than the first one because they constrain the values of the variables D and D1 stronger than necessary. For making both terms in our example identical, it is only important that D and D1 have the same value, although this value can be anything. Matching in Prolog always results in the *most general* instantiation. This is the instantiation that commits the variables to the least possible extent, thus leaving the greatest possible freedom for further instantiations if further matching is required. As an example consider the following question:

?- date( D, M, 2001) = date( D1, may, Y1),
    date( D, M, 2001) = date( 15, M, Y).

To satisfy the first goal, Prolog instantiates the variables as follows:

D = D1
M = may
Y1 = 2001

After having satisfied the second goal, the instantiation becomes more specific as follows:

D = 15
D1 = 15
M = may
Y1 = 2001
Y = 2001

This example also shows that variables, during the execution of consecutive goals, typically become instantiated to increasingly more specific values.

The general rules to decide whether two terms, S and T, match are as follows:

(1) If S and T are constants then S and T match only if they are the same object.

(2) If S is a variable and T is anything, then they match, and S is instantiated to T. Conversely, if T is a variable then T is instantiated to S.

(3) If S and T are structures then they match only if

(a) S and T have the same principal functor, and

(b) all their corresponding components match.

The resulting instantiation is determined by the matching of the components.

The last of these rules can be visualized by considering the tree representation of terms, as in the example of Figure 2.7. The matching process starts at the root (the principal functors). As both functors match, the process proceeds to the arguments where the pairs of corresponding arguments are matched. So the whole matching process can be thought of as consisting of the following sequence of (simpler) matching operations:

triangle = triangle,
point(1,1) = X,
A = point(4,Y),
point(2,3) = point(2,Z).

The whole matching process succeeds because all the matchings in the sequence succeed. The resulting instantiation is:

X = point(1,1)
A = point(4,Y)
Z = 3

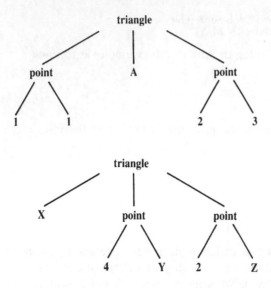

**Figure 2.7** Matching **triangle( point(1,1), A, point(2,3) ) = triangle( X, point(4,Y), point(2,Z) )**

The following example will illustrate how matching alone can be used for interesting computation. Let us return to the simple geometric objects of Figure 2.4, and define a piece of program for recognizing horizontal and vertical line segments. 'Vertical' is a property of segments, so it can be formalized in Prolog as a unary relation. Figure 2.8 helps to formulate this relation. A segment is vertical if the x-coordinates of its end-points are equal, otherwise there is no other restriction on the segment. The property 'horizontal' is similarly formulated, with

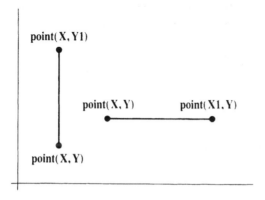

**Figure 2.8** Illustration of vertical and horizontal line segments.

only x and y interchanged. The following program, consisting of two facts, does the job:

vertical( seg( point(X1,Y1), point(X1,Y2) ) ).
horizontal( seg( point(X1,Y1), point(X2,Y1) ) ).

The following conversation is possible with this program:

?- vertical( seg( point(1,1), point(1,2) ) ).
yes
?- vertical( seg( point(1,1), point(2,Y) ) ).
no
?- horizontal( seg( point(1,1), point(2,Y) ) ).
Y = 1

The first question was answered 'yes' because the goal in the question matched one of the facts in the program. For the second question no match was possible. In the third question, Y was forced to become 1 by matching the fact about horizontal segments.

A more general question to the program is: Are there any vertical segments that start at the point (2,3)?

?- vertical( seg( point(2,3), P) ).
P = point(2,Y)

This answer means: Yes, any segment that ends at any point (2,Y), which means anywhere on the vertical line x = 2. It should be noted that Prolog's actual answer would probably not look as neat as above, but (depending on the Prolog implementation used) something like this:

P = point(2,_136)

This is, however, only a cosmetic difference. Here _136 is a variable that has not been instantiated. _136 is a legal variable name that the system has constructed during the execution. The system has to generate new names in order to rename the user's variables in the program. This is necessary for two reasons: first, because the same name in different clauses signifies different variables, and second, in successive applications of the same clause, its 'copy' with a new set of variables is used each time.

Another interesting question to our program is: Is there a segment that is both vertical and horizontal?

?- vertical( S), horizontal( S).
S = seg( point(X,Y), point(X,Y) )

This answer says: Yes, any segment that is degenerated to a point has the property of being vertical and horizontal at the same time. The answer was, again, derived simply by matching. As before, some internally generated names may appear in the answer, instead of the variable names X and Y.

## EXERCISES

**2.3** Will the following matching operations succeed or fail? If they succeed, what are the resulting instantiations of variables?

(a) **point( A, B) = point( 1, 2)**

(b) **point( A, B) = point( X, Y, Z)**

(c) **plus( 2, 2) = 4**

(d) **+(2, D) = +(E, 2)**

(e) **triangle( point(–1,0), P2, P3) = triangle( P1, point(1,0), point(0,Y) )**

The resulting instantiation defines a family of triangles. How would you describe this family?

**2.4** Using the representation for line segments as described in this section, write a term that represents any vertical line segment at $x = 5$.

**2.5** Assume that a rectangle is represented by the term **rectangle( P1, P2, P3, P4)** where the P's are the vertices of the rectangle positively ordered. Define the relation:

   **regular( R)**

which is true if R is a rectangle whose sides are vertical and horizontal.

## 2.3 Declarative meaning of Prolog programs

We have already seen in Chapter 1 that Prolog programs can be understood in two ways: declaratively and procedurally. In this and the next section we will consider a more formal definition of the declarative and procedural meanings of programs in basic Prolog. But first let us look at the difference between these two meanings again.

Consider a clause:

   **P :- Q, R.**

where P, Q and R have the syntax of terms. Some alternative declarative readings of this clause are:

   P is true if Q and R are true.
   From Q and R follows P.

Two alternative procedural readings of this clause are:

   To solve problem P, *first* solve the subproblem Q and *then* the subproblem R.
   To satisfy P, *first* satisfy Q and *then* R.

The difference between the declarative readings and the procedural ones is that the latter do not only define the logical relations between the head of the clause and the goals in the body, but also the *order* in which the goals are processed.
   Let us now formalize the declarative meaning.

The declarative meaning of programs determines whether a given goal is true, and if so, for what values of variables it is true. To precisely define the declarative meaning we need to introduce the concept of *instance* of a clause. An instance of a clause C is the clause C with each of its variables substituted by some term. A *variant* of a clause C is such an instance of the clause C where each variable is substituted by another variable. For example, consider the clause:

ancestor( X, Y) :- parent( X, Y).

Two variants of this clause are:

ancestor( A, B) :- parent( A, B).
ancestor( X1, X2) :- parent( X1, X2).

Instances of this clause are:

ancestor( peter, Z) :- parent( peter, Z).
ancestor( peter, barry) :- parent( peter, barry ).

Given a program and a goal G, the declarative meaning says:

> A goal G is true (that is, satisfiable, or logically follows from the program) if and only if:
>
> (1)  there is a clause C in the program such that
> (2)  there is a clause instance I of C such that
>> (a)  the head of I is identical to G, and
>> (b)  all the goals in the body of I are true.

This definition extends to Prolog questions as follows. In general, a question to the Prolog system is a *list* of goals separated by commas. A list of goals is true if *all* the goals in the list are true for the *same* instantiation of variables. The values of the variables result from the most general instantiation.

A comma between goals thus denotes the *conjunction* of goals: they *all* have to be true. But Prolog also accepts the *disjunction* of goals: *any one* of the goals in a disjunction has to be true. Disjunction is indicated by a semicolon. For example,

P :- Q; R.

is read: P is true if Q is true *or* R is true. The meaning of this clause is thus the same as the meaning of the following two clauses together:

P :- Q.
P :- R.

The comma binds stronger than the semicolon. So the clause:

P :- Q, R; S, T, U.

is understood as:

P :- ( Q, R); ( S, T, U).

and means the same as the clauses:

P :- Q, R.
P :- S, T, U.

The intended nesting of conjunctions and disjunctions can always be explicitly stated by parentheses.

## EXERCISES

**2.6** Consider the following program:

f( 1, one).
f( s(1), two).
f( s(s(1)), three).
f( s(s(s(X))), N) :-
    f( X, N).

How will Prolog answer the following questions? Whenever several answers are possible, give at least two.

(a)  ?- f( s(1), A).

(b)  ?- f( s(s(1)), two).

(c)  ?- f( s(s(s(s(s(s(1)))))), C).

(d)  ?- f( D, three),

**2.7** The following program says that two people are relatives if

(a)  one is an ancestor of the other, or

(b)  they have a common ancestor, or

(c)  they have a common successor:

relatives( X, Y) :-
    ancestor( X, Y).

relatives( X, Y) :-
    ancestor( Y, X).

relatives( X, Y) :-        % X and Y have a common ancestor
    ancestor( Z, X),
    ancestor( Z, Y).

relatives( X, Y) :-        % X and Y have a common successor
    ancestor( X, Z),
    ancestor( Y, Z).

Can you shorten this program by using the semicolon notation?

**2.8** Rewrite the following program without using the semicolon notation.

translate( Number, Word) :-
    Number = 1, Word = one;
    Number = 2, Word = two;
    Number = 3, Word = three.

# 2.4  Procedural meaning

The procedural meaning specifies *how* Prolog answers questions. To answer a question means to try to satisfy a list of goals. Thus the procedural meaning of Prolog is a procedure for executing a list of goals with respect to a given program. To 'execute goals' means: try to satisfy them.

Let us call this procedure **execute**. As shown in Figure 2.9, the inputs to and the outputs from this procedure are:

input: a program and a goal list
output: a success/failure indicator and an instantiation of variables

The meaning of the two output results is as follows:

(1) The success/failure indicator is 'yes' if the goals are satisfiable and 'no' otherwise. We say that 'yes' signals a *successful* termination and 'no' a *failure*.

(2) An instantiation of variables is only produced in the case of a successful termination; in the case of failure there is no instantiation.

In Chapter 1, we have already discussed informally what procedure **execute** does, under the heading 'How Prolog answers questions'. What follows in the rest of this section is just a more formal and systematic description of this process, and can be skipped without seriously affecting the understanding of the rest of the book.

Particular operations in the goal execution process are illustrated by the example in Figure 2.10. It may be helpful to study Figure 2.10 before reading the following general description.

To execute a list of goals:

$$G_1, G_2, \ldots, G_m$$

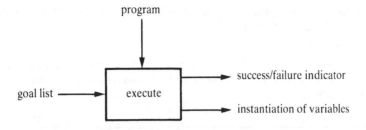

**Figure 2.9** Input/output view of the procedure that executes a list of goals.

```
PROGRAM
big( bear).                          % Clause 1
big( elephant).                      % Clause 2
small( cat).                         % Clause 3
brown( bear).                        % Clause 4
black( cat).                         % Clause 5
gray( elephant).                     % Clause 6

dark( Z) :-                          % Clause 7: Anything black is dark
   black( Z).

dark( Z) :-                          % Clause 8: Anything brown is dark
   brown( Z).

QUESTION
?- dark( X), big( X).                % Who is dark and big?
```

EXECUTION TRACE

(1) Initial goal list: **dark( X), big( X)**.

(2) Scan the program from top to bottom looking for a clause whose head matches the first goal **dark( X)**. Clause 7 found:

    **dark( Z) :- black( Z)**.

Replace the first goal by the instantiated body of clause 7, giving a new goal list:

    **black( X), big( X)**

(3) Scan the program to find a match with **black( X)**. Clause 5 found: **black( cat)**. This clause has no body, so the goal list, properly instantiated, shrinks to:

    **big( cat)**

(4) Scan the program for the goal **big( cat)**. No clause found. Therefore backtrack to step (3) and undo the instantiation X = **cat**. Now the goal list is again:

    **black( X), big( X)**

Continue scanning the program below clause 5. No clause found. Therefore backtrack to step (2) and continue scanning below clause 7. Clause 8 is found:

    **dark( Z) :- brown( Z)**.

Replace the first goal in the goal list by **brown( X)**, giving:

    **brown( X), big( X)**

(5) Scan the program to match **brown( X)**, finding **brown( bear)**. This clause has no body, so the goal list shrinks to:

    **big( bear)**

(6) Scan the program and find clause **big( bear)**. It has no body so the goal list shrinks to empty. This indicates successful termination, and the corresponding variable instantiation is:

    X = **bear**

**Figure 2.10** An example to illustrate the procedural meaning of Prolog: a sample trace of the procedure **execute**

the procedure **execute** does the following:

- If the goal list is empty then terminate with *success*.
- If the goal list is not empty then continue with (the following) operation called 'SCANNING'.

- SCANNING: Scan through the clauses in the program from top to bottom until the first clause, C, is found such that the head of C matches the first goal $G_1$. If there is no such clause then terminate with *failure*.

  If there is such a clause C of the form

  $\quad$ H :- $B_1$, . . . , $B_n$.

  then rename the variables in C to obtain a variant C' of C, such that C' and the list $G_1$, . . . , $G_m$ have no common variables. Let C' be

  $\quad$ H' :- $B_1'$, . . . , $B_n'$.

  Match $G_1$ and H'; let the resulting instantiation of variables be S.

  In the goal list $G_1$, $G_2$, . . . , $G_m$, replace $G_1$ with the list $B_1'$, . . . , $B_n'$, obtaining a new goal list

  $\quad$ $B_1'$, . . . , $B_n'$, $G_2$, . . . , $G_m$

  (Note that if C is a fact then $n = 0$ and the new goal list is shorter than the original one; such shrinking of the goal list may eventually lead to the empty list and thereby a successful termination.)

  Substitute the variables in this new goal list with new values as specified in the instantiation S, obtaining the goal list

  $\quad$ $B_1''$ , . . . , $B_n''$, $G_2'$, . . . , $G_m'$

- Execute (recursively with this same procedure) this new goal list. If the execution of this new goal list terminates with success then terminate the execution of the original goal list also with success. If the execution of the new goal list is not successful then abandon this new goal list and go back to SCANNING through the program. Continue the scanning with the clause that immediately follows the clause C (C is the clause that was last used) and try to find a successful termination using some other clause.

This procedure is written in an algorithmic notation in Figure 2.11.

When a given question has several answers, in which order are they generated by Prolog? In practice, it is often useful to know this order. The procedural meaning of Prolog determines the order. Consider the list of goals $G_1$, $G_2$ where both $G_1$ and $G_2$ have several solutions. A solution of the whole goal list is a pair: (a solution of $G_1$, a solution of $G_2$). The order in which these pairs are generated through backtracking is:

$\quad$ (1st solution of $G_1$, 1st solution of $G_2$)
$\quad$ (1st solution of $G_1$, 2nd solution of $G_2$)
$\quad$ . . .
$\quad$ (1st solution of $G_1$, last solution of $G_2$)
$\quad$ (2nd solution of $G_1$, 1st solution of $G_2$)
$\quad$ . . .
$\quad$ (last solution of $G_1$, last solution of $G_2$)

Concretely, here is a program that defines that beef, chicken and fish are kinds of meat, and red, rose and white are kinds of wine:

```
meat( beef).      meat( chicken).      meat( fish).
wine( red).       wine( rose).         wine( white).
```

**procedure** *execute (Program, GoalList, Success)*;

Input arguments:
  *Program*: list of clauses
  *GoalList*: list of goals
Output argument:
  *Success*: truth value; *Success* will become true if *GoalList* is true with respect to *Program*
Local variables:
  *Goal*: goal
  *OtherGoals*: list of goals
  *Satisfied*: truth value
  *MatchOK*: truth value
  *Instant*: instantiation of variables
  $H, H', B1, B1', \ldots, Bn, Bn'$: goals
Auxiliary functions:
  *empty(L)*: returns true if *L* is the empty list
  *head(L)*: returns the first element of list *L*
  *tail(L)*: returns the rest of *L*
  *append(L1,L2)*: appends list *L2* at the end of list *L1*
  *match(T1,T2,MatchOK,Instant)*: tries to match terms *T1* and *T2*; if succeeds
    then *MatchOK* is true and *Instant* is the corresponding instantiation of variables
  *substitute(Instant, Goals)*: substitutes variables in *Goals* according to instantiation *Instant*

**begin**
  **if** *empty*(*GoalList*) **then** *Success* := *true*
  **else**
    **begin**
      *Goal* := *head*(*GoalList*);
      *OtherGoals* := *tail*(*GoalList*);
      *Satisfied* := *false*;
      **while not** *Satisfied* **and** "*more clauses in program*" **do**
        **begin**
          *Let next clause in Program be*
            $H :\text{-} B1, \ldots, Bn.$
          *Construct a variant of this clause*
            $H' :\text{-} B1', \ldots, Bn'.$
          *match*(*Goal*,*H'*,*MatchOK*,*Instant*);
          **if** *MatchOK* **then**
            **begin**
              *NewGoals* := *append*([*B1'*, . . . ,*Bn'*], *OtherGoals*);
              *NewGoals* := *substitute*(*Instant*,*NewGoals*);
              *execute*(*Program*,*NewGoals*,*Satisfied*)
            **end**
        **end**;
      *Success* := *Satisfied*
    **end**
**end**;

**Figure 2.11** Executing Prolog goals.

Now we generate through backtracking all the combinations of meat M and wine W:

?- meat( M), wine( W).
M = beef,  W = red;
M = beef,  W = rose;
M = beef,  W = white;
M = chicken,  W = red;
M = chicken,  W = rose;
...
M = fish,  W = white;
no

Several additional remarks are in order here regarding the procedure **execute** as presented. First, it was not explicitly described how the final resulting instantiation of variables is produced. It is the instantiation S which led to a successful termination, and was possibly further refined by additional instantiations that were done in the nested recursive calls to **execute**.

Whenever a recursive call to **execute** fails, the execution returns to SCANNING, continuing at the program clause C that had been last used before. As the application of the clause C did not lead to a successful termination Prolog has to try an alternative clause to proceed. What effectively happens is that Prolog abandons this whole part of the unsuccessful execution and backtracks to the point (clause C) where this failed branch of the execution was started. When the procedure backtracks to a certain point, all the variable instantiations that were done after that point are undone. This ensures that Prolog systematically examines all the possible alternative paths of execution until one is found that eventually succeeds, or until all of them have been shown to fail.

We have already seen that even after a successful termination the user can force the system to backtrack to search for more solutions. In our description of **execute** this detail was left out.

Of course, in actual implementations of Prolog, several other refinements have to be added to **execute**. One of them is to reduce the amount of scanning through the program clauses to improve efficiency. So a practical Prolog implementation will not scan through all the clauses of the program, but will only consider the clauses about the relation in the current goal.

# EXERCISE

**2.9** Consider the program in Figure 2.10 and simulate, in the style of Figure 2.10, Prolog's execution of the question:

?- big( X), dark( X).

Compare your execution trace with that of Figure 2.10 when the question was essentially the same, but with the goals in the order:

?- dark( X), big( X).

In which of the two cases Prolog does more work before the answer is found?

## 2.5 Order of clauses and goals

### 2.5.1 Danger of indefinite looping

Consider the following clause:

p :- p.

This says that 'p is true if p is true'. This is declaratively perfectly correct, but procedurally is quite useless. In fact, such a clause can cause problems to Prolog. Consider the question:

?- p.

Using the clause above, the goal **p** is replaced by the same goal **p**; this will be in turn replaced by p, etc. In such a case Prolog will enter an infinite loop not noticing that no progress is being made.

This example is a simple way of getting Prolog to loop indefinitely. However, similar looping could have occurred in some of our previous example programs if we changed the order of clauses, or the order of goals in the clauses. In such cases Prolog tries to solve a problem in such a way that a solution is never reached, although a solution exists. Such situations are not unusual in Prolog programming. Infinite loops are, also, not unusual in other programming languages. What *is* unusual in Prolog, in comparison with other languages, is that a Prolog program may be declaratively correct, but at the same time be procedurally incorrect in that it is not able to produce an answer to a question although the answer exists. This may happen because Prolog tries to reach an answer by choosing a wrong path. And if we are unlucky, this path may be infinite.

We can usually prevent looping by reordering goals and clauses in the program. There are several other methods that preclude infinite loops, and these are more general and robust than the reordering method. These techniques will be used regularly later in the book, especially in those chapters that deal with path finding, problem solving and search. But for now, it will be instructive to consider some examples of how the order of goals and clauses affects procedural meaning.

### 2.5.2 Program variations through reordering of clauses and goals

In the family example programs of Chapter 1, there was a latent danger of producing a cycling behaviour. Our program to specify the **ancestor** relation in Chapter 1 was:

```
ancestor( Parent, Child) :-
    parent( Parent, Child).

ancestor( Ancestor, Successor) :-
    parent( Ancestor, Child),
    ancestor( Child, Successor).
```

Let us analyse some variations of this program. All the variations will clearly have the same declarative meaning, but not the same procedural meaning. According to the declarative semantics of Prolog we can, without affecting the declarative meaning, change:

(1)  the order of clauses in the program, and

(2)  the order of goals in the bodies of clauses.

The **ancestor** procedure consists of two clauses, and one of them has two goals in the body. There are, therefore, four variations of this program, all with the same declarative meaning. The four variations are obtained by:

(1)  swapping both clauses, and

(2)  swapping the goals for each order of clauses.

The corresponding four procedures, called **anc1**, **anc2**, **anc3** and **anc4**, are shown in Figure 2.12.

There are important differences in the behaviour of these four declaratively equivalent procedures. To demonstrate these differences, consider the parent relation as shown in Figure 1.1 of Chapter 1. Now, what happens if we ask whether Tom is an ancestor of Pat using the four variations of the ancestor relation:

```
% Four versions of the ancestor program

% The original version
anc1( X, Z) :-
    parent( X, Z).

anc1( X, Z) :-
    parent( X, Y),
    anc1( Y, Z).

% Variation 1: swap clauses of the original version
anc2( X, Z) :-
    parent( X, Y),
    anc2( Y, Z).

anc2( X, Z) :-
    parent( X, Z).

% Variation 2: swap goals in second clause of the original version
anc3( X, Z) :-
    parent( X, Z).

anc3( X, Z) :-
    anc3( X, Y),
    parent( Y, Z).

% Variation 3: swap goals and clauses of the original version
anc4( X, Z) :-
    anc4( X, Y),
    parent( Y, Z).

anc4( X, Z) :-
    parent( X, Z).
```

**Figure 2.12** Four versions of the ancestor program.

```
?- anc1( tom, pat).
yes
?- anc2( tom, pat).
yes
?- anc3( tom, pat).
yes
?- anc4( tom, pat).
```

In the last case Prolog cannot find the answer. This is manifested on the display by a Prolog's message such as 'Insufficient memory' or 'Stack overflow'.

Figure 1.9 in Chapter 1 showed the trace of **anc1** (in Chapter 1 called **ancestor**) produced by the above question. Figures 2.13–15 show the corresponding traces

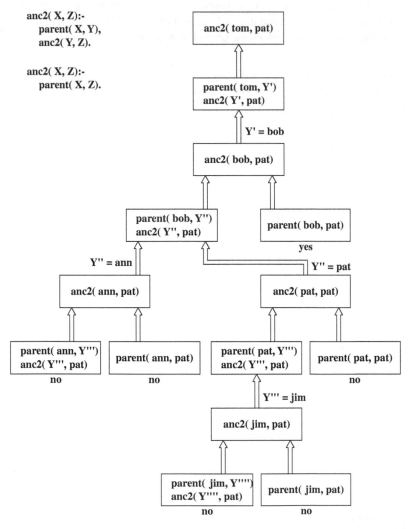

**Figure 2.13** The complete execution trace to satisfy the goal **anc2( tom, pat)**. All the alternative paths in the large left subtree fail, before the right-most path succeeds.

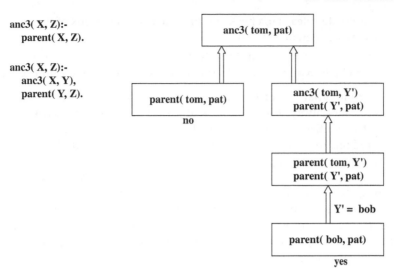

**anc3( X, Z):-**
    **parent( X, Z).**

**anc3( X, Z):-**
    **anc3( X, Y),**
    **parent( Y, Z).**

**Figure 2.14** The execution trace to satisfy the goal **anc3( tom, pat)**.

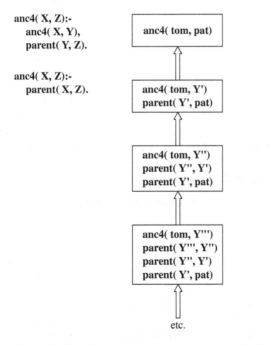

**anc4( X, Z):-**
    **anc4( X, Y),**
    **parent( Y, Z).**

**anc4( X, Z):-**
    **parent( X, Z).**

**Figure 2.15** Infinite execution trace to satisfy the goal **anc4( tom, pat)**.

for **anc2, anc3** and **anc4**. Figure 2.15 clearly shows that **anc4** is hopeless, and Figure 2.13 indicates that **anc2** is rather inefficient compared to **anc1**: **anc2** does much more searching and backtracking in the family tree.

This comparison reminds us of a general practical heuristic in problem solving: it is usually best to try the simplest idea first. In our case, all the versions of the ancestor relation are based on two ideas:

(1) the simpler idea is to check whether the two arguments of the **ancestor** relation satisfy the **parent** relation;

(2) the more complicated idea is to find somebody 'between' both people (somebody who is related to them by the **parent** and **ancestor** relations).

Of the four variations of the ancestor relation, **anc1** does simplest things first. In contrast, **anc4** always tries complicated things first. **anc2** and **anc3** are between the two extremes. Even without a detailed study of the execution traces, **anc1** should be preferred merely on the grounds of the rule 'try simple things first'. This is a general useful principle in programming.

Our four variations of the ancestor predicate can be further compared by considering the question: What types of questions can particular variations answer, and what types can they not answer? It turns out that **anc1** and **anc2** are both able to reach an answer for any type of question about ancestors; **anc4** can never reach an answer; and **anc3** sometimes can and sometimes cannot. One example in which **anc3** fails is:

?- anc3( liz, jim).

This question again brings the system into an infinite sequence of recursive calls. Thus **anc3** also cannot be considered procedurally correct.

## EXERCISE

**2.10**  Prolog implementations usually provide debugging facilities that enable the interactive tracing of the execution of goals. Such tracing gives similar insights as our diagrammatic traces in Figures 1.9 and 2.13–15. A typical use of the Prolog trace facility is as follows. Assume that you have already started your Prolog system and consulted the files with the parent relation and the versions of the ancestor relation in Figure 2.12. The interaction with  Prolog to trace the execution of the goal **anc1( tom,pat)** will look something like this (with explanatory comments added):

```
?- trace.                          % This command puts Prolog into the trace mode
yes
?- anc1( tom, pat).
    1   1 Call: anc1( tom,pat) ?    % Prolog says it started to execute anc1(...)
                                    % Now Prolog stops, user may press "enter" key
    2   2 Call: parent( tom,pat) ?  % Prolog started to execute subgoal parent(...)
                                    % User presses ''enter'' again
    2   2 Fail: parent( tom,pat) ?  % Prolog says that this subgoal has failed
    3   2 Call: parent( tom,_1035) ? % Prolog now tries 2nd clause of anc1
    3   2 Exit: parent( tom,bob) ?  % parent( tom,bob) succeeded
    4   2 Call: anc1( bob,pat) ?
    5   3 Call: parent( bob,pat) ?
    5   3 Exit: parent( bob,pat) ?
    4   2 Exit: anc1( bob,pat) ?
    1   1 Exit: anc1( tom,pat) ?    % anc1( tom,pat) succeeded
yes
```

The left column shows the consecutive numbers of the goals tried, and the numbers in the next column are the levels of 'calling' the goals (i.e. number of clause applications before a goal is reached). Compare this Prolog trace with the diagram of Figure 1.9 and find the correspondences. Trace with Prolog the goals **anc2( tom,pat)**, **anc3( tom,pat)** and **anc4( tom,pat)**. Compare these Prolog traces with Figures 2.13–15.

### 2.5.3   Combining declarative and procedural views

The foregoing section has shown that the order of goals and clauses does matter. Furthermore, there are programs that are declaratively correct, but do not work in practice. Such discrepancies between the declarative and procedural meaning may appear annoying. One may argue: Why not simply forget about the declarative meaning? This argument can be brought to an extreme with a clause such as:

    **ancestor( X, Z) :- ancestor( X, Z).**

which is declaratively correct, but is completely useless as a working program.

The reason why declarative thinking about programs should nevertheless be encouraged is that declarative descriptions are normally easier to formulate and understand than procedural descriptions. Progress in programming technology is often achieved by moving away from procedural details toward declarative views. The system itself, not the programmer, should carry the burden of filling in the procedural details. Prolog does help toward this end, although, as we have seen in this section, it only helps partially: often it does work out the procedural details itself adequately, and sometimes it does not. The philosophy adopted by many is that it is better to have at least *some* declarative meaning rather than *none* ('none' is the case in most other programming languages). The practical side of this view is that it is usually rather easy to get a working program once we have a program that is declaratively correct. Consequently, a useful practical approach that usually works is to concentrate on the declarative aspects of the problem, then test the resulting program, and if it fails procedurally try to rearrange the clauses and goals into a suitable order.

## 2.6  The relation between Prolog and logic

Prolog is related to mathematical logic, so its syntax and meaning can be specified most concisely with references to logic. Prolog is indeed often defined that way. However, such an introduction to Prolog assumes that the reader is familiar with certain concepts of mathematical logic. These concepts are, on the other hand, certainly not necessary for understanding and using Prolog as a programming tool, which is the aim of this book. For the reader who is especially interested in the relation between Prolog and logic, the following are some basic links to mathematical logic, together with some appropriate references.

Prolog's syntax is that of the *first-order predicate logic* formulas written in the so-called *clause form* (a conjunctive normal form in which quantifiers are not explicitly written), and further restricted to Horn clauses only (clauses that have at most one positive literal). Clocksin and Mellish (1987) give a Prolog program that transforms a first-order predicate calculus formula into the clause form. The procedural meaning of Prolog is based on the *resolution principle* for mechanical theorem proving introduced by Robinson in his classic paper (1965). Prolog uses a special strategy for resolution theorem proving called SLD. An introduction to the first-order predicate calculus and resolution-based theorem proving can be found in several general books on artificial intelligence (Genesereth and Nilsson 1987; Ginsberg 1993; Poole *et al*. 1998; Russell and Norvig 2010; see also Flach 1994). Mathematical questions regarding the properties of Prolog's procedural meaning with respect to logic are analysed by Lloyd (1991).

Matching in Prolog corresponds to what is called *unification* in logic. However, we avoid the word unification because matching, for efficiency reasons in most Prolog systems, is implemented in a way that does not exactly correspond to unification (see Exercise 2.11). But from the practical point of view this approximation to unification is quite adequate. Proper unification requires the so-called *occurs check*: does a given variable occur in a given term? The occurs check would make matching inefficient.

# EXERCISE

**2.11**   What happens if we ask Prolog:

?- X = f( X).

Should this request for matching succeed or fail? According to the definition of unification in logic this should fail, but what happens according to our definition of matching in Section 2.2? Try to explain why many Prolog implementations answer the question above with:

X = f(f(f(f(f(f(f(f(f(f(f(f(f( . . .

# Summary

So far we have covered a kind of basic Prolog, also called 'pure Prolog'. It is 'pure' because it corresponds closely to formal logic. Extensions whose aim is to tailor the language toward some practical needs will be covered later in the book (Chapters 3, 5, 6). Important points of this chapter are:

*   Simple objects in Prolog are *atoms, variables* and *numbers*. Structured objects, or *structures*, are used to represent objects that have several components.

*   Structures are constructed by means of *functors*. Each functor is defined by its name and arity.

*   The type of object is recognized entirely by its syntactic form.

*   The *lexical* scope of variables is one clause. Thus the same variable name in two clauses means two different variables.

*   Structures can be naturally pictured as trees. Prolog can be viewed as a language for processing trees.

*   The *matching* operation takes two terms and tries to make them identical by instantiating the variables in both terms.

- Matching, if it succeeds, results in the *most general* instantiation of variables.
- The *declarative semantics* of Prolog defines whether a goal is true with respect to a given program, and if it is true, for what instantiation of variables it is true.
- A comma between goals means the conjunction of goals. A semicolon between goals means the disjunction of goals.
- The *procedural semantics* of Prolog is a procedure for satisfying a list of goals in the context of a given program. The procedure outputs the truth or falsity of the goal list and the corresponding instantiations of variables. The procedure automatically backtracks to examine alternatives.
- The declarative meaning of programs in 'pure Prolog' does not depend on the order of clauses and the order of goals in clauses.
- The procedural meaning does depend on the order of goals and clauses. Thus the order can affect the efficiency of the program; an unsuitable order may even lead to infinite recursive calls.
- Given a declaratively correct program, changing the order of clauses and goals can improve the program's efficiency while retaining its declarative correctness. Reordering is one method of preventing indefinite looping.
- There are other more general techniques, apart from reordering, to prevent indefinite looping and thereby make programs procedurally robust.
- Concepts discussed in this chapter are:
  data objects: atom, number, variable, structure
  term
  functor, arity of a functor
  principal functor of a term
  matching of terms
  most general instantiation
  declarative semantics
  instance of a clause, variant of a clause
  procedural semantics
  executing goals

# References

Clocksin, W.F. and Mellish, C.S. (1987) *Programming in Prolog*, second edn. Berlin: Springer-Verlag.

Flach, P. (1994) *Simply Logical: Intelligent Reasoning by Example*. Chichester, UK: Wiley.

Genesereth, M.R. and Nilsson, N.J. (1987) *Logical Foundation of Artificial Intelligence*. Palo Alto, CA: Morgan Kaufmann.

Ginsberg, M. (1993) *Essentials of Artificial Intelligence*. San Francisco, CA: Morgan Kaufmann.

Lloyd, J.W. (1991) *Foundations of Logic Programming*, second edn. Berlin: Springer-Verlag.

Poole, D., Mackworth, A. and Gaebel, R. (1998) *Computational Intelligence: A Logical Approach*. Oxford University Press.

Robinson, A.J. (1965) A machine-oriented logic based on the resolution principle. *JACM* **12**: 23–41.

Russell, S. and Norvig, P. (2010) *Artificial Intelligence: A Modern Approach,* third edn. Prentice Hall.

# Chapter 3

# Lists, Operators, Arithmetic

In this chapter we will study a special notation for lists, one of the simplest and most useful structures, and some programs for typical operations on lists. We will also look at simple arithmetic and the operator notation, which often improves the readability of programs. Basic Prolog of Chapter 2, extended with these three additions, becomes a convenient framework for writing interesting programs.

## 3.1 Representation of lists

The *list* is a simple data structure widely used in non-numeric programming. A list is a sequence of any number of items, such as **ann**, **tennis**, **tom**, **skiing**. Such a list can be written in Prolog as:

> [ **ann, tennis, tom, skiing**]

As we will see in a moment, this is, just a friendlier syntax for standard Prolog terms that represent list structures. As we have already seen in Chapter 2, all structured objects in Prolog are trees. Lists are no exception to this.

How can a list be represented as a structured Prolog object? We have to consider two cases: a list is either empty or non-empty. In the first case, the list is simply written as the Prolog atom []. In the second case, the list can be viewed as consisting of two things:

(1)  the first item, called the *head* of the list;

(2)  the remaining part of the list, called the *tail*.

For our example list,

> [ **ann, tennis, tom, skiing**]

the head is **ann** and the tail is the list:

> [ **tennis, tom, skiing**]

In general, the head can be anything (any Prolog object – a constant, a variable, a tree, and also a list again). The tail has to be a list. The head and the tail are then

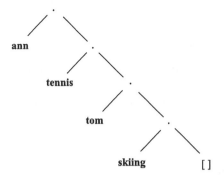

**Figure 3.1** Tree representation of the list [ ann, tennis, tom, skiing]

combined into a structure by the functor '.':

.( Head, Tail)

Since **Tail** is in turn a list, it is either empty or it has its own head and tail. Therefore, to represent lists of any length, no additional principle for structuring objects is needed. Our example list is represented in the standard Prolog notation as the term:

.( ann, .( tennis, .( tom, .( skiing, [ ] ) ) ) )

Figure 3.1 shows the corresponding tree structure. Note that the empty list appears in this tree. This is because the one but last tail is a single item list:

[ skiing]

This list has the empty list as its tail:

[ skiing] = .( skiing, [ ] )

This example shows how the general principle for structuring data objects in Prolog also applies to lists of any length. As our example also shows, however, the standard notation with dots and possibly deep nesting of subterms in the tail can produce rather confusing expressions. This is the reason why Prolog provides the friendlier notation for lists, so that they can be written as sequences of items enclosed in square brackets. A programmer can use both notations, but the square bracket notation is, of course, normally preferred. We will be aware, however, that this is only a cosmetic improvement and that our lists will be in any case internally represented as binary trees. When such terms are output they are automatically converted into the list notation. Thus the following conversation with Prolog is possible:

```
?- [a,b,c] = .(a, .(b, .(c, []))).
yes
?- List1 = [a,b,c],  List2 = .( a, .( b, .( c, [ ] ) ) ).

List1 = [a,b,c]
List2 = [a,b,c]

?- Hobbies1 = .( tennis, .( music, [ ] ) ),
   Hobbies2 = [ skiing, food],
   L = [ ann, Hobbies1, tom, Hobbies2].
```

**Hobbies1** = [ tennis, music]
**Hobbies2** = [ skiing, food)
**L** = [ ann, [tennis,music], tom, [skiing,food] ]

This example also confirms that the elements of a list can be objects of any kind; in particular they can also be lists.

It is often practical to treat the whole tail as a single object. For example, let:

**L** = [a,b,c]

Then we could write:

**Tail** = [b,c]   and   **L** = .( a, Tail)

To express this in the square bracket notation for lists, Prolog provides another notational extension, the vertical bar, which separates the head and the tail:

**L** = [ a | Tail]

The vertical bar notation is in fact more general: we can list any number of elements followed by '|' and the list of remaining items. Thus alternative ways of writing the list [a,b,c] are:

[a,b,c] = [a | [b,c] ] = [a,b | [c] ] = [a,b,c | [ ] ]

To summarize:

- A list is a data structure that is either empty or consists of two parts: a *head* and a *tail*. The tail itself has to be a list.

- Lists are handled in Prolog as a special case of binary trees. For improved readability Prolog provides a special notation for lists, thus accepting lists written as:

  [ Item1, Item2, ... ]

or

  [ Head | Tail]

or, generally,

  [ Item1, Item2, ... | Others]

## 3.2 Some operations on lists

Lists can be used to represent sets, although strictly speaking there is a difference: the order of elements in a set does not matter while the order of items in a list does; also, the same object can occur repeatedly in a list. Still, the most common operations on lists are similar to those on sets. Common operations include:

- checking whether some object is an element of a list, which corresponds to checking for the set membership;

- concatenation of two lists, obtaining a third list, which may correspond to the union of sets;

- adding a new object to a list, or deleting an object from it.

In the remainder of this section we give programs for these and some other operations on lists.

## 3.2.1 Membership

Let us implement the membership relation as:

member( X, L)

where X is an object and L is a list. The goal **member( X, L)** is true if X occurs in L. Here are some examples:

- **member( b, [a,b,c] )**   is true
- **member( b, [a,[b,c]] )**   is not true
- **member( [b,c], [a,[b,c]] )**   is true

The program for the membership relation can be based on the following observation:

X is a member of L if either:
(1)  X is the head of L, or
(2)  X is a member of the tail of L.

This can be written in two clauses:

member( X, [X | Tail] ).

member( X, [Head | Tail] ) :-
    member( X, Tail).

When programming in other languages, we usually think of **member** as a procedure to find a given item in a given list. Prolog allows several other, surprising uses of predicate **member** – uses that in other languages we normally would not even think of. We will look at these in the following examples. Let us start with the normal use:

```
?- member( b, [ a, b, c]).      % Check whether b is in [a,b,c]
yes
```

We can generate through backtracking all the members of a given list:

```
?- member( X, [ a, b, c]).       % Find such X that X is member of [a,b,c]
X = a;
X = b;
X = c;
no
```

More imaginatively, we may also reverse the question: Find lists that contain a given item, e.g. 'apple':

```
?- member( apple, L).
L = [ apple | _A] ;              % Any list that has "apple" as the head
L = [ _A, apple | _B] ;          % First item is anything, second is "apple"
L = [ _A, _B, apple | _C] ;
. . .
```

Another idea is: find lists that contain **a**, **b** and **c**:

```
?- member( a, L), member( b, L), member( c, L).
L = [ a, b, c | _A] ;
L = [ a , b,_A, c | _B] ;
L = [a,b,_A,_B,c|_C] ;
L = [ a, b, _A, _B, _C, c | _D] ;
...
```

These results may be interesting, but one might prefer the program also to generate permutations of **a**, **b** and **c**. In the query above, Prolog never gets to alternative permutations of **a**, **b** and **c** because of the order in which the solutions are generated. First, **a** is put in the list as the list's head, then **b** as the second element of the list, and then (potentially infinitely many!) lists that contain **c** are generated. Can we somehow force Prolog to generate permutations instead? Yes, we just have to fix the length of the list to three elements only:

```
?- L = [ _, _, _],          % L is any list with exactly three elements
   member( a, L), member( b, L), member( c, L).
L = [ a, b, c] ;
L = [ a, c, b] ;
L = [ b, a, c] ;
L = [ c, a, b] ;
L = [ b, c, a] ;
L = [ c, b, a] ;
no
```

As a final example of using **member**, consider a simple word-by-word translation between English and Spanish using a dictionary. Let a dictionary be represented as a list of pairs of words. Let these pairs be terms of the form

**p( EnglishWord, SpanishWord)**

Here we will define a simple dictionary as part of the query to Prolog. We can then translate 'two' into Spanish, and 'tres' into English with the query:

```
?- Dict = [ p( one, uno),  p( two, dos), p( three, tres)],    % A small dictionary
   member( p( two, Sp), Dict),                                % Translate two into Spanish
   member( p( En, tres), Dict).                               % Translate tres into English
Sp = dos,  En = three
```

What is the time complexity of our **member** procedure? This can be easily worked out by studying the execution of a query like ?- **member( d, [a,b,c,d,e,f])**. In this execution, the **member** predicate is recursively called on lists [b,c,d,e,f], then [c,d,e,f] and then [d,e,f]. This recursive call succeeds by the first clause of **member**, and thus recursion is over. Accordingly, it is easy to see that the **member** procedure scans the list linearly until the element sought for is encountered as the head of the remaining part of the list. So the time complexity is linear in the length of the list.

In the dictionary example above, using a list to represent a large dictionary will be inefficient, but for small dictionaries this does not matter.

## 3.2.2   Concatenation

For concatenating lists we will define the relation:

conc( L1, L2, L3)

Here L1 and L2 are lists, and L3 is their concatenation. For example,

conc( [a,b], [c,d], [a,b,c,d] )

is true, but

conc( [a,b], [c,d], [a,b,a,c,d] )

is false. In the definition of **conc** we will have again two cases, depending on the first argument, Ll:

(1)   If the first argument is the empty list then the second and the third arguments must be  the same list (call it L); this is expressed by the following Prolog fact:

conc( [ ], L, L).

(2)   If the first argument of **conc** is a non-empty list then it has a head and a tail and must look like this:

[X | L1]

Figure 3.2 illustrates the concatenation of [X | L1] and some list L2. The result of the concatenation is the list [X | L3] where L3 is the concatenation of Ll and L2. In Prolog this is written as:

conc( [X | L1], L2, [X | L3] ) :-
    conc( L1, L2, L3).

This program can now be used for concatenating given lists, for example:

?- conc( [a,b,c], [1,2,3], L).
L = [a,b,c,1,2,3]
?- conc( [a,[b,c],d], [a,[ ],b], L).

L = [a, [b,c], d, a, [ ], b]

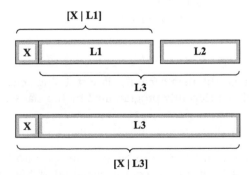

**Figure 3.2** Concatenation of lists.

Although the conc program looks rather simple it can be used flexibly in many other ways. For example, we can use conc in the inverse direction for *decomposing* a given list into two lists, as follows:

?- conc( L1, L2, [a,b,c] ).

L1 = [ ]
L2 = [a,b,c];

L1 = [a]
L2 = [b,c];

L1 = [a,b]
L2 = [c];

L1 = [a,b,c]
L2 = [ ];

no

It is possible to decompose the list [a,b,c] in four ways, all of which were found by our program through backtracking.

We can also use our program to look for a certain pattern in a list. For example, we can find the months that precede and the months that follow a given month, as in the following goal:

?- conc(Before, [may | After],
          [jan,feb,mar,apr,may,jun,jul,aug,sep,oct,nov,dec] ).

Before = [jan,feb,mar,apr]
After = [jun,jul,aug,sep,oct,nov,dec].

Further, we can find the immediate predecessor and the immediate successor of May by asking:

?- conc(_, [Month1,may,Month2 | _],
          [jan,feb,mar,apr,may,jun,jul,aug,sep,oct,nov,dec] ).

Month1 = apr
Month2 = jun

Further still, we can, for example, delete from some list, L1, everything that follows three successive occurrences of z in L1 together with the three z's. For example:

?- L1 = [a,b,z,z,c,z,z,z,d,e],      % A given list
   conc( L2, [z,z,z | _], L1).      %  L2 is L1 up to 3 z's

L1 = [a,b,z,z,c,z,z,z,d,e]
L2 = [a,b,z,z,c]

We have already programmed the membership relation. Using conc, however, the membership relation could be elegantly programmed by the clause:

member1( X, L) :-
    conc( L1, [X | L2], L).

This clause says: X is a member of list L if L can be decomposed into two lists so that the second one has X as its head. Of course, member1 defines the same relation as **member**. We have just used a different name to distinguish between the two implementations. Note that the above clause can be written using anonymous variables as:

> **member1( X, L) :-**
>     **conc( _, [X | _], L).**

It is interesting to compare both implementations of the membership relation, **member** and **member1**. **member** has a rather straightforward procedural meaning, which is as follows:

> To check whether some X is a member of some list L:
>
> (1)  first check whether the head of L is equal to X, and then
>
> (2)  check whether X is a member of the tail of L.

On the other hand, the declarative reading of **member1** is straightforward, but its procedural meaning is not so obvious. An interesting exercise is to find how **member1** actually computes something. An example execution trace will give some idea: let us consider the question:

> **?- member1( b, [a,b,c] ).**

Figure 3.3 shows the execution trace. From the trace we can infer that **member1** behaves similarly to **member**. It scans the list, element by element, until the item in question is found or the list is exhausted.

The list membership and concatenation relations are so commonly used in Prolog that they are often provided as built-in predicates in Prolog systems. In such cases, concatenation usually appears under the name **append**.

# EXERCISES

......................................................................................................................................................................

**3.1**  (a)  Write a goal, using **conc**, to delete the last three elements from a list L producing another list Ll. Hint: L is the concatenation of Ll and a three-element list.

   (b)  Write a goal to delete the first three elements and the last three elements from a list L producing list L2.

**3.2**  Define the relation

> **last( Item, List)**

so that **Item** is the last element of a list **List**. Write two versions: (a) using the **conc** relation, (b) without **conc**.

......................................................................................................................................................................

## 3.2.3  Adding an item

To add an item to a list, it is easiest to put the new item in front of the list so that it becomes the new head. If X is the new item and the list to which X is added is L then the resulting list is simply:

> **[X | L]**

So we actually need no procedure for adding a new element in front of the list. Nevertheless, if we want to define such a procedure explicitly, it can be written as the fact:

> **add( X, L, [X | L] ).**

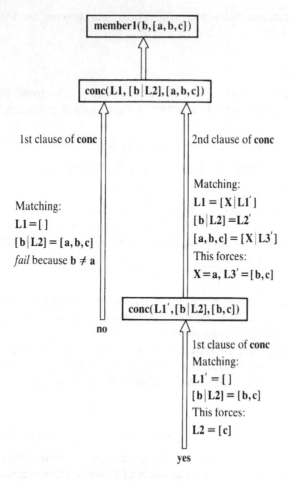

**Figure 3.3** Procedure **member1** finds an item in a given list by sequentially searching the list.

### 3.2.4  Deleting an item

Deleting an item, X, from a list, L, can be programmed as a relation

> **del( X, L, L1)**

where Ll is equal to the list L with the item X removed. The **del** relation can be defined similarly to the membership relation. We have, again, two cases:

(1)  If X is the head of the list then the result after the deletion is the tail of the list.

(2)  If X is in the tail then it is deleted from there.

> **del( X, [X | Tail], Tail).**
>
> **del( X, [Y | Tail], [Y | Tail1] ) :-**
>     **del( X, Tail, Tail1).**

Like **member**, **del** is also non-deterministic. If there are several occurrences of X in the list then **del** will be able to delete any one of them by backtracking. Of course, each alternative execution will only delete one occurrence of X, leaving the others untouched. For example:

?- del( a, [a,b,a,a], L).

L = [b,a,a];

L = [a,b,a];

L = [a,b,a];

no

**del** will fail if the list does not contain the item to be deleted. **del** can also be used in the inverse direction, to add an item to a list by inserting the new item anywhere in the list. For example, if we want to insert a at any place in the list [1,2,3] then we can do this by asking the question: What is L such that after deleting a from L we obtain [1,2,3]?

?- del( a, L, [1,2,3] ).

L = [a,1,2,3];

L = [1,a,2,3];

L = [1,2,a,3];

L = [1,2,3,a];

no

In general, the operation of inserting X at any place in some list **List** giving **BiggerList** can be defined by the clause:

**insert**( X, List, BiggerList) :-
    **del**( X, BiggerList, List).

In **member1** we elegantly implemented the membership relation by using **conc**. We can also use **del** to test for membership. The idea is simple: some X is a member of **List** if X can be deleted from **List**:

**member2**( X, List) :-
    **del**( X, List, _).

## 3.2.5  Sublist

Let us now consider the sublist relation. This relation has two arguments, a list L and a list S such that S occurs within L as its sublist. So,

sublist( [c,d,e], [a,b,c,d,e,f] )

is true, but

sublist( [c,e], [a,b,c,d,e,f] )

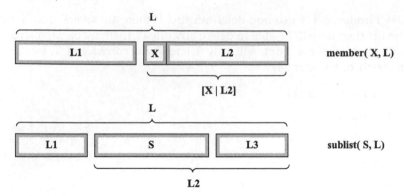

**Figure 3.4** The **member** and **sublist** relations.

is not. The Prolog program for **sublist** can be based on the same idea as **member1**, only this time the relation is more general (see Figure 3.4). Accordingly, the relation can be formulated as:

S is a sublist of L if:

(1)  L can be decomposed into two lists, Ll and L2, and
(2)  L2 can be decomposed into two lists, S and some L3.

As we have seen before, the **conc** relation can be used for decomposing lists. So the above formulation can be expressed in Prolog as:

```
sublist( S, L) :-
   conc( L1, L2, L),
   conc( S, L3, L2).
```

Of course, the **sublist** procedure can be used flexibly in several ways. Although it was designed to check if some list occurs as a sublist within another list it can also be used, for example, to find all the sublists of a given list:

?- **sublist**( S, [a,b,c] ).

S = [ ];

S = [a];

S = [a,b];

S = [a,b,c];

S = [ ];

S = [b];

...

## 3.2.6  Permutations

Sometimes it is useful to generate permutations of a given list. To this end, we will define the **permutation** relation with two arguments. The arguments are two lists such that one is a permutation of the other. The intention is to generate

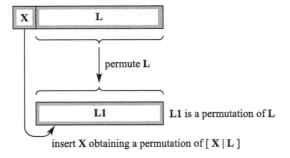

**Figure 3.5** One way of constructing a permutation of the list [X | L].

permutations of a list through backtracking using the **permutation** procedure, as in the following example:

?- **permutation**( [a,b,c], P).

P = [a,b,c];

P = [a,c,b];

P = [b,a,c];

...

The program for **permutation** can be, again, based on two cases, depending on the first list:

(1) If the first list is empty then the second list must also be empty.

(2) If the first list is not empty then it has the form [X | L], and a permutation of such a list can be constructed as shown in Figure 3.5: first permute L obtaining L1 and then insert X at any position into L1.

Prolog clauses that correspond to these two cases are:

**permutation**( [ ], [ ] ).

**permutation**( [X | L], P) :-
  **permutation**( L, L1),
  **insert**( X, L1, P).

One alternative to this program would be to delete an element, X, from the first list, permute the rest of it obtaining a list P, and then add X in front of P. The corresponding program is:

**permutation2**( [ ], [ ] ).

**permutation2**( L, [X | P] ) :-
  **del**( X, L, L1),
  **permutation2**( L1, P).

It is instructive to do some experiments with our permutation programs. Its normal use would be something like this:

?- **permutation**( [red,blue,green], P).

This would result in all six permutations, as intended:

P = [ red, blue, green];

P = [ red, green, blue];

P = [ blue, red, green];

P = [ blue, green, red];

P = [ green, red, blue];

P = [ green, blue, red];

no

Another attempt to use **permutation** is:

?- **permutation**( L, [a,b,c] ).

Our first version, **permutation**, will now instantiate L successfully to all six permutations. If the user then requests more solutions, the program would never answer 'no' because it would get into an infinite loop trying to find another permutation when there is none. Our second version, **permutation2**, will in this case find only the first (identical) permutation and then immediately get into an infinite loop. Thus, some care is necessary when using these permutation programs.

# EXERCISES

**3.3** Define two predicates

**evenlength( List) and oddlength( List)**

so that they are true if their argument is a list of even or odd length respectively. For example, the list [a,b,c,d] is 'evenlength' and [a,b,c] is 'oddlength'.

**3.4** Define the relation

**reverse( List, ReversedList)**

that reverses lists. For example, **reverse**( [a,b,c,d], [d,c,b,a] ).

**3.5** Define the predicate **palindrome( List)**. A list is a palindrome if it reads the same in the forward and in the backward direction. For example, [m,a,d,a,m].

**3.6** Define the relation

**shift( List1, List2)**

so that **List2** is **List1** 'shifted rotationally' by one element to the left. For example,

?- **shift**( [1,2,3,4,5], L1),
    **shift**( L1, L2).

produces:

L1 = [2,3,4,5,1]
L2 = [3,4,5,1,2]

**3.7** Define the relation

**translate( List1, List2)**

to translate a list of numbers between 0 and 9 to a list of the corresponding words. For example:

**translate( [3,5,1,3], [three,five,one,three] )**

Use the following as an auxiliary relation:

**means( 0, zero).   means( 1, one).   means( 2, two).   ...**

**3.8** Define the relation

**subset( Set, Subset)**

where **Set** and **Subset** are two lists representing two sets. We would like to be able to use this relation not only to check for the subset relation, but also to generate all possible subsets of a given set. For example:

```
?- subset( [a,b,c], S).
S = [a,b,c];
S = [a,b];
S = [a,c];
S = [a];
S = [b,c];
S = [b];
...
```

**3.9** Define the relation

**dividelist( List, List1, List2)**

so that the elements of **List** are partitioned between **List1** and **List2**, and **List1** and **List2** are of approximately the same length. For example:

**dividelist( [a,b,c,d,e], [a,c,e], [b,d] ).**

**3.10** Define the predicate

**equal_length( L1, L2)**

which is true if lists L1 and L2 have equal number of elements.

**3.11** Define the relation

**flatten( List, FlatList)**

where **List** can be a list of lists, and **FlatList** is **List** 'flattened' so that the elements of **List**'s sublists (or sub-sublists) are reorganized as one plain list. For example:

```
?- flatten( [a,b,[c,d],[ ],[[[e]]],f], L).
L = [a,b,c,d,e,f]
```

## 3.3 Operator notation

In mathematics we are used to writing expressions like

$2*a + b*c$

where $+$ and $*$ are operators, and 2, $a$, $b$, are arguments. In particular, $+$ and $*$ are said to be *infix* operators because they appear *between* the two arguments. Such expressions can be represented as trees, as in Figure 3.6, and can be written as Prolog terms in which $+$ and $*$ appear as functors:

+( *(2,a), *(b,c) )

Since we normally prefer to have such expressions written in the usual, infix style with operators, Prolog caters for this notational convenience. Prolog will therefore accept our expression written simply as:

2*a + b*c

This is, however, only the external representation of this object, and is equivalent to the standard form +( *( 2, a), *( b, c)). Such a term will be written out by Prolog, again, in the more readable, infix notation. Thus operators in Prolog are no more than a notational extension. If we write a + b, Prolog will handle it exactly as if it had been written as +(a,b).

In order that Prolog properly understands expressions such as a + b*c, Prolog has to know that * binds stronger than ∣ . In Prolog, the convention is that operators with lower precedence bind stronger, and the operator with the highest precedence in a term is the principal functor of the term. Therefore in Prolog, the precedence of + is defined higher than the precedence of *, and therefore * binds stronger than +. The precedence of operators decides what is the correct interpretation of an expression. For example, the expression a + b*c is understood as

+( a, *(b,c) )

and not as

*( +(a,b), c)

We can always explicitly indicate with parentheses what the intended interpretation is. The expression a + b*c means the same as a + (b*c). If the other interpretation is intended in which * is the principal functor, then the expression has to be written as (a + b)*c.

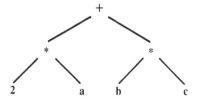

**Figure 3.6** Tree representation of the expression 2* + b*c.

A programmer can define his or her own operators. So, for example, we can define the atoms **has** and **supports** as infix operators and then write in the program facts like:

> **peter has information.**
> **floor supports table.**

These facts are exactly equivalent to:

> **has( peter, information).**
> **supports( floor, table).**

A programmer can define new operators by inserting into the program special kinds of clauses, sometimes called *directives*, which act as operator definitions. An operator definition must appear in the program before any expression containing that operator. For our example, the operator **has** can be defined by the directive:

> **:- op( 600, xfx, has).**

This tells Prolog that we want to use 'has' as an operator, whose precedence is 600 and its type is 'xfx', which is a kind of infix operator. The form of the specifier 'xfx' suggests that the operator, denoted by 'f', is between the two arguments denoted by 'x'.

Notice that operator definitions do not specify any operation or action. In principle, *no operation on data is associated with an operator* (except in very special cases). Operators are normally used, as functors, only to combine objects into structures and not to invoke actions on data, although the word 'operator' appears to suggest an action.

Operator names are atoms. An operator's precedence must be in some range which depends on the implementation. We will assume that the range is between 1 and 1200.

There are three groups of operator types which are indicated by type specifiers such as **xfx**. The three groups are:

(1) infix operators of three types:

> xfx   xfy   yfx

(2) prefix operators of two types:

> fx   fy

(3) postfix operators of two types:

> xf   yf

The specifiers are chosen so as to reflect the structure of the expression where 'f' represents the operator and 'x' and 'y' represent arguments. An 'f' appearing between the arguments indicates that the operator is infix. The prefix and postfix specifiers have only one argument, which follows or precedes the operator respectively.

There is a difference between 'x' and 'y'. To explain this we need to introduce the notion of the *precedence of argument*. If an argument is enclosed in parentheses or it is an unstructured object then its precedence is 0; if an argument is a structure then its precedence is equal to the precedence of its principal functor.

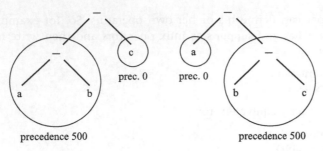

**Figure 3.7** Two interpretations of the expression a − b − c assuming that '−' has precedence 500. If '−' is of type **yfx**, then interpretation 2 is invalid because the precedence of b − c is not less than the precedence of '−'.

'x' represents an argument whose precedence must be strictly lower than that of the operator. 'y' represents an argument whose precedence is lower or equal to that of the operator.

These rules help to disambiguate expressions with several operators of the same precedence. For example, the expression

   **a − b − c**

is normally understood as (a − b) − c, and not as a − (b − c). To achieve the normal interpretation the operator '−' has to be defined as **yfx**. Figure 3.7 shows why the second interpretation is then ruled out.

As another example consider the prefix operator **not**. If **not** is defined as **fy** then the expression

   **not not p**

is legal; but if **not** is defined as **fx** then this expression is illegal because the argument to the first **not** is **not p**, which has the same precedence as **not** itself. In this case the expression has to be written with parentheses:

   **not( not p)**

For convenience, some operators are predefined in the Prolog system so that they can be readily used, and no definition is needed for them. What these operators are and what their precedences are depend on the implementation of Prolog. We will assume that this set of 'standard' operators is as if defined by the clauses in Figure 3.8. The operators in this figure are a subset of those defined in the Prolog standard, plus the operator **not**. As Figure 3.8 also shows, several operators can be declared by one clause if they all have the same precedence and if they are all of the same type. In this case the operators' names are written as a list.

The use of operators can greatly improve the readability of programs. As an example let us assume that we are writing a program for manipulating Boolean expressions. In such a program we may want to state, for example, one of de Morgan's equivalence theorems, which can in mathematics be written as:

   $\sim(A \& B) <===> \sim A \lor \sim B$

One way to state this in Prolog is by the clause:

   **equivalence( not( and( A, B)), or( not( A), not( B) ) ).**

```
:- op( 1200, xfx, [ :-, -->] ).
:- op( 1200, fx [ :-, ?-] ).
:- op( 1100, xfy, ';' ).
:- op( 1050, xfy, -> ).
:- op( 1000, xfy, ',' ).
:- op( 900, fy, [ not, \+] ).
:- op( 700, xfx, [ =, \=, ==, \==, =.. ] ).
:- op( 700, xfx, [ is, =:=, =\=, <, =<, >, >=, @<, @=<, @>, @>=] ).
:- op( 500, yfx, [ +, − ] ).
:- op( 400, yfx, [ *, /, //, mod] ).
:- op( 200, xfx, ** ).
:- op( 200, xfy, ^ ).
:- op( 200, fy, - ).
```

**Figure 3.8** A set of predefined operators.

However, it is in general a good programming practice to try to retain as much resemblance as possible between the original problem notation and the notation used in the program. In our example, this can be achieved almost completely by using operators. A suitable set of operators for our purpose can be defined as:

```
:- op( 800, xfx, <===>).      % Logical equivalence
:- op( 700, xfy, v).          % Disjunction
:- op( 600, xfy, &).          % Conjunction
:- op( 500, fy, ~).           % Negation
```

Now the de Morgan's theorem can be written as the fact:

$$\sim(A \& B) <===> \sim A \; v \sim B.$$

According to our specification of operators above, this term is understood as shown in Figure 3.9.

To summarize:

- The readability of programs can be often improved by using the operator notation. Operators can be infix, prefix or postfix.

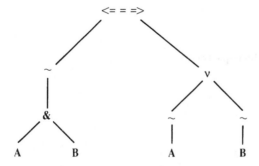

**Figure 3.9** Interpretation of the term $\sim(A \& B) <===> \sim A \; v \sim B$.

- In principle, no operation on data is associated with an operator except in special cases. Operator definitions do not define any action, they only introduce new notation. Operators, as functors, only hold together components of structures.

- A programmer can define his or her own operators. Each operator is defined by its name, precedence and type.

- The precedence is an integer within some range, usually between 1 and 1200. The operator with the highest precedence in the expression is the principal functor of the expression. Operators with lowest precedence bind strongest.

- The type of an operator depends on two things: (1) the position of the operator with respect to the arguments, and (2) the precedence of the arguments compared to the precedence of the operator itself. In a specifier like xfy, x indicates an argument whose precedence is strictly lower than that of the operator; y indicates an argument whose precedence is less than or equal to that of the operator.

# EXERCISES

**3.12** Assume the operator definitions

```
:- op( 300, xfx, plays).
:- op( 200, xfy, and).
```

Then the following two terms are syntactically legal objects:

Term1 = jimmy plays football and squash
Term2 = susan plays tennis and basketball and volleyball

How are these terms understood by Prolog? What are their principal functors and what is their structure?

**3.13** Suggest an appropriate definition of operators ('was', 'of', 'the') to be able to write clauses like

diana was the secretary of the department.

and then ask Prolog:

?- Who was the secretary of the department.

Who = diana

?- diana was What.

What = the secretary of the department

**3.14** Consider the program:

```
t( 0+1, 1+0).

t( X+0+1, X+1+0).

t( X+1+1, Z) :-
    t( X+1, X1),
    t( X1+1, Z).
```

How will this program answer the following questions if '+' is an infix operator of type **yfx** (as usual):

(a) ?- t( 0+1, A).

(b) ?- t( 0+1+1, B).

(c) ?- t( 1+0+1+1+1, C).

(d) ?- t( D, 1+1+1+0).

**3.15** In the previous section, relations involving lists were written as:

> member( Element, List),
> conc( List1, List2, List3),
> del( Element, List, NewList), . . .

Suppose that we would prefer to write these relations as:

> Element in List,
> concatenating List1 and List2 gives List3,
> deleting Element from List gives NewList, . . .

Define 'in', 'concatenating', 'and', etc. as operators to make this possible. Also, redefine the corresponding procedures.

## 3.4 Arithmetic

Some of the predefined operators can be used for basic arithmetic operations. These are:

| | |
|---|---|
| + | addition |
| − | subtraction |
| * | multiplication |
| / | division |
| ** | power |
| // | integer division |
| mod | modulo, the remainder of integer division |

Notice that this is an exceptional case in which an operator may in fact invoke an operation. But even in such cases an additional indication to perform arithmetic will be necessary. The following question is a naive attempt to request arithmetic computation:

> ?- X = 1 + 2.

Prolog will simply answer

> X = 1 + 2

and not X = 3 as one might possibly expect. The reason is simple: the expression 1 + 2 merely denotes a Prolog term where + is the functor and 1 and 2 are its arguments. The operator '=' in the question above just requires the matching of X and 1 + 2. There is nothing in the question to force Prolog to actually carry out the addition operation. A special predefined operator, **is**, is provided to circumvent this problem. The **is** operator will force evaluation. So the way to actually invoke arithmetic is:

?- X is 1 + 2.

Now the answer will be:

X = 3

The addition here was carried out by a special procedure that is associated with the operator **is**. We call such procedures *built-in procedures*, or *built-in predicates*.

Different implementations of Prolog may use somewhat different notations for arithmetic. In this book, '/' denotes real division, the operator // denotes integer division, and **mod** denotes the remainder. Accordingly, the question:

?- X is 5/2,
  Y is 5//2,
  Z is 5 mod 2.

is answered by:

X = 2.5
Y = 2
Z = 1

The left argument of the **is** operator is a simple object – a variable or a number. The right argument is an arithmetic expression composed of arithmetic operators, numbers and variables. The **is** operator will force the evaluation of the expression, and then the result of the evaluation will be matched with the object on the left of **is**. All the variables in the expression must already be instantiated to numbers at the time of execution of this goal. The precedence of the predefined arithmetic operators (see Figure 3.8) is such that the associativity of arguments with operators is the same as normally in mathematics. Parentheses can be used to indicate a different nesting of an expression. Note that +, –, *, / and // are defined as **yfx**, which means that evaluation is carried out from left to right. For example,

X is 5 – 2 – 1

is interpreted as:

X is (5 – 2) – 1

Prolog implementations also provide standard functions such as sin(X), cos(X), atan(X), log(X), exp(X), etc. These functions can appear to the right of operator **is**.

Arithmetic is also involved when *comparing* numerical values. We can, for example, test whether the product of 277 and 37 is greater than 10000 by the goal:

?- 277 * 37 > 10000.
yes

Note that, similarly to **is**, the '>' operator also forces the evaluation.

Suppose that we have in the program a relation **born** that relates the names of people with their birth years. Then we can retrieve the names of people born between 1980 and 1990 inclusive with the following question:

```
?- born( Name, Year),
   Year   >=   1980,
   Year   =<   1990.
```

The comparison operators are as follows:

| | |
|---|---|
| X > Y | X is greater than Y |
| X < Y | X is less than Y |
| X >= Y | X is greater than or equal to Y |
| X —< Y | X is less than or equal to Y |
| X =:= Y | the values of X and Y are equal |
| X =\= Y | the values of X and Y are not equal |

Notice the difference between the matching operator '=' and '=:='; for example, in the goals X = Y and X =:= Y. The first goal will cause the matching of the objects X and Y, and will, if X and Y match, possibly instantiate some variables in X and Y. There will be no evaluation. On the other hand, X =:= Y causes the arithmetic evaluation and cannot cause any instantiation of variables. These differences are illustrated by the following examples:

```
?- 1 + 2 =:= 2 + 1.
```

yes

```
?- 1 + 2 = 2 + 1.
```

no

```
?- 1 + A = B + 2.
```

A = 2
B = 1

Let us further illustrate the use of arithmetic operations by two simple examples. The first is computing the greatest common divisor; the second is counting the items in a list. Given two positive integers, X and Y, their greatest common divisor, D, can be found according to three cases:

(1)  If X and Y are equal then D is equal to X.

(2)  If X < Y then D is equal to the greatest common divisor of X and the difference Y − X.

(3)  If Y < X then do the same as in case (2) with X and Y interchanged.

It can be easily shown by an example that these three rules actually work. Choosing, for example, X = 20 and Y = 25, the above rules would give D = 5 after a sequence of subtractions.

These rules can be formulated into a Prolog program by defining a three-argument relation, say:

```
gcd( X, Y, D)
```

The three rules are then expressed as three clauses, as follows:

gcd( X, X, X).

gcd( X, Y, D) :-
  X < Y,
  Y1 is Y – X,
  gcd( X, Y1, D).

gcd( X, Y, D) :-
  Y < X,
  gcd( Y, X, D).

Of course, the last goal in the third clause could be equivalently replaced by the two goals:

X1 is X – Y,
gcd( X1, Y, D)

Our next example involves counting which requires some arithmetic. The task will be to compute the length of a list; that is, we have to count the items in the list. We will define the procedure:

length( List, N)

which will count the elements in a list **List** and instantiate N to their number. As was the case with our previous relations involving lists, it is useful to consider two cases:

(1) If the list is empty then its length is 0.

(2) If the list is not empty then **List** = [**Head** | **Tail**]; then its length is equal to 1 plus the length of the tail **Tail**.

These two cases correspond to the following program:

length( [ ], 0).

length( [_ | Tail], N) :-
  length( Tail, N1),
  N is 1 + N1.

An application of **length** can be:

?- length( [ a, b, [ c, d], e], N).
N = 4

Note that in the second clause of **length**, the two goals of the body cannot be swapped. The reason for this is that N1 has to be instantiated before the goal

N is 1 + N1

can be processed. With the built-in procedure **is**, a relation has been introduced that is sensitive to the order of processing and therefore the procedural considerations have become vital.

It is interesting to see what happens if we try to program the **length** relation without the use of **is**. Such an attempt can be:

length1( [ ], 0).

length1( [_ | Tail], N) :-
  length1( Tail, N1),
  N = 1 + N1.

Now the goal

?- length1( [ a, b, [ c, d], e], N).

will produce the answer:

N = 1 + ( 1 + ( 1 + ( 1 + 0))).

The addition was never explicitly forced and was therefore not carried out at all. But in **length1** we can, unlike in **length**, swap the goals in the second clause:

length1( [_ | Tail], N) :-
  N = 1 + N1,
  length1( Tail, N1).

This version of **length1** will produce the same result as the original version. It can also be written shorter, as follows,

length1( [_ | Tail], 1 + N) :-
  length1( Tail, N).

still producing the same result. We can, however, use **length1** to find the number of elements in a list as follows:

?- length1( [ a, b, c], N), Length is N.

N = 1 + ( 1 + ( 1 + 0))
Length = 3

Here, the predicate **length1** constructed a formula for computing the length, and then this formula was evaluated by **is**.

Finally we note that the predicate **length** is often provided as a built-in predicate. To summarize:

- Built-in procedures can be used for doing arithmetic.

- Arithmetic operations have to be explicitly requested by the built-in procedure **is**. There are built-in procedures associated with the predefined operators $+$, $-$, $*$, $/$, $//$ and **mod**.

- At the time that evaluation is carried out, all arguments must be already instantiated to numbers.

- The values of arithmetic expressions can be compared by operators such as $<$, $=<$, etc. These operators force the evaluation of their arguments.

# EXERCISES

**3.16** Define the relation

max( X, Y, Max)

so that **Max** is the greater of two numbers X and Y.

**3.17** Define the predicate

> **maxlist( List, Max)**

so that **Max** is the greatest number in the list of numbers **List**.

**3.18** Define the predicate

> **sumlist( List, Sum)**

so that **Sum** is the sum of a given list of numbers **List**.

**3.19** Define the predicate

> **ordered( List)**

which is true if **List** is an ordered list of numbers. For example,

> **ordered( [1,5,6,6,9,12] ).**

**3.20** Define the predicate

> **subsum( Set, Sum, SubSet)**

so that **Set** is a list of numbers, **SubSet** is a subset of these numbers, and the sum of the numbers in **SubSet** is **Sum**. For example:

> **?- subsum( [1,2,5,3,2], 5, Sub).**
>
> **Sub = [1,2,2];**
>
> **Sub = [2,3];**
>
> **Sub = [5];**
>
> ...

**3.21** Define the procedure

> **between( N1, N2, X)**

which, for two given integers N1 and N2, generates through backtracking all the integers X that satisfy the constraint $N1 < X < N2$.

**3.22** Define the operators 'if', 'then', 'else' and ':=' so that the following becomes a legal term:

> **if X > Y then Z := X else Z := Y**

Choose the precedences so that 'if' will be the principal functor. Then define the predicate 'if' as a small interpreter for a kind of 'if-then-else' statement of the form

> **if Val1 > Val2 then Var := Val3 else Var := Val4**

where **Val1**, **Val2**, **Val3** and **Val4** are numbers (or variables instantiated to numbers) and **Var** is a variable. The meaning of the 'if' predicate should be: if the value of **Val1** is greater than the value of **Val2** then **Var** is instantiated to **Val3**, otherwise to **Val4**. Here is an example of the use of this interpreter:

```
?-    X = 2, Y = 3,
      Val2 is 2*X,
      Val4 is 4*X,
      if Y > Val2 then Z := Y else Z := Val4,
      if Z > 5 then W := 1 else W := 0.

X = 2
Y = 3
Z = 8
W = 1
Val2 = 4
Val4 = 8
```

# Summary

......................................................................................................................................

- The list is a frequently used structure. It is either empty or consists of a *head* and a *tail* which is a list as well. Prolog provides a special notation for lists.

- Common operations on lists, programmed in this chapter, are: list membership, concatenation, adding an item, deleting an item, sublist.

- The *operator notation* allows the programmer to tailor the syntax of programs toward particular needs. Using operators the readability of programs can be greatly improved.

- New operators are defined by the directive **op**, stating the name of an operator, its type and precedence.

- In principle, there is no operation associated with an operator; operators are merely a syntactic device providing an alternative syntax for terms.

- Arithmetic is done by built-in procedures. Evaluation of an arithmetic expression is forced by the procedure **is** and by the comparison predicates <, =<, etc.

- Concepts introduced in this chapter are:

    list, head of list, tail of list
    list notation
    operators, operator notation
    infix, prefix and suffix operators
    precedence of an operator
    arithmetic built-in procedures

# Chapter 4

# Programming Examples

Prolog matching, data structures and backtracking are a powerful programming tool. In this chapter we will develop the skill of using this tool through programming examples: finding a path in a graph which can be used as a building block in many applications, planning to solve robot's tasks, planning a trip, solving cryptarithmetic problems, eight queens on the chessboard, reasoning about the meaning of words using the well-known WordNet ontology. The programming examples in this chapter can be read or skipped selectively, except Section 4.1 on path finding which is useful for subsequent programming examples.

## 4.1 Finding a path in a graph

Graph structures are a very useful abstract representation for many problems. The first example in Chapter 1 of this book involved a graph showing family relations (Figure 1.1). In general, a graph is defined by a set of nodes and a set of connections between nodes. Connections can be directed, shown as arrows, or undirected, shown as lines without arrows. Directed connections are called *arcs* or *links*, undirected connections are called *edges*. In this section we will be mainly interested in directed graphs, that is graphs with (directed) links like the one in Figure 4.1.

Here are some examples of representing problems with graphs:

- An undirected graph showing direct flights, operated by an air company, between cities. Notice that this is a rather abstract representation of flight connections – distances, locations, etc. have been abstracted away.

- A graph showing links between web pages.

- A graph representing a computer network.

- A graph representing a social structure where a link between nodes P1 and P2 means that P1 knows P2.

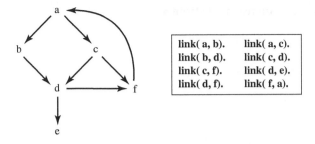

**Figure 4.1** A directed graph and its representation in Prolog.

The most common type of question concerning a graph is: Is there a path from node X to node Y? And if there is, show the path. This is an abstract version of many concrete practical questions like: How can I travel from Ljubljana to Manchester? How can a user navigate from web page X to page Y, possibly following links to intermediate pages? How many links of the type 'P1 knows P2' in a social network are needed to get from any person in the world to any other person, by following a chain of 'knows' links between people. This is known to be surprisingly small – no more than seven links.

All these concrete questions can be answered by the same algorithms that work on abstract graphs where nodes and links have no concrete meaning (as in Figure 4.1). We will here look at some basic ways of finding a path between nodes in a graph. These techniques will be implemented by short programs and will work well on (relatively) small graphs of, say, 1000 nodes. In practice, much larger graphs often occur. In artificial intelligence, there exist much more sophisticated  methods for searching large graphs. We will look at those in Part II of this book. Here we will consider basic ideas.

First, consider the predicate

    **path( StartNode, EndNode)**

which is true if there exists a path from **StartNode** to **EndNode** in the given graph. A path exists if

(1)  **StartNode** and **EndNode** are both the same node, or

(2)  there is a link from **StartNode** to a **NextNode**, and there is a path from **NextNode** to **EndNode**.

These two rules are written in Prolog as:

    **path( Node, Node).**

    **path( StartNode, EndNode) :-**
      **link( StartNode, NextNode),**
      **path( NextNode, EndNode).**

Let us try some questions with this predicate. First, is there a path from **a** to **e**:

    **?- path(a,e).**
    **yes**

Second, which nodes X are reachable from a:

```
?- path( a, X).
X = a;
X = b;
X = d;
X = e;
X = f;
X = a;
X = b;
...
```

Prolog has found that a is connected in turn to a itself, then b, then d, then e, then f, and then a again, b again, etc. The second answer X = a means that Prolog has made a complete cycle a-b-d-f-a which connects a to itself. This would be followed by X = b, X = d, etc., repeating the same answers for the second time. This complete loop will keep repeating indefinitely. Unfortunately, it is thus never found that a is also connected to c. We may ask about this explicitly:

```
?- path( a, c).
```

Prolog would enter the above-mentioned loop and stay in the loop until it runs out of memory. It would then stop and display something like 'Insufficient memory'. The reason why Prolog never gets out of the cycle can be understood by tracing the execution of our program. This would show that Prolog, starting at node a, makes one step forward according to link( a,NextNode). It finds NextNode = b, and then recursively calls path( b,c). This call again makes one step further, from b to d. Then again, it makes one step further to e. Then it tries to make another step forward from e, but that is not possible. Therefore Prolog backtracks to node d, to find an alternative step forward, this time moving from d to f, then from f to a, and then from a to b again, and then the whole loop repeats. The alternative step forward from a to c is never tried because Prolog keeps extending the cyclical path a-b-d-. . . .

The style in which our program searches a graph is called *depth-first*. Whenever there is a choice between alternatives where to continue the search, the program chooses a current deepest alternative. For example, the program starts at node a and then moves from a to b. Now it has two alternatives: either move from b to d, or from a to c. The former alternative is 'deeper' (i.e. farthest from the start of the search), therefore the move from b to d is chosen. The reason why Prolog eventually runs out of memory is that each recursive call takes some memory, because Prolog has to remember where to return in the event that backtracking occurs.

So our simple program, using the depth-first search, has a problem. It should be noted that this problem does not occur when the graph to be searched is finite and has no cyclical path. The problem can be fixed in many ways, for example by limiting the depth of search, or by checking for node repetition on the currently expanded path. All this will be done later in the book. But for now we will leave this program as is, and consider a little more interesting version of the path predicate with a third argument added:

```
path( Start, End, Path)
```

This is true if **Path** is a path between nodes **Start** and **End** in the graph. **Path** is represented as a list of nodes. So, for example:

```
?- path( a, e, Path).
Path = [ a, b, d, e]
```

This new path predicate can be defined simply by adding a third argument to our previous path program:

```
path( Node, Node, [ Node]).

path( StartNode, EndNode, [ StartNode | Rest]) :-
    link( StartNode, NextNode),
    path( NextNode, EndNode, Rest).
```

Note that there is no confusion between the two **path** predicates. Since they have different arity, they are easily distinguishable and Prolog treats them as two different predicates. Let us try the question, what are all the nodes reachable from node a:

```
?- Path( a, End, Path).
End = a, Path = [a] ;
End = b, Path = [a,b] ;
End = d, Path = [a,b,d] ;
End = e, Path = [a,b,d,e] ;
End = f, Path = [a,b,d,f] ;
End = a, Path = [a,b,d,f,a]
. . .
```

This time we can see explicitly the paths and it becomes obvious that the last answer was obtained after completing a full cycle from **a** to **a**. Again, the program keeps extending the path and never reports that node c can also be reached from **a**. Also, if we ask ?- path( a, c, P), Prolog again gets into an infinite loop and stops when all memory is exhausted. This time, however, there is an easy way round this problem. The trick consists of forcing the path to be of limited length, so that when the length has been reached during the search, the search cannot continue. To this end, we can use our **conc** predicate of Chapter 3, defined as:

```
conc( [ ], L, L).

conc( [X | L1], L2, [X | L3]) :-
    conc( L1, L2, L3).
```

Suppose we ask Prolog the following question (which might look quite pointless on first glance):

```
?- conc( L, _, _).
L = [ ];
L = [ _ ];
L = [ _, _ ];
L = [ _, _, _ ];
. . .
```

Prolog generates through backtracking general lists of increasing length. This is exactly what is needed to constrain the path length. First we construct a general path (with all the elements uninstantiated) and then ask Prolog to find a path according to this template. If a path is found then that is it, otherwise Prolog will backtrack and generate a longer path template, etc.:

```
?- conc( Path, _, _), path( a, c, Path).
Path = [ a, c];
Path = [ a, c, f, a, c];
Path = [ a, c, d, f, a, c];
. . .
```

This is a very useful programming trick that can often be used. It forces Prolog in effect to search the graph in *breadth-first* manner. In this regime, Prolog tries all the ways of finding a path of length 1, then all the paths of length 2, etc., until a path between the given nodes is found. Above we have used **conc** because it is already available as one of the frequently used predicates. A slightly more elegant way of achieving the same effect would be to define a special predicate, say **list(L)**, which is true if its argument L is a list. It can also be used to generate general lists of increasing length:

```
list( [ ]).              % Empty list is a list

list( [ _ | L]) :-       % This is also a list if
    list( L).            % L is a list
```

An equivalent question to find paths between **a** to **c** would now be:

```
?- list( Path), path( a, c, Path).
```

4.2 # Robot task planning

In this section we will illustrate the use of graph search of the previous section for simple robot task planning.

Consider a mobile robot whose task is the cleaning of a room. Figure 4.2 shows a situation in this robot's world. The robot is at the door, and there is a piece of rubbish (an empty can or a banana peel, say) in the middle of the room, and a waste basket in one of the corners of the room. We assume the robot knows how to execute basic commands like **go( door,middle)** (go from the door to the middle) or **drop** (drop whatever the robot is currently holding into the

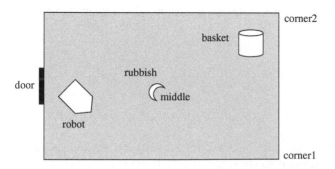

**Figure 4.2** A robot's world.

basket). To execute such commands, the robot may use its vision system, which recognizes objects and their locations.

A concrete task for the robot is specified by *goals* the robot is to achieve. Such a goal may be: rubbish in the basket. The task planning problem is to find a sequence of robot actions such that the goal of the task is achieved after executing this sequence. A plan to achieve the goal 'rubbish in basket' may be: go to the middle of the room, pick up rubbish, go to corner 2, drop rubbish into basket.

To develop such a planning program, we first have to design a representation of the robot's world, and define the 'rules of the game', that is define the possible actions the robot can perform. The current state of the robot's world is defined by three things: the positions of the robot, rubbish and basket. For example, the state shown in Figure 4.2 is determined by:

(1)  Robot at door.
(2)  Basket in corner 2.
(3)  Rubbish in the middle of room.

The positions of the robot and the basket can be any location on the floor. These locations could be defined e.g. by triples of real numbers to give the *x-y-z* coordinates. But we will here choose to refer to locations by their symbolic names like **door** or **corner2**. The location of the rubbish can, in addition, be **in_basket** or **held** (when the robot is holding the rubbish). For the rubbish, it will be useful to state explicitly in the program that some locations are on the floor. This can be done, for example, by referring to the location 'on the floor at the middle' by the Prolog term **floor(middle)**, and not just **middle**. This will make it explicit that when the rubbish is at **floor(middle)**, this is on the floor. This distinction is significant because we will allow the robot only to pick up rubbish from the floor, and not from the basket.

It is convenient to combine all the three pieces of location information into one structured object. Let us choose the word 'state' as the functor to hold the three components together. Then the state of the world of Figure 4.2 is represented by the structured object:

>  state( door, corner2, floor(middle))

If the goal of the robot's task is 'rubbish in basket', this goal can be specified by stating that the robot's plan has to bring the world into a state of the form:

>  state( _, _, in_basket)

This says that in the goal state the robot may be anywhere, the basket may be anywhere, and the rubbish must be in the basket.

Now, we have to specify the possible actions the robot can perform. These actions change the world from one state to another. We assume a 'well-behaved' robot that never drops rubbish on the floor, and never pushes rubbish around. So there are four types of actions:

>  **pickup**, pick up rubbish from floor
>  **drop**, drop rubbish into basket
>  **push( Pos1, Pos2)**, push basket from position **Pos1** to **Pos2**
>  **go( Pos1, Pos2)**, go from **Pos1** to **Pos2**

Not all actions are possible in every state of the world. For example, the action 'drop' is only possible if the robot is holding rubbish next to the basket. Such rules can be formalized in Prolog as a three-place relation named **action**:

> action( State1, Action, State2)

The three arguments of the relation specify an action thus:

> State1 $\longrightarrow$ State2
> Action

**State1** is the state before the action is executed, and **State2** is the state after the action.

The move **drop** can be defined by the Prolog fact, written here in three lines for better readability:

```
action( state( Pos, Pos, held),        % Robot and basket both at Pos, rubbish held by robot
        drop,                           % Action drop
        state( Pos, Pos, in_basket) ).  % After action: rubbish in basket
```

This clause says that after the action, both the robot and the basket remained at position **Pos**, and rubbish ended in the basket. The clause actually specifies a whole set of possible actions because it is applicable to any situation that matches the specified state before the move. Such a specification is therefore sometimes also called an *action schema*. Using Prolog variables, such schemas can be easily programmed in Prolog.

In a similar way, we can express the fact that the robot can move from any position **Pos1** to any position **Pos2** on the floor:

```
action( state( Pos1, Pos2, Pos3),
        go( Pos1, NewPos1),     % Go from Pos1 to NewPos1
        state( NewPos1, Pos2, Pos3)).
```

Note that this clause says many things, including:

- the action is 'go from some position **Pos1** to **NewPos1**'
- the locations of basket and rubbish **Pos2** and **Pos3** remain unchanged.

The robot can pick up the rubbish when both the robot and the rubbish are at the same position on the floor:

```
action( state( Pos1, Pos2, floor(Pos1),
        pickup,
        state( Pos1, Pos2, held)).
```

The remaining type of move, 'push', can be similarly specified (see Figure 4.4).

The type of question that our program will have to answer is: Can the robot, starting in some initial state, clean rubbish into basket? And if yes, what is the plan, i.e. sequence of actions, to do that. This can be formulated as a predicate

> plan( StartState, GoalState, Plan)

which is true if there exists a sequence of possible actions **Plan** that change **StartState** into **GoalState**. A plan may contain *any* number of actions, including zero actions.

The obvious idea is to represent plans as lists of actions. The request to clean the room in the state of Figure 4.2 can be stated by the question:

?- plan( state( door, corner2, floor(middle)), state( _, _, in_basket), Plan).

This requires that in the goal state, the rubbish is in the basket, and we do not care about the positions of the robot and the basket. Our program should answer with:

Plan = [ go(door,middle),  pickup,  go(middle,corner2), drop]

Note that this is like finding a path in a graph which we studied in Section 4.1. In the case of the robot, the nodes of the graph correspond to the states of the robot's world, and the links between states correspond to robot's actions that transform a state into a new state. Analogously to our program **path(StartNode,GoalNode,Path)** of Section 4.1, the definition of predicate **plan** can be based on two observations:

(1)  If goal state is equal to the start state then the goal is trivially achieved, no action is needed. We say this in Prolog by the clause:

plan( State, State, [ ]).        % Start state and goal state are equal, nothing to do

(2)  In other cases, one or more actions are necessary. The robot can achieve the goal state from any state **State1**, if there is some action **Action1** from **State1** to some state **State2**, such that the goal state can be achieved from **State2** with some further actions **RestOfPlan**. This principle is illustrated in Figure 4.3. A Prolog clause that corresponds to this is:

plan( State1, GoalState, [ Action1 | RestOfPlan]) :-
  action( State1, Action1, State2),        % Make first action resulting in State2
  plan( State2, GoalState, RestOfPlan).    % Find rest of plan from State2

The complete planning program is shown in Figure 4.4. Let us ask Prolog to achieve 'rubbish in basket' from the initial state shown in Figure 4.2:

?- plan( state(door, corner2, floor(middle)), state( Rob, Bas, in_basket), Plan).

This question specifies completely the initial state, and partially the goal state. In the goal state, we insist that the location of the rubbish is **in_basket**, but we leave the position **Rob** of the robot and **Bas** of the basket unspecified. Here is Prolog's answer:

Plan = [ go(door,middle), pickup, go(middle,corner2), drop]
Rob = corner2, Bas = corner2

This includes the plan as expected, and in addition this says that in the goal state both the robot and the basket are in corner 2.

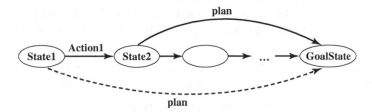

**Figure 4.3** Recursive formulation of **plan**.

```
% State of the robot's world = state( RobotLocation, BasketLocation, RubbishLocation)
% action( State, Action, NewState): Action in State produces NewState
% We assume robot never drops rubbish to floor, and never pushes rubbish around

action( state( Pos1, Pos2, floor(Pos1)),   % Robot and rubbish both at Pos1
        pickup,                            % Pick up rubbish from floor
        state( Pos1, Pos2, held)).         % Rubbish now held by robot

action( state( Pos, Pos, held),            % Robot and basket both at Pos
        drop,                              % Drop rubbish to basket
        state( Pos, Pos, in_basket)).      % Rubbish now in basket

action( state( Pos, Pos, Loc),             % Robot and basket both at Pos
        push( Pos, NewPos),                % Push basket from Pos to NewPos
        state( NewPos, NewPos, Loc)).      % Robot and basket now at NewPos

action( state( Pos1, Pos2, Loc),
        go( Pos1, NewPos1),                % Go from Pos1 to NewPos1
        state( NewPos1, Pos2, Loc)).

% plan( StartState, FinalState, Plan)

plan( State, State, [ ]).                  % To achieve State from State itself, do nothing

plan( State1, GoalState, [ Action1 | RestOfPlan]) :-
    action( State1, Action1, State2),      % Make first action resulting in State2
    plan( State2, GoalState, RestOfPlan).  % Find rest of plan
```

**Figure 4.4** A task planning program.

Let us now study *how* the planning program finds such plans. For simplicity we consider an easier question: How can the robot grasp the rubbish?

```
?- S0 = state(door, corner2, floor(middle)), plan( S0, state( _, _, held), Plan).
Plan = [ go( door,middle), pickup]
```

How did the robot find this plan? The only action possible in the initial state is **go**, which brings the robot to the new position **Pos**, where **Pos** is a *variable*. This means that the robot can go anywhere. In the resulting state **state( Pos,corner2,floor(middle))** the robot first tries to do the action **pickup** as this is the first action specified in the program. It may appear that now Prolog has to search through all possible locations **Pos**, to find that when **Pos** is equal to **middle**, the action **pickup** is possible. However, no such search through possible locations is needed here. The desired position for the robot is simply found through matching between the current goal and the Prolog fact about action **pickup**:

```
action( state( Pos, corner2, floor( middle)), Action1, SecondState) =
action( state( Pos1, Pos2, floor( Pos1)), pickup,  state( Pos1, Pos2, held)).
```

This matching requires, among other things, that:

```
Pos = Pos1, floor( middle) = floor( Pos1)
```

In other words, the rule about pickup requires that both the robot and the rubbish are at the same position. This causes the matching **Pos** = **middle**, which does the trick. So the resulting **SecondState** = **state( middle, corner2, held).**

Let us now try to find alternative plans for cleaning the room in the state of Figure 4.2. Here is what happens:

```
?- S0 = state(door, corner2, floor(middle)), plan( S0, state( _, _, in_basket), Plan).
Plan  = [ go( door, middle), pickup, go( middle, corner2), drop] ;
Plan  = [ go( door, middle), pickup, go( middle, corner2), drop, push( corner2,_A)] ;
Plan  = [ go( door, middle), pickup, go( middle, corner2), drop, push( corner2,_A),
          push( _A, _B)]
```

Here the symbols _A and _B are new variable names generated by Prolog. All the three alternative plans share the same initial part: go to middle, pickup, go to corner 2, drop. The first plan stops here, the second plan adds another action push basket to _A, and the third plan adds to this another push action. So the alternative plans are generated by simply appending to the first plan increasingly many pushing actions. This is not incorrect; all these are possible plans that achieve the goal. But it would be more interesting to also show some other, shorter alternative plans like: go to corner 2, push basket to middle, pickup, drop. Our program, as used above, will never find this alternative short plan, but will just keep lengthening the plan by arbitrarily pushing the basket around. The next plan is generated by *extending* the previous solution plan. This is the same depth-first search mechanism that we noticed in our path-finding program in Section 4.1. Figure 4.5 illustrates the robot's search space among possible plans. The search progresses in *depth-first* manner. It tends towards increasing depth along the left branch of the tree. This style of search only backtracks – returns upwards – when the current branch terminates. As the left branch can be extended by adding arbitrarily many push actions, the branch never terminates and the search will never return to shallower levels.

Can we somehow make Prolog generate alternative solutions so that all alternative shorter plans are generated before the longer ones? Yes, this can be done in several ways that will be discussed in later chapters. But here we can readily employ the simple technique that was discussed in Section 4.1 – generation of plan templates of increasing length. Using **conc** as such a generator, the question to Prolog is:

```
?- S0 = state( door, corner2, floor( middle)),   % Initial state
   conc( Plan _, _),                              % Generate plan templates, short first
   plan( S0, state( _, _, in_basket), Plan).
Plan = [ go(door,middle), pickup, go(middle,corner2), drop] ;
Plan = [ go(door,corner2), push(corner2,middle), pickup, drop)] ;
Plan = [go(door,middle), pickup, go(middle,corner2), drop, push(corner2,_A)] ;
...
```

Here two alternative 4-action plans are found first. In the first plan, the robot first goes to the middle and then to corner 2; in the second, the robot first goes to corner 2 and then pushes the box to the middle. The third plan consists of five actions. Of course, there are infinitely many plans. Longer plans are obtained just by inserting arbitrarily many go and push actions.

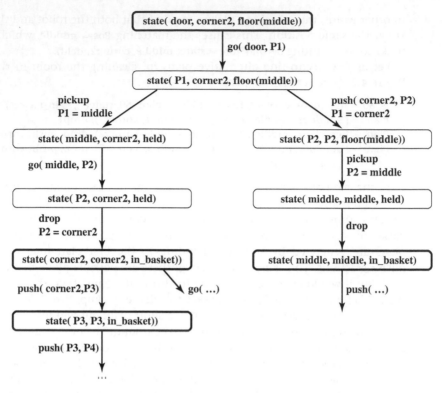

**Figure 4.5** Search for robot's plans of unlimited length by procedure **plan**. Thick ovals indicate the start state and all the goal states. Actions that are not applicable are not shown in this diagram. The search starts at the top (start state) and proceeds downwards in the depth-first manner. Alternative actions are tried in the left-to-right order, so the successful four-action plan on the left (ending with the robot and basket in corner 2) is found first. Alternative plans are found by indefinitely extending the left-hand branch of the tree. So the alternative four-action plan on the right (ending with the robot and basket in the middle of the room) is never encountered by this search.

The locations in our program so far have all been denoted by symbols like **middle** for 'the middle of the room'. Suppose that we wanted to work with numerical *x-y* coordinates in cm. Let the middle be at the point (300,200). Can we use our planning program also with locations represented this way? Yes, easily! Let us choose to represent the *x-y* points by terms of the form **point(X,Y)**. So, the position on the floor in the middle of the room would be represented by **point(300,200)**. Let the robot's *x-y* coordinates at the door be (0,200), and the basket's position in corner 2 be (600,400). Then the question to our planner is:

```
?- S0 = state( point(0,200), point(600,400), floor(point(300,200))),
   plan( S0, state( _, _, in_basket), Plan).
Plan = [ go( point(0,200), point(300,200)), pickup,
         go( point(300,200), point(600,400)), drop]
```

# EXERCISES

**4.1**  Experiment with the planning program of Figure 4.4. For example, use the program to solve the task with multiple goals: rubbish in basket, and basket in corner 1, and robot at door. What happens when using the procedure **plan** on its own, and combination of procedures **conc** and **plan**?

**4.2**  Explain why was it useful to represent the location **Pos** of the rubbish on the floor by the term **floor(Pos)** and not just **Pos** (e.g. **floor(middle)** and not just **middle**). Hint: Omit the functor **floor** in the program and correspondingly simplify the clause for action pickup. Then study what happens when asking the questions:

> ?- action( state( R, corner2, held), pickup, NewState).
> ?- plan( state( door, corner2, middle), state( _, _, in_basket), Plan).
> ?- conc( Plan, _, _), plan( state( door, corner2, middle), state( _, _, in_basket), Plan).

## 4.3  Trip planning

Suppose you are spending a holiday at Riva del Garda, the northern-most town on the shore of the lake Lago di Garda in Italy. You would like to explore by a boat trip other neighbouring towns on the northern shores of the lake, which would give you a chance to enjoy the wonderful scenery from the boat.

Figure 4.6 shows an approximate map of the area and boat connections between the towns on the lake. You would like to plan a trip according to a sight-seeing plan and the timetable of boat transfers. Say you would like something like

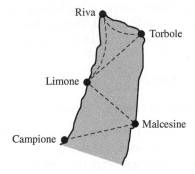

| From Riva | | | To Riva | | |
|---|---|---|---|---|---|
| Riva | 8:00 | 9:10 | Campione | – | – |
| Torbole | – | 9:25 | Malcesine | 9:00 | 10:25 |
| Limone | 8:35 | 9:55 | Limone | 9:20 | 10:50 |
| Malcesine | 8:55 | 10:15 | Torbole | 9:50 | 11:20 |
| Campione | – | – | Riva | 10:05 | 11:35 |

**Figure 4.6**  An approximate map of the northern part of lake Lago di Garda with its towns Riva, Torbole, etc., and part of a simplified timetable of boat connections between the towns. Dashed lines indicate boat routes between the towns. A dash in the timetable means that the particular route does not include the corresponding town.

this: start at Riva after 9 a.m., have a lunch break at Limone not later than 1 p.m., continue to Malcesine, spend there at least 1.5 hours for sightseeing, and then take a return route back to Riva that would include a view of Torbole from the lake. In this section we will develop a simple trip advisor that helps to find suitable schedules according to the given specifications and boat timetable.

Let us first decide on how the timetable will be represented in Prolog. Here is one possibility. We can choose to store each boat route as a list of towns and times. For example, the first column of the timetable from Riva says: depart Riva at 8:00, stop at Limone at 8:35, and immediately continue to Malcesine, arriving at 8:55. Each such boat route can be represented as one Prolog fact about the timetable relation, which will thus begin with:

> timetable( [ riva at 8:00, limone at 8:35, malcesine at 8:55 ]).
> timetable( [ riva at 9:10, torbole at 9:25, limone at 9:55, malcesine at 10:15 ]).
> . . .

For this to be syntactically legal, we have to declare two binary operators 'at' and ':' for example as:

> :- op( 100, xfx, at).
> :- op( 50, xfx, :).

The starting part of the program in Figure 4.7 shows a timetable according to our chosen representation. This is in fact only part of the actual timetable between these towns.

It will be useful to introduce some auxiliary predicates first. One such predicate is

> sail( Place1 at Time1, Place2 at Time2)

which is true if there is a direct connection between **Place1** and **Place2**, departing **Place1** at **Time1** and arriving at **Place2** at **Time2**. This is true if there is a boat route that includes the two places and times at adjacent positions in the corresponding list, which can be stated as:

> sail( PlaceTime1, PlaceTime2) :-
>   timetable( Route),
>   conc( _, [ PlaceTime1, PlaceTime2 | _ ], Route).

Here **PlaceTime1** and **PlaceTime2** are structures of the form **Place at Time**. Another useful predicate defined in Figure 4.7 is **time_diff( T1,T2, Diff)** where T1 and T2 are two given times in our chosen representation, and **Diff** is the difference in minutes between T1 and T2. For example:

> ?- time_diff( 9:50, 11:10, D).
> D = 80

The predicate **before(T1,T2)**, meaning time T1 is before T2, is also defined in Figure 4.7.

Our main predicate will be:

> schedule( Place1 at Time1, Place2 at Time2, Schedule)

This is true if **Schedule** is a list of boat transfers and boat stops between **Place1** and **Place2** at given times, that are possible according to the given timetable. A schedule

```
% Trip planner

:- op( 100, xfx, at).
:- op( 50, xfx, :).

% Part of timetable between the Northern towns of Lago di Garda

timetable( [ riva at 8:00, limone at 8:35, malcesine at 8:55 ]).
   % Start from Riva at 8:00, land in Limone at 8:35, continue to Malcesine, land at 8:55
timetable( [ riva at 9:10, torbole at 9:25, limone at 9:55, malcesine at 10:15 ]).
timetable( [ riva at 9:45, torbole at 10:00, limone at 10:30, malcesine at 10:50 ]).
timetable( [ riva at 11:45, torbole at 12:00, limone at 12:30, malcesine at 12:50 ]).
timetable( [ riva at 13:10, limone at 13:32, malcesine at 13:45 ]).
timetable( [ riva at 14:05, limone at 14:40, malcesine at 15:00 ]).
timetable( [ riva at 15:00, limone at 15:36, malcesine at 15:57, campione at 16:13 ]).
timetable( [ riva at 16:20, torbole at 16:35, limone at 17:05, malcesine at 17:25 ]).
timetable( [ riva at 18:05, torbole at 18:20, limone at 18:50, malcesine at 19:10 ]).

timetable( [ malcesine at 9:00, limone at 9:20, torbole at 9:50, riva at 10:05 ]).
timetable( [ malcesine at 10:25, limone at 10:50, torbole at 11:20, riva at 11:35 ]).
timetable( [ malcesine at 11:25, limone at 11:45, riva at 12:20 ]).
timetable( [ campione at 12:55, malcesine at 13:12, limone at 13:34, riva at 14:10 ]).
timetable( [ malcesine at 13:45, limone at 13:59, riva at 14:20 ]).
timetable( [ malcesine at 15:05, limone at 15:25, riva at 16:00 ]).
timetable( [ malcesine at 16:30, limone at 16:50, torbole at 17:20, riva at 17:35 ]).
timetable( [ malcesine at 18:15, limone at 18:35, torbole at 19:05, riva at 19:20 ]).
timetable( [ malcesine at 19:15, limone at 19:35, torbole at 20:05, riva at 20:20 ]).

% schedule( StartPLace at StartTime, EndPlace at EndTime, Schedule)

schedule( Start, Destination, [ depart( Start),  arrive( Next) | Rest]) :-
   list( Rest),                    % Rest of schedule is a list, try short schedules first
   sail( Start, Next),
   rest_schedule( Next, Destination, Rest).

rest_schedule( Place, Place, []).   % Already at destination - empty schedule

rest_schedule( CurrentPlace, Destination, [ arrive( Next) | Rest] ) :-
   sail( CurrentPlace, Next),       % Stay onboard, continue immediately to town Next
   rest_schedule( Next, Destination, Rest).

rest_schedule( Place at Time1, Destination, [ stay( Place, Time1, Time2) | Rest]) :-
          % Stay at Place until Time2
   sail( Place at Time2, _),
   before( Time1, Time2),                       % Time2 is a later departure time
   schedule( Place at Time2, Destination, Rest).    % Continue at Time2

sail( Place1, Place2) :-         % Direct connection between Place1 and Place2
   timetable( List),
   conc( _, [ Place1, Place2 | _], List).

time_diff( H1:Min1, H2:Min2, Diff) :-  % Difference in minutes between given times
   Diff is 60 * (H2 – H1) + Min2 – Min1.
```

**Figure 4.7** Planning trips by boat on Lago di Garda.

**Figure 4.7** *Contd*

```
before( Time1, Time2) :-              % Time1 is before Time2
   time_diff( Time1, Time2, Diff),
   Diff > 0.

list( [ ]).

list( [ _ | L]) :-
   list( L).
```

will be a list of events of the types: 'depart from', 'arrive at', and 'stay at'. Here is an example schedule:

```
[ depart( riva at 9:10), arrive( torbole at 9:25), arrive( limone at 9:55),
   stay( limone, 9:55, 10:30), depart( limone at 10:30), arrive( malcesine at 10:50) ]
```

This says: depart from Riva at 9:10, arrive at Torbole at 9:25 and stay on board, arrive at Limone at 9:55, disembark from ship and stay at Limone until 10:30, depart Limone at 10:30, arrive Malcesine at 10:50. Our predicate **schedule** will be implemented so that we will be able to ask Prolog to find schedules, say, from Riva at 9:10 with destination Malcesine:

```
?- schedule( riva at 9:10, malcesine at FinalTime, Schedule).
Schedule = [depart(riva at 9:10), arrive(torbole at 9:25),
             arrive(limone at 9:55), arrive(malcesine at 10:15)],
FinalTime = 10:15 ;
Schedule = [depart(riva at 9:10), arrive(torbole at 9:25),
             arrive(limone at 9:55), stay(limone,9:55,10:30),
             depart(limone at 10:30), arrive(malcesine at 10:50)],
FinalTime = 10:50 ? ;
   ...
```

The complete trip advisor program is shown in Figure 4.7. Let us here explain the predicate **schedule( StartPlace at StartTime, Destination, Schedule)**, which is defined by:

```
schedule( Start, Destination, [ depart( Start),  arrive( Next) | Rest]) :-
   list( Rest),        % Rest of schedule is a list, try short schedules first
   sail( Start, Next),
   rest_schedule( Next, Destination, Rest).
```

A schedule has to begin with a 'depart' followed by an 'arrive'. We will not allow a schedule to begin or end with 'stay'. The goal **list(Rest)** constructs through backtracking general lists (to accommodate schedules) of increasing length. This is another application of the path search technique that was introduced in Section 4.1, which ensures that short schedules are constructed before longer, possibly infinite ones. There must be a sail in the timetable from start place at start time to Next, and then the rest of the schedule must be possible from Next to Destination. The definition of predicate **rest_schedule( CurrentPlace, Destination, Rest)** consists of three Prolog clauses, each of them handling one of the three possible cases:

(1)  rest of schedule is empty, or

(2)  we stay on board and continue immediately to the next town (which requires an immediate sail in timetable from current place), or

(3)  we disembark from the ship and stay at the current place until a later sail from the current place.

Now let us ask our trip planner some questions, for example, can I travel from Campione to Riva, stay at Riva for at least 45 minutes, and return to Campione the same day?

```
?- schedule( campione at Start, campione at End, Schedule),
     member( stay( riva, T1, T2), Schedule),                       % Stay at Riva
     time_diff(T1,T2,D), D >= 45.                                  % for at least 45 min
   Schedule = [depart(campione at 12:55), arrive(malcesine at 13:12),
   arrive(limone at 13:34), arrive(riva at 14:10), stay(riva,14:10,15:0),
   depart(riva at 15:0), arrive(limone at 15:36),
   arrive(malcesine at 15:57), arrive(campione at 16:13)]
```

Consider the same question the other way round, visit Campione from Riva and return to Riva on the same day. According to our timetable this is not possible. Prolog will however not answer this question with a simple 'no'. Instead, it will indefinitely keep trying longer and longer schedules. One simple way to prevent this infinite loop is to limit the allowed length of the schedule to, say, 15. This can be done by:

```
?- length( MaxList, 15),                             % MaxList is list of 15 variables
     conc( Schedule, _, MaxList),              % Schedule cannot be longer than MaxList
     schedule( riva at Start, riva at End, Schedule),
     member( stay( campione, T1, T2), Schedule),     % Stay at Campione
     time_diff(T1,T2,D), D >= 45.                    % for at least 45 min
no
```

Now the schedule is limited to 15 events, and Prolog will quickly realize that there is no solution to this query.

Now let us ask a more complicated question: Start at Riva after 9 a.m., stay at Limone for lunch for at least 90 minutes beginning after 11:30 and before 1 p.m. and finishing before 2:30 p.m., stay at Malcesine for at least 1.5 hours, return to Riva by 18:30. This can be formulated as the following question:

```
?- schedule( riva at Start, riva at End, Schedule),      % Start at Riva, end at Riva
     member( stay(limone,TL1,TL2), Schedule),            % Include stay at Limone
     member( stay(malcesine,TM1,TM2), Schedule),         % Include stay at Malcesine
     member( arrive( torbole at _), Schedule),        % Include a view of Torbole from boat
     before( 9:00, Start),                               % Start trip after 9 am
     before( End, 18:30),                                % End trip before 6:30 pm
     before(11:30,TL1), before( TL1,13:00),        % Arive Limone between 11:30 and 13:00
     time_diff( TL1, TL2, DL), DL >= 90,                 % Stay at Limone for at least 90 min
     time_diff( TM1, TM2, DM), DM >= 90.             % Stay at Malcesine for at least 90 min
```

> Schedule = [ depart(riva at 11:45), arrive(torbole at 12:0),
> arrive(limone at 12:30), stay(limone,12:30,14:40), depart(limone at 14:40),
> arrive(malcesine at 15:0), stay(malcesine,15:0,16:30),
> depart(malcesine at 16:30), arrive(limone at 16:50),
> arrive(torbole at 17:20), arrive(riva at 17:35)]

It should be admitted that our program pays no attention to efficiency, and sometimes does much more work than necessary. For (relatively) small timetables, like ours, this does not matter. But this issue would have to be addressed in the case of larger scheduling problems. A substantial source of inefficiency is the particular way that we have been phrasing our questions to Prolog about suitable schedules. For example, our last question required that first a *complete* schedule is built, and only then it is checked whether the schedule satisfies the user's specification of times and inclusion of towns. This can be combinatorially very expensive. If a full schedule is constructed and then it turns out that there is something wrong at the beginning of the schedule, Prolog will backtrack to the beginning of the schedule only after it had tried all the alternative remainders of the schedule after the false beginning. So it will generate many remainder schedules although this is not the place where the problem occurred. In such cases, it is much better to check constraints as soon as possible to avoid futile generation of alternatives in the non-critical part of the schedule.

# EXERCISE

**4.3** Consider the following two questions that are logically equivalent:

(a) ?- schedule( riva at Start, riva at End, Schedule),
  member( arrive( malcesine at _), Schedule), before( 17:00, Start).

(b) ?- sail( riva at Start, _), before( 17:00, Start),
  schedule( riva at Start, riva at End, Schedule),
  member( arrive( malcesine at _), Schedule).

Compare the ways Prolog constructs the answer in case (a) and in case (b). Which question produces the answer more efficiently? Why? Can we simplify question (b) to:

?- before( 17:00, Start),
  schedule( riva at Start, riva at End, Schedule),
  member( arrive( malcesine at _), Schedule).

You can also measure the actual Prolog execution times when answering these questions. This can be done by a Prolog built-in predicate which is for this purpose typically called by  statistics( runtime, T). T is a list of two values: first, total execution time in milliseconds from the start of the Prolog session, and second, execution time since the previous call of statistics( runtime, _). For example:

?- statistics( runtime, T1), schedule( …), statistics( runtime, T2).

Suppose Prolog answered, among other things, T2 = [ 1315, 215]. This means that to solve the query schedule( …), Prolog needed 215 msec.

# 4.4 Solving cryptarithmetic problems

An example of a cryptarithmetic puzzle is:

```
   D O N A L D
 + G E R A L D
   ─────────────
   R O B E R T
```

The problem here is to assign decimal digits to the letters D, O, N, etc., so that the above sum is valid. All letters have to be assigned different digits, otherwise trivial solutions are possible – all letters equal zero.

We will define the predicate

**donald( ListOfLetters)**

where **ListOfLetters** is a list of variables, each of them corresponding to one of the letters in the puzzle. In the above puzzle, the list of distinct variables corresponding to the letters in the puzzle is [D,O,N,A,L,G,E,R,B,T]. This predicate, when called by the question

**?- donald( [D,O,N,A,L,G,E,R,B,T]).**        % All the distinct letters in the puzzle

will instantiate the variables **D**, **O**, **N**, etc. to distinct decimal digits so that the required summation is valid. Note that the predicate **donald** will only be able to solve our particular puzzle, but not other cryptarithmetic puzzles.

Here is a simple idea for solving the puzzle. First, assign one of available decimal digits to each of the variables in the list [ D, O, N, ...]. All the variables must be assigned different digits. Then check whether the assignment satisfies the arithmetic condition stated by the puzzle. If yes, this assignment is a solution. Otherwise Prolog will try other assignments through backtracking. A program that does this is shown in Figure 4.8. An appropriate question to Prolog which solves the puzzle and displays the solution in a reasonably clear way is:

```
?- donald( [D,O,N,A,L,G,E,R,B,T]),                        % Solve puzzle
   L1 = [D,O,N,A,L,D], L2=[G,E,R,A,L,D], L3=[R,O,B,E,R,T].  % The three lists
   A = 4
   B = 3
   ...
   L1 = [5,2,6,4,8,5]
   L2 = [1,9,7,4,8,5]
   L3 = [7,2,3,9,7,0]
```

The three lists above were introduced only for display purposes, to make the digit by digit summation obvious. Later, in Chapter 6 more practical built-in facilities for formatting the displayed information will be introduced.

A couple of comments are in order regarding the program of Figure 4.8. The program is clear and elegant. But the way the search for a solution is carried out by this program is very inefficient, so it may take several tens of seconds before the solution is found. Much more efficient search is possible which only requires a fraction of a second to solve this problem. One such solution will be presented in Chapter 6. The deficiency of the program in Figure 4.8 is that the program

```
% Solving cryptarithmetic puzzle
%              D O N A L D
%            + G E R A L D
%              -------------
%              R O B E R T

% donald( Digits): Digits is a list of digits assigned to letters in the above puzzle

donald( [D,O,N,A,L,G,E,R,B,T]) :-                    % All the letters in the puzzle
    assign( [0,1,2,3,4,5,6,7,8,9], [D,O,N,A,L,G,E,R,B,T]),   % Assign digits to letters
    100000*D + 10000*O + 1000*N +100*A + 10*L + D  +      % Number 1 plus
    100000*G + 10000*E + 1000*R + 100*A + 10*L + D  =:=   % Number 2 equals
    100000*R + 10000*O + 1000*B + 100*E + 10*R + T.       % Number 3

% assign( Digits, Vars):  Assign chosen distinct digits from list Digits to variables in list Vars

assign( _, [ ]).                         % No variable to be assigned a digit

assign( Digs, [D | Vars]) :-
    del( D, Digs, Digs1),                % Deleting D from list Digs gives Digs1
    assign( Digs1, Vars).                % Assign digits to remaining variables
```

**Figure 4.8** Solving cryptarithmetic puzzle DONALD + GERALD = ROBERT.

constructs a *complete* assignment of digits to *all* the letters, and only then is the assignment checked for arithmetic validity. A much better approach is to build only part of the assignment and then check this part immediately. For example, start by assigning digits to the right-most letters of the three numbers (D and T in our puzzle) and check that the summation is correct for this column, i.e. (D+D) mod 10 = T. If this is not true then this partial assignment should be abandoned immediately because there is no point in assigning digits to the remaining letters.

# EXERCISE

.............................................................................................

**4.4** Another drawback of our program is that it only solves the particular puzzle DONALD + GERALD = ROBERT. But to solve another famous puzzle SEND + MORE = MONEY, we would have to write another program. Of course, we can just modify the variables list and the arithmetic condition in the program. It would be more elegant, however, if our program would be more general, and capable of solving any puzzle, whereby the required arithmetic condition would be specified in the Prolog query. One way of doing this is to introduce three additional arguments to our main predicate – three lists representing the three numbers. So the main predicate would be, say,

　　**puzzle( Letters, List1, List2, List3)**

Then the question for DONALD + GERALD = ROBERT would be:

> ?- L1 = [D,O,N,A,L,D], L2 = [G,E,R,A,L,D], L3 = [R,O,B,E,R,T],
> puzzle( [D,O,N,A,L,G,E,R,B,T], L1, L2, L3).

Or a question for SEND + MORE = MONEY would be:

> ?- L1 = [0,S,E,N,D], L2 = [0,M,O,R,E], L3 = [M,O,N,E,Y],
> puzzle( [S,E,N,D,M,O,R,Y], L1, L2, L3).

Define the predicate **puzzle**. An idea: Introduce an auxiliary predicate **list_number** ( **Digits**, **N**) where **Digits** is a list of decimal digits that represents a number, and **N** is the number represented by **Digits**. For example: **list_number( [ 1,4,3], 143).**

## 4.5 The eight-queens problem

The problem here is to place eight queens on the empty chessboard in such a way that no queen attacks any other queen. A solution is shown in Figure 4.9. We will develop a program to solve this puzzle as a unary predicate

> **solution( Pos)**

which is true if and only if **Pos** represents a position with eight queens that do not attack each other. It will be interesting to compare various ideas for programming this problem. Therefore we will present three programs based on somewhat different representations of the problem.

### 4.5.1 Program 1

First, we have to choose a representation of the board position. One natural choice is to represent the position by a list of eight items, each of them corresponding to one queen. Each item in the list will specify a square of the board

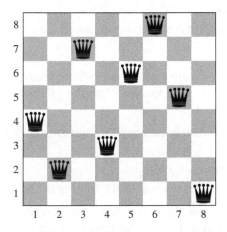

**Figure 4.9** A solution to the eight-queens problem. This position can be represented by the list [ 1/4, 2/2, 3/7, 4/3, 5/6, 6/8, 7/5, 8/1]

on which the corresponding queen is standing. Further, each square can be specified by a pair of coordinates (X and Y) on the board, where each coordinate is an integer between 1 and 8. In the program we can write such a pair as:

X/Y

where, of course, the '/' operator is not meant to indicate division, but it simply combines both coordinates together into a pair (X, Y) of coordinates, that is a square. The position in Figure 4.9 will thus be represented by the list [1/4, 2/2, 3/7, 4/3, 5/6, 6/8, 7/5, 8/1].

Having chosen this representation, the problem is to find such a list of the form:

[ X1/Y1, X2/Y2, X3/Y3, . . . , X8/Y8]

which satisfies the no-attack requirement. Our procedure **solution** will have to search for a proper instantiation of the variables X1, Y1, X2, Y2, . . . , X8, Y8. As we know that all the queens will have to be in different columns to prevent vertical attacks, we can immediately constrain the choice and so make the search task easier. We can thus fix the X-coordinates so that the solution list will fit the following, more specific template:

[ 1/Y1, 2/Y2, 3/Y3, . . . , 8/Y8]

We are interested in solutions on a board of size 8 by 8. However, in programming, the key to the solution is often in considering a more general problem. Paradoxically, it is often the case that the solution for the more general problem is easier to formulate than that for the more specific, original problem. The original problem is then simply solved as a special case of the more general problem.

The creative part of the problem is to find a suitable generalization of the original problem. In our case, a good idea is to generalize the number of queens (the number of columns in the list) from 8 to any number, including zero. The **solution** predicate can then be formulated by considering two cases:

*Case 1*   The list of queens is empty: the empty list is certainly a solution because there is nothing to attack.

*Case 2*   The list of queens is non-empty: then it looks like this:

[ X/Y | Others]

In case 2, the first queen is at some square X/Y and the other queens are at squares specified by the list **Others**. If this is to be a solution then the following conditions must hold:

(1)   There must be no attack between the queens in the list **Others**; that is, **Others** itself must also be a solution.

(2)   X and Y must be integers between 1 and 8.

(3)   A queen at square X/Y must not attack any of the queens in the list **Others**.

To program the first condition we can simply use the **solution** relation itself. The second condition can be specified as follows: Y will have to be an integer between 1 and 8. This can be stated in the program by the condition **member( Y, [1,2,3,4,5,6,7,8])**. On the other hand, we do not have to worry about X since the solution list will have to match the template in which the X-coordinates are already specified. So the template will ensure that X will be an integer between 1 and 8. We can implement the third condition as another relation, **noattack**. All this can then be written in Prolog as follows:

```
solution( [X/Y | Others] ) :-
  solution( Others),
  member( Y, [1,2,3,4,5,6,7,8] ),
  noattack( X/Y, Others).
```

It now remains to define the **noattack** relation:

**noattack( Q, Qlist)**

Again, this can be broken down into two cases:

(1) If the list **Qlist** is empty then the relation is certainly true because there is no queen to be attacked.

(2) If **Qlist** is not empty then it has the form [ **Q1** | **Qlist1**] and now two conditions must be satisfied:
   (a) the queen at **Q** must not attack the queen at **Q1**, and
   (b) the queen at **Q** must not attack any of the queens in **Qlist1**.

To ensure that a queen at some square does not attack another square is easy: the two squares must not be in the same row, the same column or the same diagonal. Our solution template guarantees that all the queens are in different columns, so it only remains to specify explicitly that:

• the Y-coordinates of the queens are different, and

• they are not in the same diagonal, either upward or downward; that is, the absolute distance between the squares in the X-direction must not be equal to the absolute distance in the Y-direction.

Figure 4.10 shows the complete program. To make the program easier to use a template list has been added. This list can be retrieved in a question for generating solutions. So we can now ask:

**?- template( S), solution( S).**

and the program will generate solutions as follows:

```
S = [ 1/4, 2/2, 3/7, 4/3, 5/6, 6/8, 7/5, 8/1];
S = [ 1/5, 2/2, 3/4, 4/7, 5/3, 6/8, 7/6, 8/1];
S = [ 1/3, 2/5, 3/2, 4/8, 5/6, 6/4, 7/7, 8/1];
...
```

These solutions are generated quickly without a noticeable delay, so the complexity of search is not problematic. It is nevertheless instructive to analyse the search complexity involved to understand that the program in fact carries out the search in a quite intelligent manner which results in relatively low complexity. As a first, rough estimate of the size of the search space, we can consider the number of all possible positions with eight queens on the board. This number is equal to the number of all possible combinations of the Y-coordinates of the eight queens. Each queen has the choice among eight possible Y-coordinates, so the total number is

```
% solution( BoardPosition) if BoardPosition is a list of non-attacking queens

solution( [ ] ).

solution( [X/Y | Others] ) :-          % First queen at X/Y, other queens at Others
   solution( Others),                  % Find solution for all other queens
   member( Y, [1,2,3,4,5,6,7,8] ),     % Choose Y coordinate of first queen
   noattack( X/Y, Others).             % First queen does not attack others

noattack( _ , [ ] ).                   % Nothing to attack

noattack( X/Y, [X1/Y1 | Others] ) :-
   Y = \ = Y1,                         % Different Y-coordinates
   Y1 – Y = \ = X1 – X,                % Different upward diagonals
   Y1 – Y = \ = X – X1,                % Different downward diagonals
   noattack( X/Y, Others).

member( Item, [Item | Rest] ).

member( Item, [First | Rest] ) :-
   member( Item, Rest).

% A solution template
template( [1/Y1,2/Y2,3/Y3,4/Y4,5/Y5,6/Y6,7/Y7,8/Y8] ).
```

**Figure 4.10** Program 1 for the eight-queens problem.

$8^8 = 16,777,216$. Fortunately, our program only searches a small fraction of this. To get a better estimate of the actual complexity of search by our program, it will be useful to study how the program actually generates alternative board positions. This is defined by the following clause in the program:

```
solution( [X/Y | Others] ) :-          % First queen at X/Y, other queens at Others
   solution( Others),                  % Find solution for all other queens
   member( Y, [1,2,3,4,5,6,7,8] ),     % Choose Y coordinate of first queen
   noattack( X/Y, Others).             % First queen does not attack others
```

Suppose that this clause is applied to finding a safe configuration of eight queens. Then the list **Others** contains seven queens' positions in columns 2, 3, ... , 8. The program first finds a solution for these seven queens, that is it places 'safely' the seven right-most queens on the board. Then it adds another queen into the left-most column by trying all the possibilities for this queen ($Y = 1$, $Y = 2$, ... ), and checks that the left-most queen does not attack any of the other seven queens. Notice that the left-most queen is only added to the board position if the remaining seven queens are already safely placed. For an unsafe configuration of the right-most seven queens, the program does not get to executing the goal **member(Y,[1,2,...])**, so many hopeless trials are thus saved. The same mechanism applies also to the other seven right-most queens, and then to the six right-most queens, etc. This leads to enormous savings in comparison with the total number of all possible positions.

Another way of looking at this is as follows. The program constructs a position by starting with the empty board, and then placing queens on the board one after another. In which column is the first queen placed, which is the second, etc.? Studying the recursive behaviour of the above clause about **solution** reveals that the first queen is placed in the right-most column, that is column 8. The first try for column 8 is Y-coordinate = 1. The second queen is then placed in the column next to the right-most one, that is column 7. The first try for column 7 is again Y-coordinate = 1. By now we have two queens on the board, one at square 8/1, and the other one at 7/1. The program *immediately* checks whether these two queens are safe, and finds they attack each other. The program now does not even try to place the remaining six queens to the left of column 7, because there is no way of completing the current position into a safe configuration. Thus all the $8^6 = 262,144$ possible placements of the remaining six queens are skipped, which saves a lot of work. The program immediately backtracks to the queen in column 7 and now tries the square 7/2. The queens at 7/2 and 8/1 again attack each other, so the placing of the remaining six queens is skipped again. Now square 7/3 is tried which turns out to be safe with respect to the queen at 8/1. Only now the program moves on to column 6 and tries to place the remaining six queens. This indicates that a lot fewer than $8^8$ placements of queens will actually be tried. It is hard to work out exactly how many queen placements will be tried before the first complete solution for eight queens is found. This is easier to answer by making our program count automatically all the trials of placing a queen on the board. Such a counter would have to be inserted just after the call **member(Y,[1,2,...])**. In Chapter 6 we will see how such a counter can be programmed. For now we just state that the number of all the queen placement trials is 876 before the first complete solution for eight queens is found.

## EXERCISE

**4.5** When searching for a solution, the program of Figure 4.10 explores alternative values for the Y-coordinates of the queens. At which place in the program is the order of alternatives defined? How can we easily modify the program to change the order in which the alternative values for Y-coordinates are tried? Experiment with different orders with the view of studying the time efficiency of the program.

## 4.5.2 Program 2

In the board representation of program 1, each solution had the form:

[ 1/Y1, 2/Y2, 3/Y3,..., 8/Y8]

because the queens were simply placed in consecutive columns. No information is lost if the X-coordinates are omitted. So a more economical representation of the board position can be used, retaining only the Y-coordinates of the queens:

[ Y1, Y2, Y3,..., Y8]

To prevent the horizontal attacks, no two queens can be in the same row. This imposes a constraint on the Y-coordinates. The queens have to occupy all the rows 1, 2,..., 8. The choice that remains is the *order* of these eight numbers. Each solution is therefore represented by a permutation of the list

[1,2,3,4,5,6,7,8]

Such a permutation, S, is a solution if all the queens are safe. So we can write:

```
solution( S) :-
   permutation( [1,2,3,4,5,6,7,8], S),
   safe( S).
```

We have already programmed the **permutation** relation in Chapter 3, but the **safe** relation remains to be specified. We can split its definition into two cases:

(1) S is the empty list: this is certainly safe as there is nothing to attack.

(2) S is a non-empty list of the form [**Queen | Others**]. This is safe if the list **Others** is safe, and **Queen** does not attack any queen in the list **Others**.

In Prolog, this is:

```
safe( [ ] ).

safe( [Queen | Others] ) :-
   safe( Others),
   noattack( Queen, Others).
```

The **noattack** relation here is slightly trickier. The difficulty is that the queens' positions are only defined by their Y-coordinates, and the X-coordinates are not explicitly present. This problem can be circumvented by a small generalization of the **noattack** relation, as illustrated in Figure 4.11. The goal

```
noattack( Queen,Others)
```

is meant to ensure that **Queen** does not attack **Others** when the X-distance between **Queen** and **Others** is equal to 1. What is needed is the generalization of the X-distance between **Queen** and **Others**. So we add this distance as a third argument of the **noattack** relation:

```
noattack( Queen, Others, Xdist)
```

Accordingly, the **noattack** goal in the **safe** relation has to be modified to:

```
noattack( Queen, Others, 1)
```

The **noattack** relation can now be formulated according to two cases, depending on the list **Others**: if **Others** is empty then there is no target and certainly no attack; if

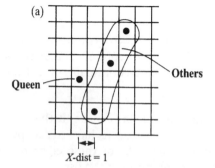
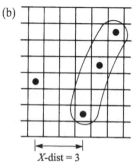

**Figure 4.11** (a) X-distance between **Queen** and **Others** is 1. (b) X-distance between **Queen** and **Others** is 3.

```
% solution( Queens): Queens is a list of Y-coordinates of eight non-attacking queens

solution( Queens) :-
   permutation( [1,2,3,4,5,6,7,8], Queens),
   safe( Queens).

permutation( [ ], [ ] ).

permutation( List, [Head | Tail]) :-
   del( Head, List, List1),             % Choose head of permuted list
   permutation( List1, Tail).           % Permute remaining elements of List

% del( Item, List, NewList): deleting Item from List gives NewList

del( Item, [Item | List], List).
del( Item, [First | List], [First | List1] ) :-
   del( Item, List, List1).


% safe( Queens): Queens is a list of Y-coordinates of non-attacking queens

safe( [ ] ).
safe( [Queen | Others] ) :-
   safe( Others),
   noattack( Queen, Others, 1).

% noattack( Queen, Queens, Dist):
%    Queen does not attack any queen in Queens at horizontal distance Dist

noattack( _, [ ], _).

noattack( Y, [Y1 | Ylist], Xdist) :-
   Y1 - Y =\= Xdist,          % Not upward diagonal attack
   Y - Y1 =\= Xdist,          % Not downward diagonal attack
   Dist1 is Xdist + 1,
   noattack( Y, Ylist, Dist1).
```

**Figure 4.12** Program 2 for the eight-queens problem.

**Others** is non-empty then **Queen** must not attack the first queen in **Others** (which is **Xdist** columns to the right of **Queen**), nor any queen in the tail of **Others** at **Xdist** + 1. This leads to the program shown in Figure 4.12.

## 4.5.3 Program 3

Our third program for the eight-queens problem will be based on the following reasoning. Each queen has to be placed on some square. Each square belongs to some column, some row, some upward diagonal and some downward diagonal of the board. Queens attack each other along columns, rows and diagonals. Therefore, to make sure that all the queens are safe, each queen must be placed

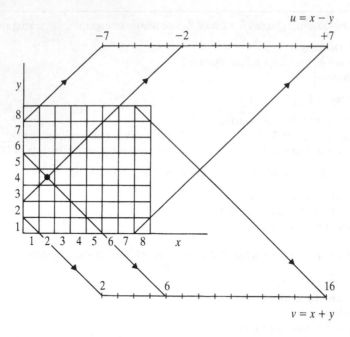

**Figure 4.13** The relation between columns, rows, upward and downward diagonals. The indicated square has coordinates: $x = 2$, $y = 4$, $u = 2 - 4 = -2$, $v = 2 + 4 = 6$.

in a *different* column, a different row, a different upward and a different downward diagonal. It is thus natural to consider a richer representation with four coordinates:

| $x$ | columns |
| $y$ | rows |
| $u$ | upward diagonals |
| $v$ | downward diagonals |

The four coordinates are not independent: given $x$ and $y$, $u$ and $v$ are determined (Figure 4.13 illustrates). For example, as:

$$u = x - y$$
$$v = x + y$$

The domains for all four dimensions are:

$\text{Dx} = [1,2,3,4,5,6,7,8]$

$\text{Dy} = [1,2,3,4,5,6,7,8]$

$\text{Du} = [-7,-6,-5,-4,-3,-2,-1,0,1,2,3,4,5,6,7]$

$\text{Dv} = [2,3,4,5,6,7,8,9,10,11,12,13,14,15,16]$

The eight-queens problem can now be stated as follows: select eight 4-tuples (X,Y,U,V) from the domains (X from Dx, Y from Dy, etc.), never using the same element twice from any of the domains. Of course, once X and Y are chosen, U and V are determined. The solution can then be, roughly speaking, as follows: given all four domains, select the position of the first queen, delete the corresponding items from

```
% solution( Ylist): Ylist is a list of Y-coordinates of eight non-attacking queens

solution( Ylist):-
    sol( Ylist,                                 % Y-coordinates of queens
        [1,2,3,4,5,6,7,8],                      % Domain for X-coordinates
        [1,2,3,4,5,6,7,8],                      % Domain for Y-coordinates
        [-7,-6,-5,-4,-3,-2,-1,0,1,2,3,4,5,6,7], % Upward diagonals
        [2,3,4,5,6,7,8,9,10,11,12,13,14,15,16] ).  % Downward diagonals

sol( [ ], [ ], Dy, Du, Dv).

sol( [Y | Ylist], [X | Dx1], Dy, Du, Dv) :-
    del( Y, Dy, Dy1),                           % Choose a Y-coordinate
    U is X-Y,                                   % Corresponding upward diagonal
    del( U, Du, Du1),                           % Remove it
    V is X + Y,                                 % Corresponding downward diagonal
    del( V, Dv, Dv1),                           % Remove it
    sol( Ylist, Dx1, Dy1, Du1, Dv1).            % Use remaining values

del( Item, [Item | List], List).

del( Item, [First | List], [First | List1] ) :-
    del( Item, List, List1).
```

**Figure 4.14** Program 3 for the eight-queens problem.

the four domains, and then use the rest of the domains for placing the rest of the queens. A program based on this idea is shown in Figure 4.14. The board position is, again, represented by a list of Y-coordinates. The key relation in this program is

    sol( Ylist, Dx, Dy, Du, Dv)

which instantiates the Y-coordinates (in **Ylist**) of the queens, assuming that the queens are placed in consecutive columns taken from **Dx**. All Y-coordinates and the corresponding U- and V-coordinates are taken from the lists **Dy**, **Du** and **Dv**. The top procedure, **solution**, can be invoked by the question:

    ?- solution( S).

This will cause the invocation of **sol** with the complete domains that correspond to the problem space of eight queens.

The **sol** procedure is general in the sense that it can be used for solving the N-queens problem (on a chessboard of size N by N). It is only necessary to properly set up the domains Dx, Dy, Du and Dv which depend on N.

Let us mechanize the generation of the domains. For that we need a procedure

    gen( N1, N2, List)

which will, for two given integers N1 and N2, produce the list:

    List = [ N1, N1 + 1, N1 + 2, ... , N2 - 1, N2]

Such a procedure is:

    gen( N, N, [N] ).

```
gen( N1, N2, [N1 | List] ) :-
  N1 < N2,
  M is N1 + 1,
  gen( M, N2, List).
```

The top level predicate, **solution**, has to be accordingly generalized to

```
solution( N, S)
```

where N is the size of the board and S is a solution represented as a list of Y-coordinates of N queens. The generalized **solution** predicate is:

```
solution( N, S) :-
  gen( 1, N, Dxy),                    % Dxy – domain for X and Y
  Nu1 is 1 – N, Nu2 is N – 1,
  gen( Nu1, Nu2, Du),
  Nv2 is N + N,
  gen( 2, Nv2, Dv),
  sol( S, Dxy, Dxy, Du, Dv).
```

For example, a solution to the twelve-queens problem is generated by:

```
?- solution( 12, S).
S = [1,3,5,8,10,12,6,11,2,7,9,4]
```

## 4.5.4 Concluding remarks

The three solutions to the eight-queens problem show how the same problem can be approached in different ways. We also varied the representation of data. Sometimes the representation was more economical, sometimes it was more explicit and partially redundant. The drawback of the more economical representation is that some information has to be recomputed whenever it is required.

At several points, the key step toward the solution was to generalize the problem. Paradoxically, by considering a more general problem, the solution became easier to formulate. This generalization principle is a kind of standard technique that can often be applied.

Of the three programs, the third one illustrates best how to approach general problems of constructing under constraints a structure from a given set of elements.

Although all three programs solve the eight-queens problem quickly, a natural question is: Which of the three programs is most efficient? In this respect, program 2 is considerably inferior while the other two programs are similar. The reason is that permutation-based program 2 constructs complete permutations while the other two programs are able to recognize and reject unsafe permutations when they are only partially constructed. Program 3 avoids some of the arithmetic computation that is essentially captured in the redundant board representation this program uses.

## EXERCISE

**4.6** Let the squares of the chessboard be represented by pairs of their coordinates of the form X/Y, where both X and Y are between 1 and 8.

(a) Define the relation **jump( Square1, Square2)** according to the knight jump on the chessboard. Assume that **Square1** is always instantiated to a square while **Square2** can be uninstantiated. For example:

?- jump( 1/1, S).

S = 3/2;

S = 2/3;

no

(b) Define the relation **knightpath( Path)** where **Path** is a list of squares that represent a legal path of a knight on the empty chessboard.

(c) Using this **knightpath** relation, write a question to find any knight's path of length 4 moves from square 2/1 to the opposite edge of the board (Y = 8) that goes through square 5/4 after the second move.

## 4.6 WordNet ontology

Consider the following four sentences:

(1) John found a keyboard and a mouse.
(2) John spotted a mouse and a hamster.
(3) John pressed the mouse button.
(4) John scared the smaller rodent.

Suppose you are told that these sentences were taken from two different stories, a pair of sentences from each of the two stories. Which pair of sentences are likely to belong to the same story, and which to the other? That is, which pairs of sentences are about the same topics? This is not difficult for a human to decide, but it requires some knowledge of the semantics of natural language. So the question is rather more difficult for a computer.

To answer such questions by a computer, one straightforward attempt is to look for common words in the given sentences. Let us just consider the nouns in the sentences. Then we may reason as follows: 'John' appears in all the sentences, so this provides no indication about which sentences belong together. 'Mouse' appears in the first three sentences, which sets them apart from sentence 4. But which of the first three sentences should be paired with sentence 4? To answer this, simple word occurrences do not suffice. The particular *senses* of words have to be considered as well. A human quickly finds that the word 'mouse' appears in two senses: first, as a computer mouse in sentences 1 and 3, and second as an animal in sentence 2. The intended senses can be guessed from the context in which 'mouse' appears. In sentence 1, the context includes the word 'keyboard' which is semantically associated with the mouse device, and in sentence 3 the context includes 'button' which is part of the mouse device (but not part of animal mouse). On the other hand, sentence 2 includes the word 'hamster' which associates better with animal mouse than with computer mouse. Sentence 4 contains 'rodent' which better associates with the animals mouse and hamster (both being rodents) than with electronic devices. So sentences 1 and 3 are likely to belong to one story, and sentences 2 and 4 to the other. We say that in the example above, the meaning of the various occurrences of the word 'mouse' was ambiguous and it had to be *disambiguated*.

In this section we will look at WordNet®, a well-known, freely available lexical database that can be used for automated disambiguation and other kinds of reasoning about the semantic relations between words, phrases, sentences or documents, including Web pages. In WordNet, English words are related to their possible meanings, which are in turn related by various semantic relations, such as similarity or generality. Intended uses of WordNet include automatic text analysis and artificial intelligence. WordNet was created and is being developed further at Princeton University under the direction of George A. Miller, a professor of psychology.

## 4.6.1  Elements of WordNet

WordNet can be viewed as a database of relations between words, their properties and meanings. There is a publicly available Prolog version of WordNet (http://wordnet.princeton.edu/wordnet/) where all these relations are defined as a (rather large) Prolog program. Each of these relations appears in a separate file named according to the following format: wn_<relation>.pl, where <relation> is the name of a WordNet relation. For example, the file wn_s.pl contains all the clauses (facts) about the relation s, and wn_hyp.pl contains all the clauses about relation hyp, etc. These relations will be explained later. Only a subset of these files will suffice for our experiments with WordNet. These files can be loaded into Prolog by:

  ?- [ wn_s, wn_g, wn_sim, wn_hyp, wn_mp, wn_mm].

We will now briefly look at what there is in WordNet and in the files defining WordNet relations. Let us first consider some types of entities that appear as arguments in these relations. These types are:

- *words*, in their basic forms (e.g. 'device', but not 'devices');
- *senses*, a word can be used in various senses, such as 'mouse' as an animal, or 'mouse' as an electronic device;
- *types* of words, like noun, verb or adjective;
- *synsets*; a synset is a set of synonymous word senses.

*Synset* is a fundamental concept in WordNet. 'Synset' is a word introduced by WordNet itself. A synset is a set of words, used in such senses that make these words synonymous. A word can be used in various senses. For example, the word 'plane' may mean:

(1)  an aircraft (noun);

(2)  an unbounded two-dimensional shape (noun, in mathematics);

(3)  to travel on the surface of water (verb);

(4)  having the property of surface without slope, like 'a plane surface' (adjective).

Each of these is a *sense* of word 'plane'. Each of these belongs to a different synset. Other words in some senses may belong to the same synset. Figure 4.15 illustrates these relations.

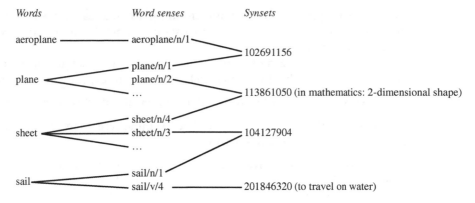

**Figure 4.15** Examples of words, word senses and synsets from WordNet. Notation like 'plane/n/2' means: sense no. 2 of the noun 'plane'.

Synsets, words and the senses of words are in WordNet defined by the relation **s**:

> s( SynsetID, WordNumber, Word, Type, Sense, Count)

The name **s** of this relation comes from 'synset'. The arguments are:

**SynsetID** = synset identifier (a number) to which **Word** with **Sense** belongs
**WordNumber** = the consecutive number of **Word** among words in this synset
**Word** = a word
**Type** = type of word like noun or verb
**Sense** = identifier (a number) of the particular sense of **Word**
**Count** = the number of occurrences of this sense of **Word** in a text corpus; this indicates how common this word sense is

Another useful relation that clarifies the meaning of a synset is:

> g( SynsetID, Explanation)

g stands for 'gloss', and **Explanation** is a glossary clarification of the meaning of **SynsetID**.

In the Prolog version of WordNet, relations like **s/6** and **g/2** are defined in files wn_s.pl and wn_g.pl respectively. So we can consult these two files by ?- [wn_s, wn_g]. Then we can, for example, retrieve the senses of word 'plane' by:

```
?- s( Synset, _, plane, Type, SenseNo, _), g( Synset, Gloss).
Synset = 102691156
Type = n
SenseNo = 5
Gloss = 'an aircraft that has a fixed wing and is powered by propellers or jets; ...';

Synset = 113861050
Type = n
SenseNo = 2
Gloss = '(mathematics) an unbounded two-dimensional shape; ...'
...
```

Two senses of 'plane' above are aircraft and mathematical concept of a plane. In addition, there are quite a few other senses of 'plane', including 'to travel on the surface of water'.

There are about a dozen other relations between synsets defined in WordNet. Here we will mention another four which will suffice for our experiments with the system:

**sim( S1, S2)**       The two synsets S1 and S2 contain adjectives with similar meaning

Let us play with **s** and **sim** a little. For example, are there words with similar meaning as the word 'comprehensive'?

```
?- s( Syn1, _, comprehensive, _, _, _),        % "comprehensive" belongs to Syn1
   sim( Syn1, Syn2),                           % synset Syn2 is similar to Syn1
   s( Syn2, _, SimilarWord, _, _, _).          % SimilarWord belongs to Syn2
SimilarWord = 'across-the-board' ;
SimilarWord = 'all-embracing' ;
SimilarWord = 'all-encompassing' ;
SimilarWord = 'all-inclusive'
...
```

There are many adjectives similar to 'comprehensive'. In Prolog's answers above, the numbers **Syn1** and **Syn2** were omitted. We can use the relation **sim** for example to change a given sentence to a sentence with a similar meaning by replacing a word in the sentence with a similar word. In the following, a sentence will be represented as a list of words. For example, the sentence 'John gave a comprehensive talk' will be represented by the list

[ john, gave, a, comprehensive, talk]

Here is a predicate that does this:

```
% rephrase( Sentence, Word, NewSentence):
%   Replace Word in Sentence by a similar word

rephrase( Sentence, Word, NewSentence) :-
   conc( Prefix, [Word | Postfix], Sentence),   % Divide Sentence into Prefix, Word and Postfix
   s( Syn1, _, Word, _, _, _),                  % Word belongs to synset Syn1
   sim( Syn1, Syn2),                            % Syn2 is similar to Syn1
   s( Syn2, _, SimilarWord, _, _, _),           % SimilarWord belongs to Syn2
   conc( Prefix, [SimilarWord | Postfix], NewSentence).   % Put together new sentence
```

Here is a query that generates such re-wordings of 'John gave a comprehensive talk':

?- rephrase( [ john, gave, a, comprehensive, talk], comprehensive, NewSentence).

Prolog generates altogether 38 new sentences. Many of them make good sense and some answers look quite clever. Here are some of these sentences:

```
NewSentence = [ john, gave, a, 'all-embracing', talk] ;
NewSentence = [ john, gave, a, 'all-inclusive', talk] ;
NewSentence = [ john, gave, a, cosmopolitan, talk] ;
NewSentence = [ john, gave, a, general, talk] ;
NewSentence = [ john, gave, a, plenary, talk] ;
NewSentence = [ john, gave, a, super, talk] ;
NewSentence = [john, gave, a, umbrella, talk] ;
...
```

There are some grammatical imperfections in the use of article 'a' (instead of 'an') which, with our present knowledge of Prolog, will have to be tolerated for now. We can try a further example:

```
?- rephrase( [ john, has, a, bad, computer], bad, NewSentence).
NewSentence = [john, has, a, nonfunctional, computer] ;
NewSentence = [john, has, a, dreadful, computer] ;
NewSentence = [john, has, a, terrible, computer] ;
NewSentence = [john, has, a, lousy, computer] ;
...
```

These are, again, only some of the many Prolog's answers.

The following relations define *hypernyms* and *meronyms*. A hypernym of a word is a more general word, e.g. 'device' is a hypernym of 'keyboard'. Meronym is roughly a part-of relation, e.g. a 'leg' is a part of a 'table'. This is more specifically called the *part meronym*. There are other types of meronyms, like *member meronym*, e.g.: a 'player' is a member of a 'team'. The corresponding predicates in WordNet are:

hyp( S1, S2)   synset S2 contains hypernyms of synset S1
mm( S1, S2)   S1 is a member meronym of S2
mp( S1, S2)   S1 is a part meronym of S2

All these relations hold between nouns.

## 4.6.2 Reasoning about the meaning of words with WordNet

Let us now return to our initial question illustrated by the four sentences 'John found a keyboard and a mouse', etc. How can we reason with WordNet about the semantic relations between the sentences? One question is, for example, what is the meaning of 'mouse' in 'John found a keyboard and a mouse'? Is it an animal mouse or a computer mouse? The idea is to look into the context in which the word appears, that is other words in the same sentence. Concretely in our example sentences, what senses of the words 'mouse' and 'keyboard', or 'mouse' and 'hamster', are connected by the WordNet relations.

The following are some examples of how relations between word senses, or synsets, are found. To run these examples, we load some of the WordNet Prolog files:

```
?- [wn_s, wn_hyp, wn_mm, wn_mp, wn_g].
```

Now we can explore how words in our sentences are related by these basic relations in WordNet. Let us consider the words 'mouse' and 'hamster' in sentence 2. What senses of these two words are related by WordNet relations? For example, do they belong to the same synset? Here is an appropriate query:

```
?- s( Syn, _, mouse, T1, Sen1, _),    % Sen1 is a sense number of mouse, Syn is the synset
   s( Syn, _, hamster, T2, Sen2, _).  % Sense Sen2 of hamster belongs to the same synset Syn
no
```

Further simple queries would show that mouse and hamster are not directly connected by any of the relations in WordNet. We can then try indirect connections, for example: do 'mouse' and 'hamster' in some sense belong to a common more general concept:

```
?- s( S1, _, mouse, _, Sens1,_),        % S1 is a synset to which "mouse" belongs
   s( S2, _, hamster, _, Sens2, _),     % S2 is a synset to which "hamster" belongs
   hyp( S1, S), hyp(S2,S),              % S1 and S2 have a common hypernym S
   s(S,_,Word, _, _, _).                % A corresponding more general word
S1 = 102330245
Sens1 = 1,
Word = rodent,
S = 102329401,
...
```

This says that 'mouse' and 'hamster' in the above senses are both kinds of rodent. We can also check the sense no. 1 of 'mouse' with the glossary:

```
?- g( 102330245, G).
G = 'any of numerous small rodents typically resembling diminutive rats ...'
```

So, WordNet's sense no. 1 of 'mouse' is an animal.

Synsets can be related by several other relations, other than **hyp**. Here is an auxiliary predicate that will help to retrieve such relationships of the kinds **hyp**, **mm** and **mp**, in any direction:

```
r0( Syn1, Syn2, rel( Rel, S1, S2) )
```

This means that synsets **Syn1** and **Syn2** are in relation **Rel**, in the direction from **S1** to **S2**. Here, either **S1** = **Syn1** and **S2** = **Syn2**, or the other way round: **S1** = **Syn2** and **S2** = **Syn1**. This depends on the direction of the relation. This predicate is defined in Figure 4.16. It can be used to see whether two synsets are in any of the relations **hyp**, **mm** or **mp**. However, we are also interested in *indirect* connections between synsets, as in the example above between 'mouse' and 'hamster' which are indirectly connected via 'rodent'. That is, we are interested in *paths* that follow the **hyp**, **mm** and **mp** relations between synsets. This is programmed in Figure 4.16 as:

```
s_path( Syn1, Syn2, Path)
```

Here **Path** connects synsets **Syn1** and **Syn2**. A path is represented as a list of relationships rel( Rel, S1, S2) where **Rel** is one of the relations **hyp**, **mm** or **mp** that hold in WordNet between synsets **S1** and **S2**. The last line of this procedure is \+ mentioned( Syn2, L), which requires that **Syn** is not a member of list L. The symbol '\+' means a kind of negation, which will be discussed in detail in Chapter 5. This requirement prevents cyclic paths and thus avoids some of the search complexity. We are only looking for non-cyclic paths between synsets because cyclic paths are of no interest in this case.

Finally, the predicate word_path( SynList, WordList) in Figure 4.16 converts a list **SynList** of relationships between synsets into a list of relationships between words and their types and senses that correspond to the synsets in **SynList**. The notation **Word/Type/Sense** means a word of type **Type** and sense number **Sense**. For example **mouse/n/4** (word 'mouse' of type noun and sense 4) means a computer mouse. For each synset in **SynList**, only one word-type-sense (a member of this synset) is included in **WordList**.

```
% r0( Syn1, Syn2, rel( Rel, S1, S2) ):
%     Syn1 and Syn2 are in relation Rel, in direction from S1 to S2

r0( Syn1, Syn2, rel( Rel, S1, S2) )  :-
   ( S1 = Syn1, S2 = Syn2;      % Choose first and second arg. of relation between Syn1 and Syn2
     S1 = Syn2, S2 = Syn1),
   ( hyp( S1, S2), Rel = hyp;    % Check hyp relation
     mm( S1, S2), Rel = mm;      % Check mm relation
     mp( S1, S2), Rel = mp       % Check mp relation
   ).

%  r( W1/T1/Sen1, W2/T2/Sen2, MaxLength, WordPath):
%     Sense Sen1 of word W1 of type T1 is related to sense Sen2 of word W2 of type T2
%     by a chain WordPath of basic relations given in WordNet;
%     chain contains at most MaxLength relations

r( W1/T1/Sen1, W2/T2/Sen2, MaxLength, WordPath)  :-
   length( MaxList, MaxLength),      % MaxList is a general list of length MaxLength
   conc( SynPath, _, MaxList),       % SynPath = list not longer than MaxLength
                                     % Shorter lists SynPath are tried first
   s( Syn1, _, W1, T1, Sen1, _),
   s( Syn2, _, W2, T2, Sen2, _),
   s_path( Syn1, Syn2, SynPath),
   word_path( SynPath, WordPath),
   mentioned( W1/T1/Sen1, WordPath),      % Word W1 mentioned in WordPath
   mentioned( W2/T2/Sen2, WordPath).      % Word W2 mentioned in WordPath

% s_path( Syn1, Syn2, Path):
%    Path connects synsets Syn1 and Syn2; Path is list of relationships rel( Rel, S1, S2)

s_path( Syn, Syn, [ ]).           % Path from synset to itself

s_path( Syn1, Syn2, [Rel | L])  :-
   s_path( Syn1, Syn, L),         % Path from Syn1 to one-but-last synset Syn on the path
   r0( Syn, Syn2, Rel),           % Last step on the path: direct relation between Syn and Syn2
   \+ mentioned( Syn2, L).        % Syn2 is not mentioned in path L

%  word_path( SynList, WordList):
%     WordList is list of relationships between triples Word/Type/Sense
%     that correspond to synsets in SynList

word_path( [], []).

word_path( [ rel(Rel,Syn1,Syn2) | SynRels], [ rel(Rel,W1/T1/Sen1,W2/T2/Sen2) | WordRels])  :-
   s( Syn1, _, W1, T1, Sen1, _),
   s( Syn2, _, W2, T2, Sen2, _),
   word_path( SynRels, WordRels).

% mentioned( X, RelationChain):  X is mentioned in list RelationChain as an argument of a relation

mentioned( X, L)  :-
   member( Rel, L),
   ( Rel = rel( _, X, _); Rel = rel( _, _, X) ).
```

**Figure 4.16** Searching for paths between words and synsets in WordNet.

We can now use our predicate **r**, defined in Figure 4.16, to analyse the likely senses of the words in our four sentences. The words of interest are 'mouse' and 'keyboard' in sentence 1, 'mouse' and 'hamster' in sentence 2, etc. We will, quite arbitrarily, assume that two words are related if there is a path of WordNet relations of length three at the most between the two words. Here is the question for sentence 1:

```
?- r( keyboard/T1/Sen1, mouse/T2/Sen2, 3, Path).   % Path of length up to 3 relations
T1 = n,
Sen1 = 1,
T2 = n,
Sen2 = 4,
Path = [rel( hyp, mouse/n/4, 'electronic device'/n/1), rel( hyp,
           'electronic device'/n/1, device/n/1), rel( hyp, keyboard/n/1, device/n/1)].
```

This says that noun 'keyboard' in sense no. 1 is connected with noun 'mouse' in sense no. 4. **Path** tells that the connection is: (1) **mouse/n/4** is a kind of **'electronic device'/n/1**, and (2) this is in turn a kind of **device/n/1**, and (3) **keyboard/n/1** is a kind of **device/n/1**. An appropriate question for sentence 2 is:

```
?- r( mouse/T1/Sen1, hamster/T2/Sen2, 3, Path).
Path = [ rel( hyp, hamster/n/1, rodent/n/1), rel( hyp, mouse/n/1, rodent/n/1)].
```

This answer tells that **mouse/n/1** and **hamster/n/1** are related by a path of length 2 because they are both a kind of **rodent/n/1**. An appropriate question for sentence 3 is:

```
?- r( mouse/T1/Sen1, button/T2/Sen2, 3, Path).
Path = [ rel( hyp, 'mouse button'/n/1, button/n/2),
           rel( mp, 'mouse button'/n/1, mouse/n/4)].
```

This says that **mouse/n/4** and **button/n/2** are related because 'mouse button'/n/1 is a kind of **button/n/2**, and 'mouse button'/n/1 is a part of **mouse/n/4** (WordNet's relation **mp** stands for 'meronym part', which is the part-of relation). For sentence 4, the only word to be analysed is 'rodent', and the only possible sense is: **rodent/n/1**. These connections are illustrated in Figure 4.17.

So far we have determined with the help of WordNet the likely senses in which the words in our sentences are used. That is, we have *disambiguated* the words' senses. This was based on connections between word senses *within* a sentence. Now the question is which sentences (with their words used in these senses) belong together. The idea now is to investigate connections between word senses that appear *between* sentences. For example, when analysing whether sentences 1 and 2 belong to the same story, we check whether **keyboard/n/1** or **mouse/n/4** from sentence 1 is connected with either **mouse/n/1** or **hamster/n/1**. Two relevant questions in this respect are:

```
?- r( keyboard/n/1, mouse/n/1, 3, Path).
no
?- r( mouse/n/1, mouse/n/4, 3, Path).
no
```

Checking all the possible pairs of word senses, our programs say that no word sense in sentence 1 is connected to any of the word senses in sentence 2. We can now proceed to analysing pairs of word senses appearing in sentences 1 and 3, then 1

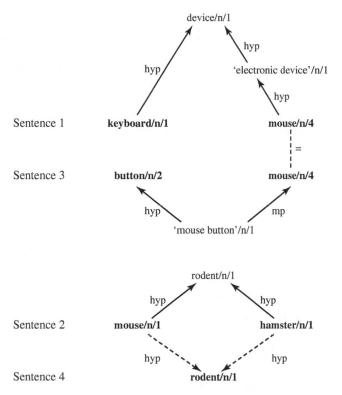

**Figure 4.17** Some WordNet relations between word senses (in bold face) in the four sentences. The notation **mouse/n/4** means word 'mouse' of type noun and sense no. 4. Words in sentences 1 and 3 form a cluster, and words in sentences 2 and 4 form another cluster.

and 4, then 2 and 3 etc. Dashed links in Figure 4.17 show the discovered 'inter-sentence' connections between word senses. Finally, examining the inter-sentence connections we determine which sentences are related. Figure 4.17 shows no connections between sentences 1 and 2, between sentences 1 and 4, and between sentences 3 and 4. On the other hand, there are inter-sentence connections between pairs of sentences 1 and 3, and 2 and 4. The conclusion is that sentences 1 and 3 belong to one story, and sentences 2 and 4 to the other story.

In this section we looked at some ideas about how an ontology like WordNet can be applied to word sense disambiguation, and to the analysis of semantic similarity of sentences or whole texts, e.g. whole documents. Such techniques can be used in semantic document clustering or document retrieval (where documents could be papers represented by their abstracts, and these would be compared for semantic similarity with user search queries). Other similar applications would include searching for relevant documents on the web. Of course, we only considered some initial ideas and played with them in a very rudimentary form. For example, we could introduce the degree of relatedness between word senses, sentences and whole documents by, say, giving more weight to shorter paths and to more common word senses. In general, the meaning of natural language is very tricky, and this difficulty is also reflected in WordNet. Some paths of relationships between words in WordNet turn out to be longer than one would intuitively expect, so the length of these paths may not be a very precise indicator of a common sense intuition about how close word senses are. Another difficulty is simply the complexity. WordNet is quite a large database and includes hundreds of thousands of Prolog facts. So serious attention would have to be paid to the efficiency of programs using WordNet.

# PROJECT

In the above examples, we analysed intra- and inter-sentence connections between words by manually asking Prolog to check the relations between pairs of word senses with the predicate **r/4**. Write a program that will perform all this automatically and partition a set of lists of words into clusters of related lists of words. A user's question to this program would be, for example:

```
?- partition( [ [ keyboard, mouse], [mouse, hamster], [ mouse, button], [rodent]],
   Cluster1, Cluster2).
Cluster1 = [ [ keyboard/n/1, mouse/n/4], [mouse/n/4, button/n/2] ]
Cluster2 = [ [ mouse/n/1, hamster/n/1], [ rodent/n/1 ]
```

*Note*: This project will become easier after learning further elements of Prolog in Chapters 5 and 6.

# Summary

The examples of this chapter illustrate some strong points and characteristic features of Prolog programming:

- Abstract path finding in a graph appears in various forms as part of many programming problems. Prolog's built-in automatic backtracking searches for a path in *depth-first* manner. We looked at a simple technique which forces Prolog to search essentially in *breadth-first* manner, which is often preferred to depth-first search.

- As in the case of eight queens, the same problem can be approached in different ways by varying the representation of the problem. Often, introducing redundancy into the representation saves computation. This entails trading space for time.

- When searching a combinatorial space of candidate solutions, it is generally best to check as soon as possible whether (partial) conditions for a solution are satisfied, before a complete candidate solution is constructed. This often leads to enormous savings in computation time. This was done, for example, in our programs 1 and 3 for the eight-queens problem, but not in the cryptarithmetic program, nor in the travel planning program.

- Often, the key step toward a solution is to generalize the problem. Paradoxically, by considering a more general problem the solution may become easier to formulate.

# Chapter 5

# Controlling Backtracking

We have already seen that a programmer can control the execution of a program through the ordering of clauses and goals. In this chapter we will look at another control facility, called 'cut', for preventing backtracking. The cut also extends the expressive power of Prolog and enables the definition of a kind of negation, called 'negation as failure' and associated with the 'closed world assumption'.

## 5.1 Preventing backtracking

Prolog will automatically backtrack if this is necessary for satisfying a goal. Automatic backtracking is a useful programming concept because it relieves the programmer of the burden of programming backtracking explicitly. On the other hand, uncontrolled backtracking may cause inefficiency in a program. Therefore we sometimes want to control, or to prevent, backtracking. We can do this in Prolog by using the 'cut' facility.

Let us first study the behaviour of a simple example program whose execution involves some backtracking. We will identify those points at which the backtracking is useless and leads to inefficiency.

Consider a regulation about the state of alert due to pollution. Figure 5.1 shows the relation between the concentration X of the pollutant and the degree of alert Y, which can be *normal*, or *alert1*, or *alert2*. The relation between X and Y can be specified by three rules:

*Rule 1*:   if X < 3 then Y = normal
*Rule 2*:   if $3 \leq X$ and X < 6 then Y = alert1
*Rule 3*:   if $6 \leq X$ then Y = alert2

This can be written in Prolog as a binary relation:

f( X, Y)

State of alert Y

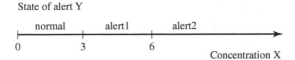

**Figure 5.1** State of alert as a function of pollution level.

as follows:

>  f( X, normal) :- X < 3.                  % Rule 1
>
>  f( X, alert1) :- 3 =< X, X < 6.          % Rule 2
>
>  f( X, alert2) :- 6 =< X.                 % Rule 3

This program, of course, assumes that X is already instantiated to a number before f(X,Y) is executed, as required by the comparison operators.

We will make two experiments with this program. Each experiment will reveal some source of inefficiency in the program, and we will remove each source in turn by using the cut mechanism.

## 5.1.1 Experiment 1

Suppose that the concentration X of the pollutant was measured, and the result was X = 2. Now an administrator, not being familiar with the regulations, may wonder whether the concentration 2 is unsafe and should be the cause of alarm. To find out about this, Prolog can be asked the question: ?- f( 2, alert1). But let us assume the user asks the following, equivalent question:

>  ?- f( 2, Y), Y = alert1.

Let us analyse how Prolog looks for an answer. When executing the first goal, f(2,Y), Y becomes instantiated to **normal**. So the second goal becomes

>  normal = alert1

which fails, and so does the whole goal list. This is straightforward, but before admitting that the goal list is not satisfiable, Prolog tries, through backtracking, two useless alternatives. The detailed trace is shown in Figure 5.2.

The three rules about the **f** relation are mutually exclusive so that one of them at most will succeed. Therefore we know that as soon as one rule succeeds there is no point in trying to use the other rules, as they are bound to fail. But Prolog of course does not know this. In the example of Figure 5.2, rule 1 has become known to succeed at the point indicated by 'CUT'. In order to prevent futile backtracking at this point we have to tell Prolog explicitly *not* to backtrack. We can do this by using the cut mechanism. The cut is written as '!' and is inserted between goals as a kind of pseudo-goal. Our program, rewritten with cuts, is:

>  f( X, normal) :- X < 3, !.
>  f( X, alert1) :- 3 =< X, X < 6, !.
>  f( X, alert2) :- 6 =< X.

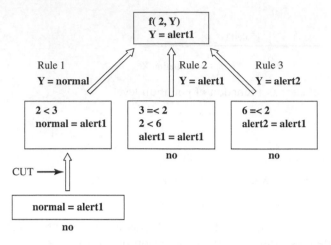

**Figure 5.2** At the point marked 'CUT' we already know that the rules 2 and 3 are bound to fail.

The cut will now prevent backtracking at the points at which it appears in the program. If we now ask:

?- f( 2, Y), Y = alert1.

Prolog will produce the same left-hand branch as in Figure 5.2. This branch will fail at the goal **normal = alert1**. Now Prolog will try to backtrack, but not beyond the point marked '!' in the program. The alternative branches that correspond to 'rule 2' and 'rule 3' will not be generated.

The new program, equipped with cuts, is in general more efficient than the original version without cuts. When the execution fails, the new program will recognize this sooner than the original program.

To conclude, we have improved the efficiency by adding cuts. If the cuts are now removed in this example, the program will still produce the same result; it will sometimes only spend more time. In our case, by introducing the cut we only changed the *procedural* meaning of the program; that is, the results of the program were not affected. We will see later that using a cut may affect the results as well.

## 5.1.2 Experiment 2

Let us now perform a second experiment with the second version of our program. Suppose we ask:

?- f( 7, Y).
Y = alert2

Let us trace what has happened. All three rules were tried before the answer was obtained. This produced the following sequence of goals:

*Try rule 1*:    7 < 3 fails, so backtrack and try rule 2 (cut was not reached)
*Try rule 2*:    3 =< 7 succeeds, but then 7 < 6 fails, backtrack and try rule 3
                  (cut was not reached)
*Try rule 3*:    6 =< 7 succeeds

This trace reveals another source of inefficiency. First it is established that $X < 3$ is not true (7 < 3 fails). The next goal is $3 =< X$ ( 3 =< 7 succeeds). But we know that once the first test has failed, the second test is bound to succeed as it is the negation of the first. Therefore the second test is redundant and the corresponding goal can be omitted. The same is true about the goal $6 =< X$ in rule 3. This leads to the following, more economical formulation of the three rules:

if $X < 3$ then $Y = $ normal,
otherwise if $X < 6$ then $Y = $ alert1,
otherwise $Y = $ alert2.

We can now omit the conditions in the program that are guaranteed to be true whenever they are executed. This leads to the third version of the program:

```
f( X, normal) :-  X < 3, !.
f( X, alert1) :-  X < 6, !.
f( X, alert2).
```

This program produces the same answers to our example questions as our original version, but it is more efficient than both previous versions. But what happens if we *now* remove the cuts? The program becomes:

```
f( X, normal) :- X < 3.
f( X, alert1) :- X < 6.
f( X, alert2).
```

This may produce multiple solutions, some of which are not correct. For example:

```
?- f( 1, Y).
Y = normal;
Y = alert1;
Y = alert2;
no
```

It is important to notice that, in contrast to the second version of the program, this time the cuts not only affect the procedural behaviour, but also change the results of the program. This may produce completely unacceptable results. Suppose $X = 2$ and the user suspects that this may correspond to **alert1**, and asks:

```
?- f( 2, alert1).
yes
```

Try to work out by tracing our program 3 how this unexpected answer is produced. Also, work out why a more careful formulation of this question still works fine:

```
?- f( 2, Y), Y = alert1.
no
```

These examples show that cut may be useful and may enable improved efficiency. But there may be problems with cut that require special attention. These will be analysed later in this chapter.

A more precise meaning of the cut mechanism is as follows:

> Let us call the 'parent goal' the goal that matched the head of the clause containing the cut. When the cut is encountered as a goal it succeeds immediately, but it commits the system to all choices made between the time the 'parent goal' was invoked and the time the cut was encountered. All the remaining alternatives between the parent goal and the cut are discarded.

To clarify this definition, consider a clause of the form:

H :- B1, B2, ..., Bm, !, ..., Bn.

Let us assume that this clause was invoked by a goal G that matched H. Then G is the parent goal. At the moment that the cut is encountered, the system has already found some solution of the goals **B1**, ..., **Bm**. When the cut is executed, this (current) solution of **B1**, ..., **Bm** becomes frozen and all possible remaining alternatives are discarded. Also, the goal G now becomes committed to this clause: any attempt to match G with the head of some other clause is precluded.

Let us apply these rules to the following example:

C :- P, Q, R, !, S, T, U.

C :- V.

A :- B, C, D.

?- A.

Here A, B, C, D, P, etc. have the syntax of terms. The cut will affect the execution of the goal C as illustrated by Figure 5.3. Backtracking will be possible within the goal list P, Q, R; however, as soon as the cut is reached, all alternative solutions of the goal list P, Q, R are suppressed. The alternative clause about C,

C :- V.

will also be discarded. However, backtracking will still be possible within the goal list S, T, U. The 'parent goal' of the clause containing the cut is the goal C in the clause:

A :- B, C, D.

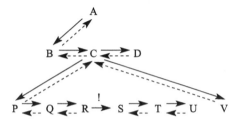

**Figure 5.3** The effect of the cut on the execution. Starting with A, the solid arrows indicate the sequence of calls; the dashed arrows indicate backtracking. There is 'one way traffic' between R and S.

Therefore the cut will only affect the execution of the goal C. On the other hand, it will be 'invisible' from goal A. So automatic backtracking within the goal list B, C, D will remain active regardless of the cut within the clause used for satisfying C.

##  5.2 Examples of using cut

### 5.2.1 Computing maximum

The procedure for finding the larger of two numbers can be programmed as the relation

    max( X, Y, Max)

where Max = X if X is greater than or equal to Y, and Max is Y if X is less than Y. This corresponds to the following two clauses:

    max( X, Y, X) :- X >= Y.

    max( X, Y, Y) :- X < Y.

These two rules are mutually exclusive. If the first one succeeds then the second one will fail. If the first one fails then the second must succeed. Therefore a more economical formulation, with 'otherwise', is possible:

If $X \geq Y$ then Max = X,
otherwise Max = Y.

This is written in Prolog using a cut as:

    max( X, Y, X) :- X >= Y, !.

    max( X, Y, Y).

It should be noted that the use of this procedure requires care. It is safe if in the goal max(X,Y,Max) the argument Max is not instantiated. The following example of incorrect use illustrates the problem:

    ?- max( 3, 1, 1).

    yes

The following reformulation of **max** overcomes this limitation:

    max( X, Y, Max) :-
      X > = Y, !, Max = X
      ;
      Max = Y.

### 5.2.2 Single-solution membership

We have been using the relation

    member( X, L)

for establishing whether X is in list L. The program was:

> member( X, [X | L] ).
>
> member( X, [Y | L] ) :- member( X, L).

This is non-deterministic: if X occurs several times then any occurrence can be found. An 'occurrence' here means that an element of L *matches* X. Let us now change **member** into a deterministic procedure which will find only the first occurrence. The change is simple: we only have to prevent backtracking as soon as X is found, which happens when the first clause succeeds. The modified program is:

> member( X, [X | L] ) :- !.
>
> member( X, [Y | L] ) :- member( X, L).

This program will generate just one solution. For example:

> ?- member( X, [a,b,c] ).
>
> X = a;
>
> no

## 5.2.3  Adding an element to a list without duplication

Often we want to add an item X to a list L so that X is added only if X is not yet in L. If X is already in L then the list remains the same because we do not want to have redundant duplicates in L. The **add** relation has three arguments:

> add( X, L, L1)

where X is the item to be added, L is the list to which X is to be added and L1 is the resulting new list. Our rule for adding can be formulated as:

> If X is a member of list L then L1 = L,
> otherwise L1 is equal to L with X inserted.

It is easiest to insert X in front of L so that X becomes the head of L1. This is then programmed as follows:

> add( X, L, L) :- member( X, L), !.
>
> add( X, L, [X | L] ).

The behaviour of this procedure is illustrated by the following example:

> ?- add( a, [b,c], L).
>
> L = [a,b,c]
>
> ?- add( X, [b,c], L).
>
> L = [b,c]
> X = b
>
> ?- add( a, [b,c,X], L).
>
> L = [b,c,a]
> X = a

Similar to the foregoing example with **max**, **add(X,L1,L2)** is intended to be called with **L2** uninstantiated. Otherwise the result may be unexpected: for example **add( a, [a], [a,a] )** succeeds.

This example is instructive because we cannot easily program the 'non-duplicate add' without the use of cut or another construct derived from the cut. If we omit the cut in the foregoing program then the **add** relation will also add duplicate items. For example:

> ?- add( a, [a,b,c], L).

> L = [a,b,c];

> L = [a,a,b,c]

So the cut is necessary here to specify the intended relation, and not only to improve efficiency. The next example also illustrates this point.

## 5.2.4  Classification into categories

Assume we have a database of results of tennis games played by members of a club. The pairings were not arranged in any systematic way, so each player just played some other players. The results are in the program represented as facts like:

> beat( tom, jim).
> beat( ann, tom).
> beat( pat, jim).

We want to define a relation

> class( Player, Category)

that ranks the players into categories. We have just three categories:

> **winner:**　　every player who won all his or her games is a winner
> **fighter:**　　any player that won some games and lost some
> **sportsman:**　any player who lost all his or her games

For example, if all the results available are just those above then Ann and Pat are winners, Tom is a fighter and Jim is a sportsman.

It is easy to specify the rule for a fighter:

> X is a fighter if
> 　there is some Y such that X beat Y and
> 　there is some Z such that Z beat X.

Now a rule for a winner:

> X is a winner if
> 　X beat some Y and
> 　X was not beaten by anybody.

This formulation contains 'not' which we will only define in the next section. So for now the formulation of **winner** appears trickier. The same problem occurs with **sportsman**. The problem can be circumvented by combining the definition of

**winner** with that of **fighter**, and using the 'otherwise' connective. Such a formulation is:

> If X beat somebody and X was beaten by somebody
>> then X is a fighter,
>> otherwise if X beat somebody
>>> then X is a winner,
>>> otherwise if X got beaten by somebody
>>>> then X is a sportsman.

This formulation can be readily translated into Prolog. The mutual exclusion of the three alternative categories is indicated by the cuts:

```
class( X, fighter) :-
   beat( X, _ ),
   beat( _, X), !.

class( X, winner) :-
   beat( X, _ ), !.

class( X, sportsman) :-
   beat( _, X).
```

Notice that the cut in the clause for **winner** is not necessary. Care is, again, needed when using such procedures containing cuts. Here is what can happen:

```
?- class( tom, C).
```

C = **fighter**;                    % As intended

no

```
?- class( tom, sportsman).
```

yes                    % Not as intended

The call of **class** is safe if the second argument is not instantiated. Otherwise we may get an unintended result.

# EXERCISES

**5.1** Let a program be:

```
p( 1).

p( 2) :- !.

p( 3).
```

Write all Prolog's answers to the following questions:

(a)  ?- p( X).

(b)  ?- p( X), p( Y).

(c)  ?- p( X), !, p( Y).

**5.2**   The following relation classifies numbers into three classes: positive, zero and negative:

> **class( Number, positive) :- Number > 0.**
>
> **class( 0, zero).**
>
> **class( Number, negative) :- Number < 0.**

Define this procedure in a more efficient way using cuts.

**5.3**   Define the procedure

> **split( Numbers, Positives, Negatives)**

which splits a list of numbers into two lists: positive ones (including zero) and negative ones. For example:

> **split( [ 3, −1, 0, 5, −2 ], [ 3, 0, 5 ], [ −1, −2 ])**

Propose two versions: one with a cut and one without.

## 5.3  Negation as failure

'Mary likes all animals but snakes'. How can we say this in Prolog? It is easy to express one part of this statement: Mary likes any X if X is an animal. This is in Prolog:

> **likes( mary, X) :- animal( X).**

But we have to exclude snakes. This can be done by using a different formulation:

> If X is a snake then 'Mary likes X' is not true,
> otherwise if X is an animal then Mary likes X.

That something is not true can be said in Prolog by using a special goal, **fail**, which always fails, thus forcing the parent goal to fail. The above formulation is translated into Prolog, using **fail**, as follows:

> **likes( mary, X) :-**
> **snake( X), !, fail.**
>
> **likes( mary, X) :-**
> **animal( X).**

The first rule here will take care of snakes: if X is a snake then the cut will prevent backtracking (thus excluding the second rule) and fail will cause the failure. These two clauses can be written more compactly as one clause:

> **likes( mary, X) :-**
> **snake( X), !, fail**
> **;**
> **animal( X).**

We can use the same idea to define the relation

> **different( X, Y)**

which is true if X and Y are different. We have to be more precise, however, because 'different' can be understood in several ways:

- X and Y are not literally the same;
- X and Y do not match;
- the values of arithmetic expressions X and Y are not equal.

Let us choose here that X and Y are different if they do not match. The key to saying this in Prolog is:

If X and Y match then **different(X,Y)** fails,
otherwise **different(X,Y)** succeeds.

We again use the cut and **fail** combination:

**different( X, X) :- !, fail.**

**different( X, Y).**

This can also be written as one clause:

**different( X, Y) :-**
  **X = Y, !, fail**
  **;**
  **true.**

**true** is a goal that always succeeds.

These examples indicate that it would be useful to have a unary predicate 'not' such that

**not( Goal)**

is true if **Goal** is not true. We will now define the **not** relation as follows:

If **Goal** succeeds then **not( Goal)** fails,
otherwise **not( Goal)** succeeds.

This definition can be written in Prolog as:

**not( P) :-**
  **P, !, fail**
  **;**
  **true.**

Henceforth, we will assume that **not** is a built-in Prolog procedure that behaves as defined here. We will also assume that **not** is defined as a prefix operator, so that we can also write the goal

**not( snake(X) )**

equivalently as:

**not snake( X)**

Some Prolog implementations, in fact, support this notation. If not, then we can always define **not** ourselves as above. Alternatively, in many Prologs, **not** Goal is written as \+ **Goal**. In this book, we will be using **not** and \+ as equivalent. The more mysterious \+ notation is also recommended in the Prolog standard for the following reason. The way that **not** ( and \+) is defined in Prolog is called *negation as failure*. According to our definition above, **not(Goal)** succeeds if **Goal** fails. This definition is based on the so-called *closed world assumption*, and does not exactly correspond to negation in mathematical logic. This difference can cause unexpected results if **not** is used without care. Closed world assumption and associated problems with **not** will be discussed later in the chapter.

Nevertheless, **not** is a useful facility and can often be used advantageously in place of cut. Our two foregoing examples can be rewritten with **not** as:

```
likes( mary, X) :-
   animal( X),
   not snake( X).

different( X, Y) :-
   not( X = Y).
```

This certainly looks better than our original formulations. It is more natural and is easier to read.

Our tennis player classification program of the previous section can also be rewritten, using **not**, in a way that is closer to the initial definition of the three categories:

```
class( X, fighter) :-
   beat( X, _ ),
   beat( _, X).

class( X, winner) :-
   beat( X, _ ),
   not beat( _, X).

class( X, sportsman) :-
   beat( _, X),
   not beat( X, _ ).
```

As another example of the use of **not**, let us reconsider program 1 for the eight-queens problem of the previous chapter (Figure 4.10). We specified the **no_attack** relation between a queen and other queens. This relation can be formulated also as the negation of the **attack** relation. Figure 5.4 shows a program modified accordingly.

```
solution( [ ] ).
solution( [X/Y | Others] ) :-
   solution( Others),
   member( Y, [1,2,3,4,5,6,7,8] ),        % Usual member predicate
   not attacks( X/Y, Others).

attacks( X/Y, Others) :-
   member( X1/Y1, Others),
   ( Y1 = Y;
     Y1 is Y + X1 − X;
     Y1 is Y − X1 + X).
```

**Figure 5.4** Another eight-queens program.

# EXERCISES

**5.4** Given two lists, **Candidates** and **RuledOut**, write a sequence of goals (using **member** and **not**) that will through backtracking find all the items in **Candidates** that are not in **RuledOut**.

**5.5** Define the set subtraction relation

   **set_difference( Set1, Set2, SetDifference)**

where all the three sets are represented as lists. For example:

   **set_difference( [a,b,c,d], [b,d,e,f], [a,c] )**

**5.6** Define the predicate

   **unifiable( List1, Term, List2)**

where **List2** is the list of all the members of **List1** that match **Term**, but are not instantiated by this matching. For example:

   **?- unifiable( [X, b, t(Y)], t(a), List).**

   **List = [X, t(Y)]**

Note that X and Y have to remain uninstantiated although the matching with **t(a)** does cause their instantiation. Hint: Use **not( Term1 = Term2)**. If **Term1 = Term2** succeeds then **not( Term1 = Term2)** fails and the resulting instantiation is undone!

## 5.4 Closed world assumption, and problems with cut and negation

Using the cut facility we get something, but not for nothing. The advantages and disadvantages of using cut were illustrated by examples in the previous sections. Let us summarize, first, the advantages:

(1) With cut we can often improve the efficiency of the program. The idea is to explicitly tell Prolog: do not try other alternatives because they are bound to fail.

(2) Using cut we can specify mutually exclusive rules; so we can express rules of the form:

   *if* condition P *then* conclusion Q

   *otherwise* conclusion R

   In this way, cut enhances the expressive power of the language.

The reservations against the use of cut stem from the fact that we can lose the valuable correspondence between the declarative and procedural meaning of programs. If there is no cut in the program we can change the order of clauses and goals, and this will only affect the efficiency or termination of the program, not the declarative meaning. On the other hand, in programs with cuts, a change in the order of clauses may affect the declarative meaning. This means that we can get different results. The following example illustrates:

**p :- a, b.**

**p :- c.**

The declarative meaning of this program is: p is true if and only if a and b are both true or c is true. This can be written as a logic formula:

p <===> (a & b) ∨ c

We can change the order of the two clauses and the declarative meaning remains the same. Let us now insert a cut:

**p :- a, !, b.**

**p :- c.**

The declarative meaning is now:

p <===> (a & b) ∨ (∼a & c)

If we swap the clauses,

**p :- c.**

**p :- a, !, b.**

then the meaning becomes:

p <===> c ∨ (a & b)

The important point is that when we use the cut facility we have to pay more attention to the procedural aspects. Unfortunately, this additional difficulty increases the probability of a programming error.

In our examples in the previous sections we have seen that sometimes the removal of a cut from the program can change the declarative meaning of the program. But there were also cases in which the cut had no effect on the declarative meaning. The use of cuts of the latter type is less delicate, and therefore cuts of this kind are sometimes called 'green cuts'. From the point of view of readability of programs, green cuts are 'innocent' and their use is quite acceptable. When reading a program, green cuts can simply be ignored.

In contrast, cuts that do affect the declarative meaning are called 'red cuts'. Red cuts are the ones that make programs hard to understand, and they should be used with special care.

Cut is often used in combination with a special goal, **fail**. In particular, we defined the negation (**not**) of a goal as the failure of the goal. The negation, so defined, is just a special, more restricted way of using cut. For reasons of clarity we will prefer to use **not** instead of the cut–fail combination (whenever possible), because the negation is intuitively clearer than the cut–fail combination.

It should be noted that **not** may also cause problems, and so should also be used with care. The problem is that **not**, as defined here, does not correspond exactly to negation in mathematics. Let us consider an example – a single clause program:

**round( ball).**

Let us ask this program:

?- round( ball).

yes

Prolog says 'yes' which means: 'Yes, it logically follows from the program that ball is round.' Now, let us ask:

?- round( earth).

no

By 'no' Prolog actually means to say: 'It is not possible to derive from the program that Earth is round, so I don't know.' Prolog's 'no' is to be understood as 'don't know, there is not enough information in the program to prove this goal'. Finally, let us ask:

?- not round( earth).

yes

It should be noted that, according to Prolog's answers to the previous two questions, this last answer is not quite appropriate. Namely, here 'yes' does not mean that 'not round(earth)' logically follows from the program. Prolog's 'yes' here is the result of the particular definition of negation in Prolog, that is negation as failure. Inference by negation as failure is based on the 'closed world assumption' (abbreviated CWA). According to CWA, every Prolog program is assumed to state *everything* that is true in the world described by the program. Accordingly, everything that is not stated by the program (or is not derivable from the program) is assumed to be false, and consequently, its negation is assumed true. The program states **round(ball)**, but says nothing about Earth. Therefore, relying on CWA, Prolog infers that **round(earth)** is false, and further **not round(earth)** must be true.

This deserves special care because in everyday life we do not normally assume that 'the world is closed'. When we do not explicitly state in a program that Earth is round, we do not really mean to imply that Earth is not round.

Another aspect that requires special care is the quantification of variables under **not**. To illustrate this aspect, consider the following program about restaurants:

good_standard( jeanluis).

expensive( jeanluis).

good_standard( francesco).

| reasonable( Restaurant) :- | % A restaurant is reasonably priced if |
|    not expensive( Restaurant). | % it is not expensive |

The usual question of interest is:

?- good_standard( X), reasonable( X).

Prolog will answer:

X = francesco

If we ask apparently the same question

?- reasonable( X), good_standard( X).

then Prolog will answer:

**no**

Why did Prolog not find Francesco this time? This looks like a bug, although it accidentally conveys an instructive message unrelated to Prolog: it is better to first consider quality before price and not the other way round! The reader is invited to trace the program to understand why we get different answers when asking what seems to be a logically equivalent question. The key difference between both questions is that the variable X is, in the first case, already instantiated when **reasonable( X)** is executed, whereas X in **reasonable( X)** is not yet instantiated in the second case. In the first case, the negated goal is **not expensive(francesco)**, whereas in the second case the negated goal is **not expensive(X)**. The general hint is: **not Goal** works safely if the variables in **Goal** are instantiated at the time **not Goal** is called. Otherwise we may get unexpected results for reasons explained in the sequel.

The problem with uninstantiated negated goals arises from unfortunate change of the quantification of variables in negation as failure. In the usual interpretation in Prolog, the question:

?- **expensive( X).**

means: Does there *exist* X such that **expensive( X)** is true? If yes, what is X? So X is *existentially* quantified. Accordingly Prolog answers X = **jeanluis**. But the following question may produce a surprise:

?- **not expensive( X).**

**no**

The question is not interpreted as: Does there exist X such that **not expensive(X)**? The expected answer might be X = **francesco**. But Prolog answers 'no' because negation as failure changes the quantification to universal. The question **not expensive(X)** is interpreted as:

not( exists X such that **expensive( X))**

This is equivalent to:

For *all* X: not **expensive( X)**

That is: Is it true that nobody is expensive? This explains why Prolog answers **no**. As already stated, to avoid such possible surprises due to subtleties in quantification of variables, it is usually a good idea to ensure that the variables under a negated goal are instantiated before this goal is executed. Without variables, there can be no confusion about their quantification.

We have discussed in detail problems with cut, which also indirectly occur in **not**. The intention of the discussion has been to warn users about the necessary care, not to discourage the use of cut. Cut is useful and often necessary. And after all, the kind of complications that are incurred by cut in Prolog commonly occur when programming in other languages as well.

## Summary

- The cut facility prevents backtracking. It is used both to improve the efficiency of programs and to enhance the expressive power of the language.

- Efficiency is improved by explicitly telling Prolog (with cut) not to explore alternatives that we know are bound to fail.

- Cut makes it possible to formulate mutually exclusive conclusions through rules of the form:

  *if* Condition *then* Conclusion1 *otherwise* Conclusion2

- Cut makes it possible to introduce *negation* as *failure*: **not** Goal is defined through the failure of Goal.

- Two special goals are sometimes useful: **true** always succeeds, **fail** always fails.

- There are also some reservations against cut: inserting a cut may destroy the correspondence between the declarative and procedural meaning of a program. Therefore, it is part of good programming style to use cut with care and not to use it without reason.

- **not** defined through failure does not exactly correspond to negation in mathematical logic. Negation as failure makes the closed world assumption (CWA). Therefore, the use of **not** also requires special care.

- **not** appears to change the usual quantification of variables in Prolog goals, which may result in unintended results. To avoid this, it is often useful to ensure that the variables in a negated goal get instantiated before the goal is executed.

- In many Prologs, **not** is written as '\+'

## References

The distinction between 'green cuts' and 'red cuts' was proposed by van Emden (1982). Le (1993) proposed a different negation for Prolog which is mathematically advantageous, but computationally more expensive.

Le, T.V. (1993) *Techniques of Prolog Programming*. John Wiley & Sons.
van Emden, M. (1982) Red and green cuts. *Logic Programming Newsletter*: 2.

# Chapter 6

# Built-in Predicates

Prolog implementations usually include a large number of built-in predicates. In this chapter we look at a 'classical' repertoire of built-in predicates that are also part of Prolog standard. These features enable the programming of operations that are not possible using only the features introduced so far. One set of such predicates manipulates terms: testing whether some variable has been instantiated to an integer, taking terms apart, constructing new terms, etc. Another useful set of procedures manipulates the 'database': they add new clauses to the program or remove existing ones. Another set of built-in predicates generates sets of solutions, yet another enables input and output of data.

   The built-in predicates largely depend on the implementation of Prolog. However, the predicates discussed in this chapter are provided by many Prolog implementations. Various implementations provide additional features.

## 6.1   Testing the type of terms

### 6.1.1   Predicates *var, nonvar, atom, integer, float, number, atomic, compound*

Terms may be of different types: variable, integer, atom, etc. If a term is a variable then it can be, at some point during the execution of the program, instantiated or uninstantiated. Further, if it is instantiated, its value can be an atom, a structure, etc. It is sometimes useful to know what the type of this value is. For example, we may want to add the values of two variables, X and Y, by:

   Z is X + Y

Before this goal is executed, X and Y have to be instantiated to numbers. If we are not sure that X and Y will indeed be instantiated to numbers at this point then we should check this in the program before arithmetic is done.

To this end we can use the built-in predicate **number**. number( X) is true if X is a number or if it is a variable whose value is a number. We say that X must 'currently stand for' a number. The goal of adding X and Y can then be protected by the following test on X and Y:

..., number( X), number( Y), Z is X + Y, ...

If X and Y are not both numbers then no arithmetic will be attempted. So the number goals 'guard' the goal Z is X + Y before meaningless execution.

Built-in predicates of this sort are: **var, nonvar, atom, integer, float, number, atomic, compound**. Their meaning is as follows:

| | |
|---|---|
| var( X) | succeeds if X is currently an uninstantiated variable |
| nonvar( X) | succeeds if X is not a variable, or X is an already instantiated variable |
| atom( X) | is true if X currently stands for an atom |
| integer( X) | is true if X currently stands for an integer |
| float( X) | is true if X currently stands for a real number |
| number( X) | is true if X currently stands for a number |
| atomic( X) | is true if X currently stands for a number or an atom |
| compound( X) | is true if X currently stands for a compound term (a structure) |

The following example questions to Prolog illustrate the use of these built-in predicates:

?- var( Z), Z = 2.

Z = 2

?- Z = 2, var( Z).

no

?- integer( Z), Z = 2.

no

?- Z = 2, integer( Z), nonvar( Z).

Z = 2

?- atom( 3.14).

no

?- atomic( 3.14).

yes

?- atom( = => ).

yes

?- atom( p(1)).

no

?- compound ( 2 + X).

yes

We will illustrate the need for **atom** by an example. We would like to count how many times a given atom occurs in a given list of objects. To this purpose we will define a procedure:

count( A, L, N)

where A is the atom, L is the list and N is the number of occurrences. The first attempt to define count could be:

count( _, [ ], 0).

count( A, [A | L], N) :- !,
   count( A, L, N1),             % N1 = number of occurrences in tail
   N is N1 + 1.

count( A, [_ | L], N) :-
   count( A, L, N).

Now let us try to use this procedure on some examples:

?- count( a, [a,b,a,a], N).

N = 3

?- count( a, [a,b,X,Y], Na).

Na = 3

. . .

?- count( b, [a,b,X,Y], Nb).

Nb = 3

. . .

?- L = [a, b, X, Y], count( a, L, Na), count( b, L, Nb).

Na = 3
Nb = 1
X = a
Y = a

. . .

In the last example, X and Y both became instantiated to a and therefore we only got Nb = 1; but this is not what we had in mind. We are interested in the number of real occurrences of the given *atom*, and not in the number of terms that *match* this atom. According to this more precise definition of the count relation we have to check whether the head of the list is an atom. The modified program is as follows:

count( _, [ ], 0).

count( A, [B | L], N) :-
   atom( B), A = B, !,       % B is atom A?
   count( A, L, N1),        % Count in tail
   N is N1 + 1
   ;
   count( A, L, N).          % Otherwise just count the tail

The following, more complex programming exercise in solving cryptarithmetic puzzles makes use of the **nonvar** predicate.

## 6.1.2  A cryptarithmetic puzzle using *nonvar*

We have tackled the cryptarithmetic puzzle DONALD + GERALD = ROBERT in Section 4.4. We wrote an elegant program that solves the puzzle, but we also noted that the program was rather inefficient. Here we will write a much more efficient program in which the digit-by-digit summation will be implemented. The built-in predicate **nonvar** will enable the new approach. Also, the new program will be more flexible in that it will work for any cryptarithmetic puzzle.

We will define a relation

   sum( N1, N2, N)

where N1, N2 and N represent the three numbers of a given cryptarithmetic puzzle. The goal **sum**(N1,N2,N) is true if there is an assignment of digits to the letters such that N1 + N2 = N. Each number will be represented as a list of decimal digits. For example, the number 225 would be represented by the list [2,2,5]. As these digits are not known in advance, an uninstantiated variable will stand for each digit. Using this representation, the problem can be depicted as:

   [D,O,N,A,L,D]
 + [G,E,R,A,L,D]
 = [R,O,B,E,R,T]

The task is to find such an instantiation of the variables D, O, N, etc., for which the sum is valid. When the **sum** relation has been programmed, the puzzle can be stated to Prolog by the question:

   ?- sum( [D,O,N,A,L,D], [G,E,R,A,L,D], [R,O,B,E,R,T ]).

To define the **sum** relation on lists of digits, we have to implement the actual rules for doing summation in the decimal number system. The summation is done digit by digit, starting with the right-most digits, continuing toward the left, always taking into account the carry digit from the right. It is also necessary to maintain a set of available digits; that is, digits that have not yet been used for instantiating variables already encountered. So, in general, besides the three numbers N1, N2 and N, some additional information is involved, as illustrated in Figure 6.1:

- carry digit before the summation of the numbers;
- carry digit after the summation;
- set of digits available before the summation;
- remaining digits, not used in the summation.

To formulate the **sum** relation we will use, once again, the principle of generalization of the problem: we will introduce an auxiliary, more general relation, **sum1**. **sum1** has some extra arguments, which correspond to the foregoing additional information:

   sum1( N1, N2, N, C1, C, Digits1, Digits)

Number1 = $[D_{11}, D_{12}, \ldots, D_{1i}, \ldots]$
Number2 = $[D_{21}, D_{22}, \ldots, D_{2i}, \ldots]$
Number3 = $[D_{31}, D_{32}, \ldots, D_{3i}, \ldots]$

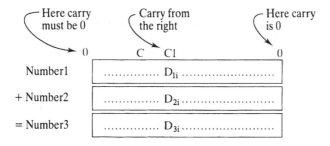

**Figure 6.1** Digit by digit summation. The relations at the indicated ith digit position are: $D_{3i} = (C1 + D_{1i} + D_{2i}) \bmod 10$; $C = (C1 + D_{1i} + D_{2i}) \operatorname{div} 10$.

N1, N2 and N are our three numbers, as in the **sum** relation, C1 is carry from the right (before summation of N1 and N2), and C is carry to the left (after the summation). The following example illustrates:

?- **sum1( [H,E], [6,E], [U,S], 1, 1, [1,3,4,7,8,9], Digits).**

H = 8
E = 3
S = 7
U = 4
Digits = [1,9]

This corresponds to the following summation:

```
1 ←    ←1
   8 3
   6 3
   ―――
   4 7
```

As Figure 6.1 shows, C1 and C have to be 0 if N1, N2 and N are to satisfy the **sum** relation. **Digits1** is the list of available digits for instantiating the variables in N1, N2 and N; **Digits** is the list of digits that were not used in the instantiation of these variables. Since we allow the use of any decimal digit in satisfying the **sum** relation, the definition of **sum** in terms of **sum1** is as follows:

**sum( N1, N2, N) :-**
    **sum1( N1, N2, N, 0, 0, [0,1,2,3,4,5,6,7,8,9], _).**

The burden of the problem has now shifted to the **sum1** relation. This relation is, however, general enough that it can be defined recursively. We will assume, without loss of generality, that the three lists representing the three numbers are of equal length. Our example problem, of course, satisfies this constraint; if not, a 'shorter' number can be prefixed by zeros.

The definition of **sum1** can be divided into two cases:

(1) The three numbers are represented by empty lists. Then:

  **sum1**( [ ], [ ], [ ], C, C, **Digs, Digs**).

(2) All three numbers have some left-most digit and the remaining digits on their right. So they are of the form:

  [D1 | N1],  [D2 | N2],  [D | N]

In this case two conditions must be satisfied:

  (a) The three numbers N1, N2 and N have to satisfy the **sum1** relation, giving some carry digit, C2, to the left, and leaving some unused subset of decimal digits, **Digs2**.

  (b) The left-most digits D1, D2 and D, and the carry digit C2 have to satisfy the relation indicated in Figure 6.1: C2, D1 and D2 are added giving D and a carry to the left. This condition will be formulated in our program as the relation **digitsum**.

Translating this case into Prolog we have:

```
sum1( [D1 | N1], [D2 | N2], [D | N], C1, C, Digs1, Digs) :-
  sum1( N1, N2, N, C1, C2, Digs1, Digs2),
  digitsum( D1, D2, C2, D, C, Digs2, Digs).
```

It only remains to define the **digitsum** relation in Prolog. There is one subtle detail that involves the use of the metalogical predicate **nonvar**. D1, D2 and D have to be decimal digits. If any of them is not yet instantiated then it has to become instantiated to one of the digits in the list **Digs2**. This digit has to be deleted from the set of available digits. If D1, D2 or D is already instantiated then, of course, the set of available digits will remain the same. This is realized in the program as a non-deterministic deletion of an item from a list. If this item is non-variable then nothing is deleted (no instantiation occurs). This is programmed as:

```
del_var( Item, List, List) :-
  nonvar( Item), !.                    % Item already instantiated

del_var( Item, [Item | List], List).   % Delete the head

del_var( Item, [A | List], [A | List1]) :-
  del_var( Item, List, List1).         % Delete Item from tail
```

A complete program along these lines for cryptarithmetic puzzles is shown in Figure 6.2. The program also includes the definition of two puzzles. The question to Prolog about DONALD, GERALD and ROBERT, using this program, would be:

  ?- **puzzle1**( N1, N2, N), **sum**( N1, N2, N).

Sometimes this puzzle is made easier by providing part of the solution as an additional constraint that D be equal 5. The puzzle in this form can be communicated to Prolog using **sum1**:

```
% Solving cryptarithmetic puzzles
sum( N1, N2, N) :-                        % Numbers represented as lists of digits
    sum1( N1, N2, N,
         0, 0,                            % Carries from right and to left both 0
         [0,1,2,3,4,5,6,7,8,9], _).       % All available digits

sum1( [ ], [ ], [ ], C, C, Digits, Digits).

sum1( [D1 | N1], [D2 | N2], [D | N], C1, C, Digs1, Digs) :-
    sum1( N1, N2, N, C1, C2, Digs1, Digs2),
    digitsum( D1, D2, C2, D, C, Digs2, Digs).

digitsum( D1, D2, C1, D, C, Digs1, Digs) :-
    del_var( D1, Digs1, Digs2),           % Select an available digit for D1
    del_var( D2, Digs2, Digs3),           % Select an available digit for D2
    del_var( D, Digs3, Digs),             % Select an available digit for D
    S is D1 + D2 + C1,
    D is S mod 10,                        % Remainder
    C is S // 10.                         % Integer division

del_var( A, L, L) :-
    nonvar( A), !.                        % A already instantiated

del_var( A, [A | L], L).                  % Delete the head

del_var( A, [B | L], [B | L1]) :-
    del_var( A, L, L1).                   % Delete from tail
% Some puzzles
puzzle1( [D,O,N,A,L,D],
         [G,E,R,A,L,D],
         [R,O,B,E,R,T] ).

puzzle2( [0,S,E,N,D],
         [0,M,O,R,E],
         [M,O,N,E,Y] ).
```

**Figure 6.2** A program for cryptarithmetic puzzles.

```
?- sum1( [5,O,N,A,L,5],
         [G,E,R,A,L,5],
         [R,O,B,E,R,T],
         0, 0, [0,1,2,3,4,6,7,8,9], _).
```

It is interesting that in both cases there is only one solution. That is, there is only one way of assigning digits to letters.

# EXERCISES

**6.1** Write a procedure **simplify** to symbolically simplify summation expressions with numbers and symbols (lower-case letters). Let the procedure rearrange the expressions so that all the symbols precede numbers. These are examples of its use:

?- simplify( 1 + 1 + a, E).

E = a + 2

?- simplify( 1 + a + 4 + 2 + b + c, E).

E = a + b + c + 7

?- simplify( 3 + x + x, E).

E = 2*x + 3

**6.2** Define the procedure:

    **add_to_tail( Item, List)**

to store a new element into a list. Assume that all of the elements that can be stored are non-variables. **List** contains all the stored elements followed by a tail that is not instantiated and can thus accommodate new elements. For example, let the existing elements stored be **a**, **b** and **c**. Then

    **List = [a, b, c | Tail]**

where **Tail** is a variable. The goal

    **add_to_tail( d, List)**

will cause the instantiation

    **Tail = [d | NewTail]**   and   **List = [a, b, c, d | NewTail]**

Thus the structure can, in effect, grow by accepting new items. Define also the corresponding membership relation.

## 6.2  Constructing and decomposing terms: =.., *functor, arg, name*

There are three built-in predicates for decomposing terms and constructing new terms: **functor**, **arg** and '=..'. We will first look at =.., which is written as an infix operator and reads as 'univ'. The goal

    **Term =.. L**

is true if L is a list that contains the principal functor of **Term**, followed by its arguments. The following examples illustrate:

    ?- f( a, b) =.. L.

    L = [f, a, b]

    ?- T =.. [rectangle, 3, 5].

    T = rectangle( 3, 5)

    ?- Z =.. [p, X, f(X,Y)].

    Z = p( X, f(X,Y) )

Why would we want to decompose a term into its components – its functor and its arguments? Why construct a new term from a given functor and arguments? The following example illustrates the need for this.

Let us consider a program that manipulates geometric figures. Figures are squares, rectangles, triangles, circles, etc. They can, in the program, be represented as terms such that the functor indicates the type of figure, and the arguments specify the size of the figure, as follows:

```
square( Side)
triangle( Side1, Side2, Side3)
circle( R)
```

One operation on such figures can be enlargement. We can implement this as the predicate

```
enlarge( Fig, Factor, Fig1)
```

where Fig and Fig1 are geometric figures of the same type (same functor), and the parameters of Fig1 are those of Fig multiplied by Factor. For simplicity, we will assume that all the parameters of Fig are already known; that is, instantiated to numbers, and so is Factor. One way of programming the enlarge relation is:

```
enlarge( square(A), F, square(A1) ) :-
   A1 is F*A.

enlarge( circle(R), F, circle(R1) ) :-
   R1 is F*R1.

enlarge( rectangle(A,B), F, rectangle(A1,B1) ) :-
   A1 is F*A, B1 is F*B.

...
```

This works, but it is awkward when there are many different figure types. We have to foresee all types that may possibly occur. Thus, we need an extra clause for each type although each clause says essentially the same thing: take the parameters of the original figure, multiply all the parameters by the factor, and make a figure of the same type with new parameters.

One (unsuccessful) attempt to handle, at least, all one-parameter figures with one clause could be:

```
enlarge( Type(Par), F, Type(Par1) ) :-
   Par1 is F*Par.
```

However, this is normally not allowed in Prolog because the functor has to be an atom; so the variable Type would not be accepted syntactically as a functor. The correct method is to use the predicate '=..'. Then the enlarge procedure can be stated completely generally, for any type of object, as follows:

```
enlarge( Fig, F, Fig1) :-
   Fig =.. [Type | Parameters],
   multiplylist( Parameters, F, Parameters1),
   Fig1 =.. [Type | Parameters1].
```

multiplylist( [ ], _, [ ] ).

multiplylist( [X | L], F, [X1 | L1] ) :-
   X1 is F*X, multiplylist( L, F, L1).

Our next example of using the '=..' predicate comes from symbolic manipulation of formulas where a frequent operation is to substitute some subexpression by another expression. We will define the relation

   substitute( Subterm, Term, Subterm1, Term1)

as follows: if all occurrences of **Subterm** in **Term** are substituted by **Subterm1** then we get **Term1**. For example:

   ?- substitute( sin(x), 2*sin(x)*f(sin(x)), t, F).

   F = 2*t*f(t)

By 'occurrence' of **Subterm** in **Term** we will mean something in **Term** that *matches* **Subterm**. We will look for occurrences from top to bottom. So the goal

   ?- substitute( a+b, f( a, A+B), v, F).

will produce

   F = f( a, v),        A = a,        B = b

and not

   F = f( a, v + v),       A = a + b,       B = a + b

In defining the **substitute** relation we have to consider the following decisions depending on the case:

   If **Subterm** = **Term** then **Term1** = **Subterm1**;
   otherwise if **Term** is 'atomic' (not a structure)
      then **Term1** = **Term** (nothing to be substituted),
      otherwise the substitution is to be carried out on the arguments of **Term**.

These rules can be converted into a Prolog program, shown in Figure 6.3.

Here is an example of using the **substitute** predicate. Suppose we have symbolic expressions like x*sin((x+y)/2), and we would like to evaluate such an expression for some given numerical values of the symbols in the expression, for example x = 1 and y = 2.14. This can be implemented as a predicate like:

   eval( Exp, SymbolValues, Val)

which computes the value **Val** of symbolic expression **Exp** for the values of the symbols given in the list **SymbolValues**. For example:

   ?- eval( x*sin((x+y)/2), [ x = 1, y = 2.14], V).

   V = 0.9999996829318346        % V is the value of the expression for x=1 and y=2.14

Here is a definition of **eval**, using **substitute**:

   eval( Exp, SymbolValues, Val) :-
      subst_symbols( Exp, SymbolValues, Exp1),      % Substitute symbols by their values
      Val is Exp1.

```
% substitute( Subterm, Term, Subterm1, Term1):
%  if all occurrences of Subterm in Term are substituted with Subterm1 then we get Term1.

% Case 1: Substitute whole term
substitute( Term, Term, Term1, Term1) :- !.

% Case 2: Nothing to substitute if Term atomic
substitute( _, Term, _, Term) :-
   atomic( Term), !.

% Case 3: Do substitution on arguments
substitute( Sub, Term, Sub1, Term1) :-
   Term =.. [F | Args],                % Get arguments
   substlist( Sub, Args, Sub1, Args1), % Perform substitution on them
   Term1 =.. [F | Args1].              % Construct Term1

substlist( _, [ ], _, [ ] ).

substlist( Sub, [Term | Terms], Sub1, [Term1 | Terms1] ) :-
   substitute( Sub, Term, Sub1, Term1),
   substlist( Sub, Terms, Sub1, Terms1).
```

**Figure 6.3** A procedure for substituting a subterm of a term by another subterm.

```
subst_symbols( Exp, [ ], Exp).                % No symbol to substitute

subst_symbols( Exp0, [ Symbol = Number | SymbolValues], Exp) :-
   substitute( Symbol, Exp0, Number, Exp1),   % Subst. Symbol by Number giving Exp1
   subst_symbols( Exp1, SymbolValues, Exp).   % Substitute remaining symbols
```

Terms that are constructed by the '=..' predicate can, of course, also be used as goals. The advantage of this is that the program itself can, during execution, generate and execute goals of forms that were not necessarily foreseen at the time of writing the program. A sequence of goals illustrating this effect would be something like the following:

```
obtain( Functor),
compute( Arglist),
Goal =.. [Functor | Arglist],
Goal
```

Here, **obtain** and **compute** are some user-defined procedures for getting the components of the goal to be constructed. The goal is then constructed by '=..', and invoked for execution by simply stating its name, **Goal**.

An implementation of Prolog may require that all the goals, as they appear in the program, are *syntactically* either atoms or structures with an atom as the principal functor. Thus a variable, regardless of its eventual instantiation, in such a case may not be syntactically acceptable as a goal. This problem is circumvented by another built-in predicate, **call**, whose argument is the goal to be executed. Accordingly, the above example would be rewritten as:

```
...
Goal =.. [Functor | Arglist],
call( Goal)
```

Sometimes we may want to extract from a term just its principal functor or one of its arguments. We can, of course, use the '=..' predicate. But it can be neater, and also more efficient, to use one of the other two built-in procedures for manipulating terms: **functor** and **arg**. Their meaning is as follows: a goal

functor( Term, F, N)

is true if F is the principal functor of **Term** and N is the arity of F. A goal

arg( N, Term, A)

is true if A is the Nth argument in **Term**, assuming that arguments are numbered from left to right starting with 1. The following examples illustrate:

?- functor( t( f(X), X, t), Fun, Arity).

Fun = t

Arity = 3

?- arg( 2, f( X, t(a), t(b)), Y).

Y = t(a)

?- functor( D, date, 3),
    arg( 1, D, 29),
    arg( 2, D, june),
    arg( 3, D, 1982).

D – date( 29, june, 1982)

The last example shows a special application of the **functor** predicate. The goal functor(D,date,3) generates a 'general' term whose principal functor is **date** with three arguments. The term is general in that the three arguments are uninstantiated variables whose names are generated by Prolog. For example:

D = date( _5, _6, _7)

These three variables are then instantiated in the example above by the three **arg** goals.
   Related to this set of built-in predicates is the predicate **name** for constructing or decomposing atoms:

name( A, L)

is true if L is the list of ASCII codes of the characters in atom A. For example:

?- name( abc, L), name( A, [97,98,98,97]).

L = [97,98,99],   A = abba          % ASCII code of "a" is 97, of "b" is 98, etc.

## EXERCISES

**6.3** Define the predicate **ground( Term)** so that it is true if **Term** does not contain any uninstantiated variables.

**6.4** The **substitute** procedure of this section only produces the 'outer-most' substitution when there are alternatives. Modify the procedure so that all possible alternative substitutions are produced through backtracking. For example:

?- substitute( a+b, f(A+B), new, NewTerm).

A = a
B = b
NewTerm = f( new);

A = a+b
B = a+b
NewTerm = f( new+new)

Our original version only finds the first answer.

**6.5** Define the relation

subsumes( Term1, Term2)

so that **Term1** is more general than **Term2**. For example:

?- subsumes( X, c).

yes

?- subsumes( g(X), g(t(Y)) ).

yes

?- subsumes( f(X,X), f(a,b) ).

no

## 6.3 Various kinds of equality and comparison

When do we consider two terms to be equal? Until now we have introduced three kinds of equality in Prolog. The first was based on matching, written as:

X = Y

This is true if X and Y match. Another type of equality was written as:

X is E

This is true if X matches the value of the arithmetic expression E. We also had:

El =:= E2

This is true if the values of the arithmetic expressions E1 and E2 are equal. In contrast, when the values of two arithmetic expressions are not equal, we write:

E1 =\= E2

Sometimes we are interested in a stricter kind of equality: the *literal equality* of two terms. This kind of equality is implemented as another built-in predicate written as an infix operator '==':

T1 == T2

This is true if terms T1 and T2 are identical; that is, they have exactly the same structure and all the corresponding components are the same. In particular, the names of the variables also have to be the same. The complementary relation is 'not identical', written as:

T1 \== T2

Here are some examples:

?- f( a, b) == f( a, b).

yes

?- f( a, b) == f( a, X).

no

?- f( a, X) == f( a, Y).

no

?- X = Y, f( a, X) == f( a, Y).

yes

?- X \== Y.

yes

?- t( X, f(a,Y) ) == t( X, f(a,Y) ).

yes

As an example, let us redefine the relation

count( Term, List, N)

from Section 6.1. This time let N be the number of literal occurrences of the term **Term** in a list **List**:

```
count( _, [ ], 0).

count( Term, [Head | L ], N) :-
  Term == Head, !,
  count( Term, L, N1),
  N is N1 + 1
  ;
  count( Term, L, N).
```

We have already seen predicates that compare terms arithmetically, for example $X + 2 < 5$. Another set of built-in predicates compares terms alphabetically and thus defines an ordering relation on terms. For example, the goal

X @< Y

is read: term X precedes term Y. The precedence between simple terms is determined by alphabetical or numerical ordering. The precedence between structures is determined by the precedence of their principal functors. If the principal functors are equal, then the precedence between the top-most, left-most functors in the subterms in X and Y decides. Examples are:

?- paul @< peter.

yes

?- f(2) @< f(3).

yes

?- g(2) @< f(3).

no

?- g(2) @>= f(3).

yes

?- f( a, g(b), c) @< f( a, h(a), a).

yes

All the built-in predicates in this family are @<, @=<, @>, @>= with their obvious meanings.

## 6.4  Database manipulation

According to the relational model of databases, a database is a specification of a set of relations. A Prolog program can be viewed as such a database: the specification of relations is partly explicit (facts) and partly implicit (rules). Some built-in predicates make it possible to update this database during the execution of the program. This is done by adding (during execution) new clauses to the program or by deleting existing clauses. Predicates that serve these purposes are **assert**, **asserta**, **assertz** and **retract**.

A goal of the form

   **assert( C)**

always succeeds and, as its side effect, causes a clause C to be 'asserted' – that is, added to the database. A goal of the form

   **retract( C)**

does the opposite: it deletes a clause that matches C. If there is no such clause then **retract** fails.

In this way a program can modify itself during its execution. This can be useful, for example in a program that interacts with the environment and maintains the current state of the world. Consider the blocks world of Chapter 1, where part of the state of the world was specified by the relation **on(Block,Something)**. A possible state of three blocks **a**, **b** and **c** in this world can be defined by:

   on( a, b).    on( b, table).    on( c, table).

Now a robot that operates in this world executes the action **move(a,b,c)**, meaning: move block **a** from **b** to **c**. As the result of this action, **a** is on **c**, and **a** is no longer on **b**. Using **retract** and **assert**, the effects of such an action can be programmed as:

```
move( X, Y, Z)  :-     % Move X from Y to Z
   retract( on( X, Y)),  % X is no longer on Y
   assert( on( X, Z)).   % Now X is on Z
```

The program can now be made to simulate the robot's action of moving a from b to c by:

?- move( a, b, c).

The result of this will be the modified relation on as follows:

on( b, table).　　on( c, table).　　on( a, c).

Clauses of any form can be asserted or retracted. However, depending on the implementation of Prolog, it may be required that predicates manipulated through assert/retract be declared as *dynamic*, using the directive dynamic( PredicateIndicator). For example:

:- dynamic on/2.　　% Binary predicate on is "dynamic"

Predicates that are only introduced by **assert**, and not by **consult**, are automatically assumed as dynamic.

Asserted clauses do not have to be facts, they can also be rules which are used by the Prolog interpreter as usual. For example, our familiar predicate **member** can be input into Prolog by the following asserts:

?- assert( member( X, [ X | _]),
　　assert( (member( X, [ _ | L]) :- member( X, L)).

In the second assert, an extra pair of parentheses is necessary for syntactic reasons when asserting a rule (because of very high priority of the operator ':-').

The next example illustrates that **retract** is non-deterministic: a whole set of clauses can, through backtracking, be removed by a single **retract** goal. For example, we can remove all the clauses about the on/2 relation with:

:- retract( on( X, Y)), fail.

no

Here is what happened before Prolog answered 'no': first, **retract( on( X, Y))** removed the first clause of the on relation. Then **fail** forced Prolog to backtrack to **retract( on( X, Y))**, which removed the second fact about the on relation, etc. In the end, Prolog says 'no' because by that time all the backtrack choices have been exhausted (there is nothing left to retract about the on relation).

When asserting a clause, we may want to specify the position at which the new clause is inserted to the database. The predicates **asserta** and **assertz** enable us to control the position of insertion. The goal

asserta( C)

adds C at the beginning of the database. The goal

assertz( C)

adds C at the end of the database. We will assume that **assert** is equivalent to **assertz**, as usual in Prolog implementations. The following example illustrates these effects:

?- assert( p(b) ), assertz( p(c) ), assert( p(d) ), asserta( p(a) ).

yes

?- P( X).

X = a;
X = b;
X = c;
X = d

One useful application of **asserta** is to store already computed answers to questions. For example, let there be a predicate:

solve( Problem, Solution)

defined in the program. We may now ask some question and request that the answer be remembered for future questions:

?- solve( problem1, Solution),
   asserta( solve( problem1, Solution) ).

If the first goal above succeeds then the answer (**Solution**) is stored and used, as any other clause, in answering further questions. The advantage of such a 'memoization' of answers is that a further question that matches the asserted fact will normally be answered much quicker than the first one. The result now will be simply retrieved as a fact, and not computed through a possibly time-consuming process. This technique of storing derived solutions is also called 'caching'.

An extension of this idea is to use **assert** for generating all solutions in the form of a table of facts. For example, we can generate a table of products of all pairs of integers between 0 and 9 as follows: generate a pair of integers X and Y, compute Z is X*Y, assert the three numbers as one line of the product table, and then force the failure. The failure will cause, through backtracking, another pair of integers to be found and so another line tabulated, etc. The following procedure **maketable** implements this idea:

```
maketable :-
  L = [0,1,2,3,4,5,6,7,8,9],
  member( X, L),        % Choose first factor X
  member( Y, L),        % Choose second factor Y
  Z is X*Y,
  assert( product(X,Y,Z) ),
  fail.
```

The question

?- maketable.

will, of course, not succeed, but it will, as a side effect, add the whole product table to the database. After that we can ask, for example, what pairs give the product 8:

?- product( A, B, 8).

A = 1
B = 8;
A = 2
B = 4;
...

A remark on the style of programming should be made at this stage. The foregoing examples illustrate some obviously useful applications of **assert** and **retract**.

However, their use requires special care. Excessive and careless use of these facilities cannot be recommended as good programming style. By asserting and retracting we modify the program. Therefore relations that hold at some point will not be true at some other time. At different times the same questions receive different answers. A lot of asserting and retracting may thus obscure the meaning of the program. The resulting behaviour of the program may become difficult to understand, difficult to explain and difficult to trust.

## EXERCISES

**6.6** (a) Write a Prolog question to remove the whole **product** table from the database.

(b) Modify the question so that it only removes those entries where the product is 0.

**6.7** Define the relation

   copy_term( Term, Copy)

which will produce a copy of **Term** so that **Copy** is **Term** with all its variables renamed. This can be easily programmed by using **asserta** and **retract**. In some Prologs **copy_term** is provided as a built-in predicate.

## 6.5 Control facilities

So far we have covered most of the extra control facilities except **repeat**. For completeness the complete set is presented here.

- *cut*, written as '!', prevents backtracking. It was introduced in Chapter 5. A useful predicate is **once( P)** defined in terms of cut as:

   once( P) :- P, !.

   once( P) produces one solution only. The cut, nested in **once**, does not prevent backtracking in other goals.

- **fail** is a goal that always fails.
- **true** is a goal that always succeeds.
- **not( P)** is negation as failure that behaves exactly as if defined as:

   not( P) :- P, !, fail; true.

   Some problems with cut and **not** were discussed in detail in Chapter 5.

- ( P -> Q; R) is an if-then-else construct. It is read as: if **P** then **Q** else **R**. The arrow '->' is an infix operator whose priority is less than that of ';' and greater than that of a comma. For example, we can define M as the larger of X and Y (assuming that X and Y have numerical values) as:

   ( X >= Y -> M = X; M = Y)

   For example:

   ?- X = 10, member( Y, [ 5, 15]), ( X >= Y -> M = X; M = Y).
      X = 10, Y = 5, M = 10 ;

X = 10, Y = 15, M = 15 ;
no

Note that the if-then-else construct behaves as if defined by:

( P -> Q; R) :-  P, !, Q.

( P -> Q; R) :-  R.

- **call**( P) invokes a goal P. It succeeds if P succeeds.
- **repeat** is a goal that always succeeds. Its special property is that it is non-deterministic; therefore, each time it is reached by backtracking it generates another alternative execution branch. **repeat** behaves as if defined by:

**repeat.**
**repeat :- repeat.**

A typical way of using **repeat** is illustrated by the following procedure **dosquares** which reads a sequence of numbers and outputs their squares. The sequence is concluded with the atom **stop**, which serves as a signal for the procedure to terminate.

```
dosquares :-
  repeat,
  read( X),
  ( X = stop, !
  ;
    Y is X*X, write(Y),
    fail
  ).
```

## 6.6 *bagof, setof* and *findall*

We can generate, by backtracking, all the objects, one by one, that satisfy some goal. Each time a new solution is generated, the previous one disappears and is not accessible any more. However, sometimes we would prefer to have all the generated solutions  available together – for example, collected into a list. The built-in predicates **bagof**, **setof** and **findall** serve this purpose.

The goal

bagof( X, P, L)

will produce the list **L** of all the objects **X** such that a goal **P** is satisfied. Of course, this usually makes sense only if **X** and **P** have some common variables. For example, let us have these facts in the program:

age( peter, 7).
age( ann, 5).
age( pat, 8).
age( tom, 5).

Then we can obtain the list of all the children of age 5 by the goal:

?- bagof( Child, age( Child, 5), List).

List = [ ann, tom]

If, in the above goal, we leave the age unspecified, then we get, through back-tracking, three lists of children, corresponding to the three age values:

?- bagof( Child, age( Child, Age), List).

Age = 7
List = [ peter];

Age = 5
List = [ ann, tom];

Age = 8
List = [ pat];

no

We may prefer to have all of the children in one list regardless of their age. This can be achieved by explicitly stating in the call of bagof that we do not care about the value of Age as long as such a value exists. This is stated as:

?- bagof( Child, Age ^ age( Child, Age), List).

List = [ peter, ann, pat, tom]

Syntactically, '^' is a predefined infix operator of type xfy.

If there is no solution for P in the goal bagof( X, P, L), then the bagof goal simply fails. If the same object X is found repeatedly, then all of its occurrences will appear in L, which leads to duplicate items in L.

The predicate setof is similar to bagof. The goal

setof( X, P, L)

will again produce a list L of objects X that satisfy P. Only this time the list L will be ordered, and duplicate items, if there are any, will be eliminated. The ordering of the objects is according to the built-in predicate @<, which defines the ordering among terms. For example:

?- setof( Child, Age ^ age( Child, Age), ChildList),
   setof( Age, Child ^ age( Child, Age), AgeList).

ChildList = [ ann, pat, peter, tom]
AgeList = [5, 7, 8]

There is no restriction on the kind of objects that are collected. So we can, for example, construct the list of children ordered by their age, by collecting pairs of the form Age/Child:

?- setof( Age/Child, age( Child, Age), List).

List = [5/ann, 5/tom, 7/peter, 8/pat]

Another predicate of this family, similar to bagof, is findall.

findall( X, P, L)

```
findall( X, Goal, Xlist) :-
    call( Goal),                        % Find a solution
    assertz( queue(X) ),                % Assert it
    fail;                               % Try to find more solutions
    assertz( queue(bottom) ),           % Mark end of solutions
    collect( Xlist).                    % Collect the solutions

collect( L) :-
    retract( queue(X) ), !,             % Retract next solution
    ( X == bottom, !, L = [ ]           % End of solutions?
    ;
      L = [X | Rest], collect( Rest) ). % Otherwise add X and collect the rest
```

**Figure 6.4** An implementation of the **findall** relation.

produces, again, a list of objects that satisfy condition **P**. The difference with respect to **bagof** is that *all* of the objects X are collected regardless of (possibly) different solutions for variables in **P** that are not shared with **X**. This difference is shown in the following example:

> ?- findall( Child, age( Child, Age), List).

> List = [ peter, ann, pat, tom]

If there is no object X that satisfies P then **findall** will succeed with L = [ ].

If **findall** were not available as a built-in predicate then it could be programmed as follows. All solutions for P are generated by forced backtracking. Each solution is, when generated, immediately asserted into the database so that it is not lost when the next solution is found. After all the solutions have been generated and asserted, they have to be collected into a list and retracted from the database. This whole process can be imagined as all the solutions generated forming a queue. Each newly generated solution is, by assertion, added to the end of this queue. When the solutions are collected the queue dissolves. Note, in addition, that the end of this queue has to be marked, for example, by the atom 'bottom' (which, of course, should be different from any solution that is possibly expected). An implementation of **findall** along these lines is shown as Figure 6.4.

# EXERCISES

**6.8** Use **bagof** to define the relation **powerset( Set, Subsets)** to compute the set of all subsets of a given set (all sets represented as lists).

**6.9** Use **bagof** to define the relation

> copy_term( Term, Copy)

such that **Copy** is **Term** with all its variables renamed.

## 6.7   Input and output

The method of communication between the user and the program that we have been using up to now consists of user questions to the program and program answers in terms of instantiations of variables. This method of communication is simple and suffices to get the information in and out. However, it is often not sufficient because it is too rigid. Extensions to this basic communication method are needed in the following areas:

- input of data in forms other than questions – for example, in the form of English sentences,
- output of information in any format desired, and
- input from and output to any computer file or device and not just the keyboard and display.

We will now look at built-in facilities for reading data from computer files and for outputting data to files. These procedures can also be used for formatting data objects in the program to achieve a desired output representation of these objects. We will also look at facilities for reading programs and for constructing and decomposing atoms. Built-in predicates for input and output depend on the implementation of Prolog. We will study here a simple and handy repertoire of such predicates, which is part of many Prolog implementations. However, the manual should be consulted for details and specificities. Many Prolog implementations provide various additional facilities not covered here. Such extra facilities handle windows, provide graphics primitives for drawing on the screen, input information from the mouse, and so on.

### 6.7.1   Communication with files

We will first consider the question of directing input and output to files, and then how data can be input and output in different forms.

Figure 6.5 shows a general situation in which a Prolog program communicates with several files. The program can, in principle, read data from several input files, also called *input streams*, and output data to several output files, also called

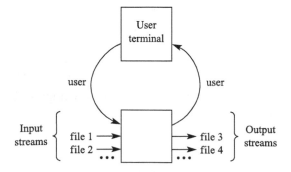

**Figure 6.5** Communication between a Prolog program and several files.

*output streams*. Data coming from the user's keyboard is treated as just another input stream. Data output on the display is, analogously, treated as another output stream. Both of these pseudo-files are referred to by the name **user**. The names of other files can be chosen by the programmer.

At any time during the execution of a Prolog program, only two files are 'active': one for input and one for output. These two files are called the *current input stream* and the *current output stream* respectively. At the beginning of execution these two streams correspond to the computer keyboard and display. The current input stream can be changed to another file, **Filename**, by the goal

   see( Filename)

Such a goal succeeds (unless there is something wrong with **Filename**) and causes, as a side effect, that input is switched from the previous input stream to **Filename**. So a typical example of using the **see** predicate is the following sequence of goals, which reads something from **file1** and then switches back to the keyboard:

   ...
   see( file1),
   read_from_file( Information),
   see( user),
   ...

The current output stream can be changed by a goal of the form:

   tell( Filename)

A sequence of goals to output some information to **file3**, and then redirect succeeding output back to the monitor, is:

   ...
   tell( file3),
   write_on_file( Information),
   tell( user),
   ...

The goal

   seen

closes the current input file. The goal

   told

closes the current output file.

We will assume here that files can only be processed sequentially although many Prolog implementations also handle files with random access. In sequential files, each request to read something from an input file will cause reading at the current position in the current input stream. After the reading, the current position will move to the next unread item. So the next request for reading will start reading at this new current position. If a request for reading is made at the end of a file, then the information returned by such a request is the atom end_of_file.

Writing is similar. Each request to output information will append this information at the end of the current output stream. It is not possible to move backward and to overwrite part of the file.

We will here only consider 'text-files' – that is, files of characters. Characters are letters, digits and special characters. Some of them are said to be non-printable because when they are output on the monitor they do not appear on the screen. They may, however, have other effects, such as spacing between columns and lines.

There are two main ways in which files can be viewed in Prolog, depending on the form of information. One way is to consider a character as the basic element of the file. Accordingly, one input or output request will cause a single character to be read or written. The built-in predicates for this are **get**, **get0** and **put**.

The other way of viewing a file is to consider bigger units of information as basic building blocks of the file. Such a natural bigger unit is a Prolog term. So each input/output request of this type transfers a whole term from the current input stream or to the current output stream respectively. Predicates for transfer of terms are **read** and **write**. Of course, in this case, the information in the file has to be in a form that is consistent with the syntax of terms.

What kind of file organization is chosen will, of course, depend on the problem. Whenever the problem specification will allow the information to be naturally squeezed into the syntax of terms, we will prefer to use a file of terms. It will then be possible to transfer a whole meaningful piece of information with a single request. On the other hand, there are problems whose nature dictates that files are viewed as sequences of characters. An example is the processing of natural language sentences, say, to generate a dialogue in English between the system and the user. In such cases, files will have to be viewed as sequences of characters that cannot be parsed into Prolog terms.

## 6.7.2 Processing files of terms

The built-in predicate **read** is used for reading terms from the current input stream. The goal

   **read( X)**

will cause the next term, T, to be read, and this term will be matched with X. If X is a variable then, as a result, X will become instantiated to T. If matching does not succeed then the goal **read( X)** fails. The predicate **read** is deterministic, so in the case of failure there will be no backtracking to input another term. Each term in the input file must be followed by a full stop and a space or carriage-return.

If **read( X)** is executed when the end of the current input file has been reached then X will become instantiated to the atom **end_of_file**.

The built-in predicate **write** outputs a term. So the goal

   **write( X)**

will output the term X on the current output file. X will be output in the same standard syntactic form in which Prolog normally displays values of variables. A useful feature of Prolog is that the **write** procedure 'knows' to display any term no matter how complicated it may be.

As an example, the following piece of program reads a term X from file **file1**, computes Y, and writes Y to file **file2**. It adds a full stop after Y so that Y can be later read from **file2** with a **read** command:

```
see( file1), read( X),
p( X, Y),                       % Compute Y that is in relation p with X
tell( file2), write( Y), write( .),    % Write full stop after Y
```

Typically, there are additional built-in predicates for formatting the output. They insert spaces and new lines into the output stream. The goal

```
tab( N)
```

causes N spaces to be output. The predicate **nl** (which has no arguments) causes the start of a new line at output.

The following examples will illustrate how the interaction between the user and the program can be implemented. Let us assume that we have a procedure that computes the cube of a number:

```
cube( N, C) :-
    C is N * N * N.
```

Suppose we want to use this for calculating the cubes of a sequence of numbers. We could do this by a sequence of questions:

```
?- cube( 5, Y).

Y = 125

?- cube( 12, Z).

Z = 1728
```

For each number, we had to type in the corresponding goal. Let us now modify this program so that the **cube** procedure will read the data from the user interactively. Now the program will keep reading data and outputting their cubes until the atom **stop** is read. The program will also prompt the user when the next number is needed by displaying 'Next item, please:'. The results will be displayed in a friendlier form like 'Cube of 5 is 125'. A conversation with this new version of **cube** would then be, for example, as follows:

```
?- cube.

Next item, please: 5.

Cube of 5 is 125

Next item, please: 12.

Cube of 12 is 1728

Next item, please: stop.

yes
```

Everything underlined above was typed in by the user. All the rest was generated by Prolog. To carry out such a conversation, the **cube** procedure can be defined as:

```
cube :-
  write( 'Next item, please':),
  read( X),
  process( X).

process( stop) :- !.

process( N) :-
  C is N * N * N,
  write( 'Cube of'), write( N), write( 'is'),
  write( C), nl,
  cube.
```

It may appear that the above **cube** procedure could be simplified. However, the following attempt to simplify is not correct:

```
cube :-
  write( 'Next item, please:'),
  ( read( stop), !                    % All done
  ;
  read( N),
  C is N * N * N,
  write( 'Cube of'), write( N), write( 'is'), write( C), nl,
  cube ).
```

The reason why this is wrong can be seen easily if we trace the program with input data 5, say. The goal **read( stop)** will fail when the number is read, and this number will be lost. The next **read** goal will input the next term, that is number 12. Another defect is that it can happen that the **stop** signal is read by the goal **read(N)**, which would then cause a request to multiply non-numeric data.

In the following we will look at some typical examples of operations that involve reading and writing. We start with displaying lists.

Besides the standard Prolog format for displaying lists, there are several other natural forms. The following procedure:

```
writelist( L)
```

outputs a list **L** so that each element of **L** is written on a separate line:

```
writelist( [ ] ).

writelist( [X | L] ) :-
  write( X), nl,
  writelist( L).
```

For example, we can display a list of lists as:

```
?- writelist( [ [a,b,c], [d,e,f], [g,h,i] ] ).

[ a, b, c]
[ d, e, f]
[ g, h, i]
```

A list of integer numbers can be shown as a bar graph. The following procedure, **bars**, will display a list in this form, assuming that the numbers in the list are sufficiently small. An example of using **bars** is:

```
?- bars( [3,4,6,5] ).
***
****
******
*****
```

The **bars** procedure can be defined as follows:

```
bars( [ ] ).

bars( [N | L] ) :-
   stars( N), nl,
   bars( L).

stars( N) :-
   N > 0,
   write( *),
   N1 is N – 1,
   stars( N1).

stars( N) :-
   N =< 0.
```

A typical sequence of goals to process a whole file, **F**, looks like this:

```
..., see( F), processfile, see( user),...
```

Here **processfile** is a procedure to read and process each term in **F**, one after another, until the end of the file is encountered. A typical schema for **processfile** is:

```
processfile :-
   read( Term),          % Assuming Term not a variable
   process( Term).

process( end_of_file) :- !.    % All done

process( Term) :-
   treat( Term),          % Process current item
   processfile.           % Process rest of file
```

Here **treat( Term)** represents whatever is to be done with each term. An example would be a procedure to display each term together with its consecutive number. Let us call this procedure **showfile**. It has to have an additional argument to count the terms read:

```
showfile( N) :-
   read( Term),
   show( Term, N).

show( end_of_file, _) :- !.    % All done

show( Term, N) :-
   write( N), tab( 2), write( Term), nl,
   N1 is N + 1,
   showfile( N1).
```

## EXERCISES

**6.10**  Let f be a file of terms. Define a procedure

> **findterm( Term)**

that displays on the monitor the first term in f that matches **Term**.

**6.11**  Let f be a file of terms. Write a procedure

> **findallterms( Term)**

that displays on the monitor all the terms in f that match **Term**. Make sure that **Term** is not instantiated in the process (which could prevent its match with terms that occur later in the file).

## 6.7.3  Processing files of characters

A character is written on the current output stream with the goal

> **put( C)**

where C is the ASCII code (a number between 0 and 127) of the character to be output. For example, the question

> **?- put( 65), put( 66), put( 67).**

causes the following output:

> **ABC**

65 is the ASCII code of 'A', 66 of 'B', 67 of 'C'.

A single character can be read from the current input stream by the goal:

> **get0( C)**

This causes the current character to be read from the input stream, and the variable C becomes instantiated to the ASCII code of this character. A variation of the predicate **get0** is **get**, which is used for reading non-blank characters. So the goal

> **get( C)**

will cause the skipping over of all non-printable characters (such as blanks) from the current input position in the input stream up to the first printable character. This character is then also read and C is instantiated to its ASCII code.

As an example of using predicates that transfer single characters let us define a procedure, **squeeze**, to do the following: read a sentence from the current input stream, and output the same sentence reformatted so that multiple blanks between words are replaced by single blanks. For simplicity we will assume that any input sentence processed by **squeeze** ends with a full stop and that words are separated simply by one or more blanks, but no other character. An acceptable input is then:

> The        robot tried        to pour wine out        of the        bottle.

The goal **squeeze** would output this in the form:

> The robot tried to pour wine out of the bottle.

The **squeeze** procedure will have a similar structure to the procedures for processing files in the previous section. First, it will read the first character, output this character, and then complete the processing depending on this character. There are three alternatives that correspond to the following cases: the character is either a full stop, a blank or a letter. The mutual exclusion of the three alternatives is achieved in the program by cuts:

```
squeeze :-
   get0( C),
   put( C),
   dorest( C).

dorest( 46) :- !.          % 46 is ASCII for full stop, all done
dorest( 32) :- !,          % 32 is ASCII for blank
   get( C),                % Skip other blanks
   put( C),
   dorest( C).

dorest( Letter) :-
   squeeze.
```

# EXERCISE

**6.12**  Generalize the **squeeze** procedure to handle commas as well. All blanks immediately preceding a comma are to be removed, and we want to have one blank after each comma.

## 6.7.4  Constructing and decomposing atoms

It is sometimes desirable to have information, read as a sequence of characters, represented in the program as an atom. The built-in predicate **name** can be used to this end. **name** relates atoms and their ASCII encodings:

> **name( A, L)**

is true if L is the list of ASCII codes of the characters in A. There are two typical uses of **name**:

(1)  given an atom, break it down into single characters;

(2)  given a list of characters, combine them into an atom.

An example of the first kind of application would be a program that deals with orders, taxis and drivers. These could be, in the program, represented by atoms such as:

> **order1, order2, driver1, driver2, taxia1, taxilux**

The following predicate:

> **taxi( X)**

tests whether an atom X represents a taxi:

```
taxi( X) :-
  name( X, Xlist),
  name( taxi, Tlist),
  conc( Tlist, _, Xlist).          % Is word 'taxi' prefix of X?
```

The next example illustrates the use of combining characters into atoms. We will define a predicate:

**getsentence( Wordlist)**

that reads a free-form natural language sentence and instantiates **Wordlist** to some internal representation of the sentence. One choice for the internal representation, which enables further processing of the sentence, is this: each word of the input sentence is represented as a Prolog atom; the whole sentence is represented as a list of atoms. For example, if the current input stream is:

Mary was pleased to see the robot fail.

then the goal **getsentence( Sentence)** will cause the instantiation:

Sentence = [ 'Mary', was, pleased, to, see, the, robot, fail]

For simplicity, we will assume that each sentence terminates with a full stop and that there are no punctuation symbols within the sentence.

The program is shown in Figure 6.6. The procedure **getsentence** first reads the current input character, **Char**, and then supplies this character to the procedure **getrest** to complete the job. **getrest** has to react properly according to three cases:

(1) **Char** is the full stop: then everything has been read.

(2) **Char** is the blank: ignore it, **getsentence** from rest of input.

(3) **Char** is a letter: first read the word, **Word**, which begins with **Char**, and then use **getsentence** to read the rest of the sentence, producing **Wordlist**. The cumulative result is the list **[Word | Wordlist]**.

The procedure that reads the characters of one word is:

**getletters( Letter, Letters, Nextchar)**

The three arguments are:

(1) **Letter** is the current letter (already read) of the word being read.

(2) **Letters** is the list of letters (starting with **Letter**) up to the end of the word.

(3) **Nextchar** is the input character that immediately follows the word read. **Nextchar** must be a non-letter character.

We conclude this example with a comment on the possible use of the **getsentence** procedure. It can be used in a program to process text in natural language. Sentences represented as lists of words are in a form that is suitable for further processing in Prolog. A simple example is to look for certain keywords in input sentences. A much more difficult task would be to grammatically parse the sentence and understand it; that is, to extract from the sentence its meaning,

```
/*
Procedure getsentence reads in a sentence and combines the words into a list of atoms.
For example
   getsentence( Wordlist)
produces
   Wordlist = [ 'Mary', was, pleased, to, see, the, robot, fail]
if the input sentence is:
   Mary was pleased to see the robot fail.
*/

getsentence( Wordlist) :-
   get0( Char),
   getrest( Char, Wordlist).

getrest( 46, [ ] ) :- !.                        % End of sentence: 46 = ASCII for '.'

getrest( 32, Wordlist) :- !,                    % 32 = ASCII for blank
   getsentence( Wordlist).                      % Skip the blank

getrest( Letter, [Word | Wordlist] :-
   getletters( Letter, Letters, Nextchar),      % Read letters of current word
   name( Word, Letters),
   getrest( Nextchar, Wordlist).

getletters( 46, [ ], 46) :- !.                  % End of word: 46 = full stop

getletters( 32, [ ], 32) :- !.                  % End of word: 32 = blank

getletters( Let, [Let | Letters], Nextchar) :-
   get0( Char),
   getletters( Char, Letters, Nextchar).
```

**Figure 6.6** A procedure to transform a sentence into a list of atoms.

represented in some chosen formalism. This is an important research area of Artificial Intelligence, and is introduced in Chapter 23.

# EXERCISES

**6.13** Define the relation

   starts( Atom, Character)

to check whether Atom starts with Character.

**6.14** Define the procedure **plural** that will convert nouns into their plural form. For example:

   ?- plural( table, X).

   X = tables

**6.15**   Write the procedure

search( KeyWord, Sentence)

that will, each time it is called, find a sentence in the current input file that contains the given **KeyWord**. **Sentence** should be in its original form, represented as a sequence of characters or as an atom (procedure **getsentence** of this section can be accordingly modified).

## 6.7.5   Reading programs

We can communicate our programs to the Prolog system by means of built-in predicates that *consult* or *compile* files with programs. The details of 'consulting' and compiling files depend on the implementation of Prolog. Here we look at some basic facilities that are available in many Prologs.

We tell Prolog to read a program from a file F with a goal of the form consult( F), for example:

?- consult( program3).

Depending on the implementation, the file name **program3** will typically have an extension like 'pl' indicating that it is a Prolog program file. The effect of this goal will be that all the clauses in file **program3** are read and loaded into the memory, so they will be used by Prolog when answering further questions from the user. Another file may be 'consulted' at some later time during the same session. Basically, the effect is again that the clauses from this new file are added into the memory. However, details depend on the implementation and other circumstances. If the new file contains clauses about a procedure defined in the previously consulted file, then the new clauses may be simply added at the end of the current set of clauses, or the previous definition of this procedure may be entirely replaced by the new one.

Several files may be consulted by the same **consult** goal, for example:

?- consult( [ program3, program4, queens]).

Such a question can also be written more simply as:

?- [ program3, program4, queens].

Consulted programs are used by a Prolog *interpreter*. If a Prolog implementation also features a *compiler*, then programs can be loaded in a compiled form. This enables more efficient execution with a typical speed-up factor of 5 or 10 between the interpreted and compiled code. Programs are loaded into memory in the compiled form by the built-in predicate **compile**, for example:

?- compile( program3).

or

?- compile( [ program4, queens, program6]).

Compiled programs are more efficiently executed, but interpreted programs are easier to debug because they can be inspected and traced by Prolog's debugging facilities. Therefore an interpreter is typically used in the program development phase, and a compiler is used with the final program.

It should be noted, again, that the details of consulting and compiling files depend on the implementation of Prolog. Usually a Prolog implementation also allows the user to enter and edit the program interactively.

# Summary

- A Prolog implementation normally provides a set of built-in procedures to accomplish several useful operations that are not possible in pure Prolog. In this chapter, such a set of predicates available in many Prolog implementations was introduced.

- The type of a term can be tested by the following predicates:

  **var( X)**          X is a (non-instantiated) variable
  **nonvar( X)**       X is not a variable
  **atom( X)**         X is an atom
  **integer( X)**      X is an integer
  **float( X)**        X is a real number
  **atomic( X)**       X is either an atom or a number
  **compound( X)**     X is a structure

- Terms can be constructed or decomposed:

  **Term =.. [ Functor | ArgumentList]**
  **functor( Term, Functor, Arity)**
  **arg( N, Term, Argument)**
  **name( Atom, CharacterCodes)**

- Terms can be compared:

  X = Y          X and Y match
  X == Y         X and Y are identical
  X \== Y        X and Y are not identical
  X =:= Y        X and Y are arithmetically equal
  X =\= Y        X and Y are not arithmetically equal
  X < Y          arithmetic value of X is less than Y (related: =<, >, >=)
  X @< Y         term X precedes term Y (related: @=<, @>, @>=)

- A Prolog program can be viewed as a relational database that can be updated by the following procedures:

  **assert( Clause)**   add **Clause** to the program
  **asserta( Clause)**  add at the beginning
  **assertz( Clause)**  add at the end
  **retract( Clause)**  remove a clause that matches **Clause**

- All the objects that satisfy a given condition can be collected into a list by the predicates:

  **bagof( X, P, L)**   L is the list of all X that satisfy condition P
  **setof( X, P, L)**   L is the sorted list of all X that satisfy condition P
  **findall( X, P, L)** similar to **bagof**

- **repeat** is a control facility that generates an unlimited number of alternatives for backtracking.

- Input and output (other than that associated with querying the program) are done using built-in procedures. This chapter introduced a simple repertoire of such procedures that can be found in many Prolog implementations.

- This repertoire assumes that files are sequential. There is the *current input stream* and the *current output stream*. The computer keyboard and display are treated as files called **user**.

- Switching between streams is done by:

| | |
|---|---|
| see( File) | **File** becomes the current input stream |
| tell( File) | **File** becomes the current output stream |
| seen | close the current input stream |
| told | close the current output stream |

- Files are read and written in two ways:

  as sequences of characters
  as sequences of terms

- Built-in procedures for reading and writing characters and terms are:

| | |
|---|---|
| read( Term) | input next term |
| write( Term) | output **Term** |
| put( CharCode) | output character with the given ASCII code |
| get0( CharCode) | input next character |
| get( CharCode) | input next 'printable' character |

- Two procedures help formatting:

| | |
|---|---|
| nl | output new line |
| tab( N) | output N blanks |

- Many Prolog implementations provide additional facilities to handle non-sequential files, windows, provide graphics primitives, input information from the mouse, etc.

## Reference to Prolog standard

For some of the predicates mentioned in this chapter, ISO standard for Prolog (Deransart *et al.* 1996) recommends different names from those used in most Prolog implementations. However, the predicates are conceptually the same, so compatibility is only a matter of renaming. The concerned predicates in this chapter are: **see(Filename)**, **tell(Filename)**, **get(Code)**, **put(Code)**, **name(Atom,CodeList)**. The corresponding predicate names in the standard are: **set_input(Filename)**, **set_output(Filename)**, **get_code(Code)**, **put_code(Code)**, **atom_codes(Atom,CodeList)**.

Deransart, P., Ed-Bdali, A. and Ceroni, L. (1996) *Prolog: The Standard.* Berlin: Springer-Verlag.

# Chapter 7

# Constraint Logic Programming

........................................................................................................

........................................................................................................

*Constraint programming* is a powerful paradigm for formulating and solving problems that can be naturally defined in terms of constraints among a set of variables. Solving such problems consists of finding such combinations of values of the variables that satisfy the constraints. This is called *constraint satisfaction*. *Constraint logic programming* (CLP) combines the constraint approach with logic programming. In CLP, constraint satisfaction is embedded into a logic programming language, such as Prolog. Programming with constraints is a kind of declarative programming and requires a special way of thinking about problems. In this chapter we introduce CLP and develop through programming examples the skill of solving problems with constraints.

## 7.1 Constraint satisfaction and logic programming

........................................................................................................

### 7.1.1 Motivation

Let us look at some initial examples that illustrate the need for CLP. Consider the query:

?- $X + 1 = 5$.

In Prolog this matching fails, so Prolog's answer is 'no'. However, if the user's intention is that X is a number and '+' is arithmetic addition, then the answer $X = 4$ would be more desirable. Using the built-in predicate is instead of '=' does not quite achieve this interpretation. But constraint logic programming (CLP) does. In the syntactic convention for CLP that we will be using, this query will be written as:

?- { $X + 1 = 5$ }.        % Numerical constraint
  $X = 4$

The constraint above is enclosed in curly brackets, which distinguishes it from the usual Prolog goals. The constraint is handled by a specialized constraint solver that 'understands' operations on real numbers, and can typically solve sets of equations or inequations of certain types.

As a next example, consider the conversion of temperature from Fahrenheit to Centigrade. For this, we may define the predicate:

```
convert( Centigrade, Fahrenheit) :-
  Centigrade is ( Fahrenheit − 32)*5/9.
```

This can be used to convert 95 degrees Fahrenheit into Centigrade:

```
?- convert( C, 95).
C = 35
```

But we cannot use this to convert from Centigrade to Fahrenheit because the built-in predicate is expects everything on the right-hand side instantiated. So in this case we get an error message like:

```
?- convert( 35, F).
Instantiation error in argument of is/2
```

To make the procedure work in both directions, we can test which of the arguments is instantiated to a number, and then use the conversion formula properly rewritten for each case. All this is much more elegant in CLP, where the same formula, interpreted as a numerical constraint, works in both directions:

```
convert( Centigrade, Fahrenheit) :-
  { Centigrade = ( Fahrenheit − 32)*5/9 }.
```

```
?- convert( 35, F).
F = 95
```

```
?- convert( C, 95).
C = 35
```

Our CLP program even works when neither of the two arguments is instantiated:

```
?- convert( C, F).
{ F = 32.0 + 1.8*C }
```

As the numerical calculation in this case is not possible, the answer is a general formula, meaning: the solution is a set of all F and C that satisfy this formula. Notice that this formula, produced by the CLP system, is a simplification of the constraint in our **convert** program.

## 7.1.2  Constraint satisfaction

In this section we will consider a general statement of constraint satisfaction problems. A constraint satisfaction problem is stated as follows:

*Given*:

(1)  a set of *variables*,

(2)  the *domains* from which the variables can take values, and

(3)  *constraints* that the variables have to satisfy.

*Find*:
An assignment of values to the variables, so that these values satisfy all the given constraints.

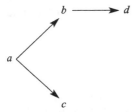

**Figure 7.1** Precedence constraints among tasks *a*, *b*, *c*, *d*.

Often there are several assignments that satisfy the constraints. In optimization problems, we can specify a criterion to choose among the assignments that satisfy the constraints.

The constraint satisfaction approach, and in particular its combination with logic programming, has proved to be a very successful tool for a large variety of problems. Typical examples come from scheduling, logistics, and resource management in production, transportation and placement. These problems involve assigning resources to activities, like machines to jobs, people to rosters, crew to trains or planes, doctors and nurses to duties and wards, etc.

Let us look at a typical example from scheduling. Let there be four tasks *a*, *b*, *c* and *d* whose durations are 2, 3, 5 and 4 hours respectively. Let there be these precedence constraints among the tasks: task *a* has to precede tasks *b* and *c*, and *b* has to precede *d* (Figure 7.1). The problem is to find the start times *Ta*, *Tb*, *Tc* and *Td* of the corresponding tasks so that the finishing time *Tf* of the schedule is minimal. Assume the earliest start time is 0.

The corresponding constraint satisfaction problem can be formally stated as follows:

Variables: *Ta*, *Tb*, *Tc*, *Td*, *Tf*
Domains: All the variables' domains are non-negative real numbers
Constraints:

| | |
|---|---|
| $Ta + 2 \leq Tb$ | (task *a* which takes 2 hours precedes *b*) |
| $Ta + 2 \leq Tc$ | (*a* precedes *c*) |
| $Tb + 3 \leq Td$ | (*b* precedes *d*) |
| $Tc + 5 \leq Tf$ | (*c* finished by *Tf*) |
| $Td + 4 \leq Tf$ | (*d* finished by *Tf*) |

Criterion: minimize *Tf*

This constraint satisfaction problem has a set of solutions which all minimize the finishing time. This set of solutions can be stated as:

$Ta = 0$
$Tb = 2$
$2 \leq Tc \leq 4$
$Td = 5$
$Tf = 9$

All the starting times are determined, except for task *c* which may start at any time in the interval between 2 and 4.

It is straightforward to solve this scheduling problem in Prolog with CLP facilities. Such CLP facilities are typically available in a Prolog system as a library of predicates that handle constraints. A typical way to load such a library into Prolog is:

```
?- use_module( library( clpr)).
Library clpr consulted
```

The result of this query is that the library is loaded that deals with constraints among real numbers, which is what we need for our CLP problem. Now all we have to do is to state the constraints among the variables representing the start times of tasks, and the optimization criterion:

```
?- { Ta =< 0,              % Task a cannot start before time 0
Ta + 2 =< Tb,              % Task b cannot start before a has finished
Ta + 2 =< Tc,              % a precedes c
Tb + 3 =< Td,              % b precedes d
Tc + 5 =< Tf,              % c finished by finishing time Tf
Td + 4 =< Tf },            % d finished by Tf
minimize( Tf).             % Look for schedules with minimal finishing time
```

Prolog's answer is:

```
Ta = 0.0
Tb = 2.0
Td = 5.0
Tf = 9.0
{Tc =< 4.0}
{Tc >= 2.0}
```

The curly brackets tell Prolog that the inequalities are to be handled as constraints by the constraint solver, and not by Prolog's own built-in predicate '=<'.

## 7.1.3 Satisfying constraints

In this section we outline some techniques used in solving sets of constraints. Constraint satisfaction problems are often depicted as graphs, called *constraint networks*. The nodes in the graph correspond to the variables, and the arcs correspond to the constraints. For each binary constraint $p(X,Y)$ between the variables $X$ and $Y$, there are two directed arcs $(X,Y)$ and $(Y,X)$ in the graph. To find a solution of a constraint satisfaction problem, various *consistency algorithms* can be used. These algorithms are best viewed as operating over constraint networks. They check the consistency of the domains of variables with respect to constraints. We show the main ideas of such algorithms below. It should be noted that we only present a consistency technique operating on binary constraints, although constraints can in general be of any arity.

Consider variables $X$ and $Y$ whose domains are $Dx$ and $Dy$ respectively. Let there be a binary constraint $p(X,Y)$ between $X$ and $Y$. The arc $(X,Y)$ is said to be *arc consistent* if for each value of $X$ in $Dx$, there is some value for $Y$ in $Dy$ satisfying the constraint $p(X,Y)$. If $(X,Y)$ is not arc consistent, then all the values in $Dx$ for which there is no corresponding value in $Dy$ may be deleted from $Dx$. This makes $(X,Y)$ arc consistent.

For example, consider the variables $X$ and $Y$ whose domains are sets of all integers between 0 and 10 inclusive, written as:

$Dx = 0..10, \quad Dy = 0..10$

Let there be the constraint $p(X,Y)$: $X + 4 \leq Y$. Now, the arc $(X,Y)$ is not arc consistent. For example, for $X = 7$ there is no value of $Y$ in $Dy$ satisfying $p(7,Y)$. To make the arc $(X,Y)$ consistent, the domain $Dx$ is reduced to $Dx = 0..6$. Similarly, the arc $(Y,X)$ can be made consistent by reducing $Dy$: $Dy = 4..10$. By such a reduction of $Dx$ and $Dy$ we do not lose any solution of the constraint problem because the discarded values clearly cannot be part of any solution.

After reducing domain $Dx$, some other arc may become inconsistent. For an arc of the form $(Z,X)$ there may be values of $Z$ for which, after reducing $Dx$, there may no longer be any corresponding value in $Dx$. Then in turn the arc $(Z,X)$ can be made consistent by correspondingly reducing the domain $Dz$. So this effect may propagate throughout the network, possibly cyclically, for some time until either all the arcs become consistent, or some domain becomes empty. In the latter case the constraints are clearly not satisfiable. In the case where all the arcs are consistent, there are again two cases:

(1) Each domain has a single value; this means we have a single solution to the constraint problem.

(2) All the domains are non-empty, and at least one domain has multiple values.

For case 2, the arc consistency, of course, does not guarantee that all possible combinations of domain values are solutions to the constraint problem. It may even be that no combination of values actually satisfies all the constraints. Therefore some combinatorial search is needed over the reduced domains to find a solution. One possibility is to choose one of the multi-valued domains and try to assign repeatedly its values to the corresponding variable. Assigning a particular value to the variable means reducing the variable's domain, possibly causing inconsistent arcs to appear again. So the consistency algorithm can be applied again to further reduce the domains of variables, etc. If the domains are finite, this will eventually result in either an empty domain, or all the domains single-valued. The search can be done differently, not necessarily by choosing a single value from a domain. An alternative policy may be to choose a non-singleton domain and split it into two approximately equal size subsets. The algorithm is then applied to both subsets.

For illustration let us consider how this algorithm may work on our scheduling example. Let the domains of all the variables be integers between 0 and 10. Figure 7.2 shows the constraint network and the trace of a constraint satisfaction algorithm. Initially, at step 'Start', all the domains are $0..10$. In each execution step, one of the arcs in the network is made consistent. In step 1, arc $(Tb,Ta)$ is considered, which reduces the domain of $Tb$ to $2..10$. Next, arc $(Td,Tb)$ is considered, which reduces the domain of $Td$ to $5..10$, etc. After step 8 all the arcs are consistent and all the reduced domains are multi-valued. As we are interested in the minimal finishing time, assigning $Tf = 9$ may now be tried (9 being the minimum value in the domain $Tf$ at this moment). Arc consistency is then executed again, reducing all the domains to singletons except the domain of $Tc$ to $2..4$.

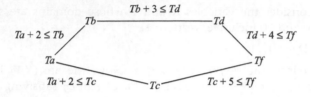

| Step | Arc | Ta | Tb | Tc | Td | Tf |
|------|-----|------|------|------|------|------|
| Start |      | 0..10 | 0..10 | 0..10 | 0..10 | 0..10 |
| 1 | (Tb,Ta) |      | 2..10 |      |      |      |
| 2 | (Td,Tb) |      |      |      | 5..10 |      |
| 3 | (Tf,Td) |      |      |      |      | 9..10 |
| 4 | (Td,Tf) |      |      |      | 5..6 |      |
| 5 | (Tb,Td) |      | 2..3 |      |      |      |
| 6 | (Ta,Tb) | 0..1 |      |      |      |      |
| 7 | (Tc,Ta) |      |      |      | 2..10 |      |
| 8 | (Tc,Tf) |      |      |      | 2..5 |      |

**Figure 7.2** Top: constraint network for the scheduling problem. Bottom: an arc consistency execution trace.

Notice how consistency techniques exploit the constraints to reduce the domains of variables as soon as new information is available. New information triggers the related constraints, which results in reduced domains of the concerned variables. Such execution can be viewed as data-driven. Constraints are active in the sense that they do not wait to be explicitly called by the programmer, but activate automatically when relevant information appears. This idea of data-driven computation is further discussed in Chapter 25 under 'Pattern-directed programming'.

## EXERCISES

**7.1** Try to execute the arc consistency algorithm with different orders of the arcs. What happens?

**7.2** Execute the arc consistency algorithm on the final state of the trace in Figure 7.2, after *Tf* is assigned value 9.

## 7.1.4 Extending Prolog to constraint logic programming

Let us now consider the relation between Prolog and constraint satisfaction. Pure Prolog itself can be viewed as a rather specific constraint satisfaction language where all the constraints are of very limited form. They are just equalities between terms. These equality constraints are checked by Prolog's matching of terms. Constraints among the arguments of a predicate are also stated in terms of other predicates, that is predicate calls in the body of a Prolog rule. But these predicate calls all eventually unfold to matching. Prolog can be extended to a 'real' CLP language by introducing other types of constraints in addition to matching. Of course, the Prolog interpreter has to be enhanced so that it can handle these other types of constraints. A CLP system that can handle arithmetic equality and inequality constraints can directly solve our example scheduling problem as stated above.

A program with constraints is interpreted roughly as follows. A list of goals may contain goals of two types: (a) the usual Prolog goals, that is calls of Prolog predicates, and (b) constraint goals, such as numerical equalities and inequalities. During the execution of such a list of goals, a set **CurrConstr** of current constraints is maintained. Initially this set is empty. The goals in the list are executed one by one in the usual order. Normal Prolog goals are processed as usual. When a constraint goal **Constr** is processed, the constraints **Constr** and **CurrConstr** are merged, giving **NewConstr**. The domain-specialized constraint solver then tries to satisfy **NewConstr**. Two basic outcomes are possible:

(a) **NewConstr** is found to be unsatisfiable, which corresponds to the goal's failure and causes backtracking;

(b) **NewConstr** is not found to be unsatisfiable, and constraints in **NewConstr** are simplified as much as possible by the constraint solver.

For example, let **CurrConstr** be { X =< 3 }. Now, if **Constr** is { X > 5} then **NewConstr** is the conjunction { X =< 3, X > 5}, which the constraint solver recognizes as unsatisfiable. If on the other hand, **Constr** is { X =< 2} then **NewConstr** is { X =< 3, X =< 2}, which is simplified by the constraint solver to **NewConstr** = { X =< 2}. The remaining goals in the list are executed with the so updated set of current constraints.

The extent of simplification depends on the current state of the information about the variables, as well as on the abilities of the particular constraint solver to use this information effectively. In fact, the power of a CLP system depends on the constraint solver's ability to simplify merged constraints. A completely impotent constraint solver would always simply add conjunctively new constraints to the existing constraints. As a result, the constraints would just keep accumulating, and such a weak constraint solver would never solve them, nor simplify them, nor recognize their unsatisfiability.

CLP systems differ in the domains and types of constraints they can process. Families of CLP techniques appear under names of the form CLP(X) where X stands for the domain. For example, in CLP(R) the domains of the variables are real numbers, and constraints are arithmetic equalities, inequalities and disequalities over real numbers. CLP(X) systems over other domains include: CLP(Z) (integers), CLP(Q) (rational numbers), CLP(B) (Boolean domains) and CLP(FD) (user-defined finite domains). Available domains and types of constraints in actual implementations largely depend on the available techniques for solving particular types of constraints. In CLP(R), for example, linear equalities and inequalities are typically available because efficient techniques exist for handling these types of constraints. On the other hand, the use of non-linear constraints is very limited.

In the remainder of this chapter we will look in more detail at CLP(R), CLP(Q) and CLP(FD) using the syntactic conventions for CLP in SICStus Prolog and SWI Prolog (see references at the end of the chapter).

## 7.2 CLP over real numbers: CLP(R), CLP(Q)

As in our examples so far, we will be using the following notational convention for CLP(R). A set of constraints is inserted into a Prolog clause as a goal enclosed in curly brackets. Individual constraints are separated by commas and semi-colons. As in Prolog, a comma means conjunction, and a semicolon means disjunction. So the conjunction of constraints Cl, C2 and C3 is written as:

{ Cl, C2, C3}

Each constraint is of the form:

**Expr1   Operator   Expr2**

Both **Expr1** and **Expr2** are usual arithmetic expressions. They may, depending on the particular CLP(R) system, also include calls to some standard functions, such as $\sin(X)$. The operator can be one of the following, depending on the type of constraint:

| | |
|---|---|
| $=$ | for equations |
| $=\backslash=$ | for disequations |
| $<$, $=<$, $>$, $>=$ | for inequations |

A typical constraint solver can handle sets of linear equations, inequations and disequations. Here are some examples:

?- { 3\*X – 2\*Y = 6, 2\*Y = X}.
X = 3.0
Y = 1.5

?- { Z =< X–2, Z =< 6–X, Z+1 = 2}.
Z = 1.0
{X >= 3.0}
{X =< 5.0}

A CLP(R) solver also includes a linear optimization facility. This finds the extreme value of a given linear expression inside the region that satisfies the given linear constraints. The built-in CLP(R) predicates for this are:

**minimize( Expr)**
**maximize( Expr)**

In these two predicates, **Expr** is a linear expression in terms of variables that appear in linear constraints. The predicates find the variable values that satisfy these constraints and respectively minimize or maximize the value of the expression. For example:

?- { X =< 5}, **maximize(X)**.
X = 5.0

?- { X = < 5, 2 =< X}, **minimize( 2\*X + 3).**
X = 2.0

?- { X >=2, Y >=2, Y =< X+1, 2\*Y =< 8–X, Z = 2\*X + 3\*Y}, **maximize(Z).**
X = 4.0
Y = 2.0
Z = 14.0

?- { X =< 5}, **minimize( X).**
no

In the last example, X was not bounded downwards, therefore the minimization goal failed.

It should be noted that minimize and maximize find the optimum within the current numerical constraints, but not over alternative solutions of Prolog goals. For example:

?- { 0 =< X}, { X =< 5; X =< 10}, **maximize(X).**
X = 5.0 ? ;
X = 10.0

The results are two maximum values for X, one for each of the two alternative executions of the disjunction in the question. So this is *not* combinatorial optimization over all the executions, which would result in only one, global maximal value X = 10.

The following CLP(R) predicates find the supremum (least upper bound) or infimum (greatest lower bound) of an expression:

**sup( Expr, MaxVal)**
**inf( Expr, MinVal)**

**Expr** is a linear expression in terms of linearly constrained variables. **MaxVal** and **MinVal** are the maximum and the minimum values that this expression takes within the region where the constraints are satisfied. Unlike with **maximize/1** and **minimize/1**, the variables in **Expr** do not get instantiated to the extreme points. For example:

?- { 2 =< X, X =< 5}, **inf( X, Min), sup( X, Max).**
Max = 5.0
Min = 2.0
{X >= 2.0}
{X =< 5.0}

?- {X >=2, Y >=2, Y =< X+1, 2\*Y =< 8 – X, Z = 2\*X + 3\*Y},
   **sup(Z,Max), inf(Z,Min), maximize(Z).**
X = 4.0
Y = 2.0
Z = 14.0
Max = 14.0
Min = 10.0

The next example further illustrates the flexibility of constraints in comparison with Prolog standard arithmetic facilities. Consider the predicate **fib( N,F)** for computing F as the Nth Fibonacci number: $F(0) = 1$, $F(1) = 1$, $F(2) = 2$, $F(3) = 3$,

F(4) = 5, etc. In general, for N > 1, F(N) = F(N − 1) + F(N − 2). Here is a Prolog definition of fib/2:

```
fib( N, F) :-
  N = 0, F = 1
  ;
  N = 1, F = 1
  ;
  N >= 2,
  N1 is N − 1, fib(N1,F1),
  N2 is N − 2, fib(N2,F2),
  F is F1 + F2.
```

An intended use of this program is:

```
?- fib( 6,F).
F = 13
```

Consider, however, a question in the opposite direction:

```
?- fib( N, 13).
```

It would be nice if the program would answer N = 6 since the 6th Fibonacci number is 13. But the above query produces an error because the goal N > 1 is executed with N uninstantiated. However, our fib/2 program can be made more flexible by rewriting it in CLP(R):

```
fib( N, F) :-
  { N = 0, F = 1}
  ;
  { N = 1, F = 1}
  ;
  { N >= 2, F = F1+F2, N1 = N–1, N2 = N–2},
  fib( N1, F1),
  fib( N2, F2).
```

This definition follows exactly the original Prolog formulation, but all the arithmetic is accomplished by CLP(R) constraints. This now enables the execution in the opposite direction: given a Fibonacci number F, what is its index N?

```
?- fib( N, 13).
N = 6
```

However, this program still gets into trouble when asked an unsatisfiable question:

```
?- fib( N, 4).
```

The program keeps trying to find two consecutive Fibonacci numbers F1 and F2 such that F1 + F2 = 4. It keeps generating larger and larger solutions for F1 and F2, all the time hoping that eventually their sum will be equal 4. It does not realize that once their sum has exceeded 4, it will only be increasing and so it can never become equal to 4. Finally this hopeless search ends in a memory overflow. It is instructive to see how this can be fixed by adding some obvious extra constraints to the fib procedure. It is easy to see that for all N, the N-th Fibonacci number F(N) ≥ N. Therefore the variables N1, F1, N2 and F2 in our program must always satisfy the constraints: F1 >= N1, F2 >= N2. These extra constraints can be added to the constraints in the third disjunct of the body of the **fib** clause. This clause then becomes:

**fib( N, F) :-**
   ...
   ;
   { N >= 2, F = F1+F2, N1 = N–1, N2 = N–2,
      F1 >= N1, F2 >= N2},                    % Computationally useful extra constraints
   **fib( N1, F1),**
   **fib( N2, F2).**

The extra constraints are logically redundant, but they enable the program to realize that the above question fails:

**?- fib( N, 4).**
**no**

The recursive calls of **fib** in effect expand the expression for F in the condition F = 4:

4 = F = F1 + F2 =
F1' + F2' + F2 =
F1'' + F2'' + F2' + F2

Each time this expression is expanded, new constraints are added to the previous constraints. At the time that the four-term sum expression is obtained, the constraint solver finds out that the accumulated constraints are a contradiction that cannot be satisfied. In particular, at that time N1 and N2 become constrained to N1 >= 3 and N2 >= 2. Consequently, F1 >= 3 and F2 >= 2, and therefore F1 + F2 cannot be equal to 4 as required in the query.

Let us briefly mention CLP(Q), a close relative to CLP(R). The difference is that in CLP(R) real numbers are approximated by floating point numbers, whereas the domain Q is rational numbers, that is quotients between two integers. They can be used as another approximation to real numbers. The domain Q may have the advantage over the domain R (represented as floating point numbers) in that the solutions of some arithmetic constraints can be stated *exactly* as quotients of integers, whereas floating point numbers are only approximations. Here is an example:

**?- { X = 2\*Y, Y = 1–X }.**

A CLP(Q) solver gives: X = 2/3, Y = 1/3. A CLP(R) solver gives something like: X = 0.666666666, Y = 0.333333333.

# EXERCISE

**7.3** Demonstrate precisely how in the example query above '?- fib(N,4).' the constraint solver may realize that the accumulated constraints are not satisfiable.

## 7.3 Example of CLP(R) programming: blocks in boxes

Consider the following problem. Let there be a given set of parcels, do they all fit into a given box; or, given a set of pallets, do they fit into a given container? And if yes, how can they be placed into the container so that they fit? We will assume that all the parcels and pallets are rectangular, and will be referring to them as blocks to be fitted into a box. For simplicity, we will also assume that all the blocks are aligned with the sides of the box. For a start we will consider the planar, two-dimensional version of the problem where all the blocks are to be arranged in the X–Y plane. So our problem is reduced to that of fitting given rectangles (referred to as 'blocks') into another rectangle (referred to as 'box'). Figure 7.3 shows an example.

We will represent the dimensions of an object in the program by the term **dim(Dx,Dy)**. Accordingly, block **b1** and box **box1** will be defined by the facts:

```
block( b1, dim( 5.0, 3.0)).
box( box1, dim( 6.0, 6.0)).
```

Figure 7.4 shows a program that solves our example problem of Figure 7.3. Let us explain the predicates in this program.

A block can be placed into the box at some position and orientation. The position of a block in the box is determined by the coordinates of the left-bottom corner of the block, relative to the left-bottom corner of the box. For example, the position of block b2 in the box is given by the term **pos(0.0,3.0)**. The position of block b3 is given by the term **pos(5.0,Y)** where there is some freedom in the value of Y: $0 \le Y \le 0.6$. Each block occupies a rectangle in the plane. Such a rectangle is specified by its position **Pos** and dimensions **Dim**, and is represented in our program by a term of the form **rect( Pos, Dim)**. In Figure 7.3, block b2 occupies the rectangle **rect( pos(0.0,3.0), dim(6.0,2.0))**.

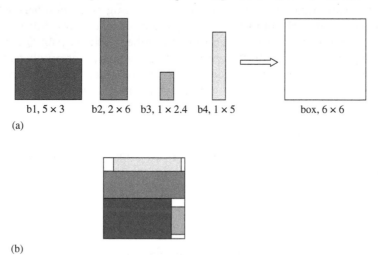

b1, 5 × 3     b2, 2 × 6   b3, 1 × 2.4   b4, 1 × 5      box, 6 × 6

(a)

(b)

**Figure 7.3** Placing blocks into a box (two-dimensional version). (a) There are four blocks b1, b2, b3, b4 of given dimensions (b1 of size 5 × 3, etc.), and a box of size 6 × 6. Do they fit into the box? (b) One solution (some of the blocks were rotated by 90 degrees).

```
% Placing blocks into a box
% This is a planar version, all blocks and boxes are rectangles
% Blocks and boxes are to be aligned with x,y axes

% block( BlockName, dim(Width, Length)):
%     specification of a block dimensions, height does not matter

block( b1, dim( 5.0, 3.0)).              % Block b1 has size 5 by 3
block( b2, dim( 2.0, 6.0)).
block( b3, dim( 1.0, 2.4)).
block( b4, dim( 1.0, 5.0)).

box( box1, dim( 6.0, 6.0)).              % Box box1 has size 6 by 6
box( box2, dim( 7.0, 5.0)).
box( box3, dim( 6.0, 5.0)).

% Representation of rectangles:
%     rect( pos(X,Y), dim(A,B)) represents a rectangle of size A by B at position pos(X,Y)

% rotate( Rectangle, RotatedRectangle):
%     Rotation of rectangle in X-Y plane, always aligned with X-Y axes

rotate( rect( Pos, Dim), rect( Pos, Dim)).          % Zero rotation
rotate( rect( Pos, dim( A, B)), rect( Pos, dim( B, A))).   % Rotated by 90 degrees

% block_rectangle( BlockName, Rectangle):
%     Rectangle is a minimal rectangle that accommodates block BlockName

block_rectangle( BlockName, rect( Pos, Dim)) :-     % Rectangle at any position
    block( BlockName, Dim0),                        % Dimensions of BlockName
    rotate( rect( Pos, Dim0), rect( Pos, Dim)).     % Block possibly rotated

% inside( Rectangle1, Rectangle2): Rectangle1 completely inside Rectangle2

inside( rect( pos( X1, Y1), dim( Dx1, Dy1)), rect( pos( X2, Y2), dim( Dx2, Dy2))) :-
    { X1 >= X2, Y1 >= Y2, X1+Dx1 =< X2+Dx2, Y1+Dy1 =< Y2+Dy2}.

% no_overlap( Rect1, Rect2):  Rectangles Rect1 and Rect2 do not overlap

no_overlap( rect( pos(X1,Y1), dim(Dx1,Dy1)), rect( pos(X2,Y2), dim(Dx2,Dy2)))  :-
    { X1 + Dx1 =< X2;  X2 + Dx2 =< X1 ;     % Rectangles left or right of each other
      Y1 + Dy1 =< Y2;  Y2 + Dy2 =< Y1 }.    % Rectangles above or below of each other

% fit( Box, Block1, Block2, Block3, Block4):
%     The 4 blocks, whose rectangles are Block1, Block2, ... fit into a box

fit( BoxName, Block1, Block2, Block3, Block4) :-
    box( BoxName, Dim), Box = rect( pos( 0.0, 0.0), Dim),
    block_rectangle( b1, Block1),  inside( Block1, Box),    % Block b1 inside Box
    block_rectangle( b2, Block2),  inside( Block2, Box),    % Block b2 inside Box
    block_rectangle( b3, Block3),  inside( Block3, Box),
    block_rectangle( b4, Block4),  inside( Block4, Box),
    no_overlap( Block1, Block2),            % No overlap between blocks b1 and b2
    no_overlap( Block1, Block3),            % No overlap between b1 and b3
    no_overlap( Block1, Block4),
    no_overlap( Block2, Block3),
    no_overlap( Block2, Block4),
    no_overlap( Block3, Block4).
```

**Figure 7.4** Fitting four blocks into a box.

A block can be placed into a box in its original orientation or after it has been rotated. We have constrained the choice of orientation to X or Y direction, so there are only two orientations possible. If a block is rotated by 90 degrees, the effect is that the block's X and Y dimensions are swapped. For example, rotating a block with dimensions **dim(5.0,3.0)** results in **dim(3.0,5.0)**. Predicate **block_rectangle( BlockName, Rectangle)** constructs for a given block a corresponding rectangle, and takes care of the two possible orientations of a block. For example:

> ?- block_rectangle( b1, Rectangle).
> Rectangle = rect( P, dim( 5.0, 3.0)) ;
> Rectangle = rect( P, dim( 3.0, 5.0))

This means block b1 will occupy a rectangle of size 5 by 3 or 3 by 5, at some unspecified position P.

To ensure that all the blocks are placed into the box safely, (1) there must be no overlap between any pair of blocks, and (2) all the blocks must be inside the box. The predicates **no_overlap** and **inside** in the program of Figure 7.4 enforce these types of conditions. inside(R1,R2) is true if rectangle R1 is completely inside rectangle R2. no_overlap(R1,R2) is true if rectangles R1 and R2 do not overlap, although they may touch. The no-overlap condition between two rectangles R1 and R2 is satisfied in any of the following four cases:

- R1 is completely to the left of R2 (no overlap in X-direction), or
- R1 is completely to the right of R2 (no overlap in X-direction), or
- R1 is completely below R2 (no overlap in Y-direction), or
- R1 is completely above R2 (no overlap in Y-direction).

These conditions are formulated as CLP(R) constraints as follows. Let rectangle R1 be of size **dim(Dx1,Dy1)** at position **pos(Px1,Py1)**, and rectangle R2 of size **dim(Dx2,Dy2)** at position **pos(Px2,Py2)**. Then the first case above (R1 left of R2) is expressed by the constraint:

> { Px1 + Dx1 =< Px2 }

The other three cases are handled analogously.

Finally, the predicate **fit( Box, Rect1, Rect2,...)** is true if all the four blocks, placed into rectangles **Rect1, Rect2, . . . ,** fit into **Box**.

Before loading the program of Figure 7.4 into Prolog, we, of course, have to load the CLP(R) library with:

> ?- use_module( library( clpr)).

For the case of our particular four blocks, the question:

> ?- fit( box1, R1, R2, R3, R4).

also produces, among other solutions, the one illustrated in Figure 7.3:

> R1 = rect( pos( 0.0, 0.0), dim( 5.0, 3.0)),
> R2 = rect( pos( 0.0, 3.0), dim( 6.0, 2.0)),
> R3 = rect( pos( 5.0, A), dim( 1.0, 2.4)),
> R4 = rect( pos( B, 5.0), dim( 5.0, 1.0)),
> { A >= 0.0 }, { A =< 0.6},
> { B >= 0.0}, {B =< 1.0}

The results presented above were slightly reformatted for better readability. The reader may also try whether the four blocks fit the boxes **box2** and **box3**.

## EXERCISES

**7.4** Run times of our program for just four blocks are trivial. However, how about larger numbers of blocks? If the program of Figure 7.4 was extended to handle any number of blocks, its complexity would grow rapidly with the number of blocks. Fortunately, our program usually recognizes many hopeless alternatives quite early, so that large subsets of hopeless alternatives are not fully explored at all. Analyse where in the program the sources of combinatorial complexity occur and work out the order of complexity in the worst case.

**7.5** The **fit/5** predicate in our program only works for four blocks. All the blocks and pairs of blocks are explicitly enumerated to check for the no-overlap requirement. Extending the program in this style for a larger number of blocks (beyond 10, say) would become too cumbersome. Re-define the **fit** predicate as:

  fit( Box, [ BlockName1/Rectangle1, BlockName2/Rectangle2, . . .])

which would work for a list of blocks of any (reasonable) length.

**7.6** Modify the program of Figure 7.4 for the case of three-dimensional blocks and boxes. The structure of the program and the main principles will remain the same, so that relatively straightforward modifications are needed: (1) dimensions and positions become three-dimensional, like **dim(5.0, 3.0, 2.0)**; (2) instead of two possible orientations of blocks, there will now be six (resulting from 90 degree rotations about three axes X, Y and Z); (3) the no-overlap condition between rectangles being 'before' or 'after' in either X or Y directions will now have to include also the two cases for the Z direction.

## 7.4 CLP over finite domains: CLP(FD)

CLP over finite domains comprises some specific mechanisms. We will here illustrate these by some typical examples, using the typical notation and predicates from the CLP(FD) library of some Prolog systems. Our examples will be completely compatible with SICStus Prolog, and largely with SWI Prolog. We will here only introduce a subset of these predicates, those needed for our examples.

Domains of variables will be sets of integers. The predicate **in/2** is used to state the domain of a variable, written as:

  X in Set

where **Set** can be:

| | |
|---|---|
| {Integer1, Integer2, . . . } | set of given integers |
| Term1 . . Term2 | set of integers between **Term1** and **Term2** |
| Set1 \/ Set2 | union of **Set1** and **Set2** |
| Set1 /\ Set2 | intersection of **Set1** and **Set2** |
| \ Set1 | complement of **Set1** |

Arithmetic constraints have the form:

**Exp1 Relation Exp2**

where **Exp1** and **Exp2** are arithmetic expressions, and **Relation** can be:

| | |
|---|---|
| #= | equal |
| #\= | not equal |
| #< | less than |
| #> | greater than |
| #=< | less or equal |
| #>= | greater or equal |

For example:

?- X in 1..5, Y in 0..4,
    X #< Y, Z #= X+Y+1.

X in 1..3
Y in 2..4
Z in 3..7

?- X in 1..5, X in \{4}.

X in (1..3) \/ {5}

Predicate **indomain(X)** assigns through backtracking possible values to X, for example:

?- X in 1..3, indomain(X).

X = 1;
X = 2;
X = 3

There are some useful predicates on lists of variables:

**domain( L, Min, Max)**

meaning: all the variables in list L have domains **Min..Max**.

**all_different( L)**

meaning: all the variables in L must have different values.

**labeling( Options, L)**

generates concrete possible values of the variables in list L. **Options** is a list of options regarding the order in which the variables in L are 'labelled'. If Options = [] then by default the variables are labelled from left to right, taking the possible values one by one from the smallest to the largest. This simplest labelling strategy will satisfy for all the examples in this chapter, although it will not always be the most efficient. Here are some examples:

?- **domain( [X,Y], 1, 2), labeling( [ ], [X,Y]).**

X=1, Y=1;
X=1, Y=2;
X=2, Y=1;
X=2, Y=2

This is how permutations can be generated using **all_different** and **labeling**:

?- L = [X,Y,Z], **domain**( L, 1, 3), **all_different**( L), **labeling**( [ ], L).

L = [1,2,3], X = 1, Y = 2, Z = 3;
L = [1,3,2], X = 1, Y = 3, Z = 2;
L = [2,1,3], X = 2, Y = 1, Z = 3;

. . .

It is easy to solve cryptarithmetic puzzles using these primitives. Consider the puzzle:

```
  D O N A L D
+ G E R A L D
  ───────────
  R O B E R T
```

Each letter above is to be substituted by a different decimal digit so that the numbers add up. Figure 7.5 shows a CLP(FD) program to solve this puzzle. The query to this program is:

?- **solve**( N1, N2, N3).

N1 = [5,2,6,4,8,5]

N2 = [1,9,7,4,8,5]

N3 = [7,2,3,9,7,0]

Figure 7.6 shows a CLP(FD) program for the familiar eight-queens problem. It is instructive to note that both programs, cryptarithmetic and eight queens, have the following basic structure: first, the domains of variables are defined, then constraints are imposed, and finally the labelling finds concrete solutions. This is a usual structure of CLP(FD) programs.

Finally, let us consider optimization problems with CLP(FD), such as the minimization of the finishing time in scheduling. Built-in CLP(FD) predicates useful for optimization are:

**minimize**( Goal, X)   and   **maximize**( Goal, X)

```
% Cryptarithmetic puzzle DONALD + GERALD = ROBERT in CLP(FD)

solve( [D,O,N,A,L,D], [G,E,R,A,L,D], [R,O,B,E,R,T]) :-
  Vars = [D,O,N,A,L,G,E,R,B,T],              % All variables in the puzzle
  domain( Vars, 0, 9),                        % They are all decimal digits
  all_different( Vars),                       % They are all different
  100000*D + 10000*O + 1000*N + 100*A + 10*L + D +
  100000*G + 10000*E + 1000*R + 100*A + 10*L + D #=
  100000*R + 10000*O + 1000*B + 100*E + 10*R + T,
  labeling( [], Vars).
```

**Figure 7.5** A cryptarithmetic puzzle in CLP(FD).

```
% 8 queens in CLP(FD)

solution( Ys) :-                          % Ys is list of Y-coordinates of queens
  Ys = [ _, _, _, _, _, _, _, _],         % There are 8 queens
  domain( Ys, 1, 8),                      % All the coordinates have domains 1..8
  all_different( Ys),                     % All different to avoid horizontal attacks
  safe( Ys),                              % Constrain to prevent diagonal attacks
  labeling( [], Ys).                      % Find concrete values for Ys

safe( []).

safe( [Y | Ys]) :-
  no_attack( Y, Ys, 1),                   % 1 = horizontal distance between queen Y and Ys
  safe( Ys).

% no_attack( Y, Ys, D):
%   queen at Y doesn't attack any queen at Ys;
%   D is column distance between first queen and other queens

no_attack( Y, [], _).

no_attack( Y1, [Y2 | Ys], D) :-
  D #\= Y1-Y2,
  D #\= Y2-Y1,
  D1 is D + 1,
  no_attack( Y1, Ys, D1).
```

**Figure 7.6** A CLP(FD) program for eight queens.

which find such a solution of **Goal** that minimizes (maximizes) the value of X. Typically **Goal** is an 'indomain' or a labelling goal. For example:

```
?- X in 1..20, V #= X*(20-X), maximize( indomain(X), V).
X = 10, V = 100
```

Another example is: find optimal values of X and Y between 1 and 20 so that the product X*Y is maximized, under the constraint that 2*X + Y does not exceed 40:

```
?- domain( [ X, Y], 1, 20),
  2*X + Y #=<40,
  maximize( labeling( [], [ X, Y]), X*Y).

X = 10,  Y = 20
```

Our simple scheduling problem of Figure 7.1 can be solved by the following query:

```
?- StartTimes = [Ta,Tb,Tc,Td,Tf],        % Tf finishing time
  domain( StartTimes, 0, 20),
  Ta + 2 #=< Tb,                          % a precedes b
  Ta + 2 #=< Tc,                          % a precedes c
  Tb + 3 #=< Td,                          % b precedes d
  Tc + 5 #=< Tf,                          % c finishes by Tf
  Td + 4 #=< Tf,                          % d finishes by Tf
  minimize( labeling( [ ], StartTimes), Tf).

StartTimes = [0,2,2,5,9]
```

Here only one optimal solution is generated.

# EXERCISES

**7.7** Measure the time needed by the program in Figure 7.5 to solve the cryptarithmetic puzzle. Then replace the labelling goal by:

    **labeling( [ff], Vars)**

The labelling option 'ff' stands for 'first fail'. That is, the variable with currently the smallest domain will be assigned a value first. Having the smallest domain, this variable is generally the most likely one to cause a failure. This labelling strategy aims at discovering inconsistency as soon as possible, thus avoiding futile search through inconsistent alternatives. Measure the execution time of the modified program. It will be helpful to use the built-in predicate to measure computation time:

    **statistics( runtime, V)**

A call of this predicate instantiates V to a list of the form [ T1, T2] where T1 is the program's run time in milliseconds since the start of the Prolog session, and T2 is the run time since the last call of **statistics(runtime, ...)**. A question to measure time **Time** to solve the puzzle is then, for example:

    **?- statistics( runtime, _), solve( ...), statistics( runtime, [ _, Time]).**

In fact, the time needed by the program to solve this puzzle will probably be too small (something like one or a few milliseconds) for reliable measurement with the **statistics** predicate. Therefore, to obtain reliable measurements, the call of **solve** should be repeated, say, a thousand times. Write also a timing predicate **repeat(Goal,N)** that N times repeats the execution of Goal.

**7.8** Generalize the eight-queens CLP(FD) program to an N queens program. For large N, a good labelling strategy for N queens is 'middle-out', which starts in the middle of the domain and then continues with values further and further away from the middle. Implement this labelling strategy and compare its efficiency experimentally with the straight labelling (as in Figure 7.6).

# Summary

- Constraint satisfaction problems are stated in terms of variables, domains of variables and constraints among the variables.
- Constraint satisfaction problems are often represented as constraint networks.
- Consistency algorithms operate on constraint networks and reduce the domains of variables.
- Constraint logic programming (CLP) combines the constraint satisfaction approach and logic programming.
- CLP systems differ in types of domains and constraints. CLP systems include CLP(R) (over real numbers), CLP(Q) (over rational numbers), CLP(Z) (over integers), CLP(FD) (over finite domains), CLP(B) (over Booleans).
- The power of a CLP system mainly depends on the power of specialized solvers that can solve systems of specific types of constraints, and possibly optimize a given measure within the constraints.

- One aspect in CLP programming is specifying constraints that are as strong as possible. The stronger the constraints, the more they reduce the search space and thus contribute to efficiency. Even adding redundant constraints may improve efficiency.

- Typical practical application areas for CLP include scheduling, logistics and resource management.

- In this chapter, CLP programs were presented for simple scheduling, packing, a cryptarithmetic puzzle and eight queens.

- Concepts discussed in this chapter are:

  constraint satisfaction problems
  constraint satisfaction
  constraint networks
  arc consistency algorithms
  constraint logic programming (CLP)
  CLP(R), CLP(Q), CLP(FD)
  branch-and-bound method

## References

Marriott and Stuckey (1998), Apt (2003) and Dechter (2003) are excellent books on techniques of constraint satisfaction and CLP programming. Rossi, van Beek and Walsh (2006) edited a multi-author collection of chapters that provides a detailed state-of-the-art on a number of key topics in constraint satisfaction. Van Hentenryck (1989) is a well-known earlier discussion of various programming techniques in CLP. Jaffar and Maher (1994) and Mackworth (1992) survey constraint solving techniques. Ongoing research in this area appears in the specialized journal *Constraints* (published by Springer), as well as in *Artificial Intelligence Journal*. The Fibonacci example in this chapter is similar to the one given by Cohen (1990).

The syntax for constraints in this chapter is as used in the SICStus Prolog (SICStus 2010). It is also largely compatible with that used in SWI Prolog (2010).

Apt, K.R. (2003) *Principles of Constraint Programming*. Cambridge: Cambridge University Press.

Cohen, J. (1990) Constraint logic programming languages. *Communications of the ACM* **33**: 52–68.

Dechter, R. (2003) *Constraint Processing*. San Francisco: Morgan Kaufmann.

Jaffar, J. and Maher, M. (1994) Constraint logic programming: a survey. *Journal of Logic Programming* **19–20**: 503–581.

Mackworth, A.K. (1992) Constraint satisfaction. In: Shapiro, S.C. (ed.) *Encyclopedia of Artificial Intelligence*, second edition. New York: Wiley.

Marriott, K. and Stuckey, P.J. (1998) *Programming with Constraints: an Introduction*. Cambridge, MA: The MIT Press.

Rossi, F., van Beek, P. and Walsh, T. (2006) *Handbook of Constraint Programming (Foundations of Artificial Intelligence)*. Elsevier Science.

SICStus Prolog (2010) http://www.sics.se/isl/sicstuswww/site/index.html

SWI Prolog (2010) http://www.swi-prolog.org/

Van Hentenryck, P. (1989) *Constraint Satisfaction in Logic Programming*. Cambridge, MA: MIT Press.

# Chapter 8

# Programming Style and Technique

In this chapter we will review some general principles of good programming and discuss the following questions in particular: How to think about Prolog programs? What are the elements of good programming style in Prolog? How to debug Prolog programs? How to make Prolog programs more efficient?

## 8.1 General principles of good programming

What is a good program? Answering this question is not trivial as there are several criteria for judging how good a program is. Generally accepted criteria include the following:

- *Correctness.* Above all, a good program should be correct. That is, it should do what it is supposed to do. This may seem a trivial, self-explanatory requirement. However, in the case of complex programs, correctness is often not attained. A common mistake when writing programs is to neglect this obvious criterion and pay more attention to other criteria, such as efficiency or external glamour of the program.

- *User-friendliness.* A good program should be easy to use and interact with.

- *Efficiency.* A good program should not needlessly waste computer time and memory space.

- *Readability.* A good program should be easy to read and easy to understand. It should not be more complicated than necessary. Clever programming tricks that obscure the meaning of the program should be avoided. The general organization of the program and its layout help its readability.

- *Modifiability.* A good program should be easy to modify and to extend. Transparency and modular organization of the program help modifiability.

- *Robustness.* A good program should be robust. It should not crash immediately when the user enters some incorrect or unexpected data. The program should, in the case of such errors, stay 'alive' and behave reasonably (should report errors).

- *Documentation*. A good program should be properly documented. The minimal documentation is the program's code including sufficient program comments, and examples of running the program.

The importance of particular criteria depends on the problem and on the circumstances in which the program is written, and on the environment in which it is used. There is no doubt that correctness has the highest priority. The issues of readability, user-friendliness, modifiability, robustness and documentation are usually given, at least, as much priority as the issue of efficiency.

There are some general guidelines for practically achieving the above criteria. One important rule is to first *think* about the problem to be solved, and only then to start writing the actual code in the programming language used. Once we have developed a good understanding of the problem and the solution is well thought through, the actual coding will be fast and easy, and there is a good chance that we will soon get a correct program.

A common mistake is to start writing the code even before the full definition of the problem has been understood. A fundamental reason why early coding is bad practice is that the thinking about the problem and the ideas for a solution should be done in terms that are most relevant to the problem. These terms are usually far from the syntax of the programming language used, and they may include natural language statements and pictorial representation of ideas.

Such a formulation of the solution will have to be transformed into the programming language, but this transformation process may not be easy. A good approach is to use the principle of *stepwise refinement*. The initial formulation of the solution is referred to as the 'top-level solution', and the final program as the 'bottom-level solution'.

According to the principle of stepwise refinement, the final program is developed through a sequence of transformations, or 'refinements', of the solution. We start with the first, top-level solution and then proceed through a sequence of solutions; these are all equivalent, but each solution in the sequence is expressed in more detail. In each refinement step, concepts used in previous formulations are elaborated to greater detail and their representation gets closer to the programming language. It should be realized that refinement applies both to procedure definitions and to data structures. In the initial stages we normally work with more abstract, bulky units of information whose structure is refined later.

Such a strategy of top-down stepwise refinement has the following advantages:

- it allows for formulation of rough solutions in terms that are most relevant to the problem;

- in terms of such powerful concepts, the solution should be succinct and simple, and therefore likely to be correct;

- each refinement step should be small enough so that it is intellectually manageable; if so, the transformation of a solution into a new, more detailed representation is likely to be correct, and so is the resulting solution at the next level of detail.

In the case of Prolog we may talk about the stepwise refinement of *relations*. If the problem suggests thinking in algorithmic terms, then we can also talk about refinement of *algorithms*, adopting the procedural point of view in Prolog.

In order to properly refine a solution at some level of detail, and to introduce useful concepts at the next lower level, we need ideas. Therefore programming is creative, especially so for beginners. With experience, programming gradually becomes less of an art and more of a craft. But, nevertheless, a major question is: How do we get ideas? Most ideas come from experience, from similar problems whose solutions we know. If we do not know a direct programming solution, another similar problem could be helpful. Another source of ideas is everyday life. For example, if the problem is to write a program to sort a list of items we may get an idea from considering the question: How would I myself sort a set of exam papers according to the alphabetical order of students?

General principles of good programming outlined in this section basically apply to Prolog as well. We will discuss some details with particular reference to Prolog in the following sections.

## 8.2  How to think about Prolog programs

One characteristic feature of Prolog is that it allows for both the procedural and declarative way of thinking about programs. The two approaches have been discussed in detail in Chapter 2, and illustrated by examples throughout the text. Which approach will be more effective and practical depends on the problem. Declarative solutions are usually easier to develop, but may lead to an inefficient program.

During the process of developing a solution we have to find ideas for reducing problems to one or more easier subproblems. An important question is: How do we find proper subproblems? There are several general principles that often work in Prolog programming. These will be discussed in the following sections.

### 8.2.1  Use of recursion

The principle here is to split the problem into cases belonging to two groups:

(1)  trivial, or 'boundary' cases;

(2)  'general' cases where the solution is constructed from solutions of (simpler) versions of the original problem itself.

In Prolog we use this technique all the time. Let us look at one more example: processing a list of items so that each item is transformed by the same transformation rule. Let this procedure be

> maplist( List, F, NewList)

where **List** is an original list, F is a transformation rule (a binary relation) and **NewList** is the list of all transformed items. The problem of transforming **List** can be split into two cases:

(1)  Boundary case: **List** = [ ]

if **List** = [ ] then **NewList** = [ ], regardless of F

(2)  General case: **List = [X | Tail]**

> To transform a list of the form [X | Tail], do:
>> transform the item X by rule F obtaining NewX, and
>> transform the list Tail obtaining NewTail;
>> the whole transformed list is [NewX | NewTail].

In Prolog:

```
maplist( [ ], _, [ ] ).

maplist( [X | Tail], F, [NewX | NewTail] ) :-
   G =.. [F, X, NewX],
   call( G),
   maplist( Tail, F, NewTail).
```

Suppose we have a list of numbers and want to compute the list of their squares. **maplist** can be used for this as follows:

```
square( X, Y) :-
   Y is X*X.

?- maplist( [2, 6, 5], square, Squares).
Squares = [ 4, 36, 25]
```

One reason why recursion so naturally applies to defining relations in Prolog is that data objects themselves often have a recursive structure. Lists and trees are such objects. A list is either empty (boundary case) or has a head and a tail that is itself a list (general case). A binary tree is either empty (boundary case) or it has a root and two subtrees that are themselves binary trees (general case). Therefore, to process a whole non-empty tree, we must do something with the root, and process the subtrees.

## 8.2.2   Generalization

It is often a good idea to generalize the original problem, so that the solution to the generalized problem can be formulated recursively. The original problem is then solved as a special case of its more general version. Generalization of a relation typically involves the introduction of one or more extra arguments. A major problem, which may require deeper insight into the problem, is how to find the right generalization.

As an example let us revisit the eight-queens problem. The original problem was to place eight queens on the chessboard so that they do not attack each other. Let us call the corresponding relation:

**eightqueens( Pos)**

This is true if **Pos** is a position with eight non-attacking queens. A good idea in this case is to generalize the number of queens from eight to N. The number of queens now becomes the additional argument:

**nqueens( Pos, N)**

The advantage of this generalization is that there is an immediate recursive formulation of the **nqueens** relation:

(1)  Boundary case: N = 0

>     To safely place zero queens is trivial.

(2)  General case: N > 0

>     To safely place N queens on the board, satisfy the following:
>     achieve a safe configuration of (N – 1) queens; and
>     add the remaining queen so that she does not attack any other queen.

Once the generalized problem has been solved, the original problem is easy:

> **eightqueens( Pos) :- nqueens( Pos, 8).**

## 8.2.3  Using pictures

When searching for ideas about a problem, it is often useful to introduce some graphical representation of the problem. A picture may help us to perceive some essential relations in the problem. Then we just have to describe what we *see* in the picture in the programming language.

The use of pictorial representations is often useful in problem solving in general; it seems, however, that it works with Prolog particularly well. The following arguments explain why:

(1)  Prolog is particularly suitable for problems that involve objects and relations between objects. Often, such problems can be naturally illustrated by graphs in which nodes correspond to objects and arcs correspond to relations.

(2)  Structured data objects in Prolog are naturally pictured as trees.

(3)  The declarative meaning of Prolog facilitates the translation of pictorial representations into Prolog because, in principle, the order in which the picture is described does not matter. We just put what we see into the program in any order. (For practical reasons of the program's efficiency this order will possibly have to be polished later.)

## 8.3  Programming style

The purpose of conforming to some stylistic conventions is:

* to reduce the danger of programming errors; and
* to produce programs that ate readable and easy to understand, easy to debug and to modify.

We will review here some ingredients of good programming style in Prolog: some general rules of good style, tabular organization of long procedures and commenting.

## 8.3.1  Some rules of good style

* Program clauses should be short. Their body should ideally contain no more than a few goals.

- Procedures should be short because long procedures are hard to understand. However, long procedures are acceptable if they have some uniform structure (this will be discussed later in this section).

- Mnemonic names for procedures and variables should be used. Names should indicate the meaning of relations and the role of data objects.

- The layout of programs is important. Spacing, blank lines and indentation should be consistently used for the sake of readability. Clauses about the same procedure should be clustered together; there should be blank lines between clauses (unless, perhaps, there are numerous facts about the same relation); each goal can be placed on a separate line. Prolog programs sometimes resemble poems for the aesthetic appeal of ideas and form.

- Stylistic conventions of this kind may vary from program to program as they depend on the problem and personal taste. It is important, however, that the same conventions are used consistently throughout the whole program.

- The cut operator should be used with care. Cut should not be used if it can be easily avoided. It is better to use, where possible, 'green cuts' rather than 'red cuts'. As discussed in Chapter 5, a cut is called 'green' if it can be removed without altering the declarative meaning of the clause. The use of 'red cuts' should be restricted to clearly defined constructs such as **not** or the selection between alternatives. An example of the latter construct is:

  *if* Condition *then* **Goal1** *else* **Goal2**

  This translates into Prolog, using cut, as:

  | | |
  |---|---|
  | **Condition, !,** | % Condition true? |
  | **Goal1** | % If yes then Goal1 |
  | ; | |
  | **Goal2** | % Otherwise Goal2 |

- The **not** procedure can also lead to surprising behaviour, as it is related to cut. We have to be well aware of how **not** is defined in Prolog. This was discussed in Chapter 5. However, if there is a dilemma between **not** and cut, the former is perhaps better than some obscure construct with cut.

- Program modification by **assert** and **retract** can grossly degrade the transparency of the program's behaviour. In particular, the same program will answer the same question differently at different times. In such cases, if we want to reproduce the same behaviour we have to make sure that the whole previous state, which was modified by assertions and retractions, is completely restored.

- The use of a semicolon may obscure the meaning of a clause. The readability can sometimes be improved by splitting the clause containing the semicolon into more clauses; but this will, possibly, be at the expense of the length of the program and its efficiency.

To illustrate some points of this section consider the relation

  **merge( List1, List2, List3)**

where **List1** and **List2** are ordered lists that merge into **List3**. For example:

  **merge( [2,4,7], [1,3,4,8], [1,2,3,4,4,7,8] )**

The following is an implementation of **merge** in bad style:

```
merge( List1, List2, List3) :-
  List1 = [ ], !, List3 = List2;              % First list empty
  List2 = [ ], !, List3 = List1;              % Second list empty
  List1 = [X | Rest1],
  List2 = [Y | Rest2],
  ( X < Y, !,
    Z = X,                                    % Z is head of List3
    merge( Rest1, List2, Rest3);
    Z = Y,
    merge( List1, Rest2, Rest3) ),
  List3 = [Z | Rest3].
```

Here is a better version which avoids semicolons:

```
merge( [ ], List, List)  :-  !.              % The cut prevents redundant solutions

merge( List, [ ], List).

merge( [X | Rest1], [Y | Rest2], [X | Rest3] ) :-
  X < Y, !,
  merge( Rest1, [Y | Rest2], Rest3).

merge( List1, [Y | Rest2], [Y | Rest3] ) :-
  merge( List1, Rest2, Rest3).
```

## 8.3.2  Tabular organization of long procedures

Long procedures are acceptable if they have some uniform structure. Typically, such a form is a set of facts when a relation is effectively defined in the tabular form. Advantages of such an organization of a long procedure are:

- Its structure is easily understood.
- Incrementability: it can be refined by simply adding new facts.
- It is easy to check and correct or modify (by simply replacing some fact independently of other facts).

## 8.3.3  Commenting

Program comments should explain in the first place what the program is about and how to use it, and only then the details of the solution method used and other programming details. The main purpose of comments is to enable the user to use the program, to understand it and to possibly modify it. Comments should describe, in the shortest form possible, everything that is essential to these ends. Under-commenting is a usual fault, but a program can also be over-commented. Explanation of details that are obvious from the program code itself is only a needless burden to the program.

Long passages of comments should precede the code they refer to, while short comments should be interspersed with the code itself. Information that should, in general, be included in comments comprises the following:

- What the program does, how it is used (for example, what goal is to be invoked and what are the expected results), examples of using the program.
- What are top-level predicates?
- How are main concepts (objects) represented?
- Execution time and memory requirements of the program.
- What are the program's limitations?
- Are there any special system-dependent features used?
- What is the meaning of the predicates in the program? What are their arguments? Which arguments are 'input' and which are 'output', if known? (Input arguments have fully specified values, without uninstantiated variables, when the predicate is called.)
- Algorithmic and implementation details.
- The following conventions are often used when describing predicates. References to a predicate are made by stating the predicate's name and its arity, written as:

      **PredicateName / Arity**

  For example, **merge( List1, List2, List3)** would be referred to as **merge/3**. The input/output modes of the arguments are indicated by prefixing arguments' names by '+' (input) or '-' (output). For example, **merge( +List1, +List2, -List3)** indicates that the first two arguments of **merge** are input, and the third one is output.

## 8.4 Debugging

When a program does not do what it is expected to do the main problem is to locate the error(s). It is easier to locate an error in a part of the program (or a module) than in the program as a whole. Therefore, a good principle of debugging is to start by testing smaller units of the program, and when these can be trusted, to test bigger modules or the whole program.

Debugging in Prolog is facilitated by two things: first, Prolog is an interactive language so any part of the program can be directly invoked by a proper question to the Prolog system; second, Prolog implementations usually provide special debugging aids. The basis for debugging aids is *tracing*. 'Tracing a goal' means that the information regarding the goal's satisfaction is displayed during execution. This information includes:

- Entry information: the predicate name and the values of arguments when the goal is invoked.
- Exit information: in the case of success, the values of arguments that satisfy the goal; otherwise an indication of failure.
- Re-entry information: invocation of the same goal caused by backtracking.

Between entry and exit, the trace information for all the subgoals of this goal can be obtained. So we can trace the execution of our question all the way down to the lowest level goals until facts are encountered. Such detailed tracing may turn out to be impractical due to the excessive amount of tracing information; therefore, the user can specify selective tracing. There are two selection mechanisms: first, suppress tracing information beyond a certain level; second, trace only some specified subset of predicates, and not all of them.

Such debugging aids are activated by system-dependent built-in predicates. A typical subset of such predicates is as follows:

**trace**

triggers exhaustive tracing of goals that follow.

**notrace**

stops further tracing.

**spy( P)**

specifies that a predicate P be traced. This is used when we are particularly interested in the named predicate and want to avoid tracing information from other goals (either above or below the level of a call of P). Several predicates can be simultaneously active for 'spying'.

**nospy( P)**

stops 'spying' P.

Tracing beyond a certain depth can be suppressed by special commands during execution. There may be several other debugging commands available, such as returning to a previous point of execution. After such a return we can, for example, repeat the execution at a greater detail of tracing.

As an example of how Prolog debugging aids may help, consider this (faulty) program for the familiar **conc** relation:

```
conc( [], L, L).
conc( [X | L1], L2, [X | L3]) :-
    conc( L1, L1, L3).
```

What is wrong here? Yes, the last line should be **conc( L1, L2, L3)**. How can Prolog help the programmer to find this? First, when we load this program with **consult(conc_program)** (assuming the program is in the file conc_program.pl), a Prolog system will typically issue a warning like: 'L2 – a singleton variable'. This means that the variable L2 only appears once in the clause. Singleton variables are not necessarily errors. But they can take any value and are thus unrelated to the other variables in the clause. Often, such variables only appear as a result of the programmer's typing errors. If such a variable can indeed take any value, it can be replaced by an anonymous variable ('_'). It is a useful practice to consistently use an anonymous variable whenever the programmer actually means 'any value' to make this explicit to the reader, and make good use of singleton error warnings. If such a convention is adopted, a warning about a singleton variable signals a typo.

Now, suppose that in our case the programmer ignored the singleton variable warning, and noticed that the program is not producing intended results, for example:

```
?- conc( [a,b], [c,d], L3).

L3 = [a,b]
```

To find the bug, the programmer may now use **trace**:

```
?- trace, conc( [a,b], [c,d], L3).
```

```
1 Call: conc( [a,b], [c,d],_533) ?          % Here the programmer types "return"
2 Call: conc( [b], [b], _1170) ?
```

At this point, it will probably become clear to the programmer that the second argument in this recursive call is wrong, which is where the error is.

## 8.5 Improving efficiency

There are several aspects of efficiency, including the most common ones, execution time and space requirements of a program. Another aspect is the time needed by the programmer to develop the program.

The traditional computer architecture is not particularly suitable for the Prolog style of program execution – that is, satisfying a list of goals. Therefore, the limitations of time and space may be experienced earlier in Prolog than in many other programming languages. Whether this will cause difficulties in a practical application depends on the problem. The issue of time efficiency is practically meaningless if a Prolog program that is run a few times per day takes 1 second of CPU time and a corresponding program in some other language, say Java, takes 0.1 seconds. The difference in efficiency will perhaps matter if the two programs take 50 minutes and 5 minutes respectively.

On the other hand, in many areas of application Prolog will greatly reduce the program development time. Prolog programs will be easier to write, to understand and to debug than in other languages. Problems that gravitate toward the 'Prolog domain' involve symbolic computation, structured data objects and relations between them, possibly combined with search. In particular, Prolog has been successfully applied in areas such as planning and scheduling, symbolic problem solving in general, databases, prototyping, implementation of programming languages, discrete and qualitative simulation, architectural design, machine learning, natural language understanding, expert systems, and other areas of artificial intelligence. On the other hand, numerical mathematics is an area for which Prolog is not a natural candidate.

With respect to the execution efficiency, executing a *compiled* program is generally more efficient than *interpreting* the program. Therefore, if the Prolog system contains both an interpreter and a compiler, then the compiler should be used if efficiency is critical.

If a program suffers from inefficiency then it can often be radically improved by improving the algorithm itself. To this end, the procedural aspects of the program have to be studied. A simple way of improving the execution efficiency is to find a better ordering of clauses of procedures, and of goals in the bodies of clauses. Another relatively simple method is to provide guidance to the Prolog system by means of cuts.

Ideas for improving the efficiency of a program usually come from a deeper understanding of the problem. A more efficient algorithm can, in general, result from improvements of two kinds:

- Improving search efficiency by avoiding unnecessary backtracking and stopping the execution of useless alternatives as soon as possible.

- Using more suitable data structures to represent objects in the program, so that operations on objects can be implemented more efficiently.

We will study both kinds of improvements by looking at examples. Yet another technique of improving efficiency will be illustrated by an example. This technique, called caching, is based on asserting into the database intermediate results that are likely to be needed again in the future computation. Instead of repeating the computation, such results are simply retrieved as already known facts.

## 8.5.1 Improving efficiency in a map colouring program

In this example, a simple idea of search reordering in map colouring will convert a practically unacceptable time complexity into a trivial one.

The map colouring problem is to assign each country in a given map one of four given colours in such a way that no two neighbouring countries are painted with the same colour. There is a theorem which guarantees that this is always possible.

Let us assume that a map is specified by the neighbour relation

   **ngb( Country, Neighbours)**

where **Neighbours** is the list of countries bordering on **Country**. So the map of Europe would be specified (in alphabetical order) as:

   **ngb( albania, [greece, macedonia, montenegro, serbia] ).**
   **ngb( andorra, [france, spain] ).**
   **ngb( austria, [czech_republic, germany, hungary, italy, liechtenstein,**
   **slovakia, slovenia, switzerland] ).**
   ...

Let a solution be represented as a list of pairs of the form

   **Country/Colour**

which specifies a colour for each country in a given map. For the given map, the names of countries are fixed in advance, and the problem is to find the values for the colours. Thus, for Europe, the problem is to find a proper instantiation of variables C1, C2, C3, etc. in the list:

   **[ albania/C1, andorra/C2, austria/C3, ... ]**

Now let us define the predicate

   **colours( Country_colour_list)**

which is true if the **Country_colour_list** satisfies the map colouring constraint with respect to a given **ngb** relation. Let the four colours be yellow, blue, red and green. The condition that no two neighbouring countries are of the same colour can be formulated in Prolog as follows:

   **colours( [ ] ).**

```
        colours( [Country/Colour | Rest] ) :-
          colours( Rest),
          member( Colour, [yellow, blue, red, green] ),
          \+ ( member( Country1/Colour, Rest), neighbour( Country, Country1) ).

        neighbour( Country, Country1) :-
          ngb( Country, Neighbours),
          member( Country1, Neighbours).
```

Here, **member( X,L)** is, as usual, the list membership relation. This will work well for simple maps, with a small number of countries. Europe might be problematic, however. One attempt to colour Europe could be as follows: first, create a list of pairs **Country/Colour** of all the countries in the map, **Colour** being a distinct uninstantiated variable for each country, and then apply the predicate **colours** on this list:

```
        ?- findall( Cntry/Colour, ngb( Cntry, _), CountryColourList),
           colours( CountryColourList).
```

However, it depends on luck whether this will work well or not. It may take just a fraction of a second to find a solution, but if the order of the countries in the list is unfortunate it may take unreasonably long, hours or more, for the search to find a legal colouring among the possibilities.

A detailed study of the way Prolog tries to satisfy the **colours** goal reveals the source of inefficiency. The order in which the countries are assigned colours corresponds to the order in the list (starting at the end), which was in our case generally independent of the neighbour relation between countries. If the order in the list does not reflect geographic neighbourhood, the colouring process starts at some end of the map, continues at some other end, etc., moving around more or less randomly. This may easily lead to a situation in which a country that is to be coloured is surrounded by many other countries, already painted with all four available colours. Then backtracking is necessary, which leads to inefficiency.

The following example illustrates a problematic order. Suppose the countries are coloured in the order:

Cn0, ... long list of countries here, ... , Cn1, Cn2, Cn3, Cn4, ...

Let country Cn0 have many neighbours, Cn1, ... , Cn4 being among them. Our program will colour the right-hand side of the list first, so these neighbours will be coloured before country Cn0. Suppose that the four neighbours have been coloured by different colours. Therefore this colouring is doomed to fail, because there is no options left for Cn0. But the program will first colour all the countries in the long list in the middle before noticing, when colouring Cn0, that this attempt has gone astray. The decisive mistake occurred quite early, but the program will only gradually backtrack to the four neighbours. Before that, it will try in vain all the possible colourings of the long list in the middle, which may result in disastrous combinatorial complexity.

It is clear, then, that the efficiency depends on the order in which the countries are coloured. Intuition suggests a simple colouring strategy that should work better than random: start with some country that has many neighbours, and then proceed to the neighbours, then to the neighbours of neighbours, etc.

For Europe, then, Germany (having most neighbours) is a good candidate to start with. Of course, when the template country/colour list is constructed, Germany has to be put at the end of the list and other countries have to be added at the front of the list. In this way the colouring algorithm, which starts at the rear end, will commence with Germany and proceed from there from neighbour to neighbour. Such a neighbour-based country/colour template has a good chance of colouring the map of Europe quickly.

We can construct a properly ordered list of countries manually, but we can also do it automatically with the following procedure **makelist**. It starts the construction with some specified country (Germany in our case) and collects the countries into a list called **Closed**. Each country is first put into another list, called **Open**, before it is transferred to **Closed**. Each time that a country is transferred from **Open** to **Closed**, its neighbours are added to **Open**.

```
makelist( List) :-
    collect( [germany], [ ], List).          % Start with Germany

collect( [ ], Closed, Closed).               % No more candidates for Closed

collect( [X | Open], Closed, List) :-
    member( X, Closed), !,                   % X has already been collected?
    collect( Open, Closed, List).            % Discard X

collect( [X | Open], Closed, List) :-
    ngb( X, Ngbs),                           % Find X's neighbours
    conc( Ngbs, Open, Open1),                % Put them to Open1
    collect( Open1, [X | Closed], List).     % Collect the Rest
```

The **conc** relation is, as usual, the list concatenation relation.

## 8.5.2  Improving efficiency of list concatenation by difference lists

In our programs so far, the concatenation of lists has been programmed as:

```
conc( [ ], L, L).

conc( [X | L1], L2, [X | L3] ) :-
    conc( L1, L2, L3).
```

This is inefficient when the first list is long. The following example explains why:

```
?- conc( [a,b,c], [d,e], L).
```

This produces the following sequence of goals:

```
conc( [a,b,c], [d,e], L)
    conc( [b,c], [d,e], L')         where L = [a | L']
        conc( [c], [d,e], L'')      where L' = [b | L'']
            conc( [ ], [d,e], L''')  where L'' = [c | L''']
            true                     where L''' = [d,e]
```

This shows that the program in effect scans the entire first list, until the empty list is encountered.

But could we not simply skip the whole of the first list in a single step and append the second list, instead of gradually working down the first list? To do this, we need to know where the end of a list is; that is, we need another representation of lists. One solution is the data structure called *difference list*. In difference list representation, a list is represented by a pair of lists. For example, the list

[a,b,c]

can be represented by the two lists:

L1 = [a,b,c,d,e]
L2 = [d,e]

Such a pair of lists, which we will for brevity choose to write as **L1-L2**, represents the 'difference' between L1 and L2. This of course only works if L2 is a suffix of L1. Note that the same list can be represented by several 'difference pairs'. So the list [a,b,c] can be represented, for example, by

[a,b,c] - [ ]

or

[a,b,c,d,e] - [d,e]

or

[a,b,c,d,e | T] - [d,e | T]

or

[a,b,c | T] - T

where T is any list. The empty list is represented by any pair of the form **L-L**.

The second member of the pair indicates the end of the list, so the end is directly accessible. This can be used for an efficient implementation of concatenation. The method is illustrated in Figure 8.1. With the help of this figure, we can reason about the concatenation of **L1** and **L2**, represented by difference lists as follows:

L1  is represented by  **A1 - Z1**
L2  is represented by  **A2 - Z2**
L3  is represented by  **A1 - Z2**

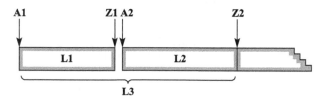

**Figure 8.1** Concatenation of lists represented by difference pairs. L1 is represented by A1 - Z1, L2 by A2 – Z2, and the result L3 by A1 - Z2 when Z1 = A2 must be true.

For A1 - Z2 to represent the concatenation, it is clear from Figure 8.1 that Z1 must be equal to A2. This can be implemented as the following conc_d predicate:

    conc_d( A1 - Z1, A2 - Z2, A1 - Z2)  :-
        Z1 = A2.

Equivalently, this can be written simply as a Prolog fact:

    conc_d( A1 - Z1, Z1 - Z2, A1 - Z2).

Let us use conc_d to concatenate the lists [a,b,c], represented by the pair [a,b,c | T1]-T1, and the list [d,e], represented by [d,e | T2]-T2:

    ?- conc_d( [a,b,c | T1] - T1, [d,e | T2] - T2, L).

The concatenation is done just by matching this goal with the clause about conc_d, giving:

    T1 = [d,e | T2]
    L  = [a,b,c,d,e | T2] - T2

Due to its efficiency, this *difference lists* technique for list concatenation is very popular, although it cannot be used as flexibly as our usual conc procedure.

### 8.5.3  Last call optimization and accumulators

Recursive calls normally take up memory space, which is only freed after the return from the call. A large number of nested recursive calls may lead to short-age of memory. In special cases, however, it is possible to execute nested recursive calls without requiring extra memory. In such a case a recursive procedure has a special form, called *tail recursion*. A tail-recursive procedure only has one recursive call, and this call appears as the *last goal* of the *last clause* in the procedure. In addition, the goals preceding the recursive call must be deterministic, so that no backtracking occurs after this last call. We can force this determinism by placing a cut just before the recursive call. Typically a tail-recursive procedure looks like this:

    p(...) :-....          % No recursive call in the body of this clause
    p(...) :-....          % No recursive call in the body of this clause
    ...
    p(...) :-
        ..., !,            % The cut ensures no backtracking
        p(...).            % Tail-recursive call

In the cases of such tail-recursive procedures, no information is needed upon the return from a call. Therefore such recursion can be carried out simply as iteration in which a next cycle in the loop does *not* require additional memory. A Prolog system will typically notice such an opportunity of saving memory and realize tail recursion as iteration. This is called *tail recursion optimization*, or *last call optimization*.

When memory efficiency is critical, tail-recursive formulations of procedures help. Often it is indeed possible to re-formulate a recursive procedure into a tail-recursive one. Let us consider the predicate for computing the sum of a list of numbers:

    sumlist( List, Sum)

Here is a simple first definition:

```
sumlist( [ ], 0).

sumlist( [ First | Rest], Sum) :-
  sumlist( Rest, Sum0),
  Sum is X + Sum0.
```

This is not tail recursive, so the summation over a very long list will require many recursive calls and therefore a lot of memory. However, we know that in a typical procedural language such summation can be carried out as a simple iterative loop. How can we make **sumlist** tail recursive and enable Prolog too to carry it out as iteration? Unfortunately we cannot simply swap the goals in the body of the second clause, because the **is** goal can only be executed *after* Sum0 has been computed. But the following is a common trick that does it:

```
sumlist( List, Sum) :-
  sumlist( List, 0, Sum).                    % Call auxiliary predicate

% sumlist( List, PartialSum, TotalSum):
%   TotalSum = PartialSum + sum over List

sumlist( [ ], Sum, Sum).                      % Total sum = partial sum

sumlist( [ First | Rest ], PartialSum, TotalSum) :-
  NewPartialSum is PartialSum + First,
  sumlist( Rest, NewPartialSum, TotalSum).
```

This is now tail recursive and Prolog can benefit from last call optimization.

The technique of making our **sumlist** procedure tail recursive as above is frequently used. To define our target predicate **sumlist/2**, we introduced an auxiliary predicate **sumlist/3**. The additional argument, **PartialSum**, enabled a tail-recursive formulation. Such extra arguments are called *accumulators*. The final result is gradually accumulated in such an accumulator during successive recursive calls.

Here is another famous example of tail-recursion formulation through introducing an accumulator argument:

```
reverse( List, ReversedList)
```

**ReversedList** has the same elements as **List**, but in the reverse order. The following is a first, straightforward attempt:

```
reverse( [ ], [ ]).

reverse( [X | Rest], Reversed) :-
  reverse( Rest, RevRest),
  conc( RevRest, [X], Reversed).              % Append X at end of RevRest
```

This is not tail recursive. Apart from that, it is also very inefficient because of the goal **conc(RevRest, [X], Reversed)**, which requires time proportional to the length of **RevRest**. Therefore, to reverse a list of length $n$, the procedure above will require time proportional to $n^2$. But, of course, a list can be reversed in linear time. Therefore, due to its inefficiency, the procedure above is also known as 'naive reverse'. A much more efficient version below introduces an accumulator:

**reverse( List, Reversed) :-**
   **reverse( List, [ ], Reversed).**

% reverse( List, PartReversed, Reversed):
%   Reversed is obtained by adding the elements of List in reverse order
%   to PartReversed

**reverse( [ ], Reversed, Reversed).**              % Nothing to add to Reversed

**reverse( [X | Rest], PartReversed, TotalReversed) :-**
   **reverse( Rest, [X | PartReversed], TotalReversed).**   % Add X to accumulator

This is efficient (time is linear in the length of list) and tail recursive.

## 8.5.4   Simulating arrays with *arg*

The list structure is the easiest representation for sets in Prolog. However, accessing an item in a list is done by scanning the list. This takes time proportional to the length of the list. For long lists this is very inefficient. Tree structures, discussed in Chapters 9 and 10, offer much more efficient access. However, often it is possible to access an element of a structure through the element's *index*. In such cases, *array* structures, provided in other programming languages, are the most effective because they enable direct access to a required element.

There is no array facility in Prolog, but arrays can be simulated to some extent by using the built-in predicates **arg** and **functor**. Here is an example. The goal:

   **functor( A, f, 100)**

makes a structure with 100 elements:

   **A = f( _, _, _, ...)**

In other languages, a typical example statement that involves direct access to an element of an array is:

   A[60] : = 1

This initializes the value of the 60th element of array A to 1. We can achieve analogous effect in Prolog by the goal:

   **arg( 60, A, 1)**

This directly accesses the 60th component of the compound term A, which as the result gets instantiated to:

   **A = f( _, ..., _, 1, _, ..., _)**       % 60th component equal 1

The point is that time needed to access the Nth component of a structure does not depend on N. Another typical example statement from other programming languages is:

   X : = A[60]

This translates into our simulated array in Prolog as:

   **arg( 60, A, X)**

This is much more efficient than having a list of 100 elements and accessing the 60th element by nested recursion down the list. However, the updating of the value of an element in a simulated array is awkward. Once the values in an array have been initialized, they can be changed, for example:

$A[60] := A[60] + 1$

A straightforward way to simulate such an update of a *single* value in an array in Prolog would be as follows: build a *whole* new structure with 100 components using **functor**, insert the new value at the appropriate place in the structure, and fill all the other components by the corresponding components of the previous structure. All this is awkward and very inefficient. One idea to improve this is to provide uninstantiated 'holes' in the components of the structure, so that future values of array elements can be accommodated in these holes. So we can, for example, store successive update values in a list in which the rest of the list is an uninstantiated variable – a 'hole' for future values. As an example consider the following updates of the value of variable X in a procedural language:

$X := 1; \quad X := 2; \quad X := 3$

These updates can be simulated in Prolog with the 'holes' technique as follows:

| | |
|---|---|
| X = [ 1 | Rest1] | % Corresponds to X : = 1, Rest1 is hole for future values |
| Rest1 = [ 2 | Rest2] | % Corresponds to X : = 2, Rest 2 is hole for future values |
| Rest2 = [ 3 | Rest3] | % Corresponds to X : = 3 |

At this point X = [ 1, 2, 3 | Rest3]. Obviously the whole history of the values of X is maintained, and the current value is the one just preceding the 'hole'. If there are many successive updates, the 'current' value gets nested deep, and the technique becomes inefficient again. A further idea, to overcome this source of inefficiency, is to throw away the previous values at the moment when a list gets too long, and start again with a list consisting of just a head and an uninstantiated tail.

In spite of these potential complications, in many cases the simulation of arrays with **arg** is simple and works well. One such example is our solution 3 for the eight-queens problem in Chapter 4 (Figure 4.14). This program places a next queen into a currently free column (X-coordinate), row (Y-coordinate), upward diagonal (U-coordinate) and downward diagonal (V-coordinate). The sets of currently free coordinates are maintained, and when a new queen is placed the corresponding occupied coordinates are deleted from these sets. The deletion of U- and V-coordinates in Figure 4.14 involves scanning the corresponding lists, which is inefficent. Efficiency can easily be improved by simulated arrays. So the set of all 15 upward diagonals can be represented by the following term with 15 components:

$Du = u(\_, \_, \_, \_, \_, \_, \_, \_, \_, \_, \_, \_, \_, \_, \_)$

Consider placing a queen at the square (X,Y) = (1,1). This square lies on the 8th upward diagonal. The fact that this diagonal is now occupied can be marked by instantiating the 8th component of **Du** to 1 (that is, the corresponding X-coordinate):

arg( 8, Du, 1)

Now **Du** becomes:

$$\textbf{Du} = \textbf{u}(\,\_,\,\_,\,\_,\,\_,\,\_,\,\_,\,\_,\, 1,\,\_,\,\_,\,\_,\,\_,\,\_,\,\_,\,\_\,)$$

If later a queen is attempted to be placed at $(X,Y) = (3,3)$, also lying on the 8th diagonal, this would require:

    **arg( 8, Du, 3)**       % Here $X = 3$

This will fail because the 8th component of **Du** is already 1. So the program will not allow another queen to be placed on the same diagonal. This implementation of the sets of upward and downward diagonals leads to a considerably more efficient program than the one in Figure 4.14.

## 8.5.5 Improving efficiency by asserting derived facts

Sometimes during computation the same goal has to be satisfied again and again. As Prolog has no special mechanism to discover such situations whole computation sequences are repeated.

    As an example consider a program to compute the Nth Fibonacci number for a given N. The Fibonacci sequence is:

    1, 1, 2, 3, 5, 8, 13, . . .

Each number in the sequence, except for the first two, is the sum of the previous two numbers. We will define a predicate

    **fib( N, F)**

to compute, for a given N, the Nth Fibonacci number, F. We count the numbers in the sequence starting with $N = 1$. The following **fib** program deals first with the first two Fibonacci numbers as two special cases, and then specifies the general rule about the Fibonacci sequence:

    **fib( 1, 1).**                % 1st Fibonacci number

    **fib( 2, 1).**                % 2nd Fibonacci number

    **fib( N, F) :-**            % Nth Fib. number, $N > 2$
      **N > 2,**
      **N1 is N - 1, fib( N1, F1),**
      **N2 is N - 2, fib( N2, F2),**
      **F is F1 + F2.**       % Nth number is the sum of its two predecessors

This program tends to redo parts of the computation. This is easily seen if we trace the execution of the following goal:

    **?- fib( 6, F).**

Figure 8.2 illustrates this computational process. For example, the third Fibonacci number, $f(3)$, is needed in three places and the same computation is repeated each time.

    This can be easily avoided by remembering each newly computed Fibonacci number. The idea is to use the built-in procedure **asserta** and to add these

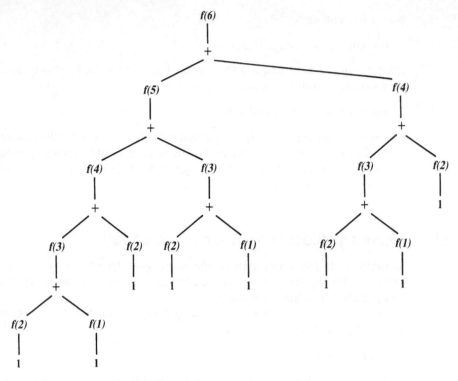

**Figure 8.2** Computation of the 6th Fibonacci number by procedure **fib**.

(intermediate) results as facts to the database. These facts have to precede other clauses about **fib** to prevent the use of the general rule in cases where the result is already known. The modified procedure, **fib2**, differs from **fib** only in this assertion:

| | |
|---|---|
| **fib2( 1, 1).** | % 1st Fibonacci number |
| **fib2( 2, 1).** | % 2nd Fibonacci number |
| **fib2( N, F) :-**<br>  **N > 2,**<br>  **N1 is N - 1, fib2( N1, F1),**<br>  **N2 is N - 2, fib2( N2, F2),**<br>  **F is F1 + F2,**<br>  **asserta( fib2( N, F) ).** | % Nth Fib. number, N > 2<br><br><br><br>% Remember Nth number |

This program will try to answer any **fib2** goal by first looking at stored facts about this relation, and only then resort to the general rule. As a result, when a goal **fib2( N, F)** is executed all Fibonacci numbers, up to the Nth number, will get tabulated. Figure 8.3 illustrates the computation of the 6th Fibonacci number by **fib2**. A comparison with Figure 8.2 shows the saving in the computational complexity. For greater N, the savings would be much more substantial.

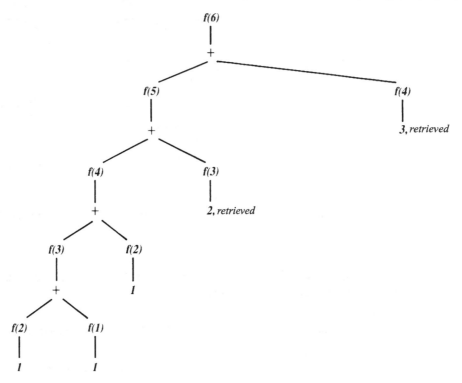

**Figure 8.3** Computation of the 6th Fibonacci number by procedure **fib2**, which remembers previous results. This saves some computation in comparison with **fib**, see Figure 8.2.

Asserting intermediate results, also called *caching*, is a standard technique for avoiding repeated computations. It should be noted, however, that in the case of Fibonacci numbers we can preferably avoid repeated computation by using another algorithm, rather than by asserting intermediate results. This other algorithm will lead to a program that is more difficult to understand, but more efficient to execute. The idea this time is not to define the Nth Fibonacci number simply as the sum of its two predecessors and leave the recursive calls to unfold the whole computation 'downwards' to the two initial Fibonacci numbers. Instead, we can work 'upwards', starting with the initial two numbers, and compute the numbers in the sequence one by one in the forward direction. We have to stop when we have computed the Nth number. Most of the work in such a program is done by the procedure:

**forwardfib( M, N, F1, F2, F)**

Here, F1 and F2 are the (M – 1)st and Mth Fibonacci numbers, and F is the Nth Fibonacci number. Figure 8.4 helps to understand the **forwardfib** relation. According to this figure, **forwardfib** finds a sequence of transformations to reach a final configuration (when M = N) from a given starting configuration. When **forwardfib**

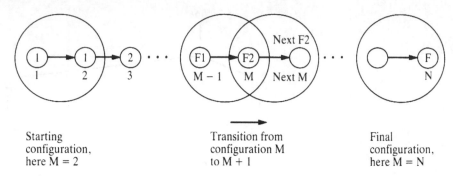

Starting
configuration,
here M = 2

Transition from
configuration M
to M + 1

Final
configuration,
here M = N

**Figure 8.4** Relations in the Fibonacci sequence. A 'configuration', depicted by a large circle, is defined by three things: an index M and two consecutive Fibonacci numbers $f(M-1)$ and $f(M)$.

is invoked, all the arguments except F have to be instantiated, and M has to be less than or equal to N. The program is:

```
fib3( N, F) :-
    forwardfib( 2, N, 1, 1, F).          % The first two Fib. numbers are 1

forwardfib( M, N, F1, F2, F2) :-
    M >= N.                              % Nth Fibonacci number reached

forwardfib( M, N, F1, F2, F) :-
    M < N,                               % Nth number not yet reached
    NextM is M + 1,
    NextF2 is F1 + F2,
    forwardfib( NextM, N, F2, NextF2, F).
```

Notice that **forwardfib** is tail recursive, and M, F1 and F2 are accumulator arguments.

## EXERCISES

**8.1** Procedures **sub1**, **sub2** and **sub3**, shown below, all implement the sublist relation. **sub1** is a more procedural definition whereas **sub2** and **sub3** are written in a more declarative style. Study the behaviour, with reference to efficiency, of these three procedures on some sample lists. Two of them behave nearly equivalently and have similar efficiency. Which two? Why is the remaining one less efficient?

```
sub1( List, Sublist) :-
    prefix( List, Sublist).

sub1( [ _ | Tail], Sublist) :-
    sub1( Tail, Sublist).                % Sublist is sublist of Tail

prefix( _, [ ] ).

prefix( [X | List1], [X | List2] ) :-
    prefix( List1, List2).
```

```
sub2( List, Sublist) :-
   conc( List1, List2, List),
   conc( List3, Sublist, List1).

sub3( List, Sublist) :-
   conc( List1, List2, List),
   conc( Sublist, _, List2).
```

**8.2** Define the relation

add_at_end( List, Item, NewList)

to add **Item** at the end of **List** producing **NewList**. Let both lists be represented by difference pairs.

**8.3** Define the relation

reverse( List, ReversedList)

where both lists are represented by difference pairs.

**8.4** Rewrite the **collect** procedure of Section 8.5.1 using difference pair representation for lists so that the concatenation can be done more efficiently.

**8.5** The following procedure computes the maximum value in a list of numbers:

```
max( [X], X).

max( [X | Rest], Max) :-
   max( Rest, MaxRest),
   (  MaxRest >= X, !, Max = MaxRest
   ;
      Max = X).
```

Transform this into a tail-recursive procedure. Hint: Introduce accumulator argument **MaxSoFar**.

**8.6** Rewrite program 3 for eight queens (Figure 4.14) using simulated array with **arg** to represent the sets of free diagonals, as discussed in Section 8.5.4. Measure the improvement in efficiency.

**8.7** Implement the updating of the value of an element of an array simulated by **functor** and **arg**, using 'holes' for future values along the lines discussed in Section 8.5.4.

# Summary

- There are several criteria for evaluating programs:
  correctness
  user-friendliness
  efficiency
  readability
  modifiability
  robustness
  documentation

- The principle of *stepwise refinement* is a good way of organizing the program development process. Stepwise refinement applies to relations, algorithms and data structures.

- In Prolog, the following techniques often help to find ideas for refinements:

  *Using recursion*: identify boundary and general cases of a recursive definition.

  *Generalization*: consider a more general problem that may be easier to solve than the original one.

  *Using pictures*: graphical representation may help to identify important relations.

- It is useful to conform to some stylistic conventions to reduce the danger of programming errors, make programs easier to read, debug and modify.

- Prolog systems usually provide program debugging aids. Trace facilities are most useful.

- There are many ways of improving the efficiency of a program. Simple techniques include:

  reordering of goals and clauses
  controlling backtracking by inserting cuts
  remembering (by **asserta**) solutions that would otherwise be computed again

- More sophisticated techniques aim at better algorithms (improving search efficiency in particular) and better data structures. Frequently used programming techniques of this kind are:

  difference lists
  tail recursion, last call optimization
  accumulator arguments
  simulating arrays with **functor** and **arg**

## References

Ross (1989) and O'Keefe (1990) explore in depth the efficiency issues, program design and programming style in Prolog. Sterling (1990) edited a collection of papers describing the design of large Prolog programs for a number of practical applications.

O'Keefe, R.A. (1990) *The Craft of Prolog*. Cambridge, MA: MIT Press.
Ross, P. (1989) *Advanced Prolog: Techniques and Examples*. Harlow: Addison-Wesley.
Sterling, L. (1990) *The Practice of Prolog*. Cambridge, MA: MIT Press.

# Chapter 9

# Operations on Data Structures

....................................................................................................................

....................................................................................................................

One fundamental question in programming is how to represent complex data objects, such as sets, and efficiently implement operations on such objects. The theme of this chapter is some frequently used data structures that belong to three big families: lists, trees and graphs. We will examine ways of representing these structures in Prolog, and develop programs for some operations on these structures, such as sorting a list, representing data sets by tree structures, storing data in trees and retrieving data from trees, and path finding in graphs.

## 9.1 Sorting lists
....................................................................................................................

A list can be sorted if there is an ordering relation between the items in the list. We will for the purpose of this discussion assume that there is an ordering relation

   gt( X, Y)

meaning that X is *greater than* Y, whatever 'greater than' means. If our items are numbers then the **gt** relation will perhaps be defined as:

   gt( X, Y) :- X > Y.

If the items are atoms then the **gt** relation can correspond to the alphabetical order, for example defined by:

   gt( X, Y) :- X @> Y.

Remember that this relation also orders compound terms.
   Let

   **sort( List, Sorted)**

denote a relation where **List** is a list of items and **Sorted** is a list of the same items sorted in the ascending order according to the **gt** relation. We will develop three definitions of this relation in Prolog, based on different ideas for sorting a list. The first idea is as follows:

To sort a list, **List:**

- Find two adjacent elements, X and Y, in **List** such that **gt(** X, Y**)** and swap X and Y in **List**, obtaining **List1**; then sort **List1**.

- If there is no pair of adjacent elements, X and Y, in **List** such that **gt(** X, Y**)**, then **List** is already sorted.

The purpose of swapping two elements, X and Y, that occur out of order, is that after the swapping the new list is closer to a sorted list. After a sufficient amount of swapping we should end up with all the elements in order. This principle of sorting is known as *bubble sort*. The corresponding Prolog procedure will be therefore called **bubblesort:**

```
bubblesort( List, Sorted) :-
    swap( List, List1), !,                    % A useful swap in List?
    bubblesort( List1, Sorted).

bubblesort( Sorted, Sorted).                  % Otherwise list is already sorted

swap( [X, Y | Rest], [Y, X | Rest] ) :-       % Swap first two elements
    gt( X, Y).

swap( [Z | Rest], [Z | Rest1] ) :-            % Swap elements in tail
    swap( Rest, Rest1).
```

Another simple sorting algorithm is *insertion sort*, which is based on the following idea:

To sort a non-empty list, **L = [X | T]:**

(1) Sort the tail T of L.
(2) Insert the head, X, of L into the sorted tail at such a position that the resulting list is sorted. The result is the whole sorted list.

This translates into Prolog as the following **insertsort** procedure:

```
insertsort( [ ], [ ] ).

insertsort( [X | Tail], Sorted) :-
    insertsort( Tail, SortedTail),            % Sort the tail
    insert( X, SortedTail, Sorted).           % Insert X at proper place

insert( X, [Y | Sorted], [Y | Sorted1] ) :-
    gt( X, Y), !,
    insert( X, Sorted, Sorted1).

insert( X, Sorted, [X | Sorted] ).
```

The sorting procedures **bubblesort** and **insertsort** are simple, but inefficient. Of the two procedures, insertion sort is the more efficient one. However, the average time that **insertsort** requires for sorting a list of length $n$ grows proportionally to $n^2$. For long lists, therefore, a much better sorting algorithm is *quicksort*. This is based on the following idea, which is illustrated in Figure 9.1.

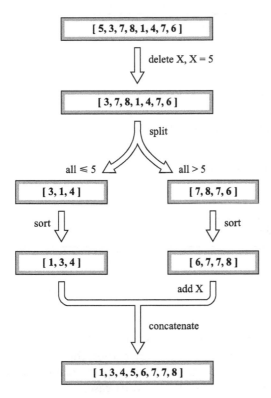

**Figure 9.1** Sorting a list by quicksort.

To sort a non-empty list, L:

(1) Delete some element X from L and split the rest of L into two lists, called **Small** and **Big**, as follows: all elements in L that are greater than X belong to **Big**, and all others to **Small**.

(2) Sort **Small** obtaining **SortedSmall**.

(3) Sort **Big** obtaining **SortedBig**.

(4) The whole sorted list is the concatenation of **SortedSmall** and [ X | **SortedBig**].

If the list to be sorted is empty then the result of sorting is also the empty list. A Prolog implementation of quicksort is shown in Figure 9.2. In this implementation, the element X that is deleted from L is simply the head of L. The splitting is programmed as a four-argument relation:

**split( X, L, Small, Big)**

The time complexity of this algorithm depends on how lucky we are when splitting the list to be sorted. If the list is split into two lists of approximately equal lengths then the time complexity of this sorting procedure is of the order

```
% quicksort( List, SortedList): sort List by the quicksort algorithm

quicksort( [ ], [ ] ).

quicksort( [X | Tail], Sorted) :-
    split( X, Tail, Small, Big),
    quicksort( Small, SortedSmall),
    quicksort( Big, SortedBig),
    conc( SortedSmall, [X | SortedBig], Sorted).

split( X, [ ], [ ], [ ] ).

split( X, [Y | Tail], [Y | Small], Big) :-
    gt( X, Y), !,
    split( X, Tail, Small, Big).

split( X, [Y | Tail], Small, [Y | Big] ) :-
    split( X, Tail, Small, Big).
```

**Figure 9.2** Quicksort.

$n \log n$ where $n$ is the length of the list to be sorted. If, on the contrary, splitting always results in one list far bigger than the other, then the complexity is in the order of $n^2$. Analysis would show that the average performance of quicksort is, fortunately, closer to the best case than to the worst case.

The program in Figure 9.2 can be further improved by a better implementation of the concatenation operation. Using the difference-pair representation of lists, introduced in Chapter 8, concatenation is reduced to triviality. To use this idea in our sorting procedure, the lists in the program of Figure 9.2 can be represented by pairs of lists of the form A-Z as follows:

> **SortedSmall**     is represented by     A1 - Z1
> **SortedBig**       is represented by     A2 - Z2

Then the concatenation of the lists **SortedSmall** and [X | **SortedBig**] corresponds to the concatenation of pairs:

> A1 - Z1        and        [X | A2] - Z2

The resulting concatenated list is represented by:

> A1 - Z2        where        Z1 = [X | A2]

The empty list is represented by any pair Z-Z. Introducing these changes systematically into the program of Figure 9.2 we get a more efficient implementation of quicksort, programmed as **quicksort2** in Figure 9.3. The procedure **quicksort** still uses the usual representation of lists, but the actual sorting is done by the more efficient **quicksort2**, which uses the difference-pair representation. The relation between the two procedures is:

```
quicksort( L, S) :-
    quicksort2( L, S - [ ] ).
```

```
% quicksort( List, SortedList): sort List with the quicksort algorithm

quicksort( List, Sorted) :-
   quicksort2( List, Sorted - [ ] ).

% quicksort2( List, SortedDiffList): sort List, result is represented as difference list

quicksort2( [], Z - Z).

quicksort2( [X | Tail], A1 - Z2) :-
   split( X, Tail, Small, Big),
   quicksort2( Small, A1 - [X | A2] ),
   quicksort2( Big, A2 - Z2).
```

**Figure 9.3** A more efficient implementation of **quicksort** using difference-pair representation for lists. Relation **split( X, List, Small, Big)** is as defined in Figure 9.2.

## EXERCISES

**9.1**  Write a procedure to merge two sorted lists producing a third list. For example:

?- merge( [2,5,6,6,8], [1,3,5,9], L).

L = [1,2,3,5,5,6,6,8,9]

**9.2**  The difference between the sorting programs of Figures 9.2 and 9.3 is in the representation of lists – the latter uses difference lists. Transformation between plain lists and difference lists is straightforward and could be mechanized. Carry out the corresponding changes systematically in the program of Figure 9.2 to transform it into the program of Figure 9.3.

**9.3**  Our **quicksort** program performs badly when the list to be sorted is already sorted or almost sorted. Analyse why.

**9.4**  Another good idea for sorting a list is the *merge-sort* algorithm. It avoids the weakness of **quicksort** that occurs when lists **Small** and **Big** happen to be of very different lengths. Merge-sort is based on dividing the list, then sorting smaller lists, and then merging these sorted smaller lists. Accordingly, to sort a list L:

- divide L into two lists, L1 and L2, of approximately equal length;
- sort L1 and L2 giving S1 and S2;
- merge S1 and S2 giving L sorted.

The complexity of merge-sort is of the order $n \log n$. Implement merge-sort and compare its efficiency with the **quicksort** program.

## 9.2  Representing sets by binary trees

A set of objects is often represented as a list. A disadvantage of using the list representation is that the set membership testing is inefficient. The predicate

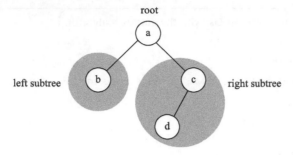

**Figure 9.4** A binary tree.

**member( X, L)** to test whether X is a member of a list L is usually programmed as:

**member( X, [X | L] ).**

**member( X, [Y | L] ) :-**
  **member( X, L).**

To find X in a list L, this procedure scans the list element by element until X is found or the end of the list is encountered. This is very inefficient in the case of long lists.

There are various tree structures for representing sets that facilitate more efficient implementation of the set membership relation. We will here consider binary trees.

A binary tree is either empty or it consists of three things:

- a root;
- a left subtree;
- a right subtree.

The root can be anything, but the subtrees have to be binary trees again. Figure 9.4 shows an example. This tree represents the set {a, b, c, d}. The elements of the set are stored as nodes of the tree. In Figure 9.4, the empty subtrees are not pictured; for example, the node b has two subtrees that are both empty.

There are many ways to represent a binary tree by a Prolog term. One simple possibility is to make the root of a binary tree the principal functor of the term, and the subtrees its arguments. Accordingly, the example tree of Figure 9.4 would be represented by:

**a( b, c(d) )**

Among other disadvantages, this representation requires another functor for each node of the tree. This can lead to trouble if nodes themselves are structured objects.

A better and more usual way to represent binary trees is as follows: we need a special symbol to represent the empty tree, and we need a functor to construct a non-empty tree from its three components (the root and the two subtrees). We will make the following choice regarding the functor and the special symbol:

- Let the atom **nil** represent the empty tree.
- Let the functor be **t** so the tree that has a root X, a left subtree L and a right subtree R is represented by the term **t( L, X, R)** (see Figure 9.5).

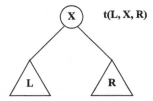

**Figure 9.5** A representation of binary trees.

In this representation, the example tree of Figure 9.4 is represented by the term:

t( t( nil, b, nil), a, t( t( nil, d, nil), c, nil) )

Let us now consider the set membership relation, here named **in**. A goal

in( X, T)

is true if X is a node in a tree T. The **in** relation can be defined by the following rules:

X is in a tree T if:

- the root of T is X, or

- X is in the left subtree of T, or

- X is in the right subtree of T.

These rules directly translate into Prolog:

in( X, t( _, X, _) ).

in( X, t( L, _, _) ) :-
    in( X, L).

in( X, t( _, _, R) ) :-
    in( X, R).

Obviously, the goal

in( X, nil)

will fail for any X.

Let us investigate the behaviour of this procedure. In the following examples, T is the tree of Figure 9.4. The goal

in( X, T)

will, through backtracking, find all the data in the set in the following order:

X = a; X = b; X = c; X = d

Now let us consider efficiency. The goal

in( a, T)

succeeds immediately by the first clause of the procedure **in**. On the other hand, the goal

in( d, T)

will cause several recursive calls of **in** before d is eventually found. Similarly, the goal

$\quad$ **in( e, T)**

will fail only after the whole tree has been searched by recursive calls of **in** on all the subtrees of T.

The time needed to find an item in a tree is generally proportional to $n$, the number of elements stored in the tree. This is, then, as inefficient as representing a set by a list. A major improvement can, however, be achieved if there is an ordering relation between the data in the set. Then the data in the tree can be ordered from left to right according to this relation. We say that a tree **t( Left, X, Right)** is ordered from left to right if:

(1)  all the nodes in the left subtree, **Left**, are less than X; and

(2)  all the nodes in the right subtree, **Right**, are greater than X; and

(3)  both subtrees are also ordered.

Such a binary tree is called a *binary dictionary*, or a binary search tree. Figure 9.6 shows an example.

The advantage of ordering is that, to search for an object in a binary dictionary, it is always sufficient to search at most one subtree. The key to this economization when searching for X is that we can by comparing X and the root immediately discard at least one of the subtrees. For example, let us search for the item 6 in the tree of Figure 9.6. We start at the root, 5, compare 6 and 5, and establish 6 > 5. As all the data in the left subtree must be less than 5, the only remaining possibility to find 6 is the right subtree. So we continue the search in the right subtree, moving to node 8, etc.

The general method for searching in the binary dictionary is:

To find an item X in a dictionary D:

- if X is the root of D then X has been found, otherwise

- if X is less than the root of D then search for X in the left subtree of D, otherwise search for X in the right subtree of D;

- if D is empty the search fails.

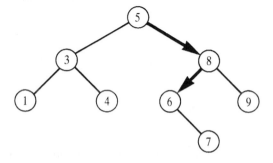

**Figure 9.6** A binary dictionary. Item 6 is reached by following the indicated path 5 → 8 → 6.

```
% in( X, Tree): X in binary dictionary Tree

in( X, t( _, X, _) ).

in( X, t( Left, Root, Right) ) :-
    gt( Root, X),                          % Root greater than X
    in( X, Left).                          % Search left subtree

in( X, t( Left, Root, Right) ) :-
    gt( X, Root),                          % X greater than Root
    in( X, Right).                         % Search right subtree
```

**Figure 9.7** Finding an item X in a binary dictionary.

These rules are programmed as the procedure **in** in Figure 9.7. The relation **gt( X, Y)** means: X is greater than Y. If the items stored in the tree are numbers then this relation is simply X > Y.

In a way, the **in** procedure itself can be also used for *constructing* a binary dictionary. For example, the following sequence of goals will construct a dictionary D that contains the elements 5, 3, 8:

   **?- in( 5, D), in( 3, D), in( 8, D).**

   **D = t( t( D1, 3, D2), 5, t( D3, 8, D4) ).**

The variables D1, D2, D3 and D4 are four unspecified subtrees. They can be anything and D will still contain the given items 3, 5 and 8. The dictionary that is constructed depends on the order of the goals in the question (Figure 9.8).

A comment is in order here on the search efficiency in dictionaries. Generally speaking, the search for an item in a dictionary is more efficient than searching in a list. What is the improvement? Let $n$ be the number of items in our data set. If the set is represented by a list then the expected search time will be proportional to its length $n$. On average, we have to scan the list up to something like

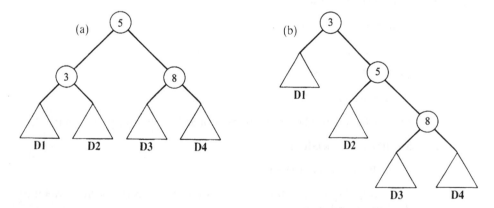

**Figure 9.8** (a) Tree D that results from the sequence of goals: **in( 5, D), in( 3, D), in( 8, D).** (b) Tree resulting from: **in( 3, D), in( 5, D), in( 8, D).**

half-way through it. If the set is represented by a binary dictionary, the search time will be roughly proportional to the height of the tree. The height of a tree is the length of a longest path between the root and a leaf in the tree. The height, however, depends on the shape of the tree.

We say that a tree is (approximately) *balanced* if, for each node in the tree, its two subtrees accommodate an approximately equal number of items. If a dictionary with $n$ nodes is nicely balanced then its height is proportional to $\log n$. We say that a balanced tree has *logarithmic complexity*. The difference between $n$ and $\log n$ is the improvement of a balanced dictionary over a list. This holds, unfortunately, only when a tree is approximately balanced. If the tree gets out of balance its performance will degrade. In extreme cases of totally unbalanced trees, a tree is in effect reduced to a list. In such a case the tree's height is $n$, and the tree's performance is equally poor as that of a list. Therefore we are always interested in balanced dictionaries. Methods of achieving this objective will be discussed in Chapter 10.

# EXERCISES

**9.5** Define the predicates

(a) **binarytree( Object)**

(b) **dictionary( Object)**

to recognize whether **Object** is a binary tree or a binary dictionary respectively, written in the notation of this section.

**9.6** Define the procedure

> **height( BinaryTree, Height)**

to compute the height of a binary tree. Assume that the height of the empty tree is 0, and that of a one-element tree is 1.

**9.7** Define the relation

> **linearize( Tree, List)**

to collect all the nodes in **Tree** into a list.

**9.8** Define the relation

> **maxelement( D, Item)**

so that **Item** is the largest element stored in the binary dictionary D.

**9.9** Modify the procedure

> **in( Item, BinaryDictionary)**

by adding the third argument, **Path**, so that **Path** is the path between the root of the dictionary and **Item**.

# 9.3 Insertion and deletion in a binary dictionary

When maintaining a dynamic set of data we may want to insert new items into the set and also delete some old items from the set. So one common repertoire of operations on a set of data, S, is:

| | |
|---|---|
| **in( X, S)** | X is a member of S |
| **add( S, X, S1)** | Add X to S giving S1 |
| **del( S, X, S1)** | Delete X from S giving S1 |

Let us now define the *add* relation. It is easiest to insert new data at the bottom level of the tree, so that a new item becomes a leaf of the tree at such a position that the ordering of the tree is preserved. Figure 9.9 shows changes in a tree during a sequence of insertions. Let us call this kind of insertion **addleaf( D, X, D1).**

Rules for adding at the leaf level are:

- The result of adding X to the empty tree is the tree **t( nil, X, nil).**

- If X is the root of D then D1 = D (no duplicate item gets inserted).

- If the root of D is greater than X then insert X into the left subtree of D; if the root of D is less than X then insert X into the right subtree.

Figure 9.10 shows a corresponding program.

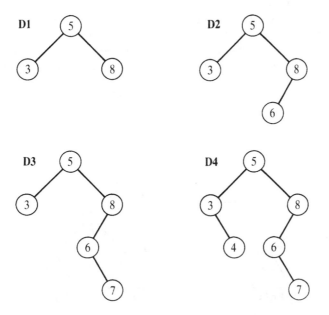

**Figure 9.9** Insertion into a binary dictionary at the leaf level. The trees correspond to the following sequence of insertions: **add( D1, 6, D2), add( D2, 7, D3), add( D3, 4, D4).**

```
% addleaf( Tree, X, NewTree):
%    inserting X as a leaf into binary dictionary Tree gives NewTree

addleaf( nil, X, t( nil, X, nil) ).

addleaf( t( Left, X, Right), X, t( Left, X, Right) ).

addleaf( t( Left, Root, Right), X, t( Left1, Root, Right) )  :-
  gt( Root, X),
  addleaf( Left, X, Left1).

addleaf( t( Left, Root, Right), X, t( Left, Root, Right1) )  :-
  gt( X, Root),
  addleaf( Right, X, Right1).
```

**Figure 9.10** Inserting an item as a leaf into the binary dictionary.

Let us now consider the *delete* operation. It is easy to delete a leaf, but deleting an internal node is more complicated. The deletion of a leaf can be in fact defined as the inverse operation of inserting at the leaf level:

```
delleaf( D1, X, D2) :-
  addleaf( D2, X, D1).
```

Unfortunately, if X is an internal node then this does not work because of the problem illustrated in Figure 9.11. X has two subtrees, **Left** and **Right**. After X is removed, we have a hole in the tree and **Left** and **Right** are no longer connected to the rest of the tree. They cannot both be directly connected to the father of X, A, because A can accommodate only one of them.

If one of the subtrees **Left** and **Right** is empty then the solution is simple: the non-empty subtree is connected to A. If they are both non-empty then one idea is as shown in Figure 9.12. The left-most node of **Right**, Y, is transferred from its current position upwards to fill the gap after X. After this transfer, the tree

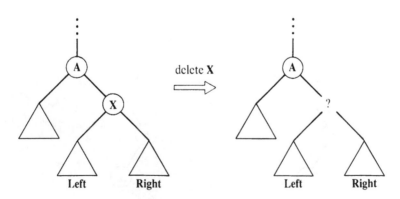

**Figure 9.11** Deleting X from a binary dictionary. The problem is how to patch up the tree after X is removed.

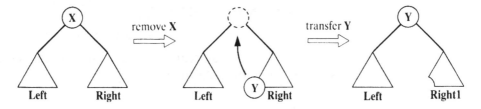

**Figure 9.12** Filling the gap after removal of X.

```
% del( Tree, X, NewTree):
%    deleting X from binary dictionary Tree gives NewTree

del( t( nil, X, Right), X, Right).

del( t( Left, X, nil), X, Left).

del( t( Left, X, Right), X, t( Left, Y, Right1) ) :-
   delmin( Right, Y, Right1).

del( t( Left, Root, Right), X, t( Left1, Root, Right) ) :-
   gt( Root, X),
   del( Left, X, Left1).

del( t( Left, Root, Right), X, t( Left, Root, Right1) ) :-
   gt( X, Root),
   del( Right, X, Right1).

% delmin( Tree, Y, NewTree):
%    delete minimal item Y in binary dictionary Tree producing NewTree

delmin( t( nil, Y, Right), Y, Right).

delmin( t( Left, Root, Right), Y, t( Left1, Root, Right) ) :-
   delmin( Left, Y, Left1).
```

**Figure 9.13** Deleting from the binary dictionary.

remains ordered. Of course, the same idea works symmetrically, with the transfer of the right-most node of **Left**.

According to these considerations, the operation to delete an item from the binary dictionary is programmed in Figure 9.13. The transfer of the left-most node of the right subtree is accomplished by the relation

   **delmin( Tree, Y, Tree1)**

where Y is the minimal (that is, the left-most) node of **Tree**, and **Tree1** is **Tree** with Y deleted.

There is another elegant solution to *add* and *delete*. The *add* relation can be defined non-deterministically so that a new item is inserted at any level of the tree, not just at the leaf level. The rules are:

> To add X to a binary dictionary D either:
>
> - add X at the root of D (so that X becomes the new root), or
>
> - if the root of D is greater than X then insert X into the left subtree of D, otherwise insert X into the right subtree of D.

The difficult part of this is the insertion at the root of D. Let us formulate this operation as a relation

   **addroot( D, X, D1)**

where X is the item to be inserted at the root of D and D1 is the resulting dictionary with X as its root. Figure 9.14 illustrates the relations between X, D and D1. The remaining question is now: What are the subtrees L1 and L2 in Figure 9.14 (or R1 and R2 alternatively)? The answer can be derived from the following constraints:

- L1 and L2 must be binary dictionaries;
- the set of nodes in L1 and L2 is equal to the set of nodes in L;
- all the nodes in L1 are less than X, and all the nodes in L2 are greater than X.

The relation that imposes all these constraints is just our **addroot** relation. Namely, if X were added as the root into L, then the subtrees of the resulting tree would be just L1 and L2. In Prolog, L1 and L2 must satisfy the goal:

   **addroot( L, X, t( L1, X, L2) )**

The same constraints apply to R1 and R2:

   **addroot( R, X, t( R1, X, R2) )**

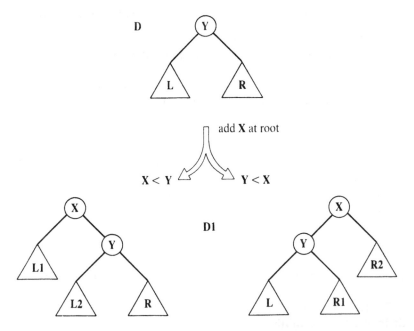

**Figure 9.14** Inserting X at the root of a binary dictionary.

```
% add( Tree, X, NewTree):
%    inserting X at any level of binary dictionary Tree gives NewTree

add( Tree, X, NewTree)  :-
    addroot( Tree, X, NewTree).                    % Add X as new root

add( t( L, Y, R), X, t( L1, Y, R) )  :-            % Insert X into left subtree
    gt( Y, X),
    add( L, X, L1).

add( t( L, Y, R), X, t( L, Y, R1) )  :-            % Insert X into right subtree
    gt( X, Y),
    add( R, X, R1).

% addroot( Tree, X, NewTree): inserting X as the root into Tree gives NewTree

addroot( nil, X, t( nil, X, nil) ).                % Insert into empty tree

addroot( t( L, Y, R), X, t( L1, X, t( L2, Y, R) ) )  :-
    gt( Y, X),
    addroot( L, X, t( L1, X, L2) ).

addroot( t( L, Y, R), X, t( t( L, Y, R1), X, R2) )  :-
    gt( X, Y),
    addroot( R, X, t( R1, X, R2) ).
```

**Figure 9.15** Insertion into the binary dictionary at any level of the tree.

Figure 9.15 shows a complete program for the 'non-deterministic' insertion into the binary dictionary.

The nice thing about this insertion procedure is that there is no restriction on the level of insertion. Therefore *add* can be used in the inverse direction in order to delete an item from the dictionary. For example, the following goal list constructs a dictionary D containing the items 3, 5, 1, 6, and then deletes 5, yielding a dictionary DD:

    add( nil, 3, D1), add( D1, 5, D2), add( D2, 1, D3),
    add( D3, 6, D), add( DD, 5, D)

## 9.4 Displaying trees

Like all data objects in Prolog, a binary tree, T, can be directly output by the built-in procedure **write**. However, the goal

    write( T)

will only output all the information, but will not graphically indicate the actual tree structure. It can be rather tiring to imagine the actual tree structure from a Prolog term that represents that tree. Therefore it is often desirable to have a tree typed out in a way that graphically indicates its structure.

There is a relatively simple method for displaying trees in such a form. The trick is to display a tree growing from left to right, and not from top to bottom

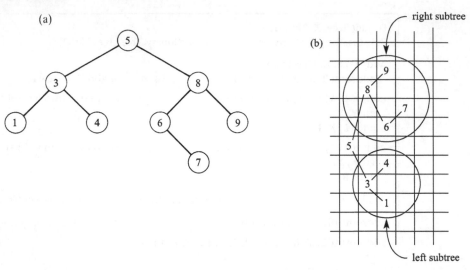

**Figure 9.16** (a) A tree as normally pictured. (b) The same tree as typed out by the procedure **show** (arcs are added for clarity).

as trees are usually pictured. The tree is rotated to the left so that the root becomes the left-most element, and the leaves are moved to the right. Figure 9.16 illustrates.

Let us define a procedure

  **show( T)**

to display a tree T in the form indicated in Figure 9.16. The principle is:

> To show a non-empty tree, T:
>
> (1)  show the right subtree of T, indented by some distance, H, to the right;
>
> (2)  write the root of T;
>
> (3)  show the left subtree of T indented by distance H to the right.

The indentation distance H, which can be appropriately chosen, is an additional parameter for displaying trees. Introducing H we have the procedure

  **show2( T, H)**

to display T indented H spaces from the left margin. The relation between the procedures **show** and **show2** is:

  **show( T) :- show2( T, 0).**

The complete program, which indents by 2, is shown in Figure 9.17. The principle of achieving such an output format can be easily adopted for displaying other types of trees.

```
% show( Tree): display binary tree

show( Tree) :-
    show2( Tree, 0).

% show2( Tree, Indent): display Tree indented by Indent

show2( nil, _ ).
show2( t( Left, X, Right), Indent) :-
    Ind2 is Indent + 2,                % Indentation of subtrees
    show2( Right, Ind2),               % Display right subtree
    tab( Indent), write( X), nl,       % Write root
    show2( Left, Ind2).                % Display left subtree
```

**Figure 9.17** Displaying a binary tree.

## EXERCISE

**9.10** Our procedure for displaying trees shows a tree in an unusual orientation, so that the root is on the left and the leaves of the tree are on the right. Write a (more difficult) procedure to display a tree in the usual orientation with the root at the top and the leaves at the bottom.

## 9.5 Graphs

### 9.5.1 Representing graphs

Graph structures are used in many applications for representing relations between various things: relations among people in social networks, among computers in computer networks, among pages on the web, items in mind maps, items in ontologies, etc. Mathematically, a graph is defined by a set of *nodes* and a set of *edges*, where each edge is a pair of nodes. When the edges are directed they are also called *arcs*. Arcs are represented by *ordered* pairs. Such a graph is a *directed* graph. The edges can be attached costs, names or any kind of labels, depending on the application. Figure 9.18 shows examples.

**Figure 9.18** (a) A graph. (b) A directed graph with costs attached to the arcs.

Graphs can be represented in Prolog in several ways. One method is to represent each edge or arc separately as one clause. The graphs in Figure 9.18 can be thus represented by sets of clauses, for example:

**connected( a, b).**
**connected( b, c).**
. . .

**arc( s, t, 3).**
**arc( t, v, 1).**
**arc( u, t, 2).**
. . .

Another method is to represent a whole graph as one data object. A graph can be thus represented as a pair of two sets: nodes and edges. Each set can be represented as a list; each edge is a pair of nodes. Let us choose the functor **graph** to combine both sets into a pair, and the functor **e** for edges. Then one way to represent the (undirected) graph in Figure 9.18 is:

**G1 = graph( [a,b,c,d], [e(a,b), e(b,d), e(b,c), e(c,d)] )**

To represent a directed graph we can choose the functors **digraph** and **a** (for arcs). The directed graph of Figure 9.18 is then:

**G2 = digraph( [s,t,u,v], [a(s,t,3), a(t,v,1), a(t,u,5), a(u,t,2), a(v,u,2)] )**

Here each arc is a triple: two nodes and the cost of the arc. If each node is connected to at least one other node then we can omit the list of nodes from the representation as the set of nodes is then implicitly specified by the list of edges.

Yet another method is to associate with each node a list of nodes that are adjacent to that node. Then a graph is a list of pairs consisting of a node plus its adjacency list. Our example graphs can then, for example, be represented by:

**G1 = [ a -> [b], b -> [a,c,d], c -> [b,d], d -> [b,c] ]**

**G2 = [ s -> [t/3], t -> [u/5, v/1], u -> [t/2], v -> [u/2] ]**

The symbols '- >' and '/' above are, of course, infix operators.

What will be the most suitable representation will depend on the application and on operations to be performed on graphs. Two typical operations are:

• find a path between two given nodes;
• find a subgraph, with some specified properties, of a graph.

Finding a *spanning tree* of a graph is an example of the latter operation. In the following sections we will look at programs for finding a path and for finding a spanning tree. We have already seen examples of path finding in Chapter 4. Here we will introduce some additional aspects of this.

## 9.5.2  Finding a path

Let G be a graph, and A and Z two nodes in G. Let us define the relation

**path( A, Z, G, P)**

where P is an acyclic path between A and Z in G. P is represented as a list of nodes on the path. If G is the graph in the left-hand side of Figure 9.18 then the following goals are true:

**path( a, d, G, [a,b,d] )**

**path( a, d, G, [a,b,c,d] )**

Since a path must not contain any cycle, a node can appear in the path at most once. One method to find a path is:

To find an acyclic path, P, between A and Z in a graph, G:

If A = Z then P = [A], otherwise
find an acyclic path, P1, from some node Y to Z, and find a path from A to Y avoiding the nodes in P1.

This formulation implies another relation: find a path under the restriction of avoiding some subset of nodes (P1 above). We will, accordingly, define another procedure:

**path1( A, Path1, G, Path)**

As illustrated in Figure 9.19, the arguments are:

- A is a node,
- G is a graph,
- **Path1** is a path in G,
- **Path** is an acyclic path in G that goes from A to the beginning of **Path1** and continues along **Path1** up to its end.

The relation between **path** and **path1** is:

**path( A, Z, G, Path) :- path1( A, [Z], G, Path).**

Figure 9.19 suggests a recursive definition of **path1**. The boundary case arises when the start node of **Path1** (Y in Figure 9.19) coincides with the start node of **Path**, A. If the start nodes do not coincide then there must be a node, X, such that:

(1)  Y is adjacent to X, and

(2)  X is not in **Path1**, and

(3)  **Path** must satisfy the relation path1( A, [X | Path1], G, Path).

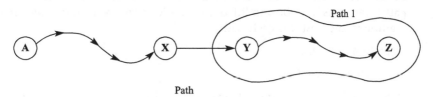

**Figure 9.19** The **path1** relation: **Path** is a path between A and Z; the last part of **Path** overlaps with **Path1**.

% path( A, Z, Graph, Path): Path is an acyclic path from A to Z in Graph

path( A, Z, Graph, Path) :-
  path1( A, [Z], Graph, Path).

path1( A, [A | Path1], _, [A | Path1] ).

path1( A, [Y | Path1], Graph, Path) :-
  adjacent( X, Y, Graph),
  \+ member( X, Path1),                 % No-cycle condition
  path1( A, [X, Y | Path1], Graph, Path).

**Figure 9.20** Finding an acyclic path, **Path**, from A to Z in **Graph**.

A complete program is shown in Figure 9.20. This program constructs a path from A to Z backwards, starting at Z. **member** is the usual list membership relation. The relation

  adjacent( X, Y, G)

means that there is an arc from X to Y in graph G. The definition of this relation depends on the representation of graphs. If G is represented as a pair of two sets, nodes and edges,

  G = graph( Nodes, Edges)

then:

  adjacent( X, Y, graph( Nodes, Edges) ) :-
    member( e(X,Y), Edges)
    ;
    member( e(Y,X), Edges).

A classical problem on graphs is to find a Hamiltonian path; that is, an acyclic path comprising all the nodes in the graph. Using **path** this can be done as follows:

  hamiltonian( Graph, Path) :-
    path( _, _, Graph, Path),
    covers( Path, Graph).

  covers( Path, Graph) :-
    \+ ( node( N, Graph), \+ member( N, Path) ).

Here, **node( N, Graph)** means: N is a node in **Graph**.

We can attach costs to paths. The cost of a path is the sum of the costs of the arcs in the path. If there are no costs attached to the arcs then we can talk about the length instead, counting 1 for each arc in the path. Our **path** and **path1** relations can be modified to handle costs by introducing an additional argument, the cost, for each path:

  path( A, Z, G, P, C)

  path1( A, P1, C1, G, P, C)

Here, C is the cost of P and C1 is the cost of P1. The relation **adjacent** now also has an extra argument, the cost of an arc. Figure 9.21 shows a path-finding program that computes a path and its cost.

```
% path( A, Z, Graph, Path, Cost):
%    Path is an acyclic path with cost Cost from A to Z in Graph

path( A, Z, Graph, Path, Cost) :-
    path1( A, [Z], 0, Graph, Path, Cost).

path1( A, [A | Path1], Cost1, Graph, [A | Path1], Cost1).

path1( A, [Y | Path1], Cost1, Graph, Path, Cost) :-
    adjacent( X, Y, CostXY, Graph),
    \+ member( X, Path1),
    Cost2 is Cost1 + CostXY,
    path1( A, [X, Y | Path1], Cost2, Graph, Path, Cost).
```

**Figure 9.21** Path-finding in a graph: **Path** is an acyclic path with cost **Cost** from A to Z in **Graph**.

This procedure can be used for finding a minimum cost path. We can find such a path between two nodes, **node1** and **node2**, in some graph **Graph** by the goals:

> path( node1, node2, Graph, MinPath, MinCost),
>
> \+ ( path( node1, node2, Graph, _, Cost), Cost < MinCost)

We can also find a maximum cost path between any pair of nodes in a graph **Graph** by the goals:

> path( _, _, Graph, MaxPath, MaxCost),
>
> \+ ( path( _, _, Graph, _, Cost), Cost > MaxCost)

It should be noted that this is a very inefficient way for finding minimal or maximal paths. This method unselectively investigates possible paths and is completely unsuitable for large graphs because of its high time complexity. The path-finding problem frequently arises in Artificial Intelligence. We will study more efficient and sophisticated methods for finding optimal paths in Chapters 11–13.

## 9.5.3 Finding a spanning tree of a graph

A graph is said to be *connected* if there is a path from any node to any other node. Let G = (V, E) be a connected graph with the set of nodes V and the set of edges E. A *spanning tree* of G is a connected graph T = (V, E') where E' is a subset of E such that:

(1) T is connected, and

(2) there is no cycle in T.

These two conditions guarantee that T is a tree. For the left-hand side graph of Figure 9.18, there are three spanning trees, which correspond to three lists of edges:

> Tree1 = [a-b, b-c, c-d]
>
> Tree2 = [a-b, b-d, d-c]
>
> Tree3 = [a-b, b-d, b-c]

Here each term of the form X-Y denotes an edge between nodes X and Y. We can pick any node in such a list as the root of a tree. Spanning trees are of interest, for example, in communication problems because they provide, with the minimum number of communication lines, a path between any pair of nodes.

We will define a procedure

　　stree( G, T)

where T is a spanning tree of G. We will assume that G is connected. We can imagine constructing a spanning tree algorithmically as follows: Start with the empty set of edges and gradually add new edges from G, taking care that a cycle is never created, until no edge can be added because it would create a cycle. The resulting set of edges defines a spanning tree. The no-cycle condition can be maintained by a simple rule: an edge can be added only if one of its nodes is already in the growing tree, and the other node is not yet in the tree. A program that implements this idea is shown in Figure 9.22. The key relation in this

```
% Finding a spanning tree of a graph
%
% Trees and graphs are represented by lists of their edges.
% For example: Graph = [a-b, b-c, b-d, c-d]

% stree( Graph, Tree): Tree is a spanning tree of Graph

stree( Graph, Tree) :-
  member( Edge, Graph),
  spread( [Edge], Tree, Graph).

% spread( Tree1, Tree, Graph): Tree1 'spreads to' spanning tree Tree of Graph

spread( Tree1, Tree, Graph) :-
  addedge( Tree1, Tree2, Graph),
  spread( Tree2, Tree, Graph).

spread( Tree, Tree, Graph) :-
  \+ addedge( Tree, _, Graph).        % No edge can be added without creating a cycle

% addedge( Tree, NewTree, Graph):
%    add an edge from Graph to Tree without creating a cycle

addedge( Tree, [A-B | Tree], Graph) :-
  adjacent( A, B, Graph),             % Nodes A and B adjacent in Graph
  node( A, Tree),                     % A in Tree
  \+ node( B, Tree).                  % A-B doesn't create a cycle in Tree

adjacent( Node1, Node2, Graph) :-
  member( Node1-Node2, Graph)
  ;
  member( Node2-Node1, Graph).

node( Node, Graph) :-                 % Node is a node in Graph if
  adjacent( Node, _, Graph).          % Node is adjacent to anything in Graph
```

**Figure 9.22** Finding a spanning tree of a graph: an 'algorithmic' program. The program assumes that the graph is connected.

program is:

spread( Tree1, Tree, G)

All the three arguments are sets of edges. G is a connected graph; Tree1 and Tree are subsets of G such that they both represent trees. Tree is a spanning tree of G obtained by adding zero or more edges of G to Tree1. We can say that 'Tree1 gets spread to Tree'.

It is interesting that we can also develop a working program for constructing a spanning tree in another, completely declarative way, by simply stating mathematical definitions. We will assume that both graphs and trees are represented by lists of their edges, as in the program of Figure 9.22. The definitions we need are:

(1)  T is a spanning tree of G if:

- T is a subset of G, and
- T is a tree, and
- T 'covers' G; that is, each node of G is also in T.

```
% Finding a spanning tree
% Graphs and trees are represented as lists of edges.

% stree( Graph, Tree): Tree is a spanning tree of Graph

stree( Graph, Tree)  :-
    subset( Graph, Tree),
    tree( Tree),
    covers( Tree, Graph).

tree( Tree)  :-
    connected( Tree),
    \+ hasacycle( Tree).

% connected( Graph): there is a path between any two nodes in Graph

connected( Graph)  :-
    \+ ( node( A, Graph), node( B, Graph), \+ path( A, B, Graph, _) ).

hasacycle( Graph)  :-
    adjacent( Node1, Node2, Graph),
    path( Node1, Node2, Graph, [Node1, X, Y | _] ).       % Path of length > 1

% covers( Tree, Graph): every node of Graph is in Tree

covers( Tree, Graph)  :-
    \+ ( node( Node, Graph), \+ node( Node, Tree) ).

% subset( List1, List2): List2 represents a subset of List1
subset( [], [] ).

subset( [X | Set], Subset)  :-                            % X not in subset
    subset( Set, Subset).

subset( [X | Set], [X | Subset])  :-                      % X included in subset
    subset( Set, Subset).
```

**Figure 9.23** Finding a spanning tree of a graph: a 'declarative' program. Relations **node** and **adjacent** are as in Figure 9.22.

(2) A set of edges T is a tree if:

- T is connected, and
- T has no cycle.

Using our **path** program of the previous section, these definitions can be stated in Prolog as shown in Figure 9.23. It should be noted that this program is rather elegant in that it closely follows a declarative mathematical definition, and does not complicate this definition by algorithmic issues; the program is, however, very inefficient.

## EXERCISES

**9.11** Consider spanning trees of graphs that have costs attached to edges. Let the **cost** of a spanning tree be defined as the sum of the costs of all the edges in the tree. Write a program to find a minimum-cost spanning tree of a given graph.

**9.12** Experiment with the spanning tree programs in Figures 9.22 and 9.23, and measure their execution times. Identify the sources of inefficiency in the second program.

## Summary

In this chapter we studied Prolog implementations of some frequently used data structures and associated operations on them. We looked at:

- Lists:

    sorting lists:
        bubble sort
        insertion sort
        quicksort

    efficiency of these procedures

- Representing sets as binary trees and binary dictionaries:

    searching for an item in a tree
    adding an item
    deleting an item
    adding as a leaf, adding as the root
    the balance of trees, how balance affects the efficiency of these operations
    displaying trees

- Graphs:

    representing graphs
    finding a path in a graph
    finding a spanning tree of a graph

# References

In this chapter we have tackled in Prolog classic topics of sorting and of maintaining data structures for representing sets. These topics are covered in general books on algorithms and data structures, for example Aho, Hopcroft and Ullman (1983), Cormen *et al.* (2009) and Gonnet and Baeza-Yates (1991). The Prolog program for insertion at any level of the binary tree (Section 9.3) was first shown to the author by M. van Emden (personal communication).

Aho, A.V., Hopcroft, J.E. and Ullman, J.D. (1983) *Data Structures and Algorithms*. Addison-Wesley.

Cormen, T.H., Leiserson, C.E., Rivest, R. and Stein, C. (2009) *Introduction to Algorithms*, third edn. Cambridge, MA: The MIT Press.

Gonnet, G.H. and Baeza-Yates, R. (1991) *Handbook of Algorithms and Data Structures in Pascal and C* (second edn). Addison-Wesley.

# Chapter 10

# Balanced Trees

In this chapter we look at advanced techniques for representing data sets by trees. The key idea is to keep the tree balanced, or approximately balanced, in order to prevent the tree from degenerating toward a list. Such tree-balancing schemes guarantee relatively fast, logarithmic-time data-access even in the worst case. Two such schemes are presented in this chapter: 2-3 trees and AVL-trees. (The knowledge of this chapter is not a prerequisite to any other chapter.)

## 10.1 2-3 trees

A binary tree is said to be height-balanced if both its subtrees are of approximately equal height, and they are also balanced. The height of a balanced tree is approximately log $n$ where $n$ is the number of nodes in the tree. The time needed to evaluate the relations **in**, **add** and **delete** on binary dictionaries grows proportionally with the height of the tree. On balanced dictionaries, then, all these operations can be done in time that is in the order of log $n$. The logarithmic growth of the complexity of the set membership testing is a definite improvement over the list representation of sets, where the complexity grows linearly with the size of the data set. However, poor balance of a tree will degrade the performance of the dictionary. In extreme cases, the binary dictionary degenerates into a list, as shown in Figure 10.1. The form of the dictionary depends on the sequence in which the data are inserted. In the best case we get a good balance with performance in the order log $n$, and in the worst case the performance is in the order $n$. Analysis shows that on average, assuming that any sequence of data is equally likely, the complexity of **in**, **add** and **delete** is still in the order log $n$. So the average performance is, fortunately, closer to the best case than to the worst case. There are, however, several rather simple schemes for keeping good balance of the tree regardless of the data sequence. Such schemes guarantee the *worst case* performance of **in**, **add** and **delete** in the order log $n$. One of them is the 2-3 tree; another scheme is the AVL-tree.

The *2-3 tree* is defined as follows: it is either empty, or it consists of a single node, or it is a tree that satisfies the following conditions:

- each internal node has two or three children, and
- all the leaves are at the same level.

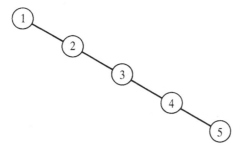

**Figure 10.1** A totally unbalanced binary dictionary. Its performance is reduced to that of a list.

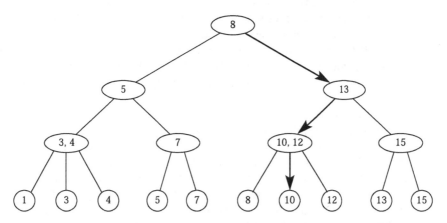

**Figure 10.2** A 2-3 dictionary. The indicated path corresponds to searching for the item 10.

A 2-3 dictionary is a 2-3 tree in which the data items are stored in the leaves, ordered from left to right. Figure 10.2 shows an example. The internal nodes contain labels that specify the minimal elements of the subtrees as follows:

- if an internal node has two subtrees, this internal node contains the minimal element of the second subtree;
- if an internal node has three subtrees then this node contains the minimal elements of the second and of the third subtree.

To search for an item, X, in a 2-3 dictionary we start at the root and move toward the bottom level according to the labels in the internal nodes. Let the root contain the labels M1 and M2. Then:

- if X < M1 then continue the search in the left subtree, otherwise
- if X < M2 then continue the search in the middle subtree, otherwise
- continue the search in the right subtree.

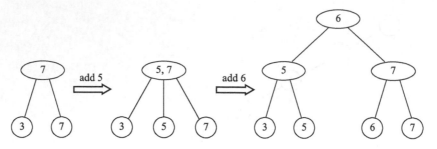

**Figure 10.3** Inserting into a 2-3 dictionary. The tree first grows in breadth and then upwards.

If the root only contains one label, M, then proceed to the left subtree if X < M, and to the right subtree otherwise. This is repeated until the leaf level is reached, and at this point X is either successfully found or the search fails.

As all the leaves are at the same level, the 2-3 tree is perfectly balanced with respect to the heights of the subtrees. All search paths from the root to a leaf are of the same length which is of the order log *n*, where *n* is the number of items stored in the tree.

When inserting new data, the 2-3 tree can also grow in breadth, not only in depth. Each internal node that has two children can accommodate an additional child, which results in the breadth-wise growth. If, on the other hand, a node with three children accepts another child then this node is split into two nodes, each of them taking over two of the total of four children. The so-generated new internal node gets incorporated further up in the tree. If this happens at the top level then the tree is forced to grow upwards. Figure 10.3 illustrates these principles.

Insertion into the 2-3 dictionary will be programmed as the relation

    **add23( Tree, X, NewTree)**

where **NewTree** is obtained by inserting X into **Tree**. The main burden of insertion will be transferred to two auxiliary relations, both called **ins**. The first one has three arguments:

    **ins( Tree, X, NewTree)**

where **NewTree** is the result of inserting X into **Tree**. **Tree** and **NewTree** have the *same height*. But, of course, it is not always possible to preserve the same height after insertion. Therefore we have another **ins** relation, with five arguments, to cater for this case:

    **ins( Tree, X, NTa, Mb, NTb)**

Here, when inserting X into **Tree**, **Tree** is split into two trees: **NTa** and **NTb**. Both **NTa** and **NTb** have the same height as **Tree**. **Mb** is the minimal element of **NTb**. Figure 10.4 shows an example.

In the program, a 2-3 tree will be represented, depending on its form, as follows:

- **nil** represents the empty tree.
- **1(X)** represents a single node tree, a leaf with item X.

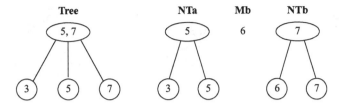

**Figure 10.4** The objects in the figure satisfy the relation **ins**( Tree, 6, NTa, Mb, NTb).

- **n2**( T1, M, T2) represents a tree with two subtrees, T1 and T2; M is the minimal element of T2.
- **n3**( T1, M2, T2, M3, T3) represents a tree with three subtrees, T1, T2 and T3; M2 is the minimal element of T2, and M3 is the minimal element of T3.

T1, T2 and T3 are all 2-3 trees.

The relation between **add23** and **ins** is: if after insertion the tree does not grow upwards then simply:

```
add23( Tree, X, NewTree) :-
    ins( Tree, X, NewTree).
```

If, however, the height after insertion increases, then **ins** determines the two subtrees, T1 and T2, which are then combined into a bigger tree:

```
add23( Tree, X, n2( T1, M, T2) ) :-
    ins( Tree, X, T1, M, T2).
```

The **ins** relation is more complicated because it has to deal with many cases: inserting into the empty tree, a single node tree, a tree of type n2 or n3. Additional subcases arise from insertion into the first, second or third subtree. Accordingly, **ins** will be defined by a set of rules so that each clause about **ins** will deal with one of the cases. Figure 10.5 illustrates some of these cases. The cases in this figure translate into Prolog as follows:

*Case a*

```
ins( n2( T1, M, T2), X, n2( NT1, M, T2) ) :-
    gt( M, X),                                  % M greater than X
    ins( T1, X, NT1).
```

*Case b*

```
ins( n2( T1, M, T2), X, n3( NT1a, Mb, NT1b, M, T2) ) :-
    gt( M, X),
    ins( T1, X, NT1a, Mb, NT1b).
```

*Case c*

```
ins( n3( T1, M2, T2, M3, T3), X, n2( NT1a, Mb, NT1b), M2, n2( T2, M3, T3) ) :-
    gt( M2, X),
    ins( T1, X, NT1a, Mb, NT1b).
```

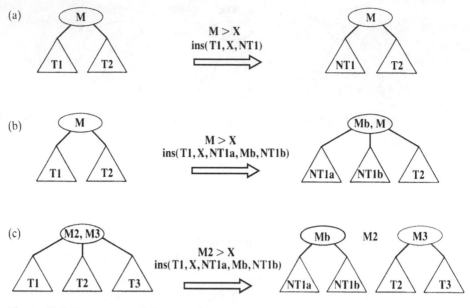

**Figure 10.5** Some cases of the **ins** relation:
(a) **ins( n2( T1, M, T2), X, n2( NT1, M, T2) );**
(b) **ins( n2( T1, M, T2), X, n3( NT1a, Mb, NT1b, M, T2) );**
(c) **ins( n3( T1, M2, T2, M3, T3), X, n2( NT1a, Mb, NT1b), M2, n2( T2, M3, T3) ).**

Figure 10.6 shows the complete program for inserting into the 2-3 dictionary. Figure 10.7 shows a program for displaying 2-3 trees.

Our program occasionally does some unnecessary backtracking. If the three-argument **ins** fails then the five-argument **ins** is called, which redoes part of the work. This source of inefficiency can easily be eliminated by, for example, redefining **ins** as:

> **ins2( Tree, X, NewTrees)**

**NewTrees** is a list of length 1 or 3, as follows:

> **NewTrees** = [ **NewTree**]   if   **ins( Tree, X, NewTree)**
>
> **NewTrees** = [ **NTa, Mb, NTb**]   if   **ins( Tree, X, NTa, Mb, NTb)**

The **add23** relation would be, accordingly, redefined as:

> **add23( T, X, T1) :-**
> **ins2( T, X, Trees),**
> **combine( Trees, T1).**

The **combine** relation has to produce a single tree, **T1**, from the list **Trees**.

% Insertion in the 2-3 dictionary

add23( Tree, X, Tree1)  :-      % Add X to Tree giving Tree1
  ins( Tree, X, Tree1).        % Tree grows in breadth

add23( Tree, X, n2( T1, M2, T2) )  :-      % Tree grows upwards
  ins( Tree, X, T1, M2, T2).

add23( nil, X, l(X) ).

ins( l(A), X, l(A), X, l(X) )  :-
  gt( X, A).

ins( l(A), X, l(X), A, l(A) )  :-
  gt( A, X).

ins( n2( T1, M, T2), X, n2( NT1, M, T2) )  :-
  gt( M, X),
  ins( T1, X, NT1).

ins( n2( T1, M, T2), X, n3( NT1a, Mb, NT1b, M, T2) )  :-
  gt( M, X),
  ins( T1, X, NT1a, Mb, NT1b).

ins( n2( T1, M, T2), X, n2( T1, M, NT2) )  :-
  gt( X, M),
  ins( T2, X, NT2).

ins( n2( T1, M, T2), X, n3( T1, M, NT2a, Mb, NT2b) )  :-
  gt( X, M),
  ins( T2, X, NT2a, Mb, NT2b).

ins( n3( T1, M2, T2, M3, T3), X, n3( NT1, M2, T2, M3, T3) )  :-
  gt( M2, X),
  ins( T1, X, NT1).

ins( n3( T1, M2, T2, M3, T3), X, n2( NT1a, Mb, NT1b), M2, n2( T2, M3, T3) )  :-
  gt( M2, X),
  ins( T1, X, NT1a, Mb, NT1b).

ins( n3( T1, M2, T2, M3, T3), X, n3( T1, M2, NT2, M3, T3) )  :-
  gt( X, M2), gt( M3, X),
  ins( T2, X, NT2).

ins( n3( T1, M2, T2, M3, T3), X, n2( T1, M2, NT2a), Mb, n2( NT2b, M3, T3) )  :-
  gt( X, M2), gt( M3, X),
  ins( T2, X, NT2a, Mb, NT2b).

ins( n3( T1, M2, T2, M3, T3), X, n3( T1, M2, T2, M3, NT3) )  :-
  gt( X, M3),
  ins( T3, X, NT3).

ins( n3( T1, M2, T2, M3, T3), X, n2( T1, M2, T2), M3, n2( NT3a, Mb, NT3b) )  :-
  gt( X, M3),
  ins( T3, X, NT3a, Mb, NT3b).

**Figure 10.6** Inserting in the 2-3 dictionary. In this program, an attempt to insert a duplicate item will fail.

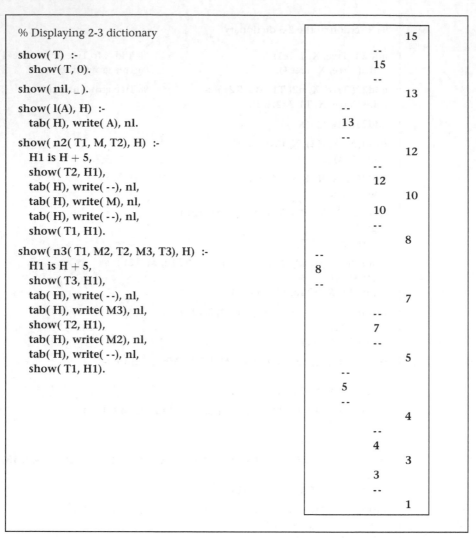

```
% Displaying 2-3 dictionary

show( T)  :-
    show( T, 0).

show( nil, _).

show( l(A), H)  :-
    tab( H), write( A), nl.

show( n2( T1, M, T2), H)  :-
    H1 is H + 5,
    show( T2, H1),
    tab( H), write( --), nl,
    tab( H), write( M), nl,
    tab( H), write( --), nl,
    show( T1, H1).

show( n3( T1, M2, T2, M3, T3), H)  :-
    H1 is H + 5,
    show( T3, H1),
    tab( H), write( --), nl,
    tab( H), write( M3), nl,
    show( T2, H1),
    tab( H), write( M2), nl,
    tab( H), write( --), nl,
    show( T1, H1).
```

```
                                15
                           --
                       15
                           --
                                13
              --
          13
              --
                                12
                   --
              12
                                10
          10
              --
                                 8
     --
 8
     --
                                 7
                   --
              7
                   --
                                 5
         --
     5
         --
                                 4
              --
          4
                                 3
          3
              --
                                 1
```

**Figure 10.7** Left: a program to display a 2-3 dictionary. Right: the dictionary of Figure 10.2 as displayed by this program.

# EXERCISES

**10.1**  Define the relation

  in( Item, Tree)

to search for **Item** in a 2-3 dictionary **Tree**.

**10.2**  Modify the program of Figure 10.6 to avoid backtracking (define relations **ins2** and **combine**).

# 10.2  AVL-trees: approximately balanced trees

AVL-tree is a binary tree that has the following properties:

(1)  Its left subtree and right subtree differ in height by 1 at the most.

(2)  Both subtrees themselves are also AVL-trees.

This definition allows for trees that are slightly out of balance. It can be shown that the height of an AVL-tree is always, even in the worst case, roughly proportional to log $n$ where $n$ is the number of nodes in the tree. This guarantees the logarithmic performance for the operations **in**, **add** and **del**.

Operations on the AVL-dictionary are essentially the same as on binary dictionaries, with some additions to maintain approximate balance of the tree. If the tree gets out of approximate balance after an insertion or deletion then some additional mechanism will get it back into the required degree of balance. To implement this mechanism efficiently, we have to maintain some additional information about the balance of the tree. Essentially we only need the difference between the heights of its subtrees, which is either $-1$, $0$ or $+1$. For the sake of simplicity of the operations involved we will, however, prefer to maintain the complete heights of trees and not only the differences.

We will define the insertion relation as:

>  **addavl( Tree, X, NewTree)**

where both **Tree** and **NewTree** are AVL-dictionaries such that **NewTree** is **Tree** with X inserted. AVL-trees will be represented by terms of the form:

>  **t( Left, A, Right) / Height**

where A is the root, **Left** and **Right** are the subtrees, and **Height** is the height of the tree. The empty tree is represented by **nil/0**. Now let us consider the insertion of X into a non-empty AVL-dictionary:

>  **Tree = t( L, A, R)/H**

We will start our discussion by only considering the case where X is greater than A. Then X is to be inserted into R and we have the following relation:

>  **addavl( R, X, t( R1, B, R2)/Hb)**

Figure 10.8 illustrates the following ingredients from which **NewTree** is to be constructed:

>  **L, A, R1, B, R2**

What can be the heights of L, R, R1 and R2? L and R can only differ in height by 1 at the most. Figure 10.8 shows what the heights of R1 and R2 can be. As only one item, X, has been inserted into R, at most one of the subtrees R1 and R2 can have the height $h + 1$.

In the case that X is less than A then the situation is analogous with left and right subtrees interchanged. Therefore, in any case, we have to construct **NewTree** from three trees (let us call them **Tree1**, **Tree2** and **Tree3**), and two single items, A and B. Let us now consider the question: How can we combine these five

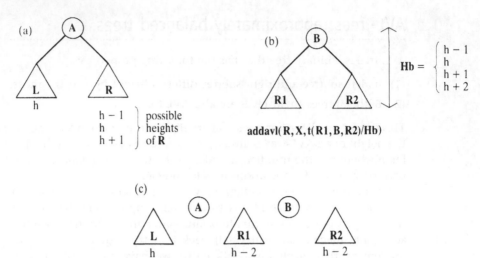

**Figure 10.8** The problem of AVL insertion: (a) AVL-tree before inserting X, X > A; (b) AVL-tree after inserting X into **R**; (c) ingredients from which the new tree is to be constructed.

ingredients to make **NewTree** so that **NewTree** is an AVL-dictionary? The order from left to right in **NewTree** has to be:

   **Tree1, A, Tree2, B, Tree3**

We have to consider three cases:

(1)  The middle tree, **Tree2**, is taller than both other trees.

(2)  **Tree1** is at least as tall as **Tree2** and **Tree3**.

(3)  **Tree3** is at least as tall as **Tree2** and **Tree1**.

Figure 10.9 shows how **NewTree** can be constructed in each of these cases. In case 1, the middle tree **Tree2** has to be decomposed and its parts incorporated into **NewTree**. The three rules of Figure 10.9 are easily translated into Prolog as a relation:

   **combine( Tree1, A, Tree2, B, Tree3, NewTree)**

The last argument, **NewTree**, is an AVL-tree constructed from five ingredients, the first five arguments. Rule 1, for example, becomes:

```
combine(
   T1/H1, A, t(T21,B,T22) / H2, C, T3/H3,              % Five ingredients
   t( t(T1/H1,A,T21)/Ha, B, t(T22,C,T3/H3)/Hc)/Hb) :-  % Their combination
   H2 > H1, H2 > H3,                                   % Middle tree is tallest
   Ha is H1 + 1,                                       % Height of left subtree
   Hc is H3 + 1,                                       % Height of right subtree
   Hb is Ha + 1.                                       % Height of the whole tree
```

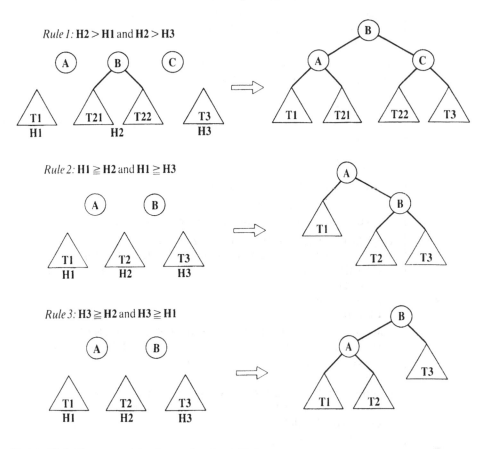

**Figure 10.9** Three combination rules for AVL-trees.

A complete **addavl** program, which also computes the heights of the tree and the subtrees, is shown as Figure 10.10.

Our program works with the heights of trees. A more economical representation is, as said earlier, possible. In fact, we only need the balance, which can only be −1, 0 or +1. The disadvantage of such economization would be, however, somewhat more complicated combination rules.

# EXERCISES

**10.3** Define the relation

    **avl( Tree)**

to test whether a binary tree **Tree** is an AVL-tree; that is, all the sibling subtrees may differ in their heights by 1 at the most. Let binary trees be represented by terms of the form **t( Left, Root, Right)** or **nil**.

```
% addavl( Tree, X, NewTree): insertion into AVL-dictionary
%     Tree = t( Left, Root, Right)/HeightOfTree
%     Empty tree = nil/0

addavl( nil/0, X, t( nil/0, X, nil/0)/1).          % Add X to empty tree
addavl( t( L, Y, R)/Hy, X, NewTree) :-             % Add X to non-empty tree
  gt( Y, X),
  addavl( L, X, t( L1, Z, L2)/_ ),                 % Add into left subtree
  combine( L1, Z, L2, Y, R, NewTree).              % Combine ingredients of NewTree
addavl( t( L, Y, R)/Hy, X, NewTree) :-
  gt( X, Y),
  addavl( R, X, t( R1, Z, R2)/_ ),                 % Add into right subtree
  combine( L, Y, R1, Z, R2, NewTree).

% combine( Tree1, A, Tree2, B, Tree3, NewTree):
%     combine Tree1, Tree2, Tree3 and nodes A and B into an AVL-tree

combine( T1/H1, A, t( T21, B, T22)/H2, C, T3/H3,
         t( t(T1/H1,A,T21)/Ha, B, t(T22,C,T3/H3)/Hc)/Hb) :-
  H2 > H1, H2 > H3,                                % Middle subtree tallest
  Ha is H1 + 1,
  Hc is H3 + 1,
  Hb is Ha + 1.
combine( T1/H1, A, T2/H2, C, T3/H3, t( T1/H1, A, t(T2/H2,C,T3/H3)/Hc)/Ha) :-
  H1 >= H2, H1 >= H3,                              % Tall left subtree
  max1( H2, H3, Hc),
  max1( H1, Hc, Ha).
combine( T1/H1, A, T2/H2, C, T3/H3, t( t(T1/H1,A,T2/H2)/Ha, C, T3/H3)/Hc) :-
  H3 >= H2, H3 >= H1,                              % Tall right subtree
  max1( H1, H2, Ha),
  max1( Ha, H3, Hc).
max1( U, V, M) :-                                  % M is 1 + max. of U and V
  U > V, !, M is U + 1
  ;
  M is V + 1.
```

**Figure 10.10** AVL-dictionary insertion. In this program, an attempt to insert a duplicate will fail. See Figure 10.9 for **combine**.

**10.4**  Trace the execution of the AVL insertion algorithm, starting with the empty tree and successively inserting 5, 8, 9, 3, 1, 6, 7. How is the root item changing during this process?

# Summary

- 2-3 trees and AVL-trees, implemented in this chapter, are types of balanced trees.
- Balanced, or approximately balanced, trees guarantee efficient execution of the three basic operations on trees: looking for an item, adding or deleting an item. All these operations can be done in time proportional to log $n$, where $n$ is the number of nodes in the tree.

# References and historical notes

2-3 trees and AVL-trees are examples of various balanced tree structures that appear as standard material in books on algorithms and data structures, such as Cormen *et al.* (2009). AVL-trees are named after their authors Adelson-Velskii and Landis who introduced the idea of balanced trees in their famous paper in 1962. Adelson-Velskii is also known as one of the authors of the first computer chess world champion program KAISSA. Operations on AVL trees are described in detail in Knuth's classic book (1998). 2-3 trees were invented by Hopcroft in 1970 (unpublished) and described in detail, among others, by Aho, Hopcroft and Ullman (1974, 1983). 2-3 trees are a special case of more general B-trees, introduced by Bayer and McCreight (1972), also described in detail in Cormen *et al.* (2009). A Prolog program for AVL-tree insertion that only uses tree-bias information (that is, the difference between the heights of the subtrees −1, 0 or +1, and not the complete height) was published by van Emden (1981).

Adelson-Velskii, G.M. and Landis, E.M. (1962) An algorithm for the organization of information, *Soviet Mathematics Doklady* **3**: 1259–1263.

Aho, A.V., Hopcroft, J.E. and Ullman, J.D. (1974) *The Design and Analysis of Computer Algorithms*. Addison-Wesley.

Aho, A.V., Hopcroft, J.E. and Ullman, J.D. (1983) *Data Structures and Algorithms*. Addison-Wesley.

Bayer, R. and McCreight, E.M. (1972) Organization and maintenance of large ordered indexes. *Acta Informatica*, **1**: 173–189.

Cormen,T.H., Leiserson, C.E., Rivest, R. and Stein, C. (2009) *Introduction to Algorithms*, third edn. Cambridge, MA: The MIT Press.

Knuth, D.E. (1998) *The Art of Computer Programming*, Volume 3: *Sorting and Searching*, second edn. Addison-Wesley.

van Emden, M. (1981) In: *Logic Programming Newsletter* 2.

# Chapter 11

# Problem-Solving as Search

····································································································

····································································································

This chapter is centred around a general scheme, called *state space*, for representing problems. A state space is a graph whose nodes correspond to problem situations, and a given problem is reduced to finding a path in this graph. We will study examples of formulating problems using the state-space approach, and discuss general methods for solving problems represented in this formalism. Problem solving involves graph searching and exploring alternatives. The basic strategies for exploring alternatives, presented in this chapter, are the depth-first search, breadth-first search and iterative deepening.

## 11.1   Introductory concepts and examples

····································································································

Let us consider the example in Figure 11.1. The problem is to find a plan for a robot to rearrange a stack of blocks as shown in the figure. The robot is only allowed to move one block at a time. A block can be grasped only when its top is clear. A block can be put on the table or on some other block. To find a required plan, we have to find a sequence of moves that accomplish the given task.

We can think of this problem as a problem of exploring among possible alternatives. In the initial problem situation we are only allowed one alternative: put block C on the table. After C has been put on the table, we have three alternatives:

- put A on table, or
- put A on C, or
- put C on A.

We will not seriously consider putting C on the table as this clearly has no effect on the situation.

As this example illustrates, we have, in such a problem, two types of concept:

(1)  Problem situations.
(2)  Legal moves, or actions, that transform problem situations into other situations.

**Figure 11.1** A blocks rearrangement problem.

Problem situations and possible moves form a directed graph, called a *state space*. A state space for our example problem is shown in Figure 11.2. The nodes of the graph correspond to problem situations, and the arcs correspond to legal transitions between states. The problem of finding a solution plan is equivalent to finding a path between the given initial situation (the start node) and some specified final situation, also called a *goal node*.

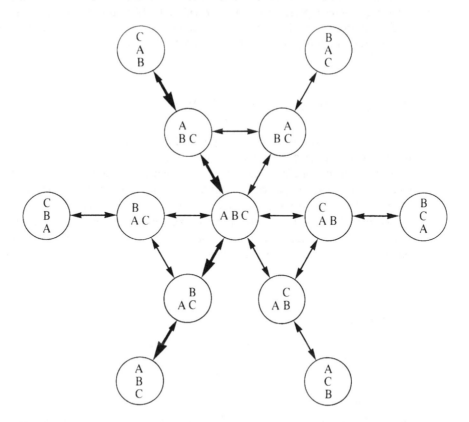

**Figure 11.2** A state-space representation of the block manipulation problem. The indicated path is a solution to the problem in Figure 11.1.

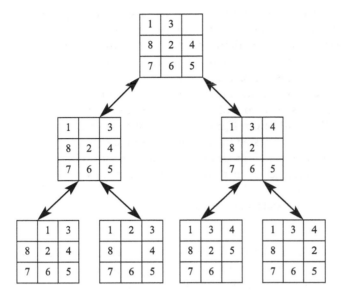

**Figure 11.3** An eight puzzle and the corresponding state-space representation.

Figure 11.3 shows another example problem: an eight puzzle and its representation as a path-finding problem. The puzzle consists of eight sliding tiles, numbered by digits from 1 to 8, and arranged in a 3 by 3 array of nine cells. One of the cells is always empty, and any adjacent tile can be moved into the empty cell. Equivalently, we can say that the empty cell is allowed to move around, swapping its place with any of the adjacent tiles. The final situation is some special arrangement of tiles, as shown for example in Figure 11.3.

It is easy to construct similar graph representations for other popular puzzles. Straightforward examples are the Tower of Hanoi, or getting fox, goose and grain across the river. In the latter problem, the boat can only hold the farmer and one other object, and the farmer has to protect the goose from the fox, and the grain from the goose. Many practical problems also naturally fit this paradigm. Among them is the travelling salesman problem, which is the formal model of many practical optimization problems. The problem is defined by a map with $n$ cities and road distances between the cities. The task is to find a shortest route from some starting city, visiting all the cities and ending in the starting city. No city, with the exception of the starting one, may appear in the tour twice.

Let us summarize the concepts introduced by these examples. The state space of a given problem specifies the 'rules of the game': nodes in the state space correspond to situations, and arcs correspond to 'legal moves', or actions, or solution steps. A particular problem is defined by:

- a state space,
- a start node,
- a goal condition (a condition to be reached); 'goal nodes' are those nodes that satisfy this condition.

We can attach costs to legal moves or actions. For example, costs attached to moving blocks in the block manipulation problem would indicate that some blocks are harder to move than others. In the travelling salesman problem, moves correspond to direct city-to-city journeys. Naturally, the costs of such moves are the distances between the cities.

In cases where costs are attached to moves, we are normally interested in minimum cost solutions. The cost of a solution is the sum of the costs of the arcs along the solution path. Even if no costs are given we may have an optimization problem: we may be interested in shortest solutions.

Before presenting some programs that implement classical algorithms for searching state spaces, let us first discuss how a state space can be represented in a Prolog program.

We will represent a state space by a relation

s( X, Y)

which is true if there is a legal move in the state space from a node X to a node Y. We will say that Y is a *successor* of X. If there are costs associated with moves then we will add a third argument, the cost of the move:

s( X, Y, Cost)

This relation can be represented in the program explicitly by a set of facts. For typical state spaces of any significant complexity this would be, however, impractical or impossible. Therefore the successor relation, s, is usually defined implicitly by stating the rules for computing successor nodes of a given node.

Another question of general importance is, how to represent problem situations, that is nodes themselves. The representation should be compact, but it should also enable efficient execution of operations required; in particular, the evaluation of the successor relation, and possibly the associated costs.

As an example, let us consider the block manipulation problem of Figure 11.1. We will consider a more general case, so that there are altogether any number of blocks that are arranged in one or more stacks. The number of stacks will be limited to some given maximum to make the problem more interesting. This may also be a realistic constraint because a robot that manipulates blocks may be only given a limited working space on the table.

A problem situation can be represented as a list of stacks. Each stack can be, in turn, represented by a list of blocks in that stack ordered so that the top block in the stack is the head of the list. Empty stacks are represented by empty lists. Allowing three stacks only, the initial situation of the problem in Figure 11.1 can be thus represented by:

[ [c,a,b], [], [] ]

A goal situation is any arrangement with the ordered stack of all the blocks. There are three such situations:

[ [a,b,c], [], [] ]

[ [], [a,b,c], [] ]

[ [], [], [a,b,c] ]

The successor relation can be programmed according to the following rule: **Situation2** is a successor of **Situation1** if there are two stacks, **Stack1** and **Stack2**, in **Situation1**, and the top block of **Stack1** can be moved to **Stack2**. As all situations are represented as lists of stacks, this is translated into Prolog as:

```
s( Stacks, [Stack1, [Top1 | Stack2] | OtherStacks] ) :-    % Move Top1 to Stack2
    del( [Top1 | Stack1], Stacks, Stacks1),                % Find first stack
    del( Stack2, Stacks1, OtherStacks).                    % Find second stack

del( X, [X | L], L).

del( X, [Y | L], [Y | L1] ) :-
    del( X, L, L1).
```

The goal condition for our example problem is:

```
goal( Situation) :-
    member( [a,b,c], Situation).
```

We will program search algorithms as a relation

```
solve( Start, Solution)
```

where **Start** is the start node in the state space, and **Solution** is a path between **Start** and any goal node. For our block manipulation problem, the corresponding call can be:

```
?- solve( [ [c,a,b], [], [] ], Solution).
```

As the result of a successful search, **Solution** becomes a list of block arrangements. This list represents a plan for transforming the initial state into a state in which all the three blocks are in one stack arranged as [a,b,c].

## 11.2 Depth-first search and iterative deepening

Given a state-space formulation of a problem, there are many approaches to finding a solution path. Two basic search strategies are: *depth-first* search and *breadth-first* search. In this section we will implement depth-first search and its variation called *iterative deepening*.

We will start the development of this algorithm and its variations with a simple idea:

To find a solution path, **Sol**, from a given node, N, to some goal node:
- if N is a goal node then **Sol** = [N], or
- if there is a successor node, N1, of N, such that there is a path **Sol1** from N1 to a goal node, then **Sol** = [ N | Sol1].

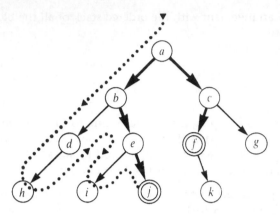

**Figure 11.4** A simple state space: *a* is the start node, *f* and *j* are goal nodes. The order in which the depth-first strategy visits the nodes in this state space is: *a, b, d, h, e, i, j*. The solution found is: [a,b,e,j]. On backtracking, the other solution is discovered: [a,c,f].

This translates into Prolog as:

```
solve( N, [N] ) :-
    goal( N).

solve( N, [ N | Sol1] ) :-
    s( N, N1),
    solve( N1, Sol1).
```

This program is an implementation of the depth-first strategy. It is called 'depth-first' because of the order in which the alternatives in the state space are explored. Whenever the depth-first algorithm is given a choice of continuing the search from several nodes, it always decides to choose a deepest one. A 'deepest' node is one that is farthest from the start node. Figure 11.4 illustrates the order in which the nodes are visited. This order corresponds to the Prolog trace when answering the question:

```
?- solve( a, Sol).
```

The depth-first search is most amenable to the recursive style of programming in Prolog. The reason for this is that Prolog itself, when executing goals, explores alternatives in the depth-first fashion.

The depth-first search is simple and easy to program, and may work well in certain cases. The eight-queens programs of Chapter 4 were, in fact, examples of depth-first search. A state-space formulation of the eight-queens problem that could be used by the **solve** procedure above can be as follows:

- nodes are board positions with zero or more queens placed in consecutive files of the board;
- a successor node is obtained by placing another queen anywhere in the next file so that she does not attack any of the existing queens;
- the start node is the empty board represented by the empty list;
- a goal node is any position with eight queens (the successor rule guarantees that the queens do not attack each other).

Representing the board position as a list of Y-coordinates of the queens, this can be programmed as:

```
s( Queens, [Queen | Queens] )  :-
    member( Queen, [1,2,3,4,5,6,7,8] ),      % Place Queen into any row
    noattack( Queen, Queens).

goal( [_, _, _, _, _, _, _, _] ).            % Position with 8 queens
```

The **noattack** relation requires that **Queen** does not attack any of the **Queens**; it can be easily programmed as in Chapter 4. The question

```
?- solve( [], Solution).
```

will produce a list of board positions with increasing number of queens. The list will end with a safe configuration of eight queens. It will also find alternative solutions through backtracking.

The depth-first search often works well, as in this example, but there are many ways in which our simple **solve** procedure can run into trouble. Whether this will actually happen or not depends on the state space. To embarrass our **solve** procedure with the problem of Figure 11.4, a slight modification of this problem is sufficient: add an arc from *h* to *d*, thus creating a cycle (Figure 11.5). The search would in this case proceed as follows: start at *a* and descend to *h* following the left-most branch of the graph. At this point, in contrast with Figure 11.4, *h* has a successor, *d*. Therefore the execution will *not backtrack* from *h*, but *proceed* to *d* instead. Then the successor of *d*, *h*, will be found, etc., resulting in cycling between *d* and *h*.

An obvious improvement of our depth-first program is to add a cycle-detection mechanism. Accordingly, any node that is already in the path from the start node to the current node should not be considered again. We can formulate this as a relation:

**depthfirst( Path, Node, Solution)**

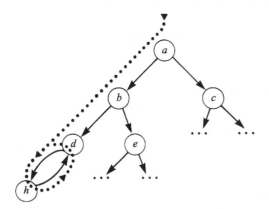

**Figure 11.5** Starting at *a*, the depth-first search ends in cycling between *d* and *h*: *a, b, d, h, d, h, d* . . . .

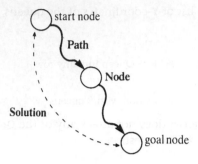

**Figure 11.6** Relation **depthfirst( Path, Node, Solution).**

As illustrated in Figure 11.6, **Node** is the state from which a path to a goal state is to be found; **Path** is a list of already visited nodes between the start node and **Node**; **Solution** is **Path** extended via **Node** to a goal node.

For the sake of ease of programming, paths will be in our program represented by lists in the *inverse* order. The argument **Path** can be used for cycle detection to prevent the algorithm from considering those successors of **Node** that have already been encountered. A corresponding depth-first search program is shown in Figure 11.7.

With the cycle-detection mechanism, our depth-first procedure will find solution paths in state spaces such as that in Figure 11.5. There are, however, state spaces in which this program will still easily get lost. Many state spaces are infinite. In such a space, the depth-first algorithm may miss a goal node, proceeding along an infinite branch of the graph. The program may then indefinitely explore this infinite part of the space, never getting closer to a goal. The eight-queens state space, as defined in this section, may seem to be susceptible to this kind of trap. However, this space is, incidentally, finite. Because by the limited choice of Y-coordinates, eight queens at most can be placed safely.

```
% solve( Node, Solution):
%    Solution is an acyclic path (in reverse order) between Node and a goal

solve( Node, Solution)  :-
    depthfirst( [], Node, Solution).

% depthfirst( Path, Node, Solution):
%    extending the path [Node | Path] to a goal gives Solution

depthfirst( Path, Node, [Node | Path] )  :-
    goal( Node).

depthfirst( Path, Node, Sol)  :-
    s( Node, Node1),
    \+ member( Node1, Path),                    % Prevent a cycle
    depthfirst( [Node | Path], Node1, Sol).
```

**Figure 11.7** A depth-first search program that avoids cycling.

```
% depthfirst2( Node, Solution, Maxdepth):
%    Solution is a path, not longer than Maxdepth, from Node to a goal

depthfirst2( Node, [Node], _ ) :-
   goal( Node).

depthfirst2( Node, [Node | Sol], Maxdepth) :-
   Maxdepth > 0,
   s( Node, Node1),
   Max1 is Maxdepth − 1,
   depthfirst2( Node1, Sol, Max1).
```

**Figure 11.8** A depth-limited, depth-first search program.

To avoid aimless infinite non-cyclic branches, we can limit the depth of search. We then define the depth-first search procedure as:

> depthfirst2( Node, Solution, Maxdepth)

The search is not allowed to go in depth beyond **Maxdepth**. This constraint can be programmed by decreasing the depth limit at each recursive call, and not allowing this limit to become negative. The resulting program is shown in Figure 11.8.

A difficulty with the depth-limited program in Figure 11.8 is that we have to guess a suitable limit in advance. If we set the limit too low – that is, less than any solution path – then the search will fail. If we set the limit too high, the search will become too complex. To circumvent this difficulty, we can execute the depth-limited search iteratively, varying the depth limit: start with a very low depth limit and gradually increase the limit until a solution is found. This technique is called *iterative deepening*. It can be implemented by modifying the program of Figure 11.8 in the following way. The **depthfirst2** procedure can be called from another procedure which would, on each recursive call, increase the limit by 1.

There is, however, a more elegant implementation based on a procedure

> path( Node1, Node2, Path)

where **Path** is an acyclic path, in reverse order, between nodes **Node1** and **Node2** in the state space. Let the path be represented as a list of nodes in the inverse order. Then **path** can be written as:

```
path( Node, Node, [Node] ).                              % Single node path

path( FirstNode, LastNode, [LastNode | Path] ) :-
   path( FirstNode, OneButLast, Path),                   % Path up to one-but-last node
   s( OneButLast, LastNode),                             % Last step
   \+ member( LastNode, Path).                           % No cycle
```

Let us find some paths starting with node a in the state space of Figure 11.4:

```
?- path( a, Last, Path).

Last = a
Path = [a];

Last = b
Path = [b,a];
```

**Last = c**
**Path = [c,a];**

**Last = d**
**Path = [d,b,a];**

...

The **path** procedure generates, for the given initial node, all possible acyclic paths of increasing length. This is exactly what we need in the iterative deepening approach: generate paths of increasing length until a path is generated that ends with a goal node. This immediately gives a depth-first iterative deepening search program:

**depth_first_iterative_deepening( Node, Solution) :-**
  **path( Node, GoalNode, Solution),**
  **goal( GoalNode).**

This technique is in fact very useful in practice, as long as the combinatorial complexity of the problem does not require the use of problem-specific heuristics. The procedure is simple and, even if it does not do anything very clever, it does not waste much time or space. In comparison with some other search strategies, such as breadth first (discussed in the next section), the main advantage of iterative deepening is that it requires relatively little memory space. At any point of execution, the space requirements are basically reduced to *one path* between the start node of the search and the current node. Paths are generated, checked and forgotten, which is in contrast to some other search procedures (like breadth-first search) that, during search, keep many candidate paths at the same time. A disadvantage of iterative deepening is the consequence of its main strength: on each iteration, when the depth limit is increased, the paths previously computed have to be recomputed and extended to the new limit. In typical search problems, however, this recomputation does not critically affect the overall computation time. Typically, most computation is done at the deepest level of search; therefore, repeated computation at upper levels adds relatively little to the total time.

## EXERCISES

**11.1** Write a depth-first search procedure (with cycle detection)

**depthfirst1( CandidatePath, Solution)**

to find a solution path **Solution** as an extension of **CandidatePath**. Let both paths be represented as lists of nodes in the inverse order, so that the goal node is the head of **Solution**.

**11.2** Write a depth-first procedure that combines both the cycle-detection and the depth-limiting mechanisms of the procedures in Figures 11.7 and 11.8.

**11.3** The procedure **depth_first_iterative_deepening/2** in this section may get into an indefinite loop if there is no solution path in the state space. It keeps searching for longer solution paths even when it is obvious that there do not exist any longer paths than those already searched. The same problem may occur when the user requests alternative solutions after all the solutions have already been found. Write an iterative deepening search program that will look for paths of length $i+1$ only if there was at least one path found of length $i$.

**11.4** Experiment with the depth-first programs of this section in the blocks world planning problem of Figure 11.1.

**11.5** Write a procedure

**show( Situation)**

to display a problem state, **Situation**, in the blocks world. Let **Situation** be a list of stacks, and a stack in turn a list of blocks. The goal

**show( [ [a], [e,d], [c,b] ] )**

should display the corresponding situation; for example, as:

```
        e    c
   a    d    b
   ===========
```

## 11.3 Breadth-first search

In contrast to the depth-first search strategy, the breadth-first search strategy chooses to first visit those nodes that are closest to the start node. This results in a search process that tends to develop more into breadth than into depth, as illustrated by Figure 11.9.

The breadth-first search is not so easy to program as the depth-first search. The reason for this difficulty is that we have to maintain a *set* of alternative candidate nodes, not just one as in depth-first search. This set of candidates is the whole growing bottom edge of the search tree. However, even this set of nodes is not sufficient if we also want to extract a solution path from the search process.

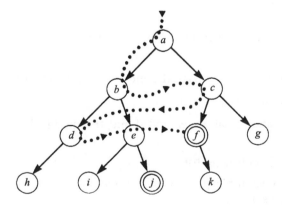

**Figure 11.9** A simple state space: $a$ is the start node, $f$ and $j$ are goal nodes. The order in which the breadth-first strategy visits the nodes in this state space is: $a$, $b$, $c$, $d$, $e$, $f$. The shorter solution [a,c,f] is found before the longer one [a,b,e,j].

Therefore, instead of maintaining a set of candidate nodes, we maintain a set of candidate *paths*. Then,

> **breadthfirst( Paths, Solution)**

is true if some path from a candidate set **Paths** can be extended to a goal node. **Solution** is such an extended path.

We will use the following representation for the set of candidate paths. The set will be represented as a list of paths, and each path will be a list of nodes in the inverse order; that is, the head will be the most recently generated node, and the last element of the list will be the start node of the search. The search is initiated with a single element candidate set:

> [ [StartNode] ]

An outline for breadth-first search is:

> To do the breadth-first search when given a list of candidate paths:
>
> - if the head of the first path is a goal node then this path is a solution of the problem, otherwise
> - remove the first path from the candidate list and generate the list of all possible one-step extensions of this path, add this list of extensions at the end of the candidate list, and execute breadth-first search on this updated list.

For our example problem of Figure 11.9, this process develops as follows:

(1) Start with the initial candidate list:

> [ [a] ]

(2) Generate extensions of path [a]:

> [ [b,a], [c,a] ]

Note that all paths are represented in the inverse order.

(3) Remove the first candidate path, [b,a], from the set and generate extensions of this path:

> [ [d,b,a], [e,b,a] ]

Add the list of extensions to the end of the candidate list:

> [ [c,a], [d,b,a], [e,b,a] ]

(4) Remove [c,a] and add its extensions to the end of the candidate list, producing:

> [ [d,b,a], [e,b,a], [f,c,a], [g,c,a] ]

In further steps, [d,b,a] and [e,b,a] are extended and the modified candidate list becomes:

> [ [f,c,a], [g,c,a], [h,d,b,a], [i,e,b,a], [j,e,b,a] ]

Now the search process encounters [f,c,a], which contains a goal node, f. Therefore this path is returned as a solution.

A program that carries out this process is shown in Figure 11.10. In this program all one-step extensions are generated by using the built-in procedure **findall**. A test to prevent the generation of cyclic paths is also made.

```
% solve( Start, Solution):
%    Solution is a path (in reverse order) from Start to a goal

solve( Start, Solution)  :-
   breadthfirst( [ [Start] ], Solution).

% breadthfirst( [ Path1, Path2, ...], Solution):
%    Solution is an extension to a goal of one of paths

breadthfirst( [ [Node | Path] | _ ], [Node | Path])  :-
   goal( Node).

breadthfirst( [Path | Paths], Solution)  :-
   extend( Path, NewPaths),
   conc( Paths, NewPaths, Paths1),
   breadthfirst( Paths1, Solution).

extend( [Node | Path], NewPaths)  :-
   findall( [NewNode, Node | Path],
            ( s( Node, NewNode), \+ member( NewNode, [Node | Path] ) ),
            NewPaths).
```

**Figure 11.10** An implementation of breadth-first search.

**member** and **conc** are the list membership and list concatenation relations respectively.

A drawback of this program is the inefficiency of the conc operation. This can be rectified by using the difference-pair representation of lists introduced in Chapter 8. The set of candidate paths would then be represented by a pair of lists, **Paths** and **Z**, written as:

Paths - Z

Introducing this representation into the program of Figure 11.10, it can be systematically transformed into the program shown in Figure 11.11. This transformation is left as an exercise for the reader.

```
% solve( Start, Solution):
%    Solution is a path (in reverse order) from Start to a goal

solve( Start, Solution)  :-
   breadthfirst( [ [Start] | Z] - Z, Solution).

breadthfirst( [ [Node | Path] | _ ] - _ , [Node | Path] )  :-
   goal( Node).

breadthfirst( [Path | Paths] - Z, Solution)  :-
   extend( Path, NewPaths),
   conc( NewPaths, Z1, Z),              % Add NewPaths at end
   Paths \== Z1,                         % Set of candidates not empty
   breadthfirst( Paths - Z1, Solution).
```

**Figure 11.11** A more efficient program than that of Figure 11.10 for the breadth-first search. The improvement is based on using the difference-pair representation for the list of candidate paths. Procedure **extend** is as in Figure 11.10.

# EXERCISES

**11.6** Let the state space be a tree with uniform branching $b$, and let the solution length be $d$. For the special case $b = 2$ and $d = 3$, how many nodes are generated in the worst case by breadth-first search and by iterative deepening (counting regenerated nodes as well)? Denote by $N(b, d)$ the number of nodes generated by iterative deepening in the general case. Find a recursive formula giving $N(b, d)$ in terms of $N(b, d - 1)$.

**11.7** Rewrite the breadth-first program of Figure 11.10 using the difference-pair representation for the list of candidate paths, and show that the result can be the program in Figure 11.11. In Figure 11.11, what is the purpose of the goal:

    Paths \== Z1

Test what happens if this goal is omitted; use the state space of Figure 11.9. The difference should only show when trying to find more solutions when there are none left.

**11.8** How can the search programs of this section be used for searching from a *starting set* of nodes instead of a single start node?

**11.9** How can the search programs of this chapter be used to search in the backward direction; that is, starting from a goal node and progressing toward the start node (or a start node in the case of multiple start nodes)? Hint: redefine the s relation. In what situations would the backward search be advantageous over the forward search?

**11.10** Sometimes it is beneficial to search *bidirectionally*; that is, to work from both ends, the start and the goal. The search ends when both ends come together. Define the search space (relation s) and the goal relation for a given graph so that our search procedures would, in effect, perform bidirectional search.

**11.11** Three search procedures **find1**, **find2** and **find3** defined below use different search strategies. Identify these strategies.

```
find1( Node, [Node]) :-
  goal( Node).

find1( Node, [Node | Path]) :-
  s( Node, Node1),
  find1( Node1, Path).

find2( Node, Path) :-
  conc( Path, _, _),                      % Usual conc/3 for list concatenation
  find1( Node, Path).

find3( Node, Path) :-
  goal( Goal),
  find3( Node, [Goal], Path).

find3( Node, [Node | Path], [Node | Path]).

find3( Node, [Node2 | Path2], Path) :-
  s( Node1, Node2),
  find3( Node, [Node1, Node2 | Path2], Path).
```

**11.12**   Study the following search program and describe its search strategy:

```
% search( Start, Path1 - Path2): Find path from start node S to a goal node
% Solution path is represented by two lists Path1 and Path2

search( S, P1 - P2)  :-
    similar_length( P1, P2),             % Lists of approximately equal lengths
    goal( G),
    path2( G, P2, N),
    path1( S, P1, N).

path1( N, [N], N).

path1( First, [First | Rest], Last)  :-
    s( First, Second),
    path1( Second, Rest, Last).

path2( N, [N], N).

path2( First, [First | Rest], Last)  :-
    s( Second, First),
    path2( Second, Rest, Last).

similar_length( List1, List2)  :-        % Lists of similar length
    equal_length( List2, List),          % Lists of equal length
    ( List1 = List; List1 = [_ | List]).
equal_length( [ ], [ ]).

equal_length( [X1 | L1], [X2 | L2])  :-
    equal_length( L1, L2).
```

**11.13**   Experiment with various search techniques in the blocks world planning problem.

**11.14**   The breadth-first programs of this chapter only check for repeated nodes that appear in the same candidate path. In graphs, a node can be reached by different paths. This is not detected by our programs, which, therefore, duplicate the search below such nodes. Modify the programs of Figures 11.10 and 11.11 to prevent this unnecessary work.

## 11.4   Analysis of basic search techniques

We will now analyse and compare the basic search techniques. First we will consider their application to searching graphs, then comment on the optimality of solutions they produce. Finally we will analyse their time and space complexity.

Examples so far might have made the wrong impression that our search programs only work for state spaces that are trees and not general graphs. However, when a graph is searched it, in effect, unfolds into a tree so that some paths are possibly copied in other parts of the tree. Figure 11.12 illustrates this. So our programs work on graphs as well, although they may unnecessarily duplicate some work in cases where a node is reached by various paths. In cases when many paths lead to the same node this may become extremely inefficient. Repetition of work can be prevented by checking for repetition of a node in *all* the candidate paths, and not only in the path in which the node was generated.

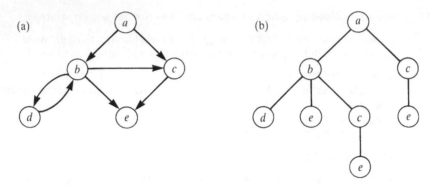

**Figure 11.12**  (a) A state space: $a$ is the start node. (b) The tree of all possible non-cyclic paths from $a$ as effectively developed by the breadth-first search program of Figure 11.10.

Of course, such checking is only possible in our breadth-first programs where alternative paths are available for checking.

Our breadth-first search programs generate solution paths, one after another, ordered according to their lengths: shortest solutions come first. This is important if optimality (with respect to length) is a concern. The breadth-first strategy is guaranteed to produce a shortest solution first. This is, of course, not true for the depth-first strategy. However, depth-first iterative deepening performs depth-first search to increasing depth limits and is thus bound to find the shortest solutions first. So iterative deepening in a way simulates breadth-first search.

Our programs do not, however, take into account any costs associated with the arcs in the state space. If the minimal cost of the solution path is the optimization criterion (and not its length) then the breadth-first search is not sufficient. The best-first search of Chapter 12 will aspire to optimize the cost.

The typical problem associated with search is the *combinatorial complexity*. For non-trivial problem domains the number of alternatives to be explored is so high that the complexity becomes most critical. It is easy to see how this happens. To simplify the analysis let us assume the state space is a tree with uniform branching $b$. That is, each node in the tree, except the leaves, has exactly $b$ successors. Assume a shortest solution path has length $d$, and there are no leaves in the tree at depth $d$ or less. The number of alternative paths of length $d$ from the start node is $b^d$. Breadth-first search will explore the number of paths of order $b^d$, $O(b^d)$. The number of candidate paths grows very fast with their length, which leads to what is called *combinatorial explosion*.

Let us now compare the complexity of the basic search algorithms. The time complexity is usually measured as the number of nodes generated by a search algorithm. The space complexity is usually measured as the maximum number of nodes that have to be stored in memory during search.

Consider breadth-first search in a tree with branching factor $b$ and a shortest solution path of length $d$. The number of nodes at consecutive levels in the tree grows exponentially with depth, so the number of nodes generated by breadth-first search is:

$$1 + b + b^2 + b^3 + \cdots$$

The total number of nodes up to the solution depth $d$ is $O(b^d)$. So the time complexity of breadth-first search is $O(b^d)$. Breadth-first search maintains all the candidate paths in memory, so its space complexity is also $O(b^d)$.

Analysis of unlimited depth-first search is less clear because it may completely miss the solution path of length $d$ and get lost in an infinite subtree. To facilitate the analysis let us consider depth-first search limited to a maximum depth $d_{\max}$ so that $d \leq d_{\max}$. Time complexity of this is $O(b^{d_{\max}})$. Space complexity is however only $O(d_{\max})$. Depth-first search only maintains the currently explored path between the start node and the current node of the search. Compared to breadth-first search, depth-first search has the advantage of much lower space complexity, and the disadvantage of no guarantee regarding the optimality.

Iterative deepening performs $(d + 1)$ depth-first searches to increasing depths: 0, 1, ..., $d$. So its space complexity is $O(d)$. It visits the start node $(d + 1)$ times, the children of the start node $d$ times, etc. In the worst case the number of nodes generated is:

$$(d+1)*1 + d*b + (d-1)*b^2 + \cdots + 1*d^b$$

This is also $O(b^d)$. In fact, the overhead, in comparison with breadth-first search, of regenerating shallow nodes, is surprisingly small. It can be shown that the ratio between the number of nodes generated by iterative deepening and those generated by breadth-first search is approximately $b/(b-1)$. For $b \geqslant 2$ this overhead of iterative deepening is relatively small in view of the enormous space advantage over breadth-first search. In this sense iterative deepening combines the best properties of breadth-first search (optimality guarantee) and depth-first search (space economy), and it is therefore in practice often the best choice among the basic search methods.

Let us also consider bidirectional search (Exercises 11.10–12). In cases when it is applicable (goal node known) it may result in considerable savings. Assume a search graph with uniform branching $b$ in both directions, and the bidirectional search is realized as breadth-first search in both directions. Let a shortest solution path have length $d$, so the bidirectional search will stop when both breadth-first searches meet, that is when they both get to half-way between the start and the goal node. That is when each of them has progressed to depth about $d/2$ from their corresponding ends. The complexity of each of them is thus roughly $b^{d/2}$. Under these favourable circumstances bidirectional search succeeds to find a solution of length $d$ needing approximately equal resources as breadth-first search would need to solve a simpler problem of length $d/2$. Table 11.1 summarizes the comparison of the basic search techniques.

The basic search techniques do not do anything clever about the combinatorial explosion. They treat all the candidates as equally promising, and do not use any problem-specific information to guide the search in a more promising direction. They are *uninformed* in this sense. Therefore, basic search techniques are not sufficient for solving large-scale problems. For such problems, problem-specific information has to be used to guide the search. Such guiding information is called *heuristic*. Algorithms that use heuristics perform *heuristic search*. The next chapter presents such a search method.

**Table 11.1** Approximate complexities of the basic search techniques. $b$ is the branching factor, $d$ is the shortest solution length, $d_{max}$ is the depth limit for depth-first search, $d \leqslant d_{max}$.

|  | Time | Space | Shortest solution guaranteed |
|---|---|---|---|
| Breadth-first | $b^d$ | $b^d$ | yes |
| Depth-first | $b^{d_{max}}$ | $d_{max}$ | no |
| Iterative deepening | $b^d$ | $d$ | yes |
| Bidirectional, if applicable | $b^{d/2}$ | $b^{d/2}$ | yes |

## Summary

- *State space* is a formalism for representing problems.
- State space is a directed graph whose nodes correspond to problem situations and arcs to possible moves. A particular problem is defined by a *start node* and a *goal condition*. A solution of the problem then corresponds to a path in the graph. Thus problem solving is reduced to searching for a path in a graph.
- Optimization problems can be modelled by attaching costs to the arcs of a state space.
- Three basic search strategies that systematically explore a state space are *depth first*, *breadth first* and *iterative deepening*.
- The depth-first search is easiest to program, but is susceptible to cycling. Two simple methods to prevent cycling are: limit the depth of search; test for repeated nodes.
- Implementation of the breadth-first strategy is more complicated as it requires maintaining the set of candidates. This can be most easily represented as a list of lists.
- The breadth-first search always finds a shortest solution path first, but this is not the case with the depth-first strategy.
- Breadth-first search requires more space than depth-first search. In practice, space is often the critical limitation.
- Depth-first iterative deepening combines the desirable properties of depth-first and breadth-first search.
- In the case of large state spaces there is the danger of *combinatorial explosion*. The basic search strategies are poor tools for combating this difficulty. Heuristic guidance is required in such cases.
- Concepts introduced in this chapter are:

  state space
  start node, goal condition, solution path
  search strategy
  depth-first search
  breadth-first search
  iterative deepening search
  bidirectional search
  heuristic search

# References

The basic search strategies are described in any general text on artificial intelligence, for example Russell and Norvig (2010). Kowalski (1980) showed how logic can be used for implementing these principles. Korf (1985) analysed the comparative advantages of iterative deepening.

Korf, R.E. (1985) Depth-first iterative deepening: an optimal admissible tree search. *Artificial Intelligence* **27**: 97–109.

Kowalski, R. (1980) *Logic for Problem Solving*. North-Holland.

Russell, S. and Norvig, P. (2010) *Artificial Intelligence: A Modern Approach*, 3rd edn. Prentice Hall.

# Chapter 12

# Heuristic Search and the A\* Algorithm

Graph searching in problem solving typically leads to the problem of combinatorial complexity due to the proliferation of alternatives. Heuristic search aspires to fight this problem efficiently. One way of using heuristic information about a problem is to compute numerical *heuristic estimates* for the nodes in the state space. Such an estimate of a node indicates how promising a node is with respect to reaching a goal node. The idea is to continue the search always from the most promising node in the candidate set. The best-first search programs of this chapter are based on this principle.

## 12.1  Best-first search

A best-first search program can be derived as a refinement of a breadth-first search program. The best-first search also starts at the start node and maintains the set of candidate paths. The breadth-first search always chooses for expansion a shortest candidate path (that is, shallowest tip nodes of the search). The best-first search refines this principle by computing a heuristic estimate for each candidate and chooses for expansion the best candidate according to this estimate.

We will from now on assume that a cost function is defined for the arcs of the state space. So $c(n,n')$ is the cost of moving from a node $n$ to its successor $n'$ in the state space.

Let the heuristic estimator be a function $f$, such that for each node $n$ of the space, $f(n)$ estimates the 'difficulty' of $n$. Accordingly, the most promising current candidate node is the one that minimizes $f$. We will use here a specially constructed function $f$ which leads to the well-known A\* algorithm. $f(n)$ will be constructed so as to estimate the cost of a best solution path from the start node, $s$, to a goal node, under the constraint that this path goes through $n$. Let us suppose that there is such a path and that a goal node that minimizes its cost is $t$. Then the estimate $f(n)$ can be constructed as the sum of two terms, as illustrated in Figure 12.1:

$$f(n) = g(n) + h(n)$$

$g(n)$ is an estimate of the cost of an optimal path from $s$ to $n$; $h(n)$ is an estimate of the cost of an optimal path from $n$ to $t$.

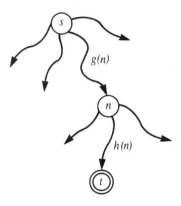

**Figure 12.1** Construction of a heuristic estimate $f(n)$ of the cost of the cheapest path from $s$ to $t$ via $n$: $f(n) = g(n) + h(n)$.

When a node $n$ is encountered by the search process we have the following situation: a path from $s$ to $n$ must have already been found, and its cost can be computed as the sum of the arc costs on the path. This path is not necessarily an optimal path from $s$ to $n$ (there may be a better path from $s$ to $n$, not yet found by the search), but its cost can serve as an estimate $g(n)$ of the minimal cost from $s$ to $n$. The other term, $h(n)$, is more problematic because the 'world' between $n$ and $t$ has not been explored by the search until this point. Therefore, $h(n)$ is typically a heuristic guess, based on the algorithm's general knowledge about the particular problem. As $h$ depends on the problem domain there is no universal method for constructing $h$. Concrete examples of how such a heuristic guess can be made will be shown later. Let us assume for now that a function $h$ is given, and concentrate on details of our best-first program.

We can imagine the best-first search to work as follows. The search process consists of a number of competing subprocesses, each of them exploring its own alternative; that is, exploring its own subtree. Subtrees have subtrees: these are explored by subprocesses of subprocesses, etc. Among all these competing processes, only one is active at each time: the one that deals with the currently most promising alternative; that is, the alternative with the lowest $f$-value. The remaining processes have to wait until the current $f$-estimates change so that some other alternative becomes more promising. Then the activity is switched to this alternative. We can imagine this activate–deactivate mechanism to work as follows: the process working on the currently top-priority alternative is given some budget and the process is active until this budget is exhausted. During this activity, the process keeps expanding its subtree and reports a solution if a goal node was encountered. The budget for this run is defined by the heuristic estimate of the closest competing alternative.

Figure 12.2 shows an example of such behaviour. Given a map, the task is to find the shortest route between the start city $s$ and the goal city $t$. In estimating the cost of the remaining route distance from a city $X$ to the goal we simply use the straight-line distance denoted by $dist(X, t)$. So:

$$f(X) = g(X) + h(X) = g(X) + dist(X, t)$$

(a)

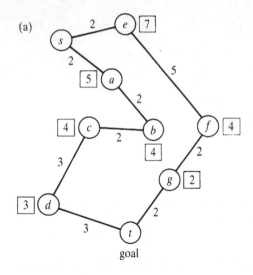

(b)

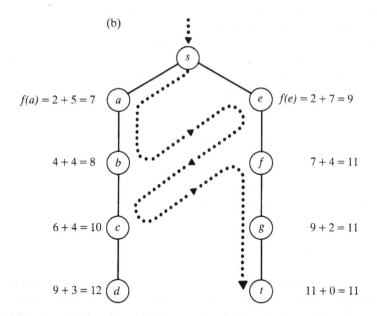

$f(a) = 2 + 5 = 7$     a          e     $f(e) = 2 + 7 = 9$

$4 + 4 = 8$     b          f     $7 + 4 = 11$

$6 + 4 = 10$     c          g     $9 + 2 = 11$

$9 + 3 = 12$     d          t     $11 + 0 = 11$

**Figure 12.2** Finding the shortest route from s to t in a map. (a) The map with links labelled by their lengths; the numbers in the boxes are straight-line distances to t. (b) The order in which the map is explored by a best-first search. Heuristic estimates are based on straight-line distances. The dotted line indicates the switching of activity between alternate paths. The line shows the ordering of nodes according to their f-values; that is, the order in which the nodes are *expanded* (not the order in which they are generated).

In this example, we can imagine the best-first search as consisting of two processes, each of them exploring one of the two alternative paths: Process 1 the path via $a$, Process 2 the path via $e$. Figure 12.2b shows how the activity switches between these two processes. In initial stages, Process 1 is more active because $f$-values along its path are lower than along the other path. At the moment that Process 1 is at $c$ and Process 2 still at $e$, the situation changes. The evaluations of the competing nodes $c$ and $e$ are:

$$f(c) = g(c) + h(c) = 6 + 4 = 10$$

$$f(e) = g(e) + h(e) = 2 + 7 = 9$$

So $f(e) < f(c)$, and now Process 2 proceeds to $f$ and Process 1 waits. Here, however,

$$f(f) = 7 + 4 = 11$$

$$f(c) = 10$$

Now $f(c) < f(f)$, therefore Process 2 is stopped and Process 1 is allowed to proceed, but only to $d$ when $f(d) = 12 > 11$. Process 2, invoked at this point, now runs smoothly up to the goal $t$.

The search thus outlined, starting with the start node, keeps generating new successor nodes, always progressing in the most promising direction according to the $f$-values. During this process, a search tree is generated whose root is the start node of the search. Our best-first search program will thus keep expanding this search tree until a solution is found. This tree will be represented in the program by terms of two forms:

(1) l( N, F/G) represents a single node tree (a leaf); N is a node in the state space, G is $g(N)$ (cost of the path found from the start node to N); F is $f(N) = G + h(N)$.

(2) t( N, F/G, Subs) represents a tree with non-empty subtrees; N is the root of the tree, **Subs** is a list of its subtrees; G is $g(N)$; F is the *updated* $f$-value of N – that is, the $f$-value of the most promising successor of N; the list **Subs** is ordered according to increasing $f$-values of the subtrees. The first element of **Subs** is the most promising subtree.

For example, consider the search in Figure 12.2 again. At the moment that the node $s$ has been expanded, the search tree consists of three nodes: the root $s$ and its children, $a$ and $e$. In our program this search tree will be represented by the term:

t( s, 7/0, [l(a,7/2), l(e,9/2)] )

The $f$-value of the root $s$ is equal to 7, that is the $f$-value of the root's most promising successor $a$. The search tree is now expanded by expanding the most promising subtree $a$. The closest competitor to $a$ is $e$ whose $f$-value is 9. Therefore, $a$ is allowed to expand as long as the $f$-value of $a$ does not exceed 9. Thus, the nodes $b$ and $c$ are generated. $f(c) = 10$, so the bound for expansion has been exceeded and alternative $a$ is no longer allowed to grow. At this moment, the search tree is:

t( s, 9/0, [l(e,9/2), t(a,10/2, [t(b,10/4, [l(c,10/6)] ) ] ) ] )

Notice that now the $f$-value of node $a$ is 10 while that of node $s$ is 9. They have been updated because new nodes, $b$ and $c$, have been generated. Now the most promising successor of $s$ is $e$, whose $f$-value is 9.

The updating of the $f$-values is necessary to enable the program to recognize the most promising subtree at each level of the search tree (that is, the tree that contains the most promising tip node). This modification of $f$-estimates leads, in fact, to a generalization of the definition of $f$. The generalization extends the definition of the function $f$ from nodes to trees. For a single node tree (a leaf), $n$, we have the original definition:

$$f(n) = g(n) + h(n)$$

For a tree, $T$, whose root is $n$, and $n$'s subtrees are $S_1$, $S_2$, etc.,

$$f(T) = \min_i f(S_i)$$

A best-first program along these lines is shown as Figure 12.3.

The key procedure is **expand**, which has six arguments illustrated in Figure 12.4:

**expand( P, Tree, Bound, Tree1, Solved, Solution)**

It expands a current (sub)tree **Tree** as long as the $f$-value of this tree remains less or equal to **Bound**. The arguments of **expand** are:

| | |
|---|---|
| **P** | Path between the start node and **Tree**. |
| **Tree** | Current search (sub)tree. |
| **Bound** | $f$-limit for expansion of **Tree**. |
| **Tree1** | **Tree** expanded within **Bound**; consequently, the $f$-value of **Tree1** is greater than **Bound** (unless a goal node has been found during the expansion). |
| **Solved** | Indicator whose value is 'yes', 'no' or 'never'; these values indicate whether a goal node has been found during expansion of **Tree**. |
| **Solution** | A solution path from the start node 'through **Tree1**' to a goal node within **Bound** (if such a goal node exists). |

**P**, **Tree** and **Bound** are 'input' parameters to **expand**; that is, they are already instantiated whenever **expand** is called. **expand** produces three kinds of results, which is indicated by the value of the argument **Solved** as follows:

(1) **Solved = yes.**
 **Solution** = a solution path found by expanding **Tree** within **Bound**.
 **Tree1** = uninstantiated.

(2) **Solved = no.**
 **Tree1** = **Tree** expanded so that its $f$-value exceeds **Bound** (Figure 12.4 illustrates)
 **Solution** = uninstantiated.

(3) **Solved = never.**
 **Tree1** and **Solution** = uninstantiated.

The last case indicates that **Tree** is a 'dead' alternative and should never be given another chance by reactivating its exploration. This case arises when the $f$-value of **Tree** is less or equal to **Bound**, but the tree cannot grow because no leaf in it has any successor at all, or such a successor would create a cycle.

Some clauses about **expand** deserve explanation. The clause that deals with the most complicated case when **Tree** has subtrees – that is,

**Tree = t( N, F/G, [T | Ts] )**

% bestfirst( Start, Solution): Solution is a path from Start to a goal

**bestfirst( Start, Solution)** :-
  expand( [ ], l( **Start**, 0/0), 9999, _, **yes**, **Solution**).      % Assume 9999 is > any f-value

% expand( Path, Tree, Bound, Tree1, Solved, Solution):
%    Path is path between start node of search and subtree Tree,
%    Tree1 is Tree expanded within Bound,
%    if goal found then Solution is solution path and Solved = yes

% Case 1: goal leaf-node, construct a solution path

**expand( P, l( N, _), _, _, yes, [N | P] )** :-
  **goal(N)**.

% Case 2: leaf-node, f-value less than Bound
% Generate successors and expand them within Bound

**expand( P, l(N, F/G), Bound, Tree1, Solved, Sol)** :-
  **F =< Bound**,
  ( **bagof( M/C, ( s(N, M, C), \+ member(M, P) ), Succ)**,
    **!**,                                % Node N has successors
    **succlist( G, Succ, Ts)**,           % Make subtrees Ts
    **bestf( Ts, F1)**,                   % f-value of best successor
    **expand( P, t(N, F1/G, Ts), Bound, Tree1, Solved, Sol)**
    **;**
    **Solved = never**                    % N has no successors – dead end
  ).

% Case 3: non-leaf, f-value less than Bound
% Expand the most promising subtree; depending on
% results, procedure continue will decide how to proceed

**expand( P, t(N, F/G, [T | Ts]), Bound, Tree1, Solved, Sol)** :-
  **F =< Bound**,
  **bestf( Ts, BF), min( Bound, BF, Bound1)**,        % Bound1 = min( Bound, BF)
  **expand( [N | P], T, Bound1, T1, Solved1, Sol)**,
  **continue( P, t(N, F/G, [T1 | Ts]), Bound, Tree1, Solved1, Solved, Sol)**.

% Case 4: non-leaf with empty subtrees
% This is a dead end which will never be solved

**expand( _, t(_, _, [ ]), _, _, never, _)** :- **!**.

% Case 5: value greater than Bound
% Tree may not grow

**expand( _, Tree, Bound, Tree, no, _)** :-
  **f( Tree, F), F > Bound**.

% continue( Path, Tree, Bound, NewTree, SubtreeSolved, TreeSolved, Solution)

**continue( _, _, _, _, yes, yes, Sol)**.

**continue( P, t(N, F/G, [T1 | Ts]), Bound, Tree1, no, Solved, Sol)** :-
  **insert( T1, Ts, NTs)**,
  **bestf( NTs, F1)**,
  **expand( P, t(N, F1/G, NTs), Bound, Tree1, Solved, Sol)**.

**Figure 12.3** An implementation of the A* algorithm.

**Figure 12.3** *Contd*

```
continue( P, t(N, F/G, [_ | Ts]), Bound, Tree1, never, Solved, Sol) :-
    bestf( Ts, F1),
    expand( P, t(N, F1/G, Ts), Bound, Tree1, Solved, Sol).

% succlist( G0, [Node1/Cost1, ...], [l(BestNode, BestF/G), ...] ):
%    make list of search leaves ordered by their f-values

succlist( _, [], [] ).

succlist( G0, [N/C | NCs], Ts) :-
    G is G0 + C,
    h( N, H),                                    % Heuristic term h(N)
    F is G + H,
    succlist( G0, NCs, Ts1),
    insert( l(N, F/G), Ts1, Ts).

% Insert T into list of trees Ts preserving order with respect to f-values

insert( T, Ts, [T | Ts] ) :-
    f( T, F), bestf( Ts, F1),
    F =< F1, !.

insert( T, [T1 | Ts], [T1 | Ts1] ) :-
    insert( T, Ts, Ts1).

% Extract f-value

f( l(_ , F/_), F).                               % f-value of a leaf

f( t(_ , F/_, _), F).                            % f-value of a tree

bestf( [T | _], F) :-                            % Best f-value of a list of trees
    f( T, F).

bestf( [], 9999).                                % No trees: bad f-value
```

says the following. First, the most promising subtree, T, is expanded. This expansion is not given the bound **Bound**, but possibly some lower value, depending on the *f*-values of the other competing subtrees, **Ts**. This ensures that the currently growing subtree is always the most promising subtree. The expansion process then switches between the subtrees according to their *f*-values. After the best candidate has been expanded, an auxiliary procedure **continue** decides what to do next; this depends on the type of result produced by this expansion. If a solution was found then this is returned, otherwise expansion continues.

The clause that deals with the case

Tree = l( N, F/G)

generates successor nodes of N together with the costs of the arcs between N and successor nodes. Procedure **succlist** makes a list of subtrees from these successor nodes, also computing their *g*-values and *f*-values as shown in Figure 12.5. The resulting tree is then further expanded as far as **Bound** permits. If, on the other hand, there were no successors, then this leaf is abandoned for ever by instantiating **Solved** = 'never'.

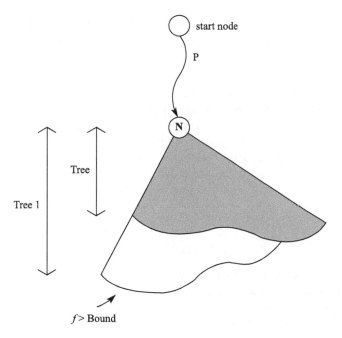

**Figure 12.4** The **expand** relation: expanding **Tree** until the $f$-value exceeds **Bound** results in **Tree1**.

Other relations are:

s( N, M, C)   M is a successor node of N in the state space; C is the cost of the arc from N to M.

h( N, H)   H is a heuristic estimate of the cost of the best path from node N to a goal node.

The program also uses the predicates **member/2** and **min/3**, assuming their usual definitions.

Application of this best-first search program to some example problems will be shown in the next section. But first some general, concluding comments on this program. It is a variation of a heuristic algorithm known in the literature as the A* algorithm (see references at the end of the chapter). A* has attracted a great

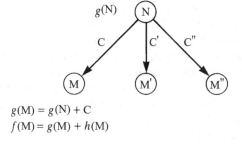

$g(M) = g(N) + C$
$f(M) = g(M) + h(M)$

**Figure 12.5** Relation between the $g$-value of node N, and the $f$- and $g$-values of its children in the search space.

deal of attention. It is one of the fundamental algorithms of the field of artificial intelligence, and probably the most famous. We will mention here an important result from the mathematical analysis of A*:

> A search algorithm is said to be *admissible* if it always produces an optimal solution (that is, a minimum-cost path) provided that a solution exists at all. Our implementation, which produces all solutions through backtracking, can be considered admissible if the *first* solution found is optimal. Let, for each node $n$ in the state space, $h^*(n)$ denote the cost of an optimal path from $n$ to a goal node. A theorem about the admissibility of A* says: an A* algorithm that uses a heuristic function $h$ such that for all nodes $n$ in the state space
>
> $$h(n) \leq h^*(n)$$
>
> is admissible.

This result is of great practical value. Even if we do not know the exact value of $h^*$ we just have to find a lower bound of $h^*$ and use it as $h$ in A*. This is sufficient guarantee that A* will produce an optimal solution.

There is a trivial lower bound, namely:

$h(n) = 0$, for all $n$ in the state space

This indeed guarantees admissibility. The disadvantage of $h = 0$ is, however, that it has no heuristic power and does not provide any guidance for the search. A* using $h = 0$ behaves similarly to the breadth-first search. It in fact reduces to the breadth-first search in the case that the arc-cost function $c(n, n') = 1$ for all arcs $(n, n')$ in the state space. The lack of heuristic power results in high complexity. We would therefore like to have $h$, which is a lower bound of $h^*$ (to ensure admissibility), and which is also as close as possible to $h^*$ (to ensure efficiency). Ideally, if we knew $h^*$, we would use $h^*$ itself: A* using $h^*$ finds an optimal solution directly, without any backtracking at all.

An important detail should be mentioned about the program of Figure 12.3. This program does avoid cyclic paths by checking whether a new node appears earlier on the same path. However, the program does not check whether a new node has been reached previously by some alternative path. This can lead to very significant inefficiency. The subtree rooted at this node will possibly be re-generated for each alternative path by which this node has been reached. Depending on the shape of state space, the number of alternative paths to the same node may grow exponentially with the depth of the node. This may result in intolerable amount of unnecessary repeated work. A common solution to avoid this is roughly as follows. When a new node is generated during search, it is checked not only whether a cycle has appeared, but also whether the same node has appeared anywhere else in the search graph so far. If yes, then the $g$ values of both copies of the node are compared. If the new copy's $g$ value is greater, then this is a clearly inferior alternative and it is immediately abandoned. If the new $g$ is lower, then the new copy of the node is retained for further exploration.

A terminological comment regarding A* is in order to clarify a possible confusion. In the literature, A* is sometimes defined so that the definition of A* already includes the property h ≤ h* from the admissibility theorem. A*, when so defined, is of course automatically admissible.

## EXERCISES

**12.1** Define the problem-specific relations **s**, **goal** and **h** for the route-finding problem of Figure 12.2. Inspect the behaviour of our A* program on this problem.

**12.2** The following statement resembles the admissibility theorem: 'For every search problem, if A* finds an optimal solution then $h(n) \leq h^*(n)$ for all nodes $n$ in the state space.' Is this correct?

**12.3** Let $h_1$, $h_2$ and $h_3$ be three admissible heuristic functions ($h_i \leq h^*$) alternatively used by A* on the same state space. Combine these three functions into another heuristic function $h$ which will also be admissible and guide the search at least as well as any of the three functions $h_i$ alone.

**12.4** A mobile robot moves in the $x$–$y$ plane among obstacles. All the obstacles are rectangles aligned with the $x$ and $y$ axes. The robot can only move in the directions $x$ and $y$, and is so small that it can be approximated by a point. The robot has to plan collision-free paths between its current position to some given goal position. The robot aims at minimizing the path length and the changes of the direction of movement (let the cost of one change of direction be equal to one unit of length travelled). The robot uses the A* algorithm to find optimal paths. Define the predicates **s( State,NewState, Cost)** and **h( State,H)** (preferably admissible) to be used by the A* program for this search problem. Assume that the goal position for the robot is defined by the predicate **goal( Xg/Yg)** where **Xg** and **Yg** are the $x$ and $y$ coordinates of the goal point. The obstacles are represented by the predicate

    **obstacle( Xmin/Ymin, Xmax/Ymax)**

where **Xmin/Ymin** is the bottom left corner of the obstacle, and **Xmax/Ymax** is its top right corner.

## 12.2 Best-first search applied to the eight puzzle

If we want to apply the best-first search program of Figure 12.3 to some particular problem we have to add problem-specific relations. These relations define the particular problem ('rules of the game') and also convey heuristic information about how to solve that problem. This heuristic information is supplied in the form of a heuristic function.

Problem-specific predicates are:

    **s( Node, Node1, Cost)**

This is true if there is an arc, costing **Cost**, between **Node** and **Node1**, in the state space.

    **goal( Node)**

is true if **Node** is a goal node in the state space.

    h( **Node, H**)

H is a heuristic estimate of the cost of a cheapest path from **Node** to a goal node.

In this and the following sections we will define these relations for two example problem domains: the eight puzzle (described in Section 11.1) and a task-scheduling problem.

Problem-specific relations for the eight puzzle are shown in Figure 12.6. A node in the state space is some configuration of the tiles on the board. In the program, this is represented by a list of the current positions of the tiles. Each position is specified by a pair of coordinates: X/Y. The order of items in the list is as follows:

(1) the current position of the empty square,

(2) the current position of tile 1,

(3) the current position of tile 2,

    . . .

The goal situation (see Figure 11.3) is defined by the clause:

    **goal**([2/2,1/3,2/3,3/3,3/2,3/1,2/1,1/1,1/2] ).

An auxiliary relation is:

    **mandist( S1, S2, D)**

D is the 'Manhattan distance' between squares S1 and S2; that is, the distance between S1 and S2 in the horizontal direction plus the distance between S1 and S2 in the vertical direction.

We want to minimize the *length* of solutions. Therefore, we define the cost of all the arcs in the state space to equal 1. In the program of Figure 12.6, three example starting positions from Figure 12.7 are also defined.

The heuristic function, *h*, is programmed as:

    **h( Pos, H)**

Pos is a board position; H is a combination of two measures:

(1) **totdist**: the 'total distance' of the eight tiles in **Pos** from their 'home squares'. For example, in the starting position of the puzzle in Figure 12.7(a), **totdist** = 4.

(2) **seq**: the 'sequence score' that measures the degree to which the tiles are already ordered in the current position with respect to the order required in the goal configuration. **seq** is computed as the sum of scores for each tile according to the following rules:

    – a tile in the centre scores 1;

    – a tile on a non-central square scores 0 if the tile is, in the clockwise direction, followed by its proper successor;

    – such a tile scores 2 if it is not followed by its proper successor.

For example, for the starting position of the puzzle in Figure 12.7(a), **seq** = 6.

/* Problem-specific procedures for the eight puzzle

Current situation is represented as a list of positions of the tiles, with first item in the list corresponding to the empty square.

Example:

| | | | | This position is represented by: |
|---|---|---|---|---|

```
3   | 1  2  3 |
2   | 8     4 |          [2/2, 1/3, 2/3, 3/3, 3/2, 3/1, 2/1, 1/1, 1/2]
1   | 7  6  5 |
      1  2  3
```

'Empty' can move to any of its neighbours, which means that 'empty' and its neighbour interchange their positions.
*/

% s( Node, SuccessorNode, Cost)

```
s( [Empty | Tiles], [Tile | Tiles1], 1)  :-        % All arc costs are 1
    swap( Empty, Tile, Tiles, Tiles1).             % Swap Empty and Tile in Tiles

swap( Empty, Tile, [Tile | Ts], [Empty | Ts] )  :-
    mandist( Empty, Tile, 1).                      % Manhattan distance = 1

swap( Empty, Tile, [T1 | Ts], [T1 | Ts1] )  :-
    swap( Empty, Tile, Ts, Ts1).

mandist( X/Y, X1/Y1, D)  :-                        % D is Manh. dist. between two squares
    dif( X, X1, Dx),
    dif( Y, Y1, Dy),
    D is Dx + Dy.

dif( A, B, D)  :-                                  % D is | A-B |
    D is A-B, D >= 0, !
    ;
    D is B-A.
```

% Heuristic estimate h is the sum of distances of each tile
% from its 'home' square plus 3 times 'sequence' score

```
h( [Empty | Tiles], H)  :-
    goal( [Empty1 | GoalSquares] ),
    totdist( Tiles, GoalSquares, D),               % Total distance from home squares
    seq( Tiles, S),                                % Sequence score
    H is D + 3*S.

totdist( [], [], 0).

totdist( [Tile | Tiles], [Square | Squares], D)  :-
    mandist( Tile, Square, D1),
    totdist( Tiles, Squares, D2),
    D is D1 + D2.
```

% seq( TilePositions, Score): sequence score

**Figure 12.6** Problem-specific predicates for the eight puzzle, to be used with the best-first search of Figure 12.3.

**Figure 12.6** *Contd*

```
seq( [First | OtherTiles], S) :-
   seq( [First | OtherTiles ], First, S).

seq( [Tile1, Tile2 | Tiles], First, S) :-
   score( Tile1, Tile2, S1),
   seq( [Tile2 | Tiles], First, S2),
   S is S1 + S2.

seq( [Last], First, S) :-
   score( Last, First, S).

score( 2/2, _, 1) :- !.                         % Tile in centre scores 1

score( 1/3, 2/3, 0) :- !.                       % Proper successor scores 0
score( 2/3, 3/3, 0) :- !.
score( 3/3, 3/2, 0) :- !.
score( 3/2, 3/1, 0) :- !.
score( 3/1, 2/1, 0) :- !.
score( 2/1, 1/1, 0) :- !.
score( 1/1, 1/2, 0) :- !.
score( 1/2, 1/3, 0) :- !.

score( _, _, 2).                                % Tiles out of sequence score 2

goal( [2/2,1/3,2/3,3/3,3/2,3/1,2/1,1/1,1/2] ).  % Goal squares for tiles

% Display a solution path as a list of board positions

showsol( [] ).

showsol( [P | L] ) :-
   showsol( L),
   nl, write( '---'),
   showpos( P).

% Display a board position

showpos( [S0,S1,S2,S3,S4,S5,S6,S7,S8] ) :-
   member( Y, [3,2,1] ),                        % Order of Y-coordinates
   nl, member( X, [1,2,3] ),                    % Order of X-coordinates
   member( Tile-X/Y,                            % Tile on square X/Y
          [' '-S0,1-S1,2-S2,3-S3,4-S4,5-S5,6-S6,7-S7,8-S8] ),
   write( Tile),
   fail                                         % Backtrack to next square
   ;
   true.                                        % All squares done

% Starting positions for some puzzles

start1( [2/2,1/3,3/2,2/3,3/3,3/1,2/1,1/1,1/2] ).  % Requires 4 steps

start2( [2/1,1/2,1/3,3/3,3/2,2/3,1/2,2/1,1/2,2/3] ).  % Requires 5 steps

start3( [2/2,2/3,1/3,3/1,1/2,2/1,3/3,1/1,3/2] ).  % Requires 18 steps

% An example query: ?- start1( Pos), bestfirst( Pos, Sol), showsol( Sol).
```

| 1 | 3 | 4 |
|---|---|---|
| 8 |   | 2 |
| 7 | 6 | 5 |

(a)

| 2 | 8 | 3 |
|---|---|---|
| 1 | 6 | 4 |
| 7 |   | 5 |

(b)

| 2 | 1 | 6 |
|---|---|---|
| 4 |   | 8 |
| 7 | 5 | 3 |

(c)

**Figure 12.7** Three starting positions for the eight puzzle: (a) requires four steps; (b) requires five steps; (c) requires 18 steps.

The heuristic estimate, H, is computed as:

$$H = \textbf{totdist} + 3 * \textbf{seq}$$

This heuristic function works well in the sense that it very efficiently directs the search toward the goal. For example, when solving the puzzles of Figure 12.7(a) and (b), no node outside the shortest solution path is ever expanded before the first solution is found. This means that the shortest solutions are found directly in these cases without any backtracking. Even the difficult puzzle of Figure 12.7(c) is solved almost directly. A drawback of this heuristic is, however, that it is not admissible: it does not guarantee that the shortest solution path will always be found before any longer solution. The $h$ function used does not satisfy the admissibility condition: $h \leqslant h^*$ for all the nodes. For example, for the initial position in Figure 12.7(a),

$$h = 4 + 3 * 6 = 22, h^* = 4$$

On the other hand, the 'total distance' measure itself is admissible: for all positions:

$$\textbf{totdist} \leq h^*$$

This inequality can be easily proved by the following argument: if we relaxed the problem by allowing the tiles to climb on top of each other, then each tile could travel to its home square along a trajectory whose length is exactly the Manhattan distance between the tile's initial square and its home square. So the optimal solution in the relaxed puzzle would be exactly of length **totdist**. In the original problem, however, there is interaction between the tiles and they have to avoid each other. This can prevent the tiles from moving along the shortest trajectories, which ensues our optimal solution's length be equal or greater than **totdist**. This means that A* using heuristic function $h = \textbf{totdist}$ is guaranteed to find shortest solutions for eight puzzles. This property is so attractive that **totdist** alone is indeed usually employed when experimenting with A*-like algorithms in the eight or fifteen puzzle domains.

# EXERCISE

**12.5** Modify the best-first search program of Figure 12.3 to count the number of nodes generated in the search. One easy way is to keep the current number of nodes asserted as a fact, and update it by **retract** and **assert** whenever new nodes are generated. Experiment with various heuristic functions for the eight puzzle with respect to their heuristic power, which is reflected in the number of nodes generated.

## 12.3 Best-first search applied to scheduling

Let us consider the following task-scheduling problem. We are given a set of *tasks*, $t_1$, $t_2$, ..., with their execution times $D_1$, $D_2$, ... respectively. The tasks are to be executed on a set of $m$ identical *processors*. Any task can be executed on any processor, but each processor can only execute one task at a time. There is a precedence relation between tasks which tells what tasks, if any, have to be completed before some other task can be started. The scheduling problem is to assign tasks to processors so that the precedence relation is not violated and that all the tasks together are processed in the shortest possible time. The time that the last task in a schedule is completed is called the *finishing time* of the schedule. We want to minimize the finishing time over all permissible schedules.

Figure 12.8 shows such a task-scheduling problem and two permissible schedules, one of which is optimal. This example shows an interesting property of optimal schedules; namely, that they may include 'idle time' for processors. In the optimal schedule of Figure 12.8, processor 2 after having executed task $t_2$ waits for two time units although it could start executing task $t_7$.

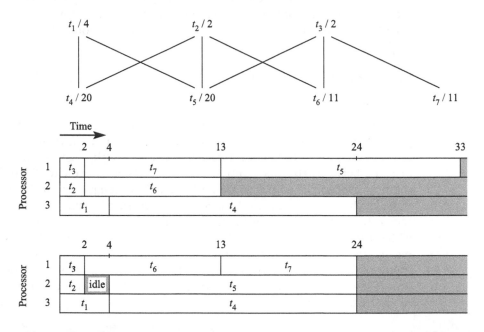

**Figure 12.8** A task-scheduling problem with seven tasks and three processors. The top part of the diagram shows the task precedence relation and the duration of the tasks. Task $t_5$, for example, requires 20 time units, and its execution can only start after three other tasks, $t_1$, $t_2$ and $t_3$, have been completed. Two permissible schedules are shown; an optimal one with the finishing time 24, and a suboptimal one with the finishing time 33. In this problem any optimal schedule has to include idle time. Adapted from Coffman/Denning, *Operating Systems Theory*, © 1973, p. 86, Prentice Hall, Englewood Cliffs, New Jersey.

One way to construct a schedule is roughly as follows. We start with the empty schedule (with void time slots for each processor) and gradually insert tasks one by one into the schedule until all the tasks have been inserted. Usually there are alternatives at any such insertion step because there are several candidate tasks waiting to be processed. Therefore, the scheduling problem is one of search. Accordingly, we can formulate the scheduling problem as a state-space search problem as follows:

- states are partial schedules;
- a successor state of some partial schedule is obtained by adding a not yet scheduled task to this schedule; another possibility is to leave a processor that has completed its current task idle;
- the start state is the empty schedule;
- any schedule that includes all the tasks in the problem is a goal state;
- the cost of a solution (which is to be minimized) is the finishing time of a goal schedule;
- accordingly, the cost of a transition between two (partial) schedules whose finishing times are $F_1$ and $F_2$ respectively is the difference $F_2 - F_1$.

Some refinements are needed to this rough scenario. First, we decide to fill the schedule according to increasing times so that tasks are inserted into the schedule from left to right. Also, each time a task is added, the precedence constraint has to be checked. Further, there is no point in leaving a processor idle indefinitely if there are still some candidate tasks waiting. So we decide to leave a processor idle only until some other processor finishes its current task, and then consider again assigning a task to it.

Now let us decide on the representation of problem situations – that is, partial schedules. We need the following information:

(1) list of waiting tasks and their execution times,

(2) current engagements of the processors;

We will also add for convenience:

(3) the finishing time of the (partial) schedule; that is, the latest end-time of the current engagements of the processors.

The list of waiting tasks and their execution times will be represented in the program as a list of the form:

[ Task1/D1, Task2/D2, . . . ]

The current engagements of the processors will be represented by a list of tasks currently being processed; that is, pairs of the form:

**Task/FinishingTime**

There are $m$ such pairs in the list, one for each processor. We will always add a new task to a schedule at the moment that the first current execution is completed. To this end, the list of current engagements will be kept ordered according to increasing finishing times. The three components of a partial schedule (waiting tasks, current engagements and finishing time) will be combined in the program into a single expression of the form:

WaitingList * ActiveTasks * FinishingTime

In addition to this information we have the precedence constraint, which will be specified in the program as a relation:

prec( TaskX, TaskY)

Now let us consider a heuristic estimate. We will use a rather straightforward heuristic function, which will not provide a very efficient guidance to the search algorithm. The function will be admissible and will hence guarantee an optimal schedule. It should be noted, however, that a much more powerful heuristic would be needed for large scheduling problems.

Our heuristic function will be an optimistic estimate of the finishing time of a partial schedule completed with all currently waiting tasks. This optimistic estimate will be computed under the assumption that two constraints on the actual schedule be relaxed:

(1)  remove the precedence constraint;

(2)  allow (unrealistically) that a task can be executed in a distributed fashion on several processors, and that the sum of the execution times of this task over all these processors is equal to the originally specified execution time of this task on a single processor.

Let the execution times of the currently waiting tasks be $D_1, D_2, \ldots$, and the finishing times of the current processors engagements be $F_1, F_2, \ldots$. Such an optimistically estimated finishing time, *Finall*, to complete all the currently active and all the waiting tasks, is:

$$Finall = \left( \sum_i D_i + \sum_j F_j \right) \Big/ m$$

where $m$ is the number of processors. Let the finishing time of the current partial schedule be:

$$Fin = \max_j (F_j)$$

Then the heuristic estimate H (an extra time needed to complete the partial schedule with the waiting tasks) is:

if *Finall* > *Fin* then $H = Finall - Fin$ else $H = 0$

A complete program that defines the state-space relations for task scheduling as outlined above is shown in Figure 12.9. The figure also includes a specification of the particular scheduling problem of Figure 12.8. These definitions can now be used by the best-first search program of Figure 12.3. One of the optimal solutions produced by best-first search in the thus specified problem space is an optimal schedule of Figure 12.8.

/* Problem-specific relations for task scheduling

Nodes in the state space are partial schedules specified by:

[ WaitingTask1/D1, WaitingTask2/D2, ...] * [ Task1/F1, Task2/F2, ...] * FinTime

The first list specifies the waiting tasks and their durations; the second list specifies the currently executed tasks and their finishing times, ordered so that F1 ≦ F2, F2 ≦ F3 .... Fintime is the latest completion time of current engagements of the processors.

*/

% s( Node, SuccessorNode, Cost)

```
s( Tasks1 * [_/F | Active1] * Fin1, Tasks2 * Active2 * Fin2, Cost) :-
    del( Task/D, Tasks1, Tasks2),                          % Pick a waiting task
    \+ ( member( T/_, Tasks2), before( T, Task) ),         % Check precedence
    \+ ( member( T1/F1, Active1), F < F1, before( T1, Task) ),   % Active tasks too
    Time is F + D,                                         % Finishing time of activated task
    insert( Task/Time, Active1, Active2, Fin1, Fin2),
    Cost is Fin2 - Fin1.

s( Tasks * [_/F | Active1] * Fin, Tasks * Active2 * Fin, 0) :-
    insertidle( F, Active1, Active2).                      % Leave processor idle

before( T1, T2) :-                                         % Task T1 before T2
    prec( T1, T2).                                         % according to precedence

before( T1, T2) :-
    prec( T, T2),
    before( T1, T).

insert( S/A, [T/B | L], [S/A, T/B | L], F, F) :-           % Task lists are ordered
    A =< B, !.

insert( S/A, [T/B | L], [T/B | L1], F1, F2) :-
    insert( S/A, L, L1, F1, F2).

insert( S/A, [], [S/A], _, A).

insertidle( A, [T/B | L], [idle/B, T/B | L] ) :-           % Leave processor idle
    A < B, !.                                              % until first greater finishing time

insertidle( A, [T/B | L], [T/B | L1] ) :-
    insertidle( A, L, L1).

del( A, [A | L], L).                                       % Delete item from list

del( A, [B | L], [B | L1] ) :-
    del( A, L, L1).

goal( [] * _ * _).                                         % Goal state: no task waiting
```

% Heuristic estimate of a partial schedule is based on an
% optimistic estimate of the final finishing time of this
% partial schedule extended by all the remaining waiting tasks.

**Figure 12.9** Problem-specific predicates for the task-scheduling problem. The particular scheduling problem of Figure 12.8 is also defined by its precedence graph and an initial (empty) schedule as a start node of search.

**Figure 12.9** *Contd*

```
h( Tasks * Processors * Fin, H) :-
   totaltime( Tasks, Tottime),            % Total duration of waiting tasks
   sumnum( Processors, Ftime, N),         % Ftime is sum of finishing times
                                          % of processors, N is their number

   Finall is ( Tottime + Ftime)/N,
   ( Finall > Fin, !, H is Finall – Fin
     ;
     H = 0
   ).
totaltime( [ ], 0).
totaltime( [_/D | Tasks], T) :-
   totaltime( Tasks, T1),
   T is T1 + D.
sumnum( [ ], 0, 0).
sumnum( [_/T | Procs], FT, N) :-
   sumnum( Procs, FT1, N1),
   N is N1 + 1,
   FT is FT1 + T.
% A task-precedence graph
prec( t1, t4).   prec( t1, t5).   prec( t2, t4).   prec( t2, t5).
prec( t3, t5).   prec( t3, t6).   prec( t3, t7).
% A start node
start( [t1/4, t2/2, t3/2, t4/20, t5/20, t6/11, t7/11] * [idle/0, idle/0, idle/0] * 0).
% An example query: ?- start( Problem), bestfirst( Problem, Sol).
```

## PROJECT

In general, scheduling problems are known to be combinatorially difficult. Our simple heuristic function does not provide very powerful guidance. Propose other functions and experiment with them.

## Summary

- Heuristic information can be used to estimate how far a node is from a nearest goal node in the state space. In this chapter we considered the use of numerical heuristic estimates.
- The *best-first* heuristic principle guides the search process so as to always expand the node that is currently the most promising according to the heuristic estimates. The well-known A* algorithm that uses this principle was programmed in this chapter.

- To use A* for solving a concrete problem, a state space, a goal predicate and a heuristic function have to be defined. For complex problems, the difficult part is to find a good heuristic function.

- The *admissibility* theorem helps to establish whether A*, using a particular heuristic function, will always find an optimal solution.

- In this chapter best-first search was applied to the eight puzzle problem and a task-scheduling problem.

- Concepts discussed in this chapter are:

  heuristic estimates
  heuristic search
  best-first search
  algorithm A*
  admissibility of search algorithms, admissibility theorem

## References and historical notes

The best-first search program of this chapter is a variation of many similar algorithms of which A* is the most popular. Descriptions of A* can be found in general text books on artificial intelligence, such as Russell and Norvig (2010), and Nilsson (1998). Doran and Michie (1966) originated the best-first search guided by distance-to-goal estimate. The admissibility theorem was discovered by Hart, Nilsson and Raphael (1968). In the literature, the property $h \leqslant h^*$ is sometimes included in the definition of A*. An excellent and rigorous treatment of many variations of best-first search algorithms and related mathematical results is provided by Pearl (1984).

The eight puzzle was used in artificial intelligence as a test problem for studying heuristic principles by several researchers – for example, Doran and Michie (1966) and Michie and Ross (1970).

Our task-scheduling problem and its variations arise in numerous applications in which servicing of requests for resources is to be planned. Our example task-scheduling problem in Section 12.3 is borrowed from Coffman and Denning (1973).

Finding good heuristics is important and difficult, therefore the study of heuristics is one of the central themes of artificial intelligence. There are, however, also some limitations on how far we can get in the refinement of heuristics. It may appear that to solve any combinatorial problem efficiently we only have to find a powerful heuristic. However, there are problems (including many scheduling problems) for which no general heuristic exists that would guarantee both efficiency and admissibility in all cases. Many theoretical results that pertain to this limitation issue are collected in Garey and Johnson (1979).

Coffman, E.G. and Denning, P.J. (1973) *Operating Systems Theory*. Prentice Hall.

Doran, J. and Michie, D. (1966) Experiments with the graph traverser program. *Proc. Royal Society of London* **294(A)**: 235–259.

Garey, M.R. and Johnson, D.S. (1979) *Computers and Intractability*. W.H. Freeman.

Hart, P.E., Nilsson, N.J. and Raphael, B. (1968) A formal basis for the heuristic determination of minimum cost paths. *IEEE Transactions on Systems Sciences and Cybernetics* **SSC-4(2)**: 100–107.

Michie, D. and Ross, R. (1970) Experiments with the adaptive graph traverser. *Machine Intelligence* **5**: 301–308.

Nilsson, N.J. (1998) *Artificial Intelligence: A New Synthesis.* San Francisco, CA: Morgan Kaufmann Publishers.

Pearl, J. (1984) *Heuristics: Intelligent Search Strategies for Computer Problem Solving.* Addison-Wesley.

Russell, S.J. and Norvig, P. (2010) *Artificial Intelligence: A Modern Approach,* third edn. Prentice Hall.

# Best-First Search: Minimizing Time and Space

......................................................................................................................................................

......................................................................................................................................................

Typically, the time and space complexity of the A* algorithm grows exponentially with the depth of search. In practical applications, it depends on the particular circumstances which of the two resources is more critical: time or space. In many practical situations space is more critical. Several variations of the A* algorithm have been developed that save space, at the expense of time. In this chapter we will look at two space-saving techniques in the context of best-first search: IDA* (iterative deepening A*), and RBFS (recursive best-first search). In some situations, on the other hand, time is the critical resource. This happens when the problem-solver is working under  real-time circumstances. The algorithm has to produce answers quickly, at the time when they are needed by an online application, even if they are way off optimal. One of such algorithms is RTA* (real-time A*), also described in this chapter.

## 13.1   Time and space complexity of the A* algorithm

......................................................................................................................................................

Heuristic guidance in best-first search typically reduces the search to visiting only a small part of the problem space. This can be viewed as the reduction of effective branching of search tree. If the 'average' branching in the problem space is $b$, then heuristic guidance effectively results in average branching $b'$ where $b'$ is typically substantially less than $b$. This means that heuristic guidance typically reduces the search effort very significantly. In fact, the savings typically grow exponentially with the depth of search.

In spite of such a drastic reduction of search effort, the order of the complexity of A* (and our implementation of it in Figure 12.3) is still exponential in the depth of search. This holds for both time and space complexity because the algorithm maintains all the generated nodes in the memory. In practical applications, it depends on the particular circumstances which of the two resources is more critical: time or space. Perhaps, in most practical situations space is more critical. A* may use up all the available memory in a matter of minutes. After that the search practically cannot proceed although the user would find it acceptable that the algorithm would run for hours or even days. Suppose we want to construct a timetable for the whole school for the next semester that will start in a month. Then we would not mind the program running for days to produce a really good timetable. The situation is quite different if the program's decisions are needed in real time, practically immediately, for example by a robot that has to react quickly by performing appropriate actions in a changing world. Then a suboptimal action is usually better than no action at all. In such a situation the program's runtime is critical as it has to produce a decision in real time.

Several variations of the A* algorithm have been developed that save space, at the expense of time. The basic idea is similar to depth-first iterative deepening discussed in Chapter 11. Space requirements are reduced from exponential to linear in the depth of search. The price is the increase of algorithm's runtime because many nodes in the search space have to be re-generated again and again. In situations at the other extreme, when the best-first search algorithm has to produce solutions in real time, short runtimes are typically achieved by sacrificing the optimality of solutions.

In the following sections we will look at two space-saving techniques in the context of best-first search. The first of them is called IDA* (iterative deepening A*); the second one appears under the name RBFS (recursive best-first search). Then we will consider the RTA* algorithm (real-time A*) as a representative of search algorithms that minimize computation time at the expense of the quality of solutions.

## 13.2 IDA* – iterative deepening A* algorithm

IDA* is similar to depth-first iterative deepening, with the following difference. In iterative deepening, depth-first searches are performed to increasing depth limits. On each iteration the depth-first search is bounded by the current depth limit. In IDA*, however, the successive depth-first searches are bounded by the current limit in the *values* of the nodes (heuristic $f$-values of the nodes). So the basic search mechanism in IDA* is again depth-first, which has very low space complexity. IDA* can be stated as follows:

Bound := f(StartNode);
**Repeat**
    perform depth-first search starting with StartNode, subject to
        condition that a node N is expanded only if $f(N) \leq$ Bound;
    **if** this depth-first search encounters a goal node
        **then** signal 'solution found',
    **else**
        compute NewBound as the minimum of the $f$-values of
        the nodes reached just outside Bound:
            NewBound = min{ $f(N)$ | N generated by this search, $f(N) >$ Bound}
        Bound := NewBound
    **until** solution found.

To illustrate this algorithm, consider IDA* applied to the route-finding problem (Figure 12.2b; let $f(s) = 6$). IDA* proceeds as follows:

Bound $= f(s) = 6$
Perform depth-first search limited by $f \leq 6$. This search expands $s$, generating $a$
and $e$, and finds:

$f(a) = 7 >$ Bound
$f(e) = 9 >$ Bound

NewBound $= \min\{ 7, 9\} = 7$
Perform depth-first search limited by $f \leq 7$, starting with node $s$.
The nodes just outside this bound are $b$ and $e$.
NewBound $= \min \{ f(b), f(e)\} = \min\{ 8, 9\} = 8$
From now on, the bound changes as follows: 9 $(f(e))$, 10 $(f(c))$, 11 $(f(f ))$. For
each of these values, depth-first search is performed.
When depth-first search is performed with Bound $= 11$, solution is found.

This example is only intended to illustrate how IDA* works, although the example
makes the algorithm look awkward because of repeated depth-first searches.
However, in large search problems IDA*'s space economy could be very beneficial
while the overheads of repeated searches could be quite acceptable. How bad these
overheads are depends on the properties of the search space, in particular on the
properties of the evaluation function $f$. The favourable cases are those when many
nodes have equal $f$-values. In such cases each successive depth-first search explores
many new nodes, more than the number of regenerated nodes. So the overhead is
comparatively small. Unfavourable cases are those when the $f$-values tend not to be
shared among many nodes. In the extreme case each node has a different $f$-value.
Then many successive $f$-bounds are needed, and each new depth-first search will
only generate one new node whereas all the rest will be the regeneration of the
already generated (and forgotten) nodes. In such extreme cases the overheads of
IDA* are of course unacceptable.

Another property of interest of IDA* regards the admissibility. Let $f(N)$ be
defined as $g(N) + h(N)$ for all nodes N. If $h$ is admissible ($h(N) \leq h^*(N)$ for all N)
then IDA* is guaranteed to find an optimal solution.

A possible drawback of IDA* is that it does not guarantee that the nodes are
explored in the best-first order (i.e. the order of increasing $f$-values). Suppose now
that $f$ is an evaluation function not necessarily of the form $f = g + h$. If function $f$
is not monotonic then the best-first order is not guaranteed. Function $f$ is said to
be *monotonic* if its value monotonically increases along the paths in the state space.
That is: $f$ is monotonic if for all pairs of nodes N and N': if $s$(N, N') then $f$(N) $\leq$
$f$(N'). The reason for a non best-first order is that with non-monotonic $f$, the $f$-
bound may become so large that nodes with different $f$-values will be expanded for
the first time by this depth-first search. This depth-first search will keep expanding
nodes as long as they are within the $f$-bound, and will not care about the order
in which they are expanded. This may lead IDA* to find a suboptimal solution
even in cases when A*, using the same evaluation function, is guaranteed to find
an optimal solution. In principle we are always interested in best-first order because
we expect that the function $f$ reflects the quality of solutions.

One easy way of implementing IDA* in Prolog is shown in Figure 13.1. This
program largely exploits Prolog's backtracking mechanism. The $f$-bound is maintained as a fact of the form

**next_bound( Bound)**

```
% idastar( Start, Solution):
%    Perform IDA* search; Start is the start node, Solution is solution path

idastar( Start, Solution) :-
    retract( next_bound(_)), fail          % Clear next_bound
    ;
    asserta( next_bound( 0)),              % Initialize bound
    idastar0( Start, Solution).

idastar0( Start, Sol) :-
    retract( next_bound( Bound)),          % Current bound
    asserta( next_bound( 99999)),          % Initialize next bound
    f( Start, F),                          % f-value of start node
    df( [Start], F, Bound, Sol)            % Find solution; if not, change bound
    ;
    next_bound( NextBound),
    NextBound < 99999,                     % Bound finite
    idastar0( Start, Sol).                 % Try with new bound

% df( Path, F, Bound, Sol):
%    Perform depth-first search within Bound
%    Path is the path from start node so far (in reverse order)
%    F is the f-value of the current node, i.e. the head of Path

df( [N | Ns], F, Bound, [N | Ns]) :-
    F =< Bound,
    goal( N).                              % Succeed: solution found

df( [N | Ns], F, Bound, Sol) :-
    F =< Bound,                            % Node N within f-bound
    s( N, N1), \+ member( N1, Ns),         % Expand N
    f( N1, F1),
    df( [N1,N | Ns], F1, Bound, Sol).

df( _, F, Bound, _) :-
    F > Bound,                             % Beyond Bound
    update_next_bound( F),                 % Just update next bound
    fail.                                  % and fail

update_next_bound( F) :-
    next_bound( Bound),
    Bound =< F, !                          % Do not change next bound
    ;
    retract( next_bound( Bound)), !,       % Lower next bound
    asserta( next_bound( F)).
```

**Figure 13.1** An implementation of the IDA* algorithm.

which is updated through **assert** and **retract**. On each iteration, the bound for depth-first search is retrieved from this fact. Then (through **retract** and **assert** on this fact), the bound for the next iteration is initialized to 99999. That is a large value assumed greater than any possible $f$-value. The depth-first search is programmed to only allow the expanding of a node N if $f(N) \leq$ Bound. If, on the other hand,

$f(N) >$ Bound then the value $f(N)$ is compared to NextBound (stored under **next_bound(NextBound)**). If $f(N) <$ NextBound then the **next_bound** fact is updated to store $f(N)$.

## EXERCISES

**13.1** Construct an example state space and the function $f$ for which IDA* would not expand nodes in the best-first order.

**13.2** Apply the IDA* program of Figure 13.1 to the eight puzzle using the definitions of the successor relation **s/3** and **totdist/3** as in Figure 12.6. Use just total distance (**totdist/3**) as the heuristic function $h$ (to ensure admissibility). Define also the predicate **f/2** (needed by the IDA* program) so that $f(N) = g(N) + h(N)$. To enable the computation of $g(N)$, keep the $g$-value of a node explicitly as part of the representation of the node (e.g. N = G:**TilePositions**). Experiment with the eight puzzles defined in Figure 12.6. Try also the start state [1/2,3/3,3/1,1/3,3/2,1/1,2/3,2/ 1,2/2]. Compare the execution times and lengths of solutions found by A* (using heuristic function of Figure 12.6) and IDA* (using just total distance).

## 13.3 RBFS – recursive best-first search

IDA* is a valuable idea and very easy to implement, but in unfavourable situations the overheads of re-generating nodes become unacceptable. Therefore a better, although more complicated space-saving technique is the so-called RBFS ('recursive best-first search'). RBFS is very similar to our A* program of Figure 12.3 (which also is recursive in the same sense as RBFS!). The difference between our A* program and RBFS is that A* keeps in memory *all* the already generated nodes whereas RBFS only keeps the current search path and the sibling nodes along this path. When RBFS temporarily suspends the search of a subtree (because it no longer looks the best), it 'forgets' that subtree to save space. So RBFS's space complexity is (as in IDA*) only linear in the depth of search. The only thing that RBFS remembers of such an abandoned subtree is the updated $f$-value of the root of the subtree. The $f$-values are updated through backing-up the $f$-values in the same way as in the A* program. To distinguish between the 'static' evaluation function $f$ and these backed-up values, we write (for a node N):

$f(N) =$ value of node N returned by the evaluation function (always the same during search)
$F(N) =$ backed-up $f$-value (changes during search because it depends on the descendent nodes of N)

$F(N)$ is defined as follows:

$F(N) = f(N)$ if N has (never) been expanded by the search
$F(N) = \min\{ F(N_i) \mid N_i$ is a child of N$\}$

As the A* program, RBFS also explores subtrees within a given $f$-bound. The bound is determined by the $F$-values of the siblings along the current search path (the smallest *F*-value of the siblings, that is the *F*-value of the closest competitor to the current node). Suppose that a node N is currently the best node in the search tree (i.e. has the lowest *F*-value). Then N is expanded and N's children are explored up to some *f*-bound Bound. When this bound is exceeded (manifested by $F(N) >$ Bound) then all the nodes generated below N are 'forgotten'. However, the updated value $F(N)$ is retained and is used in deciding about how to continue search.

The *F*-values are not only determined by backing-up the values from a node's children, but can also be *inherited* from the node's parents. Such inheritance occurs as follows. Let there be a node N which is about to be expanded by the search. If $F(N) > f(N)$ then we know that N must have already been expanded earlier and $F(N)$ was determined from N's children, but the children have then been removed from the memory. Now suppose a child $N_i$ of N is generated again and $N_i$'s static value $f(N_i)$ is also computed again. Now $F(N_i)$ is determined as follows:

if $f(N_i) < F(N)$ **then** $F(N_i) = F(N)$ **else** $F(N_i) = f(N_i)$

This can be written shorter as:

$$F(N_i) = \max\{F(N), f(N_i)\}$$

Thus in the case $f(N_i) < F(N)$, $N_i$'s *F*-value is inherited from $N_i$'s parent N. This is justified by the following argument: when $N_i$ was generated (and removed) earlier, the value $F(N_i)$ was necessarily $\geq F(N)$. Otherwise, by the back-up rule, $F(N)$ would have been smaller.

To illustrate how RBFS works, consider the route-finding problem of Figure 12.2. Figure 13.2 shows selected snapshots of the current path (including the siblings along the path) kept in the memory. The search keeps switching (as in A*) between the alternative paths. However, when such a switch occurs, the previous path is removed from the memory to save space. In Figure 13.2, the numbers written next to the nodes are the nodes' *F*-values. At snapshot (A), node *a* is the best candidate node ($F(a) < F(e)$). Therefore the subtree below *a* is searched with Bound = 9 (i.e. $F(e)$, the closest – the only competitor). When this search reaches node *c* (snapshot B), it is found that $F(c) = 10 >$ Bound. Therefore this path is (temporarily) abandoned, the nodes *c* and *b* removed from the memory and the value $F(c) = 10$ backed-up to node *a*, so $F(a)$ becomes 10 (snapshot C). Now *e* is the best competitor ($F(e) = 9 < 10 = F(a)$), and its subtree is searched with Bound = $10 = F(a)$. This search stops at node *f* because $F(f) = 11 >$ Bound (snapshot D). Node *e* is removed, and $F(e)$ becomes 11 (snapshot E). Now the search switches to *a* again with Bound = 11. When *b* is regenerated, it is found that $f(b) = 8 < F(a)$. Therefore node *b* inherits its *F*-value from node *a*, so $F(b)$ becomes 10. Next *c* is regenerated and *c* also inherits its *F*-value from *b*, so $F(c)$ becomes 10. The Bound = 11 is exceeded at snapshot F, the nodes *d*, *c* and *b* are removed and $F(d) = 12$ is backed-up to node *a* (snapshot G). Now the search switches to node *e* and runs smoothly to the goal *t*.

Let us now formulate the RBFS algorithm more formally. The algorithm is centred around the updating of the *F*-values of nodes. So a good way to formulate the algorithm is by defining a function:

*NewF*( N, *F*(N), *Bound*)

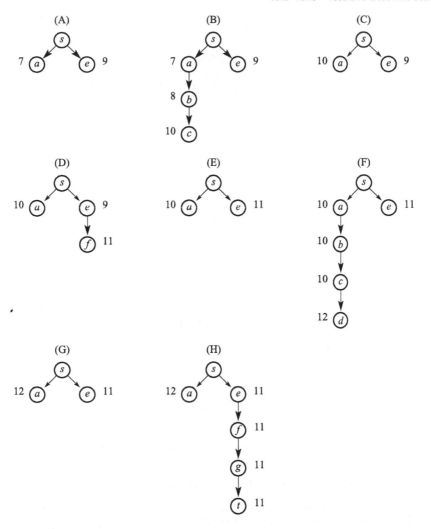

**Figure 13.2** The trace of the RBFS algorithm on the route problem of Figure 12.2. The figures next to the nodes are the nodes' *F*-values (which change during search).

where N is a node whose current *F*-value is *F*(N). The function carries out the search within Bound, starting with node N, and computes the new *F*-value of N, *NewF*, resulting from this search. The new value is determined at the moment that the bound is exceeded. If, however, a goal is found before this, then the function terminates, signalling success as a side effect. The function *NewF* is defined in Figure 13.3.

A Prolog implementation of RBFS is shown in Figure 13.4. This program is similar to the A* program of Figure 12.3. The heart of the program is the procedure

**rbfs( Path, SiblingNodes, Bound, NewBestFF, Solved, Solution)**

```
function NewF( N, F(N), Bound)
    begin
        if F(N) > Bound then NewF := F(N)
        else if goal(N) then exit search with success
        else if N has no children then NewF := infinity (dead end)
        else
           begin
             for each child Nᵢ of N do
                 if f(N) < F(N) then F(Nᵢ) := max( F(N), f(Nᵢ))
                 else F(Nᵢ) := f(Nᵢ);
             sort children Nᵢ in increasing order of their F-values;
             while F(N₁) ≤ Bound and F(N₁) < infinity do
                 begin
                     Bound1 := min( Bound, F-value of best sibling of N₁);
                     F(N₁) := NewF( N₁, F(N₁), Bound1);
                     reorder nodes N₁, N₂, ... according to new F(N₁)
                 end
             NewF := F(N₁)
    end
```

**Figure 13.3** The updating of *F*-values in RBFS search.

```
% Linear-space best-first search; the RBFS algorithm
% The program assumes 99999 is greater than any f-value

% bestfirst( Start, Solution): Solution is a path from Start to a goal

bestfirst( Start, Solution)  :-
    rbfs( [ ], [ (Start, 0/0/0) ], 99999, _, yes, Solution).

% rbfs( Path, SiblingNodes, Bound, NewBestFF, Solved, Solution):
%    Path = path so far in reverse order
%    SiblingNodes = children of head of Path
%    Bound = upper bound on F-value for search from SiblingNodes
%    NewBestFF = best f-value after searching just beyond Bound
%    Solved = yes, no, or never
%    Solution = solution path if Solve = yes
%
%    Representation of nodes: Node = ( State, G/F/FF)
%    where G is cost till State, F is static f-value of State,
%    FF is backed-up value of State

rbfs( Path, [ (Node, G/F/FF) | Nodes], Bound, FF, no, _)  :-
    FF > Bound, !.
```

**Figure 13.4** A best-first search program that only requires space linear in the depth of search (RBFS algorithm).

**Figure 13.4** *Contd*

```
rbfs( Path, [ (Node, G/F/FF) | _], _, _, yes, [Node | Path]) :-
  F = FF,                           % Only report solution once, when first reached; then F=FF
  goal( Node).

rbfs( _, [], _, _, never, _) :- !.          % No candidates, dead end!

rbfs( Path, [ (Node, G/F/FF) | Ns], Bound, NewFF, Solved, Sol) :-
  FF =< Bound,                      % Within Bound: generate children
  findall( Child/Cost,
          ( s( Node, Child, Cost), \+ member( Child, Path)),
          Children),
  inherit( F, FF, InheritedFF),             % Children may inherit FF
  succlist( G, InheritedFF, Children, SuccNodes),   % Order children
  bestff( Ns, NextBestFF),                  % Closest competitor FF among siblings
  min( Bound, NextBestFF, Bound2), !,
  rbfs( [Node | Path], SuccNodes, Bound2, NewFF2, Solved2, Sol),
  continue(Path, [(Node,G/F/NewFF2)|Ns], Bound, NewFF, Solved2, Solved, Sol).

% continue( Path, Nodes, Bound, NewFF, ChildSolved, Solved, Solution)

continue( Path, [N | Ns], Bound, NewFF, never, Solved, Sol) :- !,
  rbfs( Path, Ns, Bound, NewFF, Solved, Sol).     % Node N a dead end

continue( _, _, _, _, yes, yes, Sol).

continue( Path, [ N | Ns], Bound, NewFF, no, Solved, Sol) :-
  insert( N, Ns, NewNs), !,                 % Ensure siblings are ordered by values
  rbfs( Path, NewNs, Bound, NewFF, Solved, Sol).

succlist( _, _, [], []).

succlist( G0, InheritedFF, [Node/C | NCs], Nodes) :-
  G is G0 + C,
  h( Node, H),
  F is G + H,
  max( F, InheritedFF, FF),
  succlist( G0, InheritedFF, NCs, Nodes2),
  insert( (Node, G/F/FF), Nodes2, Nodes).

inherit( F, FF, FF) :-                     % Child inherits father's FF if
  FF > F, !.                               % father's FF greater than father's F

inherit( F, FF, 0).

insert( (N, G/F/FF), Nodes, [ (N, G/F/FF) | Nodes]) :-
  bestff( Nodes, FF2),
  FF =< FF2, !.

insert( N, [N1 | Ns], [N1 | Ns1]) :-
  insert( N, Ns, Ns1).

bestff( [ (N, F/G/FF) | Ns], FF).          % First node – best FF

bestff( [], 99999).                        % No nodes – FF = 'infinite'
```

which carries out the RBFS algorithm. The arguments are:

| | |
|---|---|
| **Path** | Path so far from start node of search in reverse order. |
| **SiblingNodes** | The children of the last node in the path so far, i.e. the head of **Path**. |
| **Bound** | Upper bound on *F*-values for extending the search from **SiblingNodes**. |
| **NewBestFF** | The best *F*-value after extending search just beyond **Bound**. |
| **Solved** | Indicates the success of search below **SiblingNodes** (**Solved** = yes if a goal was found, **no** if search went just beyond **Bound**, **never** if this is a dead end). |
| **Solution** | Solution path if **Solve** = yes, otherwise undefined. |

The representation of the nodes includes, besides a state in the state space also the path costs, *f*-values and *F*-values as follows:

**Node** = ( **State**, G/F/FF)

where **G** is the cost of the path from the start state to **State**, **F** is static value *f*(State), and **FF** is the current backed-up value *F*(State). It should be noted that variable **F** in the program denotes an *f*-value, and **FF** in the program denotes an *F*-value. The procedure **rbfs** carries out the search below **SiblingNodes** within **Bound**, and computes **NewBestFF** according to the function *NewF* in Figure 13.3.

Let us summarize the important properties of the RBFS algorithm. First, its space complexity is linear in the depth of search. The price for this is the time needed to regenerate already generated nodes. However, these overheads are substantially smaller than in IDA*. Second, like A* and unlike IDA*, RBFS expands the nodes in the best-first order even in the case of a non-monotonic *f*-function.

# EXERCISES

**13.3** Consider the route-finding problem of Figure 12.2. How many nodes are generated by A*, IDA* and RBFS on this problem (counting also the regenerated nodes)?

**13.4** Consider the state space in Figure 13.5. Let *a* be the start node and *l* the goal node. Give the order in which nodes are generated (including regeneration) by the RBFS

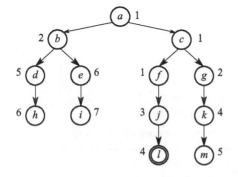

**Figure 13.5** A state space; the numbers next to the nodes are the nodes' *f*-values; *l* is the goal node.

algorithm. How are the backed-up values $F(b)$ and $F(c)$ changing during this process?

**13.5** Inheritance of $F$-values in RBFS saves time (prevents unnecessary regeneration of nodes). Explain how. Hint: Consider the search by RBFS of the binary tree in which for each node its $f$-value is equal to the depth of the node in the tree. Study the execution of RBFS with and without inheritance of $F$-values on this state space up to depth 8.

**13.6** Compare the A*, IDA* and RBFS programs on the eight-puzzle problems. Measure execution times and the number of nodes generated during search, including the regenerated nodes (add node counters to the programs).

# 13.4 RTA* – real-time A* algorithm

Consider a robot that uses the A* algorithm for planning its tasks. The robot receives a specification of a task in terms of goals to be achieved. Then the robot starts A* to work out a detailed optimal plan of robot's actions for achieving the goals. The robot waits until A* produces a complete solution plan, and then starts executing the plan. This is fine as long as the search problem solved by A* is not too complex. For complex problems, however, this approach will be completely inappropriate as the robot may have to wait for hours before a plan is ready to be executed. In a real-time environment, this would be unacceptable. The robot, or any agent in general, has to make a decision about its next action quickly, even in cases when the complete solution is not yet known. Notice that such a situation does not only occur when a physical agent is to act in a changing world. Suppose we are using A* to compute a schedule for a complex scheduling problem. It may easily take too long (like years, or much more) to compute an optimal schedule with, say, A* or RBFS. In such a case, it is not possible to wait until a complete solution emerges. It is better to irreversibly make some scheduling decisions before the complete schedule has been worked out, and continue the computation of the rest of the schedule from there.

In this section we will look at a search algorithm that is more suitable for such a real-time environment. This approach is known as RTA*, which stands for 'real-time A*'. The name RTA* for this algorithm may not be the most appropriate, but this name has become established in the literature.

To describe the RTA* algorithm, it is easiest if we assume a physical agent, a robot, whose actions cause moving between the physical states of the agent and its environment. The robot starts at some state and wants to reach a given goal state. Instead of working out a complete solution path between the start state and a goal state, the idea of RTA* is just to perform some relatively inexpensive lookahead which stops well before a goal state is found. A lookahead limited by a fixed depth D means to effectively generate all the nodes that can be reached from the current state in no more than D steps. Then the tip nodes of this lookahead search are evaluated, and their values are backed up to the immediate successors of the current physical state of the robot. The robot then makes an actual physical move to the best looking immediate successor state, and continues the planning and execution from this next state. We will denote the

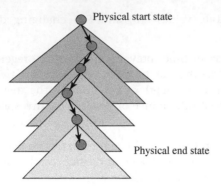

Physical start state

Physical end state

**Figure 13.6** The RTA* method. The circles represent the physical states of the robot and its environment, and the arrows represent the actions actually executed by the robot. The  triangles represent the robot's 'lookahead' – the depth-limited planning, which is the robot's 'thinking' about the consequences of available actions.

evaluation function for states as $f$, as usual. The function $f$ can be defined as the sum $f = g + h$ as in A*. So for a given state $s$, $f(s)$ is the value of $s$ in terms of how costly it will be to reach a goal state from $s$. The lower $f$ is, the better. $g(s)$ is the cost of the path from the current physical state to state $s$, and $h(s)$ is an estimate of the cost of the rest of the path to the goal. As illustrated in Figure 13.6, the solving of a task by RTA* thus consists of the following procedure:

Let *current_state* be the initial physical state of the robot and its environment;  While *current_state* is not a goal state repeat the following two steps:

(1) 'Planning': find the most promising successor state of *current_state* by a fixed depth lookahead.

(2) 'Execution': physically perform the action that brings the robot from the current state to the most promising successor state; update *current_state* to become this successor state.

By splitting the task into planning and execution, RTA* can solve much larger problems than A*, although suboptimally. RTA* only peforms local optimization, within the current lookahead. This may be myopic and may produce decisions that will later turn to be inferior. However, as they have already been executed by the robot, they cannot be retracted.

In the RTA* algorithm, there are two distinguishing states: (a) the *start state*, which is the robot's physical state where the solving of the task begins; and (b) the *current state*, which is the actual physical state of the robot after some actions have possibly been executed. The values $f(s)$ and $g(s)$ for a state s are measured relative to the current state (and not relative to the start state). So $g(s)$ is the cost of path from the current state to $s$. *Visited states* are states that have been physically visited, that is the robot has moved to these states during the execution of RTA*.

Figure 13.7 shows a sketch of the RTA* algorithm. Here are some further details of this algorithm. The depth of lookahead $d$ is a parameter of the

Let current state $s$ := start_state;

While goal not found do:

        Plan: evaluate successors of $s$ by lookahead of fixed depth $d$;

        *best_s* := successor with min. backed-up f value;

        *second_best_f* := f value of the second best successor;

        Store $s$ among 'visited nodes' and store f(s) := *second_best_f*;

        Execute: current state $s$ := *best_s*;

        If s is a goal node then goal has been found, exit the while loop.

**Figure 13.7** RTA* algorithm.

algorithm. The lookahead can be done by the depth-first search to limited depth $d$. A node $n$ encountered during this lookahead is assigned its heuristic $h$ value as follows:

- if goal($n$) then return $h(n) = 0$, don't search beyond $n$
- if visited($n$) then return $h(n)$ = previously stored $f(n)$, don't search beyond $n$
- if $n$ is at lookahead horizon (that is at search-depth limit) then evaluate $n$ statically by heuristic function $h(n)$
- if $n$ is not at lookahead horizon then generate $n$'s successors and back up $f$-value from them

Notice that for a visited node $s$, its $f$-value is stored as $f(s) = f(second\_best\_successor)$. This may look strange – why not store the $f$-value of the best successor? The reason is as follows (see Figure 13.8). If the best successor (according to the lookahead) *best_s* subsequently turns out as a bad decision, the robot may at some later point return to state $s$. This time the robot should not repeat the same bad decision, but should consider $s$'s second best successor. Otherwise, the problem-solver would find *best_s* as the most promising successor again, possibly make the same bad decision and repeat the same loop.

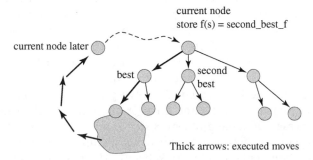

**Figure 13.8** Illustration of why RTA* stores the second best $f$-value. If the move from current state to its best successor was a mistake, the robot may complete a loop shown by thick arrows, and become confronted by the same decision next time round. This time the robot should avoid the same mistake.

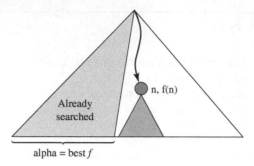

alpha = best $f$

**Figure 13.9** Alpha pruning: if evaluation function $f$ is monotonic then the subtree rooted at node $n$ can be pruned, that is disregarded during the lookahead.

If evaluation function $f$ is monotonic then another improvement is possible, called *alpha pruning*. This idea is a simpler version of the so-called  alpha-beta pruning in game tree search, which will be discussed later in the chapter on game playing. During lookahead done by depth-limited depth-first search, the nodes at the search horizon are evaluated in the order from left to right. RTA* maintains the best $f$-value encountered so far during this lookahead. Let this value be denoted as *alpha*. Let now a node $n$ be encountered before the look-ahead horizon; if $f(n) \geq alpha$ then subtree of $n$ can be pruned. The reason is that all the descendants of $n$ will have $f$-values greater or equal $f(n)$, and none of them will possibly improve on the best $f$ value so far (see Figure 13.9). Many evaluation functions are monotonic, for example the Manhattan distance based evaluation in the eight puzzle. Therefore alpha pruning may lead to significant speed ups.

Figure 13.10 shows a Prolog implementation of RTA* that also performs alpha-pruning. This program maintains the set of visited nodes by asserting these nodes, together with their 'second-best' $f$-values, under the predicate **visited/2**. Before RTA* search starts, all the previously stored visited nodes are retracted by the built-in predicate **retractall**. The best $f$-value so far is also maintained through **assert** and **retract**. The lookahead depth limit is a parameter of the program stored as the asserted fact about the predicate **lookahead_depth**.

A further development of RTA* is LRTA*, which stands for 'Learning RTA*'. LRTA* learns in a way to become better at solving problems from the same domain. This can be done by successively solving multiple problem instances with different start states and the same goal, or the same problem in multiple trials. In the latter case, the same problem is solved several times (trials) whereby the programs' 'experience' accumulates by remembering 'deep' heuristic values (that is values of states obtained by lookahead). These values are transferred between trials as a table of visited nodes with their backed-up heuristic values. In such a table used by LRTA*, the *best* successors' $f$ are stored (rather than the second best $f$ as in RTA*). Best $f$ is the appropriate information to be transferred *between* trials, whereas second best is appropriate *within* a single trial.

```
% Real-time A*

% rta( StartNode, SolutionPath)

rta( StartNode, [StartNode | Rest])  :-
  retractall( visited( _, _)),              % Retract all previously stored visited nodes
  rta( [StartNode | Rest]).                 % Perform RTA* search to find a solution path

% rta( [Node | Rest]):  find a solution path from Node to a goal state

rta( [ Node])  :-
  goal( Node).

rta( [ Node, BestSucc | Rest])  :-
  setof( F/Cost/Succ,
      H^( s( Node, Succ, Cost), h( Succ, H), F is Cost + H),
      SuccList),              % Successor nodes ordered according to shallow F
  best( SuccList, none, 999999, 999999, _/C/BestSucc, SecondBestF),
  DeepH is C + SecondBestF,
  update_visited( Node, DeepH),             % Store Node's second best f value
  rta( [BestSucc | Rest]).

% best( NodeList, BestSoFar, BestFsoFar, SecondBestFsoFar, BestNode, SecondBestF):
%   BestNode is the best node among NodeList according to fixed depth lookahead

best( [], BestSoFar, _, SecondBestF, BestSoFar, SecondBestF)  :-  !.

best( [Node | Nodes], BestSoFar, BestFsoFar, SecondBestFsoFar, BestNode, SecondBestF)  :-
  lookahead_depth( D),
  lookahead( Node, DeepF, D, SecondBestFsoFar),       % Obtain "deep" F by D-move lookahead
  (
    DeepF < BestFsoFar, !,                  % New best
    best( Nodes, Node, DeepF, BestFsoFar, BestNode, SecondBestF)
    ;
    DeepF < SecondBestFsoFar, !,            % New second best
    best( Nodes, BestSoFar, BestFsoFar, DeepF, BestNode, SecondBestF)
    ;
    best( Nodes, BestSoFar, BestFsoFar, SecondBestFsoFar, BestNode, SecondBestF)
  ).

update_visited( Node, DeepH)  :-            % DeepH is Node's heuristic value for next encounter
  retractall( visited( Node, _)),           % Retract previous value if any
  asserta( visited( Node, DeepH)).

% lookahead( ShallowF/G/Node, DeepF, LookaheadDepth, Bound)
%   DeepF is Node's F-value after lookahead to LookaheadDepth
%   In case of monotonic F, alpha-pruning is possible when current F >= Bound
%   Alpha-pruning is not implemented in this version

lookahead( ShallowF/G/Node, DeepF, LookaheadDepth, Bound)  :-
  asserta( bestF( Bound)),        % We have to improve on Bound else alpha-prune
  lookahead( ShallowF/G/Node, LookaheadDepth),
  retract( bestF( DeepF)).
```

**Figure 13.10** An implementation of RTA*. To change the depth limit for lookahead after the program has been consulted, **lookahead_depth/1** has first to be retracted, and then a new definition asserted.

**Figure 13.10** *Contd*

```
lookahead( _/G/Node, D)  :-
   (
      goal( Node), !, DeepF = G                         % Goal node
      ;
      visited( Node, DeepH), !, DeepF is G + DeepH      % Already visited
      ;
      D = 0, !, h( Node, H), DeepF is G + H             % Lookahead depth reached
   ),
   update_bestF( DeepF).
lookahead( _/G/Node, D)  :-                             % Here lookahead depth not yet reached
   s( Node, ChildNode, Cost),
   G1 is G + Cost,
   h( ChildNode, H1), F1 is G1 + H1,
   bestF( Bound), F1 < Bound,        % Child's F must be lower than Bound, else alpha-prune
   D1 is D - 1,
   lookahead( _/G1/ChildNode, D1),
   fail                              % Look at other successor nodes
   ;
   true.
update_bestF( F)  :-
   bestF( BestFsoFar),
   BestFsoFar =< F, !                % Do not change best F
   ;
   retract( bestF( _)), !,
   asserta( bestF( F)).              % Update best F

% lookahead_depth( SearchDepthLimit): lookahead depth, to be set by user
:- asserta( lookahead_depth( 1)).    % Depth limit for lookahead set to 1, for example
```

## Summary

- The time and space requirements of A* typically grow exponentially with solution length. In practical applications, space is often more critical than time. Special techniques for best-first search aim at saving space at the expense of time, or saving time at the expense of the quality of solutions.

- IDA* is a simple space-efficient best-first search algorithm based on a similar idea as iterative deepening. Overheads due to node regeneration in IDA* are acceptable in cases when many nodes in the state space have equal *f*-values. When the nodes tend not to share *f*-values the overheads become unacceptable.

- RBFS is a more sophisticated space-efficient best-first search algorithm that generally regenerates fewer nodes than IDA*.

- The space requirements of both IDA* and RBFS are very modest. They only grow linearly with the depth of search.

- The RTA* algorithm is a real-time version of A*, used in situations where quick decisions are needed even if they may be suboptimal.

- Concepts discussed in this chapter are:

    algorithms IDA*, RBFS and RTA*
    space-efficiency of best-first search
    monotonicity of evaluation function
    real-time best-first search

## References

Richard Korf contributed the key ideas of the algorithms of this chapter. An early description of IDA* appeared in Korf (1985). The RBFS algorithm was introduced and analysed by Korf (1993), and RTA* in Korf (1990). Russell and Norvig (2010) discuss further ideas for space-bounded search.

Korf, R.E. (1985) Depth-first iterative-deepening: an optimal admissible tree search. *Artificial Intelligence* **27**: 97–109.
Korf, R.E. (1990) Real-time heuristic search, *Artificial Intelligence* **42**: 189–211.
Korf, R.E. (1993) Linear-space best-first search. *Artificial Intelligence* **62**: 41–78.
Russell, S.J. and Norvig, P. (2010) *Artificial Intelligence: A Modern Approach,* third edn. Prentice Hall.

# Chapter 14

# Problem Decomposition and AND/OR Graphs

AND/OR graphs are a suitable representation for problems that can be naturally decomposed into mutually independent subproblems. Examples of such problems include route finding, design, symbolic integration, game playing, theorem proving, etc. In this chapter we will develop programs for searching AND/OR graphs, including a heuristically guided best-first AND/OR search.

## 14.1 AND/OR graph representation of problems

In Chapters 11–13, problem solving was centred around the state-space representation of problems. Accordingly, problem solving was reduced to finding a path in a state-space graph. Another representation, the AND/OR graph representation, more naturally suits certain kinds of problems. This representation relies on the decomposition of problems into subproblems. Decomposition into subproblems is advantageous if the subproblems are mutually independent, and can therefore be solved independently of each other.

Let us illustrate this with an example. Consider the problem of finding a route in a road map between two cities, as shown in Figure 14.1. We will disregard path lengths for the moment. The problem could, of course, be formulated as path finding in a state space. The corresponding state space would look just like the map: the nodes in the state space correspond to cities, the arcs correspond to direct connections between cities, arc costs correspond to distances between cities. However, let us construct another representation of this problem, based on a natural decomposition of the problem.

In the map of Figure 14.1, there is also a river. Let us assume that there are only two bridges at which the river can be crossed, one bridge at city $f$ and the other at city $g$. Obviously, our route will have to include one of the bridges; so it will have to go through $f$ or through $g$. We have, then, two major alternatives:

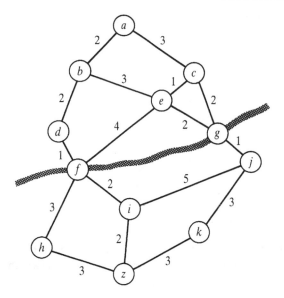

**Figure 14.1** Finding a route from *a* to *z* in a road map. The river has to be crossed at *f* or *g*. An AND/OR representation of this problem is shown in Figure 14.2.

To find a path between *a* and *z*, find *either*

(1) a path from *a* to *z* via *f*, *or*
(2) a path from *a* to *z* via *g*.

Each of these two alternative problems can now be decomposed as follows:

(1) To find a path from *a* to *z* via *f*:
   1.1 find a path from *a* to *f*, *and*
   1.2 find a path from *f* to *z*.
(2) To find a path from *a* to *z* via *g*:
   2.1 find a path from *a* to *g*, *and*
   2.2 find a path from *g* to *z*.

To summarize, we have two main alternatives for solving the original problem: (1) via *f* or (2) via *g*. Further, each of these alternatives can be *decomposed* into two subproblems (1.1 and 1.2, or 2.1 and 2.2 respectively). What is important here is that (in both alternatives) each of the subproblems can be solved independently of the other. Such a decomposition can be pictured as an *AND/OR graph* (Figure 14.2). Notice the curved arcs which indicate the AND relationship between subproblems. Of course, the graph in Figure 14.2 is only the top part of a corresponding AND/OR tree. Further decomposition of subproblems could be based on the introduction of additional intermediate cities.

What are goal nodes in such an AND/OR graph? Goal nodes correspond to subproblems that are trivial or 'primitive'. In our example, such a subproblem would be 'find a route from *a* to *c*', for there is a direct connection between cities *a* and *c* in the road map.

Some important concepts have been introduced in this example. An AND/OR graph is a directed graph in which nodes correspond to problems, and arcs

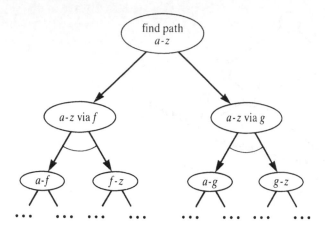

**Figure 14.2** An AND/OR representation of the route-finding problem of Figure 14.1. Nodes correspond to problems or subproblems, and curved arcs indicate that all (both) subproblems have to be solved.

indicate relations between problems. There are also relations among arcs themselves. These relations are AND and OR, depending on whether we have to solve just one of the successor problems or several (see Figure 14.3). In principle, a node can issue both AND-related arcs and OR-related arcs. We will, however, assume that each node has either only AND successors or only OR successors. Each AND/OR graph can be transformed into this form by introducing auxiliary OR nodes if necessary. Then, a node that only issues AND arcs is called an AND node; a node that only issues OR arcs is called an OR node.

In the state-space representation, a solution to the problem was a path in the state space. What is a solution in the AND/OR representation? A solution, of course, has to include all the subproblems of an AND node. Therefore, a solution is not a path any more, but it is a *tree*. Such a solution tree, T, is defined as follows:

- the original problem, P, is the root node of T;
- if P is an OR node then exactly one of its successors (in the AND/OR graph), together with its own solution tree, is in T;
- if P is an AND node then all of its successors (in the AND/OR graph), together with their solution trees, are in T.

**Figure 14.3** (a) To solve P solve any of $P_1$ or $P_2$ or ... (b) To solve Q solve all $Q_1$ and $Q_2$...

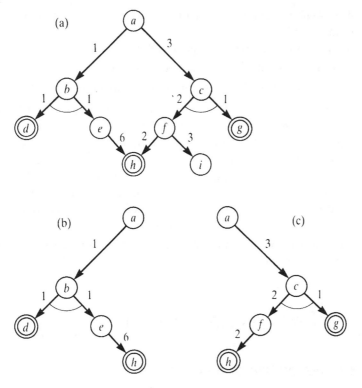

**Figure 14.4** (a) An AND/OR graph: *d*, *g* and *h* are goal nodes; *a* is the problem to be solved. (b) and (c) Two solution trees whose costs are 9 and 8 respectively. The cost of a solution tree is here defined as the sum of all the arc costs in the solution tree.

Figure 14.4 illustrates this definition. In this figure, there are costs attached to arcs. Using costs we can formulate an optimization criterion. We can, for example, define the cost of a solution graph as the sum of all the arc costs in the graph. As we are normally interested in the minimum cost, the solution graph in Figure 14.4(c) will be preferred.

But we do not have to base our optimization measure on the costs of arcs. Sometimes it is more natural to associate costs with nodes rather than arcs, or with both arcs and nodes.

To summarize:

- AND/OR representation is based on the philosophy of decomposing a problem into subproblems.

- Nodes in an AND/OR graph correspond to problems; links between nodes indicate relations between problems.

- A node that issues OR links is an OR node. To solve an OR node, one of its successor nodes has to be solved.

- A node that issues AND links is an AND node. To solve an AND node, all of its successors have to be solved.

- For a given AND/OR graph, a particular problem is specified by two things:
  – a start node, and
  – a goal condition for recognizing goal nodes.

- *Goal nodes* (or 'terminal' nodes) correspond to trivial (or 'primitive') problems.

- A solution is represented by a *solution graph*, a subgraph of the AND/OR graph.

- The state-space representation can be viewed as a special case of the AND/OR representation in which all the nodes are OR nodes.

- To benefit from the AND/OR representation, AND-related nodes should represent subproblems that can be solved independently of each other. The independency criterion can be somewhat relaxed, as follows: there must exist an ordering of AND subproblems so that solutions of subproblems that come earlier in this ordering are not destroyed when solving later subproblems. This will be illustrated by the Tower of Hanoi example in the next section.

- Costs can be attached to arcs or nodes or both in order to formulate an optimization criterion.

 ## 14.2 Examples of AND/OR representation

### 14.2.1 AND/OR representation of route finding

For the shortest route problem of Figure 14.1, an AND/OR graph including a cost function can be defined as follows:

- OR nodes are of the form X-Z, meaning: find a shortest path from X to Z.

- AND nodes are of the form

  X-Z via Y

  meaning: find a shortest path from X to Z under the constraint that the path goes through Y.

- A node X-Z is a goal node (primitive problem) if X and Z are directly connected in the map.

- The cost of each goal node X-Z is the given road distance between X and Z.

- The costs of all other (non-terminal) nodes are 0.

The cost of a solution graph is the sum of the costs of all the nodes in the solution graph (in our case, this is just the sum over the terminal nodes). For the problem of Figure 14.1, the start node is *a-z*. Figure 14.5 shows a solution tree of cost 9. This tree corresponds to the path [a,b,d,f,i,z]. This path can be reconstructed from the solution tree by visiting all the leaves in this tree in the left-to-right order.

### 14.2.2 The Tower of Hanoi problem

The Tower of Hanoi problem, shown in Figure 14.6, is another classic example of effective application of the AND/OR decomposition scheme. For simplicity, we will

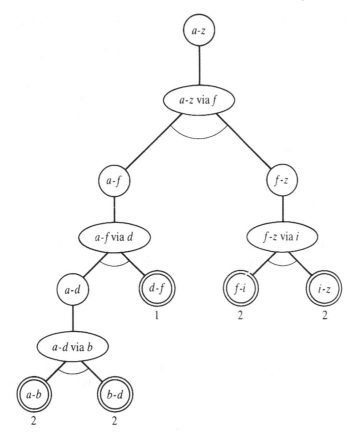

**Figure 14.5** The cheapest solution tree for the route problem of Figure 14.1 formulated as an AND/OR graph.

**Figure 14.6** The Tower of Hanoi problem.

consider a simple version of this problem, containing three disks only:

There are three pegs, 1, 2 and 3, and three disks, *a*, *b* and *c* (*a* being the smallest and *c* being the biggest). Initially, all the disks are stacked on peg 1. The problem is to transfer them all on to peg 3. Only one disk can be moved at a time, and no disk can ever be placed on top of a smaller disk.

This problem can be viewed as the problem of achieving the following set of goals:

(1)  Disk *a* on peg 3.

(2)  Disk *b* on peg 3.

(3)  Disk *c* on peg 3.

These goals are, unfortunately, not independent. For example, disk *a* can immediately be placed on peg 3, satisfying the first goal. This will, however, prevent the fulfilment of the other two goals (unless we undo the first goal again). Fortunately, there is a convenient ordering of these goals so that a solution can easily be derived from this ordering. The ordering can be found by the following reasoning: goal 3 (disk *c* on peg 3) is the hardest because moving disk *c* is subject to most constraints. A good idea that often works in such situations is: try to achieve the hardest goal first. The logic behind this principle is: as other goals are easier (not as constrained as the hardest) they can hopefully be achieved without the necessity of undoing this hardest goal.

The problem-solving strategy that results from this principle in our task is:

First satisfy the goal 'disk *c* on peg 3',
then satisfy the remaining goals.

But the first goal cannot immediately be achieved: disk *c* cannot move in the initial situation. Therefore, we first have to prepare this move and our strategy is refined to:

(1)  Enable moving disk *c* from 1 to 3.

(2)  Move disk *c* from 1 to 3.

(3)  Achieve remaining goals: *a* on 3, and *b* on 3.

Disk *c* can only move from 1 to 3 if both *a* and *b* are stacked on peg 2. Then, our initial problem of moving *a*, *b* and *c* from peg 1 to peg 3 is reduced to three subproblems:

To move *a*, *b* and *c* from 1 to 3:

(1)  move *a* and *b* from 1 to 2, *and*

(2)  move *c* from 1 to 3, *and*

(3)  move *a* and *b* from 2 to 3.

Problem 2 is trivial (one-step solution). The other two subproblems can be solved independently of problem 2 because disks *a* and *b* can be moved regardless of the position of disk *c*. To solve problems 1 and 3, the same decomposition principle can be applied (disk *b* *is* the hardest this time). Accordingly, problem 1 is reduced to three trivial subproblems:

To move *a* and *b* from 1 to 2:

(1)  move *a* from 1 to 3, *and*

(2)  move *b* from 1 to 2, *and*

(3)  move *a* from 3 to 2.

## 14.2.3  AND/OR formulation of game playing

Games like chess and checkers can naturally be viewed as problems, represented by AND/OR graphs. Such games are called two-person, perfect-information games, and we will assume here that there are only two possible outcomes: WIN or LOSS. (We can think of games with three outcomes – WIN, LOSS and DRAW – as also

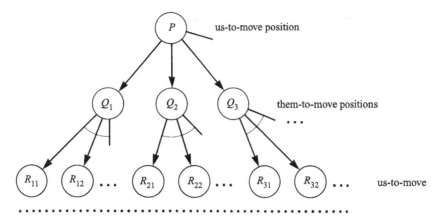

**Figure 14.7** An AND/OR formulation of a two-person game; the players are 'us' and 'them'.

having just two outcomes: WIN and NO-WIN.) As the two players move in turn we have two kinds of positions, depending on who is to move. Let us call the two players 'us' and 'them', so the two kinds of positions are: 'us-to-move' positions and 'them-to-move' positions. Assume that the game starts in an us-to-move position $P$. Each alternative us-move in this position leads to one of them-to-move positions $Q_1, Q_2, \ldots$ (Figure 14.7). Further, each alternative them-move in $Q_1$ leads to one of the positions $R_{11}, R_{12}, \ldots$. In the AND/OR tree of Figure 14.7, nodes correspond to positions, and arcs correspond to possible moves. Us-to-move levels alternate with them-to-move levels. To win in the initial position, $P$, we have to find a move from $P$ to $Q_i$, for some $i$, so that the position $Q_i$ is won. Thus, $P$ is won if $Q_1$ or $Q_2$ or $\ldots$ is won. Therefore position $P$ is an OR node. For all $i$, position $Q_i$ is a them-to-move position, so if it is to be won for us it has to be won after *each* them-move. Thus $Q_i$ is won if all $R_{i1}$ and $R_{i2}$ and $\ldots$ are won. Accordingly, all them-to-move positions are AND nodes. Goal nodes are those positions that are won by the rules of the game; for example, their king checkmated in chess. Those positions that are lost by the rules of the game correspond to unsolvable problems. To solve the game we have to find a solution tree that guarantees our victory regardless of the opponent's replies. Such a solution tree, then, is a complete strategy for winning the game: for each possible continuation that can be chosen by the opponent, there is a move in such a strategy tree that forces a win.

## 14.3 Basic AND/OR search procedures

In this section we will only be interested in finding *some* solution of the problem, regardless of its cost. So for the purposes of this section we can ignore the costs of links or nodes in an AND/OR graph.

The simplest way of searching AND/OR graphs in Prolog is to use Prolog's own search mechanism. This happens to be trivial as Prolog's procedural meaning itself is nothing but a procedure for searching AND/OR graphs. For example, the

AND/OR graph of Figure 14.4 (ignoring the arc costs) can be specified by the following clauses:

a :- b.          % a is an OR node with two successors, b and c

a :- c.

b :- d, e.       % b is an AND node with two successors, d and e

e :- h.

c :- f, g.

f :- h; i.       % f is an OR node

d.   g.   h.     % d, g and h are goal nodes

To see whether problem a can be solved we can simply ask:

?- a.

Now Prolog will automatically search the graph of Figure 14.4 in the depth-first fashion and answer 'yes', after having visited that part of the search graph corresponding to the solution tree in Figure 14.4(b).

The advantage of this approach to programming AND/OR search is its simplicity. There are disadvantages, however:

- We only get an answer 'yes' or 'no', not a solution tree as well. We could reconstruct the solution tree from the program's trace, but this can be awkward and insufficient if we want a solution tree explicitly accessible as an object in the program.

- This program is hard to extend so as to be able to handle costs as well.

- If our AND/OR graph were a general graph, containing cycles, then Prolog with its depth-first strategy could enter an indefinite recursive loop.

Let us rectify these deficiencies gradually. We will first define our own depth-first search procedure for AND/OR graphs.

To begin with, we will change the representation of AND/OR graphs in the program. For that we will introduce a binary relation represented in the infix notation with the operator '--->'. For example, node a linked to its two OR successors will be represented by the clause:

a ---> or: [b,c].

The symbols '--->' and ':' are both infix operators that can be defined by:

:- op( 600, xfx, --->).

:- op( 500, xfx, :).

The complete AND/OR graph of Figure 14.4 is thus specified by the clauses:

a ---> or : [b,c].

b ---> and : [d,e].

c ---> and : [f,g].

e ---> or : [h].

f ---> or : [h,i].

goal( d). goal( g). goal( h).

The depth-first AND/OR procedure can be constructed from the following principles:

> To solve a node, N, use the following rules:
>
> (1)  If N is a goal node then it is trivially solved.
>
> (2)  If N has OR successors then solve one of them (attempt them one after another until a solvable one is found).
>
> (3)  If N has AND successors then solve all of them (attempt them one after another until they have all been solved).
>
> If the above rules do not produce a solution then assume the problem cannot be solved.

A corresponding program can be as follows:

```
solve( Node) :-
   goal( Node).

solve( Node) :-
   Node ---> or : Nodes,          % Node is an OR node
   member( Node1, Nodes),         % Select a successor Node1 of Node
   solve( Node1).

solve( Node) :-
   Node ---> and : Nodes,         % Node is an AND node
   solveall( Nodes).              % Solve all Node's successors

solveall( [ ] ).

solveall( [Node | Nodes] ) :-
   solve( Node),
   solveall( Nodes).
```

**member** is the usual list membership relation.

This program still has the following disadvantages:

- it does not produce a solution tree, and

- it is susceptible to infinite loops, depending on the properties of the AND/OR graph (cycles).

The program can easily be modified to produce a solution tree. We have to modify the **solve** relation so that it has two arguments:

```
solve( Node, SolutionTree)
```

Let us represent a solution tree as follows. We have three cases:

(1)  If **Node** is a goal node then the corresponding solution tree is **Node** itself.

(2)  If **Node** is an OR node then its solution tree has the form:

```
Node ---> Subtree
```

where **Subtree** is a solution tree for one of the successors of **Node**.

(3)  If **Node** is an AND node then its solution tree has the form:

> Node - - -> and : Subtrees

where **Subtrees** is the list of solution trees of all of the successors of **Node**.

For example, in the AND/OR graph of Figure 14.4, the first solution of the top node *a* is represented by:

> a - - -> b - - -> and : [d, e - - -> h]

The three forms of a solution tree correspond to the three clauses about our **solve** relation. So our initial **solve** procedure can be altered by simply modifying each of the three clauses; that is, by just adding solution tree as the second argument to **solve**. The resulting program is shown as Figure 14.8. An additional procedure in this program is **show** for displaying solution trees. For example, the solution tree of Figure 14.4 is displayed by **show** in the following form:

> a - - -> b - - -> d
>          e - - -> h

The program of Figure 14.8 is still prone to infinite loops. One simple way to prevent infinite loops is to keep trace of the current depth of the search and prevent the program from searching beyond some depth limit. We can do this by simply introducing another argument to the **solve** relation:

> solve( Node, SolutionTree, MaxDepth)

As before, **Node** represents a problem to be solved, and **SolutionTree** is a solution not deeper than **MaxDepth**. **MaxDepth** is the allowed depth of search in the graph. In the case that **MaxDepth** = 0 no further expansion is allowed; otherwise, if **MaxDepth** > 0 then **Node** can be expanded and its successors are attempted with a lower depth limit **MaxDepth** – 1. This can easily be incorporated into the program of Figure 14.8. For example, the second clause about **solve** becomes:

```
solve( Node, Node - - -> Tree, MaxDepth) :-
    MaxDepth > 0,
    Node - - -> or : Nodes,                % Node is an OR node
    member( Node1, Nodes),                 % Select a successor Node 1 of Node
    Depth1 is MaxDepth – 1,                % New depth limit
    solve( Node1, Tree, Depth1).           % Solve successor with lower limit
```

This depth-limited, depth-first procedure can also be used in the iterative deepening regime, thereby simulating the breadth-first search. The idea is to do the depth-first search repetitively, each time with a greater depth limit, until a solution is found. That is, try to solve the problem with depth limit 0, then with 1, then with 2, etc. Such a program is:

```
iterative_deepening( Node, SolTree) :-
    trydepths( Node, SolTree, 0).    % Try search with increasing depth limit, start with 0

trydepths( Node, SolTree, Depth) :-
    solve( Node, SolTree, Depth)
    ;
    Depth1 is Depth + 1,                   % Get new depth limit
    trydepths( Node, SolTree, Depth1).     % Try higher depth limit
```

```
% Depth-first AND/OR search

% solve( Node, SolutionTree):
%   find a solution tree for Node in an AND/OR graph

solve( Node, Node) :-                 % Solution tree of goal node is Node itself
   goal( Node).

solve( Node, Node ---> Tree) :-
   Node ---> or : Nodes,              % Node is an OR node
   member( Node1, Nodes),             % Select a successor Node1 of Node
   solve( Node1, Tree).

solve( Node, Node ---> and : Trees)  :-
   Node ---> and : Nodes,             % Node is an AND node
   solveall( Nodes, Trees).           % Solve all Node's successors

% solveall( [Node1, Node2, ...], [SolutionTree1, SolutionTree2, ...] )

solveall( [], [] ).

solveall( [Node | Nodes], [Tree | Trees] ) :-
   solve( Node, Tree),
   solveall( Nodes, Trees).

show( Tree) :-                        % Display solution tree
   show( Tree, 0).                    % Indented by 0

% show( Tree, H): display solution tree indented by H

show( Node ---> Tree, H) :- !,
   write( Node), write( ' ---> '),
   H1 is H + 7,
   show( Tree, H1).

show( and : [T], H) :- !,            % Display single AND tree
   show( T).

show( and : [T | Ts], H) :- !,       % Display AND list of solution trees
   show( T, H),
   tab( H),
   show( and : Ts, H).

show( Node, H) :-
   write( Node), nl.
```

**Figure 14.8** Depth-first search for AND/OR graphs. This program does not avoid infinite cycling. Procedure **solve** finds a solution tree and procedure **show** displays such a tree. **show** assumes that each node only takes one character on output.

As with iterative deepening in state space (see Chapter 11), a disadvantage of this breadth-first simulation is that the program researches top parts of the search space each time that the depth limit is increased. On the other hand, the important advantage as compared with genuine breadth-first search is space economy.

## EXERCISES

**14.1** Complete the depth-limited, depth-first AND/OR search program according to the procedure outlined in this section.

**14.2** Define in Prolog an AND/OR space for the Tower of Hanoi problem and use this definition with the search procedures of this section.

**14.3** Consider some simple two-person, perfect-information game without chance and define its AND/OR representation. Use a depth-first AND/OR search program to find winning strategies in the form of AND/OR trees.

 **Best-first AND/OR search**

### 14.4.1 Heuristic estimates and the search algorithm

The basic search procedures of the previous section search AND/OR graphs systematically and exhaustively, without any heuristic guidance. For complex problems such procedures are too inefficient due to the combinatorial complexity of the search space. Heuristic guidance that aims to reduce the complexity by avoiding useless alternatives becomes necessary. The heuristic guidance introduced in this section will be based on numerical heuristic estimates of the difficulty of problems in the AND/OR graph. The program that we shall develop is an implementation of the algorithm known as AO*. It can be viewed as a generalization of the A* best-first search program for the state-space representation of Chapter 12.

Let us begin by introducing an optimization criterion based on the costs of arcs in the AND/OR graph. First, we extend our representation of AND/OR graphs to include arc costs. For example, the AND/OR graph of Figure 14.4 can be represented by the following clauses:

a - - -> or : [b/1, c/3].

b - - -> and : [d/1, e/1].

c - - -> and : [f/2, g/1].

e - - -> or : [h/6].

f - - -> or : [h/2, i/3].

goal( d). goal( g). goal( h).

We shall define the cost of a solution tree as the sum of all the arc costs in the tree. The optimization objective is to find a minimum-cost solution-tree. For illustration, see Figure 14.4 again.

It is useful to define the *cost of a node* in the AND/OR graph as the cost of the node's optimal solution tree. So defined, the cost of a node corresponds to the difficulty of the node.

We shall now assume that we can estimate the costs of nodes (without knowing their solution trees) in the AND/OR graph with some heuristic function $h$.

Such estimates will be used for guiding the search. Our heuristic search program will begin the search with the start node and, by expanding already visited nodes, gradually grow a search tree. This process will grow a *tree* even in cases where the AND/OR graph itself is not a tree; in such a case the graph unfolds into a tree by duplicating parts of the graph.

The search process will at any time of the search select the 'most promising' candidate solution tree for the next expansion. Now, how is the function $h$ used to estimate how promising a candidate solution tree is? Or, how promising a node (the root of a candidate solution tree) is?

For a node $N$ in the search tree, $H(N)$ will denote its estimated difficulty. For a tip node $N$ of the current search tree, $H(N)$ is simply $h(N)$. On the other hand, for an interior node of the search tree we do not have to use function $h$ directly because we already have some additional information about such a node; that is, we already know its successors. Therefore, as Figure 14.9 shows, for an interior OR node $N$ we approximate its difficulty as:

$$H(N) = \min_i(cost(N, N_i) + H(N_i))$$

where $cost(N, N_i)$ is the cost of the arc from $N$ to $N_i$. The minimization rule in this formula is justified by the fact that, to solve $N$, we just have to solve one of its successors.

The difficulty of an AND node $N$ is approximated by:

$$H(N) = \sum_i(cost(N, N_i) + H(N_i))$$

We say that the $H$-value of an interior node is a 'backed-up' estimate.

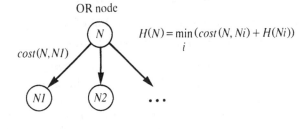

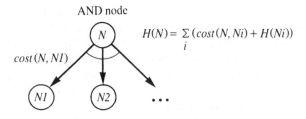

**Figure 14.9** Estimating the difficulty, $H$, of problems in the AND/OR graph.

In our search program, it will be more practical to use (instead of the $H$-values) another measure, $F$, defined in terms of $H$, as follows. Let a node $M$ be the predecessor of $N$ in the search tree, and the cost of the arc from $M$ to $N$ be $cost(M, N)$, then we define:

$$F(N) = cost(M, N) + H(N)$$

Accordingly, if $M$ is the parent node of $N$, and $N_1, N_2, \ldots$ are $N$'s children, then:

$$F(N) = cost(M, N) + \min_i F(N_i), \qquad \text{if } N \text{ is an OR node}$$

$$F(N) = cost(M, N) + \sum_i F(N_i), \qquad \text{if } N \text{ is an AND node}$$

The start node $S$ of the search has no predecessor, but let us choose the cost of its (virtual) incoming arc as 0. Now, if $h$ for all goal nodes in the AND/OR graph is 0, and an optimal solution tree has been found, then $F(S)$ is just the cost of this solution tree (that is, the sum of all the costs of its arcs).

At any stage of the search, each successor of an OR node represents an alternative candidate solution subtree. The search process will always decide to continue the exploration at that successor whose $F$-value is minimal. Let us return to Figure 14.4 again and trace such a search process when searching the AND/OR graph of this figure. Initially, the search tree is just the start node $a$, and then the tree grows until a solution tree is found. Figure 14.10 shows some snapshots taken during the growth of the search tree. We shall assume for simplicity that $h = 0$ for all the nodes. Numbers attached to nodes in Figure 14.10 are the $F$-values of the nodes (of course, these change during the search as more information is accumulated). Here are some explanatory remarks to Figure 14.10.

Expanding the initial search tree (snapshot A) produces tree B. Node $a$ is an OR node, so we now have two candidate solution subtrees: $b$ and $c$. As $F(b) = 1 < 3 = F(c)$, alternative $b$ is selected for expansion. Now, how far can alternative $b$ be expanded? The expansion can proceed until either:

(1) the $F$-value of node $b$ has become greater than that of its competitor $c$, or

(2) it has become clear that a solution tree has been found.

So candidate $b$ starts to grow with the upper bound for $F(b)$: $F(b) \leq 3 = F(c)$. First, $b$'s successors $d$ and $e$ are generated (snapshot C) and the $F$-value of $b$ is increased to 3. As this does not exceed the upper bound, the candidate tree rooted in $b$ continues to expand. Node $d$ is found to be a goal node, and then node $e$ is expanded, resulting in snapshot D. At this point $F(b) = 9 > 3$, which stops the expansion of alternative $b$. This prevents the process from realizing that $h$ is also a goal node and that a solution tree has already been generated. Instead, the activity now switches to the competing alternative $c$. The bound on $F(c)$ for expanding this alternative is set to 9, since at this point $F(b) = 9$. Within this bound the candidate tree rooted in $c$ is expanded until the situation of snapshot E is reached. Now the process realizes that a solution tree (which includes goal nodes $h$ and $g$) has been found, and the whole process terminates. Notice that the cheaper of the two possible solution trees was reported a solution by this process – that is, the solution tree in Figure 14.4(c).

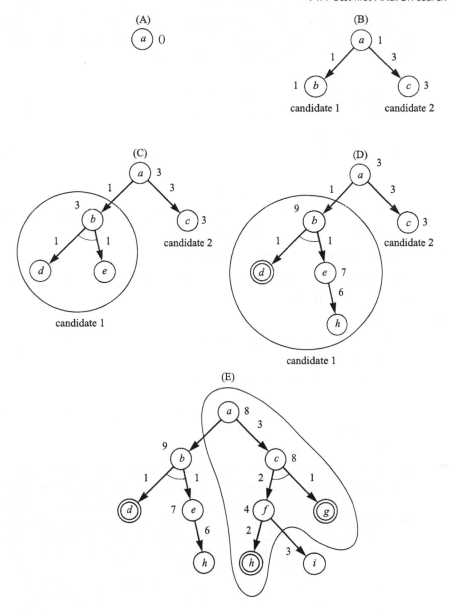

**Figure 14.10** A trace of a best-first AND/OR search (using $h = 0$) solving the problem of Figure 14.4.

## 14.4.2 Search program

A program that implements the ideas of the previous section is given in Figure 14.12. Before explaining some details of this program, let us consider the representation of the search tree that this program uses.

There are several cases, as shown in Figure 14.11. The different forms of the search tree arise from combining the following possibilities with respect to the tree's size and 'solution status':

- Size:

   (1) the tree is either a single node tree (a leaf), or

   (2) it has a root and (non-empty) subtrees.

- Solution status:

   (1) the tree has already been discovered to be solved (the tree is a solution tree), or

   (2) it is still just a *candidate* solution tree.

The principal functor used to represent the tree indicates a combination of these possibilities. This can be one of the following:

**leaf      solvedleaf      tree      solvedtree**

Further, the representation comprises some or all of the following information:

- root node of the tree,
- *F*-value of the tree,
- the cost C of the arc in the AND/OR graph pointing to the tree,
- list of subtrees,
- relation among subtrees (AND or OR).

The list of subtrees is always ordered according to increasing *F*-values. A subtree can already be solved. Such subtrees are accommodated at the end of the list.

Now to the program of Figure 14.12. The top-level relation is

**andor( Node, SolutionTree)**

where **Node** is the start node of the search. The program produces a solution tree (if one exists) with the aspiration that this will be an optimal solution. Whether it will really be a cheapest solution depends on the heuristic function *h* used by the algorithm. There is a theorem that talks about this dependence on *h*. The theorem is similar to the admissibility theorem about the state-space, best-first search of Chapter 12 (algorithm A*). Let $COST(N)$ denote the cost of a cheapest solution tree of a node N. If for each node N in the AND/OR graph the heuristic estimate $h(N) \leq COST(N)$ then **andor** is guaranteed to find an optimal solution. If *h* does not satisfy this condition then the solution found may be suboptimal. A trivial heuristic function that satisfies the admissibility condition is $h = 0$ for all the nodes. The disadvantage of this function is, of course, lack of heuristic power.

The key relation in the program of Figure 14.12 is:

**expand( Tree, Bound, Tree1, Solved)**

**Tree** and **Bound** are 'input' arguments, and **Tree1** and **Solved** are 'output' arguments. Their meaning is:

| | |
|---|---|
| **Tree** | is a search tree that is to be expanded. |
| **Bound** | is a limit for the *F*-value within which **Tree** is allowed to expand. |
| **Solved** | is an indicator whose value indicates one of the following three cases: |

*Case 1*: Search leaf

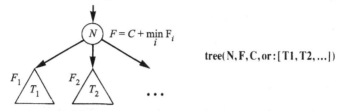

leaf( N, F, C )

*Case 2*: Search tree with OR subtrees

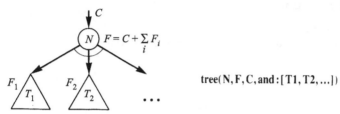

tree( N, F, C, or : [ T1, T2, ... ] )

*Case 3*: Search tree with AND subtrees

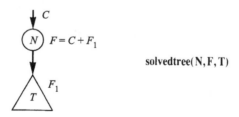

tree( N, F, C, and : [ T1, T2, ... ] )

*Case 4*: Solved leaf

solvedleaf ( N, F )

*Case 5*: Solution tree rooted at OR node

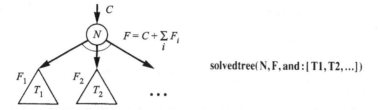

solvedtree( N, F, T )

*Case 6*: Solution tree rooted at AND node

solvedtree( N, F, and : [ T1, T2, ... ] )

**Figure 14.11** Representation of the search tree.

```
/* BEST-FIRST AND/OR SEARCH

This program only generates one solution. This solution is guaranteed to be a cheapest one if the
heuristic function used is a lower bound of the actual costs of solution trees.

Search tree is either:

tree( Node, F, C, SubTrees)                    tree of candidate solutions

leaf( Node, F, C)                              leaf of a search tree

solvedtree( Node, F, SubTrees)                 solution tree

solvedleaf( Node, F)                           leaf of solution tree

C is the cost of the arc pointing to Node

F = C + H, where H is the heuristic estimate of an optimal solution subtree rooted in Node

SubTrees are always ordered so that:

(1) all solved subtrees are at the end of a list;
(2) other (unsolved subtrees) are ordered according to ascending F-values.
*/

:- op( 500, xfx, :).

:- op( 600, xfx, --->).

andor( Node, SolutionTree) :-
    expand( leaf( Node, 0, 0), 9999, SolutionTree, yes).          % Assuming 9999 > any F-value

% Procedure expand( Tree, Bound, NewTree, Solved)
% expands Tree with Bound producing NewTree whose
% 'solution-status' is Solved

% Case 1: bound exceeded

expand( Tree, Bound, Tree, no) :-
    f( Tree, F), F > Bound, !.                 % Bound exceeded

% In all remaining cases F ≦ Bound
% Case 2: goal encountered

expand( leaf( Node, F, C), _, solvedleaf( Node, F), yes) :-
    goal( Node), !.

% Case 3: expanding a leaf

expand( leaf( Node, F, C), Bound, NewTree, Solved) :-
    expandnode( Node, C, Tree1), !,
    expand( Tree1, Bound, NewTree, Solved)
    ;
    Solved = never, !.                         % No successors, dead end

% Case 4: expanding a tree
```

Figure 14.12 Best-first AND/OR search program.

**Figure 14.12** *Contd*

```
expand( tree( Node, F, C, SubTrees), Bound, NewTree, Solved) :-
  Bound1 is Bound - C,
  expandlist( SubTrees, Bound1, NewSubs, Solved1),
  continue( Solved1, Node, C, NewSubs, Bound, NewTree, Solved).

% expandlist( Trees, Bound, NewTrees, Solved)
% expands tree list Trees with Bound producing
% NewTrees whose 'solved-status' is Solved

expandlist( Trees, Bound, NewTrees, Solved) :-
  selecttree( Trees, Tree, OtherTrees, Bound, Bound1),
  expand( Tree, Bound1, NewTree, Solved1),
  combine( OtherTrees, NewTree, Solved1, NewTrees, Solved).

% 'continue' decides how to continue after expanding a tree list

continue( yes, Node, C, SubTrees, _, solvedtree( Node, F, SubTrees), yes) :-
  backup( SubTrees, H), F is C + H, !.

continue( never, _, _, _, _, _, never) :- !.

continue( no, Node, C, SubTrees, Bound, NewTree, Solved) :-
  backup( SubTrees, H), F is C + H, !,
  expand( tree( Node, F, C, SubTrees), Bound, NewTree, Solved).

% 'combine' combines results of expanding a tree and a tree list

combine( or : _, Tree, yes, Tree, yes) :- !.            % OR list solved

combine( or : Trees, Tree, no, or : NewTrees, no) :-
  insert( Tree, Trees, NewTrees), !.                    % OR list still unsolved

combine( or : [ ], _, never, _, never) :- !.            % No more candidates

combine( or : Trees, _, never, or : Trees, no) :- !.    % There are more candidates

combine( and : Trees, Tree, yes, and : [Tree | Trees], yes) :-
  allsolved( Trees), !.                                 % AND list solved

combine( and : _, _, never, _, never) :- !.             % AND list unsolvable

combine( and : Trees, Tree, YesNo, and : NewTrees, no) :-
  insert( Tree, Trees, NewTrees), !.                    % AND list still unsolved

% 'expandnode' makes a tree of a node and its successors

expandnode( Node, C, tree( Node, F, C, Op : SubTrees) ) :-
  Node ---> Op : Successors,
  evaluate( Successors, SubTrees),
  backup( Op : SubTrees, H), F is C + H.

evaluate( [ ], [ ] ).

evaluate( [Node/C | NodesCosts], Trees) :-
  h( Node, H), F is C + H,
  evaluate( NodesCosts, Trees1),
  insert( leaf( Node, F, C), Trees1, Trees).

% 'allsolved' checks whether all trees in a tree list are solved
```

▶

**Figure 14.12** *Contd*

```
allsolved( [ ] ).

allsolved( [Tree | Trees] ) :-
    solved( Tree),
    allsolved( Trees).

solved( solvedtree( _, _, _) ).

solved( solvedleaf( _, _) ).

f( Tree, F) :-                              % Extract F-value of a tree
    arg( 2, Tree, F), !.                    % F is the 2nd argument in Tree

% insert( Tree, Trees, NewTrees) inserts Tree into
% tree list Trees producing NewTrees

insert( T, [ ], [T] ) :- !.

insert( T, [T1 | Ts], [T, T1 | Ts] ) :-
    solved( T1), !.

insert( T, [T1 | Ts], [T1 | Ts1] ) :-
    solved( T),
    insert( T, Ts, Ts1), !.

insert( T, [T1 | Ts], [T, T1 | Ts] ) :-
    f( T, F), f( T1, F1), F =< F1, !.

insert( T, [T1 | Ts], [T1 | Ts1] ) :-
    insert( T, Ts, Ts1).

% 'backup' finds the backed-up F-value of AND/OR tree list

backup( or : [Tree | _], F) :-              % First tree in OR list is best
    f( Tree, F), !.

backup( and : [ ], 0) :- !.

backup( and : [Tree1 | Trees], F) :- !.
    f( Tree1, F1),
    backup( and : Trees, F2),
    F is F1 + F2, !.

backup( Tree, F) :-
    f( Tree, F).

% Relation selecttree( Trees, BestTree, OtherTrees, Bound, Bound1):
% OtherTrees is an AND/OR list Trees without its best member BestTree;
% Bound is expansion bound for Trees, Bound1 is
% expansion bound for BestTree

selecttree( Op : [Tree], Tree, Op : [ ], Bound, Bound) :- !.      % The only candidate

selecttree( Op : [Tree | Trees], Tree, Op : Trees, Bound, Bound1) :-
    backup( Op : Trees, F),
    ( Op = or, !, min( Bound, F, Bound1);
      Op = and, Bound1 is Bound - F).

min( A, B, A) :- A < B, !.

min( A, B, B).
```

(1) **Solved = yes: Tree** can be expanded within bound so as to comprise a solution tree **Tree1**;

(2) **Solved = no: Tree** can be expanded to **Tree1** so that the *F*-value of **Tree1** exceeds **Bound**, and there was no solution subtree before the *F*-value overstepped **Bound**;

(3) **Solved = never: Tree** is unsolvable.

**Tree1** is, depending on the cases above, either a solution tree, an extension of **Tree** just beyond **Bound**, or uninstantiated in the case **Solved = never**.

Procedure

   **expandlist( Trees, Bound, Trees1, Solved)**

is similar to **expand**. As in **expand**, **Bound** is a limit of the expansion of a tree, and **Solved** is an indicator of what happened during the expansion ('yes', 'no' or 'never'). The first argument is, however, a *list* of trees (an AND list or an OR list):

   **Trees = or : [T1, T2, . . . ]** or **Trees = and : [T1, T2, . . . ]**

**expandlist** selects the most promising tree T (according to *F*-values) in **Trees**. Due to the ordering of the subtrees this is always the first tree in **Trees**. This most promising subtree is expanded with a new bound **Bound1**. **Bound1** depends on **Bound** and also on the other trees in **Trees**. If **Trees** is an OR list then **Bound1** is the lower of **Bound** and the *F*-value of the next best tree in **Trees**. If **Trees** is an AND list then **Bound1** is **Bound** minus the sum of the *F*-values of the remaining trees in **Trees**. **Trees1** depends on the case indicated by **Solved**. In the case **Solved = no**, **Trees1** is the list **Trees** with the most promising tree in **Trees** expanded with **Bound1**. In the case **Solved = yes**, **Trees1** is a solution of the list **Trees** (found within **Bound**). If **Solved = never**, **Trees1** is uninstantiated.

The procedure **continue**, which is called after expanding a tree list, decides what to do next, depending on the results of **expandlist**. It either constructs a solution tree, or updates the search tree and continues its expansion, or signals 'never' in the case that the tree list was found unsolvable.

Another procedure,

   **combine( OtherTrees, NewTree, Solved1, NewTrees, Solved)**

relates several objects dealt with in **expandlist**. **NewTree** is the expanded tree in the tree list of **expandlist**, **OtherTrees** are the remaining, unchanged trees in the tree list, and **Solved1** indicates the 'solution-status' of **NewTree**. **combine** handles several cases, depending on **Solved1** and on whether the tree list is an AND list or an OR list. For example, the clause

   **combine( or : _, Tree, yes, Tree, yes).**

says: in the case that the tree list is an OR list, and the just expanded tree was solved, and its solution tree is **Tree**, then the whole list has also been solved, and its solution is **Tree** itself. Other cases are best understood from the code of **combine** itself.

For displaying a solution tree, a procedure similar to **show** of Figure 14.8 can be defined. This procedure is left as an exercise for the reader.

## 14.4.3 Example of problem-defining relations: route finding

Let us now formulate the route-finding problem as an AND/OR search so that this formulation can be directly used by our **andor** procedure of Figure 14.12. We shall assume that the road map is represented by a relation

  s( City1, City2, D)

meaning that there is a direct connection between City1 and City2 of distance D. Further, we shall assume there is a relation

  key( City1 - City2, City3)

meaning: to find a route from City1 to City2 we should consider paths that go through City3 (City3 is a 'key point' between City1 and City2). For example, in the map of Figure 14.1, *f* and *g* are key points between *a* and *z*:

  key( a-z, f).    key( a-z, g).

We shall implement the following principles of route finding:
  To find a route between two cities X and Z:

  (1) if there are key points Y1, Y2, . . . between X and Z then find either

    • route from A to Z via Y1, or
    • route from A to Z via Y2, or

  (2) if there is no key point between X and Z then simply find some neighbour city Y of X such that there is a route from Y to Z.

We have, then, two kinds of problems that will be represented as:

(1)  **X-Z**       find a route from X to Z
(2)  **X-Z via Y**   find a route from X to Z through Y

Here 'via' is an infix operator with precedence higher than that of '-' and lower than that of '--->'. The corresponding AND/OR graph can now be implicitly defined by the following piece of program:

  :- op( 560, xfx, via).

  % Expansion rule for problem X-Z when
  % there are key points between X and Z,
  % costs of all arcs are equal 0

  X-Z ---> or : ProblemList
    :- bagof( ( X-Z via Y)/0, key( X-Z, Y), ProblemList), !.

  % Expansion rule for problem X-Z with no key points

  X-Z ---> or : ProblemList
    :- bagof( ( Y-Z)/D, s( X, Y, D), ProblemList).

  % Reduce a 'via problem' to two AND-related subproblems
    X-Z via Y ---> and : [( X-Y)/0, ( Y-Z)/0].

  goal( X-X).                    % To go from X to X is trivial

The function *h* could be defined, for example, as the air distance between cities.

# EXERCISES

**14.4** Let an AND/OR graph be defined by:

a - - -> or:[b/1,c/2].

b - - -> and:[d/1,e/1].

c - - -> and:[e/1,f/1].

d - - -> or:[h/6].

e - - -> or:[h/2].

f - - -> or:[h/4,i/2].

goal(h).         goal(i).

Draw all the solution trees and calculate their costs. Suppose this graph is searched by the AO* algorithm, where the start node is *a*, and the heuristic *h*-values of the nodes *b*, *d*, *e*, *h* and *i* are all 0. Give the intervals for the values $h(c)$ and $h(f)$ that allow AO* to find the optimal solution.

**14.5** Write a procedure

**show2( SolutionTree)**

to display a solution tree found by the **andor** program of Figure 14.12. Let the display format be similar to that of the **show** procedure of Figure 14.8, so that **show2** can be written as a modification of **show**, using a different tree representation. Another useful modification would be to replace the goal **write( Node)** in **show** by a user-defined procedure

**writenode( Node, H)**

which outputs **Node** in some suitable form, and instantiates H to the number of characters that **Node** takes if output in this form. H is then used for proper indentation of subtrees.

# Summary

- AND/OR graph is a formalism for representing problems. It naturally suits problems that are decomposable into independent subproblems. Game playing is an example of such problems.
- Nodes of an AND/OR graph are of two types: AND nodes and OR nodes.
- A concrete problem is defined by a start node and a goal condition. A solution of a problem is represented by a solution graph.
- Costs of arcs and nodes can be introduced into an AND/OR graph to model optimization problems.
- Solving a problem, represented by an AND/OR graph, involves searching the graph. The depth-first strategy searches the graph systematically and is easy to program. However, it may suffer from inefficiency due to combinatorial explosion.

- Heuristic estimates can be introduced to estimate the difficulty of problems, and the best-first heuristic principle can be used to guide the search. Implementing this strategy is more difficult.

- Prolog programs for depth-first search, depth-first iterative deepening and best-first search of AND/OR graphs were developed in this chapter.

- Concepts introduced in this chapter are:

  AND/OR graphs
  AND arcs, OR arcs
  AND nodes, OR nodes
  solution graph, solution tree
  arc costs, node costs
  heuristic estimates in AND/OR graphs, backed-up estimates
  depth-first search in AND/OR graphs
  iterative deepening in AND/OR graphs
  best-first search in AND/OR graphs

## References

AND/OR graphs and related search algorithms are part of the classical artificial intelligence problem-solving and game-playing machinery. An early example of their application is a symbolic integration program (Slagle 1963). Prolog itself does AND/OR search. AND/OR graphs can be found in general books on artificial intelligence (Russell and Norvig 2010). Our best-first AND/OR program is a variation of an algorithm known as AO*. Formal properties of AO* (including its admissibility) have been studied by several authors; Pearl (1984) gives a comprehensive account of these results.

Pearl, J. (1984) *Heuristics: Intelligent Search Strategies for Computer Problem Solving*. Addison-Wesley.

Russell, S.J. and Norvig, P. (2010) *Artificial Intelligence: A Modern Approach*, third edn. Prentice Hall.

Slagle, J.R. (1963) A heuristic program that solves symbolic integration problems in freshman calculus. In: *Computers and Thought* (Feigenbaum, E. and Feldman, J., eds). McGraw-Hill.

# Chapter 15

## Knowledge Representation and Expert Systems

An expert system is a program that behaves like an expert for some problem domain. It uses domain-specific knowledge, and it should be capable of *explaining* its decisions and the underlying reasoning. Typically, an expert system is expected to be able to deal with uncertain and incomplete information. In this chapter we will review basic concepts in representing knowledge and building expert systems.

## 15.1 Functions and structure of an expert system

An *expert system* is a program that behaves like an expert in some, usually narrow, domain of application. Typical applications include tasks such as medical diagnosis, locating equipment failures, or interpreting measurement data. Expert systems have to be capable of solving problems that require expert knowledge in the application domain. They should possess that knowledge in some form. Therefore they are also called *knowledge-based systems*. However, not every knowledge-based system can be considered an expert system. We take the view that an expert system also has to be capable, in some way, of *explaining* its behaviour and its decisions to the user, as human experts do. Such an explanation feature is especially necessary in uncertain domains (like medical diagnosis) to enhance the user's confidence in the system's advice, or to enable the user to detect a possible flaw in the system's reasoning. Therefore, expert systems have to have a friendly user-interaction capability that will make the system's reasoning transparent to the user.

An additional feature that is typically required of an expert system is the ability to deal with uncertainty and incompleteness. Information about the problem to be solved can be incomplete or unreliable; relations in the problem domain can be approximate. For example, we may not be quite sure that some symptom is present in the patient, or that some measurement data are absolutely correct; some drug *may* cause some problem, but *usually* does not. All this requires reasoning with uncertainty.

To build an expert system we have, in general, to develop the following functions:

- *problem-solving* function capable of using domain-specific knowledge – this may require *dealing with uncertainty*;

- *user-interaction* function, which includes explanation of the system's intentions and decisions during and after the problem-solving process.

Each of these functions can be very complicated, and may depend on the domain of application and practical requirements. Various intricate problems may arise in the design and implementation. This involves the representation of knowledge and associated reasoning. In this chapter we will develop a framework of basic ideas that can be further refined.

It is convenient to divide the development of an expert system into three main modules, as illustrated in Figure 15.1:

(1) a knowledge base,

(2) an inference engine,

(3) a user interface.

A *knowledge base* comprises the knowledge that is specific to the domain of application, including such things as simple facts about the domain, rules or constraints that describe relations or phenomena in the domain, and possibly also methods, heuristics and ideas for solving problems in this domain. An *inference engine* knows how to actively use the knowledge in the base. A *user interface* caters for smooth communication between the user and the system, also providing the user with an insight into the problem-solving process carried out by the inference engine. It is convenient to view the inference engine and the interface as one module, usually called an *expert system shell*, or simply a *shell* for brevity.

The foregoing scheme separates knowledge from algorithms that use the knowledge. This division is suitable for the following reasons: the knowledge base clearly depends on the application. On the other hand, the shell is, in principle at least, domain independent. Thus a rational way of developing expert systems for several applications consists of developing a shell that can be used universally, and then to plug in a new knowledge base for each application. Of

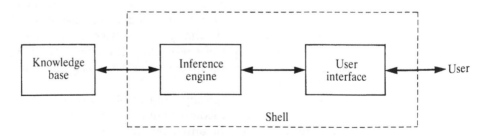

**Figure 15.1** The structure of expert systems.

course, all the knowledge bases will have to conform to the same formalism that is 'understood' by the shell. According to practical experience in complex expert systems the scenario with one shell and many knowledge bases will not work quite so smoothly unless the application domains are indeed very similar. Nevertheless, even if modifications of the shell from one domain to another are necessary, at least the main principles can be retained.

This chapter presents some basic expert systems techniques. In particular, we will look at representing knowledge with if-then rules, basic inference mechanisms in rule-based expert systems (such as forward or backward chaining), enhancing rule-based representation with uncertainty, semantic networks and frame-based representation of knowledge. Bayesian networks are the most common formalism for representing uncertain knowledge. They will be the topic of the next chapter.

## 15.2   Representing knowledge with if-then rules

In principle, any consistent formalism in which we can express knowledge about some problem domain can be considered for use in an expert system. However, the language of *if-then* rules, also called *production* rules, is traditionally the most popular formalism for representing knowledge in expert systems. In general, such rules are conditional statements, but they can have various interpretations. Examples are:

- *if* precondition P *then* conclusion C;
- *if* situation S *then* action A;
- *if* conditions C1 and C2 hold *then* condition C does not hold.

If-then rules usually turn out to be a natural form of expressing knowledge, and have the following desirable features:

- *Modularity*: each rule defines a small, relatively independent piece of knowledge.
- *Incrementability*: new rules can be added to the knowledge base relatively independently of other rules.
- *Modifiability* (as a consequence of modularity): old rules can be changed relatively independent of other rules.
- Support system's *transparency*.

This last property is an important and distinguishing feature of expert systems. By transparency of the system we mean the system's ability to explain its decisions and solutions. If-then rules facilitate answering the following basic types of user's questions:

(1)  'How' questions: *How* did you reach this conclusion?

(2)  'Why' questions: *Why* are you interested in this information?

Mechanisms, based on if-then rules, for answering such questions will be discussed later.

If-then rules often define logical relations between concepts of the problem domain. Purely logical relations can be characterized as belonging to 'categorical knowledge', 'categorical' because they are always meant to be absolutely true. However, in some domains, such as medical diagnosis, 'soft' or probabilistic knowledge prevails. It is 'soft' in the sense that empirical regularities are usually only valid to a certain degree (often but not always). In such cases if-then rules may be modified by adding a probabilistic qualification to their logical interpretation. For example:

*if* condition A *then* conclusion B follows *with certainty* F

Figures 15.2, 15.3 and 15.4 give an idea of the variety of ways of expressing knowledge by if-then rules. They show example rules from three different knowledge-based systems: MYCIN for medical consultation, AL/X for diagnosing equipment failures and AL3 for problem solving in chess.

In general, if you want to develop a serious expert system for some chosen domain then you have to consult actual experts for that domain and learn a great deal about it yourself. Extracting some understanding of the domain from experts and literature, and moulding this understanding into a chosen knowledge-representation formalism is called *knowledge elicitation*. This is, as a rule, a complex effort that we cannot go into here. But we do need some domain and a small knowledge base as material to carry out our examples in this chapter. Consider the toy knowledge base shown in Figure 15.5. It is concerned with

---

**if**
    1 the infection is primary bacteremia, and
    2 the site of the culture is one of the sterilesites, and
    3 the suspected portal of entry of the organism is the gastrointestinal tract
**then**
    there is suggestive evidence (0.7) that the identity of the organism is bacteroides.

---

**Figure 15.2** An if-then rule from the MYCIN system for medical consultation (Shortliffe 1976). The parameter 0.7 says to what degree the rule can be trusted.

---

**if**
    the pressure in V-01 reached relief valve lift pressure
**then**
    the relief valve on V-01 has lifted [$N = 0.005, S = 400$]
**if**
    NOT the pressure in V-01 reached relief valve lift pressure, and the relief valve on V-01 has lifted
**then**
    the V-01 relief valve opened early (the set pressure has drifted) [$N = 0.001, S = 2000$]

---

**Figure 15.3** Two rules from an AL/X demonstration knowledge base for fault diagnosis (Reiter 1980). $N$ and $S$ are the 'necessity' and 'sufficiency' measures. $S$ estimates to what degree the condition part of the rule *suffices* to infer the conclusion part. $N$ estimates to what degree the truth of the condition part is *necessary* for the conclusion to be true.

> **if**
>     1 there is a hypothesis, $H$, that a plan $P$ succeeds, and
>     2 there are two hypotheses,
>        $H_1$, that a plan $R_1$ refutes plan $P$, and
>        $H_2$, that a plan $R_2$ refutes plan $P$, and
>     3 there are facts: $H_1$ is *false*, and $H_2$ is *false*
> **then**
>     1 generate the hypothesis, $H_3$, that the combined plan '$R_1$ or $R_2$' refutes plan $P$,
>        and
>     2 generate the fact: $H_3$ *implies* not($H$)

**Figure 15.4** A rule for plan refinement in chess problem solving from the AL3 system (Bratko 1982).

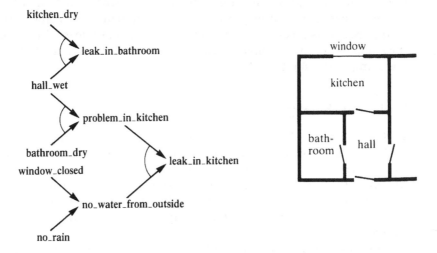

**Figure 15.5** A toy knowledge base to diagnose leaks in water appliances in the flat shown.

diagnosing the problem of water leaking in a flat. A problem can arise either in the bathroom or in the kitchen. In either case, the leakage also causes a problem (water on the floor) in the hall. Apart from its overall naivety, this knowledge base only assumes single faults; that is, the problem may be in the bathroom or the kitchen, but not in both of them at the same time. This knowledge base is shown in Figure 15.5 as an *inference network*. Nodes in the network correspond to propositions and links correspond to rules in the knowledge base. Arcs that connect some of the links indicate the conjunctive connection between the corresponding propositions. Accordingly, the rule about a problem in the kitchen in this network is:

    *if* hall_wet *and* bathroom_dry *then* problem_in_kitchen

The network representation of Figure 15.5 is, in fact, an AND/OR graph as discussed in Chapter 14. This indicates the relevance of AND/OR representation of problems in the context of rule-based expert systems.

## 15.3 Forward and backward chaining in rule-based systems

Once knowledge is represented in some form, we need a reasoning procedure to draw conclusions from the knowledge base. There are two basic ways of reasoning with if-then rules:

- backward chaining, and
- forward chaining.

Both of these procedures are very easily implemented in Prolog. In fact, procedures for searching AND/OR graphs, presented in Chapter 14, can be used here. On the other hand, there is often an emphasis in expert systems on the style of search, from its semantic point of view, in relation to the human reasoning; that is, it is desirable to sequence the reasoning in ways that humans find natural in the domain of application. This is important when interaction with the user occurs during the reasoning process and we want to make this process transparent to the user. This section sketches, in Prolog, the basic reasoning procedures as they appear in the context of expert systems, although they are similar to searching AND/OR graphs.

### 15.3.1 Backward chaining

With our example knowledge base of Figure 15.5, reasoning in the backward chaining style may proceed as follows. We start with a hypothesis – for example, **leak_in_kitchen** – then we reason backwards in the inference network. To confirm the hypothesis, we need **problem_in_kitchen** and **no_water_from_outside** to be true. The former is confirmed if we find that the hall is wet and the bathroom is dry. The latter is confirmed, for example, if we find that the window was closed.

This style of reasoning is called backward chaining because we follow a chain of rules backwards from the hypothesis (**leak_in_kitchen**) to the pieces of evidence (**hall_wet**, etc.). This is trivially programmed in Prolog – this is, in fact, Prolog's own built-in style of reasoning. The straightforward way is to state the rules in the knowledge base as Prolog rules:

```
leak_in_bathroom :-
  hall_wet,
  kitchen_dry.

problem_in_kitchen :-
  hall_wet,
  bathroom_dry.

no_water_from_outside :-
  window_closed
  ;
  no_rain.

leak_in_kitchen :-
  problem_in_kitchen,
  no_water_from_outside.
```

The observed pieces of evidence can be stated as Prolog facts:

```
hall_wet.
bathroom_dry.
window_closed.
```

The hypothesis can now be checked by:

```
?- leak_in_kitchen.
yes
```

Using Prolog's own syntax for rules, as in the foregoing, has certain disadvantages however:

(1) This syntax may not be the most suitable for a user unfamiliar with Prolog; for example, the domain expert should be able to read the rules, specify new rules and modify them.

(2) The knowledge base is not syntactically distinguishable from the rest of the program; a more explicit distinction between the knowledge base and the rest of the program may be desirable.

It is easiest to tailor the syntax of expert rules to our taste by using Prolog operator notation. For example, we can choose to use 'if', 'then', 'and' and 'or' as operators, appropriately declared as:

```
:- op( 800, fx, if).
```

```
:- op( 700, xfx, then).
```

```
:- op( 300, xfy, or).
```

```
:- op( 200, xfy, and).
```

This suffices to write our example rules of Figure 15.5 as:

```
if
   hall_wet and kitchen_dry
then
   leak_in_bathroom.

if
   hall_wet and bathroom_dry
then
   problem_in_kitchen.

if
   window_closed or no_rain
then
   no_water_from_outside.
. . .
```

Let the observable findings be stated as a procedure **fact**:

```
fact( hall_wet).
```

```
fact( bathroom_dry).
```

```
fact( window_closed).
```

```
% A simple backward chaining rule interpreter

:- op( 800, fx, if).
:- op( 700, xfx, then).
:- op( 300, xfy, or).
:- op( 200, xfy, and).

is_true( P) :-
    fact( P).

is_true( P) :-
    if Condition then P,              % A relevant rule
    is_true( Condition).              % whose condition is true

is_true( P1 and P2) :-
    is_true( P1),
    is_true( P2).

is_true( P1 or P2) :-
    is_true( P1)
    ;
    is_true( P2).
```

**Figure 15.6** A backward chaining interpreter for if-then rules.

Of course, we now need a new interpreter for rules in the new syntax. Such an interpreter can be defined as the procedure

   is_true( P)

where proposition **P** is either given in procedure **fact** or can be derived using rules. The new rule interpreter is given in Figure 15.6. Note that it still does backward chaining in the depth-first manner. The interpreter can now be called by the question:

   ?- is_true( leak_in_kitchen).

   yes

A major practical disadvantage of the simple inference procedures in this section is that the user has to state all the relevant information as facts in advance, before the reasoning process is started. So the user may state too much or too little. Therefore, it would be better for the information to be provided by the user interactively in a dialogue when it is needed. A simple example of such a dialogue facility will be programmed in Section 15.4.

## 15.3.2  Forward chaining

In backward chaining we start with a hypothesis (such as leak in the kitchen) and work backwards, according to the rules in the knowledge base, toward easily confirmed findings (such as the hall is wet). Sometimes it is more natural to reason in the opposite direction, from the 'if' part to the 'then' part. Forward chaining does

```
% Simple forward chaining in Prolog

forward :-
  new_derived_fact( P),                        % A new fact
  !,
  write( 'Derived: '), write( P), nl,
  assert( fact( P)),
  forward                                      % Continue
  ;
  write( 'No more facts').                     % All facts derived

new_derived_fact( Concl) :-
  if Cond then Concl,                          % A rule
  \+ fact( Concl),                             % Rule's conclusion not yet a fact
  composed_fact( Cond).                        % Condition true?

composed_fact( Cond) :-
  fact( Cond).                                 % Simple fact

composed_fact( Cond1 and Cond2) :-
  composed_fact( Cond1),
  composed_fact( Cond2).                       % Both conjuncts true

composed_fact( Cond1 or Cond2) :-
  composed_fact( Cond1)
  ;
  composed_fact( Cond2).
```

**Figure 15.7** A forward chaining rule interpreter.

not start with a hypothesis, but with some confirmed findings. Once we have observed that the hall is wet and the bathroom is dry, we conclude that there is a problem in the kitchen; also, having noticed the kitchen window is closed, we infer that no water came from the outside; this leads to the final conclusion that there is a leak in the kitchen.

Programming simple forward chaining in Prolog is still easy if not exactly as trivial as backward chaining. Figure 15.7 shows a forward chaining interpreter, assuming that rules are, as before, in the form:

  **if Condition then Conclusion**

where Condition can be an AND/OR expression. For simplicity we assume throughout this chapter that rules do not contain variables. This interpreter starts with what is already known (stated in the **fact** relation), derives all conclusions that follow from this and adds (using **assert**) the conclusions to the **fact** relation. For **assert** to work, in some Prologs the predicate **fact** has to be declared as dynamic by:

  **:- dynamic( fact/1).**

Our example knowledge base is run by this interpreter thus:

**?- forward.**

**Derived: problem_in_kitchen**
**Derived: no_water_from_outside**
**Derived: leak_in_kitchen**
**No more facts**

## 15.3.3    Forward chaining vs backward chaining

If-then rules form chains that, in Figure 15.5, go from left to right. The elements on the left-hand side of these chains are input information, while those on the right-hand side are derived information:

input information → ⋯ → derived information

These two kinds of information have a variety of names, depending on the context in which they are used. Input information can be called *data* (for example, measurement data) or *findings* or *manifestations*. Derived information can be called *hypotheses* to be proved, or *causes* of manifestations, or *diagnoses*, or *explanations* that explain findings. So chains of inference steps connect various types of information, such as:

data → ⋯ → goals
evidence → ⋯ → hypotheses
findings, observations → ⋯ → explanations, diagnoses
manifestations → ⋯ → diagnoses, causes

Both forward and backward chaining involve search, but they differ in the direction of search. Backward chaining searches from goals to data, from diagnoses to findings, etc. In contrast, forward chaining searches from data to goals, from findings to explanations or diagnoses, etc. As backward chaining starts with goals we say that it is *goal driven*. Similarly, since forward chaining starts with data we say that it is *data driven*.

An obvious question is: Which is better, forward or backward chaining? The answer depends on the problem. If we want to check whether a particular hypothesis is true then it is more natural to chain backward, starting with the hypothesis in question. On the other hand, if there are many competing hypotheses, and there is no reason to start with one rather than another, it may be better to chain forward. In particular, forward chaining is more natural in monitoring tasks where the data are acquired continuously and the system has to detect whether an anomalous situation has arisen; a change in the input data can be propagated in the forward chaining fashion to see whether this change indicates some fault in the monitored process or a change in the performance level. In choosing between forward or backward chaining, simply the shape of the rule network can also help. If there are a few data nodes (the left flank of the network) and many goal nodes (right flank) then forward chaining looks more appropriate; if there are few goal nodes and many data nodes then vice versa.

Expert tasks are usually more intricate and call for a combination of chaining in both directions. In medicine, for example, some initial observations in the patient typically trigger doctor's reasoning in the forward direction to generate some initial diagnostic hypothesis. This initial hypothesis has to be confirmed or rejected by additional evidence, which is done in the backward chaining style. In our example of Figure 15.5, observing the hall wet may trigger the following inference steps:

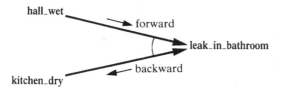

# EXERCISE

**15.1** Write a program that combines forward and backward chaining in the style discussed in this section.

 ## Generating explanation

There are standard ways of generating explanation in rule-based systems. Two usual types of explanation are called 'how' and 'why' explanation. Let us consider first the 'how' explanation. When the system comes up with an answer, the user may ask: *How* did you find this answer? The typical explanation consists of presenting the user with the trace of *how* the answer was derived. Suppose the system has just found that there is a leak in the kitchen and the user is asking 'How?'. The explanation can be along the following line:

Because:

(1)  there is a problem in the kitchen, which was concluded from hall wet and bathroom dry, and
(2)  no water came from outside, which was concluded from window closed.

Such an explanation is in fact a *proof tree* of how the final conclusion follows from rules and facts in the knowledge base. Let '<=' be defined as an infix operator. Then we can choose to represent the proof tree of a proposition **P** in one of the following forms, depending on the case:

(1)  If **P** is a fact then the whole proof tree is just **P** itself.

(2)  If **P** was derived using a rule

   **if Cond then P**

then the proof tree is

   **P <= ProofCond**

where **ProofCond** is a proof tree of **Cond**.

(3)  Let **P1** and **P2** be propositions whose proof trees are **Proof1** and **Proof2**. If **P** is **P1 and P2** then the proof tree is **Proof1 and Proof2**. If **P** is **P1 or P2** then the proof tree is either **Proof1** or **Proof2**.

```
% is_true( P, Proof) Proof is a proof that P is true

:- op( 800, xfx, <=).

is_true( P, P) :-
   fact( P).

is_true( P, P <= CondProof) :-
   if Cond then P,
   is_true( Cond, CondProof).

is_true( P1 and P2, Proof1 and Proof2) :-
   is_true( P1, Proof1),
   is_true( P2, Proof2).

is_true( P1 or P2, Proof) :-
   is_true( P1, Proof)
   ;
   is_true( P2, Proof).
```

**Figure 15.8** Generating proof trees as 'how' explanation.

Constructing proof trees in Prolog is straightforward and can be achieved by refining the predicate **is_true** of Figure 15.6 according to the three cases above. Figure 15.8 shows such a modified **is_true** predicate. Notice that proof trees of this kind are essentially the same as solution trees for problems represented by AND/OR graphs. Displaying proof trees in some user-friendly format can be programmed similarly to displaying AND/OR solution trees.

In contrast to 'how' explanation, the 'why' explanation is required *during* the reasoning process, not at the end of it. This requires user interaction with the reasoning process. The system asks the user for information at the moment that the information is needed. When asked, the user may answer 'Why?', thus triggering the 'why' explanation. Consider again the leaks knowledge base of Figure 15.5. Now suppose that the facts like **fact( hall_wet)** are not given in advance, but they are to be acquired from the user during the interactive reasoning process. We will now program such an interactive expert system shell, including the 'why' explanation, capable of the following dialogue with the user (user's answers are in italic):

?- is_true( leak_in_kitchen, How_explanation).

Is it true:hall_wet?

Please answer yes, no, or why
|: *yes.*

Is it true:bathroom_dry?
Please answer yes, no, or why
|: *yes.*

Is it true:window_closed?
Please answer yes, no, or why
|: *no.*

Is it true:no_rain?
Please answer yes, no, or why
|: *why*.                % User doesn't know about rain, so wants to learn why rain matters

To explore whether no_water_from_outside is true, using rule
if window_closed or no_rain then no_water_from_outside
  To explore whether leak_in_kitchen is true, using rule
  if problem_in_kitchen and no_water_from_outside then leak_in_kitchen

Is it true:no_rain?
Please answer yes, no, or why
|: *yes*.
How_explanation =
    (leak_in_kitchen <=
        (problem_in_kitchen <= (hall_wet <= was_told)
                            and (bathroom_dry <= was_told))
        and (no_water_from_outside <= (no_rain <= was_told)))

The display of **How_explanation** here was manually formatted for readability. In the answer to the user's how-question, the chain of two rules was displayed that connect the current goal **no_rain** with the original goal **leak_in_kitchen**.

To enable the 'real-time' querying the user about goals, some kinds of goals will be declared as *askable*, meaning that they can be asked of the user. This is added to the knowledge base as:

    askable( hall_wet).

    askable( kitchen_dry).

    . . .

Whenever the program during backward chaining encounters such a goal P, the program may ask the user whether P is true. Then the user may answer by 'yes', 'no' or 'why'. The latter answer means the user is wondering why this piece of information is needed. This is particularly natural in situations when the user does not know an answer and would need to spend some effort to find out about the answer.

In the case that the user says 'yes', the program asserts into the program the clause **fact(P)**. Also in the case of answer 'yes' or 'no', the program asserts the clause **already_asked(P)** to avoid asking the same question in the future. In the case of 'why', an appropriate explanation consists of a chain of rules connecting G with the original goal (**leak_in_kitchen** in our example). Figure 15.9 presents an interactive expert system shell implemented along these lines.

The program in Figure 15.9 is rather simplistic. For example, it would not work well in cases when a goal asked of the user contains variables, like **temperature(City,T)**. In such cases, the user, in addition to answering 'yes', would also have to specify concrete values of the variables for which the goal is true. The mechanism of querying the user, and of storing the answers would be more sophisticated and complicated. An expert system shell in Prolog that does this can be found in Bratko (2001).

```
% Interaction with user and why and how explanation
:- op( 800, xfx, <=).
% is_true( P, Proof): Proof is a proof that P is true
is_true( P, Proof) :-
  explore( P, Proof, []).

% explore( P, Proof, Trace):
%    Proof is an explanation for P, Trace is a chain of rules between P's ancestor goals
explore( P, P, _) :-
  fact( P).                                    % P is a fact

explore( P1 and P2, Proof1 and Proof2, Trace) :- !,
  explore( P1, Proof1, Trace),
  explore( P2, Proof2, Trace).

explore( P1 or P2, Proof, Trace) :- !,
  (
    explore( P1, Proof, Trace)
  ;
    explore( P2, Proof, Trace)
  ).

explore( P, P <= CondProof, Trace) :-
  if Cond then P,                              % A rule relevant to P
  explore( Cond, CondProof, [ if Cond then P | Trace]).

explore( P, Proof, Trace) :-
  askable( P),                                 % P may be asked of user
  \+ fact( P),                                 % P not already known fact
  \+ already_asked( P),                        % P not yet asked of user
  ask_user( P, Proof, Trace).

ask_user( P, Proof, Trace) :-
  nl, write( 'Is it true:'), write( P), write(?), nl, write( 'Please answer yes, no, or why'), nl,
  read( Answer),
  process_answer( Answer, P, Proof, Trace).    % Process user's answer

process_answer( yes, P, P <= was_told, _) :-   % User told P is true
  asserta( fact(P)),
  asserta( already_asked( P)).

process_answer( no, P, _, _) :-
  asserta( already_asked( P)),                 % Make sure not to ask again about P
  fail.                                        % User told P is not true

process_answer( why, P, Proof, Trace) :-       % User requested why-explanation
  display_rule_chain( Trace, 0), nl,
  ask_user( P, Proof, Trace).                  % Ask about P again

display_rule_chain( [], _).

display_rule_chain( [if C then P | Rules], Indent) :-
  nl, tab( Indent), write( 'To explore whether '), write( P), write(' is true, using rule'),
  nl, tab( Indent), write( if C then P),
  NextIndent is Indent + 2,
  display_rule_chain( Rules, NextIndent).

:- dynamic already_asked/1.
```

**Figure 15.9** Interactive expert system shell with how and why explanation.

## 15.5   Introducing uncertainty

### 15.5.1   A simple uncertainty scheme

In the foregoing discussion, the representation assumes problem domains that are *categorical*; that is, answers to all questions are either true or false, not somewhere between. As data, rules were also categorical: 'categorical implications'. However, many expert domains are not categorical. Typical expert behaviour is full of guesses (although highly articulated) that are usually true, but there can be exceptions. Both data about a particular problem and general rules can be less than certain. We can model uncertainty by assigning some qualification, other than just true or false, to assertions. Such qualification can be expressed by descriptors – for example, *true, highly likely, likely, unlikely, impossible*. Alternatively, the degree of belief can be expressed by a real number in some interval – for example, between 0 and 1 or −5 and +5. Such numbers are known by a variety of names, such as 'certainty factor', 'measure of belief' or 'subjective probability'. The most principled possibility is to use probabilities because of their solid mathematical foundation. However, correct reasoning with probabilities according to the probability calculus is typically more demanding than the reasoning in simpler, *ad hoc* uncertainty schemes.

We will discuss the use of probabilities in association with Bayesian networks in Chapter 16. In this section we will extend our rule-based representation with a simpler uncertainty scheme that only very roughly approximates probabilities. Each proposition will be added a number between 0 and 1 as a certainty qualification. We will choose to represent this as a pair of the form:

> **Proposition : CertaintyFactor**

This notation applies to rules as well. So the following form defines a rule and the degree of certainty to which the rule is valid:

> **if Condition then Conclusion : Certainty.**

In any representation with uncertainty we need a way of combining the certainties of propositions and rules. For example, let there be two propositions $P1$ and $P2$ whose certainties are $C1$ and $C2$. What is the certainty of logical combinations $P1$ *and* $P2$, $P1$ *or* $P2$? The following is one simple scheme for combining certainties. Let $P1$ and $P2$ be propositions, and $c(P1)$ and $c(P2)$ denote their certainties. Then:

$$c(P1 \ and \ P2) = min(c(P1), c(P2))$$
$$c(P1 \ or \ P2) = max(c(P1), c(P2))$$

If there is a rule

> **if P1 then P2 : C**

then

$$c(P2) = c(P1) * C$$

For simplicity we assume that no more than one rule ever bears on the same assertion. If there were two rules bearing on the same assertion in the knowledge

```
% Rule interpreter with certainties
% certainty( Proposition, Certainty)

certainty( P, Cert) :-
  given( P, Cert).

certainty( Cond1 and Cond2, Cert) :-
  certainty( Cond1, Cert1),
  certainty( Cond2, Cert2),
  min( Cert1, Cert2, Cert).

certainty( Cond1 or Cond2, Cert) :-
  certainty( Cond1, Cert1),
  certainty( Cond2, Cert2),
  max( Cert1, Cert2, Cert).

certainty( P, Cert) :-
  if Cond then P : C1,
  certainty( Cond, C2),
  Cert is C1 * C2.
```

**Figure 15.10** An interpreter for rules with certainties.

base, they could be transformed using the *or* operator into equivalent rules that satisfy this assumption. Figure 15.10 shows a rule interpreter for this uncertainty scheme. The interpreter assumes that the user specifies the certainty estimates for the observables (left-most nodes in the rule network) by the relation

**given( Proposition, Certainty)**

Now we can 'soften' some rule in our knowledge base of Figure 15.5. For example:

**if**
  **hall_wet and bathroom_dry**
**then**
  **problem_in_kitchen : 0.9.**

A situation in which the hall is wet, the bathroom is dry, the kitchen is not dry, the window is not closed and we think that there was no rain but are not quite sure can be specified as:

| | |
|---|---|
| **given( hall_wet, 1).** | % Hall is wet |
| **given( bathroom_dry, 1).** | % Bathroom is dry |
| **given( kitchen_dry, 0).** | % Kitchen is not dry |
| **given( no_rain, 0.8).** | % Probably no rain, but not sure |
| **given( window_closed, 0).** | % Window not closed |

Now we can ask about a leak in the kitchen:

**?- certainty( leak_in_kitchen, C).**
**C = 0.8**

This is obtained as follows. The facts that the hall is wet and the bathroom is dry indicate a problem in the kitchen with certainty 0.9. Since there was some possibility of rain, the certainty of **no_water_from_outside** is 0.8. Finally, the certainty of **leak_in_kitchen** is min(0.8,0.9) = 0.8.

## 15.5.2 Difficulties in handling uncertainty

The question of handling uncertain knowledge has been historically much researched and debated. Typical controversial issues were the usefulness of probability theory in handling uncertainty in expert systems on the one hand and drawbacks of *ad hoc* uncertainty schemes on the other. Our ultra-simple approach in Section 15.5.1 belongs to the latter, and can be easily criticized. For example, suppose the certainty of *a* is 0.5 and that of *b* is 0. Then in our scheme the certainty of *a or b* is 0.5. Now suppose that the certainty of *b* increases to 0.5. In our scheme this change will not affect the certainty of *a or b* at all, which is counter-intuitive.

Many schemes for handling uncertainty that do not quite respect the axioms of probability have been proposed, used and investigated. The most common problem in such schemes typically stems from ignoring some dependences between propositions. For example, let there be a rule:

*if a or b then c*

The certainty of *c* should not only depend on the certainty of *a* and *b*, but also on any correlation between *a* and *b*; that is, whether they tend to occur together or they depend on each other in some other way. Completely correct treatment of these dependencies is more complicated than it had often been considered practical, and may require information that is not normally available. The difficulties were therefore often dodged by making the assumption of *independence* of events, such as *a* and *b* in the rule above. Under such independence assumption,

$$p(c) = p(a) + p(b) - p(a) * p(b)$$

where $p(a)$ denotes the probability of *a*, etc. Unfortunately, the independence assumption is not generally justifiable. In practice it is often simply not true, and may therefore lead to incorrect and counter-intuitive results. The generally correct formula is:

$$p(c) = p(a) + p(b) - p(a) * p(b|a)$$

This requires the knowledge of the conditional probability $p(b|a)$, that is the probability of *b* given that *a* is true. It has often been admitted that such departures from mathematically sound handling of uncertainty may be unsafe in general, but it has also been argued that they are solutions that work in practice. Along with this, it has been argued that probability theory, although mathematically sound, is impractical and not really appropriate for the following reasons:

- Human experts seem to have trouble thinking in terms of actual probabilities; their likelihood estimates do not quite correspond to probabilities as defined mathematically.

- Mathematically correct probabilistic treatment requires either information that is not available or some simplification assumptions that are not really quite justified in a practical application. In the latter case, the treatment would become mathematically unsound again.

To illustrate these difficulties, consider the computation of the probability of a more complex conjunction of events:

$$p(a\ b\ c\ d\ e) = p(a) * p(b\,|\,a) * p(c\,|\,a\ b) * p(d\,|\,a\ b\ c) * p(e\,|\,a\ b\ c\ d)$$

Obviously, complicated conditional probabilities are required. These are typically hard to obtain in reality. If the probabilities are estimated from data, a lot of data is required. The number of possible conditions in conditional probabilities grows exponentially with the number of variables (we have to take into account any combination of the variables and their negations). So the situation becomes exponentially more complex with the number of variables.

Conversely, there have been equally eager arguments in favour of mathematically well-justified approaches based on the probability theory. Both of the foregoing objections regarding probability have been convincingly answered in favour of probability theory. In *ad hoc* schemes that 'work in practice', dangers clearly arise from simplifications that involve unsafe assumptions. In the next chapter we introduce *Bayesian networks* – a representation that allows correct treatment of probability and at the same time enables relatively economical treatment of dependences.

## EXERCISE

**15.2**  Let an expert system approximate the probability of the union of two events by the same formula as in our simple uncertainty scheme:

$$p(A\ or\ B) \approx \max(p(A),p(B))$$

Under what condition does this formula give probabilistically correct results? In what situation does the formula make the greatest error, what is the error?

## 15.6 Semantic networks and frames

In this section we look at two other frameworks with a long tradition in AI for representing knowledge: *semantic networks* and *frames*. These differ from rule-based representations in that they are directed to representing, in a structured way, large sets of facts. The set of facts is structured and possibly compressed: facts can be abstracted away when they can be reconstructed through inference. Both semantic networks and frames use the mechanism of inheritance in a similar way as in object-oriented programming.

Semantic networks and frames can be easily implemented in Prolog. Essentially, this amounts to adopting, in a disciplined way, a particular style of programming and organizing a program.

## 15.6.1 Semantic networks

A semantic network consists of entities and relations between the entities. It is customary to represent a semantic network as a graph. There are various types of semantic network with various conventions, but usually nodes of the graph correspond to entities, while relations are shown as links labelled by the names of relations. Figure 15.11 shows such a network. The relation name **isa** stands for 'is a'. This network represents the following facts:

- A bird is a kind of animal.
- Flying is the normal moving method of birds.
- An albatross is a bird.
- Albert is an albatross, and so is Ross.

Notice that **isa** sometimes relates a class of objects with a superclass of the class (animal is a superclass of bird, i.e. a bird is a kind of animal), and sometimes an *instance* of a class with the class itself (Albert is an albatross).

A network of this kind is immediately translated into Prolog facts; for example, as:

```
isa( bird, animal).
isa( ross, albatross).
moving_method( bird, fly).
moving_method( kiwi, walk).
```

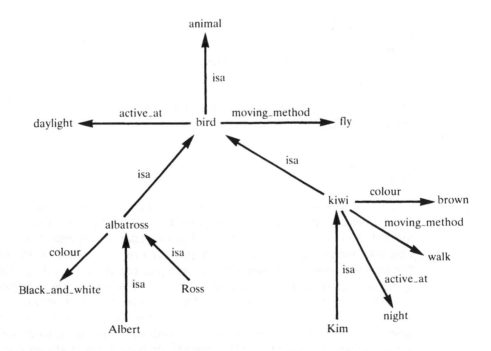

**Figure 15.11** A semantic network.

In addition to these facts, which are explicitly stated, some other facts can be inferred from the network. Ways of inferring other facts are built into a semantic network type representation as part of the representation. A typical built-in principle of inference is *inheritance*. So, in Figure 15.11, the fact 'albatross flies' is inherited from the fact 'birds fly'. Similarly, through inheritance, we have 'Ross flies' and 'Kim walks'. Facts are inherited through the **isa** relation. In Prolog, we can state that the method of moving is inherited as:

```
moving_method( X, Method) :-
    isa ( X, SuperX),                    % Climb isa hierarchy
      moving_method( SuperX, Method).
```

It is a little awkward to state a separate inheritance rule for each relation that can be inherited. Therefore, it is better to state a more general rule about facts: facts can be either explicitly stated in the network or inherited:

```
fact( Fact) :-                           % Fact not a variable; Fact = Rel( Arg1, Arg2)
    Fact, !.                             % Fact explicitly given – do not inherit

fact( Fact) :-
    Fact = . . [ Rel, Arg1, Arg2],
    isa( Arg1, SuperArg),                % Climb isa hierarchy
    SuperFact =. . [ Rel, SuperArg, Arg2],
    fact( SuperFact).
```

Our semantic network can now be asked some questions:

```
?- fact( moving_method( kim, Method) ).

Method = walk
```

This was inherited from the explicitly given fact that kiwis walk. On the other hand:

```
?- fact( moving_method( albert, Method) ).

Method = fly
```

This was inherited from the class **bird**. Note that in climbing up the **isa** hierarchy, the inherited fact is the one encountered first.

## 15.6.2  Frames

The frame representation of knowledge can be viewed as a predecessor of the idea of object oriented programming. In frame representation, facts are clustered around objects. 'Object' here means either a concrete physical object or a more abstract concept, such as a class of objects, or even a situation. Good candidates for representation by frames are, for example, the typical meeting situation or game conflict situation. Such situations have, in general, some common stereotype structure that can be filled with details of a particular situation.

A *frame* is a data structure whose components are called *slots*. Slots have names and accommodate information of various kinds. So, in slots, we can find simple values, references to other frames, or procedures that can compute the slot value from other information. A slot may also be left unfilled. Unfilled slots can be filled through inference. As in semantic networks, the most common principle of inference is inheritance. When a frame represents a class of objects (such as albatross) and another frame represents a superclass of this class (such as bird), then the class frame can inherit values from the superclass frame.

Some knowledge about birds can be put into frames as follows:

FRAME: bird
a_kind_of: animal
moving_method: fly
active_at: daylight

This frame stands for the class of all birds. Its three slots say that birds are a kind of animal (animal is a superclass of bird), that a typical bird flies and that a bird is active during daylight. Here are the frames for two subclasses of bird – albatross and kiwi:

FRAME: albatross
a_kind_of: bird
colour: black_and_white
size: 115

FRAME: kiwi
a_kind_of: bird
moving_method: walk
active_at: night
colour: brown
size: 40

Albatross is a very typical bird and it inherits the flying ability and daylight activity from the frame bird. Therefore, nothing is stated about **moving_method** and **active_at** in the albatross frame. On the other hand, kiwi is a rather untypical bird, and the usual **moving_method** and **active_at** values for birds have to be overruled in the case of the kiwi. We can also have a particular *instance* of a class; for example, an albatross called Albert:

FRAME: Albert
instance_of: albatross
size: 120

Notice the difference between the two relations **a_kind_of** and **instance_of**. The former is the relation between a class and a superclass, while the latter is the relation between a member of a class and the class.

The information in our example frames can be represented in Prolog as a set of facts, one fact for each slot value. This can be done in various ways. We will choose the following format for these facts:

**Frame_name( Slot, Value)**

The advantage of this format is that now all the facts about a particular frame are collected together under the relation whose name is the name of the frame itself. Figure 15.12 gives some frames in this format.

```
% A frame is represented as a set of Prolog facts:
%    frame_name( Slot, Value)
% where Value is either a simple value or a procedure

% Frame bird: the prototypical bird

bird( a_kind_of, animal).
bird( moving_method, fly).
bird( active_at, daylight).

% Frame albatross: albatross is a typical bird with some
% extra facts: it is black and white, and it is 115 cm long

albatross( a_kind_of, bird).
albatross( colour, black_and_white).
albatross( size, 115).

% Frame kiwi: kiwi is a rather untypical bird in that it
% walks instead of flies, and it is active at night

kiwi( a_kind_of, bird).
kiwi( moving_method, walk).
kiwi( active_at, night).
kiwi( size, 40).
kiwi( colour, brown).

% Frame albert: an instance of a big albatross

albert( instance_of, albatross).
albert( size, 120).

% Frame ross: an instance of a baby albatross

ross( instance_of, albatross).
ross( size, 40).

% Frame animal: slot relative_size obtains its value by
% executing procedure relative_size

animal( relative_size, execute( relative_size( Object, Value), Object, Value) ).
```

**Figure 15.12** Some frames.

To use such a set of frames, we need a procedure for retrieving facts about slot values. Let us implement such a fact retriever as a Prolog procedure

value( Frame, Slot, Value)

where **Value** is the value of slot **Slot** in frame **Frame**. If the slot is filled – that is, its value is explicitly stated in the frame – then this is the value; otherwise the value is obtained through inference – for example, inheritance. To find a value by inheritance, we have to move from the current frame to a more general frame according to the **a_kind_of** relation or **instance_of** relation between frames. Such a move leads to a 'parent frame' and the value may be found in this frame explicitly, or through further inheritance. This direct retrieval or retrieval by inheritance can be stated in Prolog as:

```
value( Frame, Slot, Value) :-
    Query = . . [ Frame, Slot, Value],
    Query, !.                              % Value directly retrieved

value( Frame, Slot, Value) :-
    parent( Frame, ParentFrame),           % A more general frame
    value( ParentFrame, Slot, Value).

parent( Frame, ParentFrame) :-
    ( Query = . . [ Frame, a_kind_of, ParentFrame]
      ;
      Query = . . [ Frame, instance_of, ParentFrame] ),
    Query.
```

This is sufficient to find values from frames in Figure 15.12, as in the questions:

```
?- value( albert, active_at, AlbertTime).
AlbertTime = daylight
```

```
?- value( kiwi, active_at, KiwiTime).
KiwiTime = night
```

Let us now consider a more complicated case of inference when a procedure for *computing* the value is given in the slot instead of the value itself. For example, one slot for all animals could be their relative size with respect to the typical size of a grown-up instance of their species. Stated in percentages, for the two albatrosses in Figure 15.12, the relative sizes are: Albert 104 percent, Ross 35 percent. These figures are obtained as the ratio (in percentage) between the size of the particular individual and the typical size of the individual's class. For Ross, this is:

$$40/115 * 100\% = 34.78\%$$

Thus, the value for the slot **relative_size** is obtained by executing a procedure. This procedure is universal for all the animals, so it is rational to define the slot **relative_size** in the frame **animal** and fill this slot by the corresponding procedure. The frame interpreter **value** should now be able to answer the question:

```
?- value( ross, relative_size, R).
```

```
R = 34.78
```

The way this result is obtained should be something like the following. We start at the frame **ross** and, seeing no value for **relative_size**, climb up the chain of relations **instance_of** (to get to frame **albatross**), **a_kind_of** (to get to frame **bird**) and **a_kind_of** again, to get finally to frame **animal**. Here we find the procedure for computing relative size. This procedure needs the value in slot **size** of frame **ross**. This value can be obtained through inheritance by our existing **value** procedure. It remains to extend the procedure **value** to handle the cases where a procedure in a slot is to be executed. Before we do that, we need to consider how such a procedure can be (indirectly) represented as the content of a slot. Let the procedure for computing the relative size be implemented as a Prolog predicate:

```
relative_size( Object, RelativeSize) :-
    value( Object, size, ObjSize),
    value( Object, instance_of, ObjClass),
    value( ObjClass, size, ClassSize),
    RelativeSize is ObjSize/ClassSize * 100.    % Percentage of class size
```

We can now fill the slot **relative_size** in frame **animal** with the call of this procedure. In order to prevent the arguments **Object** and **RelativeSize** getting lost in communication between frames, we also have to state them as part of the **relative_size** slot information. The contents of this slot can all be put together as one Prolog term; for example, as:

```
execute( relative_size( Object, RelSize), Object, RelSize)
```

The **relative_size** slot of frame **animal** is then specified by:

```
animal( relative_size, execute( relative_size( Obj, Val), Obj, Val)).
```

Now we are ready to modify the procedure **value** to handle procedural slots. First, we have to realize that the information found in a slot can be a procedure call; therefore, it has to be further processed by carrying out this call. This call may need, as arguments, slot values of the original frame in question. In our example, this original frame was **ross**. Our old procedure **value** forgets about this frame while climbing up to more general frames. Therefore, we have to introduce the original frame as an additional argument. The following piece of program does this:

```
value( Frame, Slot, Value) :-
    value( Frame, Frame, Slot, Value).

% Directly retrieving information in slot of (super)frame

value( Frame, SuperFrame, Slot, Value) :-
    Query =. . [ SuperFrame, Slot, Information],
    Query,                                       % Value directly retrieved
    process( Information, Frame, Value), !.      % Information is either a value
                                                 % or a procedure call

% Inferring value through inheritance

value( Frame, SuperFrame, Slot, Value) :-
    parent( SuperFrame, ParentSuperFrame),
    value( Frame, ParentSuperFrame, Slot, Value).

% process( Information, Frame, Value)

process( execute( Goal, Frame, Value), Frame, Value) :- !,
    Goal.
process( Value, _, Value).                       % A value, not procedure call
```

With this extension of our frame interpreter we have got close to the programming paradigm of object oriented programming. Although the terminology in that paradigm is usually different, the computation is essentially based on triggering the execution of procedures that belong to various frames.

Of the many subtleties of inference among frames, we have not addressed the question of *multiple inheritance*. This problem arises when a frame has more than one 'parent' frame (according to the relation **instance_of** or **a_kind_of**). Then, an inherited slot value may potentially come from more than one parent frame and the question of which one to adopt arises. Our procedure **value**, as it stands, simply takes the first value encountered, found by the depth-first search among the frames that potentially can supply the value. However, other strategies or tie-breaking rules may be more appropriate.

# EXERCISES

**15.3** Trace the execution of the query

```
?- value( ross, relative_size, Value).
```

to make sure you understand clearly how information is passed throughout the frame network in our frame interpreter.

**15.4** Let geometric figures be represented as frames. The following clauses represent a square s1 and a rectangle r2 and specify the method for computing the area of a figure:

```
s1( instance_of, square).
s1( side, 5).
r2( instance_of, rectangle).
r2( length, 6).
r2( width, 4).

square( a_kind_of, rectangle).
square( length, execute( value(Obj,side,L), Obj, L)).
square( width, execute( value(Obj,side,W), Obj, W)).
rectangle( area, execute( area(Obj,A), Obj, A)).

area( Obj, A) :-
   value( Obj, length, L), value( Obj, width, W),
   A is L*W.
```

How will the frame interpreter programmed in this section answer the question:

```
?- value( r2, length, A), value( s1, length, B), value( s1, area, C).
```

# Summary

- Typical functions required of an expert system are: solving problems in a given domain, explaining the problem-solving process, and handling uncertain and incomplete information.

- It is convenient to view an expert system as consisting of two modules: a shell and a knowledge base. A shell, in turn, consists of an inference mechanism and a user interface.

- Building an expert system shell involves decisions regarding the knowledge representation formalism, the inference mechanism, the user interaction facility and the treatment of uncertainty.

- If-then rules, or production rules, are a popular form of representing knowledge in expert systems.
- Two basic ways of reasoning in rule-based systems are: backward and forward chaining.
- Two usual types of explanation are associated with user's questions 'How? ' and 'Why?'. A proof tree can be used as a 'how' explanation. A chain of rules between the current question and the main question can be used as a 'why' explanation.
- Reasoning with uncertainty can be incorporated into the basic rule representation, and forward or backward chaining schemes. However, such additions to rules may make unjustified assumptions that simplify the probabilistic dependences between the variables in the domain.
- Other traditional knowledge representation schemes, suitable for representing large sets of facts in a structured way, are semantic networks and frames. Here facts can be directly retrieved or inferred through built-in mechanisms such as inheritance.
- In this chapter, stylized Prolog implementations were developed for backward and forward chaining, generating proof trees, interaction with the user and why-explanation, interpreting rules with uncertainty, reasoning in belief networks, inheritance in semantic networks and frames.
- Concepts discussed in this chapter are:

  > expert systems
  > knowledge base, expert system shell, inference engine
  > if-then rules, production systems
  > backward chaining, forward chaining
  > data driven inference
  > goal driven inference
  > 'how' explanation, 'why' explanation
  > categorical knowledge, uncertain knowledge
  > semantic networks
  > frames
  > inheritance

## References

General books on artificial intelligence, such as Russell and Norvig (2010), Luger (2009) and Poole and Mackworth (2010), include substantial coverage of knowledge representation and reasoning. The coverage of knowledge representation usually also includes ontologies. An *ontology* is a formal specification of domain-level concepts possibly in terms of logic, that is in terms of constants, functions and predicates. Jackson (1999) is one of a number of introductory texts on expert systems that includes a description of some well-known and historically important systems. An early and influential expert system MYCIN is described by Shortliffe (1976). Buchanan and Shortliffe (1984) is a collection of papers related to the MYCIN experiments. Pearl (1988) is a classic book on uncertainty and probabilistic reasoning in expert systems. Shafer and Pearl (1990) is a collection of papers on reasoning about uncertainty. Minsky (1975) is the classic paper on frame-type representation. Various approaches to knowledge representation for common sense reasoning, including time and space, are described by Davis (1990). Some of the examples in this chapter are taken from Bratko (1982), Reiter (1980) and Shortliffe (1976).

Bratko, I. (1982) Knowledge-based problem-solving in AL3. In: *Machine Intelligence 10* (Hayes, J.E., Michie, D. and Pao, Y.H., eds). Ellis Horwood.

Bratko, I. (2001) *Prolog Programming for Artificial Intelligence,* third edn. Pearson Education.

Buchanan, B.G. and Shortliffe, E.H. (eds) (1984) *Rule-based Expert Systems: The MYCIN Experiments of the Stanford Heuristic Programming Project.* Addison-Wesley.

Davis, E. (1990) *Representations of Commonsense Knowledge.* San Mateo, CA: Morgan Kaufmann.

Jackson, P. (1999) *Introduction to Expert Systems*, third edn. Harlow: Addison-Wesley.

Luger, G.F. (2009) *Artificial Intelligence,* fifth edn. Harlow: Addison-Wesley.

Minsky, M. (1975) A framework for representing knowledge. In: *The Psychology of Computer Vision* (Winston, P., ed.). McGraw-Hill.

Pearl, J. (1988) *Probabilistic Reasoning in Intelligent Systems: Networks of Plausible Inference.* San Mateo, CA: Morgan Kaufmann.

Poole, D. and Mackworth, A.(2010) *Computational Intelligence: A Logical Approach.* Oxford University Press.

Reiter, J. (1980) *AL/X: An Expert System Using Plausible Inference.* Oxford: Intelligent Terminals Ltd.

Russell, S. and Norvig, P. (2010) *Artificial Intelligence: A Modern Approach,* third edn. Prentice Hall.

Shafer, G. and Pearl, J. (eds) (1990) *Readings in Uncertain Reasoning.* San Mateo, CA: Morgan Kaufmann.

Shortliffe, E. (1976) *Computer-based Medical Consultations: MYCIN.* Elsevier.

# Chapter 16

# Probabilistic Reasoning with Bayesian Networks

Bayesian networks, also called belief networks, provide a way of using the probability calculus for handling uncertainty in knowledge representation. Bayesian networks enable economical handling of probabilistic dependencies, exploiting independences, and natural representation of causality. In this chapter we will study how dependences and independences between variables are stated by Bayesian networks, and implement a method for computing conditional probabilities for Bayesian network models.

## 16.1 Probabilities, beliefs and Bayesian networks

The main question addressed by *Bayesian networks*, also called *belief networks*, is: How to handle uncertainty correctly, in a principled and practical way? We already noted in Chapter 15 that these two goals of mathematical correctness and practicality are hard to achieve together, but Bayesian networks offer a good solution.

Let us first define a framework for discussion. We will be assuming that a state of the world is defined by a vector of variables that randomly take values from their domains (sets of their possible values). We will in all our examples limit the discussion to Boolean random variables only, whose possible values are true or false. For example, 'burglary' and 'alarm' are such variables. Variable 'alarm' is true when the alarm is sounding, and 'burglary' is true when the house has been broken into. Otherwise these variables are false. A state of such a world at some time is completely specified by giving the values of all the variables at this time. It should be noted that the limitation to Boolean variables is not significant. It will be quite obvious how to apply the approach to multi-valued domains.

When variables are Boolean, it is natural to consider them as *events*. For example, event 'alarm' happens when variable alarm = true.

An agent (a human or an expert system) usually cannot tell for sure whether such a variable is true or false. So instead the agent can only reason about the *probability* that a variable is true. Probabilities in this context are used as a measure of the agent's beliefs. The agent's beliefs, of course, depend on how much the agent knows about the world. Therefore such beliefs are also called *subjective probabilities*, meaning that they 'belong to the subject'. 'Subjective' here does not mean 'arbitrary'. Although these probabilities model an agent's subjective beliefs, they still conform to the calculus of probability theory.

Let us introduce some notation. Let $X$ and $Y$ be propositions, then:

$X \wedge Y$     is the conjunction of $X$ and $Y$ (also written as $XY$)
$X \vee Y$     is the disjunction of $X$ and $Y$
$\sim X$        is the negation of $X$

$p(X)$ denotes the probability that proposition $X$ is true. $p(X \mid Y)$ denotes the *conditional* probability that $X$ is true given that $Y$ is true.

A typical question about the world is: Given that the values of some variables have been observed, what are the probabilities of specific values of some other variables of interest? Or, given that some events have been observed, what are the probabilities of some other events? For example, alarm sounding has been observed, what is the probability that burglary has occurred?

The main difficulty is how to handle dependences among variables in the problem. Let there be $n$ binary variables in the problem, then $2^n - 1$ numbers are needed to define the complete probability distribution among the $2^n$ possible states of the world. This is usually too many! It is not only impractical and computationally expensive. It is usually impossible to make reasonable estimates of all these probabilities because there is not enough information available.

In fact, usually not all these probabilities are necessary. The complete probability distribution does not make any assumptions regarding independence among the variables. But it is usually unnecessary to be so cautious. Fortunately, some things *are* independent after all.

Therefore, to make the probabilistic approach practical, we have to exploit these independences. We need economical means of stating dependences among the variables, and at the same time benefit (in terms of complexity) from those things that actually are independent.

Bayesian networks provide an elegant way of declaring how things depend on each other, and what things are independent of each other. In Bayesian networks this can be stated in a natural and intuitive way.

Figure 16.1 shows an example Bayesian network about a burglary alarm system. The intention is that the sensor may be triggered by a burglar when the

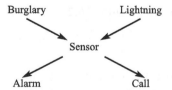

**Figure 16.1** A Bayesian network. When a burglar breaks into the house, he is likely to trigger the sensor. The sensor is in turn supposed to trigger a sound alarm and start an automatic phone call with a warning. A powerful electric storm may also trigger the sensor.

house is broken into. However, a vigorous bolt of lightning may also trigger the sensor. The sensor is supposed to trigger a sound alarm and a warning phone call. A typical question that such a Bayesian network helps to answer is something like: Suppose the weather is fine and we hear the alarm. Given these two facts, what is the probability of burglary?

The structure of this Bayesian network indicates some probabilistic dependences, as well as independences. It says, for example, that burglary is independent of lightning. If, however, it becomes known that alarm is true, then under this condition the probability of burglary is no longer independent of lightning.

In our example network, it is intuitively obvious that links in the network indicate causality. Burglary is a cause of triggering the sensor. The sensor may in turn cause an alarm. So the structure of the network allows us to reason like this: if alarm is true then burglary becomes likely as it is one of the causes that explain the alarm. If then we learn there was a heavy storm, burglary becomes less likely. Alarm is explained by another cause, lightning, so the first possible cause becomes less likely.

In this example the reasoning was both *diagnostic* and *predictive*: knowing alarm is true (consequence, or symptom of burglary), we inferred *diagnostically* that it might have been caused by burglary. Then we learned about the storm, and inferred *predictively* that it might have caused the alarm.

Let us now define more formally what exactly is stated by the links in a Bayesian network. What kind of probabilistic inferences can we make given a Bayesian network?

First, we define that a node $Z$ is a *descendant* of node $X$ if there is a path, following directed links in the network, from $X$ to $Z$.

Now suppose that $Y_1, Y_2, \ldots$ are the parents of $X$ in a Bayesian network. By definition, the Bayesian network implies the following relation of probabilistic independence: $X$ is independent of $X$'s non-descendants given $X$'s parents. So to compute the probability of $X$, it is sufficient to take into account $X$'s descendants and $X$'s parents $Y_1, Y_2$, etc. All the possible effects of other variables on $X$ are accumulated through $X$'s parents. This can be illustrated by our example network of Figure 16.1. Suppose we know that the sensor is on (*Sensor* = true), and we are interested in the probability of *Alarm*. All other nodes in the network are *Alarm*'s non-descendants, and given that *Alarm*'s parents are known (*Sensor* is the only parent), the probability of *Alarm* does not depend on any other variable. Formally:

$$p(\text{ Alarm } | \text{ Burglary } \land \text{ Lightning } \land \text{ Sensor } \land \text{ Call}) = p(\text{ Alarm } | \text{ Sensor})$$

Let us clarify this by another example, see Figure 16.2. In this network, the following simplification is possible:

$$p(\text{ } c \text{ } | \text{ } a \land b) = p(\text{ } c \text{ } | \text{ } b)$$

According to the above rule about independencies, $c$ is independent of $c$'s non-decendants given $c$'s parents. $b$, the only parent of $c$ is given, so $c$ is independent of $a$. On the other hand, the following example shows that the application of the rule about independence requires care. Can

$$p(\text{ } c \text{ } | \text{ } b \land d \land f)$$

**Figure 16.2** How can the conditional probabilities be simplified in this Bayesian network? $p(c \mid a \wedge b)$ can be simplified to $p(c \mid b)$; $p(c \mid b \wedge d \wedge f)$ cannot be simplified.

be simplified? $f$ is $c$'s non-descendant, so it would be tempting to simplify this probability to $p(c \mid b \wedge d)$. This is, however, not possible. To be safe, the condition 'given X's parents' in the rule about independence on non-descendents has to be interpreted as 'given X's parents and nothing else'. In our last example, $d$ is also given and therefore $f$ cannot be neglected. Assuming that the links in the network all indicate positive influences, the following intuitive reasoning demonstrates why not. $c$ causes $d$, so knowing $d$ is true makes c more likely. On the other hand, $e$ also causes $d$, so if $e$ is true then $c$ is 'less needed' as a cause of $d$. In our case, $e$ is not given, but $f$ is given. Knowing that $f$ is true makes $e$ more likely, and that in turn makes $c$ less likely.

The structure of a Bayesian network thus states dependences and independences between variables. This meaning of the links in a network turns out to provide a practical means to (a) define probabilistic relations (both dependencies and independencies) among the variables in a world, and (b) answer questions about this world.

The links in a Bayesian network have natural causal interpretation. It should be noted, however, that links do not necessarily represent causes. Even if the links are directed the other way round, from consequences to causes, the network may still be probabilistically correct. Later we will look at this again.

To complete the representation of a probabilistic model by a Bayesian network, we have to, in addition to specifying the structure, also specify some probabilities, that is give some actual numbers. The probabilities are required as follows. For the nodes that have no parents ('root causes'), a priori probabilities are specified. In our case burglary and lightning are root causes. For other nodes X, we have to specify the conditional probabilities of the form:

$p(X \mid$ State of X's parents)

In the network of Figure 16.1, *Sensor* has two parents: *Burglary* and *Lightning*. There are four possible combined states of the two parents: *Burglary* and *Lightning*, *Burglary* and not *Lightning*, etc. These states will be written as logical formulas *Burglary* $\wedge$ *Lightning*, *Burglary* $\wedge$ $\sim$*Lightning*, etc. So the complete specification of this Bayesian network can be:

$p(Burglary) = 0.001$
$p(Lightning) = 0.02$
$p(Sensor \mid Burglary \wedge Lightning) = 0.9$
$p(Sensor \mid Burglary \wedge \sim Lightning) = 0.9$
$p(Sensor \mid \sim Burglary \wedge Lightning) = 0.1$

$p(Sensor \mid {\sim}Burglary \wedge {\sim}Lightning) = 0.001$
$p(Alarm \mid Sensor) = 0.95$
$p(Alarm \mid {\sim}Sensor) = 0.001$
$p(Call \mid Sensor) = 0.9$
$p(Call \mid {\sim}Sensor) = 0.0$

This complete specification comprises ten probabilities. If the structure of the network (stating the independences) were not provided, the complete specification would require $2^5 - 1 = 31$ probabilities. There are $2^n$ possible states of a world comprising $n$ Boolean variables. The network structure plus 10 numbers convey information equivalent to 31 numbers. So the structure by its implicit definition of some independences in this network saves 21 numbers. In networks with more nodes the savings could of course be much greater.

How much can be saved depends on the problem. If every variable in the problem depends on everything else, then of course no saving is possible. However, if the problem does permit savings, then the savings will depend on the structure of a Bayesian network. Different Bayesian networks can be drawn for the same problem, but some networks are better than others. The general rule is that good networks respect causality between the variables. So we should make a directed link from $X$ to $Y$ if $X$ causes $Y$. For example, in the burglary domain, although it is possible to reason from alarm to burglary, it would lead to an awkward network if we started constructing the network with a link from alarm to burglary. That would require more links in the network. Also it would be more difficult to estimate the required probabilities in a 'non-causal' direction, such as $p(burglary \mid alarm)$. It is the nodes with many parents that require much data to be specified. A conditional probability of a node is required for every possible state combination of all the parents. The number of possible states grows exponentially with the number of parents.

# EXERCISES

**16.1** Often it is possible to make interesting *qualitative* inferences about probabilities in a Bayesian network without knowing exact numerical values of probabilities in the network. Consider the network in Figure 16.3a. Let both $a$ and $c$ be very rare events, and let all the links in the network correspond to the causality between events. So $p(b \mid a) \gg p(b \mid {\sim}a)$. Also $d$ is much more likely when $b$ and/or $c$ happen. Determine the relation ($<$, $>$, or $=$) between the following probabilities:

(a) $p(a) : p(a \mid c)$ (Which is larger, $p(a)$ or $p(a \mid c)$ )

(b) $p(a) : p(a \mid d)$

(c) $p(a \mid d) : p(a \mid cd)$

(d) $p(d \mid bc) : p(d \mid abc)$

**16.2** Consider the Bayesian network in Figure 16.3b. The structure of the network enables the simplification of some conditional probabilities. For example, $p( e \mid a \wedge c) = p( e \mid c)$. Here, the condition part $a \wedge c$ was simplified into $c$. In the conditional probabilities below, how can the condition parts be simplified as much as possible by considering the structure of this Bayesian network?

(a)                              (b)

**Figure 16.3** Two Bayesian networks.

(a)  $p(c \mid \sim a \wedge b \wedge e)$

(b)  $p(c \mid \sim a \wedge b \wedge d \wedge e)$

(c)  $p(c \mid \sim b \wedge d \wedge e)$

## 16.2 Some formulas from probability calculus

In the following we recall some formulas from the probability calculus that will be useful for reasoning in Bayesian networks. Let $X$ and $Y$ be propositions. Then:

$$p(\sim X) = 1 - p(X)$$

$$p(X \wedge Y) = p(X)\, p(Y \mid X) = p(Y)\, p(X \mid Y)$$

$$p(X \vee Y) = p(X) + p(Y) - p(X \wedge Y)$$

$$p(X) = p(X \wedge Y) + p(X \wedge \sim Y) = p(Y)\, p(X \mid Y) + p(\sim Y)\, p(X \mid \sim Y)$$

Propositions $X$ and $Y$ are said to be *independent* if $p(X \mid Y) = p(X)$ and $p(Y \mid X) = p(Y)$. That is: knowing $Y$ does not affect the belief in $X$ and vice versa. If $X$ and $Y$ are independent then:

$$p(X \wedge Y) = p(X)\, p(Y)$$

Propositions $X$ and $Y$ are *disjoint* if they cannot both be true at the same time: $p(X \wedge Y) = 0$ and $p(X \mid Y) = 0$ and $p(Y \mid X) = 0$.

Let $X_1, \ldots, X_n$ be propositions; then:

$$p(X_1 \wedge \ldots \wedge X_n) = p(X_1)\, p(X_2 \mid X_1)\, p(X_3 \mid X_1 \wedge X_2) \ldots p(X_n \mid X_1 \wedge \ldots \wedge X_{n-1})$$

If all $X_i$ are independent of each other then this simplifies into:

$$p(X_1 \wedge \ldots \wedge X_n) = p(X_1)\, p(X_2)\, p(X_3) \ldots p(X_n)$$

Finally, we will need Bayes' theorem:

$$p(X \mid Y) = p(X) \frac{p(Y \mid X)}{p(Y)}$$

This formula, which follows from the law for conjunction $p(X \wedge Y)$ above, is useful for reasoning between causes and effects. Considering burglary as a cause of alarm, it is natural to think in terms of what proportion of burglaries trigger alarm. That is $p(\text{alarm} \mid \text{burglary})$. But when we hear the alarm, we are interested in knowing the probability of its cause, that is: $p$(burglary | alarm). Bayes' formula helps:

$$p(\text{burglary} \mid \text{alarm}) = p(\text{burglary}) \frac{p(\text{alarm} \mid \text{burglary})}{p(\text{alarm})}$$

A variant of Bayes' theorem takes into account background knowledge $B$. It allows us to reason about the probability of a hypothesis $H$, given evidence $E$, all in the presence of background knowledge $B$:

$$p(H \mid E \wedge B) = p(H \mid B) \frac{p(E \mid H \wedge B)}{p(E \mid B)}$$

## 16.3  Probabilistic reasoning in Bayesian networks

In this section we will implement a program that computes conditional probabilities in Bayesian networks. Given a Bayesian network, we would like this interpreter to answer queries of the form: What is the probability of some propositions, given some other propositions? Example queries are:

$p($ burglary | alarm$) = ?$
$p($ burglary $\wedge$ lightning$) = ?$
$p($ burglary | alarm $\wedge \sim$lightning$) = ?$
$p($ alarm $\wedge \sim$call | burglary$) = ?$

The interpreter will derive an answer to any of these questions by recursively applying the following rules:

(1)  Probability of conjunction:

$$\text{p}( X_1 \wedge X_2 \mid Cond) = p( X_1 \mid Cond) * p( X_2 \mid X_1 \wedge Cond)$$

(2)  Probability of a certain event:

$$p( X \mid Y_1 \wedge \ldots \wedge X \wedge \ldots ) = 1$$

(3)  Probability of impossible event:

$$p( X \mid Y_1 \wedge \ldots \wedge \sim X \wedge \ldots ) = 0$$

(4)  Probability of negation:

$$p( \sim X \mid Cond) = 1 - p(X \mid Cond)$$

(5)  If condition involves a descendant of $X$ then use Bayes' theorem:

If $Y$ is a descendant of $X$ in the Bayesian network then use the general form of Bayes' formula:
$$p(X \mid Y \wedge Cond) = p(X \mid Cond) * p(Y \mid X \wedge Cond) / p(Y \mid Cond)$$

(6)  Cases when condition $Cond$ does not involve a descendant of $X$:

(a)  If $X$ has no parents then $p(X \mid Cond) = p(X)$, $p(X)$ given in the network

(b) If $X$ has parents *Parents* then

$$p(X \mid Cond) = \sum_{S \in possible\_states(Parents)} p(X \mid S)p(S \mid Cond)$$

As an example consider the question: What is the probability of burglary given alarm?

$p(\text{burglary} \mid \text{alarm}) = ?$

By rule 5 above:

$p(\text{burglary} \mid \text{alarm}) = p(\text{burglary}) * p(\text{alarm} \mid \text{burglary}) / p(\text{alarm})$

By rule 6:

$p(\text{alarm} \mid \text{burglary}) = p(\text{alarm} \mid \text{sensor}) \, p(\text{sensor} \mid \text{burglary}) +$
$\qquad\qquad\qquad\quad p(\text{alarm} \mid \sim\text{sensor}) \, p(\sim\text{sensor} \mid \text{burglary})$

By rule 6:

$p(\text{sensor} \mid \text{burglary}) =$
$\quad p(\text{sensor} \mid \text{burglary} \wedge \text{lightning}) \, p(\text{burglary} \wedge \text{lightning} \mid \text{burglary}) +$
$\quad p(\text{sensor} \mid \sim\text{burglary} \wedge \text{lightning}) \, p(\sim\text{burglary} \wedge \text{lightning} \mid \text{burglary}) +$
$\quad p(\text{sensor} \mid \text{burglary} \wedge \sim\text{lightning}) \, p(\text{burglary} \wedge \sim\text{lightning} \mid \text{burglary}) +$
$\quad p(\text{sensor} \mid \sim\text{burglary} \wedge \sim\text{lightning}) \, p(\sim\text{burglary} \wedge \sim\text{lightning} \mid \text{burglary})$

Using rules 1, 2, 3 and 4 at various places, and the conditional probabilities given in the network, we have:

$p(\text{sensor} \mid \text{burglary}) = 0.9 * 0.02 + 0 + 0.9 * 0.98 + 0 = 0.9$
$p(\text{alarm} \mid \text{burglary}) = 0.95 * 0.9 + 0.001 * (1 - 0.9) = 0.8551$

Using rules 1, 4 and 6 several times we get:

$p(\text{alarm}) = 0.00467929$

Finally:

$p(\text{burglary} \mid \text{alarm}) = 0.001 * 0.8551 / 0.00467929 = 0.182741$

The reasoning along these lines is implemented by the program in Figure 16.4. The conjunction $X_1 \wedge X_2 \wedge \ldots$ of propositions is represented by a list of the propositions [X1,X2, ... ]. The negation $\sim$X is represented by the Prolog term **not** X. The main predicate in this program is:

**prob( Proposition, Cond, P)**

where **P** is the conditional probability of **Proposition** given **Cond**. The program expects a Bayesian network to be represented by the following relations:

**parent( ParentNode, Node):** defines the structure of the network
**p( X, ParentsState, P):** P is the conditional probability of X given the state of the parents
    **ParentsState**
**p(X, P):** X is a root node and P is its probability

Figure 16.5 defines the Bayesian network of Figure 16.1 using these predicates. The following conversation with the Bayesian network program of Figure 16.4 and the

```
% Reasoning in Bayesian networks

% Bayesian network is represented by relations:
%    parent( ParentNode, Node)
%    p( Node, ParentStates, Prob):
%        Prob is conditional probability of Node given
%        values of parent variables ParentStates, for example:
%        p( alarm, [ burglary, not earthquake], 0.99)
%    p( Node, Prob):
%        probability of node without parents
%    prob( Event, Condition, P):
%        probability of Event, given Cond, is P;
%        Event is a variable, its negation, or a list
%        of simple events representing their conjunction

:- op( 900, fy, not).                              % Prefix operator 'not'

prob( [X | Xs], Cond, P)  :- !,                    % Probability of conjunction
    prob( X, Cond, Px),
    prob( Xs, [X | Cond], PRest),
    P is Px * PRest.

prob( [], _, 1)  :- !.                             % Empty conjunction

prob( X, Cond, 1)  :-
    member( X, Cond), !.                           % Cond implies X

prob( X, Cond, 0)  :-
    member( not X, Cond), !.                       % Cond implies X is false

prob( not X, Cond, P)  :- !,                       % Probability of negation
    prob( X, Cond, P0),
    P is 1 - P0.

% Use Bayes rule if condition involves a descendant of X

prob( X, Cond0, P)  :-
    delete( Y, Cond0, Cond),
    predecessor( X, Y), !,                         % Y is a descendant of X
    prob( X, Cond, Px),
    prob( Y, [X | Cond], PyGivenX),
    prob( Y, Cond, Py),
    P is Px * PyGivenX / Py.                        % Assuming Py > 0

% Cases when condition does not involve a descendant

prob( X, Cond, P)  :-
    p( X, P), !.                                    % X a root cause - its probability given

prob( X, Cond, P)  :- !,
    findall( (CONDi,Pi), p(X,CONDi,Pi), CPlist),    % Conditions on parents
    sum_probs( CPlist, Cond, P).
```

**Figure 16.4** An interpreter for Bayesian networks.

**Figure 16.4** *cont.*

```
% sum_probs( CondsProbs, Cond, WeightedSum)
%    CondsProbs is a list of conditions and corresponding probabilities,
%    WeightedSum is weighted sum of probabilities of Conds given Cond

sum_probs( [], _, 0).

sum_probs( [ (COND1,P1) | CondsProbs], COND, P) :-
   prob( COND1, COND, PC1),
   sum_probs( CondsProbs, COND, PRest),
   P is P1 * PC1 + PRest.

predecessor( X, not Y) :- !,                      % Negated variable Y
   predecessor( X, Y).

predecessor( X, Y) :-
   parent( X, Y).

predecessor( X, Z) :-
   parent( X, Y),
   predecessor( Y, Z).

member( X, [X | _]).

member( X, [_ | L]) :-
   member( X, L).

delete( X, [X | L], L).

delete( X, [Y | L], [Y | L2]) :-
   delete( X, L, L2).
```

```
% Bayesian network 'sensor'

parent( burglary, sensor).              % Burglary tends to trigger sensor
parent( lightning, sensor).             % Strong lightning may trigger sensor
parent( sensor, alarm).
parent( sensor, call).

p( burglary, 0.001).
p( lightning, 0.02).
p( sensor, [ burglary, lightning], 0.9).
p( sensor, [ burglary, not lightning], 0.9).
p( sensor, [ not burglary, lightning], 0.1).
p( sensor, [ not burglary, not lightning], 0.001).
p( alarm, [ sensor], 0.95).
p( alarm, [ not sensor], 0.001).
p( call, [ sensor], 0.9).
p( call, [ not sensor], 0.0).
```

**Figure 16.5** A specification of the Bayesian network of Figure 16.1 as expected by the program of Figure 16.4.

network of Figure 16.5 is possible. Suppose we receive a warning phone call, so we want to know about burglary:

?- prob( burglary, [call], P).
P = 0.232137

Now we learn there was a heavy storm, so:

?- prob( burglary, [call, lightning], P).
P = 0.00892857

As the warning call can be explained by strong lightning, burglary becomes much less likely. However, if the weather was fine then burglary becomes more likely:

?- prob( burglary, [call, not lightning], P).
P = 0.473934

It should be noted that our implementation of Bayesian networks aimed at a short and clear program. As a result, the program is rather inefficient. This is no problem for small Bayesian networks like the one defined by Figure 16.5, but it would be for a larger network. The problem is that, roughly, the computational complexity of reasoning with Bayesian networks grows exponentially with the number of parents of a node in the network because of the summation over all possible states of the parents. The number of possible states grows exponentially with the number of parents.

## EXERCISES

**16.3** For the Bayesian network of Figure 16.3b, express the conditional probability $p(b|c)$ in terms of probabilities that must be given by the definition of this network.

**16.4** The program below specifies a Bayesian network according to the conventions used in the program of Figure 16.4.

parent(a,c). parent(b,c). parent(b,d). parent(c,e).

| | |
|---|---|
| p(a, 0.1). | % p(a) = 0.1 |
| p(b, 0.2). | |
| p(c, [a,b], 0.5). | % p(c \| a ∧ b) = 0.5 |
| p(c, [not a, b], 0.0). | % p( c \| ~a ∧ b) = 0.0 |
| p(c, [a, not b], 0.9). | |
| p(c, [not a, not b], 0.4). | |
| p(d, [b], 0.9). | |
| p(d, [not b], 0.1). | |
| p(e, [c], 0.6). | |
| p(e, [not c], 0.1). | |

In questions (a)–(c), estimate without numerical calculation which of the mentioned probabilities is greater:

(a)  $p(a)$ or $p(a \mid e)$?

(b)  $p(c \mid a)$ or $p(c \mid ad)$?

(c)  $p(e)$ or $p(e \mid d)$?

Calculate the probabilities:

(d) $p(a \mid bc) = ?$

(e) $p(a \mid c) = ?$

(f) Run the program of Figure 16.4 to check your answers to the questions (a)–(e).

## 16.4 d-separation

In this section we look into the concept of *d-separation* (dependency-directed separation) which is helpful in determining conditional independences in a Bayesian network.

Let $E$ be a subset of the variables (nodes) in a Bayesian network. We will refer to this set as 'evidence set' or 'evidence nodes'. Evidence nodes correspond to the variables that are given, that is their values are known. These variables represent the evidence from which we try to infer other probabilities in the network conditioned on the evidence. The question that d-separation answers is, which variables in the network are conditionally independent given this evidence?

d-separation between nodes in a Bayesian network, given an evidence set, is defined in terms of topological properties of the network so that if two nodes are d-separated they are conditionally independent. Let $V_i$, $V_j$ be two variables in the network. Nodes $V_i$ and $V_j$ are conditionally independent given set $E$ if $E$ d-separates $V_i$ and $V_j$. This means:

$$p(V_i \wedge V_j \mid E) = p(V_i \mid E) * p(V_j \mid E)$$

Set $E$ d-separates $V_i$, $V_j$ if all (undirected) paths between $V_i$ and $V_j$ are 'blocked' by $E$. A path between $V_i$ and $V_j$ is *blocked* by the nodes $E$ if there is a 'blocking node' $V_b$ in $E$ on the path. $V_b$ blocks the path if one of the following cases holds (see Figure 16.6):

Case 1: $V_b$ is in set $E$ and both arcs on the path lead out of $V_b$, or

Case 2: $V_b$ is in set $E$ and one arc on the path leads into $V_b$ and one out, or

Case 3: Neither $V_b$ nor any descendant of $V_b$ is in $E$, and both arcs on the path lead into $V_b$

The three cases correspond to the following relations respectively: (1) $V_b$ is a common cause of $V_i$ and $V_j$, (2) $V_b$ is a more direct cause of $V_j$ than $V_i$ is, and (3) $V_b$ is a common consequence of $V_i$ and $V_j$.

We can illustrate the three cases by examples from the network in Figure 16.1. Sensor is a common cause of both Alarm and Call, so according to case 1 Sensor blocks the path between Alarm and Call. In calculating conditional probabilities, this enables the following simplification:

$$p ( \text{Call} \mid \text{Alarm} \wedge \text{Sensor}) = p ( \text{Call} \mid \text{Sensor})$$

Considering the path from Burglary to Call, Sensor is a more direct cause of Call than Burglary is. Therefore Sensor blocks this path, which enables the simplification:

$$p ( \text{Call} \mid \text{Burglary} \wedge \text{Sensor}) = p ( \text{Call} \mid \text{Sensor})$$

Case 1: $V_b$ is a common cause, and $V_b$ is in set $E$

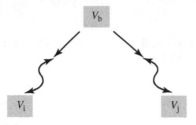

Case 2: $V_b$ is a 'closer, more direct cause' of $V_j$ than $V_i$ is; $V_b$ is in set $E$

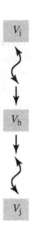

Case 3: $V_b$ is a common consequence of $V_i$ and $V_j$; $V_b$ is not in $E$, nor is $V_d$ and any other descendant of $V_b$

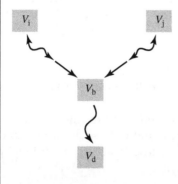

**Figure 16.6** Three cases when a node $V_b$ blocks a path between nodes $V_i$ and $V_j$. Arrows indicate directed links in the network, double-arrowed curves indicate undirected paths in the network.

Sensor is a common consequence of Burglary and Lightning, and so are Alarm and Call. Therefore Burglary and Lightning are independent only if none of the nodes Alarm, Call and Sensor is in the evidence set.

## EXERCISE

**16.5** Find all evidence sets E that d-separate $a$ and $d$ in Figure 16.3b.

## Summary

- In the probabilistic approach to the handling of uncertainty in knowledge representation, a major problem is how to cope with numerous conditional probabilities. An economical way is needed to state (conditional) dependences and independences among the variables in the problem.

- *Bayesian networks* provide an elegant way of declaring how variables depend on each other, and under what conditions variables are independent.

- The structure of a Bayesian network implies statements of probabilistic independence as follows: a node is independent of the node's non-descendants given the node's parents.

- Links in a Bayesian network most naturally correspond to causal relations between variables. However, a Bayesian network may still correctly (although possibly less elegantly) represent probabilistic (in)dependences even if links do not correspond to causality.

- The concept of d-separation helps in determining conditional independences between variables.

- In this chapter we developed a program for probabilistic reasoning in Bayesian networks. This largely relies on the Bayes formula for conditional probabilities.

- Concepts discussed in this chapter:

    Bayesian networks, belief networks
    Bayes formula
    d-separation

### References

There are a number of books on Bayesian networks. Pearl (1988) is a frequently referenced book on uncertainty and probabilistic reasoning based on Bayesian networks. Jensen (2002) and Darwiche (2009) are among more recent books on this topic. The book by Neapolitan (2004) covers the foundations of Bayesian networks and also methods that enable Bayesian networks to be automatically constructed from data. Shafer and Pearl (1990) is a collection of important papers on reasoning about uncertainty. General books on artificial intelligence, such as Russell and Norvig (2010), typically include sections on Bayesian networks.

Darwiche, A. (2009) *Modeling and Reasoning with Bayesian Networks*. Cambridge University Press.

Jensen, F.V. (2002) *Bayesian Networks and Decision Graphs*. Berlin: Springer-Verlag.

Neapolitan, R.E. (2004) *Learning Bayesian Networks*. Prentice-Hall.

Pearl, J. (1988) *Probabilistic Reasoning in Intelligent Systems: Networks of Plausible Inference*. San Mateo, CA: Morgan Kaufmann.

Russell, S. and Norvig, P. (2010) *Artificial Intelligence: A Modern Approach,* third edn. Prentice Hall.

Shafer, G. and Pearl, J. (eds) (1990) *Readings in Uncertain Reasoning*. San Mateo, CA: Morgan Kaufmann.

# Chapter 17

# Planning

Planning is a topic of traditional interest in artificial intelligence. It involves reasoning about the effects of actions and the sequencing of available actions to achieve a given goal. In this chapter we develop several simple planners that illustrate the principles of planning.

## 17.1 Representing actions

Figure 17.1 shows an example of a planning task. It can be solved by searching in a corresponding state space, as discussed in Chapter 11. However, here the problem will be represented in a way that makes it possible to reason explicitly about particular effects of actions among which the planner can choose. This will help the planner to determine whether an action is relevant to a goal to be achieved.

Actions change the current state of the planning world, thereby causing the transition to a new state. However, an action does not normally change everything in the current state, just some component(s) of the state. A good representation should therefore take into account this 'locality' of the effects of actions. To facilitate the reasoning about such local effects of actions, a state will be represented as a list of relationships that are currently true. Of course, we choose to mention only those relationships that pertain to the planning problem. For planning in the blocks world, such relationships are:

   on( Block, Object)

and

   clear( Object)

The latter condition requires that there is nothing on the top of **Object**. In planning in the blocks world, such a relationship is important because a block to be moved

**Figure 17.1** A planning problem in the blocks world: find a sequence of actions that achieve the goals: *a* on *b*, and *b* on *c*. These actions transform the initial state (on the left) into a final state (on the right).

must be clear, and a block or place to which the block is moved must also be clear. **Object** can be a block or a place. In our example, *a*, *b* and *c* are blocks, and 1, 2, 3 and 4 are places. The initial state of the world in Figure 17.1 can then be represented by the list of relationships:

[ clear( 2), clear( 4), clear( b), clear( c), on( a, 1), on( b, 3), on(c, a)]

Notice that we distinguish between a relation and a relationship. For example, **on( c, a)** is a relationship; that is, a *particular instance* of the relation **on**. Relation **on** is, on the other hand, the set of all **on** relationships.

Each available action is defined in terms of its precondition and its effects. For example, consider the action of moving block *b* from location 3 to block *c*, denoted by **move(b,3,c)**. For this action to be possible, both *b* and *c* must be clear, and *b* must be on 3. After this action is executed, *b* is on *c* and 3 becomes clear. If **move(b,3,c)** is executed in the initial state in Figure 17.1 then a new state is obtained:

[ on(b,c), clear(3), clear( 2), clear( 4), clear( b), on( a, 1), on(c, a)]

The action added the relationships **on(b,c)** and **clear(3)**, and deleted **on(b,3)** and **clear(c)**.

The effects of an action can be positive and negative. A positive effect *adds* some relationship to the current state, a negative effect *deletes* some relationship from the current state. The way of defining a planning domain in terms of actions' preconditions and effects is referred to as STRIPS-like representation, after the early planner STRIPS used in the famous Shakey robot project (Fikes and Nilsson 1971).

We will be using in this chapter the following version of this representation. Each action is specified by three things:

(1) *precondition*: a condition that has to be satisfied in a situation for the action to be possible;

(2) *add-list*: a list of relationships that the action establishes in the situation – these conditions become true after the action is executed;

(3) *delete-list*: a list of relationships that the action destroys.

Preconditions will be defined by the predicate:

**can( Action, Cond)**

which says: **Action** can only be executed in a situation in which condition **Cond** holds. The effects of an action will be defined by two predicates:

    **adds( Action, AddRels)**
    **deletes( Action, DelRels)**

Here **AddRels** is a list of relationships that Action establishes. After **Action** is executed in a state, **AddRels** is added to the state to obtain the new state. **DelRels** is a list of relationships that **Action** destroys. These relationships are removed from the state to which **Action** is applied.

For our blocks world actions will be of the form:

    **move( Block, From, To)**

where **Block** is the block to be moved, **From** is the block's current position and **To** is its new position. A complete definition of this action is given in Figure 17.2.

---

% Definition of action move( Block, From, To) in blocks world

% can( Action, Condition): Action possible if Condition true

**can( move( Block, From, To), [ clear( Block), clear( To), on( Block, From)] )  :-**
    **block( Block),**              % Block to be moved
    **object( To),**               % 'To' is a block or a place
    **To \== Block,**            % Block cannot be moved to itself
    **object( From),**           % 'From' is a block or a place
    **From \== To,**             % Move to new position
    **Block \== From.**         % Block not moved from itself

% adds( Action, Relationships): Action establishes Relationships

**adds( move(X,From,To), [ on(X,To), clear(From)]).**

% deletes( Action, Relationships): Action destroys Relationships

**deletes( move(X,From,To), [ on(X,From), clear(To)]).**

**object( X)  :-**               % X is an object if
  **place( X)**              % X is a place
  **;**                      % or
  **block( X).**              % X is a block

% A blocks world

**block( a).**
**block( b).**
**block( c).**

**place( 1).**
**place( 2).**
**place( 3).**
**place( 4).**

% A state in the blocks world
%
%        c
%      a   b
%     = = = =
% place  1  2  3  4

**state1( [ clear(2), clear(4), clear(b), clear(c), on(a,1), on(b,3), on(c,a) ] ).**

---

**Figure 17.2** A definition of the planning domain for the blocks world.

A definition of possible actions for a planning problem implicitly defines the space of all possible plans. Such a space will also be referred to as a *planning domain*.

The goal of a plan is stated in terms of relationships that are to be established. For the blocks world task in Figure 17.1, the goal can be stated as the list of relationships:

[ on( a, b), on( b, c)]

In the next section we will show how such a representation can be used in a process known as 'means-ends analysis' by which a plan can be derived.

## EXERCISES

**17.1** Extend the blocks world definition of Figure 17.2 to include other types of objects, such as pyramids, balls and boxes. Add the corresponding extra condition 'safe-to-stack' in the **can** relation. For example, it is not safe to stack a block on a pyramid; a ball can be safely put into a box, but not on a block (it might roll off).

**17.2** Define the planning domain for the cleaning robot of Section 4.2 where the actions are 'go', 'push', 'pickup' and 'drop'.

## 17.2 Deriving plans by means-ends analysis

Consider the initial state of the planning problem in Figure 17.1. Let the goal be: **on( a, b)**. The planner's problem is to find a plan – that is, a sequence of actions – that achieves this goal. A typical planner would reason as follows:

(1) Find an action that achieves **on( a, b)**. By looking at the **adds** predicate, it is found that such an action has the form

move( a, From, b)

for any **From**. Such an action will certainly have to be part of the plan, but we cannot execute it immediately in our initial state.

(2) Now enable the action **move( a, From, b)**. Look at the **can** predicate to find the action's precondition. This is:

[ clear( a), clear( b), on( a, From)]

In the initial state we already have **clear(b)** and **on( a, From)** (where **From** = 1). But **clear(a)** is not true in the initial state. So this is a remaining precondition to be made true to enable **move(a,1,b)**. Now the planner concentrates on **clear(a)** as the new goal to be achieved.

(3) Look at the **adds** relation again to find an action that achieves **clear( a)**. This is any action of the form

move( Block, a, To)

The precondition for this action is:

[ clear( Block), clear( To), on( Block, a)]

This is satisfied in our initial situation if:

**Block** = c   **and**   **To** = 2

So **move**( c, a, 2) can be executed in the initial state, resulting in a new state. This new state is obtained from the initial state by removing from the initial state all the relationships that the action deletes, and adding all the relationships that the action adds. This produces the new state:

[ clear( a), clear( b), clear( c), clear( 4), on( a, 1), on( b, 3), on( c, 2)]

Now the action **move**( a, 1, b) can be executed, which achieves the final goal **on**( a, b). The plan found can be written as the list:

[ move( c, a, 2), move( a, 1, b)]

This style of reasoning is called *means-ends analysis*. The means are the available actions, the ends are the goals to be achieved. Notice that in the foregoing example a correct plan was found immediately, without any backtracking. The example thus illustrates how the reasoning about goals and effects of actions directs the planning process in a proper direction. Unfortunately, it is not true that backtracking can always be avoided in this way. On the contrary, combinatorial complexity due to search among alternative actions is typical of planning. It should be admitted that even our example, that we solved without search (no backtracking), would require search if the problem definition in Figure 17.2 was used strictly. Namely, this definition requires that actions are fully instantiated, i.e. contain no variables. Therefore in our example there would still be search among alternative instantiations that would result from satisfying the condition **object(From)**, etc.

What is the advantage of means-ends planning in comparison with simple state-space search? Means-ends reasoning draws the planner to considering only those actions that pertain to the current goals. This can be illustrated by slightly extending the domain definition of Figure 17.2. Let the blocks be painted. Each block's vertical faces are of different colours: red, green, blue and yellow. If a block is rotated about the vertical axis and viewed from the side (as in Figure 17.1) then the block, from the perspective of the observer, changes its colour. To take the colours of blocks into account, we need another relationship as part of the state description: **colour(Block,Colour)**, saying that **Block** is currently seen to be of colour **Colour**. Let us add the actions of the form **rotate(Block,Colour,NewColour)** to the domain definition. The precondition for such an action is **clear(Block)** (so that the robot can grasp the block) and **colour(Block,Colour)**. The effect of such an action is that **Block** changes its colour from **Colour** to **NewColour**. We now have actions of type **move** and of type **rotate**.

Now suppose that the goal is **on(a,b)** again. The state space search would generate *all* possible actions in the initial state, and then again all possible actions in the next states. That is, the search would consider both the possible **move** actions and **rotate** actions. In contrast to this, a means-ends planner would only look at actions that achieve the goal **on(a,b)**, and then the actions that establish the preconditions of such actions. The preconditions are of the forms **on(_,_)** and **clear(_)**, but never of the form **colour(_,_)**. Therefore the means-ends analysis

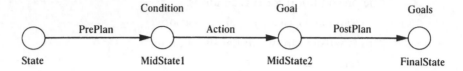

**Figure 17.3** One way of means-ends planning.

would find no reason to consider rotational actions when solving this task. The effect of this is that the search space of the means-ends planner is considerably smaller than that of the state-space search. In effect, the means-ends planner would manage, in this case, to abstract away everything that has to do with the colors because it is not relevant.

One way of planning by means-ends analysis is illustrated in Figure 17.3. It can be stated as follows:

To solve a list of goals **Goals** in state **State**, leading to state **FinalState**, do:

If all the **Goals** are true in **State** then **FinalState** = **State**. Otherwise do the following steps:

(1)  Select a still unsolved goal **Goal** in **Goals**.

(2)  Find an action **Action** that adds **Goal** to the current state.

(3)  Enable **Action** by solving the precondition **Condition** of **Action**, giving **MidState1**.

(4)  Apply **Action** to **MidState1**, giving **MidState2** (in **MidState2**, **Goal** is true).

(5)  Solve **Goals** in **MidState2**, leading to **FinalState**.

This is programmed in Prolog in Figure 17.4 as the procedure:

> plan( State, Goals, Plan, FinalState)

**State** and **FinalState** are the initial and final states of the plan respectively. **Goals** is the list of goals to be achieved and **Plan** is a list of actions that achieve the goals. It should be noted that this planning program assumes a definition of the planning domain in which all the actions and goals are fully instantiated; that is, they do not contain any variables. For the blocks world, this instantiation is forced by the predicate **can** defined in Figure 17.2. Variables would require more complicated treatment which will be discussed later.

In the second clause of the procedure **plan**, there is the goal conc(Plan,_,_). This goal forces the planner to search among plans in the iterative deepening fashion: plans of increasing lengths are searched so that all the plans of length $n$ are tried before trying plans of length $n + 1$.

The planner can now be used to find a plan for placing block $a$ on $b$, starting in the initial state of Figure 17.1, as follows:

> ?- Start = [ clear( 2), clear( 4), clear( b), clear( c), on( a, 1), on( b, 3), on( c, a)],
>     plan( Start, [ on( a, b)], Plan, FinState).
>
> Plan = [ move( c, a, 2), move( a, 1, b)]
> FinState = [ on( a, b), clear( 1), on( c, 2), clear( a), clear( 4), clear( c), on( b, 3)]

```
% A simple means-ends planner
% plan( State, Goals, Plan, FinalState)

plan( State, Goals, [ ], State) :-              % Plan empty
    satisfied( State, Goals).                   % Goals true in State

plan( State, Goals, Plan, FinalState) :-
    conc( Plan, _, _),                          % Try plans of increasing length
    conc( PrePlan, [Action | PostPlan], Plan),  % Divide Plan to PrePlan, Action and PostPlan
    select( State, Goals, Goal),                % Select a goal
    achieves( Action, Goal),                    % Relevant action
    can( Action, Condition),
    plan( State, Condition, PrePlan, MidState1),     % Enable Action
    apply( MidState1, Action, MidState2),            % Apply Action
    plan( MidState2, Goals, PostPlan, FinalState).   % Achieve remaining goals

% satisfied( State, Goals): Goals are true in State

satisfied( State, [ ]).

satisfied( State, [Goal | Goals]) :-
    member( Goal, State),
    satisfied( State, Goals).

select( State, Goals, Goal) :-
    member( Goal, Goals),
    \+ member( Goal, State).                    % Goal not satisfied already

% achieves( Action, Goal): Goal is in add-list of Action

achieves( Action, Goal) :-
    adds( Action, Goals),
    member( Goal, Goals).

% apply( State, Action, NewState): Action executed in State produces NewState

apply( State, Action, NewState) :-
    deletes( Action, DelList),
    delete_all( State, DelList, State1), !,
    adds( Action, AddList),
    conc( AddList, State1, NewState).

% delete_all( L1, L2, Diff) if Diff is set-difference of L1 and L2

delete_all( [ ], _, [ ]).

delete_all( [X | L1], L2, Diff) :-
    member( X, L2), !,
    delete_all( L1, L2, Diff).

delete_all( [X | L1], L2, [X | Diff]) :-
    delete_all( L1, L2, Diff).
```

**Figure 17.4** A simple means-ends planner.

This is smooth, the shortest plan was found as one should expect from iterative deepening search. However, further experiments with our planner reveal a surprising difficulty. Let us try the task in Figure 17.1. The initial state in Figure 17.1 is defined by the predicate **state1** in Figure 17.2. So the task of Figure 17.1 can be solved by:

>    ?- state1( Start), plan( Start, [ on( a, b), on( b, c)], Plan, _).

This produces a surprising answer:

>    **Plan** = [ move( c, a, 2), move( b, 3, a), move( b, a, c), move( a, 1, b) ]

The second move above is superfluous and makes no sense. Let us investigate how it came to be included in the plan at all and why even the breadth-first search, realized as iterative deepening, resulted in a plan longer than optimal: four actions when three would suffice.

We have to answer two questions. First, what reasoning led the planner to construct the funny plan above? Second, why did the planner not find the optimal plan in which the mysterious **move( b, 3, a)** is not included? Let us start with the first question. The last move, **move( a, 1, b)**, achieves the goal **on( a, b)**. The first three moves achieve the precondition for **move( a, 1, b)**, in particular the condition **clear( a)**. The third move clears *a*, and part of the precondition for the third move is **on( b, a)**. This is achieved by the second move, **move( b, 3, a)**. The first move clears *a* to enable the second move. This explains the reasoning behind our awkward plan and also illustrates what sort of exotic ideas may appear during means-ends planning.

The second question is: Why after **move( c, a, 2)** did the planner not immediately consider **move( b, 3, c)**, which leads to the optimal plan? The reason is that the planner was working on the goal **on( a, b)** all the time. The action **move( b, 3, c)** is completely superfluous to this goal and hence not tried. Our four-step plan achieves **on( a, b)** and, by chance, also **on( b, c)**. So **on( b, c)** is a result of luck and not of any purposeful effort by the planner. Blindly pursuing just the goal **on( a, b)** and relevant preconditions, the planner saw no reason for **move( b, 3, c)** before **move( b, 3, a)**.

It follows from the above example that the means-ends mechanism of planning as implemented in our planners is *incomplete*. It does not suggest all relevant actions to the planning process. The reason for this lies in its *locality*. The planner only considers those actions that pertain to the current goal and disregards other goals until the current goal is achieved. Therefore, it does not (unless by accident) produce plans in which actions that pertain to different goals are interleaved. In the literature, this limited planning mechanism is referred to as *linear planning*. The goals are achieved one by one in a linear order. The key to completeness that ensures that optimal plans *are* within the search space, is to enable interaction between different goals. This will be done in the next section through the mechanism of *goal regression*.

One deficiency of our simple planner is that it occasionally includes actions in the plan which destroy already achieved goals. To prevent this, the mechanism of *goal protection* is sometimes added to the planner. This mechanism keeps track of the goals already achieved and avoids actions that destroy these 'protected' goals. Unfortunately, it is not always possible to construct a plan without temporarily destroying a protected goal and then re-achieving it. So the use of goal protection is limited.

# EXERCISES

**17.3** Trace by hand the means-ends planning process for achieving **on( a, 3)** from the initial situation of Figure 17.1.

**17.4** The natural places where domain-specific planning knowledge can be introduced into our planner are the predicates **select** and **achieves**. They select the next goal to be attempted (determining the order in which goals are achieved) and the action to be tried. Redefine these two predicates for the blocks world, so that the goals and actions are more intelligently selected. For this purpose, it is useful to add the current state **State** as an extra argument to the predicate **achieves**.

## 17.3 Goal regression

Suppose we want a set of goals **Goals** to be true in some state S. Let the state just before S be S0 and the action in S0 be A. Now let us ask the question: What goals **Goals0** have to be true in S0 to ensure **Goals** are true in S? This question is illustrated by:

state S0: Goals0 $\xrightarrow{A}$ state S: Goals

So, given **Goals** and A, what is the set **Goals0**? **Goals0** must have the following properties:

(1) Action A must be possible in S0, therefore **Goals0** must include the preconditions for A.

(2) For each goal G in **Goals** either:

    – action A adds G, or

    – G is in **Goals0** and A does not delete G.

Determining **Goals0** from given **Goals** and action A is called *regressing* **Goals** *through* action A. Of course, this is of interest only for those actions A that achieve some goal G in **Goals**. The relations between various sets of goals and conditions in goal regression are illustrated in Figure 17.5.

The mechanism of goal regression can be used for planning in the following way:

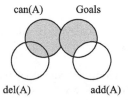

**Figure 17.5** Relations between various sets of conditions in goal regression through action A. The shaded area represents the resulting regressed goals **Goals0**: **Goals0** = **can**(A) ∪ **Goals** – **add**(A). Notice that the intersection between **Goals** and the delete-list of A must be empty.

> To achieve a list of goals **Goals** from some initial situation **StartState**, do:
>
> If **Goals** are true in **StartState** then the empty plan suffices;
> Otherwise select a goal G in **Goals** and an action A that achieves G; then regress **Goals** through A obtaining **NewGoals** and find a plan for achieving **NewGoals** from **StartState**.

This can be improved for better efficiency by observing that some combinations of goals are impossible. For example, **on(a,b)** and **clear(b)** cannot be true at the same time. This can be formulated as the relation

   **impossible( Goal, Goals)**

which says that **Goal** is not possible in combination with goals **Goals**; that is, both **Goal** *and* **Goals** can never be achieved because they are incompatible. For our blocks world, such incompatible combinations can be defined as follows:

   **impossible( on( X, X), _ ).**                  % Block cannot be on itself

   **impossible( on( X, Y), Goals) :-**
      **member( clear( Y), Goals)**
      ;
      **member( on( X, Y1), Goals), Y1 \== Y**      % Block cannot be in two places
      ;
      **member( on( X1, Y), Goals), X1 \== X.**     % Two blocks cannot be in same place

   **impossible( clear( X), Goals) :-**
      **member( on( _, X), Goals).**

A planner based on goal regression as outlined here is programmed in Figure 17.6. This program considers candidate plans in the breadth-first style (or iterative deepening) when shorter plans are tried first. This is ensured by the goal

   **conc( PrePlan, [Action], Plan)**

in the procedure **plan**. This planner finds the optimal, three-step plan for the problem of Figure 17.1.

```
% A means-ends planner with goal regression
% plan( State, Goals, Plan)

plan( State, Goals, [ ]) :-
   satisfied( State, Goals).              % Goals true in State

plan( State, Goals, Plan) :-
   conc( PrePlan, [Action], Plan),        % Divide plan achieving breadth-first effect
   select( State, Goals, Goal),           % Select a goal
   achieves( Action, Goal),
   can( Action, Condition),               % Ensure Action contains no variables
   preserves( Action, Goals),                % Protect Goals
   regress( Goals, Action, RegressedGoals),  % Regress Goals through Action
   plan( State, RegressedGoals, PrePlan).
```

**Figure 17.6** A planner based on goal regression. The planner performs an iterative deepening search.

**Figure 17.6** *contd*

```
satisfied( State, Goals) :-
    delete_all( Goals, State, [ ]).                  % All Goals in State

select( State, Goals, Goal) :-                       % Select Goal from Goals
    member( Goal, Goals).                            % A simple selection principle

achieves( Action, Goal) :-
    adds( Action, Goals),
    member( Goal, Goals).

preserves( Action, Goals) :-                         % Action does not destroy Goals
    deletes( Action, Relations),
    \+ ( member( Goal, Relations),
        member( Goal, Goals) ).

regress( Goals, Action, RegressedGoals) :-           % Regress Goals through Action
    adds( Action, NewRelations),
    delete_all( Goals, NewRelations, RestGoals),
    can( Action, Condition),
    addnew( Condition, RestGoals, RegressedGoals).   % Add precond., check imposs.

% addnew( NewGoals, OldGoals, AllGoals):
%    AllGoals is the union of NewGoals and OldGoals
%    NewGoals and OldGoals must be compatible

addnew( [ ], L, L).

addnew( [Goal | _ ], Goals, _ ) :-
    impossible( Goal, Goals),                        % Goal incompatible with Goals
    !,
    fail.                                            % Cannot be added

addnew( [X | L1], L2, L3) :-
    member( X, L2), !,                               % Ignore duplicate
    addnew( L1, L2, L3).

addnew( [X | L1], L2, [X | L3]) :-
    addnew( L1, L2, L3).

% delete_all( L1, L2, Diff): Diff is set-difference of lists L1 and L2

delete_all( [ ], _, [ ]).

delete_all( [X | L1], L2, Diff) :-
    member( X, L2), !,
    delete_all( L1, L2, Diff).

delete_all( [X | L1], L2, [X | Diff]) :-
    delete_all( L1, L2, Diff).
```

# EXERCISE

**17.5**   Trace the planning process, based on goal regression, for achieving on( a, b) from the initial situation of Figure 17.1. Suppose the plan is:

[ move( c, a, 2), move( a, 1, b)]

If the goal-list after the second action of the plan is [ on( a, b)], what are the regressed goal-lists before the second move and before the first move?

## 17.4 Combining regression planning with best-first heuristic

The planners developed thus far only use a very basic search strategy: breadth-first search (realized as iterative deepening). This strategy is completely uninformed in the sense that it does not use any domain-specific knowledge in choosing among alternatives. Consequently, our planners are in general very inefficient. There are several ways of introducing heuristic guidance, based on domain knowledge, into our planners. Some natural places where domain-specific planning knowledge can be introduced into the planners are as follows:

- relation select( State, Goals, Goal), which decides in what order the goals are attempted. For example, a piece of useful knowledge about building block structures is that, at any time, every block has to be supported, and therefore structures have to be built in the bottom-up order. A heuristic selection rule based on this would say: the 'top-most' on relations should be achieved last (that is, they should be selected first by the goal regression planner as it builds plans backwards). Another heuristic would suggest that the selection of those goals that are already true in the initial situation should be deferred.

- relation achieves( Action, Goal), which chooses among alternative actions that achieve the given goal will be tried first. Some actions seem better, for example, because they achieve several goals simultaneously; alternatively, through experience, we may be able to tell that some action's precondition will be easier to satisfy than others.

- decision about which of the alternative regressed goal sets to consider next: continue working on the one that looks easiest, because that one will probably be accomplished by the shortest plan.

This last possibility indicates how our planner can be made to search in a best first manner. This involves heuristically estimating the difficulty of alternative goal sets. Among alternative goal sets, the one that looks easiest is regressed first.

To use our best-first search programs of Chapters 12 and 13, we have to specify the corresponding state space and a heuristic function; that is, we have to define the following:

(1) A successor relation between the nodes in the state space s( Node1, Node2, Cost).

(2) The goal nodes of the search by relation goal( Node).

(3) A heuristic function by relation h( Node, HeuristicEstimate).

(4) The start node of the search.

One way is that goal sets correspond to nodes in the state space. Then, in the state space there will be a link between two goal sets Goals1 and Goals2 if there is an action A such that:

(1) A adds some goal in Goals1,

(2) A does not destroy any goal in Goals1, and

(3) **Goals2** is the result of regressing **Goals1** through action A, as already defined by predicate **regress** in Figure 17.6:

> regress( Goals1, A, Goals2)

For simplicity we will assume that all the actions have the same cost, and will accordingly assign cost 1 to all the links in the state space. Thus the successor relation will look like this:

```
s( Goals1, Goals2, 1) :-
    member( Goal, Goals1),              % Select a goal
    achieves( Action, Goal),            % A relevant action to achieve Goal
    can( Action, Condition),
    preserves( Action, Goals1),
    regress( Goals1, Action, Goals2).
```

The goal condition for this state space is: a goal set that is true in the initial situation of the plan is a goal node of the state-space search. That means the goal set is a subset of the initial state. The start node for state-space search is the list of goals to be achieved by the plan.

Although the representation above contains all the essential information, it has a small deficiency. This is due to the fact that our best-first search program finds a solution path as a sequence of states and does not include actions between states. For example, the sequence of states (i.e. goal-lists) for achieving on( a, b) in the initial situation in Figure 17.1 is:

```
[ [ clear( c), clear( 2), on( c, a), clear( b), on( a, 1)],    % True in initial situation
  [ clear( a), clear( b), on( a, 1)],                          % True after move(c,a,2)
  [ on( a, b)] ]                                               % True after move(a,1,b)
```

Notice that the best-first program returns the solution path in the inverse order. In our case this is in fact an advantage because plans are built in the backward direction, so the inverse sequence returned by the search program corresponds to the actual order in the plan. It is, however, awkward that the actions are not explicitly mentioned in the plan, although they could be reconstructed from the differences between adjacent goal-lists. But we can easily get actions explicitly into the solution path. We only have to add, to each state, the action that follows the state. So nodes of the state space become pairs of the form:

> Goals –> Action

The state-space implementation in Figure 17.7 contains this representational detail. This implementation uses a very crude heuristic function. This is simply the number of yet unsatisfied goals in the goal-list. Even if this is a very simplistic estimate of the difficulty of a goal set it works much better than no heuristic at all.

The state-space definition in Figure 17.7 can now be used by the best-first programs of Chapters 12 and 13 as follows. We have to consult the planning problem definition in terms of relations **adds**, **deletes** and **can** (Figure 17.2 for the blocks world). We also have to supply the relation **impossible** and the relation **start**, which describes the initial situation of the plan. For the situation in Figure 17.1, this is:

> start( [ on( a, 1), on( b, 3), on( c, a), clear( b), clear( c), clear( 2), clear( 4)].

```
% State-space representation of means-ends planning with goal regression

:- op( 300, xfy, ->).

s( Goals -> NextAction, NewGoals -> Action, 1) :-      % All costs are 1
    member( Goal, Goals),
    achieves( Action, Goal),
    can( Action, Condition),
    preserves( Action, Goals),
    regress( Goals, Action, NewGoals).

goal( Goals -> Action) :-
    start( State)                              % User-defined initial situation
    satisfied( State, Goals).                  % Goals true in initial situation

h( Goals -> Action, H) :-                      % Heuristic estimate
    start( State),
    delete_all( Goals, State, Unsatisfied),    % Unsatisfied goals
    length( Unsatisfied, H).                   % Number of unsatisfied goals
```

**Figure 17.7** A state-space definition for means-ends planning based on goal regression. Predicates **satisfied, achieves, preserves, regress, addnew** and **delete_all** are as defined in Figure 17.6.

To solve the task of Figure 17.1 by our means-ends best-first planner, we can now call the best-first procedure by:

> ?- bestfirst( [ on( a, b), on( b, c)] -> stop, Plan).

The null action **stop** is added here because in our representation each goal-list must be followed, at least syntactically, by an action. But [ on( a, b), on( b, c)] is the final goal-list of the plan, which is not followed by any actual action. The solution is presented by the following list of goal-lists and actions between them:

> Plan = [
> [ clear( 2), on( c, a), clear( c), on( b, 3), clear( b), on( a, 1)] -> move( c, a, 2),
> [ clear( c), on( b, 3), clear( a), clear( b), on( a, 1)] -> move( b, 3, c),
> [ clear( a), clear( b), on( a, 1), on( b, c)] -> move( a, 1, b),
> [ on( a, b), on( b, c)] -> stop]

Although this best-first planner uses the simple-minded heuristic estimates, it is fast compared with our other planners.

# EXERCISES

**17.6** Consider the simple heuristic function for the blocks world of Figure 17.7. Does this function satisfy the condition of the admissibility theorem for best-first search? (See Chapter 12 for the admissibility theorem.)

**17.7** The example heuristic function for the blocks world developed in this chapter simply counts the goals to be achieved. This is very crude as some goals are clearly more difficult than others. For example, it is trivial to achieve on( a, b) if blocks *a* and *b* are already clear, whereas it is difficult if *a* and *b* are buried under high stacks of other blocks. Therefore, a better heuristic function would try to estimate the difficulty of individual goals – for example, take into account the number of blocks to be removed before the block of interest could be moved. Propose such better heuristic functions and experiment with them.

**17.8**  Modify the planning state-space definition of Figure 17.7 to introduce the cost of actions:

> s( State1, State2, Cost)

The cost can, for example, depend on the weight of the object moved and the distance by which it is moved. Use this definition to find minimal cost plans in the blocks world.

## 17.5  Uninstantiated actions and goals

The planners developed in this chapter are implemented in programs made as simple as possible to illustrate the principles. No thought has been given to their efficiency. By choosing better representations and corresponding data structures, significant improvements in efficiency are possible. Our planners can also be enhanced by allowing uninstantiated variables in goals and actions. This is briefly discussed in this section.

All our algorithms were greatly simplified by the requirement that all the goals for the planner should always be completely instantiated. This requirement was attained by an appropriate definition of the planning domain (relations **adds**, **deletes** and **can**). In Figure 17.2, for example, the complete instantiation of variables is forced by the **can** relation, defined as:

> can( move( Block, From, To), [ clear( Block), clear( To), on( Block, From)] ) :-
>   block( Block),
>   object( To),
>   . . .

Goals like **block( Block)** above force the instantiation of variables. This may lead to the generation of numerous irrelevant alternative moves that are considered by the planner. For example, consider the situation in Figure 17.1 when the planner is asked to achieve the goal **clear( a)**. The relation **achieves** proposes this general move to achieve **clear( a)**:

> move( Something, a, Somewhere)

Then the precondition is found by:

> can( move( Something, a, Somewhere), Condition)

This forces, through backtracking, various alternative instantiations of **Something** and **Somewhere**. So all the following moves are considered before the one that works is found:

> move( b, a, 1)
> move( b, a, 2)
> move( b, a, 3)

```
move( b, a, 4)
move( b, a, c)
move( c, a, 1)
move( c, a, 2)
```

A more powerful representation that avoids this inefficiency would allow unin-stantiated variables in goals. For the blocks world, for example, one attempt to define such an alternative predicate **can** would simply be:

```
can( move( Block, From, To), [ clear( Block), clear( To), on( Block, From)] ).
```

Now consider the situation in Figure 17.1 and the goal **clear( a)** again. Relation **achieves** again proposes the action:

```
move( Something, a, Somewhere)
```

This time, when **can** is evaluated, the variables remain uninstantiated, and the precondition list is:

```
[ clear( Something), clear( Somewhere), on( Something, a)]
```

Notice that this goal-list, which the planner now has to attempt, contains variables. The goal-list is satisfied immediately in the initial situation if:

```
Something = c, Somewhere = 2
```

The key to this improvement in efficiency, where the right move was found virtually without search, is that uninstantiated moves and goals stand for *sets* of alternative moves and goals. Their instantiation is deferred until later, when it becomes clear what their values should be. On the other hand, the specification in Figure 17.2 forces immediate instantiation of actions and thereby also goals in action preconditions.

The foregoing example demonstrates the power of representation with vari-ables. However, this method is not without complications. First, the fore-going attempt to define **can** is inadequate because it allows, in the situation of Figure 17.1, the move:

```
move( c, a, c)
```

As a result we get a situation where block *c* is on itself! Thus, a better definition of **can** would not allow a block to be moved to itself, as well as other similar restrictions. Here is such a definition:

```
can(move( Block, From, To),
   [ clear( Block), clear( To), on( Block, From), different( Block, To),
     different( From, To), different( Block, From)] ).
```

Here **different( X, Y)** means that X and Y do not denote the same object. A condition like **different( X, Y)** does not depend on the state of the world. So it cannot be made true by an action, but it has to be checked by evaluating the corresponding predicate. One way to handle such quasi goals is to add the following extra clause to the procedure **satisfied** in our planners:

```
satisfied( State, [Goal | Goals]) :-
   holds( Goal),                          % Goal independent of State
   satisfied( Goals).
```

Accordingly, predicates like **different**( X, Y) would have to be defined by the procedure **holds**:

    **holds**( **different**( X, Y))

This definition could be along the following lines:

- If X and Y do not match then **different**( X, Y) holds.

- If X and Y are literally the same (X == Y) then this condition is false, and it will always be false regardless of further actions in the plan. Such conditions could then be handled in a similar way as goals declared in the relation **impossible**.

- Otherwise X and Y match, but are not literally the same. So we cannot tell at the moment. The decision whether they denote the same object or not should be postponed until X and Y become further instantiated.

As illustrated by this example, the evaluation of conditions like **different**( X, Y) that are independent of the state sometimes has to be deferred. Therefore, it would be practical to maintain such conditions as an extra argument of the procedure **plan** and handle them separately from those goals that are achieved by actions.

    This is not the only complication introduced by variables. For example, consider the move:

    **move**( a, 1, X)

Does this move delete the relation **clear**( b)? Yes, if X = b, and not, if **different**( X, b). This means that we have two possibilities, and the corresponding two alternatives are associated with the value of X: in one alternative, X is equal to b; in the other, an extra condition **different**( X, b) is added. One practical way of implementing all this would be to use the facilities of constraint logic programming (CLP) so that these additional conditions would be handled as constraints in CLP.

## 17.6 Partial order planning

One deficiency of our planners is that they consider all possible orderings of actions even when the actions are completely independent. As an example, consider the planning task of Figure 17.8 where the goal is to build two stacks of blocks from two disjoint sets of blocks that are already well separated. The two stacks can be built independently of each other by two plans, one for each stack:

    Plan1 = [ move( b, a, c), move( a, 1, b)]
    Plan2 = [ move( e, d, f), move( d, 8, e)]

**Figure 17.8** A planning task consisting of two independent subtasks.

The important point is that these two plans do not interact with each other. Therefore, only the order of actions *within* each plan is important; it does not matter in which order the two plans are executed – first P1 and then P2, or first P2 and then P1, or it is even possible to switch between them and execute a bit of one and then a bit of the other. For example, this is an admissible execution sequence:

[ move( b, a, c), move( e, d, f), move( d, 8, e), move( a, 1, b)]

If two robots are available, P1 and P2 can also be executed in parallel. In spite of this, our planners would, in the planning process, potentially consider all 24 permutations of the four actions, although there are essentially only four alternatives – two permutations for each of the two constituent plans. This problem arises from the fact that our planners strictly insist on *complete* ordering of actions in a plan. An improvement then would be to allow, in the cases when the order does not matter, the precedence between actions to remain unspecified. Thus our plans would be *partially ordered sets* of actions, instead of totally ordered sequences. Planners that allow partial ordering are called *partial order planners* (sometimes also *non-linear planners*).

Let us look at a rough idea of how partial-order plans could be constructed, by considering the example of Figure 17.1 again. The following is a sketch of how a non-linear planner may solve this problem. Analysing the goals **on( a, b)** and **on( b, c)**, the planner concludes that the following two actions will have to be included into the plan:

M1 = **move( a, X, b)**
M2 = **move( b, Y, c)**

There is no other way of achieving the two goals. But the order in which these two actions are to be executed is not yet specified. Now consider the preconditions of the two actions. The precondition for **move( a, X, b)** contains **clear( a)**. This is not satisfied in the initial situation; therefore, we need an action of the form:

M3 = **move( U, a, V)**

This has to precede the move M1, so we now have a constraint on the order of the actions:

**before( M3, M1)**

Now we check whether M2 and M3 can be the same move that achieves the objectives of both. This is not the case, so the plan will have to include three different moves. Now the planner has to answer the question: Is there a permutation of the three moves [ M1, M2, M3] such that M3 precedes M1, the permutation is executable in the initial situation and the overall goals are satisfied in the resulting state? Due to the precedence constraint, only three out of altogether six permutations are taken into account:

[ M3, M1, M2]
[ M3, M2, M1]
[ M2, M3, M1]

The second of these satisfies the execution constraint by the instantiation: U = c, V = 2, X = 1, Y = 3. As can be seen from this example, the combinatorial complexity cannot be completely avoided by partial order planning, but it can be alleviated.

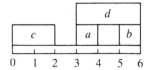

**Figure 17.9** A planning task in another blocks world: Achieve on( a, c), on( b, c), on( c, d).

In Chapter 18 we will develop a partial order planning program, and implement another method, called GRAPHPLAN, that also produces a kind of partial order plans.

# PROJECTS

Develop a program, using the techniques of this chapter, for planning in a more interesting variation of the simple blocks world used throughout this chapter. Figure 17.9 shows an example task in this new world. The new world contains blocks of different sizes and the stability of structures has to be taken into account. To make the problem easier, assume that blocks can only be placed at whole-numbered positions, and they always have to be properly supported, so that they are always stable. Also assume that they are never rotated by the robot and the move trajectories are simple: straight up until the block is above any other block, then horizontally, and then straight down. Design specialized heuristics to be used by this planner.

A robot world, more realistic and interesting than the one defined in Figure 17.2, would also comprise perception actions by a camera or touch sensor. For example, the action look( Position, Object) would recognize the object seen by the camera at **Position** (that is, instantiate variable **Object**). In such a world it is realistic to assume that the scene is not completely known to the robot, so it will possibly include, in its plan, actions whose only purpose is to acquire information. This can be further complicated by the fact that some measurements of this kind cannot be done immediately, as some objects cannot be seen (bottom objects cannot be seen by a top-view camera). Introduce other relevant goal relations and modify our planners if necessary.

Modify the goal regression planner of Figure 17.6 so that it will correctly handle variables in goals and actions, according to the discussion in Section 17.5.

# Summary

- In planning, available actions are represented in a way that enables explicit reasoning about their effects and their preconditions. This can be done by stating, for each action, its precondition, its add-list (relationships the action establishes) and delete-list (relationships the action destroys). Such representations are referred to as STRIPS-like representations.
- *Means-ends* derivation of plans is based on finding actions that achieve given goals and enabling the preconditions for such actions.

- *Goal protection* is a mechanism that prevents a planner destroying goals already achieved.
- Means-ends planning involves search through the space of relevant actions. The usual search techniques therefore apply to planning as well: depth-first, breadth-first, iterative deepening and best-first search.
- To reduce search complexity, domain-specific knowledge can be used at several stages of means-ends planning, such as: which goal in the given goal-list should be attempted next; which action among the alternative actions should be tried first; heuristically estimating the difficulty of a goal-list in best-first search.
- *Goal regression* is a process that determines which goals have to be true before an action, to ensure that given goals are true after the action. Planning with goal regression typically involves backward chaining of actions.
- Allowing uninstantiated variables in goals and actions can make planning more efficient; however, on the other hand, it significantly complicates the planner.
- Partial order planning recognizes the fact that actions in plans need not be always totally ordered. Leaving the order unspecified whenever possible allows economical treatment of sets of equivalent permutations of actions.
- Concepts discussed in this chapter are:

  action precondition, add-list, delete-list
  means-ends principle of planning
  goal protection
  goal regression
  partial order planning

## References and historical notes

The early studies of basic ideas of means-ends problem solving and planning in artificial intelligence were done by Newell, Shaw and Simon (1960). These ideas were implemented in the celebrated program GPS (General Problem Solver) whose behaviour is studied in detail in Ernst and Newell (1969). Another historically important planning program is STRIPS (Fikes and Nilsson 1971; 1993), which can be viewed as an implementation of GPS. STRIPS introduced the representation of the planning domain by the relations **adds**, **deletes** and **can**, which is also used in this chapter and is the basis for many further developments in planning. Two other logic-based representations for planning (not discussed in this chapter) are situation calculus (Kowalski 1979) and event calculus (Kowalski and Sergot 1986; Shanahan 1997). The mechanisms of STRIPS, and various related ideas and refinements, are described in Nilsson (1980), where the elegant formulations of planning in logic by Green and Kowalski are also presented. Warren's (1974) program WARPLAN is an early interesting planner written in Prolog. It can be viewed as another implementation of STRIPS, refined in a certain respect. The WARPLAN program appeared in other places in the literature – for example, in Coelho and Cotta (1988). WARPLAN consists of less than a hundred lines of Prolog code, and is therefore often mentioned in the literature as an illustration of the particular compactness of programs often achieved in Prolog. The planning programs in this book further illustrate this compactness. Waldinger (1977) studied phenomena of interaction among conjunctive goals, among them also the principle of goal regression. Goal regression corresponds to determining the *weakest precondition* used in proving program correctness. Difficulties that a planner with goal protection may have with the problem of Figure 17.1 are known in the literature as the Sussman anomaly (see, for example, Waldinger 1977). Early developments of partial order planning are Sacerdoti (1977) and Tate (1977). Allen, Hendler and Tate (1990) edited a collection of classic papers on planning to that date. Ghallab *et al.* (2004) is an excellent book on planning that covers all major developments. The general books on AI by Russell and Norvig (2010) and by Poole *et al.* (1998) include substantial material on planning. High quality papers on planning appear in the *Artificial Intelligence* journal: see, for example, AIJ volume 76 (1995), a special issue on planning and scheduling. Partial order planning and GRAPHPLAN will be studied in Chapter 18 where references relevant to these topics are given.

In our treatment in this chapter, we assumed that all the information about the domain and the current state of the world is known to the planner, there is no uncertainty, and the effects of executing actions are always as expected. In the real world, these assumptions may not be true. For example, in robotics all of the mentioned complications typically occur. Ghallab *et al.* (2004) and Russell and Norvig (2010) also present methods that address these complications.

*Artificial Intelligence* Vol. **76**. (1995) Special issue on Planning and Scheduling.

Allen, J., Hendler, J. and Tate, A. (eds) (1990) *Readings in Planning*. San Mateo, CA: Morgan Kaufmann.

Coelho, H. and Cotta, J.C. (1988) *Prolog by Example*. Berlin: Springer-Verlag.

Ernst, G.W. and Newell, A. (1969) GPS: *A Case Study in Generality and Problem Solving*. New York: Academic Press.

Fikes, R.E. and Nilsson, N.J. (1971) STRIPS: a new approach to the application of theorem proving to problem solving. *Artificial Intelligence* 2: 189–208.

Fikes, R.E. and Nilsson, N.J. (1993) STRIPS, a retrospective. *Artificial Intelligence* **59**: 227–232.

Ghallab, M., Nau, D. and Traverso, P. (2004) *Automated Planning: Theory and Practice*. Elsevier/ Morgan Kaufmann.

Kowalski, R. (1979) *Logic for Problem Solving*. North-Holland.

Kowalski, R. and Sergot, M. (1986) A logic-based calculus of events. *New Generation Computing* **4**: 67–95.

Newell, A., Shaw, J.C. and Simon, H.A. (1960) Report on a general problem-solving program for a computer. *Information Processing: Proc. Int. Conf. on Information Processing*. Paris: UNESCO.

Nilsson, N.J. (1980) *Principles of Artificial Intelligence*. Palo Alto, CA: Tioga; also Berlin: Springer-Verlag.

Poole, D., Mackworth, A. and Goebel, R. (1998) *Computational Intelligence: A Logical Approach*. Oxford University Press.

Russell, S. and Norvig, P. (2010) *Artificial Intelligence: A Modern Approach,* third edn. Prentice Hall.

Sacerdoti, E.D. (1977) *A Structure for Plans and Behavior*. New York: Elsevier.

Shanahan, M. (1997) *Solving the Frame Problem: Mathematical Investigation of the Common Sense Law of Inertia*. Cambridge, MA: MIT Press.

Tate, A. (1977) Generating project networks. *Proc. IJCAI 77*. Cambridge, MA.

Waldinger, R.J. (1977) Achieving several goals simultaneously. In: *Machine Intelligence* **8** (Elcock, E.W. and Michie, D., eds). Chichester: Ellis Horwood. Distributed by Wiley.

Warren, D.H.D. (1974) *WARPLAN: A System for Generating Plans*. University of Edinburgh: Department of Computational Logic, Memo 76.

# Chapter 18

# Partial Order Planning and GRAPHPLAN

In this chapter we discuss planning techniques that produce plans as partially ordered sets of actions. We will implement two approaches. The first is called partial order planning, or POP for short. The second is based on the GRAPHPLAN technique which employs the so-called planning graphs. These graphs enable efficient representation of possible sequences of actions by accumulating 'mutually exclusive' constraints that state which actions and which conditions cannot occur at the same time. This approach is well known for its computational efficiency.

## 18.1 Partial order planning

Consider a simple planning domain illustrated by Figure 18.1. There are a number of robots that move in a rectangular grid. Each cell of the grid can accommodate one robot at the most, so the robots have to avoid each other. The robots may move simultaneously. Possible actions in this world are of the form

> go( Robot, Cell1, Cell2)

which means that **Robot** moves from **Cell1** to **Cell2**. Allowed moves are Manhattan-like: a robot may move into an unoccupied adjacent cell in directions left, right, up or down, but not diagonally. A state of the world is defined by a set of relationships of two types:

> at( Robot, Cell1)   and   clear( Cell2)

which means: **Robot** is in **Cell1**, and **Cell2** is unoccupied. So at(a,1) means that robot a is in cell 1. On the other hand, the fact that cell 1 is not clear will be denoted by the negation, written as ~clear(1). In the sequel, such elementary properties of a state will be also called *literals* or (simple) *conditions*.

Suppose that the initial situation in such a robot world is as shown in Figure 18.1, and that the goals of a plan are: { at(a,2), at(c,6)}. A partially ordered plan (POP) for this task is a set of three actions {A1, A2, A3}, where A1 = go(a,1,2),

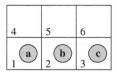

**Figure 18.1** Three robots a, b and c moving in a 3 by 2 grid. The cells of the grid are numbered 1, ... , 6. A robot may move into a horizontally or vertically adjacent unoccupied cell, e.g. **go(a,1,4)**.

A2 = **go(b,2,5)**, A3 = **go(c,3,6)** and there is the ordering constraint: **before(A2,A1)**. Any linearization of this plan, written as a Prolog list, makes a schedule that solves the task. There are three linearizations in our case:

[ A2, A1, A3],    or    [ A2, A3, A1],    or    [ A3, A2, A1]

Another possible schedule for this plan is the variation of the last two schedules so that A2 and A3 are executed in parallel.

The robots-on-grid domain is formally specified in Figure 18.2. The planning domain representation is similar to that used in Chapter 17. The difference is that the two predicates **adds(Action,PositiveEffects)** and **deletes(Action,NegativeEffects)** are replaced by a single predicate:

**effects( Action, Effects)**

where **Effects** is a list of both positive and negative effects of **Action**. The relationships that **Action** deletes from the current state appear negated in the list **Effects**. For example, after the move **go(Robot,A,B)**, **clear(B)** is no longer true. This is stated by including the literal **~clear(B)** in **Effects**.

In Figure 18.2, the predicate

**inconsistent( Literal1, Literal2)**

defines pairs of inconsistent literals, that is literals that cannot be both true at the same time.

We will now look at the POP planning algorithm. Each partial order plan, or POP, is defined by:

- a set of actions $\{A_i, A_j, ...\}$
- a set of ordering constraints like before($A_i$, $A_j$ ) ($A_i$ is before $A_j$)
- a set of *causal links*.

Causal links are of the form:

causes( $A_i$, P, $A_j$)

This is read as: action $A_i$ achieves condition P for action $A_j$. The intuition behind this is: P is one of the preconditions for action $A_j$, and action $A_i$ (partially) enables action $A_j$ by achieving P. Of course, for this to work $A_i$ has to occur before $A_j$. An example of a causal link for the domain of Figure 18.1 is:

causes( go(b,2,5), clear(2), go(a,1,2))

The action **go(b,2,5)** causes **clear(2)** for action **go(a,1,2)**.

```
% A planning domain: robots a, b and c move in grid 3 by 2

:- op( 100, fx, ~).                          % Operator for negated conditions

% Precondition of action: robot R goes from cell A to B

can( go(R,A,B), [ at(R,A), clear(B)]) :-
 robot(R), adjacent(A,B).

% Effects of action go( Robot, CellA, CellB):
%    After the action at(Robot,CellB) and clear(CellA) become true,
%    and at(Robot,CellA) and clear(CellB) become false

effects( go(R,A,B), [ at(R,B), clear(A), ~at(R,A), ~clear(B)]).

robot(a).    robot(b).    robot(c).

adjacent(A,B) :-                             % Cells A and B are adjacent in the grid
 n(A,B); n(B,A).


% n( A, B):  Cells A and B are "ordered" neighbours

n(1,2).  n(2,3).  n(4,5).  n(5,6).  n(1,4).  n(2,5).  n(3,6).

% inconsistent( G1, G2): goals G1 and G2 inconsistent

inconsistent( G, ~G).                        % Negated goals always inconsistent
inconsistent( ~G, G).

inconsistent( at(R,C1), at(R,C2)) :-
  C1 \== C2.        % Robot cannot be at different places at the same time

inconsistent( at(_,C), clear(C)).   % A cell cannot be both clear and occupied at a time
inconsistent( clear(C), at(_,C)).

inconsistent( at(R1,C), at(R2,C)) :-  % Two robots cannot be in the same cell at a time
  R1 \== R2.

state0( [ at(a,1), at(b,2), at(c,3), clear(4), clear(5), clear(6)]). % The state of Fig. 18.1
```

**Figure 18.2** A planning domain specification for the robots-on-grid world of Figure 18.1.

The purpose of a causal link **causes(A,P,B)** is to 'protect' condition **P** in the time interval between actions **A** and **B**. That is to ensure that no action that destroys **P** is inserted into the plan between actions **A** and **B**. We say that action **C** *conflicts with* the causal link **causes(A,P,B)** if **C**'s effect is to make **P** false. If such an action **C** is added to the plan, such a conflict is resolved by additional ordering constraints: **before(C,A)**, or **before(B,C)**. This ensures that **C** is outside the time interval between actions **A** and **B** (see Figure 18.3).

A plan is *consistent* if there is no cycle in the ordering constraints and no conflict between actions and causal links. For example, a plan that contains **before(A,B)** and **before(B,A)** contains a cycle, it is therefore not consistent, and obviously impossible to execute. Consistent POPs have an important property: *every* linearization of a consistent plan is a total-order solution, that is every total-order schedule consistent with the constraints is executable.

A POP planning algorithm based on the concepts introduced in the previous paragraphs is as follows. The algorithm searches a space of partial order plans. This space

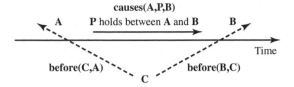

**Figure 18.3** If action C conflicts with the causal link **causes(A,P,B)** then insert C either before A or after B, to make sure P is preserved in the interval between A and B.

is a search graph (a state space) whose nodes are POPs. Before defining the successor relation between the nodes (POPs), let us define the start node. The start node of search is the POP that contains just two virtual actions called **Start** and **Finish**, with the constraint **before(Start,Finish)**. The precondition of action **Start** is just true (i.e. always satisfied), and the precondition of Finish is the conjunction of the user-specified goals of the plan. All these preconditions are 'open' in the sense that currently the plan does not ensure that they are true at the time of action **Finish**. The effects of **Start** are all the literals that are true in the given start state of the plan. So the virtual action **Start** formally establishes that just after **Start** everything is true that is known to be true in the start state of the plan. All other actions A that will be inserted into the POP will be constrained to occur in time between **Start** and **Finish**: **before( Start, A)** and **before(A,Finish)**.

We say that an action A in a POP has an *open* precondition P if P is among A's preconditions, and it is not ensured in the POP that P holds at the time that A is executed. Such an open precondition can be 'closed' by, for example, inserting an action, whose effect is P, before action A. Of course, it also has to be ensured by appropriate ordering constraints that P stays true until A happens. This leads to the following definition of the successor relations between POPs in the search space. Let **Plan** be a partially ordered plan. A successor of **Plan** is a refinement of **Plan** such that this refinement 'closes' one of the open preconditions in **Plan**. A successor of **Plan** is obtained as follows:

- Select an action A in **Plan**, such that A has an open precondition P
- Find an action B that achieves P
- B may be an existing action in **Plan**, or a new action not yet in **Plan**; if action B is new then add B to **Plan** and constrain: **before(Start,B)** and **before(B,A)**
- Add to **Plan** the causal link **causes(B,P,A)**
- Add appropriate ordering constraints to resolve all conflicts between:
  - (a) the new causal link and all the existing actions in **Plan**, and
  - (b) action B (if it is a new action) and the existing causal links in **Plan**.

A POP with no open precondition is a solution to our planning problem. Any linearization of such a POP is a total-order plan that guarantees that all the specified goals of the plan are true just before the last, virtual action **Finish**. Of course, as already mentioned, actions in such a POP can also be executed in parallel as long as such an execution schedule does not violate the ordering constraints in the POP.

# EXERCISE

**18.1** Use the POP algorithm to construct a partial order plan for the 3-robot, 6-cell problem of Figure 18.1, with the goal **at(a,3)**.

 ## An implementation of partial order planning

Our implementation of POP planning will be based on the following outline. We will use elements of CLP(FD) (constraint logic programming over finite domains, see Chapter 7) to handle the ordering constraints. The use of CLP for this is, of course, not necessary, but it will be convenient and will lead to a short program. The structures used to represent a POP will slightly differ in details from the general standard outline of POP planning in the previous section. A POP will be represented by the term **pop( Actions, OpenPreconditions, TrueConditions, Finish)**. As the formal setting of the planning problem does not involve real times, actions will be assigned discrete time points represented by integers. These time points will just be the indexes of actions that will respect the ordering constraints, and **Finish** (finishing time of the plan) will be the highest index, that is the latest symbolic time point. This time information together with the corresponding ordering constraints between time points will accomplish a similar role to that of causal links between actions and literals. Therefore there will be no need for causal links in our implementation. The remaining three components of a plan are three sets, all represented as Prolog lists:

> **Actions**, partially ordered set of actions included so far in the plan.
> **OpenConditions**, set of outstanding goals (open preconditions) yet to be achieved by the plan.
> **TrueConditions**, set of conditions already achieved by **Actions**.

Initially, list **Actions** is empty, **OpenConditions** are the given goals of the plan, and **TrueConditions** are the literals that are true in start state. All items in these sets are attached times (integers – symbolic time points). For each action, there is a time attached to the action at which the action will be executed. Each of the open conditions has a time attached to it stating when the condition has to be true. That is, the condition is needed as a precondition of an action that will happen at that time. Each literal in **TrueConditions** is accompanied by a time interval saying when the literal is guaranteed to hold during the execution of the plan. In the program, all these sets will be represented by lists as follows:

> Actions = [Action1: Time1, Action2: Time2, ... ]
> OpenConditions = [ Goal1:Time1, Goal2: Time2, ... ]
> TrueConditions = [ Cond1: Time1/Time2, ... ]

In **TrueConditions**, a time interval between two times **Time1** and **Time2** is denoted by the term **Time1/Time2**. For example, consider the three-robot domain of Figure 18.1. Let the goals of the plan be: robot **a** at cell 2, and robot **c** at cell 6.

The corresponding initial values of the three lists are:

> Actions = [ ]
> OpenConds = [ at(a,2): Finish, at(c,6): Finish]
> TrueConds = [ at(a,1): Start/Ta, at(b,2): Start/Tb, at(c,3): Start/Tc, clear(4): Start/Td, ...]

Here **Start** and **Finish** are the start time and finishing time of the plan. In our representation, relying on CLP(FD), the virtual actions 'Start' and 'Finish' are not needed. The start time **Start** and finishing time **Finish** of the plan will suffice. Notice that additional time points Ta, Tb, Tc, etc. were introduced to represent the upper ends of the time intervals in which at(a,1), at(b,2), at(c,3), etc. hold respectively. CLP(FD) constraints on these times are also set: Start < Ta Ta =< Finish, Start < Tb, Tb =< Finish, etc. In the program, according to CLP(FD) notational conventions in Prolog (see Chapter 7), these constraints will be written as: Start #< Ta, Ta #=< Finish, etc.

We will now roughly follow what the planner does when putting together a plan, but will leave out some details. The planner first selects an open condition, say **at(a,2)**, and deletes it from **OpenConds**. It then does the following:

- Choose an action that achieves at(a,2), say go(a,1,2), and 'stamps' it with a time T1;
- Add 'time-stamped' preconditions of go(a,1,2):T1, at(a,1):T1 and clear(2):T1, to OpenConds;
- Add the achieved goal at(a,2):T1/Finish to TrueConds (T1/Finish means that this goal will be true between the times T1 and Finish; that is, the goal will be protected until the end of the plan);
- Add the other effect of go(a,1,2):T1, clear(1):T1/T2, to TrueConds. Note that clear(1) does not have to hold until Finish. It will hold till some time T2 and for now there is no constraint regarding T2 other than T1 .

The three lists are now:

> Actions = [ go(a,1,2): T1]
> OpenConds = [ at(a,1):T1, clear(2):T1, at(c,6): Finish]
> TrueConds = [ at(a,2):T1/Finish, clear(1):T1/T2, at(a,1): Start/Ta, ...]

The planner will also set CLP(FD) constraints on the times: Start < T1, T1 < Finish, T1 < T2 and T2 =< Finish.

Let the planner now select the open condition **clear(2):T1**, and find an action that achieves **clear(2)**, say go(b,2,5):T3. T3 must be before T1 to achieve **clear(2)** in time for action go(a,1,2):T1. After adding the preconditions for go(b,2,5) to **OpenConds**, and updating **TrueConds**, the three lists become:

> Actions = [ go(b,2,5):T3, go(a,1,2): T1]
> OpenConds = [ at(b,2):T3, clear(5):T3, at(a,1):T1, clear(2):T1, at(c,6): Finish]
> TrueConds = [ clear(2):T3/T4, at(b,5):T3/T5, at(a,2):T1/Finish, clear(1):T1/T2, at(a,1): Start/Ta, ...]

Also, the additional time constraints are set: T3 < T1, Start < T3, T3 < Finish, T3 < T4, T4 =< Finish, T3 < T5, T5 =< Finish. Two additional time points T4 and T5 were introduced as the upper ends of the time intervals in which **clear(2)** and **at(b,5)** will be true. Considering now **OpenConds** and **TrueConds**, all the open conditions may already be true (appearing in **TrueConds**) except **at(c,6):Finish**. An action that achieves **at(c,6)** is **go(c,3,6)**. After adding this action to **Actions**, and updating **OpenConds** and **TrueConds** accordingly, the three lists become:

> Actions = [ go(c,3,6):T6, go(b,2,5):T2, go(a,1,2): T1]
> OpenGoals = [ at(c,3):T6, clear(6):T6, at(b,2):T3, clear(5):T3, at(a,1):T1, clear(2):T1]
> TrueConds = [ at(c,6):T6/Finish, clear(3):T6/T7, clear(2):T3/T4, at(b,5):T3/T5,
> at(a,2):T1/Finish, clear(1):T1/T2, at(a,1): Start/Ta, ...]

Among others, the time constraints regarding T6 are also added: **Start** < T6 and T6 =< **Finish**.

At this moment, the planner realizes that all the **OpenConds** are implied by **TrueConds** after satisfying the relevant ordering constraints. Namely, all the goals appear in **TrueConds**, and all the relevant time constraints are satisfiable. Thus the complete plan now appears in **Actions** whose times have to satisfy the ordering constraints:

- Actions = [ go(c,3,6):T6, go(b,2,5):T3, go(a,1,2): T1]

- Constraints: **Start** < T6 < **Finish**, **Start** < T3 < T1 < **Finish**

This means that **go(b,2,5)** has to be executed before **go(a,1,2)**, and **go(c,3,6)** may be executed at any time before **Finish**, regardless of the other two actions.

Our trace of the planner's search was simplified in several respects. Whenever there was a choice among open preconditions, or among actions to achieve a chosen condition, we 'guessed' the right choice. The algorithm actually has to search among these alternatives. Another important detail that we omitted above is the checking for consistency among conditions when new conditions are added to **TrueConds**. For example, let a new condition to be added be **at(a,2):T1**, where there is already the condition **clear(2):T2/T3** in **TrueConds**. The conditions **clear(2)** and **at(a,2)** are not consistent, so they cannot be true at the same time. Therefore, to ensure the consistency of the plan, the planner has to resolve this conflict by adding the ordering constraints which ensure that there is no overlap between these inconsistent conditions. In this case, the time T1 must be either before T2, or after T3: T1 < T2, or T3 < T1.

The planning algorithm illustrated by the example trace above is shown in Figure 18.4. The algorithm is non-deterministic in the sense that it contains statements like: 'choose an action', 'do either ... or ...'. A non-deterministic algorithm is assumed that it always makes a right guess, for example selects a right goal and chooses a right action. The actual program will, of course, have to search among these alternatives. Our program will perform iterative deepening search.

In the POP algorithm above, the effects of actions are added to **TrueConds** as literals with time intervals, for example **Goal:Time1/Time2**. This means that **Goal** will become true at **Time1** (or, more precisely, 'just after' **Time1**, after the action that causes it) and will stay true in the interval between **Time1** and some yet unspecified time **Time2**. **Time**, when **Goal** is needed, has to be within this interval, so: **Time1** < **Time** =< **Time2**. This is because **Action:Time1** was added to the plan to achieve **Goal** that has to be true at **Time**. Therefore **Goal** has to be protected until **Time**. Once **Goal:Time1/Time** is added to **TrueConds**, no action that destroys **Goal** will be allowed in **Plan** at any time between **Time1** and **Time**.

The time and precedence constraints will be handled in the program through CLP(FD) (see Chapter 7). The domains of time variables will be intervals of integers. The precise conventions about the handling of time in the program will

Given:

        Initial state **S0** = [ Cond1, Cond2, ...]   (conditions that are true in initial state)

        Goals of plan **Goals** = [ Goal1, Goal2, ...]

Find:

        Partially ordered plan **Plan** = [ Action1:Time1, Action2:Time2, ...]

begin

        TrueConds := [ Cond1:0/T1, Cond2:0/T2, ...]

                (these conditions are true at time 0 until some times **T1, T2, ...**)

        OpenConds := [ Goal1:Finish, Goal2:Finish, ...]   (all goals true at time **Finish**, 0 < **Finish**)

        Plan := [ ]     (start with empty plan – no action yet)

        while   **TrueConds**  do not entail **OpenGoals**  do

                select an open goal **Goal:Time** in **OpenConds**;

                delete **Goal:Time** from **OpenConds**;

                do either

                    if  **Goal:T1/T2** is in **TrueCond** then constrain T1 < Time =< T2

                        (in this case **Goal** is already achieved if the two constraints are satisfiable)

                or       (add a new action to plan)

                  begin

                    choose **Action** that achieves **Goal**;

                    add **Action:Time1** to **Plan**;  constrain  Time1 < Time;

                    let [ Cond1, Cond2, ...] be the effects, other than **Goal**, of **Action**;

                    add [ Goal:Time1/Time2, Cond1:Time1/T21, Cond2:Time1/T22, ...] to TrueConds;

                    set constraints Time1 < Time =<Time2;

                    set appropriate time constraints to prevent any conflict between literals in

                      **TrueConds** and **Action**;

                    let [ PreCond1, PreCond2, ...] be preconditions of **Action**;

                    add [ Precond1:Time1, PreCond2:Time1, ...] to **OpenConds**

                end

        end_while

        (Note: Plan now contains a set of actions and their execution times that achieve Goals)

end

**Figure 18.4** A partial order planning algorithm. Some obvious constraints are not stated explicitly, for example all the actions must occur between start time 0 and finishing time **Finish**.

be as follows. All actions occur at integer times. This incurs no loss of generality because the actions have no durations. Their (partial) order in time is all that matters. Each action takes a 'small' amount of time, when the action's effects become true. For example, let the action **move(b,2,5)** occur at time = 1, written in the program as **move(b,2,5):1**. This requires that the preconditions of this move are true at time = 1, which will be written in the program as: **at(b,2):1, clear(5):1**. The effects of the action will not yet be true at time 1, but 'just after' 1. The effects will stay true at least until the next time point, i.e. time = 2.

Figure 18.5 shows a partial order planning program written according to the above design. This program performs iterative deepening search in the space of POPs. The current 'depth limit' means the maximal number of actions in the plan. So the planner in the first place minimizes the number of actions in the plan, and then the finishing time for the given set of actions. The program finally instantiates, within the accumulated ordering constraints, all the action

```
% Partial Order Planner, using CLP(FD) and iterative deepening search
%
%   Partially ordered plan = pop( Actions, OpenConditions, TrueConditions, FinishingTime)
%
%   Actions = [ Action1:Time1, Action2:Time2, ...]    Actions and their execution times
%   OpenConditions = [ Cond1:Time1, Cond2:Time2, ...]
%   TrueConds = [ Cond1:Time11/Time12, Cond2:Time21/Time22, ... ]
%   Note: Ordering constraints are implemented as CLP(FD) constraints

:- use_module(library(clpfd)).           % Load library for CLP(FD)
:- op( 100, fx, ~).                       % Notation for negative effects of an action

% plan( StartState, Goals, Plan, Finish):
%   Plan is partially ordered plan that achieves Goals from StartState at time Finish

plan( StartState, Goals, Plan) :-
    add_intervals( 0, StartState, TrueConds, Finish),    % StartState true at time 0
    add_times( Finish, Goals, OpenConds),                % Goals should be true at time Finish
    EmptyPlan = pop( [ ], OpenConds, TrueConds, Finish),  % No actions in initial plan
    MaxActions in 0..100,                                % Maximally 100 actions in plan
    indomain( MaxActions),                               % Enforce iterative deepening search
    Finish in 1..MaxActions,                             % Domain for finishing time of Plan
    depth_first( EmptyPlan, SolutionPath, MaxActions),   % Search in space of POP's
    once( indomain( Finish)),                            % Minimize finishing time
    conc( _, [Plan], SolutionPath).                      % Working plan is last element of solution path

% s( POP, NewPOP): successor relation between partially ordered plans
%     NewPOP is POP with the first open condition in POP achieved

s( pop( Acts, [Cond:Time | OpenPs], TrueConds, Fin), pop( Acts, OpenPs, TrueConds, Fin)) :-
    member( Cond:Time1/Time2, TrueConds),        % Cond already true between Time1 and Time2
    Time1 #< Time, Time #=< Time2.               % Constrain Time to interval Time1/Time2

s( pop( Acts, [Cond:Time | OpenPs0], TrueConds0, Fin),
   pop( [Action1:Time1 | Acts], OpenPs, TrueConds, Fin))  :-
   effects( Action1, Effects),                   % Look for action that may achieve Cond
   del( Cond, Effects, RestEffects),             % Cond in Effects, that is Action1 achieves Cond
   can( Action1, PreConds1),                     % Preconditions for Action1
   0 #< Time1,  Time1 #< Time,                   % Action1 must occur after 0 and before Time
   add_times( Time1, PreConds1, NewOpenPs),              % Add Time1 to all preconditions
   add_intervals( Time1, RestEffects, RestEffectsTimes, Fin),  % Add  time intervals to all effects
   Time #=< Time2,                               % Achieved condition must be true until Time
   add_conds( [ Cond:Time1/Time2 | RestEffectsTimes], TrueConds0, TrueConds),
        % Add effects to TrueConds0
   conc( NewOpenPs, OpenPs0, OpenPs).            % Add preconditions of Action to goals

% add_conds( Conds, TrueConds, NewTrueConds):
%     Add conditions Conds to list TrueConds, and set corresponding precedence constraints

add_conds( [], TrueConds, TrueConds).

add_conds( [ CondTime | Conds], TrueConds0, TrueConds) :-
    no_conflict( CondTime, TrueConds0),          % No conflict between CondTime and TrueConds0
    add_conds( Conds, [ CondTime | TrueConds0], TrueConds).
```

**Figure 18.5** Partial order planning program.

**Figure 18.5** *contd*

```
% no_conflict( CondTime, TrueConds0):
%    Set constraints to ensure no conflict between CondTime and TrueConds0

no_conflict( _, []).

no_conflict( CondTime, [Cond1Time1 | TrueConds]) :-
  no_conflict1( CondTime, Cond1Time1),
  no_conflict( CondTime, TrueConds).

no_conflict1( CondA:Ta1/Ta2, CondB:Tb1/Tb2) :-
  inconsistent( CondA, CondB), !,      % CondA inconsistent with CondB
  ( Ta2 #=< Tb1; Tb2 #=< Ta1 )         % Ensure no time overlap between CondA and CondB
  ;
  true.                     % Case when CondA consistent with CondB - no constraint needed

% add_times( Time, Conds, TimedConds)

add_times( _, [], []).

add_times( Time, [Cond | Conds], [Cond:Time | TimedConds]) :-
  add_times( Time, Conds, TimedConds).

% add_intervals( Time, Conds, TimedConds, Finish):
%    every condition in Conds true from Time till some later time

add_intervals( _, [], [], _).

add_intervals( Time, [Cond | Conds], [Cond:Time/Time2 | TimedConds], Finish) :-
  Time #< Time2, Time2 #=< Finish,        % Cond true from Time until Time2 =< Finish
  add_intervals( Time, Conds, TimedConds, Finish).

% depth_first( POP, SolutionPath, MaxActionsInPOP):
%   Depth-first search, with respect to number of actions, among partially ordered plans

depth_first( POP, [POP], _) :-
  POP = pop( _, [], _, _).               % No open preconditions - this is a working plan

depth_first( First, [First | Rest], MaxActions) :-
  First = pop( Acts, _, _, _),
  length( Acts, NActs),
  ( NActs < MaxActions, !       % # actions in plan is below MaxActions
   ;
   Second = pop( Acts, _, _, _) ),   % # actions in plan at maximum, no action may be added
  s( First, Second),
  depth_first( Second, Rest, MaxActions).

% Display all possible execution schedules of a partial order plan

show_pop( pop( Actions, _, _, _)) :-
    instantiate_times( Actions),        % Instantiate times of actions for readability
    setof( T:A, member( A:T, Actions), Sorted),   % Sort actions according to times
    nl, write('Actions = '), write( Sorted),      % Write schedule
    fail                                          % Backtrack to produce other schedules
    ;
    nl, nl.                             % All schedues produced

% instantiate_times( Actions): instantiate times of actions respecting ordering constraints

instantiate_times( []).

instantiate_times( [_:T | Acts]) :-
  indomain( T),                % A value in domain of T
  instantiate_times( Acts).
```

times that are still not completely determined by the minimization of the finishing time. The program writes out all the possible execution schedules. This may be impractically many in some cases.

To find plans in our example domain illustrated by Figure 18.1, the programs of Figures 18.2 and 18.5 are to be read into Prolog. The latter program also loads the CLP(FD) library. Also the definitions of the frequently used predicates for lists (member/2, conc/3, del/3) have to be loaded. Then a question may be:

?- state0(S), plan(S, [at(a,3)], P), show_pop(P).
Actions = [1:go(b,2,5), 1:go(c,3,6), 2:go(a,1,2), 3:go(a,2,3)]
Actions = [1:go(b,2,5), 2:go(a,1,2), 2:go(c,3,6), 3:go(a,2,3)]

Here the procedure show_pop displayed the POP P as alternative lists of actions. The actions are prefixed by their times to achieve the ordering of lists according to time. The plan comprises four actions and constraints like go(b,2,5) occurs before go(a,1,2). This gives rise to two execution schedules shown in the Prolog's answer above. The actions with the same time, such as go(b,2,5) and go(c,3,6) can be executed in any order, or in parallel. A more interesting task is to find a plan for swapping the positions of robots a and c:

?- state0(S), plan(S, [ at(a,3), at(c,1)], P), show_pop(P).
Actions = [1:go(c,3,6), 2:go(c,6,5), 3:go(c,5,4), 4:go(b,2,5), 5:go(a,1,2), 6:go(a,2,3),
            6:go(c,4,1)]

The resulting plan has only one shortest schedule in which the last two actions may be executed in parallel. The program execution time for this planning task is well below 1 second.

# EXERCISES

**18.2**  Experiment with the POP program of this section in robots-on-grid domains with larger grids and more robots, and observe how the program's execution time depends on the size of the problem.

**18.3**  Extend the planning domain definition of Figures 18.1 and 18.2 to a Sokoban-like domain. In this domain, there are boxes in the grid, in addition to robots. Like a robot, a box occupies a whole cell. A robot at a cell adjacent to a box can push the box to the next cell. Unlike with the usual Sokoban rules, if boxes are aligned in adjacent cells, the robot can push a whole column of boxes. Experiment with our POP planner in this domain, study the time complexity of the tasks in this domain, and observe if any cooperation patterns between the robots emerge.

**18.4**  In our treatment, we assumed the classic formulation of the planning problem where actions have no durations. They happen instantaneously, so their effects appear practically at the same times as the actions. Our representation of ordering constraints with CLP(FD) easily enables us to take into account the durations of actions. If an action executed at time T takes 5 time units to execute, its effects will become true at T+5. Extend the planning domain representation of Figure 18.2 to allow the specification of actions' durations (as integers), and modify the program of Figure 18.5 to take into account the durations and to minimize the actual plan finishing time.

## 18.3 GRAPHPLAN

The GRAPHPLAN planning method generates partially ordered plans that are represented by sequences of *levels of actions*. Each level consists of actions that can be executed in arbitrary order, including parallel execution. In our implementation, such sequences of levels will be represented by lists of lists. As an example, consider the robots-on-grid domain of Figure 18.1, and assume that the goals of the plan are **at(a,2)** and **at(c,6)**. The solution plan consists of three actions: **go(a,1,2)**, **go(b,2,5)** and **go(c,3,6)**. These actions cannot be executed arbitrarily: **go(b,2,5)** must occur before **go(a,1,2)**. To respect this constraint, in GRAPHPLAN the three actions are organized in two levels. For our example, there are two such plans, **Plan1** and **Plan2**, written as lists of lists:

> **Plan1** = [ [ go(b,2,5), go(c,3,6)], [ go(a,1,2)] ]
> **Plan2** = [ [ go(b,2,5)], [ go(a,1,2), go(c,3,6)] ]

**Plan1** says: first execute the actions **go(b,2,5)** and **go(c,3,6)** in any order or in parallel, and then execute **go(a,1,2)**. **Plan2** says: first execute **go(b,2,5)**, and then in any order the actions **go(a,1,2)** and **go(c,3,6)**. In general, the representation of partially ordered plans by levelled plans often has computational advantages: it is compact and enables efficient computation.

The GRAPHPLAN method employs the so-called *planning graphs*. Levelled plans of actions can eventually be extracted from a planning graph. A planning graph is a structure that roughly represents what may happen when sequences of actions are applied to the initial state of a planning problem. In a planning graph, nodes are organized into levels as illustrated by Figure 18.6. From left to right, the first level nodes correspond to state literals, the second level nodes correspond to actions, the third level corresponds to state literals, the next level again to actions, etc.

The left-most level corresponds to the start state of the planning problem. It consists of the literals that are true in the start state. The second level consists of actions that may be executed in the start state. That is, the preconditions of these actions are included in the start level. The third level consists of literals that result from the actions in the second level, that is effects of the actions. Consider the sequence of three adjacent levels in a planning graph: **StateLevel**, followed by **ActionLevel**, followed by **NextStateLevel**. Roughly, the intuition behind this is as follows. **StateLevel** consists of preconditions of the actions in **ActionLevel**, and **NextStateLevel** consists of the effects of the actions in **ActionLevel**. The arcs between the items of consecutive levels indicate which literals in particular are the preconditions of which actions, and which literals

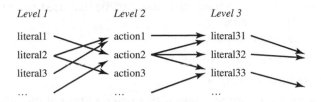

*Level 1*      *Level 2*      *Level 3*

literal1     action1  ⟶  literal31
literal2     action2  ⟶  literal32
literal3     action3     literal33
...          ...         ...

**Figure 18.6** The structure of a planning graph.

are the effects of which actions. An arc of form 'Literal → Action' means that Literal is a precondition of Action. An arc of form 'Action → Literal' means that Literal is an effect of Action. All the items of a level belong to the same time unit. The left-to-right order of levels corresponds to increasing times.

An action level may contain actions as defined by the planning domain definition. In addition to these actions, it also contains so-called *persistence actions*. Persistence actions are virtual actions that preserve literals from the previous state level. If a literal is true in a state level, and no action in the next action level affects this literal, then the literal will be true in the next state level. Each literal **P** has its own persistence action denoted by **persist(P)**. The precondition of **persist(P)** is **P**, and the effect is also **P**.

Figure 18.7 shows part of the planning graph for the robots-on-grid domain and the start state of Figure 18.1. Let us look at the top-left corner of this figure. The literal **at(a,1)** is a precondition of the actions **persist(at(a,1))** and **go(a,1,4)**. The (only) effect of **persist(at(a,1))** is **at(a,1)**. Two effects of **go(a,1,4)** are **at(a,4)** and **~at(a,1)**. There are two other effects of **go(a,1,4)**: **c(1)** and **~c(4)**. They are also part of this planning graph, but they are not shown in Figure 18.7 for space reasons (like many other literals and actions).

The literals **at(a,1)** and **~at(a,1)** are *inconsistent* because they cannot both be true at the same time, that is at the same level. Therefore we say that the actions **persist(at(a,1))** and **go(a,1,4)** have inconsistent effects. The GRAPHPLAN algorithm thus infers that the two actions cannot both actually happen at the same time. Such pairs of actions that belong to the same level are said to be *mutually exclusive*, or *mutex* for short. Only one of them may actually happen, or none of them. That means that a plan extracted from the planning graph of Figure 18.7 may, at this level, include **persist(at(a,1))** or **go(a,1,4)** or neither of these two actions. We will associate a Boolean variable with each action and each literal in the planning graph. Such a variable indicates whether an action is actually included in the plan at its level, or whether a literal is actually true at its level. We will call such variables *indicator* variables, or simply *indicators*, because they indicate the presence of an action or literal in the plan. For example, the action's **persist(at(a,1))** indicator is **PAa1**, and the action's **go(a,1,4)** indicator is **Ma14** (see Figure 18.7). The fact that these actions are mutex can be stated by a logical constraint between the indicator variables: PAa1 ∧ Ma14 ⇒ false (PAa1 ∧ Ma14 implies false). This can be written alternatively using negation as: ~ ( PAa1 ∧ Ma14).

Now, consider the pair of actions **go(a,1,4)** and **go(b,2,5)**. These two actions are not mutex and therefore they can both be included in the plan at the same level. This means that they can be actually executed in any order: first **go(a,1,4)** and then **go(b,2,5)** or vice versa, or even in parallel. Looking at Figure 18.1, obviously both robots **a** and **b** can move upwards simultaneously. As already stated, the actions that belong to the same level of a plan can be executed in any (partial) order, with any degree of parallelism.

In general, two actions are mutex if:

(a) Their preconditions are inconsistent, or

(b) Their effects are inconsistent, or

(c) An effect of one action is inconsistent with a precondition of the other action, or vice versa. This case of mutex actions is called *interference*.

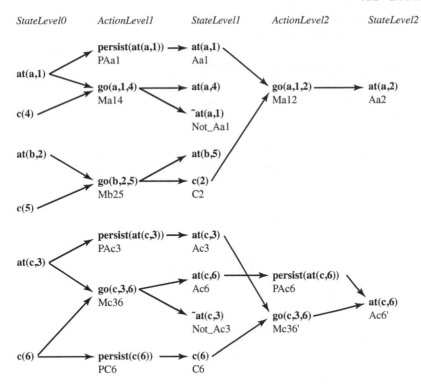

*StateLevel0*   *ActionLevel1*   *StateLevel1*   *ActionLevel2*   *StateLevel2*

**Figure 18.7** Part of planning graph for the robots-on-grid problem of Figure 18.1. For space and clarity reasons, many actions and literals are omitted, especially at the rightmost StateLevel2. The goals of the plan are **at(a,2)** and **at(c,6)**. Some actions and literals are accompanied by their 'indicator variables', for example action **go(a,1,4)** has the indicator variable Ma14. These variables are named mnemonically to indicate their associated action or literal. Indicator variables are Boolean variables that indicate whether their corresponding actions (literals) actually happen (are actually true). For example, if Ma14 is true then **go(a,1,4)** is actually included in the plan. If Ma14 is false then **go(a,1,4)** is not actually included (does not happen). If Aa1 is true then **at(a,1)** is true, else false. Some actions or literals occur at several levels in the graph, **at(c,6)** for example. For distinction, their indicator variables are Ac6 and Ac6'.

Some pairs of literals are always inconsistent, for example P and ~P. In addition to these, there are also domain-specific inconsistencies. In our robot domain, examples of such inconsistencies are: a cell cannot be occupied and clear at the same time, or a robot cannot be at two different places at the same time. There may also be domain-specific mutex actions. For example, a robot cannot simultaneously move to two different locations. In our planner, the user will have a chance to state such domain-specific inconsistencies as part of the planning domain definition. The inconsistencies just mentioned can be stated by the following Prolog clauses:

**inconsistent( at(_,C), c(C)).**          % A cell cannot be both clear and occupied at a time
**inconsistent( at(R,C1), at(R,C2)) :-**
  **C1 \== C2.**          % Robot cannot be at different places at a time
**inconsistent( go(R,P1,P2), go(R,P3,P4)) :-**
  **P1 \== P3; P2 \== P4.**          % A robot can only make one move at a time

Now assume that the planning graph (partly) shown in Figure 18.7 has already been constructed. How can a partial order plan be extracted from such a planning graph?

The goals of the plan are **at(a,2)** and **at(c,6)**. These literals appear in *StateLevel2*, and their indicator variables are Aa2 and Ac6'. For the goals to be achieved by an extracted plan, both Aa2 and Ac6' must be true. Let us now consider how Aa2 can be ensured true in the graph of Figure 18.7. There is only one action, **go(a,1,2)**, that achieves **at(a,2)**. Therefore we have this relation:

$$\text{Ma12} \Longleftrightarrow \text{Aa2},$$

and since Aa2=true, Ma12 must also be true. The preconditions of **go(a,1,2)** are **at(a,1)** and **c(2)**. Therefore we have the following logical relation between the corresponding indicator variables:

$$\text{Ma12} \Longrightarrow \text{Aa1} \wedge \text{C2}$$

Since Ma12 is true, both Aa1 and C2 must be true. The only action that results in **at(a,1)** is **persist(at(a,1))**. Therefore

$$\text{PAa1} \Longleftrightarrow \text{Aa1}$$

Since Aa1 is true, PAa1 must be true. Now since **persist(at(a,1))** and **go(a,1,4)** are mutex because of inconsistent effects, Ma14 must be false. Since the only action that achieves **c(2)** is **m(b,2,5)**, Mb25 must be true.

Until now we have been looking at the upper part of the planning graph of Figure 18.7. So far we have inferred that, to ensure the goal **at(a,2)**, the action indicator variables must be: Ma14 = false, and all of PAa1, Mb25 and Ma12 are true. Now let us turn to the bottom part of the planning graph.

The goal **at(c,6)** has to be true, which can be achieved by **persist(at(c,6))** or **go(c,3,6)**. These two actions are mutex, so there are two possibilities:

(a)  PAc6 = true, and Mc36' = false, or

(b)  PAc6 = false, and Mc36' = true

Further reasoning with the constraints on remaining indicator variables in the bottom part of the planning graph eventually gives two possibilities:

(a)  PAc6 = true, and Mc36' = false, and Mc36 = true, and PAc3 = false, or

(b)  PAc6 = false, and Mc36' = true, PAc3 = true, and Mc36 = false

Combining this with the solution for the upper part of the graph, and ignoring the persist actions, gives two GRAPHPLAN plans: action **go(b,2,5)** at the first level of the plan, **go(a,1,2)** at the second level, and **go(c,3,6)** at either first or second level. These are our familiar two levelled plans.

This whole procedure of finding relatively simple plans looks rather complicated. Nevertheless, there are two items of good news. First, the construction of planning graphs can be done relatively efficiently, in time polynomial in the length of the plan. A planning graph is not yet a solution plan. A plan still has to be extracted from the planning graph. As we saw in the foregoing example, one way of extracting a plan is by satisfying the set of logical constraints between the indicator variables. Second, although this task is generally complex, there are efficient constraint satisfaction algorithms that work efficiently on average.

Let us summarize important points that the above example helped to illustrate. The literals that appear at a state level of the planning graph may be actually true at that level, but they are not guaranteed to be true. The truth of a literal depends on the constraints among the literal and other literals and actions in the graph. Some literals and actions are mutex, so if one of them is true the other one must be false. It is necessary to solve the corresponding Boolean constraints to see which literals may be made true by selecting actions for inclusion into a plan. However, if a literal does not appear at a level then it definitely cannot be true at that level. This also holds for actions. If an action does not appear at an action level, then this action definitely cannot be part of a plan at that level. In brief, literals that appear at a state level are only *potentially* true, and actions that appear at an action level can only *potentially* appear in a plan at that level.

A planning graph can be used in several ways. As illustrated by the foregoing example, a plan can be found by solving the corresponding Boolean constraint satisfaction problem. The implementation of GRAPHPLAN in the next section will be based on this approach. Alternatively, a planning graph can be used as a source of heuristics for other planning methods. For example, if a goal literal does not appear in the first N state levels of the planning graph, the planning problem cannot be solved in up to N − 1 time steps (that is N − 1 levels of sets of concurrently executable actions).

The obvious construction of a planning graph is by starting with the state level which corresponds to the start state of the planning problem. Then continue with an action level which includes actions that are potentially executable in this state level, and construct the next state level that contains the effects of these actions, etc. We finish with a state level in which all goal literals appear and can also all be demonstrated to be true simultaneously. Alternatively, we may start with the goal level and work backward in the style of goal regression until we have generated a state level in which all the start state literals are true. In the event that our planning problem is unsolvable, there is a question: can we somehow detect when to stop expanding the planning graph because the situation has become hopeless? The answer is yes, but the test is not simple. Basically, the algorithm should stop when two successive state levels become equivalent. However, it is not enough to check whether the sets of literals at both levels are the same. The sets of literals may be the same, but at the more recent level the sets of alternative satisfiable literals may be larger than those of the previous level. So what counts are the sets of satisfiable literals. When these are the same at two consecutive state levels this means there will be no further progress.

## 18.4 Implementation of GRAPHPLAN

In the program in Figure 18.8, a planning graph is represented as a list of lists:

**PlanningGraph** = [ **StateLevN, ActionLevN, StateLevN1,** ...]

**StateLevelN** and **ActionLevelN** are the most recently generated levels. So the last element of **PlanningGraph** represents the initial state of the planning problem. The levels are lists:

**StateLevel** = [ **P1/TP1, P2/TP2,** ...]
**ActionLevel** = [ **A1/TA1,** ...]

A term of the form **P/TP** represents a literal **P** and its indicator variable **TP**, and similar for actions **A/TA**. The program basically starts with a planning graph that only contains the start state level, and then carries out the following loop:

(1)  Suppose the current planning graph be **PlanGraph** = [ **StateLevel | RestOfGraph**], where **StateLevel** is the most recent state level.

(2)  Check if all the goals of the plan are satisfiable in **StateLevel**.

(3)  If yes, then extract a plan from **PlanGraph** (just take all the actions whose indicators are true and omit all persist actions), and stop.

(4)  If the goals of the plan are not all satisfiable then expand **PlanGraph** with another action level and state level, obtaining **NewPlanGraph**, and recursively repeat the loop.

Boolean indicator variables and constraints between them are simulated as CLP(FD) variables and constraints. In this simulation, integer 0 means false, and any integer greater than 0 means true. For actions, the indicators in CLP(FD) will have integer domains {0,1}. For an indicator TA, this is specified in the program code as:

**TA in 0..1**

Indicators for literals have integer domains not constrained to a particular interval. A literal indicator **TP** will be either 1 (meaning literal **P** is true), or defined by a CLP(FD) constraint of the form T #= TA1 + TA2 + ..., where TA1, TA2, ..., are action indicators. In the program, these variables appear in CLP(FD) constraints of these forms:

| | |
|---|---|
| **TP #> 0** | requires that literal **P** is true (**TP** is **P**'s indicator). |
| **TA #=< TP** | TA implies TP (**P** is **A**'s precondition; **A** may only happen if **P** is true). |
| **T1*T2 #= 0** | T1 and T2 cannot be both true (mutually exclusive actions or literals). |
| **TP #= TP0 + TA** | This is used when **P** is an effect of **A**: if **A** happens **P** is true. |

In the last case, **TP0** is of the form TA1 + TA2 + .... . So **TP** is the sum of action indicators. All these actions cause **P** as one of their effects. This states that if all the action indicators TA1, TA2, etc. are false then **P** is false, else at least one cause of **P** is true and so **TP** #> 0, meaning that **P** is true.

Constraints are added as soon as new literals or actions are added to the planning graph. Eventually, the satisfiability of the accumulated constraints is tested by 'labelling' of all action indicators, which is written in the program as:

**labeling( [ ], AVars)**

```
%   GRAPHPLAN planner with CLP(FD)

%   Representation of a planning graph:

%       PlanningGraph = [ StateLevN, ActionLevN, StateLevN1, ...] where N1 = N-1
%       Level N is the most recently generated level
%       StateLevel = [ L1/TL1, L2/TL2, ...] , TL1, TL2, ... are Boolean indicator  variables of L1, L2, ...
%       ActionLevel = [ A1/TA1, ...], TA1 is Bolean indicator variable of A1

:- op( 100, fx, ~).        % Negation of literal

% plan( StartState, Goals, Plan)

plan( StartState, Goals, Plan) :-
    findall( P/1, member( P, StartState), StartLevel),           % Start level of planning graph
    setof( action( A, PreCond, Effects), (effects( A, Effects), can( A, PreCond)), AllActions),
                   % AllActions is a list of all available actions in the planning domain
    graphplan( [StartLevel], Goals, Plan, AllActions).

graphplan( [ StateLevel | PlanGraph], Goals, Plan, AllActs) :-
    satisfied( StateLevel, Goals),                               % Goals true in StateLevel
    extract_plan( [ StateLevel | PlanGraph], Plan)
    ;
    expand( StateLevel, ActionLevel, NewStateLev, AllActs),  % Generate new action and state levels
    graphplan( [ NewStateLev, ActionLevel, StateLevel | PlanGraph ], Goals, Plan, AllActs).

% satisfied( StateLevel, Goals): Goals are true in StateLevel

satisfied( _, []).

satisfied( StateLevel, [G | Goals]) :-
    member( G/TG, StateLevel),
    TG #> 0,                    % G must be true
    satisfied( StateLevel, Goals).

% extract_plan( PlanningGraph, Plan):
%    Extract sequence of "parallel action levels", omit "persist" actions from PlanningGraph

extract_plan( [ _ ], []).         % Just single state level, no-action plan

extract_plan( [ _, ActionLevel | RestOfGraph], Plan) :-
    collect_vars( ActionLevel, AVars),
    labeling( [ ], AVars),
    findall( A, ( member( A/1, ActionLevel), A \= persist(_) ), Actions),   % Actions to be executed
    extract_plan( RestOfGraph, RestOfPlan),
    conc( RestOfPlan, [Actions], Plan).

% expand( StateLevel, ActionLevel, NextStateLevel, AllActs) :
%    Given StateLevel, find set of possible actions ActionLevel from AllActs and
%    NextStateLevel through ActionLevel. Also set up Boolean constraints
%    among literals and actions. These constraints are necessary for actions
%    performed on StateLevel to result in NextStateLevel
```

▶

**Figure 18.8** An implementation of GRAPHPLAN.

**Figure 18.8** *contd*

```
expand( StateLev, ActionLev, NextStateLev, AllActs) :-
  add_actions( StateLev, AllActs, [ ], ActionLev1, [ ], NextStateLev1),
  findall( action( persist(P), [P], [P]), member( P/_, StateLev), PersistActs),
                                              % All persist actions for StateLev
  add_actions( StateLev, PersistActs, ActionLev1, ActionLev, NextStateLev1, NextStateLev),
  mutex_constr( ActionLev),                % Set up mutex constraints between actions
  mutex_constr( NextStateLev).             % Set up mutex constr. between literals

% add_actions( StateLev, Acts, ActLev0, ActLev, NextStateLev0, NextStateLev):
%    ActLev = ActLev0 + Acts that are potentially possible in StateLev
%    NextStateLev = NextStateLev0 + effects of Acts that are potentially possible in StateLev
%    Set up constraints between actions in ActLev and both state levels

add_actions( _, [ ], ActionLev, ActionLev, NextStateLev, NextStateLev).

add_actions( StateLev, [ action( A, PreCond, Effects) | Acts], ActLev0, ActLev, NextLev0,
  NextLev) :-
  TA in 0..1,                              % Boolean indicator variable for action A
  includes( StateLev, PreCond, TA),        % A is potentially possible in StateLev
  add_effects( TA, Effects, NextLev0, NextLev1), !,
  add_actions( StateLev, Acts, [A/TA | ActLev0], ActLev, NextLev1, NextLev)
  ;
  add_actions( StateLev, Acts, ActLev0, ActLev, NextLev0, NextLev).

% includes( StateLev, PreCond, TA):
%    All preconditions of action A whose indicator variable is TA are included in StateLev

includes( _, [ ], _).

includes( StateLev, [P | Ps], TA) :-
  member( P/T, StateLev),
  TA #=< T,                                % If action A occurs then P must be true
  includes( StateLev, Ps, TA).

% add_effects( TA, Effects, StateLev, ExpandedStateLev):
%    Add effects of action A to StateLev giving ExpandedStateLevel, constrain TA and state literals

add_effects( _, [ ], StateLev, StateLev).

add_effects( TA, [P | Ps], StateLev0, ExpandedState) :-
  ( del( P/TP, StateLev0, StateLev1), !,
    NewTP #= TP+TA,
    StateLev = [ P/NewTP | StateLev1]                % Add support of action for P
  ;
    StateLev = [P/TA | StateLev0], !                 % Truth of P equivalent to TA
  ),
  add_effects( TA, Ps, StateLev, ExpandedState).

% mutex_constr( List):
%    For all pairs P1, P2 in List: if P1, P2 are mutex then set constraint  ~(P1 and P2)
%    P's are either literals or actions
%    Conditions or actions can be mutex because they are inconsistent
%    Actions can also be mutex because of interference
```

**Figure 18.8** *contd*

```
mutex_constr( []).

mutex_constr( [P | Ps]) :-
  mutex_constr1( P, Ps),
  mutex_constr( Ps).

% mutex_constr1( P, Ps):
%   set up mutex constr. between P and all P1 in Ps

mutex_constr1( _, [ ]).

mutex_constr1( P/T, [ P1/T1 | Rest]) :-
  ( mutex( P, P1),  !, T * T1 #= 0        % T and T1 cannot be both true
    ;
    true
  ),
  mutex_constr1( P/T, Rest).

mutex( P, ~P) :- !.              % Negated conditions are always mutually exclusive

mutex( ~P, P) :- !.

mutex( A, B) :-                  % Domain-specific pair of inconsistent literals or actions
  inconsistent( A, B), !.        % Defined by the user in planning domain definition

% Actions A1, A2 mutually exclusive due to interference;
% that is action A1's effect is inconsistent with A2's precondition, or vice versa

mutex( A1, A2) :-
  ( can( A1, Precond), effects( A2, Effects)
    ;
    can( A2, Precond), effects( A1, Effects)
  ),
  member( P1, Precond),
  member( P2, Effects),
  mutex( P1, P2), !.

% collect_vars( Level, List_of_vars): collect into a list all the truth variables in Level

collect_vars( [], []).

collect_vars( [ X/V | Rest], Vars) :-
  ( X \= persist(_), var( V), !, Vars = [V | RestVars ]   % Include V if V is "non-persist" variable
    ;
    Vars = RestVars),
  collect_vars( Rest, RestVars).                          % Collect rest of variables
```

where **AVars** is the list of all the action indicators. The 'labelling' of action indicators only is sufficient because the literal indicators are all defined in terms of action indicators.

The program can now be used as follows. First load the CLP(FD) library with (this detail depends on the Prolog implementation):

```
?- use_module(library(clpfd)).
```

Then read into Prolog the programs of Figures 18.8 (GRAPHPLAN), a definition of a planning domain (for example Figure 18.2, robots-on-grid domain), and the definition of frequently used predicates (including **member/2**, **del/3**). A definition of the 'persist' action should be included in the domain definition (Figure 18.2):

    can( persist(P), [P]).
    effects( persist(P), [P]).

Now suppose that the start state of the robots is the state shown in Figure 18.1 (defined under **state0** predicate in Figure 18.2), and the goal of the plan is to swap the positions of robots a and c. The corresponding question to Prolog, and Prolog's answer are:

    ?- state0(S), plan( S, [ at(a,3), at(c,1)], Plan).
    S = [at(a,1),at(b,2),at(c,3),clear(4),clear(5),clear(6)],
    Plan = [[go(a,1,4)],[go(b,2,1),go(a,4,5)],[go(c,3,2),go(b,1,4),go(a,5,6)],[go(c,2,1),go(a,6,3)]]

This plan contains 8 actions that are arranged into 4 levels. This means the plan can be executed in 4 time steps. It is interesting to compare this plan with the one obtained with the POP planner in Section 18.2. The POP contains 7 actions only, but their execution requires 6 time steps. The differences are due to different criteria that our GRAPHPLAN and POP planner minimize. POP minimizes the number of actions in the plan, whereas GRAPHPLAN minimizes the number of levels in the plan.

# EXERCISE

**18.5** Experiment with the POP planner and GRAPHPLAN program of this chapter in various planning domains (like robots on grid, blocks world, Sokoban), and compare the solutions and efficiency of both planners.

# Summary

- A *partial order plan*, or POP for short, is defined by a set of actions and a set of ordering constraints between actions.
- Partial order planning rests on the least commitment principle in the sense that the execution order of the actions in a plan is kept as flexible as possible, and so the ordering constraints are kept to a minimum.
- A partial order planning algorithm searches the space of (partly completed) POPs. The algorithm maintains a set of 'causal links'. Each causal link specifies that some action A achieves a condition P for an action B, where P is a precondition of B. These links are used to ensure that another action does not destroy this precondition before action B occurs. Such conflicts between actions and conditions are resolved by setting ordering constraints between actions.
- In this chapter we implemented a POP planner that handles the ordering constraints by means of CLP(FD) constraints in Prolog.

- The GRAPHPLAN method generates partially ordered plans represented as sequences of levels of actions, called 'levelled plans'. A level of actions consists of actions that can be executed in parallel or in any order.

- A planning graph is a structure that represents in a relatively compact manner all possible sequences of states and actions starting from some start state. A planning graph consists of interchanging levels of actions and state literals. If two actions or two literals that belong to the same level cannot occur (or be true) at the same time, they are said to be *mutually exclusive*, or *mutex* for short. There are constraints between actions and state literals that indicate the mutex relations, and possibly other relations between actions and literals.

- A literal that appears at a state level *may* be true at that level; however, this is not guaranteed. Similarly, an action that appears at an action level may *potentially* be part of a plan. However, if a literal does not appear at a state level then it definitely cannot be true at that level. This also holds for actions.

- A planning graph can be constructed relatively efficiently, in time polynomial in the length of the plan. A plan can be extracted from a planning graph by satisfying the set of constraints among literals and actions. An alternative use of a planning graph is as a source of heuristic information for, say a heuristic state-space planner. Planners that use planning graphs in one way or another are generally among the most competitive.

- In this chapter, a GRAPHPLAN planner was implemented in which a set of Boolean constraints are solved as CLP(FD) constraints in Prolog.

## References and historical notes

Early developments of partial order planning are Sacerdoti's (1975; 1977) planner NOAH, and Tate's (1975; 1977) planner NONLIN. The GRAPHPLAN approach was introduced by Blum and Furst (1995; 1997). Partial order planning dominated the field of planning for 20 years until the planning graph technique was invented with an immediate effect of drastically improving the efficiency of planning. Weld published two excellent survey papers on planning in 1994 and 1999. The first one concentrates on partial order planning, while the second reflects the sudden shift of attention to GRAPHPLAN and SATPLAN (another successful planning approach that relies on translation of the planning problem to a satisfiability problem). About 2000, in another important development the much earlier state-space approach was revived with powerful heuristics that made state-space search very competitive with other approaches (e.g. Hoffmann and Nebel 2001). All this is also reflected in the most successful programs in International Planning Competitions that are associated with the ICAPS conferences (Int. Conferences on Automated Planning and Scheduling). Although in terms of computational efficiency, partial order planning now seems to be inferior, it still has several other advantages. These include natural extensions to the handling of actual time and durations of actions, and natural treatment of distributed or multi-agent planning. Also, plans generated by this approach are easier to understand by humans which is very desirable in some applications. All these developments in planning are covered comprehensively in the excellent book by Ghallab, Nau and Traverso (2004). Russell and Norvig (2010) also provide an excellent treatment of these topics in their general AI book.

Blum, A.L. and Furst, M.L. (1995; 1997) Fast Planning through Planning Graph Analysis. *Proc. IJCAI'95*, pp. 1636–1642. Extended version appeared in *Artificial Intelligence* **90**: 281–300 (1997).

Ghallab, M., Nau, D. and Traverso, P. (2004) *Automated Planning: Theory and Practice*. Elsevier/Morgan Kaufmann.

Hoffmann, J. and Nebel, B. (2001) The FF planning system: fast plan generation through heuristic search. *JAIR* **14:** 253–302.

Russell, S. and Norvig, P. (2010) *Artificial Intelligence: A Modern Approach,* third edn. Prentice Hall.

Sacerdoti, E.D. (1975) The nonlinear nature of plans. *Proc. IJCAI'75*, pp. 206–214.

Sacerdoti, E.D. (1977) *A Structure for Plans and Behavior*. Elsevier/North-Holland.

Tate, A. (1975) *Using Goal Structure to Direct Search in a Problem Solver*. PhD thesis, University of Edinburgh.

Tate, A. (1977) Generating project networks. *Proc. IJCAI 77*. Cambridge, MA.

Weld, D.S. (1994) An introduction to least commitment planning. *AI Magazine* **15:** 17–61.

Weld, D.S. (1999) Recent advances in AI planning. *AI Magazine* **20:** 93–122.

# Chapter 19

# Scheduling, Simulation and Control with CLP

In this chapter we look at applications of constraint logic programming (CLP) to scheduling and simulation. In a simulation program electric circuit structure will be automatically translated into a set of CLP(R) constraints. It will be possible to run this simulation program not only for the analysis of the circuit, as usual, but also for the design of the circuit. A simulator of dynamic systems will translate a system's model into a set of CLP(R) constraints. These constraints will be possible to run not only in the usual forward simulation manner, but also in the backward manner: given the final state of the system, run time backward to find the initial state. Or, given the goal of the system's behaviour, find the best control sequence that brings the system from the initial state to a state that achieves the goal. We will use the facilities of CLP introduced in Chapter 7.

## 19.1 Scheduling with CLP

### 19.1.1 Problem representation

Scheduling problems considered in this section comprise the following elements:

- A set of tasks $T_1, \ldots, T_n$.
- Durations $D_1, \ldots, D_n$ of the tasks.
- Precedence constraints given as the relation

    prec( $T_i$, $T_j$)

    which says that the task $T_i$ has to be completed by the time $T_j$ can start.
- A set of $m$ processors that are available for executing the tasks.
- Resource constraints: which tasks may be executed by which processors (which processors are suitable for a particular task).

The problem is to find a schedule whose finishing time is minimal. A schedule assigns a processor to each task, and states the starting time for each task. Of course, a schedule has to satisfy all the precedence and resource constraints: each task has to be executed by a suitable processor, and no processor can execute two tasks at the same time. The variables in the corresponding CLP formulation of the scheduling problem are: start times S1, ..., Sn, and names P1, ..., Pn of the processors assigned to tasks.

An easy special case of this scheduling problem is when there is no constraint on resources. In this case resources are assumed unlimited, so there is a free processor always available to do any task at any time. Therefore, in this case only the constraints corresponding to the precedences among the tasks have to be satisfied. These can be stated in a straightforward way. Suppose we have a precedence constraint regarding tasks a and b: prec(a,b). Let the duration of task a be Da, and the starting times of a and b be Sa and Sb. To satisfy the precedence constraint, Sa and Sb have to satisfy the constraint:

{ Sa + Da =< Sb }

In addition we require that no task Ti may start before time 0, and all the tasks must be completed by the finishing time FinTime of the schedule:

{ Si >= 0, Si + Di = < FinTime }

We will specify a particular scheduling task by the following predicates:

tasks( [Task1/Duration1, Task2/Duration2, ... ])

This gives the list of all the task names and their durations.

prec( Task1, Task2)

This specifies the precedence between tasks Task1 and Task2.

resource( Task, [ Proc1, Proc2, ... ])

This states that Task can be carried out by any of the processors Proc1, Proc2, etc. Notice that this is a similar scheduling problem specification as used in Chapter 12, where a best-first heuristic search was applied to find a best schedule. The formulation here is in fact a little more general. In Chapter 12 resource constraints only consisted of the limited number of processors, but they were all suitable for any task.

## 19.1.2 Scheduling without resource constraints

We will first consider the simple case with no resource constraints. One simple way of solving this kind of scheduling problem was shown in Chapter 7, but that solution would be very awkward for large problems. The program in Figure 19.1 is a more general realization of the same idea. This program assumes a definition of a concrete scheduling problem using the representation described above. The main predicate is:

schedule( Schedule, FinTime)

where Schedule is a best schedule for the problem specified by the predicates tasks and prec. FinTime is the finishing time of this schedule. The representation of a schedule is:

Schedule = [ Task1/Start1/Duration1, Task2/Start2/Duration2, ... ]

```
% Scheduling with CLP with unlimited resources

schedule( Schedule, FinTime) :-
  tasks( TasksDurs),
  precedence_constr( TasksDurs, Schedule, FinTime),        % Construct precedence constraints
  minimize( FinTime).

precedence_constr( [], [], FinTime).

precedence_constr( [T/D | TDs], [T/Start/D | Rest], FinTime) :-
  { Start >= 0,                                            % Earliest start at 0
    Start + D =< FinTime},                                 % Must finish by FinTime
  precedence_constr( TDs, Rest, FinTime),
  prec_constr( T/Start/D, Rest).

prec_constr( _, []).

prec_constr( T/S/D, [T1/S1/D1 | Rest]) :-
  ( prec( T, T1), !, { S+D =< S1}                          % Case when task T precedes T1
  ;
    prec( T1, T), !, { S1+D1 =< S}                         % Case when task T1 precedes T
  ;
    true ),                                                % Case of no precedence constr. between T and T1
  prec_constr( T/S/D, Rest).

% List of tasks to be scheduled

tasks( [ t1/5, t2/7, t3/10, t4/2, t5/9]).

% Precedence constraints

prec( t1, t2).   prec( t1, t4).   prec( t2, t3).   prec( t4, t5).
```

**Figure 19.1** Scheduling with precedence constraints and no resource constraints.

The procedure **schedule** basically does the following:

(1) Construct the inequality constraints between the starting times in the schedule, corresponding to the precedences among the tasks.

(2) Minimize the finishing time within the constructed inequality constraints.

As all the constraints are linear inequalities, this amounts to a linear optimization problem – a built-in facility in CLP(R).

The predicate

    **precedence_constr( TasksDurations, Schedule, FinTime)**

constructs the constraints among the start times of the tasks in **Schedule**, and the schedule's finishing time **FinTime**. The predicate

    **prec_constr( Task/Start/Duration, RestOfSchedule)**

constructs the constraints between the start time **Start** of **Task** and the start times in **RestOfSchedule**, so that these constraints on start times correspond to the precedence constraints among the tasks.

The program in Figure 19.1 also comprises the definition of a simple scheduling problem with five tasks. The scheduler is executed by the question:

```
?- schedule( Schedule, FinTime).
FinTime = 22,
Schedule = [t1/0/5,t2/5/7,t3/12/10,t4/S4/2,t5/S5/9],
{S5 = < 13}
{S4 >= 5}
{S4 - S5 =< -2}
```

For tasks **t4** and **t5** there is some freedom regarding their start times. All the start times **S4** and **S5** for **t4** and **t5** within the indicated intervals achieve optimal finishing time of the schedule. The other three tasks (**t1**, **t2** and **t3**) are on the *critical path* and their starting times cannot be moved.

## 19.1.3  Scheduling with resource constraints

Now let us consider the more difficult type of scheduling problems, those with resource constraints. For example, in the scheduling problem in Chapter 12 (Section 12.3), there were three processors altogether. Although any of the processors can execute any of the tasks, this constraint means that three tasks at the most may be processed at the same time.

This time we have to deal with two types of constraints:

(1)  Precedences between tasks, and

(2)  Resource constraints.

The precedence constraints can be handled in the same way as in the program of Figure 19.1. Now consider the resource constraints. Handling resource constraints involves assigning some processor to each task. This can be done by introducing, for each task **Ti**, another variable **Pi** whose possible values are the names of the processors. Correspondingly we will slightly extend the representation of a schedule to:

Schedule =  [ Task1/Proc1/Start1/Dur1, Task2/Proc2/Start2/Dur2, . . . ]

where **Proc1** is the processor assigned to **Task1**, **Start1** is the starting time of **Task1** and **Dur1** is its duration. Using this representation of a schedule, we will now develop the program in Figure 19.2 as an extension of the program of Figure 19.1. Our main predicate is again:

schedule( BestSchedule, BestTime)

which finds a schedule with the minimum finishing time **BestTime**. Inequality constraints on start times due to precedences between tasks are again constructed by the predicate

precedence_constr( TasksDurations, Schedule, FinTime)

This is almost the same as in Figure 19.1. The only slight difference is due to the different representation of a schedule.

Let us now deal with resource constraints. This cannot be done so efficiently as with precedence constraints. To satisfy resource constraints, an optimal

```
% Scheduling with CLP with limited resources

schedule( BestSchedule, BestTime)  :-
  tasks( TasksDurs),
  precedence_constr( TasksDurs, Schedule, FinTime),  % Set up precedence inequalities
  initialize_bound,                                  % Initialize bound on finishing time
  assign_processors( Schedule, FinTime),             % Assign processors to tasks
  minimize( FinTime),
  update_bound( Schedule, FinTime),
  fail                                               % Backtrack to find more schedules
  ;
  bestsofar( BestSchedule, BestTime).                % Final best

% precedence_constr( TasksDurs, Schedule, FinTime):
%   For given tasks and their durations, construct a structure Schedule
%   comprising start time variables. These variables and finishing time FinTime
%   are constrained by inequalities due to precedences.

precedence_constr( [], [], FinTime).

precedence_constr( [T/D | TDs], [T/Proc/Start/D | Rest], FinTime)  :-
  { Start >= 0,                                      % Earliest start at 0
    Start + D =< FinTime },                          % Must finish by FinTime
  precedence_constr( TDs, Rest, FinTime),
  prec_constr( T/Proc/Start/D, Rest).

prec_constr( _, []).

prec_constr( T/P/S/D, [T1/P1/S1/D1 | Rest])  :-
  ( prec( T, T1), !, { S+D =< S1}
  ;
    prec( T1, T), !, { S1+D1 =< S}
  ;
    true ),
  prec_constr( T/P/S/D, Rest).

% assign_processors( Schedule, FinTime):
%   Assign processors to tasks in Schedule

assign_processors( [], FinTime).

assign_processors( [T/P/S/D | Rest], FinTime)  :-
  assign_processors( Rest, FinTime),
  resource( T, Processors),                          % T can be executed by any of Processors
  member( P, Processors),                            % Choose one of suitable processors
  resource_constr( T/P/S/D, Rest),                   % Impose resource constraints
  bestsofar( _, BestTimeSoFar),
  { FinTime < BestTimeSoFar }.                        % New schedule better than best so far
```

**Figure 19.2** A CLP(R) scheduling program for problems with precedence and resource constraints.

**Figure 19.2** *contd*

```
% resource_constr( ScheduledTask, TaskList):
%   Construct constraints to ensure no resource conflict
%   between ScheduledTask and TaskList

resource_constr( _, []).

resource_constr( Task, [Task1 | Rest]) :-
   no_conflict( Task, Task1),
   resource_constr( Task, Rest).

no_conflict( T/P/S/D, T1/P1/S1/D1) :-
   P \== P1, !              % Different processors
   ;
   prec( T, T1), !          % Already constrained
   ;
   prec( T1, T), !          % Already constrained
   ;
   { S + D =< S1            % Same processor, no time overlap
   ;
   S1 + D1 =< S}.

initialize_bound :-
   retract(bestsofar(_,_)), fail
   ;
   assert( bestsofar( dummy_schedule, 9999)).   % Assuming 9999 > any finishing time

% update_bound( Schedule, FinTime):
%   update best schedule and time

update_bound( Schedule, FinTime) :-
   retract( bestsofar( _, _)), !,
   assert( bestsofar( Schedule, FinTime)).

% List of tasks to be scheduled

tasks( [t1/4,t2/2,t3/2, t4/20, t5/20, t6/11, t7/11]).

% Precedence constraints

prec( t1, t4).   prec( t1, t5).   prec( t2, t4).   prec( t2, t5).
prec( t2, t6).   prec( t3, t5).   prec( t3, t6).   prec( t3, t7).

% resource( Task, Processors):
%   Any processor in Processors suitable for Task

resource( _, [1,2,3]).    % Three processors, all suitable for any task
```

assignment of processors to tasks is needed. This requires a search among possible assignments, and there is no general way to do this in polynomial time. In general, the time complexity of finding best assignments of processors to tasks grows exponentially with the number of tasks. In the program of Figure 19.2, this search is done according to the branch-and-bound method, roughly as follows. Alternative schedules are non-deterministically constructed one by one (generate a schedule and fail). The best schedule so far is asserted in the database as a fact. Each time a new schedule is constructed, the best-so-far is updated.

When a new schedule is being constructed, the best-so-far finishing time is used as an upper bound on the finishing time of the new schedule. As soon as it is found that a new, partially built schedule cannot possibly better the best-so-far time, the new schedule is abandoned.

This is implemented in Figure 19.2 as follows. Procedure **assign_processors** non-deterministically assigns suitable processors to tasks, one at a time. Assigning a processor to a task results in additional constraints on start times, to ensure that there is no time overlap between tasks assigned to the same processor. So each time a processor is assigned to a task, the partial schedule is refined. Each time a partial schedule is so refined, it is checked whether it has any chance of bettering the best schedule so far. For the current partial schedule to have any such chance, **FinTime** has to be less than the best time so far. In the program this is done by constraining:

{ FinTime < BestTimeSoFar }

If this constraint is incompatible with the other current constraints, then this partial schedule has no hope. As more resource constraints will have to be satisfied to complete the schedule, the actual finishing time may eventually only become worse. So if **FinTime** < **BestTimeSoFar** is not satisfiable, then the partial schedule is abandoned; otherwise another task is assigned a processor, etc. Whenever a complete schedule is built, its finishing time is guaranteed to be less than the best finishing time found so far. Therefore the best-so-far is updated. Finally, when the best-so-far cannot be bettered, the search stops. Of course, this algorithm only produces one of possibly many best schedules.

It should be noted that this process has high combinatorial complexity due to the exponential number of possible assignments of processors to tasks. Bounding the current partial schedule by **BestTimeSoFar** leads to abandoning whole sets of bad schedules before they are completely built. How much computation time is saved by this depends on how good the upper bound is. If the upper bound is tight, bad schedules will be recognized and abandoned at an early stage thus saving more time. So the sooner some good schedule is found, the sooner a tight upper bound is applied and more search space is pruned away.

Figure 19.2 also includes the specification, according to our representation convention, of the scheduling problem of Figure 12.8. The question to schedule this problem is:

?- schedule( Schedule, FinTime).

FinTime = 24

Schedule = [ t1/3/0/4, t2/2/0/2, t3/1/0/2, t4/3/4/20, t5/2/4/20, t6/1/2/11, t7/1/13/11]

Task **t1** is executed by processor 3 starting at time 0, task **t2** by processor 2 starting at 0, etc. There is one more point of interest in this scheduling problem. All the three available processors are equivalent, so permuting the assignments of the processors to the tasks has no effect. Therefore it makes no sense to search through all the permutations as they should give the same results. We could avoid these useless permutations by, for example, fixing processor 1 to task **t7**, and limiting the choice for task **t6** to processors 1 and 2 only. This can be done easily by changing the predicate **resource**. Although this is in general a good idea, it turns out that it is not worth doing in this particular exercise. Although this would reduce the number of possible assignments by a factor of 6, the time saving is, possibly surprisingly, insignificant. The reason is that, once an optimal schedule is found, this gives a tight upper bound on the finishing time, and then other possible processor assignments are abandoned very quickly.

## EXERCISES

**19.1** Experiment with the program in Figure 19.2. Try different resource specifications, aiming at removing useless permutations, and timing the program's running times. What are the improvements?

**19.2** The program in Figure 19.2 initializes the upper bound on the finishing times (**bestsofar**) to a high value that is obviously a gross overestimate. This makes sure that an optimal schedule is within the bound, and will be found by the program. This policy, although safe, is inefficient because such a loose upper bound does not constrain the search well. Investigate different policies of initializing and changing the upper bound, for example, starting with a very low bound and increasing it if necessary (if no schedule exists within this bound). Compare the run times of various policies. Measure the run time for the case when the bound is immediately set to the true minimal finishing time.

## 19.2 A simulation program with constraints

Numerical simulation can be sometimes done very elegantly with CLP(R). It is particularly appropriate when a simulated system can be viewed as consisting of a number of components and connections among the components. Electrical circuits are examples of such systems. Resistors and capacitors are examples of components. Real-valued parameters and variables are associated with components, such as electrical resistances, voltages and currents. Such a setting fits well the style of constraint programming. The laws of physics impose constraints on the variables associated with components. Connections between components impose additional constraints. So to carry out numerical simulation with CLP(R) for a family of systems, such as electrical networks, we have to define the laws for the types of components in the domain, and the laws for connecting components. These laws are stated as constraints on variables. To simulate a concrete system from such a family, we then have to specify the concrete components and connections in the system. This will cause the CLP interpreter to set up the constraints for the complete system, and carry out the simulation by satisfying the constraints. Of course, this approach is effective if the types of constraint in the simulated domain are handled efficiently by our particular CLP system.

In this section we will apply this approach to the simulation of electrical circuits consisting of resistors, diodes and batteries. The relations between voltages and currents in such circuits are piecewise linear. Given that our CLP(R) system efficiently handles linear equations and inequations, it is a suitable tool for simulating such circuits.

Figure 19.3 shows our components and connections, and the corresponding constraints enforced by the components and connections. We can define these

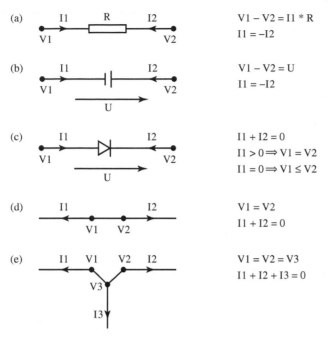

(a)
$$V1 - V2 = I1 * R$$
$$I1 = -I2$$

(b)
$$V1 - V2 = U$$
$$I1 = -I2$$

(c)
$$I1 + I2 = 0$$
$$I1 > 0 \Rightarrow V1 = V2$$
$$I1 = 0 \Rightarrow V1 \leq V2$$

(d)
$$V1 = V2$$
$$I1 + I2 = 0$$

(e)
$$V1 = V2 = V3$$
$$I1 + I2 + I3 = 0$$

**Figure 19.3** Components and connections for electrical circuits, and the corresponding constraints; (a) resistor; (b) battery; (c) diode; (d, e) connection between two or three terminals.

elements in a CLP(R) program as follows. A resistor has some resistance R and two terminals T1 and T2. The variables associated with each terminal are the electrical potential V and the current I (directed into the resistor). So a terminal T is a pair (V,I). The lawful behaviour of the resistor can then be defined by the predicate:

> **resistor( (V1,I1), (V2,I2), R) :-**
> **{ I1 = − I2, V1−V2 = I1 ∗ R}.**

The behaviour of the battery can be defined similarly, as shown in the program of Figure 19.4. The figure also gives a definition of the diode.

For connections, it is best to define the general case when any number of terminals are connected:

> **conn( [ Terminal1, Terminal2, . . . ])**

The voltages at all the terminals must be equal, and the sum of the currents into all of the terminals must be equal to 0.

It is now easy to compose circuits to be simulated. Figure 19.5 shows some circuits. The figure also gives definitions of these circuits executable by our simulator in CLP(R). Consider circuit (a). The following example illustrates that our simulator can, to some extent, also be used for design, not only for simulation. In the definition of predicate **circuit_a** in Figure 19.5, we have chosen to make the terminal **T21** one of the arguments of this predicate. This makes it possible to 'read' the voltage and current at this point in the circuit. The potential at terminal T2 is fixed to 0, the battery has 10 V, but the resistors are left unspecified (they also are arguments of **circuit_a**).

```
% Electric circuit simulator in CLP(R)

% resistor( T1, T2, R):
%   R = resistance; T1, T2 its terminals

resistor( (V1,I1), (V2,I2), R) :-
  { I1 = −I2, V1−V2 = I1 * R }.

% diode( T1, T2):
%   T1, T2 terminals of a diode
%   Diode open in direction from T1 to T2

diode( (V1,I1), (V2,I2) ) :-
  { I1 + I2 = 0},
  { I1 > 0, V1 = V2          % Diode open

  ;

  I1 = 0, V1 =< V2}.         % Diode closed

battery( (V1,I1), (V2,I2), Voltage) :-
  { I1 + I2 = 0, Voltage = V1 − V2 }.

% conn( [T1,T2, . . .]):
%   Terminals T1, T2, . . . connected
%   Therefore all electrical potentials are equal, and sum of currents = 0

conn( Terminals) :-
  conn( Terminals, 0).

conn( [ (V,I) ], Sum) :-
  { Sum + I = 0 }.

conn( [ (V1,I1), (V2,I2) | Rest], Sum) :-
  { V1 = V2, Sum1 = Sum + I1},
  conn( [ (V2, I2) | Rest], Sum1).
```

**Figure 19.4** Constraints for some electrical components and connections.

Consider the question: What should the resistors be so that the voltage at terminal T21 is 6 V and the current is 1 A?

```
?- circuit_a( R1, R2, (6, 1)).
R1 = 4.0
R2 = 6.0
```

Let us now consider the more complex circuit (b). A question may be: Given the battery voltage 10 V, what are the electrical potentials and the current at the 'middle' resistor R5?

```
?- circuit_b(10, _, _, _, _, T51, T52).
T51 = ( 7.340425531914894, 0.0425531914893617)
T52 = ( 5.212765957446809, −0.0425531914893617)
```

So the potentials at the terminals of R5 are 7.340 V and 5.213 V respectively, and the current is 0.04255 A.

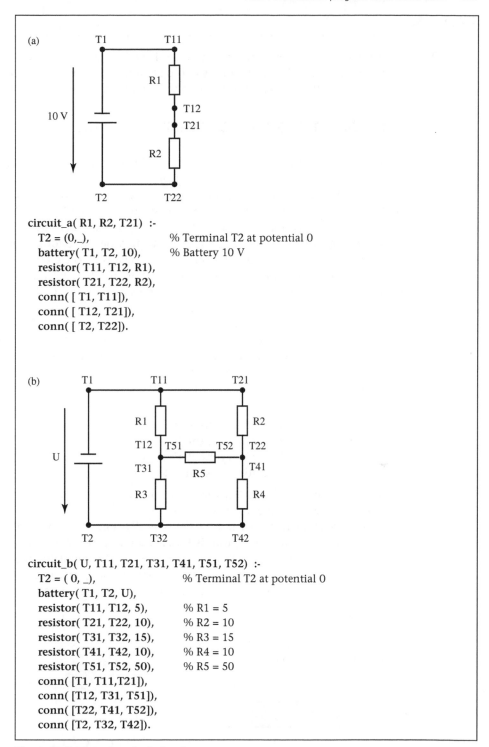

```
circuit_a( R1, R2, T21) :-
   T2 = (0,_),                  % Terminal T2 at potential 0
   battery( T1, T2, 10),        % Battery 10 V
   resistor( T11, T12, R1),
   resistor( T21, T22, R2),
   conn( [ T1, T11]),
   conn( [ T12, T21]),
   conn( [ T2, T22]).
```

```
circuit_b( U, T11, T21, T31, T41, T51, T52) :-
   T2 = ( 0, _),                % Terminal T2 at potential 0
   battery( T1, T2, U),
   resistor( T11, T12, 5),      % R1 = 5
   resistor( T21, T22, 10),     % R2 = 10
   resistor( T31, T32, 15),     % R3 = 15
   resistor( T41, T42, 10),     % R4 = 10
   resistor( T51, T52, 50),     % R5 = 50
   conn( [T1, T11,T21]),
   conn( [T12, T31, T51]),
   conn( [T22, T41, T52]),
   conn( [T2, T32, T42]).
```

**Figure 19.5** Two electrical circuits.

## EXERCISE

**19.3** Experiment with the program in Figure 19.4. Define other circuits. For example, extend the circuit of Figure 19.5(b) by adding a diode in series with resistor R5. How does this affect the voltage at T51? Try also the opposite orientation of the diode.

## 19.3 Simulation and control of dynamic systems

In dynamic systems, the values of the variables in the system change in time. Consider the spring and mass system in Figure 19.6. Let X denote the position of the block. When X = 0, the spring is at rest length, exerting no force on the block. V will denote the velocity of the block. Suppose that initially X = 1 and V = 0, so the block is not moving, and the spring is extended and is pulling the block back towards X = 0. The spring is exerting a negative force F on the block which causes a negative acceleration A < 0. Negative acceleration causes V to become negative, and the block starts moving to the left. It crosses X = 0 and continues moving to the left. When X < 0, the spring is pulling the block to the right, but due to inertia the block is still moving left for some time. As the surface is very smooth, imagine it is ice, we will neglect friction. Under such conditions, the block will reach X = −1, and then start moving to the right, and so on. So when the only force acting on the block is that of the spring, the block will keep oscillating between X = −1 and +1.

A physics model of this system can be stated in terms of differential equations as follows:

$F = - k * X$     (k is the coefficient of the spring)
$A = F/m$     (m is the mass of the block)
$dX/dt = V$     (Velocity V is time derivative of X)
$dV/dt = A$     (Acceleration A is time derivative of V)

In the sequel, we will for simplicity consider the case m = 1 and k = 1. Also we will omit units like kg from the notation.

A numerical simulator of such a system typically starts with some initial time $T_0$, say $T_0 = 0$, and an initial state, that is initial values of the system variables. In our example, the initial state was X(0) = 1, V(0) = 0. The simulator then iteratively increases time in small steps DT, say DT = 0.01 second, and computes the next state by making numerical approximations, for example for spring and block:

$T_{i+1} = T_i + DT$
$A(T_i) = −X(T_i)$
$X(T_{i+1}) = X(T_i) + V(T_i) *DT$
$V(T_{i+1}) = V(T_i) + A(T_i) * DT$

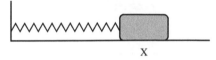

X

**Figure 19.6** The spring and mass system. The block slides left or right on a frictionless surface.

This is a simple method for numerically solving a differential equation. It is an approximation, but its error is often tolerable. In general, the error is small if time step DT is small.

This can be programmed in Prolog as the predicate

simulate( InitialState, Behaviour)

which means: starting with InitialState, the simulation produces the system's Behaviour which is a list of system's states until the end of the simulation run. The simulation will end when a user-defined predicate stop is true.

```
simulate( State, [State]) :-
    stop( State).                        % User-defined stopping criterion

simulate( State, [State | Rest]) :-
    transition( State, NextState),       % Transition to next state, defined by system model
    simulate( NextState, Rest).
```

Each system state can be represented as a list of system variable values. The state of the system usually contains those variables that determine the future behaviour of the system, X and V in our case. For convenience we will also include time T as part of the state. The transition predicate depends on the simulated system, and can be viewed as a model of the system. For the spring-mass system, the system's variables are X and V. So a state will be represented by a list [T,X,V]. Then a model of this system can be defined as:

```
transition( [ T1, X1, V1], [ T2, X2, V2]) :-
    time_step( DT),              % Simulation time-step
    T2 is T1 + DT,               % Next time point
    A1 is −X1,                   % Approx. acceleration in interval T1..T2
    V2 is V1 + A * DT,           % Velocity change due to acceleration
    X2 is X1 + V1 * DT.          % X change due to velocity
```

We have to add a definition of time step and stopping condition as, say:

```
time_step( 0.01).
```

```
stop( [ Time, _, _]) :-
    Time >= 9.999999.            % Run for 10 seconds, allow for numerical error
```

We are ready to run our simulation example from time 0 to time 10 with:

```
?- simulate( [0.0, 1.0, 0.0], Behaviour).
```

```
Behaviour = [ [ 0.0, 1.0, 0.0], . . .]
```

This is basically the usual approach to numerical simulation of dynamic systems. It is useful of course, but limited by the fixed order of numerical calculation according to increasing time. For example, we cannot run the simulator backwards: given a final state, what is the initial state? Or, more interestingly, can we use the simulator to answer a *control* type question like: I can affect the block with an external force F (in addition to the spring force) of magnitude, say, between −1 and 1. I want to bring the block from X = 0 to X ≥ 3. How should F change in time to achieve the objective X ≥ 3 as soon as possible?

Such questions cannot be, at least directly, answered by our rigid simulator that computes state by state in the time order. However, our simulator can be easily made more flexible by implementing the relations between the variables as CLP(R) constraints. Then the numerical calculations can be done in any order. Our predicate **simulate** above is in fact already capable of executing such CLP(R) models, so just a system's model, i.e. **transition** predicate, has to be re-written with constraints. This is straightforward:

```
transition( [ T1, X1, V1], [ T2, X2, V2]) :-
    time_step( DT),                         % Simulation time-step
    { T2 = T1 + DT,                         % Next time point
      A1 = -X1,                             % Approx. acceleration in interval T1..T2
      V2 = V1 + A * DT,                     % Velocity change due to acceleration
      X2 = X1 + V1 * DT }.                  % X change due to velocity
```

This can now be easily used for simulation in reverse order of time, or for asking other questions like: The block starts at $X0 = 0$, and reaches $X = 1$ in 1 second, what should be the initial velocity V0 at time 0? We make sure the simulation ends at time 1 by:

```
stop( [ T, _, _]) :- T >= 0.999999.        % Final time is 1 second, allow numerical error
```

Then we run the simulator with initial state [ 0.0, 0.0, V0] and require that the last state of the simulation is of the form [ T, 1.0, V]:

```
?- simulate( [ 0.0, 0.0, V0], Beh),
    conc( _, [ [ _, 1.0, _] ], Beh).        % In the final state X = 1.0
V0 = 1.182493564
```

So the initial velocity should be about 1.18.

It should be noted that this increased flexibility of our simulator due to the use of CLP does not come without a price. The simulator now sets up constraints in the form of equations or inequalities and then solves them. Of course, this may be much more time consuming than running a straightforward simulation where a next state is always numerically computed from time point to time point. Also, the CLP(R) simulation has to take into account the capabilities of the underlying constraint solver. This is typically limited to linear equalities or inequalities, and non linear constraints have to be handled by other means.

In a CLP(R) formulation of the **transition** relation, we can easily improve the model numerically, to compute the next state more accurately than the foregoing straightforward model. The difference will be in the numerical integration between the current time point and the next time point. For example, in our computation model, average acceleration A in the time interval between successive time points $T_i$ and $T_{i+1}$ is approximated by:

$$A = -X(T_i)$$

This formula assumes that average acceleration due to spring force between $T_i$ and $T_{i+1}$ is constant, as if X was constant during the whole time interval. Instead, a better approximation takes the average of the accelerations at $T_i$ and $T_{i+1}$:

$$A = -(X(T_i) + X(T_{i+1}))/2$$

This is easily stated in the program as the CLP(R) constraint { $A = -(X1 + X2)/2$ }, although at the time the constraint is executed X2 is not yet known. An equivalent formulation using Prolog's built-in **is** predicate would be more complicated. Similarly, a better formula for the next X value is:

$$X(T_{i+1}) = X(T_i) + DT * (V(T_i) + V(T_{i+1}))/2$$

A numerically more accurate **transition** predicate is thus:

```
transition( [ T1, X1, V1], [ T2, X2, V2]) :-
  time_step( DT),
  { T2 = T1 + DT,                  % Next time point
    A = -(X1 + X2)/2               % Approx. average acceleration in interval X1..X2
    V2 = V1 + A*DT,                % Velocity increases due to acceleration A
    X2 = X1 + (V1 + V2)/2*DT }.    % X change due to average velocity in interval
```

Now let us extend our spring-and-mass model to enable the computation of control. An external control force F, acting on the block, is included in the model as another component of the system's state. This force is assumed to be constant, $F_i$, during the interval $(T_i, T_{i+1})$. The formula for acceleration now also has to take $F_i$ into account:

$$A = F_i - (X(T_i) + X(T_{i+1}))/2$$

This is easily stated in the program as a CLP(R) constraint. Figure 19.7 shows such an extended spring-and-mass model together with the top-level simulator and the predicate **show_behaviour(B)**. This procedure displays the behaviour resulting from

```
% simulate( InitialState, Behaviour):
%    Starting with InitialState, simulation produces Behaviour
%    Behaviour is a sequence of system's states until end of simulation
%    Time is included as part of the system's state

simulate( State, [State]) :-
  stop( State).              % User-defined stopping criterion

simulate( State, [State | Rest]) :-
  transition( State, NextState),    % Transition to next state, defined by system model
  simulate( NextState, Rest).

% Spring and block system model with control force applied to the block
% This model assumes that spring coefficient K = 1, and mass = 1
% System's state variables are X (position of mass), V (velocity of mass)
% X = 0 when the spring is at rest position (exerts no force on mass)
%   Also included as part of the state are time T and external force F

transition( [ T1, X1, V1, F1], [ T2, X2, V2, F2]) :-
  control( [T1,X1,V1,F1]),          % Impose constraints on control force F
  time_step( DT),
  { T2 = T1 + DT,                   % Next time point
    A = F1 - (X1 + X2)/2,           % Approx. average acceleration in interval X1..X2
    V2 = V1 + A*DT,                 % Velocity increases due to acceleration A
    X2 = X1 + (V1 + V2)/2*DT}.      % X change due to average velocity in interval
```

**Figure 19.7** A simulator for dynamic systems with a model of spring-and-mass system including external control force, with which it is possible to control the system.

**Figure 19.7** *contd*

```
time_step( 0.1).                        % Simulation time step

state0( [0.0, 0.0, 0.0, _]).            % State at time 0, with X = 0, V = 0

stop( [ T, X, V, F]) :-
    { X >= 3.0},                        % Stop when X reaches 3
    maximize(X)                         % Find control to maximize X at this point
    ;
    { T > 20}.                          % Alternatively, give up at time 20

% Control rule that determines constraints on control force

control( [ _, _, _, F]) :-
    { -1.0 =< F, F =< 1.0}.   % Control with limited force: choose force in interval -1..1

% show_behaviour( Behaviour): write Behaviour in tabular form, one row per time point

show_behaviour( []).

show_behaviour( [S | L]) :-
    show_state(S),
    show_behaviour( L).

show_state( [ ]) :-
    nl.

show_state( [X | Xs]) :- !,
    round3(X,Xr),             % Round X to 3 decimals
    write(Xr), write('\t'),   % Write Xr and move to next tab position
    show_state( Xs).

round3( X, Y) :-              % Y is X rounded to 3 decimal digits after the decimal point
    number(X), !,
    Y is round(1000*X)/1000
    ;
    Y = X.                    % Here X is not a number
```

a simulation run in a tabular form, so that each output line corresponds to a time point and shows the values of the system's variables at that time.

In Figure 19.7, the control force is determined in the program by the predicate:

```
control( [T,X,V,F])
```

This predicate would typically implement a control rule (or 'control strategy') which determines the control force F depending on the other state variables. In our case, however, we want the program itself to find the values for F at each simulation time point so that the system will move from state $X = 0$ and $V = 0$ to a goal state where $X \geq 3$. Let the control force be limited to the interval $-1$ to $+1$. This is stated by the control predicate as:

```
control( [ _, _, _, F]) :-
    { -1.0 = < F, F = < 1.0}.
```

The goal of control can be stated in the stopping condition:

```
stop( [ T, X, V, F]) :-
    { X >= 3.0},
    maximize(X).
```

This says that simulation stops as soon as the condition $X \geq 3$ can be satisfied, and when this happens we also want to maximize X which reflects the criterion that we want to achieve (the goal $X \geq 3$) as soon as possible. For efficiency, it is appropriate that the time step is increased to 0.1. Prolog can now be asked to compute the control force to achieve the goal of control:

```
?- simulate( [0.0,0.0,0.0,_], B), show_behaviour(B).
```

The results show that the goal is achieved at time 4.8 seconds when $X = 3.082$ and $V = 1.085$. The output simulation behaviour shows that control force F is $-1.0$ between time 0.0 and 1.6, and from then on F = 1. So, the block first has to be pushed to the left, away from the goal, to accumulate some energy in the spring. Only then the force direction changes to the right. It is interesting that a naive approach to controlling this system by always pushing to the right, towards the goal (F is always 1) would actually fail to ever reach $X = 3$. In this case, the block would be oscillating between $X = 0$ and 2. If the available control force was weaker, like $|F| \leq 0.5$, then the force would have to change direction more than once, to achieve the goal by an increasing oscillation.

These examples show some flexibility of simulation using CLP(R). Again, there are limitations in what the CLP(R) system can handle. For example, a usual criterion in optimal control is the minimization of the time integral of the square of control force. This corresponds to the minimization of the sum of $F_i^2$ over all i. This criterion is non-linear and its implementation in CLP(R) would not be so straightforward.

# Summary

In this chapter, CLP programs were presented for scheduling and for numerical simulation and control. We applied the branch-and-bound method for combinatorial optimization of a schedule. In two case studies on simulation, we developed: (a) a static simulator for electrical circuits of arbitrary structure, and (b) a simulator for a dynamic system; it was shown how control can be automatically synthesized so that the system achieves a given goal in time.

# Chapter 20

# Machine Learning

By learning, a program improves its performance at future tasks. A weather forecast program may learn from past weather data to predict weather in the future. In a medical application, a program may learn from past patient records to diagnose new patients. A robot may learn about its environment through performing experiments. Of the forms of learning, learning concepts from examples is the most common and best understood. Learning algorithms depend on the language in which the learned concepts are represented. In this chapter we develop programs that learn concepts represented by if-then rules and decision trees. We also look at learning from noisy data, when examples possibly contain errors.

## 20.1 Introduction

There are many forms of learning. For a start, let us consider some possibilities regarding the interaction between the learning program ('learner') and a human user or the program's environment in general ('teacher'). In this respect, learning can range from 'learning by being told' to 'learning by discovery'. In the former case, the learner is explicitly told what is to be learned. In this sense, programming is a kind of learning by being told. The main burden in this type of learning is on the teacher although the learner's task can also be difficult as it may not be easy to understand what the teacher had in mind. So learning by being told may require intelligent communication including a learner's model of the teacher. At the other extreme, in learning by discovery, the learner autonomously discovers new concepts merely from unstructured observations or by planning and performing experiments in the environment. There is no teacher involved here and all the burden is on the learner. The learner's environment plays the role of a teacher, or an oracle.

Between these two extremes lies another form of learning: learning from examples. Here the initiative is distributed between the teacher and the learner. The teacher provides examples for learning and the learner is supposed to make generalizations about the examples – that is, find a kind of theory, explaining the given examples.

As an illustration of learning from examples consider Figure 20.8. This is an image that a robot receives from its camera. There are a number of objects like a key or a nut in the image, and we want the robot to learn to recognize these objects. So the robot has to learn to distinguish keys from nuts, scissors from pens, etc. The intended result of learning is that, when the robot is shown a new object, the robot is able to classify this object into one of the five possible classes: nut, pen, key, etc. To help the robot in learning, we provide for each of the objects in Figure 20.8 the class to which the object belongs. The way the robot may now learn is roughly as follows. The robot's basic vision system extracts descriptive features of the objects' silhouettes: size, shape, and the number of holes. Then the robot tries to find features, or combinations of features, that distinguish between different classes. For example, the nuts all have compact shape and have one hole. The pens' silhouettes are long and have no holes. The robot may generalize these observations and speculate that all the nuts in the world have one hole, and all the pens have none. To distinguish between nuts and pens, then, it suffices to consider just the number of holes in their silhouettes.

The learner's task to generalize from examples can be difficult. The teacher can help the learner by selecting good training examples and by describing the examples in a language that permits formulating elegant general rules. In a sense, learning from examples exploits the known empirical observation that experts (that is 'teachers') find it easier to produce good examples than to provide explicit and complete general theories. Learning from examples is also called *inductive learning*. Inductive learning is the most researched kind of learning in artificial intelligence and this research has produced many solid results. From examples, several types of task can be learned: one can learn to diagnose a patient or a plant disease, to predict weather, to predict the biological activity of a new chemical compound, to determine the biological degradability of chemicals, to predict mechanical properties of steel on the basis of its chemical characteristics, to make better financial decisions, to control a dynamic system, or to improve efficiency in solving symbolic integration problems.

Machine learning techniques have been applied to all these particular tasks and many others. Practical methods exist that can be effectively used in complex applications. One application scenario is in association with knowledge acquisition for expert systems. Knowledge is acquired automatically from examples, thus helping to alleviate the knowledge-acquisition bottleneck. Another way of applying machine learning methods is *knowledge discovery in databases* (KDD), or *data mining*. Data in a database are used as examples for inductive learning to discover interesting patterns in large amounts of data. For example, it can be found with data mining, that in a supermarket a customer who buys spaghetti is likely also to buy Parmesan cheese.

In this chapter we will be mostly concerned with learning concepts from examples. We will first define the problem of learning concepts from examples more formally. To illustrate key ideas we will then follow a detailed example of learning concepts represented by semantic networks. Then we will look at induction of rules and decision trees.

##  The problem of learning concepts from examples

### 20.2.1 Concepts as sets

The problem of learning concepts from examples can be formalized as follows. Let $U$ be a universal set of objects – that is, all of the objects that the learner may encounter. There is, in principle, no limitation on the size of $U$. A concept $C$ can be formalized as a subset of objects in $U$. To learn concept $C$ means to learn to recognize objects in $C$. In other words, once $C$ is learned, the system is able, for any object $X$ in $U$, to recognize whether $X$ is in $C$.

This definition of concept is sufficiently general to enable the formalization of such diverse concepts as an arch, a certain disease, arithmetic multiplication, or the concept of poisonous:

- The concept of poisonous: For example, in the world $U$ of mushrooms, the concept 'poisonous' is the set of all poisonous mushrooms.

- The concept of an arch in the blocks world: The universal set $U$ is the set of all structures made of blocks in a blocks world. Arch is the subset of $U$ containing all the arch-like structures and nothing else.

- The concept of multiplication: The universal set $U$ is the set of tuples of numbers. *Mult* is the set of all triples of numbers $(a, b, c)$ such that $a * b = c$. More formally:

  $$Mult = \{(a, b, c) \mid a * b = c\}$$

  For example, the triple ( 2, 3, 6) is in concept *Mult*, and (2, 5, 6) is not.

- The concept of a certain disease $D$: $U$ is the set of all possible patient descriptions in terms of some chosen repertoire of features. $D$ is the set of all those descriptions of patients that suffer from the disease in question.

### 20.2.2 Examples and hypotheses

To introduce some terminology, consider the following, hypothetical problem of learning whether a mushroom is edible or poisonous. We have collected a number of example mushrooms and for each of them we have an expert opinion. Suppose that each mushroom is (unrealistically simply!) described just by its height and its width. We say that each of our example objects has two *attributes*: height and width, in centimetres. In our case both attributes are numerical. In addition, for each example mushroom its *class* is also given: poisonous or edible. The class of an object is sometimes also called the *label*. From the point of view of the concept 'edible', the two class values are appropriately abbreviated into '+' (edible) and '−' (not edible). Accordingly, the given edible mushrooms are *positive examples* for the concept 'edible'. The given poisonous mushrooms are *negative examples* for the concept 'edible'.

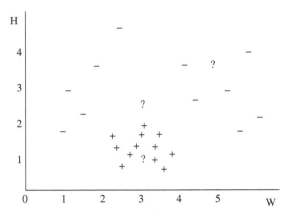

**Figure 20.1** Examples for learning about mushrooms. The attributes are W (width) and H (height) of a mushroom. The pluses indicate examples of edible mushrooms, the minuses examples of poisonous ones. The three mushrooms labelled by '?' are new, unknown cases to be classified as 'edible' or 'poisonous'.

Figure 20.1 shows our learning data. To learn about mushrooms, then, means being able to classify a new mushroom into one of the two classes '+' or '−'. Suppose now that we have a new mushroom whose attributes are: W = 3.0, H = 0.9. This mushroom is marked with '?' in Figure 20.1. Is it edible or poisonous? Looking at the examples in Figure 20.1, most people would say 'edible' without much thought. Of course, there is no guarantee that this mushroom actually is edible, and there may be a surprise. So this classification is still a *hypothesis*. However, this hypothesis seems very likely because the attribute values of this mushroom are similar to those of many known edible mushrooms, and dissimilar to all the poisonous ones. In general, the main assumption in machine learning is that objects that look similar in some way, also belong to the same class. Generally, the world appears to be kind in that this similarity assumption is usually true in real life, and this is what makes machine learning from examples possible and effective. However, how one determines that two objects are similar and others are not is another question. What is the best measure of similarity, either explicit or implicit? This depends on the domain of learning, and learning systems differ significantly in this respect.

For the same reason of similarity, another mushroom with W = 5 and H = 3.5 would quite obviously seem to be poisonous. However, a mushroom with W = 3.0 and H = 2.5 is hard to decide and any classification seems both reasonable and risky.

Usually the result of learning is a *concept description*, or a *classifier* that will classify new objects. Such a classifier can be stated in various ways, using various formalisms. These formalisms are alternatively called *concept description languages* or *hypothesis languages*. The reason for calling them *hypothesis* languages is that they describe the learner's hypotheses, on the basis of the learning data, about the *target concept*. Usually the learner can never be completely sure that a hypothesis, induced from the data, exactly corresponds to the target concept. In most practical applications, the learned description is only an approximation to the target concept.

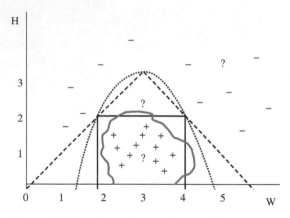

**Figure 20.2** Four hypotheses about edible mushrooms: hypothesis 1 solid black line, hypothesis 2 dashed line, hypothesis 3 dotted line, hypothesis 4 thick grey line.

Here are three possible hypotheses that can be induced from the mushroom data (see Figure 20.2):

Hypothesis 1:    If $2 < W$ and $W < 4$ and $H < 2$
then 'edible' else 'poisonous'

Hypothesis 2:    If $H > W$ then 'poisonous'
else if $H > 6 - W$ then 'poisonous'
else 'edible'

Hypothesis 3:    If $H < 3 - (W - 3)^2$ then 'edible' else 'poisonous'

All three hypotheses are stated in the form of if-then rules. Another popular hypothesis language in machine learning in AI is that of decision trees. Hypothesis 1 is represented as a decision tree shown in Figure 20.3. Internal nodes of the tree are labelled by attributes, the leaves by classes and branches correspond to attribute values. For example, the left-most branch corresponds to $W < 2$. The left-most leaf says that a mushroom that falls into this leaf is poisonous (class '−'). An object falls into a particular leaf if the object satisfies all the conditions along the path from the

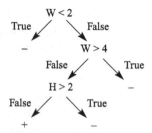

**Figure 20.3** Hypothesis 1 represented by a decision tree. Internal nodes of the tree are labelled by attributes, the leaves by classes, and branches correspond to attribute values. For example, the left-most branch corresponds to $W < 2$. The left-most leaf says that a mushroom that falls into this leaf is poisonous (class '−'). An object falls into a particular leaf if the object satisfies all the conditions along the path from the root to the leaf.

root to the leaf. For example, a mushroom with W = 3.0 and H = 0.9 is classified by this tree as follows. We start at the root, where the condition is W < 2. For our mushroom, W = 3.0, and the condition at the root is false. So we proceed to the right branch to the condition W > 4. For our mushroom, this is false, and we proceed to the next condition H > 2. Our mushroom has H = 0.9, therefore we proceed to the left branch and end up in the leaf labelled '+ '. The tree says our mushroom is edible!

All the four hypotheses in Figure 20.2 are *consistent* with the data: they classify all the learning objects into the same class as given in the examples. However, there are differences between the hypotheses when classifying new objects. According to hypotheses 1 and 4, a mushroom with W = 3 and H = 2.5 is classi-fied as poisonous; according to hypotheses 2 and 3, this mushroom is edible. From the point of view of the concept 'edible', hypothesis 1 is said to be *more specific* than hypotheses 2 and 3. Hypotheses 2 and 3 are said to be *more general* than hypothesis 1. The set of edible mushrooms according to hypothesis 1 is a subset of those edible according to hypothesis 2 or 3. On the other hand, hypothesis 2 is neither more general nor more specific than hypothesis 3.

A hypothesis does not have to be easily representable by a mathematical for-mula as was the case with hypotheses 1, 2 and 3. Hypothesis 4, in contrast, has a rather irregular shape. This is also quite a legitimate hypothesis, and is consistent with the data, but it is awkward to represent concisely. It could be represented by a table specifying this irregular borderline between edible and poisonous mush-rooms. However, such a representation might not be allowed by a particular learning system (possibly because it takes too much space), and this would make it impossible to induce by such a system.

### 20.2.3  Description languages for objects and concepts

For any kind of learning we need a language for describing objects and a lan-guage for describing concepts (hypothesis language). In general we distinguish between two major kinds of description:

- *relational descriptions* and
- *attribute-value descriptions*.

In a relational description, an object is described in terms of its components and the relations between them. A relational description of an arch may say the following: an arch is a structure consisting of three components (two posts and a lintel); each component is a block; both posts support the lintel; the posts do not touch. Such a description is *relational* because it talks about relations between components. On the other hand, in an attribute-value description we describe an object in terms of its global features. Such a description is a vector of attribute values. An attribute description may, for example, mention the attributes length, height and colour. So an attribute-value description of a particular arch may be: length = 9 m, height = 7 m, colour = yellow.

Attribute-value descriptions are a special case of relational descriptions. Attributes can be formalized as components of an object. So an attribute-value description is always easily translated into a relational description language. On the other hand, transforming a relational description into an attribute-value description is often awkward and sometimes impossible.

Description languages that can be used in machine learning are of course similar to those that can be used for representing knowledge in general. Some formalisms often used in machine learning are:

* attribute-value vectors to represent objects;
* if-then rules to represent concepts;
* decision trees to represent concepts;
* semantic networks;
* predicate logic of various types (for example, Prolog).

Semantic networks, if-then rules and decision trees will be used later in this chapter. Using predicate logic in machine learning is called *inductive logic programming* (ILP). ILP is the topic of Chapter 21.

## 20.2.4  Accuracy of hypotheses

The problem of learning from examples is usually formulated as follows. There is some target concept C that we want to learn about. There is some hypothesis language L in which we can state hypotheses about C. No definition of C is known, and the only source of information for learning about C is a set of classified examples. Usually, examples are pairs (Object, Class) where Class says what concept Object belongs to. The aim of learning is to find a formula H in the hypothesis language L so that H corresponds as well as possible to the target concept C. However, how can we know how well H corresponds to C? The only way to estimate how well H corresponds to C is to use the example set S. We can evaluate how well H performs on the example set S. If H usually classifies the examples in S correctly (that is, into the same classes as given in the examples), then we may hope that H will classify other, new objects correctly as well. So one sensible policy is to choose, among possible hypotheses, one that re-classifies all the example objects into the same class as given in the set S. Such a hypothesis is said to be *consistent* with the data. A consistent hypothesis has 100 percent classification accuracy on the learning data. Of course, we are more interested in a hypothesis's predictive accuracy. How well does the hypothesis predict the class of new objects, those not given in S? The prediction accuracy is the probability of correctly classifying a randomly chosen object in the domain of learning. Possibly surprisingly, it sometimes turns out that hypotheses that achieve the highest accuracy on the learning data S will not stand the best chance of also achieving the highest accuracy on new data, outside S. This observation pertains particularly to the case of learning from noisy data when the learning data contain errors. This will be discussed in Section 20.6.

The most usual criterion of success in inductive machine learning is the predictive accuracy of the induced hypothesis. How accurately will the induced classifier classify new objects? Ways of estimating the accuracy of induced hypotheses will be discussed in Section 20.7. However, there are other criteria of success, most notably the criterion of *comprehensibility* or 'understandability' of induced hypotheses. How meaningful is an induced hypothesis to a human expert? This aspect will also be discussed in more detail in Section 20.7.

## 20.2.5    Bias in machine learning and Ockham's razor

Usually, there are several hypotheses that seem to fit the learning data well. For the mushrooms example, we have seen four hypotheses that all look reasonable, but of course there are many more. There is a question, why would the learning system prefer one of them over the others?

To make this choice, a learning system needs a *bias*. This is a criterion that decides how to make such choices among competing hypotheses. So the system may in principle prefer more general hypotheses to more specific ones, or just the opposite. More precisely, such kind of bias is called *preference bias*. Examples of preference bias in machine learning are: maximally general hypothesis, maximally specific hypothesis, maximal estimated prediction accuracy, minimal description length (MDL), maximally compressive hypothesis, etc. According to the MDL bias, the system prefers hypotheses whose encodings are as short as possible. This may be associated with a complicated question of how to obtain a minimum length encoding, but intuitively this is quite a sensible criterion: we prefer short and simple hypotheses over long and complicated. Among our four mushroom hypotheses, hypothesis 1 looks obviously simpler than hypothesis 4. The criterion of maximally compressive hypothesis is related to MDL. A hypothesis is *compressive* in the sense that it is a shorter representation of the given examples. Once we have a hypothesis that is consistent with the learning data, we no longer need the data. The information contained in the learning examples can be reconstructed from the hypothesis. So a short hypothesis may substitute thousands of examples. In this sense a hypothesis consistent with the examples can be viewed as a compressed representation of the examples.

The preference for short hypotheses is also similar to a much older and more general principle called Ockham's razor. William of Ockham (also spelled Occam) was a fourteenth century English philosopher who strongly argued in favour of simplicity: 'Entities should not be multiplied unnecessarily.' This principle has been adopted in science as: Given two explanations of the data, all other things being equal, the simpler explanation is preferable. Or, given two scientific theories about the same observed phenomenon, the simpler one should be preferred (unless there is some other reason to believe the opposite). Ockham's razor is also a useful principle in general, and in engineering in particular.

In machine learning this principle is also reflected in the methods for learning from noisy data. In particular, we will later in this chapter look at the technique of pruning decision trees, where smaller trees are often more accurate than larger trees.

A fascinating question that has been discussed is whether there is something much deeper behind Ockham's razor, in addition to mere convenience. Namely, is it the case that nature itself prefers short and simple laws, so that short and simple scientific theories about natural phenomena have greater chance to be true? There is no definitive answer, but the practice of machine learning provides some empirical evidence in favour of this thesis.

Another type of bias in machine learning is *language bias*. A learning system uses a language for describing hypotheses. A hypothesis language may be limited, so that some hypotheses cannot even be expressed in that language. Therefore, many hypotheses are simply out of scope already at the start of learning.

For example, consider such a limited hypothesis language that only allows the separation boundary between positive and negative examples to be a straight line. None of our four mushroom hypotheses can be represented by such a restricted language. In fact, there is even no hypothesis at all in this (linear separation) language that would be consistent with the mushroom data. To represent a hypothesis consistent with the data, we need at least two straight line segments (hypothesis 2 in Figure 20.2).

## 20.3 Learning relational descriptions: a detailed example

In this section we look largely informally at a detailed example of learning relational descriptions. This example is concerned with learning in the blocks world and helps to develop the understanding of some key principles in learning.

Learning about structures in the blocks world, and about arches in particular, was introduced as a study domain by Winston (1975) in his early work in machine learning. Our treatment will basically, although not entirely, follow Winston's program called ARCHES. Although ARCHES is not a state-of-the-art learning program, it is a good illustration of some important mechanisms involved in learning.

The program ARCHES can be made to learn the concept of an arch from examples as shown in Figure 20.4. The given examples are processed sequentially and the learner gradually updates the current hypothesis about the arch concept. In the case of Figure 20.4, after all four examples have been processed by the

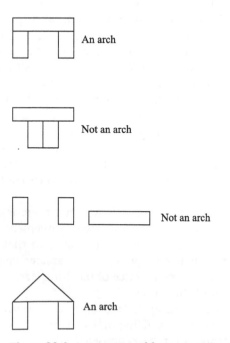

**Figure 20.4** A sequence of four examples and counter-examples for learning the concept of arch.

learner, the hypothesis (that is, the learner's final understanding of an arch) may informally look like this:

(1)  An arch consists of three parts; let us call them **post1**, **post2** and **lintel**.

(2)  **postl** and **post2** are rectangles; **lintel** can be a more general figure, a kind of polygon, for example (this may be concluded from examples 1 and 4 in Figure 20.4).

(3)  **postl** and **post2** must not touch (this can be concluded from the negative example 2).

(4)  **post1** and **post2** must support **lintel** (this can be concluded from the negative example 3).

In general, when a concept is learned by sequentially processing the learning examples, the learning process proceeds through a sequence of hypotheses, $H_1$, $H_2$, etc., about the concept that is being learned. Each hypothesis in this sequence is a further refined approximation to the target concept and is the result of the examples seen so far. After the next example is processed, the current hypothesis is updated resulting in the next hypothesis. This process can be stated as the following algorithm:

To learn a concept C from a given sequence of examples $E_1$, $E_2$, ... , $E_n$ (where $E_1$ must be a positive example of C) do:

(1)  Adopt $E_1$ as the initial hypothesis $H_1$ about C.

(2)  Process all the remaining examples: for each $E_i$ ($i = 2, 3, ...$) do:

2.1  Match the current hypothesis $H_{i-1}$ with $E_i$; let the result of matching be some description D of the differences between $H_{i-1}$ and $E_i$.

2.2  Act on $H_{i-1}$ according to D and according to whether $E_i$ is a positive or a negative example of C. The result of this is a refined hypothesis $H_i$ about C.

The final result of this procedure is $H_n$, which represents the system's understanding of the concept C as learned from the given examples. In an actual implementation, steps 2.1 and 2.2 need some refinements. These are complicated and vary between different learning systems. To illustrate some ideas and difficulties, let us consider in more detail the case of learning about the arch from the examples in Figure 20.4.

First, we have to become more specific about the representation. The ARCHES program uses semantic networks to represent both learning examples and concept descriptions. Figure 20.5 shows examples of such semantic networks. These are graphs in which nodes correspond to entities and links indicate relations between entities.

The first example, represented by a semantic network, becomes the current hypothesis of what an arch is (see $H_1$ in Figure 20.5). The three circles in the middle layer correspond to the three parts of an arch: the left post, the lintel and the right post.

The second example ($E_2$ in Figure 20.5) is a negative example of an arch. It is easy to match $E_2$ to $H_1$. As both networks are very similar it is easy to establish

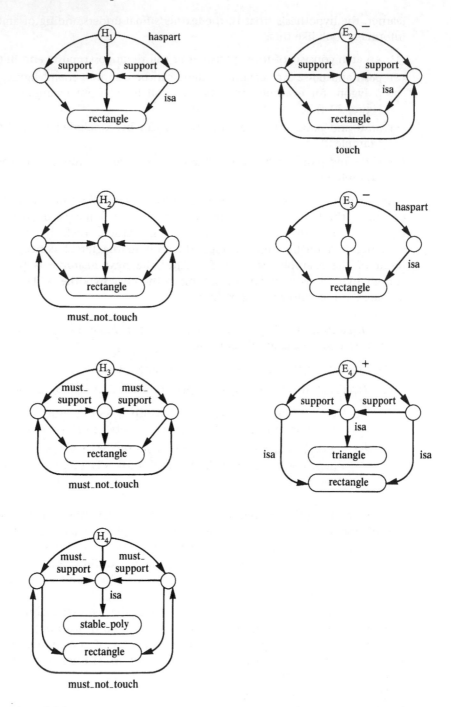

**Figure 20.5** Evolving hypotheses about the arch. At each stage the current hypothesis $H_i$ is compared with the next example $E_{i+1}$ and the next, refined hypothesis $H_{i+1}$, is produced.

the correspondence between the nodes and links in $H_1$ and $E_2$. The result of matching shows the difference D between $H_1$ and $E_2$. The difference is that there is an extra relation, **touch**, in $E_2$. Since this is the only difference, the system concludes that this must be the reason why $E_2$ is not an arch. The system now updates the current hypothesis $H_1$ by applying the following general heuristic principle of learning:

*if*
> example is negative and
> example contains a relation R which is not in the current hypothesis H

*then*
> forbid R in H (add **must_not_R** in H)

The result of applying this rule on $H_1$ will be a new hypothesis $H_2$ (see Figure 20.5). Notice that the new hypothesis has an extra link **must_not_touch**, which imposes an additional constraint on a structure should it be an arch. Therefore we say that this new hypothesis $H_2$ is *more specific* than $H_1$.

The next negative example in Figure 20.4 is represented by the semantic network $E_3$ in Figure 20.5. Matching this to the current hypothesis $H_2$ reveals two differences: two **support** links, present in $H_2$, are not present in $E_3$. Now the learner has to make a guess between three possible explanations:

(1)  $E_3$ is not an arch because the *left* **support** link is missing, or

(2)  $E_3$ is not an arch because the *right* **support** link is missing, or

(3)  $E_3$ is not an arch because *both* **support** links are missing.

Accordingly, the learner has to choose between the three possible ways of updating the current hypothesis. Let us assume that the learner's mentality is more radical than conservative, thus favouring explanation 3. The learner will thus assume that *both* **support** links are necessary and will therefore convert both **support** links in $H_2$ into **must_support** links in the new hypothesis $H_3$ (see Figure 20.5). The situation of missing links can be handled by the following condition-action rule, which is another general heuristic about learning:

*if*
> example is negative and
> example does not contain a relation R which is present in the
> current hypothesis H

*then*
> require R in the new hypothesis (add **must_R** in H)

Notice again that, as a result of processing a negative example, the current hypothesis has become still more specific since further necessary conditions are introduced: two **must_support** links. Notice also that the learner could have chosen a more conservative action; namely, to introduce just one **must_support** link instead of two. Obviously, then, the individual learning style can be modelled through the set of condition-action rules the learner uses to update the current hypothesis. By varying these rules the learning style can be varied between conservative and cautious to radical and reckless. This is another example of bias in a learning program. In our example, the program made a more radical decision that led to a

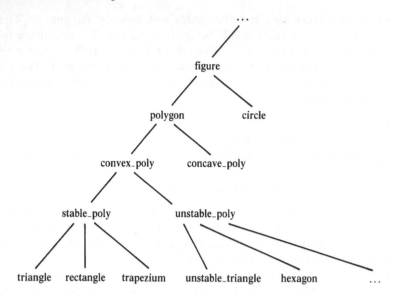

**Figure 20.6** A hierarchy of concepts.

more specific hypothesis than necessary. We say that this program is biased so that it prefers more specific hypotheses than more general ones. Another way of dealing with the three alternatives would be to keep all three of them as possible candidates, and see later which one turns out to be better. This would lead to a search among alternatives, and would lead to the typical problem of combinatorial complexity.

The last example, $E_4$, in our training sequence is again positive. Matching the corresponding semantic networks $E_4$ to $H_3$ shows the difference: the top part is a triangle in $E_4$ and a rectangle in $H_3$. The learner might now redirect the corresponding **isa** link in the hypothesis from rectangle to a new object class: **rectangle_or_triangle**. An alternative reaction in a learning program is based on a predefined hierarchy of concepts. Suppose that the learner has, as the domain-specific background knowledge, a taxonomy of concepts, as in Figure 20.6. Having found that, according to this taxonomy, rectangle and triangle are both a kind of stable polygon, the learner may update the current hypothesis to obtain $H_4$ (see Figure 20.5).

Notice that this time a positive example has been processed which resulted in a more general new hypothesis (stable polygon instead of rectangle). We say that the current hypothesis was *generalized*. The new hypothesis now allows the top part to be a trapezium although no example of an arch with a trapezium was ever shown to the learner. If the system is now shown the structure in Figure 20.7 and asked to classify it, it would declare it as an arch since it completely satisfies the system's final understanding of an arch – that is, the hypothesis $H_4$.

Here are some important points illustrated by the foregoing example:

- The procedure for matching an object to a hypothesis depends on the hypothesis language and learning system. Matching is often complicated and can be computationally complex. For example, in the case of semantic networks used

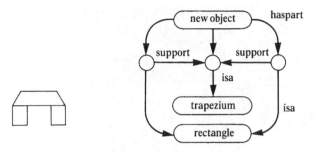

**Figure 20.7** Left: a new object; right: its representation. This object matches the concept definition $H_4$ of the arch in Figure 20.5, using the concept hierarchy of Figure 20.6.

as a hypothesis language, we may have to try all possible candidate correspondences between the nodes in the two networks that are being matched to establish the best fit.

- Given two hypotheses, one of them may be more general than the other, or more specific than the other; or they cannot be compared with respect to their generality or specificity.

- Modifications of a hypothesis during the learning process enhance either: the generality of the hypothesis in order to make the hypothesis match a given positive example; or the specificity of the hypothesis in order to prevent the hypothesis from matching a negative example.

- Concept modification principles for a given learning system can be represented as condition-action rules. By means of such rules, the 'mentality' of the learning system can be modelled, ranging from conservative to reckless. The 'mentality' of a program is a kind of bias in machine learning.

The second edition of this book (Bratko, *Prolog Programming for Artificial Intelligence*, Addison-Wesley 1990) includes a Prolog implementation of learning relational descriptions as discussed in this section. Here we omit this implementation, although the ARCHES program is a very good illustration of fundamental concepts in machine learning. However, there are learning algorithms that have established themselves as more effective learning tools for practical applications. These include the learning of if-then rules (Section 20.4) and decision trees (Section 20.5). We return to the learning of relational descriptions in the next chapter, using the framework of inductive logic programming. There we develop a more general relational learning program which we also apply to the ARCHES problem as an example.

## 20.4 Learning simple if-then rules

### 20.4.1 Describing objects and concepts by attributes

In this section we look at a kind of learning where examples and hypotheses are described in terms of a set of attributes. In principle, attributes can be of various types, depending on their possible values. So an attribute can be numerical or

**Figure 20.8** A photograph of some objects belonging to five classes.

non-numerical. Further, if the attribute is non-numerical, its set of values can be ordered or unordered. We will limit ourselves to non-numerical attributes with unordered value sets. Such a set is typically small, containing a few values only.

An object is described by specifying concrete values of the attributes in the object. Such a description is then a vector of attribute values.

Figure 20.8 shows some objects that will be used as an illustration in this section. These objects belong to five classes: nut, screw, key, pen and scissors. Suppose that these objects have been shown to a vision system. Their image has been captured by a camera and further processed by a vision program. The vision program then extracts the attribute values for each object from the camera image. In our case, the attributes are: the size, the shape and the number of holes in an object. Let the possible values of these attributes be:

size: small, large
shape: long, compact, other
holes: none, 1, 2, 3, many

Assume that the vision system extracted the three attribute values for each object. Figure 20.9 shows the attribute definitions and these examples represented as a set of Prolog clauses of the form:

**example( Class, [ Attribute1 = Vall, Attribute2 = Val2, ...]).**

Now assume that these examples are communicated to a learning program that is supposed to learn about the five classes. The result of learning will be a description of the classes in the form of rules that can be used for classifying new objects. The format of rules is exemplified by the following possible rules for the classes **nut** and **key:**

**nut  <== [[ size = small, holes = 1]]**

```
attribute( size,      [ small, large]).
attribute( shape,     [ long, compact, other]).
attribute( holes,     [ none, 1, 2, 3, many]).

example( nut,      [ size = small,  shape = compact,  holes = 1]).
example( screw,    [ size = small,  shape = long,     holes = none]).
example( key,      [ size = small,  shape = long,     holes = 1]).
example( nut,      [ size = small,  shape = compact,  holes = 1]).
example( key,      [ size = large,  shape = long,     holes = 1]).
example( screw,    [ size = small,  shape = compact,  holes = none]).
example( nut,      [ size = small,  shape = compact,  holes = 1]).
example( pen,      [ size = large,  shape = long,     holes = none]).
example( scissors, [ size = large,  shape = long,     holes = 2]).
example( pen,      [ size = large,  shape = long,      holes = none]).
example( scissors, [ size = large,  shape = other,    holes = 2]).
example( key,      [ size = small,  shape = other,    holes = 2]).
```

**Figure 20.9** Attribute definitions and examples for learning to recognize objects from their silhouettes (from Figure 20.8).

The meaning of this rule is:

> An object is a nut if
>   its size is small and
>   it has 1 hole.

A possible rule for class **key** is:

> **key** <== [[ **shape = long, holes = 1**], [ **shape = other, holes = 2**]]

This means:

> An object is a key if
>   its shape is long and
>   it has 1 hole
>   or
>   its shape is 'other' and
>   it has 2 holes.

The general form of such rules is:

> **Class** <= = [ **Conj1, Conj2,** ...]

where **Conj1, Conj2,** etc., are lists of attribute values of the form:

> [ **Att1 = Val1, Att2 = Val2,** ...]

A class description [ **Conj1, Conj2,** ...] is interpreted as follows:

(1) an object matches the description if the object satisfies at least one of **Conj1, Conj2,** etc.;

(2) an object satisfies a list of attribute values **Conj** if all the attribute values in **Conj** are as in the object.

For example, an object described by:

[ size = small, shape = long, holes = 1]

matches the rule for **key** by satisfying the first attribute-value list in the rule. Thus attribute values in **Conj** are related conjunctively: none of them may be contradicted by the object. On the other hand, the lists **Conj1**, **Conj2**, etc., are related disjunctively: at least one of them has to be satisfied.

The matching between an object and a concept description can be stated in Prolog as:

```
match( Object, Description) :-
  member( Conjunction, Description),
  satisfy( Object, Conjunction).

satisfy( Object, Conjunction) :-
  \+ (
        member( Att = Val, Conjunction),      % Value in concept
        member( Att = ValX, Object),          % and value in object
        ValX \== Val).                        % are different
```

Notice that this definition allows for partially specified objects when some attribute value may be unspecified – that is, not included in the attribute-value list. In such a case this definition assumes that the unspecified value satisfies the requirement in **Conjunction**.

## 20.4.2 Inducing rules from examples

Now we will consider how rules can be constructed from a set of examples. As opposed to the arches example of the previous section, a class description will not be constructed by processing the examples sequentially one-by-one. Instead, all the examples will be processed 'in one shot'. This is also called *batch learning* as opposed to *incremental learning*. In practice, batch learning is more common.

The main requirement here will be that the constructed class description matches exactly the examples belonging to the class. That is, the description is satisfied by all the examples of this class and no other example.

When an object matches a description, we say that the description *covers* the object. Thus we have to construct a description for the given class that covers all the examples of this class and no other example. Such a description is said to be *complete* and *sound*: complete because it covers all the positive examples and sound because it covers no negative example.

A widely used approach to constructing a consistent hypothesis as a set of if-then rules is the *covering algorithm* shown in Figure 20.10. It is called the 'covering' algorithm because it gradually covers all the positive examples of the concept learned. The covering algorithm starts with the empty set of rules. It then iteratively induces rule by rule. No rule may cover any negative example, but has to cover some positive examples. Whenever a new rule is induced, it is added to the hypothesis, and the positive examples covered by the rule are removed from the example set. The next rule is induced with this new, reduced example set, and so on until all the positive examples are covered.

```
To induce a list of rules RULELIST for a set S of classified examples, do:

RULELIST := empty;
E := S;
while  E  contains positive examples  do
  begin
    RULE := InduceOneRule(E);
    Add RULE to RULELIST;
    Remove from E all the examples covered by RULE
  end
```

**Figure 20.10** The covering algorithm. Procedure InduceOneRule(E) generates a rule that covers some positive examples and no negative ones.

The covering algorithm in Figure 20.10 insists on consistent rules. The induced rules have to cover *all* the positive examples and *no* negative one. In practice, especially when learning from noisy data, relaxed variants of the covering algorithm are used. In such variants, the algorithm may finish before all the positive examples are covered. Also, the procedure InduceOneRule may be allowed to cover some negative examples in addition to positive ones, provided that the covered positive examples have a sufficiently convincing majority.

Figure 20.11 gives an implementation of the covering algorithm. The procedure

**learn( Examples, Class, Description)**

in this program constructs a consistent description for **Class** and **Examples**. It works roughly as follows:

To cover all the examples of class **Class** in **Examples** do:

if no example in **Examples** belongs to **Class** then
   **Description** = [ ] (all positive examples covered),
otherwise **Description** = [Conj | Conjs] where **Conj** and **Conjs**
   are obtained as follows:

(1) construct a list **Conj** of attribute values that covers at least one positive example of **Class** and no example of any other class;

(2) remove from **Examples** all the examples covered by **Conj** and cover the remaining, uncovered objects by description **Conjs**.

Each attribute-value list is constructed by the procedure:

**learn_conj( Examples, Class, Conjunction)**

The attribute-value list **Conjunction** emerges gradually, starting with the empty list and adding to this list conditions of the form:

**Attribute** − **Value**

Notice that, in this way, the attribute-value list becomes more and more specific (it covers fewer objects). The attribute-value list is acceptable when it becomes so specific that it only covers positive examples of **Class**.

```
% Learning of simple if-then rules

:- op( 300, xfx, <==).

% learn( Class): collect learning examples into a list, construct and
% output a description for Class, and assert the corresponding rule about Class

learn( Class) :-
   bagof( example( ClassX, Obj), example( ClassX, Obj), Examples),   % Collect examples
   learn( Examples, Class, Description),                             % Induce rule
   nI, write( Class), write('<=='), nI,                             % Output rule
   writelist( Description),
   assert( Class <== Description).                                  % Assert rule

% learn( Examples, Class, Description):
%    Description covers exactly the examples of class Class in list Examples

learn( Examples, Class, [ ]) :-
   \+ member( example( Class, _ ), Examples).        % No example to cover

learn( Examples, Class, [Conj | Conjs]) :-
   learn_conj( Examples, Class, Conj),
   remove( Examples, Conj, RestExamples),            % Remove examples that match Conj
   learn( RestExamples, Class, Conjs).               % Cover remaining examples

% learn_conj( Examples, Class, Conj):
%    Conj is a list of attribute values satisfied by some examples of class Class and
%    no other class

learn_conj( Examples, Class,[ ]) :-
   \+ ( member( example( ClassX, _ ) Examples),      % There is no example
   ClassX \ == Class), !.                            % of different class

learn_conj( Examples, Class, [Cond | Conds]) :-
   choose_cond( Examples, Class, Cond),              % Choose attribute value
   filter( Examples, [ Cond], Examples1),
   learn_conj( Examples1, Class, Conds).

choose_cond( Examples, Class, AttVal) :-
   findall( AV/Score, score( Examples, Class, AV, Score), AVs),
   best( AVs, AttVal).                               % Best score attribute value

best( [ AttVal/_], AttVal).

best ( [ AV0/S0, AV1/S1 | AVSlist], AttVal) :-
   S1 > S0, !,                                       % AV1 better than AV0
   best( [AV1/S1 | AVSlist], AttVal)
   ;
   best( [AV0/S0 | AVSlist], AttVal).

% filter( Examples, Condition, Examples1):
%    Examples1 contains elements of Examples that satisfy Condition
```

**Figure 20.11**  A program that induces if-then rules.

**Figure 20.11** *contd*

```
filter( Examples, Cond, Examples1) :-
  findall( example( Class, Obj),
          ( member( example( Class, Obj), Examples), satisfy( Obj, Cond)),
          Examples1).

% remove( Examples, Conj, Examples1):
%    removing from Examples those examples that are covered by Conj gives Examples1

remove( [ ], _, [ ]).

remove( [example( Class, Obj) | Es], Conj, Es1) :-
  satisfy( Obj, Conj), !,                      % First example matches Conj
  remove( Es, Conj, Es1).                      % Remove it

remove( [E | Es], Conj, [E | Es1]) :-          % Retain first example
  remove( Es, Conj, Es1).


satisfy( Object, Conj) :-
  \+ ( member( Att = Val, Conj),
       member( Att = ValX, Object),
       ValX \ == Val).

score( Examples, Class, AttVal, Score) :-
  candidate( Examples, Class, AttVal),         % A suitable attribute value
  filter( Examples, [ AttVal], Examples1),     % Examples1 satisfy condition Att = Val
  length( Examples1, N1),                       % Length of list
  count_pos( Examples1, Class, NPos1),         % Number of positive examples
  NPos1 > 0,                                    % At least one positive example
  Score is (NPos1 + 1) / (N1 + 2).             % Laplace probability estimate

candidate( Examples, Class, Att = Val) :-
  attribute( Att, Values),                      % An attribute
  member( Val, Values),                         % A value
  suitable( Att = Val, Examples, Class).

suitable( AttVal, Examples, Class) :-          % At least one negative example
  member( example( ClassX, ObjX), Examples),   % must not match AttVal
  ClassX \ == Class,                            % Negative example
  \+ satisfy( ObjX, [ AttVal]), !.             % that does not match

% count_pos( Examples, Class, N):
%    N is the number of positive examples of Class

count_pos( [ ], _, 0).

count_pos( [example( ClassX,_ ) | Examples], Class, N) :-
  count_pos( Examples, Class, N1),
  ( ClassX = Class, !, N is N1 + 1; N = N1).

writelist( [ ]).

writelist( [X | L]) :-
  tab( 2), write( X), nl,
  writelist( L).
```

The process of constructing such a conjunction is highly combinatorial. Each time a new attribute-value condition is added, there are almost as many alternative candidates to be added as there are attribute-value pairs. It is not easy to immediately see which of them is the best. In general, we would like to cover all the positive examples with as few rules as possible, and with as short rules as possible. Thus learning can be viewed as a search among possible descriptions with the objective of minimizing the length of the concept description. Because of the high combinatorial complexity of this search, we normally have to resort to some heuristic. The program in Figure 20.11 relies on a heuristic scoring function that is used locally. At each point, only the best-estimated attribute value is added to the list, immediately disregarding all other candidates. The search is thus reduced to a deterministic procedure without any backtracking. This is also called *greedy search* or *hill-climbing*. It is 'greedy' because it always chooses the best-looking alternative. However, in such search there is a risk of missing the shortest concept description.

Our heuristic scoring function is based on the following intuition: a useful attribute-value condition should discriminate well between positive and negative examples. Also, we are interested in *general* rules. That is, rules that cover many examples. Thus, a rule should cover as many positive examples as possible and as few negative examples as possible. Figure 20.12 shows the construction of such a heuristic scoring function. This function is in our program implemented as the procedure:

> **score( Examples, Class, AttributeValue, Score)**

**Score** is the probability of a positive case in the area denoted by ATTVAL. The rationale is that this probability is the accuracy of future predictions by the rule that covers the subspace ATTVAL. How can this probability be estimated? Let $n$ be the number of positive examples in ATTVAL, and $N$ the number of all examples in ATTVAL. This is our sample for estimating the probability of **Class** in the subspace covered by the rule. A simple estimate of this probability is $n/N$. This is fine for large $N$. But for small $N$, this is problematic because it depends too much on chance. A more reliable estimate is therefore the Laplace estimate of probability,

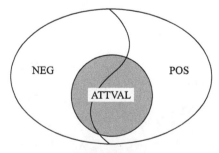

**Figure 20.12** Heuristic scoring of an attribute value. POS is the set of positive examples of the class to be learned; NEG is the set of negative examples of this class. The shaded area, ATTVAL, represents the set of objects that satisfy the attribute-value condition. The heuristic score of this attribute value is the probability of a positive case in the subspace denoted by ATTVAL.

which will be discussed in more detail later, in Section 20.6 on learning decision trees from noisy data. According to the Laplace estimate, Score is defined as:

$$\text{Score} = \frac{n+1}{N+2}$$

The program in Figure 20.11 can be run to construct some class descriptions for the examples in Figure 20.9 with the query:

```
?- learn( nut), learn( key), learn( scissors).
nut <==
   [ shape = compact, holes = 1]
key <==
   [ shape = other, size = small]
   [ holes = 1, shape = long]
scissors <==
   [ holes = 2, size = large]
```

The procedure **learn** also asserts rules about the corresponding classes in the program. These rules can be used to classify new objects. A corresponding recognition procedure that uses the learned descriptions is:

```
classify( Object, Class) :-
   Class <== Description,          % Learned rule about Class
   member( Conj, Description),     % A conjunctive condition
   satisfy( Object, Conj).         % Object satisfies Conj
```

## 20.5 Induction of decision trees

### 20.5.1 Basic tree induction algorithm

Induction of decision trees is probably the most widespread approach to machine learning. In this case, hypotheses are represented by decision trees. Induction of trees is efficient and easy to program.

Figure 20.13 shows a decision tree that can be induced from the example data of Figure 20.9 (that is, the objects in Figure 20.8). Internal nodes in the tree are labelled with attributes. The leaves of the tree are labelled with classes or the symbol 'null'. 'null' indicates that no learning example corresponds to that leaf. Branches in the tree are labelled with attribute values. In classifying an object, a path is traversed in the tree starting at the root node and ending at a leaf. At each internal node, we follow the branch labelled by the attribute value in the object. For example, an object described by:

```
[ size = small, shape = compact, holes = 1]
```

would be, according to this tree, classified as a nut (following the path: **holes** = 1, **shape** = **compact**). Notice that, in this case, the attribute value **size** = **small** is not needed to classify the object.

In comparison with if-then rules to describe classes, discussed in the previous section, trees are a more constrained representation. This has both advantages and disadvantages. Some concepts are more awkward to represent with trees than with rules: although every rule-based description can be translated into a

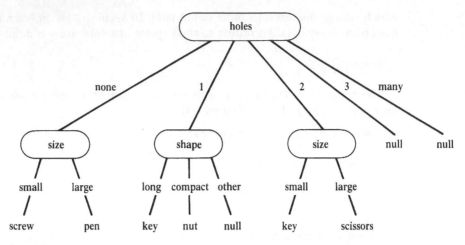

**Figure 20.13** A decision tree induced from examples of Figure 20.9 (shown graphically in Figure 20.8).

corresponding decision tree, the resulting tree may have to be much lengthier than the rule-based description. This is an obvious disadvantage of trees.

On the other hand, the fact that trees are more constrained reduces the combinatorial complexity of the learning process. This may lead to substantial improvement in the efficiency of learning. Decision tree learning is one of the most efficient forms of learning. It should be noted, however, that computational efficiency of learning is only one criterion of success in learning, as will be discussed later in this chapter.

The basic tree induction algorithm is as shown in Figure 20.14. The algorithm aims at constructing a smallest tree consistent with the learning data. However, search among all such trees is prohibitive because of combinatorial complexity. Therefore the common approach to tree induction is heuristic, without a guarantee of optimality. The algorithm in Figure 20.14 is greedy in the sense that it

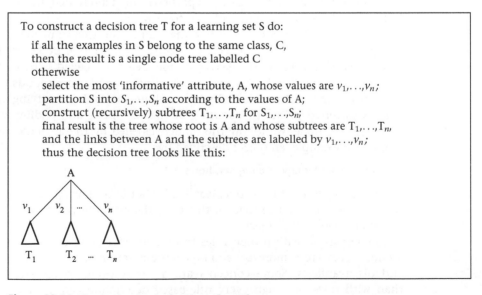

**Figure 20.14** The basic tree induction algorithm.

always chooses 'the most informative' attribute, and it never backtracks. There is no guarantee of finding a smallest tree. On the other hand, the algorithm is fast and has been found to work well in practical applications.

Even in its simplest implementation, this basic algorithm needs some refinements:

(1) If S is empty then the result is a single-node tree labelled 'null'.

(2) Each time a new attribute is selected, only those attributes that have not yet been used in the upper part of the tree are considered.

(3) If S is not empty, and not all the objects in S belong to the same class, and there is no attribute left to choose, then the result is a single-node tree. It is useful to label this node with the list of all the classes represented in S, together with their relative frequencies in S. Such a tree is sometimes called a *class probability tree*, instead of a decision tree. In such a case, the set of available attributes is not sufficient to distinguish between class values of some objects (objects that belong to different classes have exactly the same attribute values).

(4) We have to specify the criterion for selecting the 'most informative' attribute. This will be discussed in the next section.

## 20.5.2  Selecting 'the best' attribute

Criteria for selecting 'the best' attribute are a much investigated topic in machine learning. Basically, these criteria measure the 'impurity', with respect to class, of a set of examples. A good attribute should split the examples in subsets as pure as possible. For example, let there be 10 examples in a learning set. Six of the examples belong to class '+', and four to class '−'. There are two binary attributes, A with values $a_1$ and $a_2$, and B with values $b_1$ and $b_2$. Figure 20.15 shows what happens if we choose A or B as the root attribute of the decision tree. Which attribute does a better job? An ideal attribute would split the set of examples into completely pure subsets, one with '+' examples only, and the other with '−' only. Neither A nor B is ideal, but B comes much closer to this goal because B's two subsets are much purer than those of A. In B's left subset, class '+' has an 83 percent majority, and in B's right subset, '−' has a 75 percent majority. In both subsets of A, the majority class only has 60 percent majority. In fact, attribute A appears to be useless because it made no contribution in terms of purity with respect to the original set of 10 examples.

One approach to attribute selection exploits ideas from information theory. Such a criterion can be developed as follows. To classify an object, a certain amount of information is needed. After we have learned the value of some attribute of the object, we only need some remaining amount of information to

**Figure 20.15** Attribute B is better than A because B splits the example set into much purer subsets than A does.

classify the object. This remaining amount will be called the 'residual information'. Of course, residual information should be smaller than the initial information. The 'most informative' attribute is the one that minimizes the residual information. The amount of information is determined by the well-known *entropy* formula. For a domain exemplified by the learning set S, the average amount of information $I$ needed to classify an object is given by the entropy measure:

$$I = -\sum_c p(c)\log_2 p(c)$$

where $c$ stands for classes and $p(c)$ is the probability that an object in S belongs to class $c$. This formula nicely corresponds to the intuition about impurity. For a completely pure set, the probability of one of the classes is 1, and 0 for all other classes. For such a set, information $I = 0$. On the other hand, information $I$ is maximal in the case that the probabilities of all the classes are equal.

After applying an attribute A, the set S is partitioned into subsets according to the values of A. The residual information $I_{res}$ is then equal to the weighted sum of the amounts of information for the subsets:

$$I_{res}(A) = -\sum_v p(v) \sum_c p(c \mid v)\log_2 p(c \mid v)$$

where $v$ stands for the values of A, $p(v)$ is the probability of value $v$ in set S, and $p(c \mid v)$ is the conditional probability of class $c$ given that attribute A has value $v$. The probabilities $p(v)$ and $p(c \mid v)$ are usually approximated by statistics on set S.

Further refinements can be made to the information-theoretic criterion given above. A defect of this criterion is that it tends to favour attributes with many values. Such an attribute will tend to split the set S into many small subsets. If these subsets are very small, with just a few examples, they will tend to be pure anyway, regardless of the genuine correlation between the attribute and the class. The straightforward $I_{res}$ will thus give such an attribute undeserved credit. One way of rectifying this is *information gain ratio*. This ratio takes into account the amount of information $I(A)$ needed to determine the value of an attribute A:

$$I(A) = -\sum_v p(v)\log_2 (p(v))$$

$I(A)$ will tend to be higher for attributes with more values. Information gain ratio is defined as:

$$GainRatio(A) = \frac{Gain(A)}{I(A)} = \frac{I - I_{res}(A)}{I(A)}$$

The attribute to choose is the one that has the highest gain ratio.

Another idea of circumventing the problem with many-valued attributes is the *binarization* of attributes. An attribute is *binarized* by splitting the set of its values into two subsets. As a result, the splitting results in a new (binary) attribute whose two values correspond to the two subsets. When such a subset contains more than one value, it can be split further into two subsets, giving rise to another binary attribute, etc. Such a 'subsidiary' attribute can be used further down the tree. When choosing a good split, the criterion generally is to maximize the information gain of the obtained binary attribute. After all the attributes have been made binary, the problem of comparing many-valued attributes with few-valued attributes disappears. The straightforward residual information criterion gives a fair comparison of the (binary) attributes.

There exist other sensible measures of impurity, like the Gini index, defined by:

$$Gini = \sum_{i \neq j} p(i)p(j) = 1 - \sum_{i} p(i)^2$$

where $i$ and $j$ are classes. After applying attribute A, the resulting Gini index is:

$$Gini(A) = \sum_{v} p(v) \sum_{i \neq j} p(i \mid v)p(j \mid v)$$

where $v$ stands for values of A and $p(i \mid v)$ denotes the conditional probability of class $i$ given that attribute A has value $v$.

It should be noted that impurity measures are used here to assess the effect of a single attribute. Therefore, the criterion 'most informative' is *local* in the sense that it does not reliably predict the combined effect of several attributes applied jointly. The basic tree induction algorithm is based on this local minimization of impurity. Therefore this algorithm is greedy again, as was the case with our rule learning algorithm. As mentioned earlier, global optimization would be computationally much more expensive.

# EXERCISES

**20.1** Consider the problem of learning from objects' silhouettes (Figure 20.9). Calculate the entropy of the whole example set with respect to class, the residual information for attributes 'size' and 'holes', the corresponding information gains and gain ratios. Estimate the probabilities needed in the calculations simply by the relative frequencies, e.g. $p(nut) = 3/12$ or $p(nut \mid holes{=}1) = 3/5$.

**20.2** Disease D occurs in 25 percent of all the cases. Symptom S is observed in 75 percent of the patients suffering from disease D, and only in one sixth of other cases. Suppose we are building a decision tree for diagnosing disease D, so the classes are just D (person has D) and ~D (does not have D). S is one of the attributes. What are the information gain and gain ratio of attribute S?

## 20.5.3  Implementing decision-tree learning

Let us now sketch a Prolog procedure to induce decision trees:

    **induce_tree( Attributes, Examples, Tree)**

where **Tree** is a decision tree induced from **Examples** using attributes in list **Attributes**. If the examples and attributes are represented as in Figure 20.9, we can collect all the examples and available attributes into lists, used as arguments for our induction procedure:

```
induce_tree( Tree) :-
    findall( example( Class, Obj), example( Class, Obj), Examples),
    findall( Att, attribute( Att, _ ), Attributes),
    induce_tree( Attributes, Examples, Tree).
```

The form of the tree depends on the following three cases:

(1) **Tree** = **null** if the example set is empty.

(2) **Tree** = **leaf( Class)** if all of the examples are of the same class **Class**.

(3) **Tree** = **tree( Attribute, [ Val1: SubTree1, Val2 : Subtree2, ...])** if examples belong to more than one class, **Attribute** is the root of the tree, **Val1, Val2,...** are **Attribute's** values, and **SubTree1, SubTree2, ...** are the corresponding decision subtrees.

These three cases are handled by the following three clauses:

```
% induce_tree( Attributes, Examples, Tree)

induce_tree( _ , [ ], null) :- !.                          % No examples

induce_tree( _ , [example( Class, _ ) | Examples], leaf( Class)) :-
    \+ ( member( example( ClassX, _ ), Examples),          % No other example
        ClassX \== Class), !.                              % of different class

induce_tree( Attributes, Examples, tree( Attribute, SubTrees)) :-
    choose_attribute( Attributes, Examples, Attribute),    % Best attribute
    del( Attribute, Attributes, RestAtts),                 % Delete Attribute
    attribute( Attribute, Values),
    induce_trees( Attribute, Values, RestAtts, Examples, SubTrees).
```

**induce_trees** induces decision **SubTrees** for subsets of **Examples** according to **Values** of **Attribute**:

```
% induce_trees( Att, Vals, RestAtts, Examples, SubTrees)

induce_trees( _, [ ], _, _, [ ] ).                         % No values, no subtrees

induce_trees( Att, [Val1 | Vals], RestAtts, Exs, [Val1 : Tree1 | Trees]) :-
    attval_subset( Att = Val1, Exs, ExampleSubset),
    induce_tree( RestAtts, ExampleSubset, Tree1),
    induce_trees( Att, Vals, RestAtts, Exs, Trees).
```

**attval_subset( Attribute = Value, Examples, Subset)** is true if **Subset** is the subset of examples in **Examples** that satisfy the condition **Attribute = Value**:

```
attval_subset( AttributeValue, Examples, ExampleSubset) :-
    findall( example( Class, Obj),
        ( member( example( Class, Obj), Examples),
          satisfy( Obj, [ AttributeValue])),
        ExampleSubset).
```

The predicate **satisfy( Object, Description)** is defined as in Figure 20.11. The predicate **choose_attribute** selects the attribute that discriminates well among the classes. This involves the impurity criterion. The following clause minimizes the chosen impurity measure using **setof**. **setof** will order the available attributes according to increasing impurity:

```
choose_attribute( Atts, Examples, BestAtt) :-
    setof( Impurity/Att,
        ( member( Att, Atts), impurity1 ( Examples, Att, Impurity)),
        [ MinImpurity/BestAtt | _ ] ).
```

Predicate

**impurity1( Examples, Attribute, Impurity)**

implements a chosen impurity measure. **Impurity** is the combined impurity of the subsets of examples after dividing the list **Examples** according to the values of **Attribute**.

We leave the completion of this program as an exercise.

# EXERCISES

**20.3** Implement a chosen impurity measure by writing the **impurity1** predicate. This measure can be, for example, the residual information content or Gini index as discussed previously in this section. For the examples in Figure 20.9 and attribute size, use of the Gini index as impurity measure gives:

```
?- Examples = ...                        % Examples from Figure 20.9
   impurity1( Examples, size, Impurity).
   Impurity = 0.647619
```

Approximating probabilities by relative frequencies, **Impurity** is calculated as follows:

$$
\begin{aligned}
\text{Impurity} &= Gini(\text{ size}) \\
&= p(\text{small}) * (p(\text{nut} \mid \text{small}) * p(\text{screw} \mid \text{small}) + \dots) + p(\text{large}) * (\dots) \\
&= 7/12 * (3/7 * 2/7 + \dots) + 5/12 * (\dots) \\
&= 7/12 * 0.653061 + 5/12 * 0.64 \\
&= 0.647619
\end{aligned}
$$

**20.4** Complete the tree induction program of this section and test it on some learning problem, for example the one in Figure 20.9. Note that the procedure **choose_attribute**, using **setof**, is very inefficient and can be improved. Also add a procedure

show( DecisionTree)

for displaying decision trees in a readable form. For the tree in Figure 20.13, a suitable form is:

```
holes
  none
    size
      small ==>  screw
      large ==>  pen
  1
    shape
      long ==>  key
      compact ==>  nut
      other ==>  null
  2
    size
      small ==>  key
      large ==>  scissors
  3 == >  null
  many ==>  null
```

## 20.6 Learning from noisy data and tree pruning

In many applications the data for learning are imperfect. One common problem is errors in attribute values and class values. In such cases we say that the data are *noisy*. Noise of course makes the learning task more difficult and requires special mechanisms. In the case of noise, we usually abandon the consistency requirement that induced hypotheses correctly reclassify the learning examples. We allow the learned hypothesis to misclassify some of the learning objects. This concession is sensible because of possible errors in the data. We hope the mis-classified learning objects are those that contain errors. Misclassifying such objects only indicates that erroneous data have in fact been successfully ignored.

Inducing decision trees from noisy data with the basic tree induction algorithm has two problems: first, induced trees unreliably classify new objects and, second, induced trees tend to be large and thus hard to understand. It can be shown that some of this tree complexity is just the result of noise in the learning data. The learning algorithm, in addition to discovering genuine regularities in the problem domain, also traces noise in the data.

As an example, consider a situation in which we are to construct a subtree of a decision tree, and the current subset of objects for learning is S. Let there be 100 objects in S, 99 of them belonging to class C1 and one of them to class C2. Knowing that there is noise in the learning data and that all these objects have the same values of the attributes already selected up to this point in the decision tree, it seems plausible that the class C2 object is in S only as a result of an error in the data. If so, it is best to ignore this object and simply return a leaf of the decision tree labelled with class C1. Since the basic tree induction algorithm would in this situation further expand the decision tree, we have, by stopping at this point, in effect *pruned* a subtree of the complete decision tree.

Tree pruning is the key to coping with noise in tree induction programs. A program may effectively prune decision trees by using some criterion that indicates whether to stop expanding the tree or not. The stopping criterion would typically take into account the number of examples in the node, the prevalence of the majority class at the node, to what extent an additional attribute selected at this node would reduce the impurity of the example set, etc.

This kind of pruning, accomplished through stopping the tree expansion, is called *forward pruning* as opposed to another kind of pruning, called *post-pruning*. Post-pruning is done after the learning program has first constructed the *complete* decision tree consistent with the data. Then parts of the tree that seem unreliable are pruned away. This is illustrated in Figure 20.16. After the bottom parts of the tree are removed, the accuracy of the tree on new data may increase. This may appear paradoxical because by pruning we in fact throw away some information. How can accuracy increase after that?

This can be explained by that we are actually pruning the unreliable parts of the tree, those that contribute to the tree's misclassification errors most. These are the parts of the tree that mainly trace noise in the data and not the genuine regularities in the learning domain. Intuitively it is easy to see why the bottom parts of the tree are the least reliable. Our top-down tree induction algorithm takes into account all the learning data when building the top of the tree. When

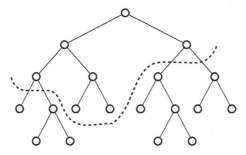

**Figure 20.16** Pruning of decision trees. After pruning, the accuracy may increase.

moving down the tree, the learning data get fragmented among the subtrees. So the lower parts of the tree are induced from less data. The smaller the data set, the greater the danger that it is critically affected by noise. This is why the lower parts of the tree are generally less reliable.

Of the two types of pruning, forward pruning and post-pruning, the latter is considered better because it exploits the information provided by the complete tree. Forward pruning, on the other hand, only exploits the information in the top part of the tree.

Post-pruning starts at the bottom of the tree, prunes (some of) the leaves, and continues to prune upwards until it decides it has pruned enough. The big question is, how to decide exactly when to prune and when not to prune. If we prune too little then our tree will overfit the data. It will also fit the noise in the data. If we prune too much then we may also throw away healthy information and the accuracy will decrease. Figure 20.17 shows a typical dependence between the size of the tree and its accuracy. Two kinds of accuracy are shown in the figure: accuracy on learning data, and accuracy on new data. The accuracy *vs* size dependence in Figure 20.17 is actually a simplification. In reality, there are several trees of the same size and different accuracy. Anyway, this simplification suffices to illustrate the main points. Accuracy on learning data never decreases with the size of the tree. A larger tree can better fit the data. But it is the accuracy on *new* data that we are mainly interested in. Generally, for small trees this

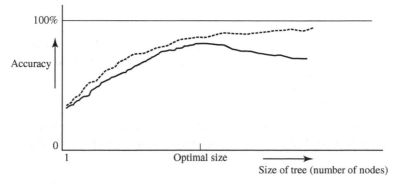

**Figure 20.17** Relation between the size of a decision tree and the tree's accuracy. Dotted curve: accuracy on learning data; solid line: accuracy on new data.

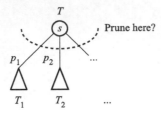

**Figure 20.18** Deciding about pruning.

accuracy also increases with the size of the tree. However, unlike the accuracy on learning data, the accuracy on new data usually reaches an optimum at the tree's optimal size. Trees larger than this tend to overfit the data and their accuracy on new data decreases with the size of the tree again. In post-pruning, we start with a large tree, completely consistent with the data, and with pruning we keep reducing the size of the tree. Looking at Figure 20.17, it would seem very easy to decide when to stop pruning: it is exactly at the size where accuracy is maximal. The problem is, however, that in reality we do not have a diagram like one in Figure 20.17 available for our learning data. So, how can we know that we have not pruned too little or too much? This is an intricate question and there are several methods that offer different, more or less satisfactory answers. We will now look at one method of post-pruning, known as *minimal error pruning*.

The key decision in post-pruning is whether to prune the subtrees below a given node or not. Figure 20.18 illustrates the situation. $T$ is a decision tree whose root is node $s$, $T_1$, $T_2$, ... are $T$'s subtrees, and $p_i$ are the probabilities of a random object passing from $s$ to subtree $T_i$. $T$ can be in turn a subtree of a larger decision tree. The question is to decide whether to prune below $s$ (i.e. remove the subtrees $T_1$, ... ), or not to prune. We here formulate a criterion based on the minimization of the expected classification error. We assume that the subtrees $T_1$, ... have already been optimally pruned using the same criterion on their subtrees.

The classification *accuracy* of a decision tree $T$ is the probability that $T$ will correctly classify a randomly chosen new object. The classification *error* of $T$ is the opposite, i.e. the probability of incorrect classification. Let us analyse the error for the two cases:

(1) If $T$ is pruned just below $s$ then $s$ becomes a leaf. $s$ is then labelled with the most likely class $C$ at $s$, and everything in this leaf is classified into class $C$. The error at $s$ is the probability that a random object that falls into $s$ belongs to a class other than $C$. This is called the *static error* at $s$:

$$e(s) = p(\text{class} \neq C \mid s)$$

(2) If the tree is not pruned just below $s$, then its error is the weighted sum of the errors $E(T_1)$, $E(T_2)$, ... of the optimally pruned subtrees $T_1$, $T_2$, ... :

$$p_1E(T_1) + p_2E(T_2) + \ldots$$

This is called the *backed-up error*.

The decision rule about pruning below s then is: if the static error is less than or equal to the backed-up error then prune, otherwise do not prune. Accordingly we can define the error of the optimally pruned tree $T$ as:

$$E(T) = \min(e(s), \sum_i p_i E(T_i))$$

Of course, if $T$ has no subtrees then simply $E(T) = e(s)$.

The remaining question is how to estimate the static error $e(s)$, which boils down to the probability of the most likely class $C$ at node $s$? The evidence we can use for this estimate is the set of examples that fall into node $s$. Let this set be $S$, the total number of examples in $S$ be $N$, and the number of examples of class $C$ be $n$. Now, the estimate of the probability of $C$ at $s$ is, in fact, an intricate problem. Most people would immediately propose that we just take the proportion $n/N$ (relative frequency) of class $C$ examples at node $s$. This is reasonable if the number of examples at $s$ is large, but obviously becomes debatable if this number is small. For instance let there be just one example at $s$. Then the proportion of the most likely class is $1/1 = 100$ percent, and the error estimate is $0/1 = 0$. But given that we only have one example at $s$, this estimate is statistically completely unreliable. Suppose we were able to get another learning example at $s$, and that this example was of another class. This single additional example would then drastically change the estimate from 100 to 50 percent!

Another good illustration of the intricacies in estimating probabilities is the outcome of a flip of a particular coin. Suppose that in the first experiment with the coin we get the head. The relative frequency now gives that the probability of the head is 1. This is completely counterintuitive because our *a priori* expectation is that this probability is 0.5. Even if this coin is not quite 'honest', the probability of the head should still be close to 0.5, and the estimate 1 is obviously inappropriate. This example also indicates that the probability estimate should depend not only on the experiments, but also on the prior expectation about this probability.

Obviously we need a more elaborate estimate than relative frequency. We here present one such estimate, called *m*-estimate, that has a good mathematical justification. According to the *m*-estimate, the expected probability of event $C$ is:

$$p = \frac{n + p_a m}{N + m}$$

Here $p_a$ is the *a priori* probability of $C$, and $m$ is a parameter of the estimate. $m$ is chosen by domain expert as explained below. The formula is derived using the Bayesian approach to probability estimation. Roughly, the Bayesian procedure assumes that there is some, possibly very vague, *a priori* knowledge about the probability of event $C$. This prior knowledge is stated as the prior probability distribution for event $C$. Then experiments are performed giving additional information about the probability of $C$. Prior probability distribution is updated with this new, experimental information, using Bayes' formula for conditional probability. The *m*-estimate formula above gives the expected value $p$ of this distribution. So the formula allows us to take into account the prior expectation about the probability of $C$, which is useful if we have some background knowledge about $C$ in addition to the given examples. This prior expectation is in the $m$-estimate formula expressed by $p_a$ and $m$, as discussed below.

The $m$-estimate formula can be rewritten as:

$$p = p_a * \frac{m}{N+m} + \frac{n}{N} * \frac{N}{N+m}$$

This provides a nice interpretation of the $m$-estimate: probability $p$ is simply equal to the a priori probability $p_a$, modified by the evidence coming from $N$ examples. If there are no examples then $N = 0$ and $p = p_a$. If there are many examples ($N$ very large) then $p = n/N$. Otherwise $p$ is between these two values. The strength of the prior probability is varied by the value of parameter $m$ ($m \geq 0$): the larger $m$, the greater the relative weight of the prior probability.

Parameter $m$ has a specially useful interpretation in dealing with noisy data. If the domain expert believes that the data are very noisy and the background knowledge is trustworthy, then he or she will set $m$ high (e.g. $m = 100$, giving much weight to prior probability). If on the other hand the learning data are trustworthy and the prior probability less so then $m$ will be set low (e.g. $m = 0.2$, thus giving much weight to the data). In practice, to avoid the uncertainty with appropriate setting of parameter $m$, we can try various values for $m$. In this way a sequence of differently pruned trees is obtained, each tree being optimal with respect to a different value of $m$. Such a sequence of trees can then be studied by the domain expert, who may be able to decide which of the trees make more sense.

There is now one remaining and non-trivial question: How to determine the prior probability $p_a$? If there is expert knowledge available then this should be used in setting $p_a$. If not, the commonly used technique is to determine the prior probabilities by statistics on the complete learning data (not just the fragment of it at node $s$), using simply the relative frequency estimate on the complete, large set. An alternative (often inferior to this) is to assume that all the classes are a priori equally likely and have uniform prior probability distribution. This assumption leads to a special case of the $m$-estimate, known as the *Laplace estimate*. If there are $k$ possible classes altogether, then for this special case we have:

$$p_a = 1/k, \quad m = k$$

So the Laplace probability estimate is:

$$p = \frac{n+1}{N+k}$$

This is handy because it does not require parameters $p_a$ and $m$. On the other hand, it is based on the usually incorrect assumption of the classes being a priori equally likely. Also, it does not allow the user to take into account the estimated degree of noise.

Figure 20.19 shows the pruning of a decision tree by minimum-error pruning, using the $m$-estimate. There are three classes x, y and z in this learning problem, whose prior probabilities are 0.4 for class x, 0.3 for class y, and 0.3 for class z. In this tree, the class frequencies of the examples falling into nodes are inserted into the nodes. For example, the left-most leaf of the tree has class frequencies

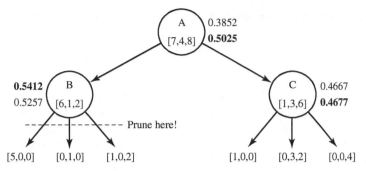

**Figure 20.19** Minimal-error pruning of a decision tree. Triples of numbers in square brackets are the numbers of class x, y and z examples that fall into the corresponding nodes. The other numbers attached to the nodes are accuracy estimates. For internal nodes, the first number is a static accuracy estimate and the second number is a backed up estimate. The higher of the two numbers (in bold face) is propagated upwards.

[5,0,0], meaning that there are five examples of class x in this leaf, and no example of any other class. Let us choose $m = 8$. The $m$-estimates of probabilities of the three classes for this leaf are:

$p(\text{ x } | \text{ leftmost\_leaf}) = (n_x + m * p_{x0}) / (N + m) = (5 + 8 * 0.4) / (5 + 8) = 0.6308$
$p(\text{ y } | \text{ leftmost\_leaf}) = (0 + 8 * 0.3) / (5 + 8) = 0.1846$
$p(\text{ z } | \text{ leftmost\_leaf}) = (0 + 8 * 0.3) / (5 + 8) = 0.1846$

Accordingly, the most likely class in this leaf is x, and all the objects falling into this leaf will be classified into class x. Now we proceed to the next leaf, that is the middle child of node B:

$p(\text{ x } | \text{ middle\_leaf}) = (0 + 8 * 0.4) / (1 + 8) = 0.3556$
$p(\text{ y } | \text{ middle\_leaf}) = (1 + 8 * 0.3) / (1 + 8) = 0.3778$
$p(\text{ z } | \text{ middle\_leaf}) = (0 + 8 * 0.3) / (1 + 8) = 0.2667$

According to these estimates, class y is the most likely, and the leaf will classify into y. The estimates for the right leaf of node B are:

$p(\text{ x } | \text{ right\_leaf}) = (1 + 8 * 0.4) / (3 + 8) = 0.3818$
$p(\text{ y } | \text{ right\_leaf}) = (0 + 8 * 0.3) / (3 + 8) = 0.2182$
$p(\text{ z } | \text{ right\_leaf}) = (2 + 8 * 0.3) / (3 + 8) = 0.4$

This leaf will classify into class z. The backed up accuracy at node B is the weighted sum of the accuracies of the leaves:

$\text{Backed\_up\_accuracy(B)} = 5/9 * 0.6308 + 1/9 * 0.3778 + 3/9 * 0.4 = 0.5257$

Static accuracy at node B is the probability of the most probable class at B. This is x:

$\text{Static\_accuracy(B)} = p(\text{ x } | \text{ B}) = (6 + 8 * 0.4) / (9 + 8) = 0.5412$

As backed up accuracy is lower than static accuracy at B, the decision is to prune the successor nodes of B. Next, pruning continues at node C. Here the backed up accuracy is 0.4677 which is slightly better than static accuracy at C which is 0.4667.

Therefore there is no pruning below C. Now we turn to node A, the root. Here we have:

Backed_up_accuracy(A) $= 9/19*0.5412 + 10/19*0.4677 = 0.5025$
Static_accuracy(A) $= 0.3852$

Static accuracy at A is the probability of z which is the most probable class at A according to the $m$-estimate. It is much better not to prune here. Finally, optimally pruned tree according to this pruning method has accuracy 0.5025, which is somewhat better than 0.4, that is the prior probability of the *a priori* most likely class x.

The use of $m$-estimate for estimating the error at the nodes of a decision tree can be criticized on the following grounds. The $m$-estimate formula assumes that the available data are a random sample. However, this is not true for the data subsets at the nodes of a decision tree. During tree construction, the data subsets at the nodes of a tree have been selected by the attribute selection criterion among possible partitions, according to the attributes, of the learning data. In spite of this theoretical reservation, experience has shown that minimal-error pruning with $m$-estimate works well in practice. When exploring data with decision trees, experimenting with various values of parameter $m$ for pruning is particularly useful.

The minimum-error pruning strategy can in principle use any approach to estimating errors. In any case, the expected error of the pruned tree will be minimized. Of course, a pruned tree thus obtained is only optimal with respect to the particular error estimates. One alternative approach to estimating errors is to partition the available learning data $S$ into two subsets: 'growing set' and 'pruning set'. The growing set is used to build a complete decision tree consistent with the 'growing' data. The pruning set is used just to measure the error at the nodes of the tree, and then prune so as to minimize this error. Since the pruning set is independent of the growing set, we can simply classify the examples in the pruning set by the decision tree and count the tree's errors. This gives an estimate of predictive accuracy on new data. The approach with a pruning set is sensible when the learning data are ample. However, it is at a disadvantage when the learning data are scarce. In such a case, holding out a pruning set means even less data for growing the tree.

# EXERCISES

**20.5** A volcano ejects lava completely randomly. In long-term statistics, the volcano was, on average, active one day in ten days and inactive the remaining days. In the most recent 30 days it was active 25 days. This recently increased activity was taken into account by experts in the forecast for the next day. The radio news said that the probability of the volcano being active the next day was at least 30 percent. The prediction on TV quoted the probability between 50 and 60 percent. Both experts, on radio and TV, were known to use the $m$-estimate method. How can the difference in their estimates be explained?

**20.6** Write a procedure

**prunetree( Tree, PrunedTree)**

that prunes a decision tree **Tree** according to the minimum-error pruning method discussed in this section. The leaves of **Tree** contain class frequency information represented as lists of integers. Use the Laplace estimate in the program. Let the number of classes be stored in the program as a fact: **number_of_classes( K)**.

## 20.7 Success of learning

We started this chapter by considering the ARCHES style of learning relational descriptions. ARCHES is a good illustration of the main principles and ideas in learning. Also, its sequential style of processing examples is perhaps closer to human learning than the one-shot learning in the other two approaches discussed in this chapter. On the other hand, the learning of attribute-value descriptions, in the form of either rules or trees, is simpler and better understood than learning relational descriptions. Therefore, the simpler approaches have until now enjoyed more attention and success in practical applications.

Learning is inherently a combinatorial process. It involves search among possible hypotheses. This search can be heuristically guided. It can also be significantly constrained by the 'linguistic bias'; that is, the effect of the hypothesis language only allowing certain forms of hypotheses to be constructed. Both our algorithms for learning if-then rules and decision trees were very strongly heuristically guided – for example, by the impurity criterion. Therefore, these algorithms are efficient, although in our Prolog implementation (Figure 20.11) the evaluation of such a heuristic itself is not efficiently implemented. These heuristics require the computation of certain statistics for which Prolog is not the most suitable.

In general, the success of learning is measured by several criteria. In the following sections we will look at some usual criteria, and discuss the benefits of tree pruning in the view of these criteria.

### 20.7.1 Criteria for success of learning

Here are some usual criteria for measuring the success of a learning system:

- *Classification accuracy*: This is usually defined as the percentage of objects correctly classified by the induced hypothesis H. We distinguish between two types of classification accuracy:
  (1) Accuracy on new objects; that is, those not contained in the training set S.
  (2) Accuracy on the objects in S. (Of course, this is only interesting when inconsistent hypotheses are allowed.)
- *Comprehensibility* (understandability) of the induced hypothesis H: It is often important for the generated description to be comprehensible in order to tell the user something interesting about the application domain. Such a description can also be used by people directly, without machine help, as an enhancement to a person's own knowledge. In this sense, machine learning is one approach to computer-aided synthesis of new knowledge. Donald Michie (1986) was an early proponent of this idea which is now commonly exploited, often under the terms

*data mining* or KDD (knowledge discovery in data). The comprehensibility criterion is also very important when the induced descriptions are used in an expert system whose behaviour has to be easy to understand.

- *Computational complexity*: What are the required computer resources in terms of time and space? Usually, we distinguish between two types of complexity:
  (1) Generation complexity (resources needed to induce a concept description from examples).
  (2) Execution complexity (complexity of classifying an object using the induced description).

## 20.7.2 Estimating the accuracy of learned hypotheses

The usual question after learning has been done is: How well will the learned hypothesis predict the class in new data? Of course, when new data become available, this accuracy can simply be measured by classifying the new objects and comparing their true class with the class predicted by the hypothesis. The difficulty is that we would like to estimate the accuracy *before* any new data become available.

The usual approach to estimating the accuracy on new data is to randomly split the available data into two sets: *training set* and *test set*. Then we run the learning program on the training set, and test the induced hypothesis on the test set as if this was new, future data. This approach is simple and unproblematic if a lot of data is available. A common situation is, however, shortage of data. Suppose we are learning to diagnose in a particular area of medicine. We are limited to the data about past patients, and the amount of data cannot be increased. When the amount of learning data is small, this may not be sufficient for successful learning. The shortage of data is then aggravated by holding out part of the data as a test set.

When the number of learning examples is small, the results of learning and testing are susceptible to large statistical fluctuations. They depend heavily on the particular split into a training set and test set. To alleviate this statistical uncertainty, the learning and testing is repeated a number of times (typically, ten times), each time for a different random split. The accuracy results are then averaged and their variance gives an idea of the stability of the estimate.

An elaboration of this type of repetitive testing is *k-fold cross-validation*. Here the complete learning set is randomly split into $k$ subsets. Then the learning and testing is repeated for each of the subsets as follows: the $i$th subset is removed from the data, the rest of the data is used as a training set, and the $i$th subset is then used for testing the induced hypothesis. The $k$ accuracy results so obtained are averaged and their variance is computed. There is no particular method to choose $k$, but the choice $k = 10$ is the most usual in machine learning experiments.

A particular case of cross-validation arises when the subsets only contain one element. In each iteration, the learning is done on all the data but one example, and the induced hypothesis is tested on the remaining example. This form of cross-validation is called 'leave-one-out'. It is sensible when the amount of available data is particularly small.

### 20.7.3   How pruning affects accuracy and transparency of decision trees

Pruning of decision trees is of fundamental importance because of its beneficial effects when dealing with noisy data. Pruning affects two measures of success of learning: first, the classification accuracy of a decision tree on new objects and, second, the transparency of a decision tree. Let us consider both of these effects of pruning.

The comprehensibility of a description depends on its structure and size. A well-structured decision tree is easier to understand than a completely unstructured tree. On the other hand, if a decision tree is small (consisting of just ten or so nodes) then it is easy to understand regardless of its structure. Since pruning reduces the size of a tree, it contributes to the comprehensibility of a decision tree. As has been shown experimentally in many noisy domains, such as medical diagnosis, the reduction of tree size can be dramatic. The number of nodes is reduced to, say, 10 percent of their original number, while retaining at least the same level of classification accuracy.

Tree pruning can also improve the classification accuracy of a tree. This effect of pruning may appear counter-intuitive since, by pruning, we throw away some information, and it would seem that as a result some accuracy should be lost. However, in the case of learning from noisy data, an appropriate amount of pruning normally improves the accuracy. This phenomenon can be explained in statistical terms: statistically, pruning works as a sort of noise suppression mechanism. By pruning, we eliminate errors in learning data that are due to noise, rather than throw away healthy information.

*Projects*

Carry out a typical project in machine learning research. This consists of implementing a learning algorithm, and testing its accuracy on experimental data sets using the 10-fold cross-validation. If you use a tree learning method, you may investigate how tree pruning affects the accuracy on new data. Investigate the effect of minimal error pruning when varying the value of parameter $m$ in $m$-estimate. Many real-life learning data sets are electronically available for such experiments from the well-known UCI Repository for Machine Learning (University of California at Irvine; http://archive.ics.uci.edu/ml/). Another common type of machine learning project is to compare the performance of selected learning methods on chosen data sets. This is usually done by using freely available software platforms for machine learning that contain implementations of many learning methods (for example Orange, www.ailab.si/orange/, or Weka, www.cs.waikato.ac.nz/ml/weka/).

## Summary

- Machine learning takes many forms along several dimensions, including: learning by being told, learning from examples, learning by discovery; learning from attribute-value data or from relational data; learning various types of descriptions, including if-then rules, decision trees, neural networks, relational descriptions; learning data can be processed sequentially (incremental learning) or all in one shot (batch learning). Learning concepts from examples is also called inductive learning. Inductive learning from attribute-value data has attained most success in practical applications and is most common.

- Learning from examples involves:

  objects and concepts as sets;
  positive and negative examples of concept to be learned;
  hypotheses about target concept;
  hypothesis language.

- The goal of learning from examples is to construct a hypothesis that 'explains' sufficiently well the given examples. Hopefully such a hypothesis will accurately classify future examples as well. A hypothesis is *consistent* with the learning examples if it classifies all the learning data as given in the examples.

- The inductive learning process involves search among possible hypotheses. This is inherently combinatorial. To reduce computational complexity, typically this process is heuristically guided.

- During its construction, a hypothesis may be generalized or specialized. Normally, the final hypothesis is a generalization of the positive examples.

- *Preference bias* is a criterion for choosing among competing hypotheses. *Language bias a priori* excludes some, typically many, hypotheses from consideration.

- Ockham's razor is a well-known principle that argues for simplicity. In machine learning it is applied as a criterion that favours simple hypotheses.

- Programs developed in this chapter are:

  A program that learns if-then rules from examples defined by attribute-value vectors.
  A program that learns decision trees from examples defined by attribute-value vectors.

- The pruning of decision trees is a powerful approach to learning from noisy data. Minimal-error pruning method was presented in detail.

- Difficulty of estimating probabilities from small samples was discussed, and the $m$-estimate was introduced. A special case of $m$-estimate is the Laplace estimate.

- Criteria for assessing the success of a method of learning from examples include:

  accuracy of induced hypotheses;
  comprehensibility of learned concept descriptions;
  computational efficiency both in inducing a hypothesis from data, and in classifying new objects with the induced hypothesis.

- The expected accuracy of learned hypotheses on new data is usually estimated by *cross-validation*. Ten-fold cross-validation is the most common. The leave-one-out method is a special form of cross-validation.

- Concepts discussed in this chapter are:

  machine learning
  learning concepts from examples, inductive learning
  data mining, knowledge discovery in data (KDD)
  hypothesis languages

relational descriptions
attribute-value descriptions
generality and specificity of hypotheses
generalization and specialization of descriptions
bias in machine learning, preference bias, language bias
Ockham's razor (also spelled Occam's razor)
ARCHES-type learning of relational descriptions
learning of if-then rules
top-down induction of decision trees
learning from noisy data
tree pruning, post-pruning, minimal-error pruning
estimating probabilities
cross-validation

## References and notes on other approaches

The books by Bishop (2007), Mitchell (1997), and Witten and Frank (2005) are excellent textbooks on machine learning (ML). Kononenko and Kukar (2007) cover remarkably many topics of ML in a compact way. In Michalski, Bratko and Kubat (1998), ML applications are presented in a variety of areas, ranging from engineering to medicine, biology and music. Michie *et al.* (1994) is a well-known empirical evaluation of many learning methods on many learning problems. Current research in machine learning is published in the AI literature, most notably in the journals *Machine Learning, Journal of Machine Learning Research, Artificial Intelligence* and *Journal of Artificial Intelligence Research*, and at annual conferences ICML (Int. Conf. on Machine Learning), ECML (European Conf. on Machine Learning), COLT (Computational Learning Theory) and ALT (Algorithmic Learning Theory). Many classical papers on ML are included in Michalski, Carbonell and Mitchell (1983, 1986) and Kodratoff and Michalski (1990). Gillies (1996) investigates implications of the technical developments in ML and its applications regarding a traditional controversy in the philosophy of science.

Many data sets for experimentation with new ML methods are electronically available from the UCI Repository (University of California at Irvine; http://archive.ics.uci.edu/ml/). There are ML environments that comprise collections of ML methods. Excellent, freely available such systems are Orange (www.ailab.si/orange/), and Weka (www.cs.waikato.ac.nz/ml/weka/). The latter is connected to the Witten and Frank (2005) book.

Our example of learning relational descriptions (Section 20.3) follows the ideas of an early learning program ARCHES (Winston 1975). The program in Section 20.4 that constructs if-then rules is a simple version of the AQ-type learning. The AQ family of learning programs was developed by Michalski and his co-workers (for example, Michalski 1983). CN2 is a well-known algorithm for learning if-then rules (Clark and Niblett 1989). CN2 is based on AQ, but Clark and Niblett carefully retained only the simple and most useful of many ideas from AQ, while omitting complications with diminishing return. The popularity of CN2 and its various refinements is largely due to this rational design choice. ABCN2 (Argument-based CN2; Možina *et al.* 2007) is an extension of CN2 towards learning from 'argumented' examples, where a domain expert can help the learning program by providing arguments as an explanation for selected examples.

Induction of decision trees is one of the most widely used approaches to learning, also known under the name TDIDT (top-down induction of decision trees, coined by Quinlan 1986). The popular, reference implementation known as C4.5 is documented in Quinlan (1993). TDIDT learning was much influenced by Quinlan's early program ID3, Iterative Dichotomizer 3 (Quinlan 1979), and tree induction is therefore often simply referred to as ID3. Tree induction was also studied outside AI by Breiman and his co-workers (1984), who independently discovered several pertinent mechanisms, including pruning of decision trees. The technique of minimal-error tree pruning was introduced by Niblett and Bratko (1986) and improved with the *m*-estimate in Cestnik and Bratko (1991). Esposito *et al.* (1997) carried out detailed experimental comparison of various methods of tree pruning. Structuring decision trees to improve their transparency was studied by Shapiro (1987).

Machine learning is an enormous field. Let us mention some of the many interesting approaches and developments in machine learning that could not be covered in this chapter.

An early attempt at machine learning is Samuel's (1959) learning program that played the game of checkers. This program improved its position-evaluation function through the experience it obtained in the games it played.

Mitchell (1982) developed the influential idea of *version space* as an attempt to handle economically the search among alternative concept descriptions.

In *reinforcement learning* (Sutton and Barto 1998) the learner explores its environment by performing actions and receiving rewards from the environment. In learning to act so as to maximize the reward, the difficulty is that the reward may be *delayed*, so it is not clear which particular actions are to be blamed for success or failure.

In *instance-based* learning, related to *case-based reasoning* (Kolodner 1993), the learner reasons about a given case by comparing it to similar previous cases. Aha *et al.* (2005) edited a collection of review papers on the topic.

*Neural networks* (covered by most books on ML; Haykin (2008) is a comprehensive treatment) is a large area of learning which aspires to some extent to resemble biological learning. The learning occurs through adjustment of numerical weights associated with artificial neurons in the network. Neural networks have not been at the centre of AI because they lack explicit symbolic representation of what has been learned. Hypotheses resulting from neural learning can be very good predictors, but are generally hard to understand and interpret by humans.

*Support Vector Machine* (SVM; developed by Vapnik and colleagues) is a very powerful classification learning method, probably the most practical to use if you do not know much about specific properties of the learning domain. SVM is probably the first and easiest off the shelf tool to try on a new data set. Roughly, 'support vectors' are special data points that define 'the safest' separation between data points of different classes. This aims at maximizing the accuracy on new data. Cristianini and Shawe-Taylor (2000) is a textbook on SVMs.

An interesting approach to learning is *explanation-based learning* (e.g. Mitchell *et al.* 1986), also known as *analytical learning*. Here the learning system uses background knowledge to 'explain' a given example by a deductive process. As a result, background knowledge gets compiled into a more efficiently executable form. One approach to explanation-based generalization is programmed in Chapter 25 of this book as a kind of meta-programming exercise.

Some learning programs learn by *autonomous discovery*. They discover new concepts through exploration, making their own experiments. A celebrated example of this kind of program is AM, Automatic Mathematician (Lenat 1982). AM, for example, starting with the concepts of set and 'bag', discovered the concepts of number, addition, multiplication, prime number, etc. Shrager and Langley (1990) edited a collection of papers on ML for scientific discovery. *Discovery Science* is an annual conference for this area.

Logic formalisms are used as a hypothesis language in the approach to learning called inductive logic programming (ILP), which is studied in the next chapter of this book.

The mathematical theory of learning is also known as COLT (computational learning theory; e.g. Kearns and Vazirani 1994, Vapnik 1998). It is concerned with questions like: How many examples are needed so that it is likely to attain some specified accuracy of the induced hypothesis? What are various theoretical complexities of learning for different classes of hypothesis languages?

In our treatment in this chapter, the learning data were assumed to be labelled: each learning example was labelled by its class. This learning setting is called *supervised learning* in the sense that there is a 'supervisor' (or 'teacher') who provided the class information. The opposite is *unsupervised learning* where only non-labelled example data points are given, but there is no class information. *Clustering* is an approach to unsupervised learning, aiming at partitioning the given data set into clusters so that similar objects end up in the same cluster (Everitt *et al.* 2001).

Aha, D.W., Marling, C. and Watson, I. (2005) *The Knowledge Engineering Review*, special issue on case-based reasoning, Volume 20 (3). Cambridge University Press.

Bishop, C.M. (2007) *Pattern Recognition and Machine Learning*. Springer-Verlag.

Breiman, L., Friedman, J.H., Olshen, R.A. and Stone, C.J. (1984) *Classification and Regression Trees*. Belmont, CA: Wadsworth Int. Group.

Cestnik, B. and Bratko, I. (1991) On estimating probabilities in tree pruning. *Proc. European Conf. on Machine Learning*, Porto, Portugal. Berlin: Springer-Verlag.

Clark, P. and Niblett, T. (1989) The CN2 induction algorithm. *Machine Learning* 3: 262–284.

Cristianini, N. and Shawe-Taylor, J. (2000) *An introduction to Support Vector Machines and other kernel-based learning methods*. Cambridge University Press.

Esposito, F., Malerba, D. and Semeraro, G. (1997) A comparative analysis of methods for pruning decision trees. *IEEE Trans. Pattern Analysis and Machine Intelligence* 19: 416–491.

Everitt, B.S., Landau, S. and Leese, M. (2001) *Cluster Analysis*, 4th edn. Arnold Publishers.

Gillies, D. (1996) *Artificial Intelligence and Scientific Method*. Oxford University Press.

Haykin, S. (2008) *Neural Networks: A Comprehensive Foundation*. Prentice Hall.

Kearns, M.J. and Vazirani, U.V. (1994) *An Introduction to Computational Learning Theory*. Cambridge, MA: MIT Press.

Kodratoff, Y. and Michalski, R.S. (1990) *Machine Learning: An Artificial Intelligence Approach*, Vol. III. Morgan Kaufmann.

Kolodner, J.L. (1993) *Case-Based Reasoning*. San Francisco, CA: Morgan Kaufmann.

Kononenko, I. and Kukar, M. (2007) *Machine Learning and Data Mining: Introduction to Principles and Algorithms*. Chichester, UK: Horwood.

Lenat, D.B. (1982) AM: discovery in mathematics as heuristic search. In: *Knowledge-Based Systems in Artificial Intelligence* (Davis, R. and Lenat, D.B., eds). McGraw-Hill.

Michalski, R.S. (1983) A theory and methodology of inductive learning. In: *Machine Learning: An Artificial Intelligence Approach* (Michalski, R.S., Carbonell, J.G. and Mitchell, T.M., eds). Tioga Publishing Company.

Michalski, R.S., Bratko, I., and Kubat, M. (eds) (1998) *Machine Learning and Data Mining: Methods and Applications*. Wiley.

Michalski, R.S., Carbonell, J.G. and Mitchell, T.M. (eds) (1983) *Machine Learning: An Artificial Intelligence Approach*. Palo Alto, CA: Tioga Publishing Company.

Michalski, R.S., Carbonell, J.G. and Mitchell, T.M. (eds) (1986) *Machine Learning: An Artificial Intelligence Approach*, Volume II. Los Altos, CA: Morgan Kaufmann.

Michie, D. (1986) The superarticulacy phenomenon in the context of software manufacture. *Proc. of the Royal Society, London, A* 405: 189–212. Also reprinted in *Expert Systems: Automating Knowledge Acquisition* (Michie, D. and Bratko, I.). Harlow, England: Addison-Wesley.

Michie, D., Spiegelhalter, D.J. and Taylor, C.C. (1994) *Machine Learning, Neural and Statistical Classification*. Hertfordshire, UK: Ellis Horwood.

Mitchell, T.M. (1982) Generalization as search. *Artificial Intelligence* 18: 203–226.

Mitchell, T.M. (1997) *Machine Learning*. McGraw-Hill.

Mitchell, T.M., Keller, R.M. and Kedar-Cabelli, S.T. (1986) Explanation-based generalisation: a unifying view. *Machine Learning* 1: 47–80.

Možina, M., Žabkar, J. and Bratko, I. (2007) Argument based machine learning. *Artificial Intelligence* **171**: 922–937.

Niblett, T. and Bratko, I. (1986) Learning decision rules in noisy domains. In: *Research and Development in Expert Systems III* (Bramer, M.A., ed.). Cambridge University Press.

Orange environment for machine learning (www.ailab.si/orange/)

Quinlan, J.R. (1979) Discovering rules by induction from large collections of examples. In: *Expert Systems in the Microelectronic Age* (Michie, D., ed.). Edinburgh University Press.

Quinlan, J.R. (1986) Induction of decision trees. *Machine Learning* 1: 81–106.

Quinlan, J.R. (1993) *C4.5 Programs for Machine Learning*. San Mateo, CA: Morgan Kaufmann.

Samuel, A.L. (1959) Some studies in machine learning using the game of checkers. *IBM Journal of Research and Development* 3: 211–229. Also in *Computers and Thought* (Feigenbaum, E.A. and Feldman, I., eds). McGraw-Hill, 1963.

Shapiro, A. (1987) *Structured Induction in Expert Systems*. Glasgow: Turing Institute Press, in association with Addison-Wesley.

Shrager, J. and Langley, P. (1990) *Computational Models of Scientific Discovery and Theory Formation*. San Mateo, CA: Morgan Kaufmann.

Sutton, R.S. and Barto, A.G. (1998) *Reinforcement Learning: An Introduction*. Cambridge, MA: MIT Press.

Vapnik, V.N. (1998) *Statistical Learning Theory*. Wiley.

Weka environment for machine learning (www.cs.waikato.ac.nz/ml/weka/).

Winston, P.H. (1975) Learning structural descriptions from examples. In: *The Psychology of Computer Vision* (Winston, P.H., ed.). McGraw-Hill.

Witten, I.H. and Frank, E. (2005) *Data Mining: Practical Machine Learning Tools and Techniques*, second edn. Elsevier.

# Chapter 21

# Inductive Logic Programming

*Inductive logic programming* is an approach to machine learning where definitions of relations are induced from examples. In ILP, logic is used as a hypothesis language and the result of learning is usually just a Prolog program. So Prolog programs are automatically constructed from examples. For instance, the user provides some examples of how lists are sorted and how they are not, and a program for sorting lists is constructed automatically. In comparison with other approaches to machine learning, ILP provides a very general way of specifying 'background knowledge', that is knowledge known to the learner before the learning starts. The price for this flexibility in ILP is a generally high computational complexity. In this chapter we develop an ILP program, called HYPER (Hypothesis Refiner), that is capable of solving typical learning exercises in the ILP setting.

## 21.1 Introduction

Inductive logic programming (ILP) is an approach to machine learning. It is a way of learning relations from examples. In ILP, logic is used as a language for defining hypotheses. Thus the result of learning is a formula in predicate logic, usually just a Prolog program.

In this framework machine learning looks like automatic programming when the user (a 'programmer') does not write programs directly. Instead, the user only specifies by examples what the intended program is supposed to do. Examples indicate what the intended program should do, and counter examples indicate what the program should not do. In addition, the user also specifies some 'background' predicates that may be used in writing the intended, new program.

Here is an example of such automatic programming in Prolog. Suppose we already have predicates **parent(X,Y)**, **male(X)** and **female(X)**, defining some family relations as in Figure 1.1 (in Chapter 1). Now we want to find a definition of a new predicate **has_daughter(X)**. Let there be some examples about this new predicate. Suppose there are two positive examples:

   **has_daughter(tom),   has_daughter(bob)**

There are two negative examples:

> **has_daughter(pam), has_daughter(jim)**

The learning task is to find a definition of the predicate **has_daughter**(X) in terms of the predicates **parent**, **male** and **female**, so that it is true for all the given positive examples and not true for any of the given negative examples. An ILP program may come up with the following hypothesis about **has_daughter**:

> **has_daughter( X) :-**
>   **parent( X, Y),**
>   **female( Y).**

This hypothesis explains all the given examples.

Notice here the typical feature of relational learning as opposed to attribute-value learning. The property **has_daughter** of X above is defined not only in terms of X's attributes. Instead, to determine whether an object X has the property **has_daughter**, look at another object Y related to X, and check properties of Y.

Let us now introduce some technical terminology of ILP. In the foregoing example, the predicate to be learned, **has_daughter**, is called a *target predicate*. The given predicates **parent**, **male** and **female** are called *background knowledge* (BK), or *background predicates*. This is the knowledge known to the learner before the learning starts. So the background predicates determine the language in which the learner can express hypotheses about the target predicate.

We can now state the usual formulation of the ILP problem:

Given:

(1) A set of positive examples $E_+$ and a set of negative examples $E_-$, and

(2) Background knowledge BK, stated as a set of logic formulas, such that the examples $E_+$ cannot be derived from BK

Find:

A hypothesis H, stated as a set of logic formulas, such that:

(1) All the examples in $E_+$ can be derived from BK and H, and

(2) No negative example in $E_-$ can be derived from BK and H.

We also say that H, together with BK, has to *cover* all the positive examples, and *must not cover* any of the negative examples. Such a hypothesis H is said to be *complete* (covers all the positive examples) and *consistent* (does not cover any negative example).

Usually both BK and H are simply sets of Prolog clauses, that is Prolog programs. So from the viewpoint of automatic programming in Prolog this corresponds to the following. Suppose our target predicate is **p**(X) and we have, among others, a positive example **p**(a) and a negative example **p**(b). A possible conversation with program BK would be:

```
?- p(a).          % A positive example
no                % Cannot be derived from BK

?- p(b).          % A negative example
no                % Cannot be derived from BK
```

Now suppose an ILP system would be called to automatically induce an additional set of clauses H and add them to the program BK. The conversation with the so extended program BK plus H would now be:

```
?- p(a).         % A positive example
yes              % Can be derived from BK and H

?- p(b).         % A negative example
no               % Cannot be derived from BK and H
```

Well-known exercises in ILP are the automatic construction of Prolog programs to concatenate or sort lists. The programs are constructed from positive examples of how lists are concatenated or sorted, and from negative examples of how they are not. In this chapter we will develop an ILP program called HYPER, and apply it to such exercises.

Let us here consider the motivation for ILP in comparison with other, not logic-based approaches to machine learning that are essentially at the level of attribute-value learning. ILP's strength rests in the power of its hypothesis language, and the way of incorporating background knowledge into the learning process. The hypothesis language allows for relational definitions that may even involve recursion. This is usually not possible with other approaches to machine learning.

In ILP, background knowledge can in principle be any Prolog program. This enables the user to provide in a very natural way prior domain-specific knowledge to be used in learning. The use of background knowledge enables the user to develop a good problem representation and to introduce problem-specific constraints into the learning process. By contrast, attribute-value learners can typically accept background knowledge in rather limited forms only, for example in the form of relevant new attributes. In ILP on the other hand, if the problem is to learn about properties of chemical compounds, the molecular structures can be introduced as background knowledge in terms of the atoms and bonds between them. If the learning task is to automatically construct a model of a physical system from its observed behaviours, the complete mathematical apparatus that is considered relevant to the modelling domain can be included in background knowledge. If this involves the treatment of time and space, axioms of reasoning about time and space may be included as background knowledge. In a typical application of ILP, the emphasis is on the development of a good representation of examples together with relevant background knowledge. A general purpose ILP system is then applied to carry out the induction.

The power of hypothesis language and flexibility of background knowledge in ILP do not come without a price. This flexibility adds to the combinatorial complexity of the learning task. Therefore attribute-value learning, such as decision trees, is much more efficient than ILP. Therefore in learning problems where attribute-value representations are adequate, attribute-value learning is recommended for efficiency reasons.

In this chapter we will develop an ILP program called HYPER (*Hyp*othesis refi*ner*), which constructs Prolog programs through gradual refinement of some starting hypotheses. To illustrate the main ideas, we will first develop a simple and inefficient version of it, called MINIHYPER. This will then be elaborated into HYPER.

# Constructing Prolog programs from examples

## 21.2.1 Representation of a learning problem

Let us consider again the family relations example to see how hypotheses may be constructed automatically from examples. Suppose that our BK and the examples are as in Figure 21.1. The corresponding family graph is similar to the one in Figure 1.1 (in Chapter 1), with the addition that Pat has a daughter, Eve. The program developed in this section will assume the representational conventions

```
% Learning from family relations

% Background knowledge

backliteral( parent(X,Y), [X,Y]).          % A background literal with vars. [X, Y]

backliteral( male(X), [X]).

backliteral( female(X), [X]).

prolog_predicate( parent(_,_)).            % Goal parent(_,_) executed directly by Prolog
prolog_predicate( male(_)).
prolog_predicate( female(_)).

parent( pam, bob).
parent( tom, bob).
parent( tom, liz).
parent( bob, ann).
parent( bob, pat).
parent( pat, jim).
parent( pat, eve).

female( pam).
male( tom).
male( bob).
female( liz).
female( ann).
female( pat).
male( jim).
female( eve).

% Positive examples

ex( has_daughter(tom)).                     % Tom has a daughter
ex( has_daughter(bob)).
ex( has_daughter(pat)).

% Negative examples

nex( has_daughter(pam)).                     % Pam doesn't have a daughter
nex( has_daughter(jim)).

start_hyp( [ [has_daughter(X)] / [X] ] ).    % Starting hypothesis
```

**Figure 21.1** A definition of the problem of learning predicate **has_daughter**.

illustrated in Figure 21.1. The positive examples are represented by the predicate **ex(Example)**, e.g.:

> **ex( has_daughter(tom)).**              % Tom has a daughter

The negative examples are represented by the predicate **nex(Example)**, e.g.:

> **nex( has_daughter(pam)).**              % Pam does not have a daughter

The predicate **backliteral** specifies the form of literals that the ILP program may use as goals when constructing Prolog clauses. For example,

> **backliteral( parent(X,Y), [X,Y]).**

says that literals of the form **parent(X,Y)**, with the variables X and Y possibly renamed, are part of the hypothesis language. The second argument in **backliteral** is a list of the variables in the literal. Such 'background literals' can be added as goals to the body of clauses that are being constructed. Background literals are calls to BK predicates that may be specified directly in Prolog. The predicate **prolog_predicate** specifies goals that are to be directly executed by the Prolog interpreter. For example,

> **prolog_predicate( parent(X,Y)).**

says that goals that match **parent(X,Y)** are evaluated by Prolog directly, executing the BK predicate **parent**. Other goals, such as **has_daughter(tom)**, will be executed by a Prolog-like interpreter with special properties that we will implement specifically for use in ILP.

## 21.2.2  Refinement graph

Let us now consider how a complete and consistent hypothesis can be generated for the learning problem of Figure 21.1. We may start with some overly general hypothesis that is complete (covers all the positive examples), but inconsistent (also covers negative examples). Such a hypothesis will have to be specialized in a way to retain its completeness and attain consistency. This can be done by searching a space of possible hypotheses and their refinements. Each refinement takes a hypothesis H1 and produces a more specific hypothesis H2, so that H2 covers a subset of the cases covered by H1.

Such a space of hypotheses and their refinements is called a *refinement graph*. Figure 21.2 shows part of such a refinement graph for the learning problem of Figure 21.1. The nodes of this graph correspond to hypotheses, the arcs between hypotheses correspond to refinements. There is a directed arc between hypotheses H1 and H2 if H2 is a refinement of H1.

Once we have a refinement graph, the learning problem is reduced to searching this graph. The start node of search is some over-general hypothesis. A goal node of search is a hypothesis that is consistent and complete. In our example of Figure 21.2, it is sufficient that all the hypotheses are just single clauses. In general, hypotheses consist of multiple clauses.

To implement this approach we have to design two things:

(1) A *refinement operator* that will generate refinements of hypotheses (such an operator defines a refinement graph).

(2) A search procedure to carry out the search.

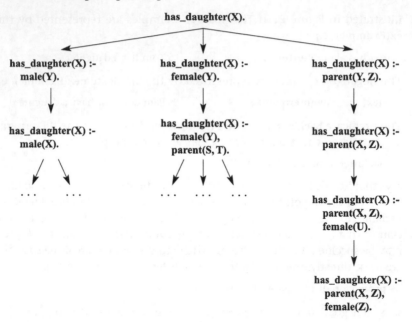

**Figure 21.2** Part of the refinement graph for the learning problem of Figure 21.1. Many possible refinements are omitted in this diagram.

In the graph of Figure 21.2, there are two types of refinement. A refinement of a clause is obtained by either:

(1)  matching two variables in the clause, or

(2)  adding a background literal to the body of the clause.

An example of the first type of refinement is:

has_daughter(X)  :-  parent(Y,Z).

is refined into

has_daughter(X)  :-  parent(X,Z).

by matching X=Y. An example of the second type of refinement is:

has_daughter(X).

is refined into

has_daughter(X)  :-  parent(Y,Z).

There are a few important points to notice. First, each refinement is a *specialization*. That is, a successor of a hypothesis in the refinement graph only covers a subset of the cases covered by the hypothesis's predecessor. Therefore it suffices that, during search, we only consider complete hypotheses. An incomplete hypothesis can never be refined into a complete one.

A second point about a refinement operator is that it has to produce sufficiently 'small' refinement steps. Otherwise a refinement operator may fail to generate the target hypothesis. Too coarse an operator may jump from a complete and inconsistent hypothesis straight to an incomplete and consistent one, over-jumping a consistent and complete hypothesis in between.

There is another type of refinement, one concerned with refining variables to structured terms. For example, the clause:

> member( X1, L1)  :-  member( X1, L3).

may be refined into

> member( X1, [X2 | L2])  :-  member( X1, L3).

where the variable **L1** is refined into the structure [X2 | L2]. For simplicity, the program MINIHYPER that we will develop in this section will not be able to handle problems that require structured terms. We will defer this until the next section when we develop a more sophisticated program HYPER.

Another point obvious from Figure 21.2 is the combinatorial complexity of refinement graphs and the ensuing search complexity. Again, in MINIHYPER we will not worry about this and simply use the uninformed iterative deepening search. This will also later be improved to a best-first search in HYPER.

## 21.2.3  Program MINIHYPER

We are now ready to start writing our first ILP program. We will choose to represent hypotheses as lists of clauses:

> Hypothesis = [Clause1, Clause2, ...]

Each clause will be represented by a list of literals (the head of the clause followed by the body literals) and the list of variables in the clause:

> Clause = [Head, BodyLiteral1, BodyLiteral2, ...] / [Var1, Var2, ...]

For example, the hypothesis

> pred(X,Y)  :-  parent(X,Y).
> pred(X,Z)  :-  parent(X,Y), pred(Y,Z).

is in this convention represented as:

> [ [pred(X1,Y1), parent(X1,Y1)] / [X1,Y1],
>   [pred(X2,Z2), parent(X2,Y2), pred(Y2,Z2)] / [X2,Y2,Z2] ]

Although it is not strictly necessary explicitly to represent the list of variables in a clause, it is handy for the implementation of hypothesis refinement by matching variables. Notice that we need different names of variables for each clause in a hypothesis because they actually are different variables.

To test whether a hypothesis covers an example we need a Prolog-like interpreter for hypotheses represented as above. To this end we will define the predicate:

> prove( Goal, Hypothesis, Answer)

that for a given **Goal** and **Hypothesis** finds **Answer** indicating whether **Goal** can be logically derived from **Hypothesis**. This predicate will basically try to prove **Goal** from **Hypothesis** in a way similar to Prolog itself. Programming this is an exercise in meta-programming which is discussed in more detail in Chapter 25. A specific difficulty in our case is the danger of infinite loops. Our refinement operator may easily generate a recursive clause like

[ p(X), p(X)]

which stands for p(X) :- p(X). This may lead to an infinite loop. We have to make our **prove** predicate immune from such loops. An easy way to do this is by limiting the length of proofs. When proving **Goal**, if the number of predicate calls reaches this limit, then the procedure **prove** will simply stop without reaching a definitive answer. The argument **Answer** of **prove** will therefore have the following possible meanings:

Answer = yes:      **Goal** has been derived from **Hypothesis** within proof limit
Answer = no:       **Goal** definitively cannot be derived from **Hypothesis** even if
                   the limit was relaxed

Answer = maybe:    proof search was terminated because maximum proof length
                   D was reached

The case 'Answer = maybe' means any one of the following three possibilities if **Goal** was executed by the standard Prolog interpreter:

(1) The standard Prolog interpreter (with no limit on proof length) would get into infinite loop.

(2) The standard Prolog interpreter would eventually find a proof of length greater than limit D.

(3) The standard Prolog interpreter would find, at some length greater than D, that this derivation alternative fails. Therefore it would backtrack to another alternative and there possibly find a proof (of length possibly no greater than D), or fail, or get into an infinite loop.

Figure 21.3 gives the program code for **prove**. The proof-length limit is specified by the predicate:

**max_proof_length( D)**

D is by default set to 6, but it can be adjusted depending on the particular learning problem. Calls of background predicates (declared with **prolog_predicate**) are simply delegated to the standard Prolog interpreter and they do not incur an increase in proof length. So only the calls of the target predicates defined in the hypothesis count.

The learning program will react to 'maybe' cautiously as follows:

(1) When proving a positive example, 'maybe' is treated as 'the example not covered'.

(2) When proving a negative example, 'maybe' is treated as not 'not covered', that is as covered.

A rationale behind this cautious interpretation of 'maybe' is that, among the possible complete hypotheses, computationally efficient ones are preferred. The answer 'maybe' at best indicates that the hypothesis is computationally inefficient, and at worst that it is incomplete.

```
% Interpreter for hypotheses
% prove( Goal, Hypo, Answ):
%    Answ = yes, if Goal derivable from Hypo in at most D steps
%    Answ = no, if Goal not derivable
%    Answ = maybe, if search terminated after D steps inconclusively

prove( Goal, Hypo, Answer) :-
  max_proof_length( D),
  prove( Goal, Hypo, D, RestD),
  (RestD >= 0, Answer = yes              % Proved
  ;
    RestD < 0, !, Answer = maybe         % Maybe, but it looks like inf. loop
  ).

prove( Goal, _ , no).                    % Otherwise Goal definitely cannot be proved

% prove( Goal, Hyp, MaxD, RestD):
%    MaxD allowed proof length, RestD 'remaining length' after proof;
%    Count only proof steps using Hyp

prove( G, H, D, D) :-
  D < 0, !.                              % Proof length overstepped

prove( [], _ , D, D) :- !.

prove( [G1 | Gs], Hypo, D0, D) :- !,
  prove( G1, Hypo, D0, D1),
  prove( Gs, Hypo, D1, D).

prove( G, _ , D, D) :-
  prolog_predicate( G),                  % Background predicate in Prolog?
  call( G).                              % Call of background predicate

prove( G, Hyp, D0, D) :-
  D0 =< 0, !, D is D0-1                   % Proof too long
  ;
  D1 is D0-1,                            % Remaining proof length
  member( Clause/Vars, Hyp),             % A clause in Hyp
  copy_term( Clause, [Head | Body] ),    % Rename variables in clause
  G = Head,                              % Match clause's head with goal
  prove( Body, Hyp, D1, D).              % Prove G using Clause
```

**Figure 21.3** A loop-avoiding interpreter for hypotheses.

The rest of the MINIHYPER program is given in Figure 21.4. The predicates in this program are as follows.

**refine( Clause, Vars, NewClause, NewVars)**
Refines a given clause **Clause** with variables **Vars** and produces a refined clause **NewClause** with new variables **NewVars**. The refined clause is obtained by matching two variables in **Vars** or by adding a new background literal to **Clause**. New literals are only added until user-defined maximal clause length is reached (defined by predicate **max_clause_length(MaxL)**).

**refine_hyp( Hyp, NewHyp)**

```
% Program MINIHYPER

% induce( Hyp):
%     induce a consistent and complete hypothesis Hyp by gradually
%     refining start hypotheses

induce( Hyp) :-
    iter_deep( Hyp, 0).                    % Iterative deepening starting with max. depth 0

iter_deep( Hyp, MaxD) :-
    write( 'MaxD = '), write( MaxD), nl,
    start_hyp( Hyp0),
    complete( Hyp0),                       % Hyp0 covers all positive examples
    depth_first( Hyp0, Hyp, MaxD)          % Depth-limited depth-first search
    ;
    NewMaxD is MaxD + 1,
    iter_deep( Hyp, NewMaxD).

% depth_first( Hyp0, Hyp, MaxD):
%     refine Hyp0 into consistent and complete Hyp in at most MaxD steps

depth_first( Hyp, Hyp, _) :-
    consistent( Hyp).

depth_first( Hyp0, Hyp, MaxD0) :-
    MaxD0 > 0,
    MaxD1 is MaxD0 − 1,
    refine_hyp( Hyp0, Hyp1),
    complete( Hyp1),                       % Hyp1 covers all positive examples
    depth_first( Hyp1, Hyp, MaxD1).

complete( Hyp) :-                          % Hyp covers all positive examples
    \+ (ex( E),                            % A positive example
        once( prove( E, Hyp, Answer)),     % Prove it with Hyp
        Answer \== yes).                   % Possibly not proved

consistent( Hyp) :-        % Hypothesis does not possibly cover any negative example
    not (nex( E),                          % A negative example
        once( prove( E, Hyp, Answer)),     % Prove it with Hyp
        Answer \== no).                    % Possibly provable

% refine_hyp( Hyp0, Hyp):
%     refine hypothesis Hyp0 into Hyp

refine_hyp( Hyp0, Hyp) :-
    conc( Clauses1, [Clause0/Vars0 | Clauses2], Hyp0),   % Choose Clause0 from Hyp0
    conc( Clauses1, [Clause/Vars | Clauses2], Hyp),      % New hypothesis
    refine( Clause0, Vars0, Clause, Vars).               % Refine the Clause

% refine( Clause, Args, NewClause, NewArgs):
%     refine Clause with arguments Args giving NewClause with NewArgs
%     Refine by unifying arguments

refine( Clause, Args, Clause, NewArgs) :-
    conc( Args1, [A | Args2], Args),       % Select a variable A
    member( A, Args2),                     % Match it with another one
    conc( Args1, Args2, NewArgs).
```

**Figure 21.4** MINIHYPER – a simple ILP program.

**Figure 21.4** *contd*

```
% Refine by adding a literal

refine( Clause, Args, NewClause, NewArgs)  :-
   length( Clause, L),
   max_clause_length( MaxL),
   L < MaxL,
   backliteral( Lit, Vars),              % Background knowledge literal
   conc( Clause, [Lit], NewClause);      % Add literal to body of clause
   conc( Args, Vars, NewArgs).           % Add literal's variables

% Default parameter settings

max_proof_length( 6).      % Max. proof length, counting calls to 'non-Prolog' pred.

max_clause_length( 3).                   % Max. number of literals in a clause
```

Refines a hypothesis **Hyp** producing **NewHyp** by non-deterministically choosing a clause in **Hyp** and refining that clause.

**induce( Hyp)**
Induces a consistent and complete hypothesis **Hyp** for the given learning problem, by iterative deepening search of the refinement graph starting with a start hypothesis (given by predicate **start_hyp(StartHyp)**).

**iter_deep( Hyp, MaxD)**
Finds a complete and consistent hypothesis **Hyp** by iterative deepening search, starting with depth-limit **MaxD** and increasing the limit until **Hyp** is found. Complete iterative-deepening search is carried out by **iter_deep(Hyp,0)**.

**depth_first( Hyp0, Hyp, MaxD)**
Performs depth-first search limited to depth **MaxD**, starting with a hypothesis **Hyp0**. If search succeeds within **MaxD** then **Hyp** is a complete and consistent hypothesis obtained in no more than **MaxD** successive refinements of **Hyp0**.

**complete( Hyp)**
True if **Hyp** covers all the given positive examples (under the 'cautious' interpretation of **Answer** in **prove/3**).

**consistent( Hyp)**
True if **Hyp** does not cover any of the given negative examples (under the cautious interpretation of **Answer** in **prove/3**).

To use MINIHYPER, the code in Figures 21.3 and 21.4 is to be loaded into Prolog, together with the frequently used predicates **member/2**, **conc/3**, **once/1** and **copy_term/2**, and a definition of the learning problem (such as the one in Figure 21.1). The parameters **max_proof_length** and **max_clause_length** can of course be redefined as appropriate for the particular learning problem.

For example, learning the predicate has_daughter(X) of Figure 21.1 looks as follows:

?- induce(H).

MaxD = 0
MaxD = 1
MaxD = 2
MaxD = 3
MaxD = 4

H = [[has_daughter(A),parent(A,B),female(B)]/[A,B]]

The increasing depth limits in iterative deepening search are displayed as MaxD = Limit. A consistent and complete hypothesis is found at refinement depth 4 (cf. Figure 21.2). If we add counters of hypotheses to the program, they would show the number of all generated hypotheses was 105, and 25 of these were refined. The resulting hypothesis H above, translated into the usual Prolog syntax is:

has_daughter(A) :- parent(A,B), female(B).

This corresponds to our target predicate.

# EXERCISE

**21.1** Experiment with MINIHYPER with modified sets of examples about has_daughter. How do these modifications affect the results?

Let us now consider a slightly more complicated learning exercise: learning the predecessor relation, using the same background knowledge as in Figure 21.1. This is more difficult because it requires a recursive definition, but this is exactly what ILP enables. We may define some positive and negative examples as follows:

ex( predecessor( pam, bob)).
ex( predecessor( pam, jim)).
ex( predecessor( tom, ann)).
ex( predecessor( tom, jim)).
ex( predecessor( tom, liz)).

nex( predecessor( liz, bob)).
nex( predecessor( pat, bob)).
nex( predecessor( pam, liz)).
nex( predecessor( liz, jim)).
nex( predecessor( liz, liz)).

'Guessing' that our target hypothesis comprises two clauses, we may define a start hypothesis as:

start_hyp( [ [predecessor(X1,Y1)] / [X1,Y1],
            [predecessor(X2,Y2)] / [X2,Y2] ] ).

The relevant background predicates are:

backliteral( parent(X,Y), [X,Y]).
backliteral( predecessor(X,Y), [X,Y]).
prolog_predicate( parent(X,Y)).

# EXERCISE

**21.2** Work out how many refinement steps are needed to obtain the target hypothesis from the start hypothesis above.

We may now try to run MINIHYPER with this problem specification, but it will turn out to be too inefficient. The search space up to the required refinement depth is large. In addition, our search procedure repeatedly generates equal hypotheses that are reachable by different refinement paths. This leads to repeated generation of large subspaces.

We will upgrade MINIHYPER to HYPER in the next section. However, we may just make the predecessor exercise possible for MINIHYPER with the following trick. To control the search complexity (not quite without 'guessing' the result of learning) we may constrain the background literals **parent(X,Y)** and **predecessor(X,Y)** to be called with the first argument X instantiated. This can be done by requiring that X be an atom by the following modified definition of background knowledge:

> **backliteral( [atom(X), parent(X,Y)], [X,Y]).**
> **backliteral( [atom(X), predecessor(X,Y)], [X,Y]).**
> **prolog_predicate( parent(X,Y)).**
> **prolog_predicate( atom(X)).**

This means that in a clause refinement a *pair* of literals is added to the clause, the first literal being **atom(X)**. In testing the completeness of such a hypothesis, the goals in the body will fail unless the argument X is instantiated (tested by **atom(X)**). This will render many useless hypotheses incomplete and they will immediately be discarded from search. The search task now becomes easier, although it may still take considerable time, in the order of minutes depending on the computer and implementation of Prolog. Eventually the goal **induce(H)** will result in:

> H = [[predecessor(A,B),[atom(A),parent(A,C)],[atom(C),predecessor(C,B)]] / [A,C,B],
>    [predecessor(D,E),[atom(D),parent(D,E)]]/[D,E]]

This is an expected definition of **predecessor.**

It is clear that MINIHYPER will soon run out of steam when faced with slightly more difficult learning problems. In the next section we will therefore make several improvements.

# EXERCISE

**21.3** Run MINIHYPER with the predecessor exercise and measure the execution time. How many hypotheses are generated, how many are refined? The 'guard' literal **atom(X)** in the background literals above is helpful, but there is a problem. At the moment that a literal pair like [**atom(X),parent(X,Y)**] is added, all the goals to it will fail (because X is a new variable not yet matched to anything else). Only after a further refinement, when X is matched to an existing variable, may such a literal succeed. So after a refinement with matching, such a hypothesis may become more *general*. This is different from the usual case when refinements produce more specific hypotheses. This anomaly in the case of **atom**(X) makes the refinement process non-monotonic: the hypotheses along a refinement path are not necessarily increasingly more specific. In this case an incomplete hypothesis may become complete after a refinement which violates the basic assumption on which the search of the hypothesis space is based! However, in this particular case the search still works. Find a sequence of refinements of *complete* hypotheses in the refinement graph that, despite this anomaly, leads to the target hypothesis.

## 21.2.4 Generalization, specialization and $\theta$-subsumption

As usual in machine learning, the space of candidate hypotheses in ILP is partially ordered by the relations 'more general than' or 'more specific than'. A hypothesis H1 is more general than H2 if H1 covers at least all the cases covered by H2. Our refinement operator corresponds to such a generality relation between hypotheses. This generality relation between hypotheses can be determined syntactically – refinements are just syntactic operations on hypotheses.

There is another generality relation frequently used in ILP, called $\theta$-subsumption. Although we will not be directly using $\theta$-subsumption in the programs in this chapter, we will introduce it here for completeness.

First let us define the notion of substitution. A *substitution* $\theta$ = {**Var1**/**Term1**, **Var2**/**Term2**, ...} is a mapping of variables **Var1**, **Var2**, etc. into terms **Term1**, **Term2**, etc. A substitution $\theta$ is applied to a clause $C$ by substituting the clause's variables by terms as specified in $\theta$. The application of substitution $\theta$ to clause $C$ is written as $C\theta$. For example:

$C$ = **has_daughter**(X) :- **parent**(X,Y), **female**(Y).
$\theta$ = { X/**tom**, Y/**liz**}
$C\theta$ = **has_daughter**(**tom**) :- **parent**(**tom**,**liz**), **female**(**liz**).

Now we can define $\theta$-subsumption. It is a generality relation between *clauses*. Clause $C_1$ $\theta$-subsumes clause $C_2$ if there is a substitution $\theta$ such that every literal in $C_1\theta$ occurs in $C_2$. For example, the clause

**parent**(X,Y).

$\theta$-subsumes the clause

**parent**(X,**liz**).

where $\theta$ = { Y/**liz** }. The clause

**has_daughter**(X) :- **parent**(X,Y).

$\theta$-subsumes the clause

**has_daughter**(X) :- **parent**(X,Y), **female**(Y).

where $\theta$ = {}. The notion of $\theta$-subsumption provides a way of syntactically checking the generality between clauses. If clause $C_1$ $\theta$-subsumes clause $C_2$ then

$C_2$ logically follows from $C_1$, so $C_1$ is more general than $C_2$. $C_1$, together with the rest of a hypothesis, enables the coverage of at least all the examples covered by $C_2$ and the rest of the hypothesis. There is a simple relation between our refinement operator and $\theta$-subsumption. The refinement operator takes a clause $C_1$ and produces clause $C_2$ so that $C_1$ $\theta$-subsumes $C_2$.

## EXERCISE

**21.4** Let there be the fact $C_0$:

> num(0).

Let clause $C_1$ be:

> num( s(X)) :- num( X).

and clause $C_2$ be:

> num( s(s(X))) :- num( X).

Is the hypothesis $\{C_0, C_1\}$ more general than hypothesis $\{C_0, C_2\}$? Does clause $C_1$ $\theta$-subsume clause $C_2$?

## 21.3 Program HYPER

We will now introduce the following improvements into the ILP program of Figure 21.4:

(1) To prevent useless refinements by inappropriate matches, the variables in clauses will be typed. Only the variables of the same type will be allowed to match in clause refinements.

(2) Handling structured terms: the refinement operator will also refine variables into terms.

(3) Distinction between input and output arguments of literals: the refinement operator will immediately take care of instantiating the input arguments.

(4) Best-first search of refinement graph instead of iterative deepening.

Let us discuss the details of these improvements.

### 21.3.1 Refinement operator

The refinement operator will be as in MINIHYPER, but enhanced with the types of arguments and distinction between input and output arguments. To introduce some syntactic conventions consider the problem definition for learning about the predicate **member(X,L)** (Figure 21.5). The clause

> backliteral( member(X,L), [L:list], [X:item] ).

```
% Problem definition for learning about member(X,L)

backliteral( member(X,L), [L:list], [X:item] ).   % Background literal

% Refinement of terms

term( list, [X|L], [ X:item, L:list]).
term( list, [], []).

prolog_predicate( fail).                           % No background predicate in Prolog

start_clause( [ member(X,L) ] / [ X:item, L:list] ).

% Positive and negative examples

ex( member( a, [a])).
ex( member( b, [a,b])).
ex( member( d, [a,b,c,d,e])).

nex( member( b, [a])).
nex( member( d, [a,b])).
nex( member( f, [a,b,c,d,e])).
```

**Figure 21.5**  Problem definition for learning list membership.

says that **member(X,L)** is a background literal (enabling recursive calls) where L is an input variable of type list, and X is an output variable of type item. The general form of defining background literals is:

**backliteral( Literal, InArgs, OutArgs)**

**InArgs** and **OutArgs** are the lists of input and output arguments respectively:

InArgs = [In1:TypeI1, In2:TypeI2, ...]
OutArgs = [Out1:TypeO1, Out2: TypeO2, ...]

where **In1, In2,** ... are the names of input variables, and **TypeI1, TypeI2,** ... are their types. Similarly the list **OutArgs** specifies the output variables and their types.

The meaning of input and output is as follows. If an argument of a literal is *input* then it is supposed to be instantiated whenever the literal is executed. In refining a clause, this means that when such a literal is added to the body of the clause, each of its input variables has to be immediately matched with some existing variable in the clause. In the example above, whenever the literal **member(X,L)** is added to a clause, the variable L has to be immediately matched with an existing variable (also of type 'list'). Such a matching should take care that the input argument is instantiated at the time the literal is executed. Output arguments *may* be matched with other variables later. So in clause refinement, the treatment of output variables is the same as the treatment of all the variables in MINIHYPER. However, the type restrictions prevent the matching of variables of different types. So X of type item cannot be matched with L of type list.

Possible refinements of variables into structured terms are defined by the predicate:

**term( Type, Term, Vars)**

This says that a variable of type **Type** in a clause can be replaced by a term **Term**. **Vars** is the list of variables and their types that occur in **Term**. So in Figure 21.5, the clauses

    **term( list, [X|L], [ X:item, L:list]).**
    **term( list, [], []).**

say that a variable of type **list** can be refined into [X|L] where X is of type **item** and L is of type **list**, or this variable is replaced by the constant [] (with no variables). We assume throughout that ':' has been introduced as an infix operator.

In Figure 21.5, the clause

    **start_clause( [ member(X,L) ] / [ X:item, L:list] ).**

declares the form of clauses in the start hypotheses in the refinement graph. Each start hypothesis is a list of up to some maximum number of (copies of) start clauses. The list of start hypotheses will be generated automatically. The maximum number of clauses in a hypothesis is defined by the predicate **max_clauses**. This can be set appropriately by the user according to specifics of the learning problem.

Let us now state the refinement operator in HYPER in accordance with the foregoing discussion. To refine a clause, perform one of the following:

(1) Match two variables in the clause, e.g. X1 = X2. Only variables of the same type can be matched.

(2) Refine a variable in the clause into a background term. Only terms defined by the predicate **term/3** may be used and the type of the variable and the type of the term have to match.

(3) Add a background literal to the clause. All of the literal's input arguments have to be matched (non-deterministically) with the existing variables (of the same type) in the clause.

As in MINIHYPER, to refine a hypothesis $H_0$, choose one of the clauses $C_0$ in $H_0$, refine clause $C_0$ into $C$, and obtain a new hypothesis $H$ by replacing $C_0$ in $H_0$ with $C$. Figure 21.6 shows a sequence of refinements when learning about **member**.

In the HYPER program, we will add to this some useful heuristics that often save complexity. First, if a clause is found in $H_0$ that alone covers a negative example, then only refinements arising from this clause are generated. The reason is that such a clause necessarily has to be refined before a consistent hypothesis is obtained. The second heuristic is that 'redundant' clauses (which contain several copies of the same literal) are discarded. And third, 'unsatisfiable clauses' are discarded. A clause is unsatisfiable if its body cannot be derived by predicate **prove** from the current hypothesis.

This refinement operator aims at producing *least specific specializations* (LSS). A specialization $H$ of a hypothesis $H_0$ is said to be *least specific* if there is no other specialization of $H_0$ more general than $H$. However, our refinement operator really only approximates LSS. This refinement operator does LSS under the constraint that the number of clauses in a hypothesis after the refinement stays the same. Without this restriction, an LSS operator would have to increase the number of clauses in a hypothesis. This would lead to a rather impractical refinement operator due to complexity. The number of clauses in a refined hypothesis could

```
member(X1,L1).
member(X2,L2).
        ↓        Refine term L1 = [X3|L3]
member(X1, [X3|L3]).
member(X2,L2).
        ↓        Match X1 = X3
member(X1, [X1|L3]).
member(X2,L2).
        ↓        Refine term L2 = [X4|L4]
member(X1, [X1|L3]).
member(X2, [X4|L4]).
        ↓        Add literal member (X5,L5) and match input L5 = L4
member(X1, [X1|L3]).
member(X2, [X4|L4])  :-  member (X5,L4).
        ↓        Match X2 = X5
member(X1, [X1|L3]).
member(X2, [X4|L4])  :-  member (X2,L4).
```

**Figure 21.6** The sequence of refinements from a start hypothesis to a target hypothesis. Notice the fourth step when a literal is added and its input argument immediately matched with an existing variable of the same type.

become very large. The limitation in our program to preserve the number of clauses in the hypothesis after its refinement is, however, not overly restrictive. If a solution requires a hypothesis with more clauses, then such a hypothesis can be generated from another start hypothesis that has a sufficient number of clauses.

## 21.3.2  Search

Search starts with a set of start hypotheses. This is the set of all possible bags of user-defined start clauses, up to some maximal number of clauses in a hypothesis. Multiple copies of a start clause typically appear in a start hypothesis. A typical start clause is something rather general and neutral, such as: **conc( L1, L2, L3)**. In search, the refinement graph is treated as a tree (if several paths lead to the same hypothesis, several copies of this hypothesis appear in the tree). The search starts with multiple start hypotheses that become the roots of disjoint search trees. Therefore strictly speaking the search space is a forest.

HYPER performs a best-first search using an evaluation function Cost(Hypothesis) that takes into account the size of a hypothesis as well as its accuracy with respect to the given examples. The cost of a hypothesis $H$ is defined heuristically as:

$$\text{Cost}(H) = w_1 * \text{Size}(H) + w_2 * \text{NegCover}(H)$$

where NegCover($H$) is the number of negative examples covered by $H$. The definition of '$H$ covers example $E$' is understood under the cautious interpretation of **Answer** in predicate **prove**. $w_1$ and $w_2$ are weights. The size of a hypothesis is defined as a weighted sum of the number of literals and number of variables in the hypothesis:

$$\text{Size}(H) = k_1 * \#\text{literals}(H) + k_2 * \#\text{variables}(H)$$

The actual code of HYPER in this chapter uses the following settings of the weights: $w_1 = 1$, $w_2 = 10$, $k_1 = 10$, $k_2 = 1$, which corresponds to:

$$\text{Cost}(H) = \#\text{variables}(H) + 10 * \#\text{literals}(H) + 10 * \text{NegCover}(H)$$

These settings are *ad hoc*, but their relative magnitudes are intuitively justified as follows. Variables in a hypothesis increase its complexity, so they should be taken into account. However, the literals increase the complexity more, hence they contribute to the cost with a greater weight. A covered negative example contributes to a hypothesis's cost as much as a literal. This corresponds to the intuition that an extra literal should at least prevent one negative example from being covered. Experiments show that, somewhat surprisingly, these weights can be varied considerably without critically affecting the search performance (see reference (Bratko 1999) at the end of this chapter).

## 21.3.3  Program HYPER

Figure 21.7 shows an implementation of the foregoing design as program HYPER. The main predicates in this program are:

**refine_hyp( Hyp0, Hyp)**
Refines hypothesis **Hyp0** into **Hyp** by refining one of the clauses in **Hyp0**.

**refine( Clause, Vars, NewClause, NewVars)**
Refines a given clause **Clause** with variables **Vars** and produces a refined clause **NewClause** with variables **NewVars**. The refined clause is obtained by matching two variables of the same type in **Vars**, or by refining a variable in **Vars** into a term, or by adding a new background literal to **Clause**.

**induce_hyp( Hyp)**
Induces a consistent and complete hypothesis **Hyp** for the given learning problem. It does best-first search by calling predicate **best_search/2**.

**best_search( Hyps, Hyp)**
Starts with a set of start hypotheses **Hyps**, generated by predicate **start_hyps/1**, and performs best-first search of the refinement forest until a consistent and complete hypothesis **Hyp** is found. It uses the cost of hypotheses as the evaluation function to guide the search. Each candidate hypothesis is combined with its cost into a term of the form **Cost:Hypothesis**. When the list of such terms is sorted (by merge sort), the hypotheses are sorted according to their increasing costs.

**prove( Goal, Hyp, Answer)**
Proof-length limited interpreter defined in Figure 21.3.

```
% Program HYPER (Hypothesis Refiner) for learning in logic

:- op( 500, xfx, :).

% induce( Hyp):
%    induce a consistent and complete hypothesis Hyp by gradually
%    refining start hypotheses

induce( Hyp) :-
    init_counts, !,                          % Initialize counters of hypotheses
    start_hyps( Hyps),                       % Get starting hypotheses
    best_search( Hyps, _:Hyp).               % Specialized best-first search

% best_search( CandidateHyps, FinalHypothesis)

best_search( [Hyp | Hyps], Hyp) :-
    show_counts,                             % Display counters of hypotheses
    Hyp = 0:H,                               % cost = 0: H doesn't cover any neg. examples
    complete(H).                             % H covers all positive examples

best_search( [C0:H0 | Hyps0], H) :-
    write('Refining hypo with cost '), write( C0),
    write(:), nl, show_hyp(H0), nl,
    all_refinements( H0, NewHs),             % All refinements of H0
    add_hyps( NewHs, Hyps0, Hyps), !,
    add1( refined),                          % Count refined hypos
    best_search( Hyps, H).

all_refinements( H0, Hyps) :-
    findall( C:H,
             ( refine_hyp(H0,H),             % H new hypothesis
               once(( add1( generated),      % Count generated hypos
                      complete(H),           % H covers all pos. exampl.
                      add1( complete),       % Count complete hypos
                      eval(H,C)              % C is cost of H
             )) ),
             Hyps).

% add_hyps( Hyps1, Hyps2, Hyps):
%    merge Hyps1 and Hyps2 in order of costs, giving Hyps

add_hyps( Hyps1, Hyps2, Hyps) :-
    mergesort( Hyps1, OrderedHyps1),
    merge( Hyps2, OrderedHyps1, Hyps).

complete( Hyp) :-                            % Hyp covers all positive examples
    \+ ( ex( P),                             % A positive example
         once( prove( P, Hyp, Answ)),        % Prove it with Hyp
         Answ \== yes).                       % Possibly not proved

% eval( Hypothesis, Cost):
%    Cost of Hypothesis = Size + 10 * # covered negative examples

eval( Hyp, Cost) :-
    size( Hyp, S),                           % Size of hypothesis
    covers_neg( Hyp, N),                     % Number of covered neg. examples
```

**Figure 21.7** The HYPER program. The procedure **prove/3** is as in Figure 21.3.

**Figure 21.7** *contd*

```
    ( N = 0, !, Cost is 0;                          % No covered neg. examples
      Cost is S + 10*N).

% size( Hyp, Size):
%    Size = k1*#literals + k2*#variables in hypothesis;
%    Settings of parameters: k1=10, k2=1

size( [], 0).

size( [Cs0/Vs0 | RestHyp], Size) :-
   length(Cs0, L0),
   length( Vs0, N0),
   size( RestHyp, SizeRest),
   Size is 10*L0 + N0 + SizeRest.

% covers_neg( H, N):
%    N is number of neg. examples possibly covered by H
%    Example possibly covered if prove/3 returns 'yes' or 'maybe'

covers_neg( Hyp, N) :-                              % Hyp covers N negative examples
   findall( 1, (nex(E), once(prove(E,Hyp,Answ)), Answ \== no), L),
   length( L, N).

% unsatisfiable( Clause, Hyp):
%    Clause can never be used in any proof, that is:
%    Clause's body cannot be proved from Hyp

unsatisfiable( [Head | Body], Hyp) :-
   once( prove( Body, Hyp, Answ)), Answ = no.

start_hyps( Hyps) :-                                % Set of starting hypotheses
   max_clauses( M),
      setof( C:H,
      (start_hyp(H,M), add1(generated),
       complete(H), add1(complete), eval(H,C)),
      Hyps).

% start_hyp( Hyp, MaxClauses):
%    A starting hypothesis with no more than MaxClauses

start_hyp( [], _).

start_hyp( [C | Cs], M) :-
   M > 0, M1 is M − 1,
   start_clause( C),                                % A user-defined start clause
   start_hyp( Cs, M1).

% refine_hyp( Hyp0, Hyp):
%    refine hypothesis Hyp0 into Hyp

refine_hyp( Hyp0, Hyp) :-
   choose_clause( Hyp0, Clause0/Vars0, Clauses1, Clauses2),   % Choose a clause
   conc( Clauses1, [Clause/Vars | Clauses2], Hyp),            % New hypothesis
   refine( Clause0, Vars0, Clause, Vars),                     % Refine chosen clause
   non_redundant( Clause),                          % No redundancy in Clause
   \+ unsatisfiable( Clause, Hyp).                  % Clause not unsatisfiable
```

►

**Figure 21.7** *contd*

```
choose_clause( Hyp, Clause, Clauses1, Clauses2) :-      % Choose Clause from Hyp
  conc( Clauses1, [Clause | Clauses2], Hyp),            % Choose a clause
  nex(E),                                               % A negative example E
  prove( E, [Clause], yes),                             % Clause itself covers E
  !                                                     % Clause must be refined
  ;
  conc( Clauses1, [Clause | Clauses2], Hyp).            % Otherwise choose any clause

% refine( Clause, Args, NewClause, NewArgs):
%    refine Clause with variables Args giving NewClause with NewArgs

% Refine by unifying arguments

refine( Clause, Args, Clause, NewArgs) :-
  conc( Args1, [A | Args2], Args),                      % Select a variable A
  member( A, Args2),                                    % Match it with another one
  conc( Args1, Args2, NewArgs).

% Refine a variable to a term

refine( Clause, Args0, Clause, Args) :-
  del( Var:Type, Args0, Args1),                         % Delete Var:Type from Args0
  term( Type, Var, Vars),                               % Var becomes term of type Type
  conc( Args1, Vars, Args).                             % Add variables in the new term

% Refine by adding a literal

refine( Clause, Args, NewClause, NewArgs) :-
  length( Clause, L),
  max_clause_length( MaxL),
  L < MaxL,
  backliteral( Lit, InArgs, RestArgs),                  % Background knowledge literal
  conc( Clause, [Lit], NewClause),                      % Add literal to body of clause
  connect_inputs( Args, InArgs),                        % Connect literal's inputs to other args.
  conc( Args, RestArgs, NewArgs).                       % Add rest of literal's arguments

% non_redundant( Clause): Clause has no obviously redundant literals

non_redundant( [_]).                                    % Single literal clause

non_redundant( [Lit1 | Lits]) :-
  \+ literal_member( Lit1, Lits),
  non_redundant( Lits).

literal_member( X, [X1 | Xs]) :-                        % X literally equal to member of list
  X == X1, !
  ;
  literal_member( X, Xs).

% show_hyp( Hypothesis):
%    Write out Hypothesis in readable form with variables names A, B, ...

show_hyp( []) :- nl.

show_hyp( [C/Vars | Cs]) :- nl,
  copy_term( C/Vars, C1/Vars1),
  name_vars( Vars1, ['A','B','C','D','E','F','G','H','I','J','K','L','M','N']),
```

**Figure 21.7** *contd*

```
    show_clause( C1),
    show_hyp( Cs), !.
  show_clause( [Head | Body]) :-
    write( Head),
    ( Body = []; write( ' :- ' ), nl ),
    write_body( Body).
  write_body( []) :-
    write('.'), !.
  write_body( [G | Gs]) :- !,
    tab( 2), write( G),
    ( Gs = [], !, write('.'), nl
      ;
      write(','), nl,
      write_body( Gs)
    ).
  name_vars( [], _).
  name_vars( [Name:Type | Xs], [Name | Names]) :-
    name_vars( Xs, Names).

% connect_inputs( Vars, Inputs):
%    Match each variable in list Inputs with a variable in list Vars

  connect_inputs( _ , []).
  connect_inputs( S, [X | Xs]) :-
    member( X, S),
    connect_inputs( S, Xs).

% merge( L1, L2, L3), all lists sorted

  merge( [], L, L) :- !.
  merge( L, [], L) :- !.
  merge( [X1|L1], [X2|L2], [X1|L3]) :-
    X1 @=< X2, !,              % X1 'lexicographically precedes' X2 (built-in predicate)
    merge( L1, [X2|L2], L3).
  merge( L1, [X2|L2], [X2|L3]) :-
    merge( L1, L2, L3).

% mergesort( L1, L2): sort L1 giving L2

  mergesort( [], []) :- !.
  mergesort( [X], [X]) :- !.
  mergesort( L, S) :-
    split( L, L1, L2),
    mergesort( L1, S1),
    mergesort( L2, S2),
    merge( S1, S2, S).

% split( L, L1, L2): split L into lists of approx. equal length

  split( [], [], []).
  split( [X], [X], []).
```

▶

**Figure 21.7** *contd*

```
split( [X1,X2 | L], [X1|L1], [X2|L2])  :-
    split( L, L1, L2).

% Counters of generated, complete and refined hypotheses

init_counts  :-
    retract( counter(_,_)), fail            % Delete old counters
    ;
    assert( counter( generated, 0)),        % Initialize counter 'generated'
    assert( counter( complete, 0)),         % Initialize counter 'complete'
    assert( counter( refined, 0)).          % Initialize counter 'refined'

add1( Counter)  :-
    retract( counter( Counter, N)), !, N1 is N+1,
    assert( counter( Counter, N1)).

show_counts  :-
    counter(generated, NG), counter( refined, NR), counter( complete, NC),
    nl, write( 'Hypotheses generated: '), write(NG),
    nl, write( 'Hypotheses refined: '), write(NR),
    ToBeRefined is NC - NR,
    nl, write( 'To be refined: '), write( ToBeRefined), nl.

% Parameter settings

max_proof_length( 6).     % Max. proof length, counting calls to preds. in hypothesis
max_clauses( 4).          % Max. number of clauses in hypothesis
max_clause_length( 5).    % Max. number of literals in a clause
```

eval( Hyp, Cost)
Evaluation function for hypotheses. Cost takes into account both the size of **Hyp** and the number of negative examples covered by **Hyp**. If **Hyp** does not cover any negative example then **Cost** = 0. In such a case **Hyp** is consistent and complete.

start_hyps( Hyps)
Generates a set **Hyps** of start hypotheses for search. Each start hypothesis is a list of up to **MaxClauses** start clauses. **MaxClauses** is defined by the user with the predicate **max_clauses**. Start clauses are defined by the user with the predicate **start_clause**.

show_hyp( Hyp)
Displays hypothesis **Hyp** in the usual Prolog format.

init_counts, show_counts, add1(Counter)
Initializes, displays and updates counters of hypotheses. Three types of hypotheses are counted separately: generated (the number of all generated hypotheses), complete (the number of generated hypotheses that cover all the positive examples), and refined (the number of all refined hypotheses).

start_clause( Clause)

User-defined start clauses, normally something very general like:

start_clause( [ member(X,L) ] / [ X:item, L:list] ).

max_proof_length(D), max_clauses(MaxClauses), max_clause_length(MaxLength)
Predicates defining the parameters: maximum proof length, maximum number of clauses in a hypothesis, and maximum number of literals in a clause. For example, for learning **member/2** or **conc/3**, MaxClauses=2 suffices. Default settings in the program of Figure 21.7 are:

max_proof_length(6).  max_clauses(4).  max_clause_length(5).

The program in Figure 21.7 also needs the frequently used predicates: **once/1, member/2, conc/3, del/3, length/2, copy_term/2**.

As an illustration let us execute HYPER on the problem of learning about the predicate **member(X,L)**. The problem definition in Figure 21.5 has to be loaded into Prolog in addition to HYPER. The question is:

?- induce(H), show_hyp(H).

During the execution HYPER keeps displaying the current counts of hypotheses (generated, refined and waiting-to-be-refined), and the hypothesis currently being refined. The final results are:

Hypotheses generated:  105
Hypotheses refined:  26
To be refined:  15

member(A,[A|B]).
member(C,[A|B]) :-
    member(C,B).

The induced hypothesis is as expected. Before this hypothesis was found, 105 hypotheses were generated all together, 26 of them were refined, and 15 of them were still in the list of candidates to be refined. The difference $105 - 26 - 15 = 64$ hypotheses were found to be incomplete and were therefore discarded immediately. The needed refinement depth for this learning problem is 5 (Figure 21.6). The total number of possible hypotheses in the refinement space defined by the (restricted) refinement operator in HYPER is several thousands. HYPER only searched a fraction of this (less than 10 percent). Experiments show that in more complex learning problems (list concatenation, path finding) this fraction is much smaller.

# EXERCISE

**21.5** Define the learning problem, according to the conventions in Figure 21.5, for learning predicate **conc(L1, L2, L3)** (list concatenation) and run HYPER with this definition. Work out the refinement depth of the target hypothesis and estimate the size of the refinement tree to this depth for a two-clause start hypothesis. Compare this size with the number of hypotheses generated and refined by HYPER.

## 21.3.4 Experiments with HYPER

HYPER with its refinement restrictions and heuristic search is much more effective than MINIHYPER. However, HYPER too is faced with the generally high complexity of learning in logic. It is interesting to explore where a boundary between feasible and infeasible learning problems lies for HYPER. The boundary can be considerably extended by cleverly designing the specification of the learning problem (background knowledge, input and output variables in background literals, set of examples). We will here look at some illustrative learning exercises with HYPER.

*Simultaneously learning two predicates odd(L) and even(L)*

HYPER can be applied without modification to *multi-predicate learning*, that is learning several predicates simultaneously where one predicate may be defined in terms of another one. This may even involve mutual recursion when the predicates learned call each other. We will here illustrate this by learning the predicates **odd(List)** and **even(List)** (true for lists of odd or even length respectively). Figure 21.8 shows a definition of this learning problem. The result of learning is:

**Hypotheses generated:** 85
**Hypotheses refined:**　16
**To be refined:**　　　29

```
even([ ]).
even([A,B|C]) :-
   even(C).
odd([A|B]) :-
   even(B).
```

```
% Inducing odd and even length for lists

backliteral( even( L), [ L:list], [ ]).
backliteral( odd( L), [ L:list], [ ]).

term( list, [X|L], [ X:item, L:list]).
term( list, [], [ ]).

prolog_predicate( fail).

start_clause([ odd( L) ] / [ L:list]).
start_clause([ even( L) ] / [ L:list]).

ex( even( [])).
ex( even( [a,b])).
ex( odd( [a])).
ex( odd( [b,c,d])).
ex( odd( [a,b,c,d,e])).
ex( even( [a,b,c,d])).

nex( even( [a])).
nex( even( [a,b,c])).
nex( odd( [])).
nex( odd( [a,b])).
nex( odd( [a,b,c,d])).
```

**Figure 21.8** Learning about odd-length and even-length lists simultaneously.

This corresponds to the target concept. However, HYPER found a definition that is not mutually recursive. By just requesting another solution (by typing a semi-colon as usual), HYPER continues the search and next finds a mutually recursive definition:

Hypotheses generated: 115
Hypotheses refined:    26
To be refined:         32

even([ ]).
odd([A|B]) :-
  even(B).
even([A|B]) :-
  odd(B).

The first, non-mutually recursive definition can be prevented by a more restrictive definition of term refinement. Such a more restrictive definition would allow lists to be refined to depth 1 only. This can be achieved by replacing type **list** with type **list(D)**, and changing the first clause about list refinement into:

term( list(D), [X|L], [ X:item, L:list(1)]) :- var(D).

This definition prevents a variable of type **list(1)** from being refined further. So terms like [X,Y|L] cannot be generated. Of course, the other clause about **term** and the **start_clause** predicate would have to be modified accordingly.

*Learning predicate path(StartNode, GoalNode, Path)*

Figure 21.9 shows a domain definition for learning the predicate **path** in a directed graph (specified by the background predicate **link/2**). The learning is accomplished smoothly, resulting in:

Hypotheses generated: 401
Hypotheses refined:    35
To be refined:         109

path(A,A,[A]).
path(A,C,[A,B|E]) :-
  link(A,B),
  path(B,C,[D|E]).

The last line of the induced definition may appear surprising, but it is in this context, in fact, equivalent to the expected **path(B,C,[B|E])** and requires one refinement step less. The fact that only 35 hypotheses were refined in this search may appear rather surprising in the view of the following facts. The refinement depth of the path hypothesis found above is 12. An estimate shows that the size of the refinement tree to this depth exceeds $10^{17}$ hypotheses! Only a tiny fraction of this is actually searched. This can be explained by the fact that the hypothesis completeness requirement constrains the search in this case particularly effectively.

*Learning insertion sort*

Figure 21.10 gives a definition for this learning problem. This definition invites debate because background knowledge is very specifically targeted at inducing

```
% Learning about path: path(StartNode,GoalNode,Path)

% A directed graph

link(a,b).
link(a,c).
link(b,c).
link(b,d).
link(d,e).

backliteral( link(X,Y), [ X:item], [ Y:item]).

backliteral( path(X,Y,L), [ X:item], [ Y:item, L:list]).

term( list, [X|L], [ X:item, L:list]).
term( list, [ ], [ ]).

prolog_predicate( link(X,Y)).

start_clause( [ path(X,Y,L)] / [X:item,Y:item,L:list] ).

% Examples

ex( path( a, a, [a])).
ex( path( b, b, [b])).
ex( path( e, e, [e])).
ex( path( f, f, [f])).
ex( path( a, c, [a,c])).
ex( path( b, e, [b,d,e])).
ex( path( a, e, [a,b,d,e])).

nex( path( a, a, [ ])).
nex( path( a, a, [b])).
nex( path( a, a, [b,b])).
nex( path( e, d, [e,d])).
nex( path( a, d, [a,b,c])).
nex( path( a, c, [a])).
nex( path( a, c, [a,c,a,c])).
nex( path( a, d, [a,d])).
```

**Figure 21.9** Learning about a path in a graph.

insertion sort. The obvious comment is that, when defining such background knowledge, we almost have to know the solution already. This, however, illustrates a typical problem with machine learning. To make the learning most effective, we have to present the learning program with as good a representation as possible, including background knowledge. This inevitably requires speculation by the user about possible solutions. In our case of sorting, the learning problem would be very hard without such a helpful definition of background knowledge. Even so this turns out to be the hardest problem among our experiments so far. The code of Figure 21.10 requires extra explanation of somewhat tricky details. In a goal sort(L1,L2), L1 is expected to be instantiated, whereas L2 is an output argument that gets instantiated after the execution of sort. To make sure that the induced sort will work with L2 uninstantiated, one of the examples is specified as:

   ex( [ sort( [c,a,b], L), L = [a,b,c] ] ).

```
% Learning sort

backliteral( sort( L, S), [L:list], [S:list]).
backliteral( insert_sorted( X, L1, L2), [X:item, L1:list], [L2:list]).

term( list, [X | L], [X:item, L:list]).
term( list, [], []).

prolog_predicate( insert_sorted( X, L0, L)).
prolog_predicate( X=Y).

start_clause( [sort(L1,L2)] / [L1:list, L2:list] ).

ex( sort( [], [])).
ex( sort( [a], [a])).
ex( [ sort( [c,a,b], L), L = [a,b,c] ] ).        % Uninstantiated 2nd arg. of sort!
ex( sort( [b,a,c], [a,b,c])).
ex( sort( [c,d,b,e,a], [a,b,c,d,e])).
ex( sort( [a,d,c,b], [a,b,c,d])).

nex( sort( [], [a])).
nex( sort( [a,b], [a])).
nex( sort( [a,c], [b,c])).
nex( sort( [b,a,d,c], [b,a,d,c])).
nex( sort( [a,c,b], [a,c,b])).
nex( sort( [], [b,c,d])).

insert_sorted( X, L, _ ) :-                      % Guarding clause: test instantiation of args.
  var(X), !, fail
  ;
  var( L), !, fail
  ;
  L = [Y|_], var(Y), !, fail.

insert_sorted( X, [], [X]) :- !.

insert_sorted( X, [Y | L], [X,Y | L]) :-
  X @< Y, !.                    % Term X lexicographically precedes term Y (built-in)

insert_sorted( X, [Y | L], [Y | L1]) :-
  insert_sorted( X, L, L1).
```

**Figure 21.10** Learning insertion sort.

This ensures that **sort** is called with L uninstantiated, so that **sort** has to *construct* (not only recognize!) the result L, and only then is this checked for correctness. Care is also needed when defining the background predicate **insert_sorted(X,L1,L2)**, to make sure that the arguments are instantiated as expected (e.g. X must not be a variable). The results are:

Hypotheses generated:  3708
Hypotheses refined:    284
To be refined:         448

```
sort([ ],[ ]).
sort([A|B],D)  :-
   sort(B,C),
   insert_sorted(A,C,D).
```

## Learning about the arch

This is similar to the relational learning example in Chapter 20, where examples are structures made of blocks (Figure 21.11), and there is a hierarchy among the types of blocks (ako(X,Y): Y is a kind of X; similar to Figure 20.6). The examples are triples of blocks. The first two blocks in a triple are the sides of an arch, the third block is the top. So one positive example is **arch(a1,b1,c1)** where **a1**, **b1** and **c1** are all rectangles, both **a1** and **b1** support **c1** and there is no touch relation between **a1** and **b1**. The blocks **a2**, **b2** and **c2** form a negative example (**nex(a2,b2,c2)**) because block **c2** is not supported by **a2** and **b2**. The blocks **a5**, **b5** and **c5** form another negative example because **c5** is not a 'stable polygon'. The arch learning problem is defined in Figure 21.12. The background predicates in this figure also include negation (\+) applied to **touch/2** and **support/2**. This background predicate is executed directly by Prolog as negation as failure, as usual. In comparison with Figure 20.4, there are a few additional negative examples to constrain the choice of consistent hypotheses. The result of learning is:

**Hypotheses generated:**  368
**Hypotheses refined:**    10
**To be refined:**         251

```
arch(A,B,C)  :-          .   % Arch consists of posts A and B, and top C
   support(B,C),              % B supports C
   \+ touch(A,B),            % A and B do not touch
   support(A,C),             % A supports C
   isa(C,stable_poly).       % C is a stable polygon
```

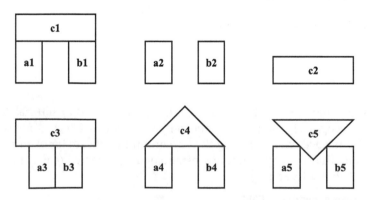

**Figure 21.11** A blocks world with two examples of an arch and three counter examples. The blocks **a1**, **b1** and **c1** form one example, the blocks **a4**, **b4** and **c4** form the other example. The blocks **a2**, **b2** and **c2** form one of the counter examples.

% Learning about arch

```
backliteral( isa(X,Y), [X:object], [ ])  :-
    member( Y, [polygon, convex_poly, stable_poly, unstable_poly, triangle,
                rectangle, trapezium, unstable_triangle, hexagon]).     % Any figure
backliteral( support(X,Y), [X:object, Y:object], [ ]).
backliteral( touch(X,Y), [X:object, Y:object], [ ]).
backliteral( \+ (G), [X:object,Y:object], [ ])  :-
    G = touch(X,Y); G = support(X,Y).

prolog_predicate( isa(X,Y)).
prolog_predicate( support(X,Y)).
prolog_predicate( touch(X,Y)).
prolog_predicate( \+ (G)).

ako( polygon, convex_poly).              % Convex polygon is a kind of polygon
ako( convex_poly, stable_poly).          % Stable polygon is a kind of convex polygon
ako( convex_poly, unstable_poly).        % Unstable polygon is a kind of convex poly.
ako( stable_poly, triangle).             % Triangle is a kind of stable polygon
ako( stable_poly, rectangle).            % Rectangle is a kind of stable polygon
ako( stable_poly, trapezium).            % Trapezium is a kind of stable polygon
ako( unstable_poly, unstable_triangle).  % Unstable triangle is a.k.o. unstable poly.
ako( unstable_poly, hexagon).            % Hexagon is a kind of unstable polygon

ako( rectangle, X)  :-
    member( X, [a1,a2,a3,a4,a5,b1,b2,b3,b4,b5,c1,c2,c3]).     % All rectangles

ako( triangle, c4).                      % Stable triangle
ako( unstable_triangle, c5).             % Triangle upside down

isa( Figure1, Figure2)  :-               % Figure1 is a Figure2
    ako( Figure2, Figure1).

isa( Fig0, Fig)  :-
    ako( Fig1, Fig0),
    isa( Fig1, Fig).

support(a1,c1).      support(b1,c1).
support(a3,c3).      support(b3,c3).        touch(a3,b3).
support(a4,c4).      support(b4,c4).
support(a5,c5).      support(b5,c5).

start_clause( [ arch(X,Y,Z)] / [X:object,Y:object,Z:object]).

ex( arch(a1,b1,c1)).
ex( arch(a4,b4,c4)).

nex( arch(a2,b2,c2)).
nex( arch(a3,b3,c3)).
nex( arch(a5,b5,c5)).
nex( arch(a1,b2,c1)).
nex( arch(a2,b1,c1)).
```

**Figure 21.12**  Learning the concept of arch.

# Summary

- Inductive logic programming (ILP) combines logic programming and machine learning.

- ILP is inductive learning using logic as the hypothesis language. ILP is also an approach to automatic programming from examples.

- In comparison with other approaches to machine learning: (1) ILP uses a more expressive hypothesis language that allows recursive definitions of hypotheses, (2) ILP allows more general form of background knowledge, (3) ILP generally has greater combinatorial complexity than attribute-value learning.

- In a *refinement graph over clauses*, nodes correspond to logic clauses, and arcs correspond to refinements between clauses.

- In a *refinement graph over hypotheses*, nodes correspond to sets of logic clauses (Prolog programs), and arcs to refinements between hypotheses.

- A refinement of a clause (a hypothesis) results in a more specific clause (hypothesis).

- A clause can be refined by: (1) matching two variables in the clause, or (2) substituting a variable with a term, or (3) adding a literal to the body of the clause.

- $\theta$-subsumption is a generality relation between clauses that can be determined syntactically based on substitution of variables.

- Program HYPER developed in this chapter induces Prolog programs from examples by searching a refinement graph over hypotheses.

- Concepts discussed in this chapter are:
  inductive logic programming
  clause refinement
  hypothesis refinement
  refinement graphs over clauses or hypotheses
  $\theta$-subsumption
  automatic programming from examples

## References and historical notes

The term inductive logic programming was introduced by Stephen Muggleton (1991). The early work in this area, before the term was actually introduced, includes Plotkin (1969), Shapiro (1983) and Sammut and Banerji (1986). The HYPER program of this chapter is based on Bratko (1999). The book by Lavrač and Džeroski (1994) is a good introduction to ILP; the book by De Raedt (2008) gives a good and more comprehensive up-to-date coverage of the field. Muggleton (1992) and De Raedt (1996) edited collections of papers on ILP. FOIL (Quinlan 1990), Progol (Muggleton 1995) and Aleph (Srinivasan 2007) are among the best-known publically available ILP systems. Bratko *et al.* (1998) review a number of applications of ILP.

Bratko, I. (1999) Refining complete hypotheses in ILP. *Inductive Logic Programming; Proc. ILP-99* (Džeroski, S. and Flach, P., eds). LNAI 1634, Springer.

Bratko, I., Muggleton, S. and Karalič, A. (1998) Applications of inductive logic programming. In: *Machine Learning and Data Mining: Methods and Applications* (Michalski, R.S., Bratko, I. and Kubat, M., eds). Chichester: Wiley.

De Raedt, L. (ed.) (1996) *Advances in Inductive Logic Programming*. Amsterdam: IOS Press.

De Raedt, L. (2008) *Logical and Relational Learning*. Springer.

Lavrač, N. and Džeroski, S. (1994) *Inductive Logic Programming: Techniques and Applications*. Chichester: Ellis Horwood.

Muggleton, S. (1991) Inductive logic programming. *New Generation Computing* **8**: 295–318.

Muggleton, S. (ed.) (1992) *Inductive Logic Programming*. London: Academic Press.

Muggleton, S. (1995) Inverse entailment and Progol. *New Generation Computing* **13**: 245–286.

Plotkin, G. (1969) A note on inductive generalisation. In: *Machine Intelligence 5* (Meltzer, B. and Michie, D, eds). Edinburgh University Press.

Quinlan, J.R. (1990) Learning logical definitions from relations. *Machine Learning* **5**: 239–266.

Sammut, C. and Banerji, R. (1986) Learning concepts by asking questions. In: *Machine Learning: An Artificial Intelligence Approach, Volume II*. (Michalski, R.S., Carbonell, J. and Mitchell, T., eds). San Mateo, CA: Morgan Kaufmann.

Shapiro, E. (1983) *Algorithmic Program Debugging*. Cambridge, MA: MIT Press.

Srinivasan, A. (2007) *The Aleph Manual*. Oxford University, Computer Laboratory (http://www.comlab.ox.ac.uk/activities/machinelearning/Aleph/aleph_toc.html).

# Chapter 22

# Qualitative Reasoning

Traditional quantitative modelling and simulation give precise numerical answers. For everyday use, such answers are often overly elaborate. When filling a bath tub, it is sufficient to know that the level of water will reach the top of the bath tub if the inflow of water is not stopped in time. We do not have to know the level precisely at any point in time. A common sense description of the tub-filling process is *qualitative*: 'The level of water will keep increasing and will eventually reach the top, which will cause overflow...'. This gives just a useful summary of a possibly large amount of quantitative information. Qualitative reasoning is an area in artificial intelligence concerned with the formalization of and algorithms for qualitative modelling and simulation of the physical world.

## 22.1  Common sense, qualitative reasoning and naive physics

### 22.1.1  Quantitative vs qualitative reasoning

Consider the bath tub in Figure 22.1. Assume the tub is initially empty, there is a constant flow from the tap, and that the drain is closed, so there is no outflow. What will happen?

To answer this question, the physicist's solution would be to write down a differential equation model of this system, and run this model by numerical simulation. The numerical simulation would produce a table with, say, 1593 rows, giving the exact values of the level of water at consecutive tabulated time points. The table would show, for example, that the level will reach the top of the tub at 62.53 cm in 159.3 seconds. For everyday use, such an elaborate answer is an overkill. A common sense answer that suffices for everyday purposes is rather something like this: 'The water level will keep increasing and will eventually reach the top. After this, water will overflow and cause a flood in the

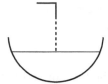

**Figure 22.1** Bath tub with some input flow and closed drain.

bathroom.' The physicist's answer was *quantitative*, giving precise numerical information. The common sense answer was *qualitative*, just giving a useful summary of the large amount of quantitative information.

The area of qualitative reasoning in artificial intelligence is concerned with the formalization of and algorithms for qualitative reasoning about the world, producing qualitative, non-numerical answers to questions that are typically answered numerically by 'proper' physics. To emphasize the contrast between the 'proper' physics as taught in schools, and the qualitative, common sense reasoning about the physical world, the qualitative physics is sometimes also called *naive physics*.

## 22.1.2 Qualitative abstraction of quantitative information

Qualitative reasoning is often viewed as an abstraction of quantitative reasoning. Accordingly, in qualitative reasoning some numerical details are discarded; instead, a rather simpler qualitative summary of these numerical details is retained. There are many ways of abstracting away from detailed numerical information. Table 22.1 gives some examples of quantitative statements and their qualitative abstractions, typical of qualitative reasoning in AI. The abstraction principles in these examples are discussed in the following paragraphs.

**Table 22.1** Examples of quantitative statements and their qualitative abstractions

| Quantitative statement | Qualitative statement |
|---|---|
| $Level(3.2 \text{ s}) = 2.6$ cm | $Level(t1) = zero .. top$ |
| $Level(3.2 \text{ s}) = 2.6$ cm | $Level(t1) = pos$ |
| $d/dt\ Level(3.2 \text{ s}) = 0.12$ m/s | $Level(t1)$ increasing |
| $Amount = Level * (Level + 5.7)$ | $M^+(Amount, Level)$ |

| Time | Amount |
|---|---|
| 0.0 | 0.00 |
| 0.1 | 0.02 |
| ... | ... |
| 159.3 | 62.53 |

$Amount(start .. end) = zero .. top/inc$

### Abstraction of numbers into symbolic values and intervals

Quantitative statement: *Level* at 3.2 s is 2.6 cm, formally written as:

Level(3.2 s) = 2.6 cm

Qualitative abstraction: *Level* at time $t1$ is between the bottom and the top of the bath tub. This may be written formally as:

Level(t1) = zero .. top

Notice here that 3.2 s has been replaced by a symbolic time point $t1$. So instead of giving exact time, this just says that there is a time point, referred to as $t1$, at which *Level* has the given qualitative value. Regarding this qualitative value, the whole set of numbers between 0 and 62.53 has been collapsed into a symbolic interval *zero .. top*. A further abstraction would be to disregard the top of the tub as an important value, and simply state: *Level* at time $t1$ is positive, written as:

Level(t1) = pos

### Abstraction of time derivatives into directions of change

Quantitative statement about the time derivative of *Level*:

$$\frac{d}{dt} Level(3.2 \text{ s}) = 0.12 \text{ m/s}$$

Qualitative abstraction: *Level* at time $t1$ is increasing.

### Abstraction of functions into monotonic relations

Quantitative statement: *Amount* = *Level* * (*Level* + 5.7)
A qualitative abstraction: For *Level* $\geq 0$, *Amount* is a monotonically increasing function of *Level*, written formally as: $M^+(Amount, Level)$. That is, if *Level* increases then *Amount* increases as well, and vice versa.

### Abstraction of increasing time sequences

A whole table giving the values of *Amount* at consecutive time points between time 0 and 159.3 s may be abstracted into a single qualitative statement: The value of *Amount* in the time interval between *start* and *end* is between *zero* and *full*, and is increasing. This can be formally written as:

Amount(start .. end) = zero .. full/inc

Qualitative reasoning is related to *qualitative modelling*. Numerical models are an abstraction of the real world. Qualitative models are often viewed as a further abstraction of numerical models. In this abstraction some quantitative information is abstracted away. For example, a quantitative model of the water flow in a river may state that the flow *Flow* depends on the level *Level* of water in the river in some complicated way which also takes into account the shape of the river bed. In a qualitative model this may be abstracted into a monotonically increasing relation:

$M^+(Level, Flow)$

This just says that the greater the level the greater the flow, without specifying this in any more concrete and detailed way. Obviously, it is much easier to design such coarse qualitative models than precise quantitative models.

## 22.1.3  Motivation and uses for qualitative modelling and reasoning

This section discusses advantages and disadvantages of qualitative modelling with respect to the traditional, quantitative modelling. Of course, there are many situations where a qualitative model, due to lack of precise numerical information, is not sufficient. However, there are also many situations in which a qualitative model has advantages.

First, qualitative modelling is easier than quantitative modelling. Precise relations among the variables in the system to be modelled may be hard or impossible to determine, but it is usually still possible to state some qualitative relations among the variables. Also, even if a complete quantitative model is known, such a model still requires the knowledge of all the, possibly many, numerical parameters in the model. For example, a numerical physiological model may require the precise electrical conductance of a neuron, its length and width, etc. These parameters may be hard or impossible to measure. Yet, to run such a numerical model, a numerical simulator will require the values of all these parameters to be specified by the user before the simulation can start. Usually the user will then make some guesses at these parameters and hope that they are not too far off their real values. But then the user will not know how far the simulation results are from the truth. The user will typically not know even if the obtained results are *qualitatively* correct. With a qualitative model, much of such guesswork can be avoided, and in the end the user will at least be sure about the qualitative correctness of the simulations. So, paradoxically, quantitative results, although more precise than qualitative results, are in greater danger of being incorrect and completely useless, because the accumulated error may become too gross. For example, in an ecological model, even without knowing the precise parameters of growth and mortality rates for the species in the model, a qualitative model may answer the question whether certain species will eventually become extinct, or possibly different species will interchange their temporal domination in time cycles. A qualitative simulator may find such an answer by finding all the possible qualitative behaviours that correspond to all possible combinations of the values of the parameters in the model.

Another point is that for many tasks, numerical precision is not required. Often it only obscures the essential properties of the system. Generic tasks in which qualitative modelling is often more appropriate include functional reasoning, diagnosis and structural synthesis. We will look at these tasks in the following paragraphs.

*Functional reasoning* is concerned with questions like: How does a device or a system work? For example:

How does the thermostat work?
How does a lock work?
How does a clock work?
How does the refrigerator attain its cooling function?
How does the heart achieve its blood-pumping function?

In all these cases we are interested in the (qualitative) mechanism of how the system works. If the numerical values of the parameters of the system change a little, usually the basic functional mechanism is still the same. All hearts are a little different, but the basic functional principle is always the same.

In a *diagnostic task* we are interested in defects that caused the observed abnormal behaviour of the system. Usually, we are only interested in those deviations from the normal state that caused a behaviour that is qualitatively different from normal.

The problem of *structural synthesis* is: Given some basic building blocks, find their combination which achieves a given function. For example, put the available components together to achieve the effect of cooling. In other words, invent the refrigerator from 'first principles'. The basic building blocks can be available technical components, or just the laws of physics, or materials with certain properties. In such design from first principles, the goal is to synthesize a structure capable of achieving some given function through some mechanism. In the early, most innovative stage of design, this mechanism is described qualitatively. Only at a later stage of design, when the structure is already known, does quantitative synthesis also become important.

The use of qualitative models requires qualitative reasoning. In the remainder of this chapter we will discuss and implement some ideas for qualitative modelling and reasoning. First, in Section 22.2, we look at static systems (where the quantities in the system do not change in time). In Section 22.3 we look at qualitative reasoning about dynamic systems, which also requires reasoning about changes in time. The mathematical basis for the approach in the latter section consists of *qualitative differential equations* (QDE), an abstraction of ordinary differential equations.

## 22.2 Qualitative reasoning about static systems

Consider simple electric circuits consisting of switches, bulbs and batteries (Figure 22.2). Switches can be open or closed (off or on), bulbs can be light or dark, blown or intact. We are interested in questions related to prediction, diagnosis or control. A diagnostic question about circuit 1 is: If the switch is on and the bulb is dark, what is the state of the bulb? Simple qualitative reasoning suffices to see that the bulb is blown.

A more interesting diagnostic question about circuit 2 is: Seeing that bulb 2 is light and bulb 3 dark, can we reliably conclude that bulb 3 is blown? Qualitative reasoning confirms that bulb 3 is necessarily blown. For bulb 2 to be light, there must be a non-zero current in bulb 2, and switch 2 must be on. If there is a non-zero current in bulb 2, there must be a non-zero voltage on bulb 2. This requires that switch 3 is off. The same non-zero voltage is on bulb 3. So with the same voltage, bulb 2 is light and bulb 3 is dark; therefore, bulb 3 must be blown.

In our qualitative model of these circuits, electric currents and voltages will just have qualitative values 'pos', 'zero' and 'neg'. The abstraction rule for converting a real number X into a qualitative value is:

if $X > 0$ then pos
if $X = 0$ then zero
if $X < 0$ then neg

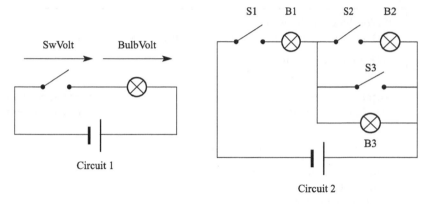

**Figure 22.2** Simple circuits made of switches, bulbs and batteries.

In standard, numerical models of electric circuits, we use some basic laws such as Kirchhoff's laws and Ohm's law. Kirchhoff's laws state that (1) the sum of all the voltages along any closed loop in a circuit is 0, and (2) the sum of all the currents into any vertex in a circuit is 0. To apply these laws in a qualitative model, we need a qualitative version of arithmetic summation. In our program, the usual arithmetic summation $X + Y = Z$ will be reduced to a qualitative summation, implemented as the predicate:

qsum( X, Y, Z)

The **qsum** relation can be defined simply by a set of facts. These state, for example, that the sum of two positive numbers is a positive number:

qsum( pos, pos, pos).

The sum of a positive and a negative number can be anything:

qsum( pos, neg, pos).
qsum( pos, neg, zero).
qsum( pos, neg, neg).

This summation is 'non-deterministic'. Due to lack of precise information, lost in the qualitative abstraction, we sometimes cannot tell what the actual result of summation is. This kind of non-determinism is rather typical of qualitative reasoning.

The program in Figure 22.3 specifies a qualitative model of our circuits, and carries out the qualitative reasoning about this model. A model of a circuit specifies the components of the circuit, and takes into account the connections among the components. The qualitative behaviour of the two types of component, switches and bulbs, is defined by the predicates:

switch( SwitchPosition, Voltage, Current)
bulb( BulbState, Lightness, Voltage, Current)

Their qualitative behaviours are simple and can be stated by Prolog facts. For example, an open switch has zero current and the voltage can be anything:

switch( off, AnyVoltage, zero).

```
% Modelling simple electric circuits
% Qualitative values of voltages and currents are: neg, zero, pos

% Definition of switch
% switch( SwitchPosition, Voltage, Current)

switch( on, zero, AnyCurrent).                    % Switch on: zero voltage
switch( off, AnyVoltage, zero).                   % Switch off: zero current

% Definition of bulb
% bulb( BulbState, Lightness, Voltage, Current)

bulb( blown, dark, AnyVoltage, zero).
bulb( ok, light, pos, pos).
bulb( ok, light, neg, neg).
bulb( ok, dark, zero, zero).

% A simple circuit consisting of a bulb, switch and battery

circuit1( SwitchPos, BulbState, Lightness)  :-
    switch( SwitchPos, SwVolt, Curr),
    bulb( BulbState, Lightness, BulbVolt, Curr),
    qsum( SwVolt, BulbVolt, pos).                 % Battery voltage = pos

% A more interesting circuit made of a battery, three bulbs and
% three switches

circuit2( Sw1, Sw2, Sw3, B1, B2, B3, L1, L2, L3)  :-
    switch( Sw1, VSw1, C1),
    bulb( B1, L1, VB1, C1),
    switch( Sw2, VSw2, C2),
    bulb( B2, L2, VB2, C2),
    qsum( VSw2, VB2, V3),
    switch( Sw3, V3, CSw3),
    bulb( B3, L3, V3, CB3),
    qsum( VSw1, VB1, V1),
    qsum( V1, V3, pos),
    qsum( CSw3, CB3, C3),
    qsum( C2, C3, C1).

% qsum( Q1, Q2, Q3):
%     Q3 = Q1 + Q2, qualitative sum over domain [pos,zero,neg]

qsum( pos, pos, pos).          qsum( pos, zero, pos).      qsum( pos, neg, pos).
qsum( pos, neg, zero).         qsum( pos, neg, neg).       qsum( zero, pos, pos).
qsum( zero, zero, zero).       qsum( zero, neg, neg).      qsum( neg, pos, pos).
qsum( neg, pos, zero).         qsum( neg, pos, neg).       qsum( neg, zero, neg).
qsum( neg, neg, neg).
```

**Figure 22.3** Qualitative modelling program for simple circuits.

A blown bulb is dark, has no current and any voltage:

    bulb( blown, dark, AnyVoltage, zero).

An intact bulb is light unless both the voltage and current in the bulb are zero. Here we are assuming that any non-zero current is sufficiently large to make a bulb light.

The voltage and the current are either both zero, both positive, or both negative. Notice that this is a qualitative abstraction of Ohm's law:

> **Voltage = Resistance * Current**

Since **Resistance** is positive, **Voltage** and **Current** must have the same sign and therefore the same qualitative value.

Once our components have been defined, it is easy to define a whole circuit. A particular circuit is defined by a predicate, such as:

> **circuit1( SwPos, BulbState, Lightness)**

Here the switch position, the state of the bulb and the lightness have been assumed to be the important properties of the circuit, hence they were made the arguments of **circuit1**. Other quantities in the circuit, such as the current in the bulb, are not visible from the outside of predicate **circuit1**. The model of the circuit consists of stating that these arguments have to obey:

(1) The laws of the bulb

(2) The laws of the switch

(3) The (qualitative) Kirchhoff's law: switch voltage + bulb voltage = battery voltage.

The physical connections between the components are also reflected in that the switch current is equal to the bulb current.

The model of circuit 2, although more complex, is constructed in a similar way.

Here are some usual types of questions that the program of Figure 22.3 answers easily.

### Prediction-type question

What will be the observable result of some 'input' to the system (switch positions), given some functional state of the system (bulbs OK or blown)? For example, what happens if we turn on all the switches, and all the bulbs are OK?

```
?- circuit2(on,on,on,ok,ok,ok,L1,L2,L3).
L1 = light
L2 = dark
L3 = dark
```

### Diagnostic-type question

Given the inputs to the system and some observed manifestations, what is the system's functional state: normal or malfunctioning; what is the failure? For example, if bulb 1 is light, bulb 3 is dark, and switch 3 is off, what are the states of the bulbs?

```
?- circuit2( _, _, off, B1, B2, B3, light, _, dark).
B1 = ok
B2 = ok
B3 = blown
```

### Control-type question

What should be the control input to achieve the desired output? For example, what should be the positions of the switches to make bulb 3 light, assuming all the bulbs are intact?

```
?- circuit2( SwPos1, SwPos2, SwPos3, ok, ok, ok, _, _, light).
SwPos1 = on
SwPos2 = on
SwPos3 = off;

SwPos1 = on
SwPos2 = off
SwPos3 = off
```

## EXERCISES

**22.1** Define the qualitative multiplication relation over signs:

    qmult( A, B, C)

where C = A*B, and A, B and C can be qualitative values pos, zero or neg.

**22.2** Define qualitative models of a resistor and a diode:

    resistor( Voltage, Current)
    diode( Voltage, Current)

The diode only allows current in one direction. In a resistor, the signs of **Voltage** and **Current** are the same. Define qualitative models of some circuits with resistors, diodes and batteries.

## 22.3 Qualitative reasoning about dynamic systems

In this section we consider an approach to qualitative reasoning about dynamic systems. The approach considered here is based on the so-called qualitative differential equations (QDE). QDEs can be viewed as a qualitative abstraction of ordinary differential equations. To develop the intuition and basic ideas of this approach, let us consider an example of filling the bath tub with an open drain (Figure 22.4). To begin with we will carry out informally some qualitative reasoning about this system. The variables we observe are: the flow into the tub, the flow out, the amount of water in the tub, and the level of water.

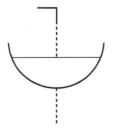

**Figure 22.4** Bath tub with open drain and constant input flow.

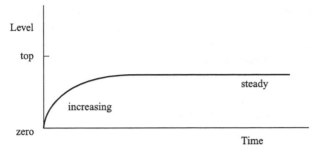

**Figure 22.5** The behaviour of water level in time.

Let the process start with an empty bath tub. The outflow at the drain depends on the level of water: the higher the level, the greater the outflow. The inflow is constant. Net flow is the difference between the inflow and outflow. Initially the level is low, the inflow is greater than the outflow, and therefore the amount of water in the tub is increasing. Therefore the level is also increasing, which causes the outflow to increase. So at some time, the outflow may become equal to the inflow. According to a precise quantitative analysis, this only happens after a 'very long' time (infinite). When this happens, both flows are at equilibrium and the level of water becomes steady. The (quantitative) time behaviour of the water level looks like the one in Figure 22.5.

The *quantitative* behaviour of the level in Figure 22.5 can be simplified into a *qualitative* behaviour as follows. Initially, the level is zero and increasing. We choose to represent this as:

**Level = zero/inc**

In the subsequent time interval, the level is between zero and top, and it is increasing. We do not qualitatively distinguish between the exact numerical values between zero and top. We take that these values are all sufficiently similar and therefore qualitatively the same. So we write:

**Level = zero..top/inc**

The next qualitative change occurs when the level stops increasing and becomes steady:

**Level = zero..top/std**

This is the final qualitative state of the water level.

We will now formalize in more detail the qualitative reasoning indicated above. First we define a *qualitative model* of the bath tub system. The variables in the system are:

**Level** = level of water
**Amount** = amount of water
**Inflow** = input flow
**Outflow** = output flow
**Netflow** = net flow (Netflow = Inflow − Outflow)

For each variable we specify its distinguished values, called *landmarks*. Typically we include minus infinity (**minf**), zero and infinity (**inf**) among the landmarks. For

**Level**, the top of the bath tub is also an important value, so we choose also to include it among the landmarks. On the other hand, as the level is always non-negative, there is no need for including **minf** among the landmarks for **Level**. The landmarks are always ordered. So for **Level** we have the following ordered set of landmarks:

   **zero < top < inf**

For **Amount** we may choose these landmarks:

   **zero < full < inf**

Now we define the dependences among the variables in the model. These dependences are called *constraints* because they constrain the values of the variables.

We will use some types of constraints typical of qualitative reasoning. One such constraint states the dependence between **Amount** and **Level**: the greater the amount of water, the greater the level. We write:

   $M_0^+($ **Amount, Level**)

In general the notation $M^+(X,Y)$ means that Y is a monotonically increasing function of X: whenever X increases, Y also increases and vice versa. $M_0^+(X,Y)$ means that Y is a monotonically increasing function of Y such that $Y(0) = 0$. We say that (0,0) is a pair of *corresponding values* for this $M^+$ relationship. Another pair of corresponding values for this $M^+$ relationship is (full,top). Notice that $M^+(X,Y)$ is equivalent to $M^+(Y,X)$.

The monotonically increasing constraint is very convenient and often greatly alleviates the definition of models. By stating $M_0^+($**Amount,Level**), we just say that the level will rise whenever the amount increases, and the level will drop whenever the amount decreases. Notice that this is true for every container of *any* shape. If instead we wanted to state the precise *quantitative* functional relation

   **Amount = f(Level)**

this would depend on the shape of the container, illustrated in Figure 22.6. Qualitatively, however, the relation between the level and the amount is always monotonically increasing, regardless of the shape of the container. So to define a qualitative model of the bath tub, we do not have to study the intricacies of the shape. This often greatly simplifies the modelling task. Our simplified, qualitative model still suffices for reliably deriving some important properties of the modelled system. For example, if there is a flow into a container with no outflow, the amount will be increasing and therefore the level will be increasing as well. So there will be some time point when the level reaches the top and water starts overflowing. All (possibly complicated) containers share this qualitative behaviour.

Similarly, the precise relation between **Outflow** and **Level** may be complicated. Qualitatively, we may simply state that it is monotonically increasing.

The types of constraints we will be using in our qualitative models are shown in Table 22.2. In the bath tub model we have the following constraints:

   $M_0^+($ **Amount, Level**)
   $M_0^+($ **Level, Outflow**)
   **sum( Outflow, Netflow, Inflow)**                    % Netflow = Inflow−Outflow
   **deriv( Amount, Netflow)**
   **Inflow = constant = inflow/std**

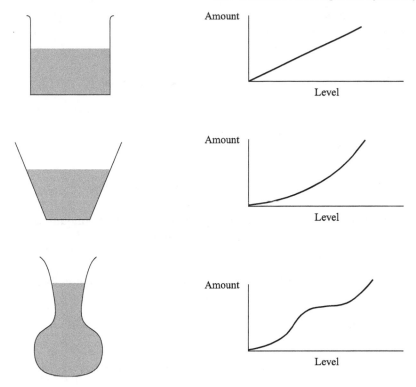

**Figure 22.6** The precise relation between the amount and the level depends on the shape of a container. However, the amount is always a monotonically increasing function of the level.

**Table 22.2** Types of qualitative constraints.

| | |
|---|---|
| $M^+(X,Y)$ | Y is a monotonically increasing function of X |
| $M^-(X,Y)$ | Y is a monotonically decreasing function of X |
| sum(X,Y,Z) | $Z = X+Y$ |
| minus(X,Y) | $Y = -X$ |
| mult(X,Y,Z) | $Z = X*Y$ |
| deriv(X,Y) | $Y = dX/dt$   (Y is time derivative of X) |

As usual, variable names start with capital letters, and constants start with lower case letters.

Sometimes it helps to illustrate the constraints by a graph. The nodes of the graph correspond to the variables in the model; the connections among the nodes correspond to the constraints. Figure 22.7 shows our bath tub model represented by such a graph.

Now let us carry out some qualitative simulation reasoning using the model in Figure 22.7. Without causing ambiguity, we will use a somewhat liberal notation. Writing **Amount**=**zero** will mean: the qualitative value of **Amount** is zero. Writing

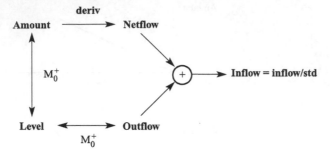

**Figure 22.7** A graphical representation of the bath tub model.

**Amount=zero/inc** will mean: the qualitative value of **Amount** is zero and it is increasing. We start with the initial condition:

Amount = zero

Due to the constraint $M_0^+$ between **Amount** and **Level** (Figure 22.7), we infer:

Level = zero

This is propagated through the other $M_0^+$ constraint to infer:

Outflow = zero

Now the constraint **Outflow + Netflow = Inflow** instantiates to:

zero + Netflow = inflow

This yields: **Netflow = inflow**

Now consider the **deriv** constraint between **Amount** and **Netflow**, that is **Netflow** is equal to the time derivative of **Amount**. Since **Netflow = inflow > zero**, we infer that **Amount** must be increasing:

Amount = zero/inc

Propagating this through the $M_0^+$ constraints we have:

Level = zero/inc
Outflow = zero/inc

Now the constraint **Outflow + Netflow = Inflow** instantiates to:

zero/inc + Netflow = inflow/std

To satisfy this constraint, **Netflow** has to be:

Netflow = inflow/dec

Thus we have the complete initial qualitative state of the bath tub:

Amount = zero/inc
Level = zero/inc
Outflow = zero/inc
Netflow = inflow/dec

Now let us consider the possible transitions to a next qualitative state of the system. We assume that all the variables behave smoothly: their values change continuously in time, and their time derivatives are continuous. Consequently, a variable that is negative cannot become positive without first becoming zero. So a negative quantity can in the next time point either stay negative or become zero. Similarly, a variable that is increasing can either stay increasing or become steady. But it cannot instantaneously become decreasing, it has to become steady first. In other words, if a variable's direction of change is 'inc' then it can either stay 'inc' or become 'std', but not 'dec'. Another constraint on possible transitions is that a changing variable cannot spend more than an instant at a landmark value. Therefore a transition from 'zero/inc' to 'zero/inc' is not possible.

The smoothness assumption is obviously reasonable in our bath tub system, at least when the level is between zero and top, so there is no water overflow. Given the smoothness constraint, the next qualitative state of **Level** is:

Level = zero..top/inc

This value, and the constraints in the model of Figure 22.7 determine the qualitative states of the other variables. So the next qualitative state of the system is:

Level = zero..top/inc
Amount = zero..full/inc
Outflow = zero..inflow/inc
Netflow = zero..inflow/dec

What are the next possible qualitative states of **Level**? There are now four possibilities:

$$Level = \begin{cases} zero..top/inc \\ zero..top/std \\ top/std \\ top/inc \end{cases}$$

In the first case **Level**'s qualitative value is the same as in the previous state. Then our model determines that the other variables also stay unchanged. So the previous qualitative state description still holds, and there is no need to introduce a new qualitative state in this case. Notice that, as in this case, a qualitative state may last for a whole time interval.

The remaining three possible transitions correspond to three alternative behaviours of the system:

(1) **Level** stops increasing and becomes steady before it has reached the top. The constraints in Figure 22.7 dictate that the other variables also become steady and there is no change from now on. So the final state of the simulation in this case is:

Level = zero..top/std
Amount = zero..full/std
Outflow = inflow/std
Netflow = zero/std

Strictly, this steady state is only reached after infinite time, but that makes no difference in our qualitative description, because it does not take into account the durations of time intervals.

(2) **Level** becomes steady exactly at the moment when it reaches the top. Although this is theoretically possible, in reality this is an unlikely coincidence. Then all

the other variables become steady, and this is again a final state of the simulation, similar to case 1.

(3) The level reaches the top and is at this moment still increasing. Then water starts flowing over the top and our model of Figure 22.7 no longer holds. At this point there is a discontinuous change into a new 'operating region'. A new model would now be needed for this new operating region. Discontinuous transition between operating regions would also require a special treatment. This will not be done here. Exiting the operating region of the model in Figure 22.7 will therefore be regarded here as another final state.

This example shows that a qualitative model may exhibit several qualitative behaviours. A real bath tub with its concrete physical parameters and a constant inflow will, of course, only behave in one of these three ways. Our qualitative model is a rather gross abstraction of reality. All the numerical information about the bath tub has been abstracted away. Therefore the qualitative simulation could not decide which of the three qualitative behaviours would correspond to an actual tub. Instead, the qualitative simulation in our case quite sensibly states that three alternatives are possible.

This section demonstrated some basic ideas for qualitative modelling and simulation. These ideas are developed into a qualitative simulation program in the next section.

## 22.4  A qualitative simulation program

Figure 22.8 shows a qualitative simulation program that executes QDE models along the lines of the previous section. The following paragraphs describe details of this implementation.

```
% An interpreter for Qualitative Differential Equations

:- op( 100, xfx, ..).
:- op( 500, xfx, :).

% landmarks( Domain, [ Land1, Land2, ...]
%    Land1, Land2 etc. are landmarks for domain Domain
%    This is part of qualitative model definition, user-defined

% correspond( Constraint):
%    Constraint specifies corresponding values for a type of constr.

correspond( sum( Dom1:zero, Dom2:zero, Dom3:zero)).

correspond( sum( Dom1:L, Dom2:zero, Dom1:L)) :-
    qmag( Dom1:L), L \== zero, not (L = _.._).       % L is nonzero landmark in Dom1

correspond( sum( Dom1:zero, Dom2:L, Dom2:L)) :-
    qmag( Dom2:L), L \== zero, \+ (L = _.._).        % L is nonzero landmark in Dom2
```

**Figure 22.8** A simulation program for qualitative differential equations. The program uses the usual list predicates **member/2** and **conc/3**.

**Figure 22.8** *contd*

```
correspond( sum( V1, V2, V3)) :-
  correspond( V1, V2, V3).                    % User-defined corr. values

% qmag( Domain:QualMagnitude)

qmag( Domain:Qm) :-
  landmarks( Domain, Lands),
  qmag( Lands, Qm).

qmag( Lands, L) :-
  member( L, Lands),
  L \== minf, L \== inf.                      % A finite landmark

qmag( Lands, L1..L2) :-                       % Interval
  conc( _, [L1,L2 | _], Lands).               % Two adjacent landmarks

% relative_qmag( Domain1:QM, Domain2:Landmark, Sign):
%    Sign is the sign of the difference between QM and Landmark
%    if QM < Landmark then Sign = neg, etc.

relative_qmag( Domain:Ma..Mb, Domain:Land, Sign) :- !,
  landmarks( Domain, Lands),
  ( compare_lands( Ma, Land, Lands, neg), Sign = neg, !
    ;
    Sign = pos
  ).

relative_qmag( Domain:M1, Domain:M2, Sign) :-
  landmarks( Domain, Lands),
  compare_lands( M1, M2, Lands, Sign), !.

% qdir( Qdir, Sign):
%    Qdir is qualitative direction of change with sign Sign

qdir( dec, neg).
qdir( std, zero).
qdir( inc, pos).

% Laws of qualitative summation
% qsum( Q1, Q2, Q3):
%    Q3 = Q1 + Q2, qualitative sum over domain [pos,zero,neg]

qsum( pos, pos, pos).
qsum( pos, zero, pos).
qsum( pos, neg, pos).
qsum( pos, neg, zero).
qsum( pos, neg, neg).
qsum( zero, pos, pos).
qsum( zero, zero, zero).
qsum( zero, neg, neg).
qsum( neg, pos, pos).
qsum( neg, pos, zero).
qsum( neg, pos, neg).
qsum( neg, zero, neg).
qsum( neg, neg, neg).
```

**Figure 22.8** *contd*

```
% qdirsum( D1, D2, D3):
%    qualitative sum over directions of change

qdirsum( D1, D2, D3)  :-
  qdir( D1, Q1), qdir( D2, Q2), qdir( D3, Q3),
  qsum( Q1, Q2, Q3).

% sum( QV1, QV2, QV3):
%    QV1 = QV2 + QV3,
%    qualitative sum over qualitative values of form Domain:Qmag/Dir
%    When called, this predicate assumes that the
%    domains of all three arguments are instantiated

sum( D1:QM1/Dir1, D2:QM2/Dir2, D3:QM3/Dir3)  :-
  qdirsum( Dir1, Dir2, Dir3),             % Directions of change: Dir1 + Dir2 = Dir3
  qmag( D1:QM1), qmag( D2:QM2), qmag( D3:QM3),
        % QM1+QM2=QM3 must be consistent with all corresponding values:
  \+ (
    correspond( sum( D1:V1, D2:V2, D3:V3)),      % V1 + V2 = V3
    relative_qmag( D1:QM1, D1:V1, Sign1),
    relative_qmag( D2:QM2, D2:V2, Sign2),
    relative_qmag( D3:QM3, D3:V3, Sign3),
    \+ qsum( Sign1, Sign2, Sign3) ).

% mplus( X, Y):
%    Y is a monotonically increasing function of X

mplus( D1:QM1/Dir, D2:QM2/Dir)  :-                % Equal directions of change
  qmag( D1:QM1), qmag( D2:QM2),
        % QM1, QM2 consistent with all corresponding values between D1, D2:
  \+ ( correspond( D1:V1, D2:V2),
       relative_qmag( D1:QM1, D1:V1, Sign1),
       relative_qmag( D2:QM2, D2:V2, Sign2),
       Sign1 \== Sign2 ).

% deriv( Var1, Var2):
%    time derivative of Var1 is qualitatively equal Var2

deriv( Dom1:Qmag1/Dir1, Dom2:Qmag2/Dir2)  :-
  qdir( Dir1, Sign1),
  qmag( Dom2:Qmag2),
  relative_qmag( Dom2:Qmag2, Dom2:zero, Sign2),    % Sign2 = sign of Qmag2
  Sign1 = Sign2.

% transition( Domain:Qmag1/Dir1, Domain:Qmag2/Dir2):
%    Variable state transitions between 'close' time points

transition( Dom:L1..L2/std, Dom:L1..L2/Dir2)  :-
  qdir( Dir2, AnySign).

transition( Dom:L1..L2/inc, Dom:L1..L2/inc).

transition( Dom:L1..L2/inc, Dom:L1..L2/std).

transition( Dom:L1..L2/inc, Dom:L2/inc)  :-
  L2 \== inf.
```

**Figure 22.8** *contd*

```
transition( Dom:L1..L2/inc, Dom:L2/std) :-
  L2 \== inf.

transition( Dom:L1..L2/dec, Dom:L1..L2/dec).

transition( Dom:L1..L2/dec, Dom:L1..L2/std).

transition( Dom:L1..L2/dec, Dom:L1/dec) :-
  L1 \== minf.

transition( Dom:L1..L2/dec, Dom:L1/std) :-
  L1 \== minf.

transition( Dom:L1/std, Dom:L1/std) :-
  L1 \== A..B.                                    % L1 not an interval

transition( Dom:L1/std, Dom:L1..L2/inc) :-
  qmag( Dom:L1..L2).

transition( Dom:L1/std, Dom:L0..L1/dec) :-
  qmag( Dom:L0..L1).

transition( Dom:L1/inc, Dom:L1..L2/inc) :-
  qmag( Dom:L1..L2).

transition( Dom:L1/dec, Dom:L0..L1/dec) :-
  qmag( Dom:L0..L1).

% system_trans( State1, State2):
%    System state transition;
%    system state is a list of variable values

system_trans( [], []).

system_trans( [Val1 | Vals1], [Val2 | Vals2]) :-
  transition( Val1, Val2),
  system_trans( Vals1, Vals2).

% legal_trans( State1, State2):
%    possible transition between states according to model

legal_trans( State1, State2) :-
  system_trans( State1, State2),
  State1 \== State2,                   % Qualitatively different next state
  legalstate( State2).                 % Legal according to model

% simulate( SystemStates, MaxLength):
%    SystemStates is a sequence of states of simulated system
%    not longer than MaxLength

simulate( [State], MaxLength) :-
  ( MaxLength = 1                      % Max length reached
  ;
    \+ legal_trans( State, _)          % No legal next state
  ) , !.
```

**Figure 22.8** *contd*

```
simulate( [State1,State2 | Rest], MaxLength) :-
  MaxLength > 1, NewMaxL is MaxLength − 1,
  legal_trans( State1, State2),
  simulate( [State2 | Rest], NewMaxL).

% simulate( InitialState, QualBehaviour, MaxLength)

simulate( InitialState, [InitialState | Rest], MaxLength) :-
  legalstate( InitialState),                          % Satisfy system's model
  simulate( [InitialState | Rest], MaxLength).

% compare_lands( X1, X2, List, Sign):
%    if X1 before X2 in List then Sign = neg
%    if X2 before X1 then Sign = pos else Sign = zero

compare_lands( X1, X2, [First | Rest], Sign) :-
  X1 = X2, !, Sign = zero
  ;
  X1 = First, !, Sign = neg
  ;
  X2 = First, !, Sign = pos
  ;
  compare_lands( X1, X2, Rest, Sign).
```

## 22.4.1 Representation of qualitative states

The variables in the model can take qualitative values from *domains*. For example, **Outflow** and **Netflow** can have a value in terms of the landmarks from the domain 'flow', defined by the bath tub model. A domain is defined by its name and its landmarks, for example:

**landmarks( flow, [ minf, zero, inflow, inf]).**

A *qualitative state* of a variable has the form:

**Domain: QMag/Dir**

**QMag** is a *qualitative magnitude*, which can be a landmark or the interval between two adjacent landmarks, written as **Land1..Land2**. **Dir** is a direction of change whose possible values are: **inc, std, dec**. Two example qualitative states of **Outflow** are:

**flow: inflow/dec**
**flow: zero..inflow/dec**

A *qualitative state of a system* is the list of qualitative states of the system's variables. For example, the initial state of the bath tub system consists of the values of the four variables **Level**, **Amount**, **Outflow** and **Netflow**:

**[ level:zero/inc, amount:zero/inc, flow:zero/inc, flow:inflow/dec ]**

A *qualitative behaviour* is a list of consecutive qualitative states.

## 22.4.2  Constraints

The program of Figure 22.8 implements three types of QDE constraints as the predicates: **deriv( X, Y)**, **sum( X, Y, Z)**, **mplus( X, Y)**. The arguments X, Y and Z are all qualitative states of variables. We look at each of these constraints in turn.

Constraint **deriv( X, Y)**: Y is qualitatively the time derivative of X. This is very simple to check: the direction of change of X has to agree with the sign of Y.

Constraint **mplus( X, Y)**: Y is a monotonically increasing function of X. Here X and Y have the form **Dx:QmagX/DirX** and **Dy:QmagY/DirY**. First, the directions of change have to be consistent: **DirX = DirY**. Second, the given corresponding values have to be respected. The technique of checking this is based on 'relative qualitative magnitudes' of X and Y (relative with respect to the pairs of corresponding values). For example, the relative qualitative magnitude of **level:zero..top** with respect to **top** is **neg**. For each pair of corresponding values, the qualitative magnitudes of X and Y are transformed into the relative qualitative magnitudes. The resulting relative qualitative magnitude of X has to be equal to that of Y.

Constraint **sum( X, Y, Z)**: X + Y = Z, where all X, Y and Z are qualitative states of variables of the form **Domain:Qmag/Dir**. Both the directions of change and the qualitative magnitudes have to be consistent with the summation constraint. First, the consistency of directions of change is checked. For example,

inc + std = inc

is true, and

inc + std = std

is false. Second, the qualitative magnitudes must be consistent with summation. In particular, they have to be consistent with respect to all the given corresponding values among X, Y and Z. The following are three examples of qualitative magnitudes satisfying the sum constraint:

flow:zero + flow:inflow = flow:inflow
flow:zero..inflow + flow:zero..inflow = flow:inflow
flow:zero..inflow + flow:zero..inflow = flow:zero..inflow

However, the following is false:

flow:zero..inflow + flow:inflow = flow:inflow

The technique of checking the consistency of qualitative magnitudes with respect to the corresponding values is as follows. First transform the given qualitative magnitudes into the relative qualitative magnitudes (relative to the corresponding values). Then check the consistency of these relative qualitative values with respect to qualitative summation. As an example consider:

sum( flow:zero..inflow/inc, flow:zero..inflow/dec, flow:inflow/std)

First, the directions of change satisfy the constraint: **inc+dec = std**. Second, consider the generally valid triple of corresponding values for summation:

correspond( sum( D1:zero, D2:Land, D2:Land))

D1 and D2 are domains, and **Land** is a landmark in **D2**. Applying this to the flow domain we have:

> correspond( sum( flow:zero, flow:inflow, flow:inflow))

Are the qualitative magnitudes in our **sum** constraint consistent with these corresponding values? To check this, the three qualitative magnitudes in the sum constraint are transformed into the relative qualitative magnitudes as follows:

> **flow:zero . . inflow** is 'pos' with respect to **flow:zero**
> **flow:zero . . inflow** is 'neg' with respect to **flow:inflow**
> **flow:inflow** is 'zero' with respect to **flow:inflow**

Now these relative qualitative magnitudes have to satisfy the constraint **qsum( pos, neg, zero)**. This is true.

The mathematical basis for this procedure for checking the **sum** constraint is as follows. Let the constraint be **sum(X,Y,Z)** with a triple of corresponding values $(x0, y0, z0)$. We can express X, Y and Z in terms of their differences from the corresponding values:

$$X = x0 + \Delta X, \quad Y = y0 + \Delta Y, \quad Z = z0 + \Delta Z$$

The sum constraint then means:

$$x0 + \Delta X + y0 + \Delta Y = z0 + \Delta Z$$

Since $x0 + y0 = z0$, it follows that $\Delta X + \Delta Y = \Delta Z$. The signs of $\Delta X$, $\Delta Y$ and $\Delta Z$ are the relative qualitative magnitudes of X, Y and Z with respect to $x0$, $y0$ and $z0$. These relative qualitative magnitudes have to satisfy the relation **qsum**.

## 22.4.3 Qualitative state transitions

A key relation in the program of Figure 22.8 is:

> transition( QualState1, QualState2)

where **QualState1** and **QualState2** are consecutive qualitative states of a variable. They both have the form: **Domain:Qmag/Dir**. The **transition** relation defines the possible transitions between qualitative states of variables, respecting the assumption about the 'smoothness' of variables. According to the smoothness assumption, the variables in the system may, within the same operating region, only change in time continuously and smoothly. For example, if a variable is approaching a landmark, it may reach the landmark, but may not jump over it. Similarly, if the direction of change of a variable is **inc**, it may remain **inc**, or become **std**, but cannot become **dec** before becoming **std** first. The **transition** predicate also makes sure that a non-steady variable can only stay at a landmark value for an instant, but not longer. Consecutive qualitative states correspond to consecutive time points that are, in principle, infinitesimally close to each other. To avoid generating infinite sequences of indistinguishable qualitative states during simulation, the simulator only generates a next system's state when there is some qualitative change with respect to the previous state. As a consequence of this, a qualitative state of the system may hold for as short as a single time point, or it may hold over a whole

```
% A bath tub model

landmarks( amount, [ zero, full, inf]).
landmarks( level, [ zero, top, inf]).
landmarks( flow, [ minf, zero, inflow, inf]).

correspond( amount:zero, level:zero).
correspond( amount:full, level:top).

legalstate( [ Level, Amount, Outflow, Netflow]) :-
    mplus( Amount, Level),
    mplus( Level, Outflow),
    Inflow = flow:inflow/std,               % Constant inflow
    sum( Outflow, Netflow, Inflow),         % Netflow = Inflow − Outflow
    deriv( Amount, Netflow),
    \+ overflowing( Level).                 % Water not over the top

overflowing( level:top .. inf/_).           % Over the top

initial( [ level: zero/inc,                 % Initial level
           amount: zero/inc,                % Initial amount
           flow: zero/inc,                  % Initial outflow
           flow: inflow/dec ] ).            % Initial inflow
```

**Figure 22.9** A qualitative model of bath tub.

time interval. Such a time interval comprises all the consecutive time points in which there is no qualitative change.

Figure 22.9 shows our bath tub model in the format expected by the simulator in Figure 22.8. The query to start the simulation from the empty bath tub, with a maximum length of 10 states, is:

```
?- initial( S), simulate( S, Behaviour, 10).
```

The first of Prolog's answers (slightly edited) to this query is:

```
S = [level:zero/inc,amount:zero/inc,flow:zero/inc,flow:inflow/dec]
Behaviour = [
  [level:zero/inc,amount:zero/inc,flow:zero/inc,flow:inflow/dec],
  [level:zero .. top/inc,amount:zero .. full/inc, flow:zero .. inflow/inc,
   flow:zero .. inflow/dec],
  [level:zero .. top/std,amount:zero .. full/std, flow:inflow/std,flow:zero/std] ]
```

Our simulator of Figure 22.8 can easily be used for running other models. Figure 22.10 shows an electric circuit with two capacitors and a resistor. Figure 22.11 shows a qualitative model of this dynamic circuit and the corresponding initial state. In the initial state, the left capacitor has some initial voltage whereas the right capacitor is empty. The query to start the simulation and the simulator's answer (slightly edited) are:

```
?- initial( S), simulate( S, Behaviour, 10).
Behaviour =
[ [volt:v0/dec,volt:zero/inc, .. ],
  [volt:zero .. v0/dec,volt:zero .. v0/inc, ... ],
  [volt:zero .. v0/std,volt:zero .. v0/std, ... ] ]
```

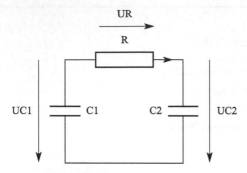

**Figure 22.10** An electric circuit with two capacitors and a resistor.

% Qualitative model of electric circuit with resistor and capacitors

landmarks( volt, [minf, zero, v0, inf]).         % Voltage on capacitors
landmarks( voltR, [minf, zero, v0, inf]).       % Voltage on resistor
landmarks( current, [minf, zero, inf]).

correspond( voltR:zero, current:zero).

legalstate( [ UC1, UC2, UR, CurrR]) :-
  sum( UR, UC2, UC1),
  mplus( UR, CurrR),             % Ohm's law for resistor
  deriv( UC2, CurrR),
  sum( CurrR, current:CurrC1, current:zero/std),   % CurrC1 = - CurrR
  deriv( UC1, current:CurrC1).       % CurrC1 = d/dt UC1

initial( [ volt:v0/dec, volt:zero/inc, voltR:v0/dec, current:zero..inf/dec]).

**Figure 22.11** A qualitative model of the circuit in Figure 22.10.

Basically this says that the voltage on capacitor C1 will be decreasing and the voltage on C2 will be increasing until both voltages become equal (the current in and voltage on the resistor become zero).

# EXERCISES

**22.3** There are two variables in the system: X and Y. Their (quantitative) time behaviours have the form:

$$X(t) = a1*\sin(k1*t), \quad Y(t) = a2*\sin(k2*t)$$

a1, a2, k1 and k2 are constant parameters of the system, all of them greater than 0. The initial time point is $t0 = 0$, so the initial qualitative state of the system is: $X(t0) = Y(t0) = $ **zero/inc**. (a) Give all the possible sequences of the first three qualitative states of this system. (b) Now suppose that there is a qualitative constraint between X and Y: $M_0^+(X,Y)$. Give all the possible sequences of the first three qualitative states of the system consistent with this constraint.

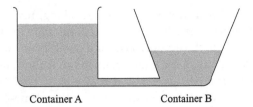

Container A          Container B

**Figure 22.12** U-tube; two containers connected by a thin pipe.

**22.4** A qualitative model of a system contains variables X, Y and Z, and the constraints:

$M_0^+(X,Y)$
sum(X,Y,Z)

The landmarks for the three variables are:

X, Y: minf, zero, inf
Z: minf, zero, landz, inf

At time t0, the qualitative value of x is x(t0) = zero/inc. What are the qualitative values Y(t0) and Z(t0)? What are the possible qualitative values of X, Y and Z in the next qualitative state of the system which holds over time interval t0..t1, until the next qualitative change? After the next qualitative change, at time t1, what are the possible new qualitative values X(t1), Y(t1) and Z(t1)?

**22.5** Define a qualitative model of the 'U-tube' system (Figure 22.12) in the form of a Prolog program expected by the simulator of Figure 22.8. In this system the two containers are connected by a thin pipe (so thin that the inertia of water flow in the pipe can be neglected). Experiment with the model and the initial state as indicated in Figure 22.12.

**22.6** Extend the simulator in Figure 22.8 by implementing other qualitative constraints that typically appear in QDEs: **minus(X,Y)** (X = −Y), **m_minus(X,Y)** (Y is a monotonically decreasing function of X), **mult(X,Y,Z)** (Z = X ∗ Y).

**22.7** Consider the following qualitative model of accelerated motion:

**landmarks( x, [ minf, zero, x1, inf]).**
**landmarks( v, [ minf, zero, v0, inf]).**

**legalstate( [ X, V]) :-**
  **V = v:_/inc,**                                      % Positive acceleration
  **deriv( X, V).**

**initial( [ x:zero .. x1/inc, v:v0/inc]).**

The qualitative simulation program of Figure 22.8 produces the following (Prolog's output slightly edited):

**?- initial( S), simulate( S, Behav, 3).**
**Behav = [ [x : zero .. x1 / inc, v : v0 / inc],**
        **[x : zero .. x1 / inc, v : v0 .. inf / inc],**
        **[x : x1 / inc, v : v0 .. inf / inc] ] ;**
**Behav = [ [x : zero .. x1 / inc, v : v0 / inc],**
        **[x : x1 / inc, v : v0 .. inf / inc],**
        **[x : x1 .. inf / inc, v : v0 .. inf / inc] ]**

The second of the two generated behaviours is, strictly speaking, not correct. The problem is in the transition between the first and the second state of the system. The first state includes **v:v0/inc**, which can only last for a single point in time (the value of an increasing variable can only be at a landmark for an instant, not longer). The second state includes **x:x1/inc**, so this is also a time-point state. However, a time-point state cannot be immediately followed by another time-point state. There has to be a time interval in between the two time points (time interval in which X would reach x1 from the interval **zero..x1**). It does not help to argue that X can be arbitrarily close to x1 in the initial state. No matter how close the initial X is to x1, there is always another real number between the initial X and x1, and X will first have to move to this number before reaching x1. How can the program in Figure 22.8 be modified to fix this deficiency? Hint: modify procedure **legal_trans**.

## 22.5 Discussion of the qualitative simulation program

Our qualitative simulator of the previous section is largely based on the QSIM algorithm (Kuipers 1986; 1994). In the interest of simplicity, there are some differences between the program in Figure 22.8 and the original QSIM algorithm: somewhat different treatment of time intervals, which simplifies the qualitative state transition table a little; not all of the constraint types have been implemented; our program does not generate new landmarks during simulation, whereas QSIM does. Regardless of these differences, the following discussion of advantages and drawbacks applies in general to this kind of simulation based on QDEs.

Let us start with some advantages. It has already been emphasized that building qualitative models is generally easier than quantitative models, and that qualitative models are more appropriate for some types of tasks. The QSIM-type qualitative simulation also has an elegant advantage over numerical simulation in that the simulation time step is adaptive, whereas in numerical simulation the time step is normally fixed. This flexibility in qualitative simulation can be particularly advantageous in comparison with fixed step numerical simulation in cases where the modelled system changes its behaviour abruptly. As an illustration of this, consider the bath tub again. When the water level is below the top, the system behaves according to the specified constraints in the model. When the level reaches the top, overflowing may begin and transition to another 'operating region' occurs. So the laws in the model change abruptly. For simulation it is therefore important to detect *exactly* the moment when the level reaches the top. In QSIM, a variable reaching its landmark is defined as a qualitative change, so the very time point when **Level=top** is automatically generated by the simulator. On the other hand, in a numerical simulator with fixed time step it will be unlikely that the level will exactly equal the top at one of the generated time points. Most likely, the next simulated level value will be either under the top, or, incorrectly, a little over the top.

Let us now discuss some problems of QSIM-type simulation. Qualitative simulation naturally appears to be computationally more economical than numerical simulation. However, paradoxically exactly the opposite may happen in practice. The reason lies in the non-determinism of qualitative simulation. Our simple bath tub model produced three different behaviours. In more complex models, the number of possible behaviours often grows exponentially with their length, which may result in combinatorial explosion. This may render qualitative simulation practically useless.

In the bath tub case, non-determinism was due to the lack of information in the model. All the three generated behaviours were consistent with the model. Real bath tubs are possible whose actual behaviours correspond to the three qualitative behaviours found by the simulator. So the simulator's results quite reasonably branch three ways. However, a more problematic kind of combinatorial branching in QSIM-type simulation is also possible. This kind of simulation may sometimes generate behaviours that do not correspond to any concrete quantitative instance of the qualitative model. Such behaviours are simply incorrect; they are inconsistent with the given qualitative model. Technically they are called *spurious behaviours*.

As an example consider a simple oscillating system consisting of a sliding block and a spring (see Figure 19.6). We assume zero friction between the block and the surface. Assume that initially at time *t*0 the spring is at its 'rest length' (X = zero) and the block has some initial velocity *v*0 to the right. Then X will be increasing and the spring will be pulling the block back, causing negative acceleration of the block, until the block stops and starts moving backwards. It will then cross zero with some negative velocity, reach the extreme position on the left, and return to X = zero. As there is no friction, we may expect that the block's velocity will be at that time *v*0 again. Now the whole cycle will be repeated. The resulting behaviour is steady oscillation.

Let us try to model this with our simulator of Figure 22.8. A quantitative model is:

$$\frac{d^2}{dt^2} X = A$$

$$A = -\frac{kX}{m}$$

X is the position of the block, A is its acceleration, *m* is its mass, and *k* is the coefficient of the spring. An appropriate qualitative model is given in Figure 22.13.

Let us execute this model from the initial state with:

?- initial( S), simulate( S, Beh, 11).

The generated behaviour **Beh** is as expected up to state 8:

[ x:minf..zero/inc, v:zero..v0/inc, a:zero..inf/dec]

Here the behaviour branches three ways. In the first branch the behaviour continues as follows:

[x:minf..zero/inc, v:v0/inc, a:zero..inf/dec]
[x:minf..zero/inc, v:v0..inf/inc, a:zero..inf/dec]
[x:zero/inc, v:v0..inf/std, a:zero/dec]

Here the velocity has reached the initial velocity *v*0 already before *X* became equal to zero. At the time when *X* = zero, velocity is already greater than *v*0. This looks

```
% Model of block on spring

landmarks( x, [ minf, zero, inf]).                    % Position of block
landmarks( v, [ minf, zero, v0, inf]).                % Velocity of block
landmarks( a, [ minf, zero, inf]).                    % Acceleration of block

correspond( x:zero, a:zero).

legalstate( [ X, V, A]) :-
    deriv( X, V),
    deriv( V, A),
    MinusA = a:_ ,
    sum( A, MinusA, a:zero/std),                      % MinusA = −A
    mplus( X, MinusA).                                % Spring pulling mass back

initial( [ x:zero/inc, v:v0/std, a:zero/dec]).
```

**Figure 22.13** A qualitative model of the block and spring system.

like a physically impossible case: the total energy in the system has increased, and the behaviour looks like an increasing oscillation. In the second branch, state 8 is followed by this:

```
[x:zero/inc, v:zero .. v0/std, a:zero/dec]
[x:zero .. inf/inc, v:zero .. v0/dec, a:minf .. zero/dec]
[x:zero .. inf/std, v:zero/dec, a:minf .. zero/std]
```

Here the block has reached $X =$ zero with velocity lower than v0. The total energy in the system here is less than in the initial state, so this appears to be a decreasing oscillation. In the third branch, state 8 is followed by:

```
[x:zero/inc, v:v0/std, a:zero/dec]
etc.
```

This corresponds to the expected case of steady oscillation.

The question is: Are the two unexpected behaviours only a consequence of lack of information in the qualitative model, or is there a problem in the simulation algorithm? It can be shown that, in fact, the model, although qualitative, contains enough information to allow the steady oscillation only. Therefore the other two behaviours, increasing and decreasing oscillations, are mathematically inconsistent with the model. They are said to be spurious. The weakness is in the simulation algorithm. The immediate question is then: Why not quickly fix the bug in the algorithm? The difficulty is that this is not a simple bug, but a complicated computational problem: How to check qualitative behaviours against *all* the constraints imposed by the model? QSIM-type simulation algorithm checks the consistency of individual states, but not also their sequences as a whole. Although improvements have been found that eliminate many spurious behaviours, a complete solution has not been discovered.

Given this drawback of the QSIM-type simulation, do we have any guarantees regarding the results of simulation? There is a theorem (Kuipers 1986) that QSIM is guaranteed to generate *all* qualitative behaviours consistent with the model. So incorrectness is limited to the opposite cases: QSIM may generate incorrect

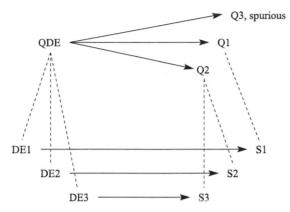

**Figure 22.14** Qualitative abstractions of differential equations and their solutions. QDE is the qualitative abstraction of three differential equations DE1, DE2 and DE3. S1, S2 and S3 are respective solutions of the three differential equations. Qualitative behaviours Q1, Q2 and Q3 are generated as solutions of QDE. Q1 is the qualitative abstraction of S1, Q2 is the abstraction of both S2 and S3. Q3 is spurious because it is not the abstraction of the solution of any corresponding differential equation.

behaviours, those not consistent with the model (spurious behaviours). Figure 22.14 illustrates the relations between the abstraction levels involved: differential equations and their solutions at the quantitative level, and QDEs and qualitative behaviours generated by QSIM at the qualitative level. Those generated behaviours that are not abstractions of any quantitative solutions are spurious.

The practical significance of the 'one sided' correctness of QSIM is the following. Suppose that a QSIM-type simulator has generated some qualitative behaviours from our model. Now we know that this set is complete in the sense that there exists no other behaviour of our modelled system that is not included among the results. We know that nothing else can happen. However, we have no guarantee that all the generated behaviours are in fact possible.

One way to eliminate spurious behaviours is to add more constraints to the model, whereby the correctness of the model should be preserved. This is not easy in general, but it is straightforward in the case of the block and spring system. We know that the energy in this system must be constant, because there is no loss of energy through friction, and there is no input of energy into the system. The total energy is the sum of kinetic and potential energy. So the energy conservation constraint is:

$$\tfrac{1}{2}mV^2 + \tfrac{1}{2}kX^2 = \text{ const.}$$

$m$ is the mass of the block, and $k$ is the coefficient of the spring. A weaker version of this constraint is sufficient for our purpose. Namely, a consequence of the above energy conservation constraint is: whenever $X = 0$, $V^2 = v_0{}^2$. An equivalent constraint is: if $V = v_0$ then $X = 0$, and if $X = 0$ then $V = v_0$ or $V = -v_0$. The following modification of the block and spring model of Figure 22.13 does not generate any spurious solutions:

```
legalstate( [ X, V, A]) :-
  deriv( X, V),
  deriv( V, A),
  MinusA = a:_ ,
  sum( A, MinusA, a:zero/std),          % MinusA = −A
  mplus( X, MinusA),                    % Spring pulling block back
  energy( X, V).                        % Weak energy conservation constraint

energy( X, V) :-
  V = v:v0/_ , !, X = x:zero/_          % If V=v0, X must be zero
  ;
  X = x:zero/_ , !, V = v:minf..zero/_  % Here V must be −v0
  ;
  true.                                 % Otherwise X non-zero, no constraint on V
```

# Summary

- 'Proper physics' solutions often comprise more numerical details than are needed for everyday purposes. Common sense, qualitative reasoning and 'naive physics' are therefore more appropriate in such cases.

- Qualitative modelling and reasoning is usually viewed as an abstraction of quantitative modelling and reasoning. Numbers are reduced to their signs, symbolic values (sometimes called *landmarks*) or intervals. Time may be simplified into symbolic time points and intervals. Time derivatives may be simplified into directions of change (increasing, decreasing or steady). Concrete functional relationships may be simplified into more vague ones, such as monotonic relationships.

- Qualitative models are easier to construct than quantitative models. Due to lack of numerical precision, qualitative models are not always sufficient, but they are generally appropriate for the tasks of diagnosis, functional reasoning, and design from 'first principles'.

- In qualitative reasoning, arithmetic operations are reduced to qualitative arithmetic. An example is qualitative summation over the signs *pos*, *zero* and *neg*. Typically, qualitative arithmetic is non-deterministic.

- Qualitative differential equations (QDE) are an abstraction of differential equations. QSIM is a qualitative simulation algorithm for models defined by QDEs. The main underlying assumption in QSIM-type simulation is that of 'smoothness': within the same 'operating region', the values of variables can only change smoothly.

- The difficulty of ensuring correctness of qualitative simulation is asymmetrical in the following sense. It is relatively easy to ensure that *all* the behaviours consistent with the given QDEs are, in fact, generated by the simulator. On the other hand, it is hard to ensure that *only* the behaviours consistent with the given QDEs are generated. This problem is known as the problem of *spurious behaviours*.

- Concepts discussed in this chapter are:

  qualitative reasoning
  qualitative modelling
  common sense and naive physics
  qualitative abstractions
  landmarks
  qualitative arithmetic
  qualitative summation
  qualitative differential equations (QDEs)
  monotonic functional constraints
  qualitative value, qualitative state of a variable
  qualitative simulation
  the QSIM algorithm
  smoothness assumption in qualitative simulation of dynamic systems
  smooth qualitative transitions
  spurious behaviours

## References and historical notes

Bobrow (1984) edited a special issue of the *Artificial Intelligence* journal entitled 'Qualitative Reasoning about Physical Systems'. Some papers in that volume became classical references in the qualitative reasoning field, such as the papers by de Kleer and Brown (1984) on *Confluences*, and by Forbus 1984 on *Qualitative Process Theory*. Although these papers are more interested in descriptions at higher levels than qualitative differential equations (QDE), they are strongly related to QDEs. QDEs can be viewed as the underlying low-level formalism to which these higher-level descriptions can be compiled. de Kleer and Williams (1991) edited another special issue on qualitative reasoning of the *Artificial Intelligence* journal. A useful selection of important papers published prior to 1990 was edited by Weld and de Kleer (1990). Faltings and Struss (1992), and Bredeweg and Struss (2003) are two other collections of papers on qualitative reasoning. A specialized forum for rapid publication of ongoing research in qualitative reasoning is the annual Workshop on Qualitative Reasoning.

The qualitative simulation program for dynamic systems in this chapter is based on the QSIM algorithm (Kuipers 1986) for QDE models. In the interest of simplicity, our program does not implement the full repertoire of qualitative constraints in QSIM, it does not introduce new landmarks during simulation, and it does not make explicit difference between time points and time intervals. Makarovič (1991), and Sacks and Doyle (1992) analyse among other, the difficulties of QSIM-style simulation. Improvements that alleviate the problem of spurious behaviours, and some other developments of QSIM, are described in Kuipers (1994). Further contributions to the treatment of spurious behaviours are Say (1998a, 1998b) and Say and Kuru (1993). Exercise 22.7 was suggested by Cem Say (personal communication).

Of course, qualitative reasoning about physical systems does not have to be based on differential equations or their direct abstraction. An approach that does not assume any underlying connection to differential equations was applied by Bratko, Mozetič and Lavrač (1989) in the modelling of a complex physiological system. A model of the heart explaining the relations between cardiac arrhythmias and ECG signals was defined in terms of logic-based qualitative descriptions. Forbus and Falkenhainer (1992), Kay *et al.* (2000), and Šuc *et al.* (2004) explore an interesting idea of combining qualitative and numerical simulation.

An important practical question is how to construct qualitative models, and can this be automated. Bratko and Šuc (2003) is a review of work on automatic learning of qualitative models from data. Automated construction of QDE models of dynamic systems from observed behaviours was first studied by Coiera (1989), followed by Bratko *et al.* (1991), Kraan *et al.* (1991), Say and Kuru (1996), and Hau and Coiera (1997). Small scale QDE-type models were synthesized from given behaviours in all these works. More recent developments in learning of QDE-type models include Coghill *et al.* (2008) and Srinivasan and King (2008). Mozetič (1987; also described in Bratko *et al.* 1989) synthesized by means of machine learning a substantial non-QDE-type qualitative model of the electrical behaviour of the heart. Kay *et al.* (2000), Šuc (2003) and Šuc *et al.* (2004) study the learning of combinations of qualitative and quantitative models.

Bredeweg *et al.* (2009) describe GARP3 (http://hcs.science.uva.nl/QRM/software/), a comprehensive publicly available system for qualitative modelling and simulation that has been frequently applied, among others, to ecological modelling.

Bobrow, D.G. (ed.) (1984) *Artificial Intelligence* **24**: Special Volume on Qualitative Reasoning about Physical Systems. Also appeared as: *Qualitative Reasoning about Physical Systems*. Cambridge, MA: MIT Press 1985.

Bratko, I., Mozetič, I. and Lavrač, N. (1989) *KARDIO: a Study in Deep and Qualitative Knowledge for Expert Systems*. Cambridge, MA: MIT Press.

Bratko, I., Muggleton, S. and Varšek, A. (1991) Learning qualitative models of dynamic systems. Proc. *Inductive Logic Programming ILP-91* (Brazdil, P., ed.), Viana do Castelo, Portugal. Also in: *Inductive Logic Programming* (Muggleton, S., ed.). London: Academic Press 1992.

Bratko, I. and Šuc, D. (2003) Learning qualitative models. *AI Magazine* **24**: 107–119.

Bredeweg, B., Linnebank, F., Bouwer, A. and Liem, J. (2009) Garp3 – Workbench for qualitative modelling and simulation. *Ecological Informatics*, **4**: 263–281 (Special issue: Qualitative models of ecological systems).

Bredeweg, B. and Struss, P. (2003, eds) *AI Magazine* **24**: Special issue on Qualitative Reasoning.

Coghill, G., Srinivasan, A. and King, D.R. (2008) Qualitative system identification from imperfect data. *Journal of Artificial Intelligence Research* **32**: 825–877.

Coiera, E. (1989) *Generating qualitative models from example behaviours*. DCS Report No. 8901, School of Computer Sc. and Eng., Univ. of New South Wales, Sydney, Australia.

de Kleer, J. and Brown, J.S. (1984) Qualitative physics based on confluences. *Artificial Intelligence Journal* **24**: 7–83.

de Kleer, J. and Williams, B.C. (eds) (1991) *Artificial Intelligence* **51**: Special Issue on Qualitative Reasoning about Physical Systems II.

Faltings, B. and Struss, P. (eds) (1992) *Recent Advances in Qualitative Physics*. Cambridge, MA: MIT Press.

Forbus, K.D. (1984) Qualitative process theory. *Artificial Intelligence* **24**: 85–168.

Forbus, K. and Falkenhainer, B.C. (1992) Self-explanatory simulations: integrating qualitative and quantitative knowledge. In: *Recent Advances in Qualitative Physics* (Faltings, B. and Struss, P., eds). Cambridge, MA: MIT Press.

Hau, D.T. and Coiera, E.W. (1997) Learning qualitative models of dynamic systems. *Machine Learning Journal* **26**: 177–211.

Kay, H., Rinner, B. and Kuipers, B. (2000) Semi-quantitative system identification. *Artificial Intelligence* **119**: 103–140.

Kraan, I.C., Richards, B.L. and Kuipers, B.J. (1991) Automatic abduction of qualitative models. *Proc. 5th Int. Workshop on Qualitative Reasoning about Physical Systems*.

Kuipers, B.J. (1986) Qualitative simulation. *Artificial Intelligence* **29**: 289–338 (also in Weld and de Kleer (1990)).

Kuipers, B.J. (1994) *Qualitative Reasoning: Modeling and Simulation with Incomplete Knowledge*. Cambridge, MA: MIT Press.

Makarovič, A. (1991) *Parsimony in Model-Based Reasoning*. Enschede: Twente University, PhD Thesis, ISBN 90-9004255-5.

Mozetič, I. (1987) The role of abstractions in learning qualitative models. *Proc. Fourth Int. Workshop on Machine Learning*, Irvine, CA: Morgan Kaufmann.

Sacks, E.P. and Doyle, J. (1992) Prolegomena to any future qualitative physics. *Computational Intelligence* **8**: 187–209.

Say, A.C.C. (1998a) L'Hôpital's filter for QSIM. *IEEE Trans. Pattern Analysis and Machine Intelligence* **20**: 1–8.

Say, A.C.C. (1998b) Improved infinity filtering in qualitative simulation. *Proc. Qualitative Reasoning Workshop 98*, Menlo Park, CA: AAAI Press.

Say, A.C.C. and Kuru, S. (1993) Improved filtering for the QSIM algorithm. *IEEE Trans. Pattern Analysis and Machine Intelligence* **15**: 967–971.

Say, A.C.C. and Kuru, S. (1996) Qualitative system identification: deriving structure from behavior. *Artificial Intelligence* **83**: 75–141.

Srinivasan, A. and King, R.D. (2008) Incremental identification of qualitative models of biological systems using inductive logic programming. *Journal of Machine Learning Research* **9**: 1475–1533.

Šuc, D. (2003) *Machine Reconstruction of Human Control Strategies*. Frontiers in Artificial Intelligence and Applications Series, Vol. 99. Amsterdam: IOS Press.

Šuc, D., Vladušič, D. and Bratko, I. (2004) Qualitatively faithful quantitative prediction. *Artificial Intelligence* **158**: 189–214.

Weld, D.S. and de Kleer, J. (1990) *Readings in Qualitative Reasoning about Physical Systems*, San Mateo, CA: Morgan Kaufmann.

# Chapter 23

# Language Processing with Grammar Rules

Many Prolog implementations provide a notational extension called DCG (definite clause grammars). This makes it very easy to implement formal grammars in Prolog. A grammar stated in DCG is directly executable by Prolog as a syntactic parser. DCG also facilitates the handling of the semantics of a language so that the meaning of a sentence can be interleaved with the syntax. This chapter shows how DCG enables elegant definitions of the syntax and meaning of non-trivial natural language sentences, such as: 'Every woman that admires a man that paints likes Monet'.

## 23.1 Grammar rules in Prolog

Grammar is a formal device for defining languages. Formally, a language is a set of sequences of symbols. Such a sequence of symbols can be abstract, without any practical meaning, or, more interestingly, it can be a statement in a programming language, or a whole program; it can also be a sentence in a natural language such as English.

One popular grammar notation is BNF (Backus-Naur form), which is commonly used in the definition of programming languages. We will start our discussion by considering BNF. A grammar comprises *production rules*. Here is a simple BNF grammar of two rules:

$$\langle s \rangle ::= a\ b$$
$$\langle s \rangle ::= a\ \langle s \rangle\ b$$

The first rule says: whenever the symbol $s$ appears in a string, it can be rewritten with the sequence $ab$. The second rule says that $s$ can be rewritten with the sequence $a$, followed by $s$, followed by $b$. In this grammar, $s$ is always enclosed by brackets '$\langle \rangle$'. This indicates that $s$ is a *non-terminal* symbol of the grammar. On the other hand, $a$ and $b$ are *terminal* symbols. Terminal symbols can never be rewritten. In BNF, the two production rules above are normally written together as one rule:

$$\langle s \rangle ::= a\ b\ |\ a\ \langle s \rangle\ b$$

But for the purpose of this chapter we will be using the expanded, longer form.

A grammar can be used to *generate* a string of symbols, called a *sentence*. The generation process always begins with some starting non-terminal symbol, *s* in our example. Then symbols in the current sequence are replaced by other strings according to the grammar rules. The generation process terminates when the current sequence does not contain any non-terminal symbol. In our example grammar, the generation process can proceed as follows. Start with:

*s*

Now by the second rule, *s* is replaced by:

*a s b*

The second rule can be used again giving:

*a a s b b*

Applying the first rule, a sentence is finally produced:

*a a a b b b*

Obviously, our grammar can generate other sentences – for example, *ab*, *aabb*, etc. In general, this grammar generates strings of the form $a^n b^n$ for $n = 1, 2, 3, \ldots$ . The set of sentences, generated by a grammar, is called the *language* defined by the grammar.

Our example grammar is simple and very abstract. However, we can use grammars to define much more interesting languages. Formal grammars are used for defining programming languages and also subsets of natural languages.

Our next grammar is still very simple, but slightly less abstract. Suppose a robot arm can be sent sequences of commands:

*up*: move one step upwards, and
*down*: move one step downwards

Here are two examples of command sequences that such a robot would accept:

*up*
*up up down up down*

Such a sequence triggers the corresponding sequence of steps performed by the robot. We will call a sequence of steps a 'move'. A move, then, consists of one step, or a step followed by a move. This is captured by the following grammar:

⟨ *move* ⟩ ::= ⟨ *step* ⟩
⟨ *move* ⟩ ::= ⟨ *step* ⟩ ⟨ *move* ⟩
⟨ *step* ⟩ ::= *up*
⟨ *step* ⟩ ::= *down*

We will use this grammar later to illustrate how the meaning can be handled within Prolog's grammar notation.

As shown earlier, a grammar generates sentences. In the opposite direction, a grammar can be used to *recognize* a given sentence. A recognizer decides whether a given sentence belongs to some language; that is, it recognizes whether the sentence can be generated by the corresponding grammar. The recognition process is essentially the inverse of generation. In recognition, the process starts with a given string of symbols, to which grammar rules are applied in the opposite direction: if the current string contains a substring, equal to the right-hand side of some rule in the grammar, then this substring is rewritten with the left-hand side of this rule. The recognition process terminates successfully when the complete given sentence has been reduced to the starting non-terminal symbol of the grammar. If there is no way of reducing the given sentence to the starting non-terminal symbol, then the recognizer rejects the sentence.

In such a recognition process, the given sentence is effectively disassembled into its constituents; therefore, this process is often also called *parsing*. To implement a grammar normally means to write a parsing program for the grammar. We will see that in Prolog such parsing programs can be written very easily. What makes this particularly elegant in Prolog is a special grammar rule notation, called DCG (definite clause grammar). Many Prolog implementations support this special notation for grammars. A grammar written in DCG is already a parsing program for this grammar. To transform a BNF grammar into DCG we only have to change some notational conventions. Our example BNF grammars can be written in DCG as follows:

```
s --> [ a], [ b].
s --> [ a], s, [ b].

move --> step.
move --> step, move.

step --> [ up].
step --> [ down].
```

Notice the differences between the BNF and DCG notations. '::=' is replaced by '-->'. Non-terminals are not in brackets any more, but terminals are in square brackets, thereby making them Prolog lists. In addition, symbols are now separated by commas, and each rule is terminated by a full stop as every Prolog clause.

In Prolog implementations that accept the DCG notation, our transformed grammars can be immediately used as recognizers or parsers of sentences. Such a parser expects sentences to be represented as difference lists of terminal symbols. (Difference-list representation was introduced in Chapter 8.) So each sentence is represented by two lists: the sentence represented is the difference between both lists. The two lists are not unique, for example:

> *aabb* can be represented by lists [ a, a, b, b] and []
> or by lists [ a, a, b, b, c] and [ c]
> or by lists [ a, a, b, b, 1, 0, 1] and [ 1, 0, 1]
> . . .

Taking into account this representation of sentences, our example DCG can be asked to recognize some sentences by questions:

```
?- s( [ a, a, b, b], []).               % Recognize string aabb

yes

?- s( [ a, a, b], []).

no
```

```
?- move( [ up, up, down], [ ]).
```

yes

```
?- move( [ up, up, left], [ ]).
```

no

```
?- move( [ up, X, up], [ ]).
```

X = up;
X = down;

no

Let us now explain *how* Prolog uses the given DCG to answer such questions. When Prolog consults grammar rules, it automatically converts them into normal Prolog clauses. In this way, Prolog converts the given grammar rules into a program for parsing sentences generated by the grammar. The following example illustrates this conversion. Our four DCG rules about robot moves are converted into four clauses:

```
move( List, Rest)  :-
   step( List, Rest).

move( List1, Rest)  :-
   step( List1, List2),
   move( List2, Rest).

step( [up | Rest], Rest).

step( [down | Rest], Rest).
```

What is actually achieved by this conversion? Let us look at the **move** procedure. The relation **move** has two arguments – two lists:

```
move( List, Rest)
```

is true if the difference of the lists **List** and **Rest** is an acceptable move. Example relationships are

```
move( [ up, down, up], [ ]).
```

or

```
move( [ up, down, up, a, b, c], [ a, b, c])
```

or:

```
move( [ up, down, up], [ down, up])
```

Figure 23.1 illustrates what is meant by the clause:

```
move( List1, Rest)  :-
   step( List1, List2),
   move( List2, Rest).
```

The clause can be read as:

> The difference of lists **List1** and **Rest** is a move if
> the difference between **List1** and **List2** is a step and
> the difference between **List2** and **Rest** is a move.

This also explains why difference-list representation is used: the pair ( **List1**, **Rest**) represents the concatenation of the lists represented by the pairs ( **List1**, **List2**) and

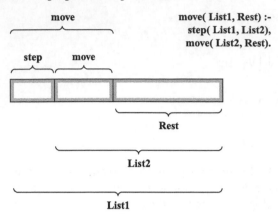

**Figure 23.1** Relations between sequences of symbols.

( List2, Rest). As shown in Chapter 8, concatenating lists in this way is much more efficient than with conc.

Now we are ready to formulate more generally the translation between DCG and standard Prolog. Each DCG rule is translated into a Prolog clause according to the following basic scheme: let the DCG rule be:

    n --> n1, n2, ..., nn.

If all n1, n2, ..., nn are non-terminals then the rule is translated into the clause:

    n( List1, Rest) :-
      n1( List1, List2),
      n2( List2, List3),
      ...
      nn( Listn, Rest).

If any of n1, n2, ..., nn is a non-terminal (in square brackets in the DCG rule) then it is handled differently. It does not appear as a goal in the clause, but is directly inserted into the corresponding list. As an example, consider the DCG rule:

    n --> n1, [ t2], n3, [ t4].

where n1 and n3 are non-terminals, and t2 and t4 are terminals. This is translated into the clause:

    n( List1, Rest) :-
      n1( List1, [t2 | List3]),
      n3( List3, [t4 | Rest]).

More interesting examples of grammars come from programming languages and natural languages. In both cases they can be elegantly implemented using DCG. Here is an example grammar for a simple subset of English:

    sentence --> noun_phrase, verb_phrase.

    verb_phrase --> verb, noun_phrase.

    noun_phrase --> determiner, noun.

    determiner --> [ a].
    determiner --> [ the].

noun --> [ cat].
noun --> [ mouse].

verb --> [ scares].
verb --> [ hates].

Example sentences generated by this grammar are:

[ the, cat, scares, a, mouse]
[ the, mouse, hates, the, cat]
[ the, mouse, scares, the, mouse]

Let us add nouns and verbs in plural to enable the generation of sentences like
[ the, mice, hate, the, cats]:

noun --> [ cats].
noun --> [ mice].

verb --> [ scare].
verb --> [ hate].

The grammar thus extended will generate the intended sentence. However, in addition, it will unfortunately also generate some unintended, incorrect English sentences, such as:

[ the, mouse, hate, the cat]

The problem lies in the rule:

sentence --> noun_phrase, verb_phrase.

This states that *any* noun phrase and verb phrase can be put together to form a sentence. But in English and many other languages, the noun phrase and verb phrase in a sentence are not independent: they have to agree in number. Both have to be either singular or plural. This is called *context dependence*. A phrase depends on the context in which it occurs. Context dependences cannot be directly handled by BNF grammars, but they can be easily handled by DCG grammars, using an extension that DCG provides with respect to BNF – namely, *arguments* that can be added to non-terminal symbols of the grammar. For example, we may add 'number' as an argument of noun phrase and verb phrase:

noun_phrase( Number)

verb_phrase( Number)

With this argument added we can easily modify our example grammar to force number agreement between the noun phrase and verb phrase:

sentence( Number) --> noun_phrase( Number), verb_phrase( Number).

verb_phrase( Number) --> verb( Number), noun_phrase( Number1).

noun_phrase( Number) --> determiner( Number), noun( Number).

noun( singular) --> [ mouse].

noun( plural) --> [ mice].

. . .

When DCG rules are read by Prolog and converted into Prolog clauses, the arguments of non-terminals are simply added to the usual two list arguments, with the convention that the two lists come last. Thus:

sentence( Number) --> noun_phrase( Number), verb_phrase( Number).

is converted into:

sentence( Number, List1, Rest)  :-
    noun_phrase( Number, List1, List2),
    verb_phrase( Number, List2, Rest).

Questions to Prolog now have to be modified accordingly so that the extra arguments are included:

?- sentence( plural, [ the, mice, hate, the, cats], [ ]).

yes

?- sentence( plural, [ the, mice, hates, the, cats], [ ]).

no

?- sentence( plural, [ the, mouse, hates, the, cat], [ ]).

no

?- sentence( Number, [ the, mouse, hates, the, cat], [ ]).

Number = singular

?- sentence( singular, [ the, What, hates, the, cat], [ ]).

What = cat;
What = mouse;
no

# EXERCISES

**23.1**  Translate into standard Prolog the DCG rule:

s --> [ a], s, [ b].

**23.2**  Write a Prolog procedure

**translate( DCGrule, PrologClause)**

that translates a given DCG rule into the corresponding Prolog clause.

**23.3**  One DCG rule in our grammar about robot moves is:

move --> step, move.

If this rule is replaced by

move --> move, step.

the language, defined by the so-modified grammar, is the same. However, the corresponding recognition procedure in Prolog is different. Analyse the difference.

What is the advantage of the original grammar? How would the two grammars handle the question:

?- move( [ up, left], []).

Handling meaning

### 23.2.1 Constructing parse trees

Let us first illustrate by an example the concept of a *parse tree*. According to our example grammar, the sentence

[ the, cat, scares, the, mice]

is parsed as shown by the parse tree of Figure 23.2. Some parts of the sentence are called *phrases* – those parts that correspond to non-terminals in the parse tree. In our example, [ the, mice] is a phrase corresponding to the non-terminal **noun_phrase**; [ scares, the, mice] is a phrase corresponding to **verb_phrase**. Figure 23.2 shows how the parse tree of a sentence contains, as subtrees, parse trees of phrases.

Here now is a definition of parse tree. The parse tree of a phrase is a tree with the following properties:

(1) All the leaves of the tree are labelled by terminal symbols of the grammar.

(2) All the internal nodes of the tree are labelled by non-terminal symbols; the root of the tree is labelled by the non-terminal that corresponds to the phrase.

(3) The parent-children relation in the tree is as specified by the rules of the grammar. For example, if the grammar contains the rule

s --> p, q, r.

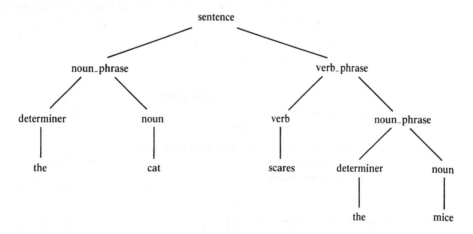

**Figure 23.2** The parse tree of the sentence 'The cat scares the mice'.

then the tree may contain the node s whose children are p, q and r:

Sometimes it is useful to have the parse tree explicitly represented in the program to perform some computation on it – for example, to extract the meaning of a sentence. The parse tree can be easily constructed by adding arguments to non-terminals in the DCG notation. We can conveniently represent a parse tree by a Prolog term whose functor is the root of the tree and whose arguments are the subtrees of the tree. For example, the parse tree for the noun phrase 'the cat' would be represented as:

> noun_phrase( determiner( the), noun( cat))

To generate a parse tree, a DCG grammar can be modified by adding to each non-terminal its parse tree as an argument. For example, the parse tree of a noun phrase in our grammar has the form:

> noun_phrase( DetTree, NounTree)

Here **DetTree** and **NounTree** are the parse trees of a determiner and a noun respectively. Adding these parse trees as arguments into our noun phrase grammar rule results in the modified rule:

> noun_phrase( noun_phrase( DetTree, NounTree)) -->
>     determiner( DetTree), noun( NounTree).

This rule can be read as:

> A noun phrase whose parse tree is **noun_phrase( DetTree, NounTree)** consists of:

- a determiner whose parse tree is **DetTree**, and
- a noun whose parse tree is **NounTree**.

We can now modify our whole grammar accordingly. To ensure number agreement, we can retain the number as the first argument and add the parse tree as the second argument. Here is part of the modified grammar:

> sentence( Number, sentence( NP, VP)) -->
>   noun_phrase( Number, NP),
>   verb_phrase( Number, VP).
>
> verb_phrase( Number, verb_phrase( Verb, NP)) -->
>   verb( Number, Verb),
>   noun_phrase( Number1, NP).
>
> noun_phrase( Number, noun_phrase( Det, Noun)) -->
>   determiner( Det),
>   noun( Number, Noun).
>
> determiner( determiner( the)) --> [ the].
>
> noun( singular, noun( cat)) --> [ cat].
>
> noun( plural, noun( cats)) --> [ cats].

When this grammar is read by Prolog it is automatically translated into a standard Prolog program. The first grammar rule above is translated into the clause:

```
sentence( Number, sentence( NP, VP), List, Rest) :-
   noun_phrase( Number, NP, List, Rest0),
   verb_phrase( Number, VP, Rest0, Rest).
```

Accordingly, a question to Prolog to parse a sentence has to be stated in this format; for example:

```
?- sentence( Number, ParseTree, [ the, mice, hate, the, cat], [ ]).

Number = plural
ParseTree = sentence( noun_phrase( determiner( the), noun( mice)),
            verb_phrase( verb( hate), noun_phrase( determiner( the),
            noun( cat))))
```

## 23.2.2 From the parse tree to the meaning

Prolog grammars are particularly well suited for the treatment of the meaning of a language, a natural language in particular. Arguments that are attached to non-terminal symbols of a grammar can be used to handle the meaning of sentences. One approach to extract the meaning involves two stages:

(1) Generate the parse tree of a given sentence.

(2) Process the parse tree to compute the meaning.

Of course this is only practical if the syntactic structure, represented by the parse tree, also reflects the semantic structure; that is, both the syntactic and semantic decomposition have similar structures. In such a case, the meaning of a sentence can be composed from the meanings of the syntactic phrases into which the sentence has been parsed.

A simple example will illustrate this two-stage method. For simplicity we will consider robot moves again. A grammar about robot moves that generates the parse tree is:

```
move( move( Step)) --> step( Step).
move( move( Step, Move)) --> step( Step), move( Move).

step( step( up)) --> [ up].
step( step( down)) --> [ down].
```

Let us define the meaning of a move as the distance between the robot's position before the move and after it. Let each step be 1 mm in either the positive or negative direction. So the meaning of the move '*up up down up*' is $1 + 1 - 1 + 1 = 2$. The distance of a move can be computed from the move's parse tree as illustrated in Figure 23.3. The corresponding arithmetic is:

$$\text{distance}('up\ up\ down\ up') =$$
$$\text{distance}('up') + \text{distance}('up\ down\ up') = 1 + 1 = 2$$

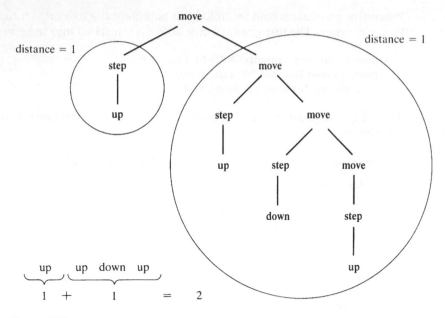

**Figure 23.3** Extracting the meaning of a move as its distance.

The following procedure computes the meaning of a move (as the corresponding distance) from the move's parse tree:

```
% meaning( ParseTree, Value)
meaning( move( Step, Move), Dist)  :-
    meaning( Step, D1),
    meaning( Move, D2),
    Dist is D1 + D2.

meaning( move( Step), Dist)  :-
    meaning( Step, Dist).

meaning( step( up), 1).

meaning( step( down), −1).
```

This can be used to compute the meaning of the move '*up up down up*' by:

```
?- move( Tree, [ up, up, down, up], [ ]), meaning( Tree, Dist).

Dist = 2
Tree = move( step( up), move( step( up), move( step( down), move( step( up)))) )
```

# EXERCISE

**23.4**  Is it possible to use this grammar and the **meaning** procedure for the inverse task; that is, to find a move with the given distance – for example:

```
?- move( Tree, Move, [ ]), meaning( Tree, 5).
```

Discuss this application.

## 23.2.3    Interleaving syntax and semantics in DCG

The DCG notation actually makes it possible to incorporate the meaning directly into a grammar, thereby avoiding the intermediate construction of the parse tree. There is another notational extension, provided by DCG, that is useful in this respect. This extension allows us to insert normal Prolog goals into grammar rules. Such goals have to be enclosed in curly brackets to make them distinguishable from other symbols of the grammar. Thus everything enclosed in curly brackets is, when encountered, executed as normal Prolog goals. This execution may, for example, involve arithmetic computation.

This feature can be used to rewrite our robot move grammar so that the meaning extraction is interleaved directly with the syntax. To do that, we have to add the meaning; that is, the move's distance as an argument of the non-terminals **move** and **step**. For example

> move( Dist)

now denotes a **move** phrase whose meaning is **Dist**. A corresponding grammar is:

> move( D) --> step( D).
> move( D) --> step( D1), move( D2), {D is D1 + D2}.
>
> step( 1) --> [ up].
> step( −1) --> [ down].

The second rule here exemplifies the curly bracket notation. This rule can be read as follows:

> A move whose meaning is **D** consists of:
>
> - a step whose meaning is **D1**, and
>
> - a move whose meaning is **D2**, where the relation **D is D1 + D2** must also be satisfied.

In fact, handling semantics by incorporating the meaning formation rules directly into a DCG grammar is so convenient that the intermediate stage of constructing the parse tree is often avoided altogether. Avoiding such an intermediate stage results in a 'collapsed' program. The usual advantages of this are a shorter and more efficient program, but there are also disadvantages: the collapsed program may be less transparent, less flexible and harder to modify.

As a further illustration of this technique of interleaving the syntax and meaning, let us make our robot example a little more interesting. Suppose that the robot can be in one of two gears: *g1* or *g2*. When a step command is received in gear *g1*, the robot will move by 1 mm up or down; in gear *g2* it will move by 2 mm. Let the whole program for the robot consist of the gear commands (to switch to gear *g1* or *g2*) and step commands, finally ending with *stop*. Example programs are:

> *stop*
> *g1 up up stop*
> *g1 up up g2 down up stop*
> *g1 g1 g2 up up g1 up down up g2 stop*

The meaning (that is, the distance) of the last program is:

> $Dist = 2 * (1 + 1) + 1 * (1 − 1 + 1) = 5$

To handle such robot programs, our existing robot move grammar has to be extended with the following rules:

```
prog( 0) --> [ stop].
prog( Dist) --> gear( _ ), prog( Dist).
prog( Dist) --> gear( G), move( D), prog( Dist1), {Dist is G * D + Dist1}.

gear( 1) --> [ g1].
gear( 2) --> [ g2].
```

##  23.3 Defining the meaning of natural language

### 23.3.1 Meaning of simple sentences in logic

Defining the meaning of natural language is an extremely difficult problem that is the subject of on-going research. An ultimate solution to the problem of formalizing the complete syntax and meaning of a language like English is far away. But (relatively small) subsets of natural languages have been successfully formalized and consequently implemented as working programs.

In defining the meaning of a language, the first question is: How will the meaning be represented? There are of course many alternatives, and good choice will depend on the particular application. The important question therefore is: What will the meaning extracted from natural language text be used for? One application is natural language access to a database. This involves answering natural language questions regarding information in the database and updating the database by new information extracted from natural language input. In such a case, the target representation of the meaning extraction process would be a language for querying and updating the database.

Logic has been accepted as a good candidate for representing the meaning of natural language sentences. In this section we will show how interpretations in logic of natural language sentences can be constructed using the DCG notation. The logical interpretations will be encoded as Prolog terms. We will only look at some interesting ideas, so many details necessary for a more general coverage will be omitted. A more complete treatment would be far beyond the scope of this book.

To start with, it is best to look at some natural language sentences and phrases and try to express in logic what they mean. Let us consider first the sentence 'John paints'. The natural way to express the meaning of this sentence in logic, as a Prolog term, is:

**paints( john)**

Notice that 'paints' here is an intransitive verb and therefore the corresponding predicate **paints** only has one argument.

Our next example sentence is 'John likes Annie'. The formalized meaning of this can be:

**likes( john, annie)**

The verb 'likes' is transitive and accordingly the predicate **likes** has two arguments.

Let us now try to define, by DCG rules, the meaning of such simple sentences. We will start with the bare syntax and then gradually incorporate the meaning into these rules. Here is a grammar that comfortably covers the syntax of our example sentences:

```
sentence --> noun_phrase, verb_phrase.

noun_phrase --> proper_noun.

verb_phrase --> intrans_verb.          % Intransitive verb
verb_phrase --> trans_verb, noun_phrase.   % Transitive verb

intrans_verb --> [ paints].
trans_verb --> [ likes].

proper_noun --> [ john].
proper_noun --> [ annie].
```

Now let us incorporate meaning into these rules. We will start with the simpler categories – noun and verb – and then proceed to the more complicated ones. Our foregoing examples suggest the following definitions. The meaning of proper noun john is simply john:

```
proper_noun( john) --> [ john].
```

The meaning of an intransitive verb like 'paints' is slightly more complicated. It can be stated as

```
paints( X)
```

where X is a variable whose value only becomes known from the context; that is, from the noun phrase. Correspondingly, the DCG rule for **paints** is:

```
intrans_verb( paints( X)) --> [ paints].
```

Let us now look at the question: How can we construct from the two meanings, john and **paints( X)**, the intended meaning of the whole sentence: **paints( john)**? We have to force the argument X of **paints** to become equal to **john**.

It may be helpful at this point to consider Figure 23.4. This shows how the meanings of phrases accumulate in the meaning of the whole sentence. To achieve the effects of the propagation of the meanings of phrases, we can first simply define that **noun_phrase** and **verb_phrase** receive their meanings from **proper_noun** and **intrans_verb** respectively:

```
noun_phrase( NP) --> proper_noun( NP).

verb_phrase( VP) --> intrans_verb( VP).
```

It remains to define the meaning of the whole sentence. Here is a first attempt:

```
sentence( S) --> noun_phrase( NP), verb_phrase( VP), {compose( NP, VP, S)}.
```

The goal **compose( NP, VP, S)** has to assemble the meanings of the noun phrase john and the verb phrase **paints( X)**. For example, this is what we want **compose** to do:

```
?- compose(john, paints(X), S).
X = john
S = paints(john)
```

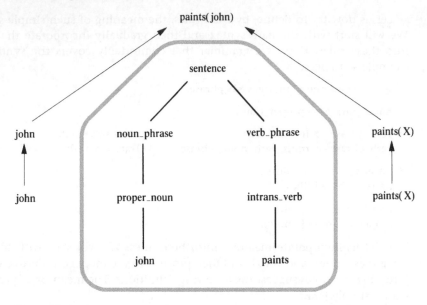

**Figure 23.4** The parse tree of the sentence 'John paints' with meaning attached to the nodes. The logical meaning of each phrase is attached to the corresponding non-terminal in the tree. The arrows indicate how the meanings of phrases accumulate.

In general, **compose(NP, VP, S)** has to find argument X in **VP**, match X = NP, and produce S = VP. The following definition does it:

```
compose( NP, VP, VP)  :-
    arg( 1, VP, NP).            % The first, i.e. the only, argument in VP in NP
```

This works, but there is a shorter method. We can avoid the extra predicate **compose** if we make the argument X in term **paints( X)** 'visible' from the outside of the term, so that it becomes accessible for instantiation. This can be achieved by redefining the meaning of **verb_phrase** and **intrans_verb** so that X becomes an extra argument:

```
intrans_verb( X, paints( X)) --> [ paints].
```

```
verb_phrase( X, VP) --> intrans_verb( X, VP).
```

This makes the argument X easily accessible and facilitates a simpler definition of the meaning of a sentence:

```
sentence( VP) --> noun_phrase( X), verb_phrase( X, VP).
```

This forces the argument X of the verb's meaning to become equal to the meaning of the noun phrase.

This technique of making parts of meanings visible is a rather common trick in incorporating meaning into DCG rules. The technique essentially works as follows. The meaning of a phrase is defined in a 'skeleton' form – for example, **paints( SomeActor)**. This defines the general form of the meaning, but leaves some of it uninstantiated (here, variable **SomeActor**). Such an uninstantiated variable serves as a slot that can be filled later depending on the meaning of other phrases in the context. This filling of slots can be accomplished by

Prolog's matching. To facilitate this, however, slots are made visible by being added as extra arguments to non-terminals. We will adopt the following convention regarding the order of these arguments: first will come the 'visible slots' of the phrase's meaning, followed by the meaning itself – for example, **verb_phrase( X, VPMeaning)**.

This technique can be applied to transitive verbs as follows. The meaning of the verb 'likes' is **likes( Somebody, Something)** (somebody likes something) where **Somebody** and **Something** are slots that should be visible from outside. Thus:

> **trans_verb( Somebody, Something, likes( Somebody, Something)) --> [ likes].**

A verb phrase with a transitive verb contains a noun phrase that provides the value for **Something**. Therefore:

> **verb_phrase( Somebody, VP) -->**
> **trans_verb( Somebody, Something, VP), noun_phrase( Something).**

The foregoing discussion has introduced some basic ideas; the DCG rules given handle but the simplest sentences. When noun phrases contain determiners like 'a' and 'every', the meaning expressions become more complicated. We will look at this in the next section.

## 23.3.2 Meaning of determiners 'a' and 'every'

Sentences that contain determiners such as 'a' are much more difficult to handle than those in the previous section. Let us consider an example sentence: 'A man paints'. It would now be a gross mistake to think that the meaning of this sentence is **paints( man)**. The sentence really says: There exists some man that paints. In logic this is phrased as:

> There exists an X such that
> X is a man and X paints.

In logic, the variable X here is said to be *existentially* quantified ('there exists'). We will choose to represent this by the Prolog term:

> **exists( X, man( X) and paints( X))**

The first argument in this term is a variable, X – the variable that is meant to be existentially quantified. **and** is assumed to be declared as an infix operator:

> **:- op( 100, xfy, and).**

The syntactic entity that dictates this logic interpretation is, possibly surprisingly, the determiner 'a'. So 'a' in a way dominates the whole sentence. To better understand how the meaning is constructed, let us look at the noun phrase 'a man'. Its meaning is:

> There exists some X such that
> X is a man.

However, in sentences where the phrase 'a man' appears, such as 'a man paints', we always want to say something else about this man (not only that he exists, but also that he paints). So a suitable form for the meaning of the noun phrase 'a man' is:

> exists( X, man( X) and Assertion)

where Assertion is some statement about X. This statement about X depends on the context; that is, on the verb phrase that follows the noun phrase 'a man'. The variable Assertion will only be instantiated when the context in which it appears becomes known.

A similar line of thought leads us to find a proper formulation of the meaning of the determiner 'a'. This determiner indicates that:

> There exists some X such that
> X has some property (for example, man( X)) and
> some further assertion about X holds (for example, paints( X)).

As a Prolog term this can be represented as:

> exists( X, Property and Assertion)

Both variables Property and Assertion are slots for meanings from the context to be plugged in. To facilitate the importation of the meanings from other phrases in context, we can, as explained in the previous section, make parts of the meaning of determiner 'a' visible. A suitable DCG rule for determiner 'a' is:

> determiner( X, Prop, Assn, exists( X, Prop and Assn)) --> [ a].

The logical meaning of the tiny determiner 'a' may seem surprisingly complicated.

Another determiner, 'every', can be handled in a similar way. Consider the sentence: 'Every woman dances'. The logic interpretation of this is:

> For all X,
> if X is a woman then X dances.

We will represent this by the following Prolog term:

> all( X, woman( X) => dances( X))

where '=>' is an infix operator denoting logical implication. Determiner 'every' thus indicates a meaning whose skeleton structure is:

> all( X, Property => Assertion)

A DCG rule that defines the meaning of determiner 'every' and makes the slots in the skeleton visible is:

> determiner( X, Prop, Assn, all( X, Prop => Assn)) --> [ every].

Having defined the meaning of determiners, we shall now concentrate on how their meaning integrates with the meanings of other phrases in the context, leading finally to the meaning of the whole sentence. We can get a first idea by looking again at the sentence 'A man paints' whose meaning is:

> exists( X, man( X) and paints( X))

We have already defined the meaning of 'a' as:

> exists( X, Prop and Assn)

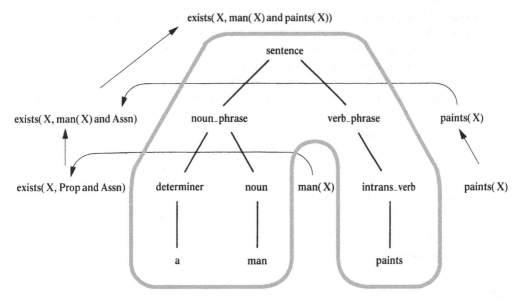

**Figure 23.5** Accumulation of meaning for the sentence 'A man paints'. Determiner 'a' dictates the overall form of the meaning of the sentence. Arrows indicate the importation of meaning between phrases.

Comparing these two meanings it is immediately obvious that the main structure of the meaning of the sentence is dictated by the determiner. The meaning of the sentence can be assembled as illustrated by Figure 23.5: start with the skeleton meaning enforced by 'a':

exists( X, Prop and Assn)

**Prop** then becomes instantiated by the noun and **Assn** by the verb phrase. The main structure of the meaning of the sentence is received from the noun phrase. Notice that this is different from the simpler grammar in the previous section where it was the verb phrase that provided the sentence's meaning structure. Again, applying the technique of making some parts of the meaning visible, the relations between meanings indicated in Figure 23.5 can be stated by the following DCG rules:

sentence( S) --> noun_phrase( X, Assn, S), verb_phrase( X, Assn).

noun_phrase( X, Assn, S) --> determiner( X, Prop, Assn, S), noun( X, Prop).

verb_phrase( X, Assn) --> intrans_verb( X, Assn).

intrans_verb( X, paints( X)) --> [ paints].

determiner( X, Prop, Assn, exists( X, Prop and Assn)) --> [ a].

noun( X, man( X)) --> [ man].

This grammar can be asked to construct the meaning of 'A man paints':

?- sentence( S, [ a, man, paints], [ ]).

S = exists( X, man( X) and paints( X))

Prolog's answer was polished by replacing a Prolog-generated variable name like _123 with X.

The grammar of the previous section handles sentences like 'John paints'. Now that we have modified our grammar we need to ensure that this new grammar that can handle 'A man paints' can also handle the simpler 'John paints'. To do this, the meaning of proper nouns has to be incorporated into the new noun phrase. The following rules accomplish this:

proper_noun( john) --> [ john].

noun_phrase( X, Assn, Assn) --> proper_noun( X).

This last rule simply says that the whole meaning of this kind of noun phrase is the same as the value in the second 'visible slot' – that is, **Assn**. This slot's value is obtained from the context (from the verb phrase) as in the question:

?- sentence( S, [ john, paints], [ ]).

S = paints( john)

## EXERCISE

**23.5** Study how our modified grammar constructs the meaning of 'John paints'. Essentially the following should happen: the meaning received from the verb phrase becomes the noun phrase's meaning, which eventually becomes the sentence's meaning.

## 23.3.3  Handling relative clauses

Nouns can be qualified by relative clauses – for example, 'Every man that paints admires Monet'. The phrase 'every man that paints' is a noun phrase in which 'that paints' is a relative clause. To cover this syntactically, our grammar rules about noun phrase can be redefined as follows:

noun_phrase --> determiner, noun, rel_clause.

rel_clause --> [ that], verb_phrase.
rel_clause --> [ ].                              % Empty relative clause

Let us now consider the meaning of such noun phrases. The sentence 'Every man that paints admires Monet' logically means:

For all X,
    if X is a man and X paints
    then X admires Monet.

This can be represented as the Prolog term:

all( X, man( X) and paints( X) => admires( X, monet))

where it is assumed that the operator 'and' binds stronger than '=>'. Thus a suitable form for the logical meaning of the noun phrase 'every man that paints' is:

all( X, man( X) and paints( X) => Assn)

In general, this form is:

all( X, Prop1 and Prop2 => Assn)

**Prop1** is determined by the noun, **Prop2** by the verb phrase of the relative clause and **Assn** by the verb phrase of the sentence. DCG rules for the noun phrase that ensure this are:

rel_clause( X, Prop1, Prop1 and Prop2) --> [ that], verb_phrase( X, Prop2).

noun_phrase( X, Assn, S) -->
   determiner( X, Prop12, Assn, S), noun( X, Prop1),
   rel_clause( X, Prop1, Prop12).

To cover the case of the empty relative clause we have to add:

rel_clause( X, Prop1, Prop1) --> [].

Figure 23.6 gives a complete DCG with the features developed in this section, including determiners 'a' and 'every', and relative clauses. This grammar is capable of extracting the logical meaning of sentences, such as:

John paints.
Every man that paints admires Monet.
Annie admires every man that paints.
Every woman that admires a man that paints likes Monet.

For example, these sentences can be submitted to our grammar as the questions:

?- sentence( Meaning1, [ every, man, that, paints, admires, monet], [ ]).

Meaning1 = all( X, man( X) and paints( X) => admires( X, monet))

?- sentence( Meaning2, [ annie, admires, every, man, that, paints], [ ]).

Meaning2 = all( X, man( X) and paints( X) => admires( annie, X))

?- sentence( Meaning3, [ every, woman, that, admires, a, man, that, paints, likes,
                monet], [ ]).

Meaning3 = all( X, woman( X) and exists( Y, ( man( Y) and paints( Y))
        and admires( X, Y)) => likes( X, monet))

A further interesting problem concerns the use of the meanings extracted from natural language input to answer questions. For example, how can we modify our program so that, after it has processed the given sentences, it can answer questions like: 'Does Annie admire anybody who admires Monet?' The answer to this logically follows from the sentences above, and we just have to make our program do some necessary reasoning. In general, we need a theorem prover to deduce answers from the meanings represented in logic. Of course, it is most practical to simply use Prolog itself as such a theorem prover. To do that we would have to translate the logical meanings into equivalent Prolog clauses. This exercise in

```
:- op( 100, xfy, and).
:- op( 150, xfy, =>).

sentence( S) -->
    noun_phrase( X, Assn, S), verb_phrase( X, Assn).

noun_phrase( X, Assn, S) -->
    determiner( X, Prop12, Assn, S), noun( X, Prop1), rel_clause( X, Prop1, Prop12).

noun_phrase( X, Assn, Assn) -->
    proper_noun( X).

verb_phrase( X, Assn) -->
    trans_verb( X, Y, Assn1), noun_phrase( Y, Assn1, Assn).

verb_phrase( X, Assn) -->
    intrans_verb( X, Assn).

rel_clause( X, Prop1, Prop1 and Prop2) -->
    [ that], verb_phrase( X, Prop2).

rel_clause( X, Prop1, Prop1) --> [].

determiner( X, Prop, Assn, all( X, Prop => Assn)) --> [ every].
determiner( X, Prop, Assn, exists( X, Prop and Assn)) --> [ a].

noun( X, man( X)) --> [ man].
noun( X, woman( X)) --> [ woman].

proper_noun( john) --> [ john].
proper_noun( annie) --> [ annie].
proper_noun( monet) --> [ monet].

trans_verb( X, Y, likes( X, Y)) --> [ likes].
trans_verb( X, Y, admires( X, Y)) --> [ admires].

intrans_verb( X, paints( X)) --> [ paints].

% Some tests

test1( Meaning)  :-
    sentence( Meaning, [ john, paints], []).

test2( Meaning)  :-
    sentence( Meaning, [ a, man, paints], []).

test3( Meaning)  :-
    sentence( Meaning, [ every, man, that, paints, admires, monet], []).

test4( Meaning)  :-
    sentence( Meaning, [ annie, admires, every, man, that, paints], []).

test5( Meaning)  :-
    sentence( Meaning, [ every, woman, that, admires, a, man, that, paints, likes,
    monet], []).
```

**Figure 23.6** A DCG handling the syntax and meaning of a small subset of natural language.

general requires some work, but in some cases such a translation is trivial. Here are some easily translatable meanings written as Prolog clauses:

**paints( john).**

**admires( X, monet)  :-**
  **man( X),**
  **paints( X).**

**admires( annie, X)  :-**
  **man( X),**
  **paints( X).**

The example query 'Does Annie admire anybody who admires Monet?' would have to be translated into the Prolog query:

**?- admires( annie, X), admires( X, monet).**

**X = john**

# EXERCISES

**23.6**  State in logic the meaning of the sentences:

(a)  Mary knows all important artists.

(b)  Every teacher who teaches French and studies music understands Chopin.

(c)  A charming lady from Florida runs a beauty shop in Sydney.

**23.7**  The grammar of Figure 23.6 can also be executed in the opposite direction: given a meaning, generate a sentence with this meaning. For example, we may try the opposite of **test5** in Figure 23.6 as follows:

**?- M = all(X,woman(X) and exists(Y,(man(Y) and paints(Y)) and admires(X,Y))**
  **=> likes(X,monet)), sentence( M, S, [ ]).**

The first Prolog's answer is:

**S = [every,woman,that,admires,a,man,that,paints,likes,monet]**
**M = all(_022C,woman(_022C) and exists(_02FC,(man(_02FC) and paints(_02FC))**
**and admires(_022C,_02FC)) => likes(_022C,monet))**

This is as expected. However, if we want another solution then we get a surprise:

**M = all(monet,woman(monet) and exists(_0364,(man(_0364) and paints(_0364))**
**and admires(monet,_0364)) => likes(monet,monet))**
**S = [monet,likes,every,woman,that,admires,a,man,that,paints]**

Explain how this was obtained, and suggest a modification of the grammar to prevent this. Hint: The problem is that the grammar allows a quantified variable (e.g. X in **all(X,...)**) to match a proper noun (**monet**); this can easily be prevented.

**23.8**  Extend the grammar of Figure 23.6 to handle composite sentences with connectives 'if', 'then', 'and', 'or', 'neither', 'nor', etc. For example: John paints and Annie sings. If Annie sings then every teacher listens.

## PROJECT

Modify the grammar of Figure 23.6 to represent the meaning of sentences as directly executable Prolog clauses. Write a program that reads natural language sentences in normal text format (not as lists) and asserts their meaning as Prolog clauses. Extend the grammar to handle simple questions in natural language which would result in a complete conversation system for a small subset of natural language. You may also consider use of the grammar to generate sentences with the given meaning as natural language answers to the user.

# Summary

- Standard grammar notations, such as BNF, can be trivially translated into the DCG notation (definite clause grammars). A grammar in DCG can be read and executed directly by Prolog as a recognizer for the language defined by the grammar.

- The DCG notation allows non-terminal symbols of the grammar to have arguments. This enables the treatment of context dependences in a grammar and direct incorporation of the semantics of a language into its grammar.

- Interesting DCG grammars have been written that cover the syntax and meaning of non-trivial subsets of natural language.

## References

Language processing and linguistic theories is one of the areas in which Prolog implementations can be particularly compact. Prototypes at least, to verify linguistic ideas and play with them, in Prolog often require practically negligible amount of coding in comparison with other languages. The DCG definitions of the syntax and meaning of natural language in this chapter follow the classical paper by Pereira and Warren (1980). In their excellent book, Pereira and Shieber (1987) give many further developments of this, including an elegant connection between the corresponding mathematical basis for defining meaning and its implementation in Prolog. Szpakowicz (1987) gives an example of applying DCG in programming language translation. Exercise 23.8 is borrowed from Kononenko and Lavrač (1988), who also give a solution. The books by Allen (1994), and Jurafsky and Martin (2008) cover a variety of topics in natural language processing. The books by Covington (1994), Gazdar and Mellish (1989), and Nugues (2006) do this using Prolog.

Allen, J.F. (1994) *Natural Language Understanding*, 2nd edn. Redwood City, CA: Benjamin/ Cummings.

Covington, M.A. (1994) *Natural Language Processing for Prolog Programmers*. Englewood Cliffs, NJ: Prentice Hall.

Gazdar, G. and Mellish, C. (1989) *Natural Language Processing in Prolog*. Harlow: Addison-Wesley.

Jurafsky, D. and Martin, J.H. (2008) *Speech and Language Processing*, 2nd edn. Prentice-Hall.

Kononenko, I. and Lavrač, N. (1988) *Prolog through Examples: A Practical Programming Guide*. Wilmslow, UK: Sigma Press.

Nugues, P.M. (2006) *An Introduction to Language Processing with Perl and Prolog*. Springer.

Pereira, F.C.N. and Shieber, S.M. (1987) *Prolog and Natural-Language Analysis*. Menlo Park, CA: CSLI – Center for the Study of Language and Information. Also available in electronic form from Microtome Publishing (2002).

Pereira, F.C.N. and Warren, D.H.D. (1980) Definite clause grammars for language analysis – a survey of the formalism and comparison with augmented transition networks. *Artificial Intelligence* **13**: 231–278.

Szpakowicz, S. (1987) Logic grammars. *BYTE* (August): 185–195.

# Chapter 24

# Game Playing

In this chapter we will consider techniques for playing two-person, perfect-information games, such as chess. For interesting games, trees of possible continuations are far too complex to be searched exhaustively, so other approaches are necessary. The usual method is based on the minimax principle, efficiently implemented as the alpha-beta algorithm. In addition to this standard technique, we will develop in this chapter a program based on the Advice Language approach for introducing pattern knowledge into a chess-playing program. This rather detailed example further illustrates how well Prolog is suited for the implementation of knowledge-based systems.

## 24.1 Two-person, perfect-information games

The kind of games that we are going to discuss in this chapter are called two-person, perfect-information games. Examples of games of this kind are chess, checkers and go. In such games there are two players that make moves alternately, and both players have the complete information of the current situation in the game. Thus this definition excludes most card games. The game is over when a position is reached that qualifies as 'terminal' by the rules of the game – for example, mate in chess. The rules also determine what is the outcome of the game that has ended in this terminal position.

Such a game can be represented by a *game tree*. The nodes in such a tree correspond to situations, and the arcs correspond to moves. The initial situation of the game is the root node; the leaves of the tree correspond to terminal positions.

In most games of this type the outcome of the game can be *win*, *loss* or *draw*. We will now consider games with just two outcomes: *win* and *loss*. Games where a draw is a possible outcome can be reduced to two outcomes: *win*, *not-win*. The two players will be called 'us' and 'them'. 'Us' can win in a non-terminal 'us-to-move' position if there is a legal move that leads to a won position. On the other hand, a non-terminal 'them-to-move' position is won for 'us' if *all* the legal moves from this position lead to won positions. These rules correspond to AND/OR tree representation of problems discussed in Chapter 14. The concepts from AND/OR trees and games correspond as follows:

| | |
|---|---|
| game positions | problems |
| terminal won position | goal node, trivially solved problem |
| terminal lost position | unsolvable problem |
| won position | solved problem |
| us-to-move position | OR node |
| them-to-move position | AND node |

Clearly, many concepts from searching AND/OR trees can be adapted for searching game trees.

A simple program that finds whether an us-to-move position is won can be defined as follows:

```
won( Pos) :-
    terminalwon( Pos).                 % A terminal won position

won( Pos) :-
    \+ terminallost( Pos),
    move( Pos, Pos1),                  % A legal move to Pos1
    \+ ( move( Pos1, Pos2),            % No opponent's move leads to a
        \+ won( Pos2) ).               % not-won position
```

The rules of the game are built into the predicates **move( Pos, Pos1)** to generate legal moves, and **terminalwon( Pos)** and **terminallost( Pos)** to recognize terminal positions that are won or lost by the rules of the game. The last rule above says, through the double negation: there is no them-move that leads to a not-won position. In other words: *all* them-moves lead to a won position for us.

As with analogous programs for searching AND/OR graphs, the above program uses the depth-first strategy. In addition, this program does not prevent cycling between positions. This may cause problems as the rules of some games allow repetition of positions. However, this repetition is often only superficial. By rules of chess, for example, after a three-fold repetition the game can be claimed a draw.

The foregoing program shows the basic principle. However, much more powerful techniques are necessary for dealing in practice with complicated games like chess or go. The combinatorial complexity of these games makes our naive search algorithm, which only stops at terminal positions of the game, completely infeasible. Figure 24.1 illustrates this point with respect to chess. The search space of astronomical proportions includes some $10^{120}$ positions. It can be argued that equal positions in the tree of Figure 24.1 occur at different places. Still, it has been shown that the number of different positions is far beyond anything manageable by foreseeable computers.

# PROJECT

Write a program to play some simple game (like *nim*) using the straightforward AND/OR search approach.

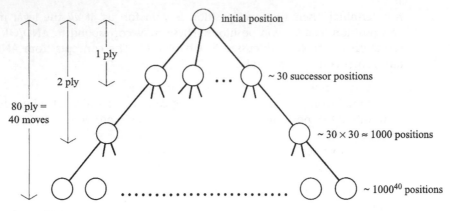

**Figure 24.1** The complexity of game trees in chess. The estimates here are based on an approximation that there are about 30 legal moves from each chess position, and that terminal positions occur at a depth of 40 moves. One move is 2 plies (1 half-move by each side).

## 24.2 The minimax principle

As searching game trees exhaustively is not feasible for interesting games, other methods that rely on searching only part of the game tree have been developed. Among these, a standard technique used in computer game playing (chess) is based on the *minimax* principle. A game tree is only searched up to a certain depth, typically a few moves, and then the tip nodes of the search tree are evaluated by some evaluation function. The idea is to assess these terminal search positions without searching beyond them, thus saving time. These terminal position estimates then propagate up the search tree according to the minimax principle. This yields position values for all the positions in the search tree. The move that leads from the initial, root position to its most promising successor (according to these values) is then actually played in the game.

Notice that we distinguish between a 'game tree' and a 'search tree'. A search tree is a part of the game tree (upper part) – that is, the part that is explicitly generated by the search process. Thus, terminal search positions do not have to be terminal positions of the game.

Much depends on the evaluation function, which, in most games of interest, has to be a heuristic estimator that estimates the winning chances from the point of view of one of the players. The higher the value the higher the player's chances are to win, and the lower the value the higher the opponent's chances are to win. As one of the players will tend to achieve a high position value, and the other a low value, the two players will be called MAX and MIN respectively. Whenever MAX is to move, he or she will choose a move that maximizes the value; in contrast, MIN will choose a move that minimizes the value. Given the values of the bottom-level positions in a search tree, this principle (called *minimax*) will determine the values of all the other positions in the search tree.

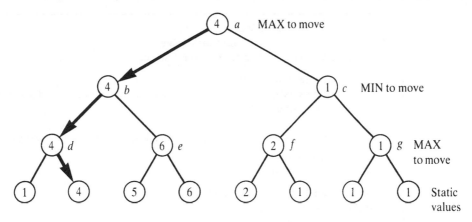

**Figure 24.2** Static values (bottom level) and minimax backed-up values in a search tree. The indicated moves constitute the *main variation* – that is, the minimax optimal play for both sides.

Figure 24.2 illustrates. In the figure, levels of positions with MAX to move alternate with those with MIN to move. The bottom-level position values are determined by the evaluation function. The values of the internal nodes can be computed in a bottom-up fashion, level by level, until the root node is reached. The resulting root value in Figure 24.2 is 4, and accordingly the best move for MAX in position *a* is *a-b*. The best MIN's reply is *b-d*, etc. This sequence of play is also called the *main variation*. The main variation defines the 'minimax-optimal' play for both sides. Notice that the value of the positions along the main variation does not vary. Accordingly, correct moves are those that preserve the value of the game.

We distinguish between the bottom-level values and the backed-up values. The former values are called 'static' since they are obtained by a 'static' evaluation function, as opposed to backed-up values that are obtained 'dynamically' by propagation of static values up the tree.

The value propagation rules can be formalized as follows. Let us denote the static value of a position $P$ by:

$v(P)$

and the backed-up value by:

$V(P)$

Let $P_1, \ldots, P_n$ be legal successor positions of $P$. Then the relation between static values and backed-up values can be defined as:

$V(P) = v(P)$       if $P$ is a terminal position in a search tree ($n = 0$)

$V(P) = \max_i V(P_i)$       if $P$ is a MAX-to-move position

$V(P) = \min_i V(P_i)$       if $P$ is a MIN-to-move position

```
% minimax( Pos, BestSucc, Val):
%    Pos is a position, Val is its minimax value;
%    best move from Pos leads to position BestSucc

minimax( Pos, BestSucc, Val) :-
   moves( Pos, PosList), !,                    % Legal moves in Pos produce PosList
   best( PosList, BestSucc, Val)
   ;
   staticval( Pos, Val).                        % Pos has no successors: evaluate statically

best( [ Pos], Pos, Val) :-
   minimax( Pos, _, Val), !.

best( [Pos1 | PosList], BestPos, BestVal) :-
   minimax( Pos1, _, Val1),
   best( PosList, Pos2, Val2),
   betterof( Pos1, Val1, Pos2, Val2, BestPos, BestVal).

betterof( Pos0, Val0, Pos1, Val1, Pos0, Val0) :-      % Pos0 better than Pos1
   min_to_move( Pos0),                                % MIN to move in Pos0
   Val0 > Val1, !                                     % MAX prefers the greater value
   ;
   max_to_move( Pos0),                                % MAX to move in Pos0
   Val0 < Val1, !.                                    % MIN prefers the lesser value

betterof( Pos0, Val0, Pos1, Val1, Pos1, Val1).        % Otherwise Pos1 better than Pos0
```

**Figure 24.3** A straightforward implementation of the minimax principle.

A Prolog program that computes the minimax backed-up value for a given position is shown in Figure 24.3. The main relation in this program is

   minimax( Pos, BestSucc, Val)

where **Val** is the minimax value of a position **Pos**, and **BestSucc** is the best successor position of **Pos** (the move to be played to achieve **Val**). The relation

   moves( Pos, PosList)

corresponds to the legal-move rules of the game: **PosList** is the list of legal successor positions of **Pos**. The predicate **moves** is assumed to fail if **Pos** is a terminal search position (a leaf of the search tree). The relation

   best( PosList, BestPos, BestVal)

selects the 'best' position **BestPos** from a list of candidate positions **PosList**. **BestVal** is the value of **BestPos**, and hence also of **Pos**. 'Best' is here either maximum or minimum, depending on the side to move.

## 24.3 The alpha-beta algorithm: an efficient implementation of minimax

The program in Figure 24.3 systematically visits *all* the positions in the search tree, up to its terminal positions in a depth-first fashion, and statically evaluates *all* the terminal positions of this tree. Usually not all this work is necessary in order to correctly compute the minimax value of the root position. Accordingly, the search algorithm can be economized. The improvement can be based on the following idea: Suppose that there are two alternative moves; once one of them has been shown to be clearly inferior to the other, it is not necessary to know *exactly* how much inferior it is for making the correct decision. For example, we can use this principle to reduce the search in the tree of Figure 24.2. The search process here proceeds as follows:

(1) Start with position *a*.

(2) Move down to *b*.

(3) Move down to *d*.

(4) Take the maximum of *d*'s successors yielding $V(d) = 4$.

(5) Backtrack to *b* and move down to *e*.

(6) Consider the first successor of *e* whose value is 5. At this point MAX (who is to move in *e*) is guaranteed at least the value of 5 in position *e* regardless of other (possibly better) alternatives from *e*. This is sufficient for MIN to realize that, at node *b*, the alternative *e* is inferior to *d*, even without knowing the exact value of *e*.

On these grounds we can neglect the second successor of *e* and simply assign to *e* an *approximate* value 5. This approximation will, however, have no effect on the computed value of *b* and, hence, of *a*.

The celebrated *alpha-beta algorithm* for efficient minimaxing is based on this idea. Figure 24.4 illustrates the action of the alpha-beta algorithm on our example tree of Figure 24.2. As Figure 24.4 shows, some of the backed-up values are approximate. However, these approximations are sufficient to determine the root value precisely. In the example of Figure 24.4, the alpha-beta principle reduces the search complexity from eight static evaluations (as originally in Figure 24.2) to five static evaluations.

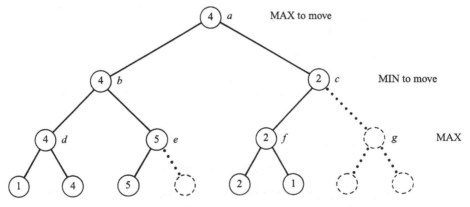

**Figure 24.4** The tree of Figure 24.2 searched by the alpha-beta algorithm. The alpha-beta search prunes the nodes shown by dotted lines, thus economizing the search. As a result, some of the backed-up values are inexact (nodes *c*, *e*, and *f*; compare with Figure 24.2). However, these approximations suffice for determination of the root value and the main variation correctly.

As said before, the key idea of the alpha-beta pruning is to find a 'good enough' move, not necessarily the best, that is sufficiently good to make the correct decision. This idea can be formalized by introducing two bounds, usually denoted *Alpha* and *Beta*, on the backed-up value of a position. The meaning of these bounds is: *Alpha* is the minimal value that MAX is already guaranteed to achieve, and *Beta* is the maximal value that MAX can hope to achieve. From MIN's point of view, *Beta* is the worst value for MIN that MIN is guaranteed to achieve. Thus, the actual value (that is to be found) lies between *Alpha* and *Beta*. If a position has been shown to have a value that lies outside the *Alpha-Beta* interval then this is sufficient to know that this position is not in the main variation, without knowing the exact value of this position. We only have to know the exact value of this position if this value is between *Alpha* and *Beta*. Formally, we can define a 'good enough' backed-up value $V(P, Alpha, Beta)$ of a position $P$, with respect to *Alpha* and *Beta*, as any value that satisfies the following requirements:

$$V(P, Alpha, Beta) < Alpha \quad \text{if} \quad V(P) < Alpha$$

$$V(P, Alpha, Beta) = V(P) \quad \text{if} \quad Alpha \leqq V(P) \leqq Beta$$

$$V(P, Alpha, Beta) > Beta \quad \text{if} \quad V(P) > Beta$$

Obviously we can always compute the exact value $V(P)$ of a root position $P$ by setting the bounds as follows:

$$V(P, -infinity, +infinity) = V(P)$$

Figure 24.5 shows a Prolog implementation of the alpha-beta algorithm. The main relation is

**alphabeta( Pos, Alpha, Beta, GoodPos, Val)**

where **GoodPos** is a 'good enough' successor of **Pos**, so that its value **Val** satisfies the requirements stated above:

**Val** $= V(Pos, Alpha, Beta)$

The procedure

**boundedbest( PosList, Alpha, Beta, GoodPos, Val)**

finds a 'good enough' position **GoodPos** in the list **PosList** so that the backed-up value **Val** of **GoodPos** is a good enough approximation with respect to **Alpha** and **Beta**.

The alpha-beta interval may get narrower (but never wider!) at deeper recursive calls of the alpha-beta procedure. The relation

**newbounds( Alpha, Beta, Pos, Val, NewAlpha, NewBeta)**

defines the new interval ( **NewAlpha, NewBeta**). This is always narrower than or equal to the old interval ( **Alpha, Beta**). So at deeper levels in the search tree, the *Alpha-Beta* bounds tend to shrink, and positions at deeper levels are evaluated with tighter bounds. Narrower intervals allow for grosser approximations, and thus more tree pruning. An interesting question is now: How much effort does the alpha-beta algorithm save compared with the exhaustive minimax search program of Figure 24.3?

```
% The alpha-beta algorithm

alphabeta( Pos, Alpha, Beta, GoodPos, Val) :-
  moves( Pos, PosList), !,
  boundedbest( Poslist, Alpha, Beta, GoodPos, Val);
  staticval( Pos, Val).                        % Static value of Pos

boundedbest( [Pos | PosList], Alpha, Beta, GoodPos, GoodVal) :-
  alphabeta( Pos, Alpha, Beta, _, Val),
  goodenough( PosList, Alpha, Beta, Pos, Val, GoodPos, GoodVal).

goodenough( [], _, _, Pos, Val, Pos, Val) :- !.    % No other candidate

goodenough( _, Alpha, Beta, Pos, Val, Pos, Val) :-
  min_to_move( Pos), Val > Beta, !;           % Maximizer attained upper bound
  max_to_move( Pos), Val < Alpha, !.          % Minimizer attained lower bound

goodenough( PosList, Alpha, Beta, Pos, Val, GoodPos, GoodVal) :-
  newbounds( Alpha, Beta, Pos, Val, NewAlpha, NewBeta),    % Refine bounds
  boundedbest( PosList, NewAlpha, NewBeta, Pos1, Val1),
  betterof( Pos, Val, Pos1, Val1, GoodPos, GoodVal).

newbounds( Alpha, Beta, Pos, Val, Val, Beta) :-
  min_to_move( Pos), Val > Alpha, !.          % Maximizer increased lower bound

newbounds( Alpha, Beta, Pos, Val, Alpha, Val) :-
  max_to_move( Pos), Val < Beta, !.           % Minimizer decreased upper bound

newbounds( Alpha, Beta, _, _, Alpha, Beta).   % Otherwise bounds unchanged

betterof( Pos, Val, Pos1, Val1, Pos, Val) :-   % Pos better than Pos1
  min_to_move( Pos), Val > Val1, !;
  max_to_move( Pos), Val < Val1, !.

betterof( _, _, Pos1, Val1, Pos1, Val1).       % Otherwise Pos1 better
```

**Figure 24.5** An implementation of the alpha-beta algorithm.

The efficiency of the alpha-beta search depends on the order in which positions are searched. It is advantageous to consider strong moves for each side first. It is easy to demonstrate by examples that if the order is unfortunate then the alpha-beta procedure will have to visit *all* the positions visited by the exhaustive minimax search. That means that in the worst case alpha-beta will have no advantage over the exhaustive minimax search. If the order is favourable, however, savings can be significant. Let $N$ be the number of terminal search positions statically evaluated by the exhaustive minimax algorithm. It has been proved that in the best case, when the strongest move is always considered first, the alpha-beta algorithm will only have to statically evaluate $\sqrt{N}$ positions.

On a similar note, this same result is relevant in a practical aspect in tournament play. In a tournament, a chess-playing program is usually given a certain amount of time for computing the next move in the game, and the depth to which the program can search will depend on this amount of time. The alpha-beta algorithm will be able, in the best case, to search *twice as deep* as the exhaustive minimax search. Experience in computer game playing shows that the ability to search deeper is very important. Between two programs, each using the same evaluation function, the program that searches deeper will play better.

The economization effect of the alpha-beta algorithm can also be expressed in terms of the effective branching factor (number of branches stemming from each internal node) of the search tree. Assume that the game tree has a uniform branching factor $b$. Due to the pruning effect, alpha-beta will only search some of the branches, thus effectively reducing the branching factor. The reduction is, in the best case, from $b$ to $\sqrt{b}$. In chess-playing programs the effective branching factor due to the alpha-beta pruning becomes about 6 compared to the total of about 30 legal moves. A less optimistic view on this result is that in chess, even with alpha-beta, deepening the search by 1 ply (one half-move) increases the number of terminal search positions by a factor of about 6.

## PROJECT

Consider a two-person game (for example, some non-trivial version of tic-tac-toe). Write game-definition relations (legal moves and terminal game positions) and propose a static evaluation function to be used for playing the game with the alpha-beta procedure.

##  24.4    Minimax-based programs: refinements and limitations

The minimax principle, together with the alpha-beta algorithm, is the basis of many successful game-playing programs, most notably chess programs. The general scheme of such a program is: perform the alpha-beta search on the current position in the game, up to some fixed depth limit (dictated by the time constraints imposed by tournament rules), using a game-specific evaluation function for evaluating the terminal positions of the search. Then execute the best move (according to alpha-beta) on the play board, accept the opponent's reply, and start the same cycle again.

The two basic ingredients, then, are the alpha-beta algorithm and a heuristic evaluation function. To build a good program for a complicated game like chess many refinements to this basic scheme are needed. We will briefly review some standard techniques.

Much depends on the evaluation function. If we had a perfect evaluation function we would only have to consider the immediate successors of the current position, thus practically eliminating search. But for games like chess, any evaluation function of practically acceptable computational complexity will necessarily be just a heuristic estimate. This estimate is based on 'static' features of the position (for example, the number of pieces on the board) and will therefore be more reliable in some positions than in others. Consider for example such a material-based evaluation function for chess and imagine a position in which White is a knight up. This function will, of course, assess the position in White's favour. This is fine if the position is quiescent, Black having no violent threat at his disposal. On the other hand, if Black can capture the White's queen on the next move, such an evaluation can result in a disastrous blunder, as it will not be able to perceive the position *dynamically*. Clearly, we can better trust the static evaluation in quiescent positions than in turbulent positions in which each side has direct threats of capturing the opponent's pieces. Obviously, we should use the static evaluation only in quiescent positions. Therefore a standard trick is to extend the search in turbulent positions beyond the depth limit until a quiescent position is reached. In particular, this extension includes sequences of piece captures in chess.

Another refinement is *heuristic pruning*. This aims at achieving a greater depth limit by disregarding some less promising continuations. This technique will prune branches in addition to those that are pruned by the alpha-beta technique itself. Therefore this entails the risk of overlooking some good continuation and incorrectly computing the minimax value.

Yet another technique is *progressive deepening*. The program repeatedly executes the alpha-beta search, first to some shallow depth, and then increases the depth limit on each iteration. The process stops when the time limit has been reached. The best move according to the deepest search is then played. This technique has the following advantages:

- enables the time control; when the time limit is reached there will always be some best move found so far;

- the minimax values of the previous iteration can be used for preliminary ordering of positions on the next iteration, thus helping the alpha-beta algorithm to search strong moves first.

Progressive deepening entails some overhead (researching upper parts of the game tree), but this is relatively small compared with the total effort.

A known problem with programs that belong to this general scheme is the 'horizon effect'. Imagine a chess position in which the program's side inevitably loses a knight. But the loss of the knight can be delayed at the cost of a lesser sacrifice, a pawn say. This intermediate sacrifice may push the actual loss of the knight beyond the search limit (beyond the program's 'horizon'). Not seeing the eventual loss of the knight, the program will then prefer this variation to the quick death of the knight. So the program will eventually lose *both* the pawn (unnecessarily) and the knight. The extension of search up to a quiescent position can alleviate the horizon effect.

There is, however, a more fundamental limitation of the minimax-based programs, which lies in the limited form of the domain-specific knowledge they use. This becomes very conspicuous when we compare the best chess programs with human chess masters. Strong programs search millions (and more) of positions before deciding on the move to play. It is known from psychological studies that human masters typically search just a few tens of positions, at most a few hundred. Despite this apparent inferiority, a chess master may still offer some resistance to a program. The masters' advantage lies in their knowledge, which far exceeds that contained in the programs. Games between machines and strong human players show that the enormous advantage in the calculating power cannot always completely compensate for the lack of knowledge.

Knowledge in minimax-based programs takes three main forms:

- evaluation function,
- tree-pruning heuristics,
- quiescence heuristics.

The evaluation function reduces many aspects of a game situation into a single number, and this reduction can have a detrimental effect. A good player's understanding of a game position, on the contrary, spans many dimensions. Let us consider an example from chess: an evaluation function will evaluate a position as equal simply by stating that its value is 0. A master's assessment of the same position can be much more informative and indicative of a further course of the game. For example, Black is a pawn up, but White has a good attacking initiative that compensates the material, so chances are equal.

In chess, minimax-based programs usually play best in sharp tactical struggles when precise calculation of forced variations is decisive. Their weakness is more likely to show in quiet positions where their play may fall short of long-range plans that prevail in such slow, strategic games. Lack of a plan makes an impression that the program keeps wandering during the game from one idea to another. It should be noted, however, that even such subtle weaknesses are very rarely perceived in games of the present leading chess programs.

In the rest of this chapter we will consider another approach to game playing, based on introducing pattern knowledge into a program by means of 'advice'. This enables the programming of goal-oriented, plan-based behaviour of a game-playing program.

##  24.5 Pattern knowledge and the mechanism of 'advice'

### 24.5.1 Goals and move-constraints

The method of representing game-specific knowledge that we consider in this section belongs to the family of Advice Languages. In Advice Languages the user specifies, in a declarative way, what ideas should be tried in certain types of situations. Ideas are formulated in terms of goals and means of achieving the goals. An Advice Language interpreter then finds out, through search, which idea actually works in a given situation.

The fundamental concept in Advice Languages is a 'piece-of-advice'. A piece-of-advice suggests what to do (or to *try* to do) next in a certain type of position. Generally speaking, advice is expressed in terms of *goals* to be achieved, and *means* of achieving these goals. The two sides are called 'us' and 'them'; advice always refers to the 'us' point of view. Each piece-of advice has four ingredients:

- *better-goal*: a goal to be achieved;
- *holding-goal*: a goal to be maintained during play toward the better-goal;
- *us-move-constraints*: a predicate on moves that selects a subset of all legal us-moves (moves that should be considered of interest with respect to the goals specified);
- *them-move-constraints*: a predicate to select moves to be considered by 'them' (moves that may undermine the goals specified).

As a simple example from the chess endgame king and pawn vs king, consider the straightforward idea of queening the pawn by simply pushing the pawn forward. This can be expressed in the form of advice as:

- *better-goal*: pawn queened;
- *holding-goal*: pawn is not lost;
- *us-move-constraints*: pawn move;
- *them-move-constraints*: approach the pawn with the king.

## 24.5.2  Satisfiability of advice

We say that a given piece-of-advice is *satisfiable* in a given position if 'us' can force the achievement of the better-goal specified in the advice under the conditions that:

(1) the holding-goal is never violated,

(2) all the moves played by 'us' satisfy us-move-constraints,

(3) 'them' is only allowed to make moves that satisfy them-move-constraints.

The concept of a *forcing-tree* is associated with the satisfiability of a piece-of-advice. A forcing-tree is a detailed strategy that guarantees the achievement of the better-goal under the constraints specified by the piece-of-advice. A forcing-tree thus specifies exactly what moves 'us' has to play on any 'them' reply. More precisely, a forcing-tree $T$ for a given position $P$ and a piece-of-advice $A$ is a subtree of the game tree such that:

- the root node of $T$ is $P$;
- all the positions in $T$ satisfy the holding-goal;
- all the terminal nodes in $T$ satisfy the better-goal, and no internal node in $T$ satisfies the better-goal;
- there is exactly one us-move from each internal us-to-move position in $T$; and that move must satisfy the us-move-constraints;
- $T$ contains all them-moves (that satisfy the them-move-constraints) from each non-terminal them-to-move position in $T$.

Each piece-of-advice can be viewed as a definition of a small special game with the following rules. Each opponent is allowed to make moves that satisfy his or her move-constraints; a position that does not satisfy the holding-goal is won for 'them'; a position that satisfies the holding-goal and the better-goal is won for 'us'. A non-terminal position is won for 'us' if the piece-of-advice is satisfiable in this position. Then 'us' will win by executing a corresponding forcing-tree in the play.

## 24.5.3  Integrating pieces-of-advice into rules and advice-tables

In Advice Languages, individual pieces-of-advice are integrated in the complete knowledge representation schema through the following hierarchy. A piece-of-advice is part of an if-then rule. A collection of if-then rules is an *advice-table*. A set of advice-tables is structured into a hierarchical network. Each advice-table has the role of a specialized expert to deal with some specific subproblem of the whole domain. An example of such a specialized expert is an advice-table that knows how to mate in the king and rook vs king ending in chess. This table is summoned when such an ending occurs in a game.

For simplicity, we will consider a simplified version of an Advice Language in which we will only allow for one advice-table. We shall call this version Advice Language 0, or AL0 for short. Here the structure of AL0 is already syntactically tailored toward an easy implementation in Prolog.

A program in AL0 is called an *advice-table*. An advice-table is an *ordered* collection of if-then rules. Each rule has the form:

**RuleName :: if Condition then AdviceList**

**Condition** is a logical expression that consists of predicate names connected by logical connectives **and, or, not**. **AdviceList** is a list of names of pieces-of-advice. An example of a rule called 'edge_rule', from the king and rook vs king ending, can be:

**edge_rule ::**
**if their_king_on_edge and our_king_close**
**then [ mate_in_2, squeeze, approach, keeproom, divide].**

This rule says: if in the current position their king is on the edge and our king is close to their king (or more precisely, kings are less than four squares apart), then try to satisfy, in the order of preference as stated, the pieces-of-advice: 'mate_in_2', 'squeeze', 'approach', 'keeproom', 'divide'. This advice-list specifies pieces-of-advice in the decreasing order of ambition: first try to mate in two moves, if that is not possible then try to 'squeeze' the opponent's king toward a corner, etc. Notice that with an appropriate definition of operators, the rule above is a syntactically correct Prolog clause.

Each piece-of-advice will be specified by a Prolog clause of the form:

**advice( AdviceName,**
        **BetterGoal :**
        **HoldingGoal :**
        **Us_Move_Constraints :**
        **Them_Move_Constraints).**

The goals are expressions that consist of predicate names and logical connectives **and, or, not**. Move-constraints are, again, expressions that consist of predicate names and the connectives **and** and **then**: **and** has the usual logical meaning, **then** prescribes the ordering. For example, a move-constraint of the form

**MC1 then MC2**

says: first consider those moves that satisfy MC1, and then those that satisfy MC2.

For example, a piece-of-advice to mate in 2 moves in the king and rook vs king ending, written in this syntax, is:

**advice( mate_in_2,**
        **mate :**
        **not rooklost :**
        **(depth = 0) and legal then (depth = 2) and checkmove :**
        **(depth = 1) and legal).**

Here the better-goal is **mate**, the holding-goal is **not rooklost** (rook is not lost). The us-move-constraints say: at depth 0 (the current board position) try any legal move, then at depth 2 (our second move) try checking moves only. The depth is measured in plies. Them-move-constraints are: any legal move at depth 1.

In playing, an advice-table is then used by repeating, until the end of the game, the following main cycle: build a forcing-tree, then play according to this tree until the play exits the tree; build another forcing-tree, etc. A forcing-tree is generated each time as follows: take the current board position **Pos** and scan the rules in the advice-table one by one; for each rule, match **Pos** with the precondition of the rule, and stop when a rule is found such that **Pos** satisfies its precondition. Now consider the advice-list of this rule: process pieces-of-advice in this list one by one until a piece-of-advice is found that is satisfiable in **Pos**. This results in a forcing-tree that is the detailed strategy to be executed across the board.

Notice the importance of the ordering of rules and pieces-of-advice. The rule used is the first rule whose precondition matches the current position. There must be for any possible position at least one rule in the advice-table whose precondition will match the position. Thus an advice-list is selected. The first satisfiable piece-of-advice in this list is applied.

An advice-table is thus largely a non-procedural program. An AL0 interpreter accepts a position and by executing an advice-table produces a forcing-tree which determines the play in that position.

## 24.6 A chess endgame program in Advice Language 0

Implementation of an AL0-based game-playing program can be conveniently divided into three modules:

(1)  an AL0 interpreter,

(2)  an advice-table in AL0,

(3)  a library of predicates (including rules of the game) used in the advice-table.

This structure corresponds to the usual structure of knowledge-based systems as follows:

* The AL0 interpreter is an inference engine.
* The advice-table and the predicate library constitute a knowledge base.

### 24.6.1  A miniature AL0 interpreter

A miniature, game-independent AL0 interpreter is implemented in Prolog in Figure 24.6. This program also performs the user interaction during play. The central function of the program is the use of knowledge in an AL0 advice-table; that is, interpreting an AL0 advice-program for the generation of forcing-trees and their execution in a game. The basic forcing-tree generation algorithm is similar to the depth-first search in AND/OR graphs of Chapter 14; a forcing-tree corresponds to an AND/OR solution tree.

For simplicity, in the program of Figure 24.6 'us' is supposed to be White, and 'them' is Black. The program is started through the procedure

  **playgame( Pos)**

```
% A miniature implementation of Advice Language 0
%
% This program plays a game from a given starting position using knowledge
% represented in Advice Language 0

:- op( 200, xfy, [:, ::].
:- op( 220, xfy, .. ).
:- op( 185, fx, if).
:- op( 190, xfx, then).
:- op( 180, xfy, or).
:- op( 160, xfy, and).
:- op( 140, fx, not).

playgame( Pos) :-                              % Play a game starting in Pos
  playgame( Pos, nil).                         % Start with empty forcing-tree

playgame( Pos, ForcingTree) :-
  show( Pos),
  ( end_of_game( Pos),                         % End of game?
    write( 'End of game'), nl, !
    ;
    playmove( Pos, ForcingTree, Pos1, ForcingTree1), !,
    playgame( Pos1, ForcingTree1)
  ).

% Play 'us' move according to forcing-tree

playmove( Pos, Move .. FTree1, Pos1, FTree1) :-
  side( Pos, w),                               % White = 'us'
  legalmove( Pos, Move, Pos1),
  showmove( Move).

% Read 'them' move

playmove( Pos, FTree, Pos1, FTree1) :-
  side( Pos, b),
  write( 'Your move: '),
  read( Move),
  ( legalmove( Pos, Move, Pos1),
    subtree( FTree, Move, FTree1), !           % Move down forcing-tree
    ;
    write( 'Illegal move'), nl,
    playmove( Pos, FTree, Pos1, FTree1)
  ).

% If current forcing-tree is empty generate a new one

playmove( Pos, nil, Pos1, FTree1) :-
  side( Pos, w),
  resetdepth( Pos, Pos0),                      % Pos0 = Pos with depth 0
  strategy( Pos0, FTree), !,                   % Generate new forcing-tree
  playmove( Pos0, FTree, Pos1, FTree1).

% Select a forcing-subtree corresponding to Move

subtree( FTrees, Move, FTree) :-
  member( Move .. FTree, FTrees), !.
```

**Figure 24.6** A miniature implementation of Advice Language 0.

**Figure 24.6** *contd*

```
subtree( _ , _ , nil).

strategy( Pos, ForcingTree) :-            % Find forcing-tree for Pos
   Rule :: if Condition then AdviceList,  % Consult advice-table
   holds( Condition, Pos, _), !,          % Match Pos against precondition
   member( AdviceName, AdviceList),       % Try pieces-of-advice in turn
   nl, write( 'Trying'), write( AdviceName),
   satisfiable( AdviceName, Pos, ForcingTree), !.  % Satisfy AdviceName in Pos

satisfiable( AdviceName, Pos, FTree) :-
   advice( AdviceName, Advice),           % Retrieve piece-of-advice
   sat( Advice, Pos, Pos, FTree).         % 'sat' needs two positions
                                          % for comparison predicates

sat( Advice, Pos, RootPos, FTree) :-
   holdinggoal( Advice, HG),
   holds( HG, Pos, RootPos),              % Holding-goal satisfied
   sat1( Advice, Pos, RootPos, FTree).

sat1( Advice, Pos, RootPos, nil) :-
   bettergoal( Advice, BG),
   holds( BG, Pos, RootPos), !.           % Better-goal satisfied

sat1( Advice, Pos, RootPos, Move .. FTrees) :-
   side( Pos, w), !,                      % White = 'us'
   usmoveconstr( Advice, UMC),
   move( UMC, Pos, Move, Pos1),           % A move satisfying move-constr.
   sat( Advice, Pos1, RootPos, FTrees).

sat1( Advice, Pos, RootPos, FTrees) :-
   side( Pos, b), !,                      % Black = 'them'
   themmoveconstr( Advice, TMC),
   bagof( Move .. Pos1, move( TMC, Pos, Move, Pos1), MPlist),
   satall( Advice, MPlist, RootPos, FTrees).  % Satisfiable in all successors

satall( _ , [], _ , [] ).

satall( Advice, [Move .. Pos | MPlist], RootPos, [Move .. FT | MFTs] ) :-
   sat( Advice, Pos, RootPos, FT),
   satall( Advice, MPlist, RootPos, MFTs).

% Interpreting holding and better-goals:
% A goal is an AND/OR/NOT combination of predicate names

holds( Goal1 and Goal2, Pos, RootPos) :- !,
   holds( Goal1, Pos, RootPos),
   holds( Goal2, Pos, RootPos).

holds( Goal1 or Goal2, Pos, RootPos) :- !,
   ( holds( Goal1, Pos, RootPos)
     ;
     holds( Goal2, Pos, RootPos)
   ).

holds( not Goal, Pos, RootPos) :- !,
   \+ holds( Goal, Pos, RootPos).
```

►

**Figure 24.6** *contd*

```
holds( Pred, Pos, RootPos)  :-
  ( Cond =.. [ Pred, Pos]                    % Most predicates do not depend on RootPos
    ;
    Cond =.. [ Pred, Pos, RootPos] ),
  call( Cond).

% Interpreting move-constraints

move( MC1 and MC2, Pos, Move, Pos1)  :- !,
  move( MC1, Pos, Move, Pos1),
  move( MC2, Pos, Move, Pos1).

move( MC1 then MC2, Pos, Move, Pos1)  :- !,
  ( move( MC1, Pos, Move, Pos1)
    ;
    move( MC2, Pos, Move, Pos1)
  ).

% Selectors for components of piece-of-advice

bettergoal( BG : _, BG).

holdinggoal( BG : HG : _, HG).

usmoveconstr( BG : HG : UMC : _, UMC).

themmoveconstr( BG : HG : UMC : TMC, TMC).

member( X, [X | L] ).

member( X, [Y | L] )  :-
  member( X, L).
```

where **Pos** is a chosen initial position of a game to be played. If it is 'them' to move in **Pos** then the program reads a move from the user, otherwise the program consults the advice-table that is attached to the program, generates a forcing-tree and plays its move according to the tree. This continues until the end of the game is reached as specified by the predicate **end_of_game** (mate, for example).

A forcing-tree is a tree of moves, represented in the program by the following structure

> Move .. [ Reply1 .. Ftree1, Reply2 .. Ftree2, ... ]

where '..' is an infix operator; **Move** is the first move for 'us'; **Reply1**, **Reply2**, etc. are the possible 'them' replies; and **Ftree1**, **Ftree2**, etc. are forcing-subtrees that correspond to each of the 'them' replies respectively.

## 24.6.2 An advice-program for the king and rook vs king ending

A broad strategy for winning with the king and rook against the sole opponent's king is to force the king to the edge, or into a corner if necessary, and then deliver mate in a few moves. An elaboration of this broad principle is:

> While making sure that stalemate is never created or the rook left unde-
> fended under attack, repeat until mate:
>
> (1) Look for a way to mate the opponent's king in two moves.
>
> (2) If the above is not possible, then look for a way to constrain further the area
> on the chessboard to which the opponent's king is confined by our rook.
>
> (3) If the above is not possible, then look for a way to move our king closer to
> the opponent's king.
>
> (4) If none of the above pieces-of-advice 1, 2 or 3 works, then look for a way of
> maintaining the present achievements in the sense of 2 and 3 (that is,
> make a waiting move).
>
> (5) If none of 1, 2, 3 or 4 is attainable, then look for a way of obtaining a
> position in which our rook divides the two kings either vertically or
> horizontally.

These principles are implemented in detail as an AL0 advice-table in Figure 24.7.
This table can be run by the AL0 interpreter of Figure 24.6. Figure 24.8 illustrates
the meaning of some of the predicates used in the table and the way the table
works.

The predicates used in the table are:

*Goal predicates*

| | |
|---|---|
| **mate** | their king mated |
| **stalemate** | their king stalemated |
| **rooklost** | their king can capture our rook |
| **rookexposed** | their king can attack our rook before our king can get to defend the rook |
| **newroomsmaller** | area to which their king is restricted by our rook has shrunk |
| **rookdivides** | rook divides both kings either vertically or horizontally |
| **okapproachedcsquare** | our king approached 'critical square', see Figure 24.9; here this means that the Manhattan distance has decreased |
| **lpatt** | 'L-pattern' (Figure 24.9) |
| **roomgt2** | the 'room' for their king is greater than two squares |

*Move-constraints predicates*

| | |
|---|---|
| **depth** = N | move occurring at **depth** = N in the search tree |
| **legal** | any legal move |
| **checkmove** | checking move |
| **rookmove** | a rook move |
| **nomove** | fails for any move |
| **kingdiagfirst** | a king move, with preference for diagonal king moves |

The arguments of these predicates are either positions (goal predicates) or moves
(move-constraints predicates). Goal predicates can have one or two arguments. One
argument is always the current search node; the second argument (if it exists) is the
root node of the search tree. The second argument is needed in the so-called
comparison predicates, which compare in some respect the root position and the

% King and rook vs king in Advice Language 0

% Rules

edge_rule :: if    their_king_edge and kings_close
           then [ mate_in_2, squeeze, approach, keeproom,
                    divide_in_2, divide_in_3 ].

else_rule :: if    true
           then [ squeeze, approach, keeproom, divide_in_2, divide_in_3 ].

% Pieces-of-advice

advice( mate_in_2,
      mate :
      not rooklost and their_king_edge :
      (depth = 0) and legal then (depth = 2) and checkmove :
      (depth = 1) and legal).

advice( squeeze,
      newroomsmaller and not rookexposed and
      rookdivides and not stalemate :
      not rooklost :
      (depth = 0) and rookmove :
      nomove).

advice( approach,
      okapproachedcsquare and not rookexposed and not stalemate and
      (rookdivides or lpatt) and (roomgt2 or not our_king_edge) :
      not rooklost :
      (depth = 0) and kingdiagfirst :
      nomove).

advice( keeproom,
      themtomove and not rookexposed and rookdivides and okorndle and
      (roomgt2 or not okedge) :
      not rooklost :
      (depth = 0) and kingdiagfirst :
      nomove).

advice( divide_in_2,
      themtomove and rookdivides and not rookexposed :
      not rooklost :
      (depth < 3) and legal :
      (depth < 2) and legal).

advice( divide_in_3,
      themtomove and rookdivides and not rookexposed :
      not rooklost :
      (depth < 5) and legal :
      (depth < 4) and legal).

**Figure 24.7** An AL0 advice-table for king and rook *vs* king. The table consists of two rules and six pieces-of-advice.

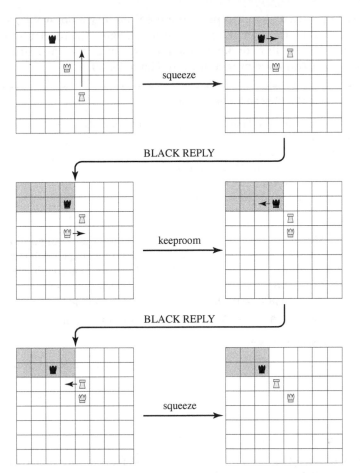

**Figure 24.8** A game fragment played by the advice-table of Figure 24.7, illustrating the method of squeezing their king toward a corner. Pieces-of-advice used in this sequence are **keeproom** (waiting move preserving 'room') and **squeeze** ('room' has shrunk). The area to which their king is confined by our rook ('room') is shadowed. After the last **squeeze**, 'room' shrinks from eight to six squares.

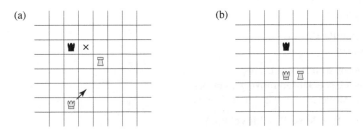

**Figure 24.9** (a) Illustration of the 'critical square' (a crucial square in the squeezing manoeuvres, indicated by a cross); the White king approaches the critical square by moving as indicated. (b) The three pieces form an L-shaped pattern.

current search position. An example is the predicate **newroomsmaller**, which tests whether the 'room' for their king has shrunk (Figure 24.8). These predicates, together with chess rules for king and rook vs king, and a board displaying procedure ( **show( Pos)** ), are programmed in Figure 24.10.

```
% Predicate library for king and rook vs king

% Position is represented by: Side .. Wx : Wy .. Rx : Ry .. Bx : By .. Depth
% Side is side to move ('w' or 'b' )
% Wx, Wy are X and Y-coordinates of White king
% Rx, Ry are X and Y-coordinates of White rook
% Bx, By are coordinates of Black king
% Depth is depth of position in search tree

% Selector relations

side( Side .._ , Side).                          % Side to move in position
wk( _ .. WK .._ , WK).                           % White king coordinates
wr( _ .._ .. WR .._ , WR).                       % White rook coordinates
bk( _ .._ .._ .._ .. BK .._ , BK).               % Black king coordinates
depth( _ .._ .._ .._ .. Depth, Depth).           % Depth of position in search tree

resetdepth( S .. W .. R .. B .. D, S .. W .. R .. B .. 0).   % Copy of position with depth 0

% Some relations between squares

n( N, N1) :-                                     % Neighbour integers 'within board'
  ( N1 is N + 1;
    N1 is N − 1),
  in( N1).

in( N) :-
  N > 0, N < 9.

diagngb( X : Y, X1 : Y1) :-                      % Diagonal neighbour squares
  n( X, X1), n( Y, Y1).

verngb( X : Y, X : Y1) :-                        % Vertical neighbour squares
  n( Y, Y1).

horngb( X : Y, X1 : Y) :-                        % Horizontal neighbour squares
  n( X, X1).

ngb( S, S1) :-                                   % Neighbour squares, first diagonal
  diagngb( S, S1);
  horngb( S, S1);
  verngb( S, S1).

end_of_game( Pos) :-
  mate( Pos).

% Move-constraints predicates
% These are specialized move generators:
% move( MoveConstr, Pos, Move, NewPos)

move( depth < Max, Pos, Move, Pos1) :-
  depth( Pos, D),
  D < Max, !.
```

**Figure 24.10** Predicate library for king and rook *vs* king.

**Figure 24.10** *contd*

```
move( depth = D, Pos, Move, Pos1) :-
  depth( Pos, D), !.

move( kingdiagfirst, w..W..R..B..D, W-W1, b..W1..R..B..D1) :-
  D1 is D + 1,
  ngb( W, W1),                        % 'ngb' generates diagonal moves first
  \+ ngb( W1, B),                     % Must not move into check
  W1 \== R.                           % Must not collide with rook

move( rookmove, w..W..Rx : Ry..B..D, Rx : Ry-R, b..W..R..B..D1) :-
  D1 is D + 1,
  coord( I),                          % Integer between 1 and 8
  ( R = Rx : I; R = I : Ry),          % Move vertically or horizontally
  R \== Rx : Ry,                      % Must have moved
  \+ inway( Rx : Ry, W, R).           % White king not in way

move( checkmove, Pos, R-Rx : Ry, Pos1) :-
  wr( Pos, R),
  bk( Pos, Bx : By),
  (Rx = Bx; Ry = By),                 % Rook and Black king in line
  move( rookmove, Pos, R-Rx : Ry, Pos1).

move( legal, w..P, M, P1) :-
  ( MC = kingdiagfirst; MC = rookmove),
  move( MC, w..P, M, P1).

move( legal, b..W..R..B..D, B-B1, w..W..R..B1..D1) :-
  D1 is D + 1,
  ngb( B, B1),
  \+ check( w..W..R..B1..D1).

legalmove( Pos, Move, Pos1) :-
  move( legal, Pos, Move, Pos1).

check( _..W..Rx : Ry..Bx : By.._ ) :-
  ngb( W, Bx : By);                   % Kings too close
  ( Rx = Bx; Ry = By),
  Rx : Ry \== Bx : By,                % Not rook captured
  \+ inway( Rx : Ry, W, Bx : By).

inway( S, S1, S1) :- !.

inway( X1 : Y, X2 : Y, X3 : Y) :-
  ordered( X1, X2, X3), !.

inway( X : Y1, X : Y2, X : Y3) :-
  ordered( Y1, Y2, Y3).

ordered( N1, N2, N3) :-
  N1 < N2, N2 < N3;
  N3 < N2, N2 < N1.

coord(1).    coord(2).    coord(3).    coord(4).
coord(5).    coord(6).    coord(7).    coord(8).

% Goal predicates

true( Pos).

themtomove( b.._ ).                   % Black = 'them' to move
```

**Figure 24.10** *contd*

```
mate( Pos) :-
  side( Pos, b),
  check( Pos),
  \+ legalmove( Pos, _, _ ).

stalemate( Pos) :-
  side( Pos, b),
  \+ check( Pos),
  \+ legalmove( Pos, _, _ ).

newroomsmaller( Pos, RootPos) :-
  room( Pos, Room),
  room( RootPos, RootRoom),
  Room < RootRoom.

rookexposed( Side .. W .. R .. B .._ ) :-
  dist( W, R, D1),
  dist( B, R, D2),
  (Side = w, !, D1 > D2 + 1
  ;
   Side = b, !, D1 > D2).

okapproachedcsquare( Pos, RootPos) :-
  okcsquaremdist( Pos, D1),
  okcsquaremdist( RootPos, D2),
  D1 < D2.

okcsquaremdist( Pos, Mdist) :-   % Manhattan distance between WK and critical square
  wk( Pos, WK),
  cs( Pos, CS),                         % Critical square
  manhdist( WK, CS, Mdist).

rookdivides( _ .. Wx : Wy .. Rx : Ry .. Bx : By .._ ) :-
  ordered( Wx, Rx, Bx), !;
  ordered( Wy, Ry, By).

lpatt( _ .. W .. R .. B .._ ) :-                % L-pattern
  manhdist( W, B, 2),
  manhdist( R, B, 3).

okorndle( _ .. W .. R .._, _ .. W1 .. R1 .._ ) :-
  dist( W, R, D),
  dist( W1, R1, D1),
  D = < D1.

roomgt2( Pos) :-
  room( Pos, Room),
  Room > 2.

our_king_edge( _ .. X : Y .._ ) :-              % White king on edge
  ( X = 1, !; X = 8, !; Y = 1, !; Y = 8).

their_king_edge( _ .. W .. R .. X : Y .._ ) :-  % Black king on edge
  ( X = 1, !; X = 8, !; Y = 1, !; Y = 8).

kings_close( Pos) :-                            % Distance between kings < 4
  wk( Pos, WK), bk( Pos, BK),
  dist( WK, BK, D),
  D < 4.
```

**Figure 24.10** *contd*

```
rooklost( _..W..B..B.._ ).                    % Rook has been captured

rooklost( b..W..R..B.._ ) :-
  ngb( B, R),                                 % Black king attacks rook
  \+ ngb( W, R).                              % White king does not defend

dist( X : Y, X1 : Y1, D) :-                   % Distance in king moves
  absdiff( X, X1, Dx),
  absdiff( Y, Y1, Dy),
  max( Dx, Dy, D).

absdiff( A, B, D) :-
  A > B, !, D is A – B;
  D is B – A.

max( A, B, M) :-
  A >= B, !, M = A;
  M = B.

manhdist( X : Y, X1 : Y1, D) :-               % Manhattan distance
  absdiff( X, X1, Dx),
  absdiff( Y, Y1, Dy),
  D is Dx + Dy.

room( Pos, Room) :-                           % Area to which B. king is confined
  wr( Pos, Rx : Ry),
  bk( Pos, Bx : By),
  ( Bx < Rx, SideX is Rx – 1; Bx > Rx, SideX is 8 – Rx),
  ( By < Ry, SideY is Ry – 1; By > Ry, SideY is 8 – Ry),
  Room is SideX * SideY, !
  ;
  Room is 64.                                 % Rook in line with Black king

cs( _..W..Rx : Ry..Bx : By.._, Cx : Cy) :-    % 'Critical square'
  ( Bx < Rx, !, Cx is Rx – 1; Cx is Rx + 1),
  ( By < Ry, !, Cy is Ry – 1; Cy is Ry + 1).

% Display procedures

show( Pos) :-
  nl,
  coord( Y), nl,
  coord( X),
  writepiece( X : Y, Pos),
  fail.

show( Pos) :-
  side( Pos, S), depth( Pos, D),
  nl, write( 'Side= '), write( S),
  write( 'Depth= '), write( D), nl.

writepiece( Square, Pos) :-
  wk( Pos, Square), !, write( 'W');
  wr( Pos, Square), !, write( 'R');
  bk( Pos, Square), !, write( 'B');
  write( '.').

showmove( Move) :-
  nl, write( Move), nl.
```

An example of how this advice-program plays is shown in Figure 24.8. The game would continue from the last position of Figure 24.8 as in the following variation (assuming 'them' moves as given in the variation). The algebraic chess notation is used where the files of the chessboard are numbered 'a', 'b', 'c', etc, and ranks are numbered 1, 2, 3, etc. For example, the move 'BK b7' means: move the Black king to the square in file 'b' and rank 7.

| | |
|---|---|
| ... | BK b7 |
| WK d5 | BK c7 |
| WK c5 | BK b7 |
| WR c6 | BK a7 |
| WR b6 | BK a8 |
| WK b5 | BK a7 |
| WK c6 | BK a8 |
| WK c7 | BK a7 |
| WR c6 | BK a8 |
| WR a6 | mate |

Some questions can now be asked. First, is this advice-program *correct* in the sense that it mates against any defence if the game starts from any king and rook vs king position? It is shown in Bratko (1978) by means of a formal proof that an advice-table, effectively the same as the one in Figure 24.7, is correct in this sense.

Another question can be: Is this advice program *optimal* in the sense that it always delivers mate in the smallest number of moves? It can easily be shown by examples that the program's play is not optimal in this sense. It is known that optimal variations (optimally played by both sides) in this ending are at most 16 moves long. Although our advice-table can be rather far from this optimum, it was shown that the number of moves needed by this advice-table is still very safely under 50. This is important because of the 50-moves rule in chess: in endgames such as king and rook vs king, the stronger side has to mate within 50 moves; if not, a draw can be claimed.

Here is a final comment on our KRK advice program. The overall mating strategy is quite logical and clear: force BK to a corner and then deliver mate. But there are some details that spoil the elegance, like 'our king approached critical square'. It should be noted that our program is only allowed a very modest amount of lookahead search. This is why such specific patterns are needed. If the program were allowed to do a little deeper lookahead search then these details would no longer be needed. It would be possible to determine correct decisions simply by search.

# PROJECT
...................................................................................................................

Consider some other simple chess endgame, such as king and pawn vs king, and write an AL0 program (together with the corresponding predicate definitions) to play this endgame.

# Summary

- Two-person games fit the formalism of AND/OR graphs. AND/OR search procedures can be therefore used to search game trees.

- The straightforward depth-first search of game trees is easy to program, but is too inefficient for playing interesting games. In such cases, the minimax principle, in association with an evaluation function and depth-limited search, offers a more feasible approach.

- The alpha-beta algorithm is an efficient implementation of the minimax principle. The efficiency of alpha-beta depends on the order in which alternatives are searched. In the best case, alpha-beta in effect reduces the branching factor of a game tree to its square root. This means that alpha-beta may be able to search within the same time limit twice as deep as straightforward minimax.

- Some refinements to the basic alpha-beta algorithm include: extending the search until a quiescent position is reached, progressive deepening and heuristic pruning.

- Numerical evaluation is a very restrictive form of applying game-specific knowledge. A more knowledge-intensive approach to game playing should provide for pattern-based knowledge. Advice Languages realize such an approach, where knowledge is represented in terms of goals and means of achieving goals.

- Programs written in this chapter are: an implementation of minimax and alpha-beta, an interpreter for Advice Language 0, and an advice-table for playing the king and rook vs king chess endgame.

- Concepts discussed in this chapter are:
  two-person, perfect-information games
  game trees
  evaluation function, minimax principle
  static values, backed-up values
  alpha-beta algorithm
  progressive deepening, heuristic pruning, quiescence heuristics
  horizon effect
  Advice Languages
  goals, constraints, piece-of-advice, advice-table

## References and historical notes

The minimax principle, implemented as the alpha-beta algorithm, is the most popularly used approach to game-playing programs, and in particular to chess programs. An early reference to the minimax principle is Shannon (1950). The development of the alpha-beta technique had a rather complicated history when several researchers independently discovered or implemented the method or at least part of it. This interesting story is described by Knuth and Moore (1975), who also present a more compact formulation of the alpha-beta algorithm using the 'neg-max' principle instead of minimax, and give a mathematical analysis of its performance. Pearl (1984) gives a comprehensive treatment of several minimax-based algorithms and their analyses. Kaindl (1990) also reviews search algorithms for games. Platt *et al.* (1996) introduce a more recent variation of alpha-beta search. There is another interesting question regarding the minimax principle: Knowing that the static evaluation is only reliable to some degree, will the minimax backed-up values be more reliable than the static values themselves? Pearl (1984) also collected early results of mathematical analyses that pertain to this question. Further papers (e.g. Luštrek *et al.* 2006) on error propagation in minimax trees explain when and why the minimax look ahead is beneficial. Nau *et al.* (2010) analyse game properties that indicate when it is best *not* to search at all.

Bramer (1983), Frey (1983), and Marsland and Schaeffer (1990) edited collections of papers on computer game playing, and chess in particular. On-going research on computer game playing is published in Advances in Computer Games conferences and a series of books resulting from these conferences (previously called Advances in Computer Chess), and in the ICGA Journal (*Journal of Int. Computer Games Association*).

The Advice Language approach to using pattern knowledge in chess was introduced by Michie, and further developed in Bratko and Michie (1980), and Bratko (1982, 1984). The king and rook vs king advice-program of this chapter is a slight modification of the advice-table that was mathematically proved correct in Bratko (1978).

Other interesting experiments in knowledge-intensive approach to chess (as opposed to search-intensive approaches) include Berliner (1977), Pitrat (1977) and Wilkins (1980). Interest in knowledge-intensive chess programming has unfortunately declined over time, due to competitive success of the search-intensive, 'brute force' approach to chess programming usually implemented as alpha-beta search. Increasing power of computer hardware made it possible to search hundreds of millions of positions per second, so the sheer power more than compensates for the lack of more subtle chess knowledge. The brute force approach culminated in 1997 in the eventual defeat of the then world leading chess player Gary Kasparov by the program Deep Blue (Hsu *et al.* 1990, Campbell *et al.* 2002), an extreme example of brute force. This win by the computer over the best human chess player was generally regarded as an immense triumph of artificial intelligence, although the true key to computer victory lay in the sheer computing power. The chess battle between humans and computers over decades was eventually decided when another famous chess program, Fritz, defeated the then world champion Vladimir Kramnik in 2006. It became clear that since then humans have stood no chance against computers at chess. Interestingly, the situation is quite different in the game of go. In go, the computer's lack of knowledge still cannot be completely compensated for by superiority in search, because of greater combinatorial complexity of go. In go, therefore, a more promising approach than alpha-beta search seems to be a more recent idea called Monte Carlo search (Coulom 2007). In Monte Carlo search, the decision with regard to the best move is based on statistics of a large number of random simulated games which all start from the current board position in the game. Paradoxically, Monte Carlo search is a further step away from knowledge-intensive game playing.

Another victory of extreme brute force is the complete solution of the game of checkers in the form of a computer generated gigantic table-base (Schaeffer *et al.* 2007). The computation of this table-base required computation resources of epic proportions, in addition to many tricks to reduce the computation. The table-base gives a best move for any checkers position and is therefore capable of perfect play. This means that the old game of checkers has been completely solved by machine.

However, the competitive successes do not remove the known shortcoming of brute-force programs: they cannot explain their play in conceptual terms. So from the points of view of explanation, commentary and teaching, the knowledge-intensive approach remains necessary. Computer-generated table-bases for chess endgames (for example, king and queen *vs* king and rook) are obscure to humans. Although they give the best move in any position of the endgame, they are of very limited use by humans. The tables lack conceptualization and they are much too large for a human to memorize. So a human player can hardly learn from such a table-base to improve his or her play in the tabulated endgame.

Guid and Bratko (2006) used chess playing programs to evaluate the performance of historical leading chess players. This enabled a comparison to be made of chess champions that never met across the board. Some results were rather surprising to many chess players and this computer-based analysis can be viewed as one step toward answering the eternal question that intrigues many chess players: Who was the best chess player of all time? Of course, this is one of those questions for which there will never be a definitive and generally agreed answer.

Berliner, H.J. (1977) A representation and some mechanisms for a problem solving chess program. In: *Advances in Computer Chess 1* (M.R.B. Clarke, ed.). Edinburgh University Press.

Bramer, M.A. (ed.) (1983) *Computer Game Playing: Theory and Practice*. Chichester: Ellis Horwood and John Wiley.

Bratko, I. (1978) Proving correctness of strategies in the AL1 assertional language. *Information Processing Letters* **7**: 223–230.

Bratko, I. (1982) Knowledge-based problem solving in AL3. In: *Machine Intelligence 10* (Hayes, J., Michie, D. and Pao, J.H., eds). Ellis Horwood (an abbreviated version also appears in Bramer 1983).

Bratko, I. (1984) Advice and planning in chess end-games. In: *Artificial and Human Intelligence* (Amarel, S., Elithorn, A. and Banerji, R., eds). North-Holland.

Bratko, I. and Michie, D. (1980) An advice program for a complex chess programming task. *Computer Journal* **23**: 353–359.

Campbell, M.S., Hoane, A.J. and Hsu, F.-H. (2002) Deep Blue, *Artificial Intelligence* **134**: 57–83.

Coulom, R. (2007) Efficient selectivity and backup operators in Monte-Carlo tree search. *Springer Lecture Notes In Computer Science Vol. 4630: Proc. 5th Int. Conf. on Computers and Games*, pp. 72–83.

Frey, P.W. (ed.) (1983) *Chess Skill in Man and Machine*, second edn. Berlin: Springer-Verlag.

Guid, M. and Bratko, I. (2006) Computer analysis of world chess champions. *ICGA Journal* **29**: 65–73.

Hsu, F.-H., Anantharaman, T.S., Campbell, M.S. and Nowatzyk, A. (1990) A grandmaster chess machine. *Scientific American* **263**: 44–50.

Luštrek, M., Gams, M. and Bratko, I. (2006) Is real-valued minimax pathological? *Artificial Intelligence* **170**: 620–642.

Kaindl, H. (1990) Tree searching algorithms. In: *Computers, Chess and Cognition* (Marsland, A.T. and Schaeffer, J., eds). Berlin: Springer-Verlag.

Knuth, D.E. and Moore, R.W. (1975) An analysis of alpha-beta pruning. *Artificial Intelligence* **6**: 293–326.

Marsland, A.T. and Schaeffer, J. (eds) (1990) *Computers, Chess and Cognition*. Berlin: Springer-Verlag.

Nau, D.S., Luštrek, M, Parker, A., Bratko, I. and Gams, M. (2010) When is it better not to look ahead? *Artificial Intelligence* **174**: 1323–1338.

Pearl, J. (1984) *Heuristics: Intelligent Search Strategies for Computer Problem Solving*. Reading, MA: Addison-Wesley.

Pitrat, J. (1977) A chess combination program which uses plans. *Artificial Intelligence* **8**: 275–321.

Plaat, A., Schaeffer, J., Pijls, W. and de Bruin, A. (1996) Best-first fixed-depth minimax algorithms. *Artificial Intelligence* **87**: 255–293.

Schaeffer, J., Burch, N., Bjornsson, Y., Kishimoto, A., Mueller, M., Lake, R., Lu, P. and Sutphen, S. (2007) Checkers is solved. *Science* **317**: 1518–1522.

Shannon, C.E. (1950) Programming a computer for playing chess. *Philosophical Magazine* **41**: 256–275.

Wilkins, D.E. (1980) Using patterns and plans in chess. *Artificial Intelligence* **14**: 165–203.

# Meta-Programming

Due to its symbol-manipulation capabilities, Prolog is a powerful language for implementing other languages and programming paradigms. In this chapter we discuss the writing of Prolog meta-interpreters – that is, interpreters for Prolog in Prolog. Such meta-interpreters extend the functionality of standard interpreter in different ways, for example to Prolog with constraints or to Prolog that reasons *abductively*, or to Prolog that queries the user. We look at a special program-compilation technique, called explanation-based generalization, that was invented as an approach to machine learning. We also develop a simple interpreter for another programming paradigm called pattern-directed programming.

## 25.1 Meta-programs and meta-interpreters

A *meta-program* is a program that takes other programs as data. Interpreters and compilers are examples of meta-programs. *Meta-interpreter* is an interpreter for a language written in that same language. So a Prolog meta-interpreter is an interpreter for Prolog, itself written in Prolog.

Due to its symbol-manipulation capabilities, Prolog is a powerful language for meta-programming. Therefore, it is often used as an implementation language for other languages. Prolog is particularly suitable as a language for rapid prototyping where we are interested in implementing new ideas quickly. This is important when we want to develop a new language or a new programming paradigm or program architecture. New ideas are rapidly implemented and experimented with. In prototyping the emphasis is on bringing new ideas to life quickly and cheaply, so that they can be immediately tested. On the other hand, there is not much emphasis on efficiency of implementation. Once the ideas are developed, a prototype may have to be re-implemented, possibly in another, more efficient programming language. Even if this is necessary, the prototype is useful because it helps to speed up the creative development stage.

Several meta-programs can be found in previous chapters of this book; for example, if-then rule interpreters of Chapter 15. They process the language of if-then rules, which is, in fact, a programming language, although programs written in it are usually called knowledge bases because of their specific contents. Another example is the interpreter for hypotheses in ILP in Chapter 21. In this chapter we show some further examples to illustrate how easily meta-programs can be written in Prolog:

- writing Prolog meta-interpreters;

- explanation-based generalization;

- implementing other programming paradigms in Prolog, in particular pattern-directed programming.

## 25.2 Prolog meta-interpreters

### 25.2.1 Basic Prolog meta-interpreter

A Prolog meta-interpreter takes a Prolog program and a Prolog goal, and executes the goal with respect to the program; that is, the meta-interpreter attempts to prove that the goal logically follows from the program. However, to be of any practical interest, the meta-interpreter must not behave exactly as the original Prolog interpreter; it has to offer some additional functionality, such as generating a proof tree or tracing the execution of programs.

We will, for simplicity, assume that the program has already been consulted by the Prolog system that executes the meta-interpreter. So our meta-interpreter can be stated as a procedure **prove** with one argument, the goal to be satisfied:

> **prove( Goal)**

The simplest Prolog meta-interpreter is trivial:

> **prove( Goal) :-**
>     **call( Goal).**

Here all the work has been delegated (by **call**) to the original Prolog interpreter, and our meta-interpreter behaves exactly like the original Prolog interpreter. This is of course of no practical value because it does not provide any additional feature. To enable features such as the generation of proof trees, we first have to reduce the 'grain size' of the interpreter. This reduction in granularity of the meta-interpreter is made possible by a built-in predicate, provided in many Prolog implementations:

> **clause( Head, Body)**

This 'retrieves' a clause from the consulted program. **Head** is the head of the retrieved clause and **Body** is its body. For a unit clause (a fact), **Body = true**. In a non-unit clause (a rule), the body can contain one or several goals. If it contains one goal, then **Body** is this goal. If the body contains several goals then they are retrieved as a pair:

> **Body** = ( FirstGoal , OtherGoals)

The comma in this term is a built-in infix operator. In the standard Prolog notation, this pair is equivalently written as:

> ,( FirstGoal, OtherGoals)

Here **OtherGoals** may again be a pair consisting of another goal and remaining goals. In a call **clause( Head, Body)**, the first argument **Head** must not be a variable. Suppose the consulted program contains the usual **member** procedure. Then the clauses of **member** can be retrieved by:

> ?- clause( member( X, L), Body).

> X = _14
> L = [_14 | _15]
> Body = true;

> X = _14
> L = [_15 | _16]
> Body = member( _14, _16)

For efficiency, in some Prologs the built-in predicate **clause/2** only retrieves clauses that belong to *dynamic* predicates. Such predicates have to be declared in the program as dynamic with a directive **dynamic** before the clauses about this predicate appear. For example, the predicate **member/2** can be declared as dynamic with the directive:

> :- dynamic member/2.

Figure 25.1 shows a basic meta-interpreter for Prolog at the level of granularity that has proved to be useful for most purposes. It should be noted, however, that this is a meta-interpreter for pure Prolog only. It does not handle built-in predicates, in particular the cut. The usefulness of this basic meta-interpreter lies in the fact that it provides a scheme that can be easily modified to obtain interesting effects. One such well-known extension results in a trace facility for Prolog. Another possibility is to prevent the Prolog interpreter from getting into infinite loops, by limiting the depth of subgoal calls (Exercise 25.2). Yet another example is an extension of Prolog to the handling of constraints, resulting in an interpreter for CLP.

```
% The basic Prolog meta-interpreter

prove( true).

prove( ( Goal1, Goal2)) :-
        prove( Goal1),
        prove( Goal2).

prove( Goal) :-
        clause( Goal, Body),
        prove( Body).
```

**Figure 25.1** The basic Prolog meta-interpreter.

# EXERCISES

**25.1** What happens if we try to execute the meta-interpreter of Figure 25.1 with itself –
for example, by:

> **?- prove( prove( member( X, [a, b, c]))).**

There is a problem because our meta-interpreter cannot execute built-in predicates
such as **clause**. How could the meta-interpreter be easily modified to be able to
execute itself, as in the query above? Another modification might be needed in that
**prove** itself would be declared as dynamic.

**25.2** Modify the meta-interpreter of Figure 25.1 by limiting the depth of Prolog's search for
proof. Let the modified meta-interpreter be the predicate **prove( Goal, DepthLimit)**,
which only succeeds if **DepthLimit** $\geq 0$. Each recursive call reduces the limit.

## 25.2.2 A tracing meta-interpreter

A first attempt to extend the basic meta-interpreter of Figure 25.1 to a tracing
interpreter is:

> **prove( true) :- !.**
>
> **prove( ( Goal1, Goal2)) :- !,**
>   **prove( Goal1), prove( Goal2).**
>
> **prove( Goal) :-**
>   **write( 'Call: '), write( Goal), nl,**
>   **clause( Goal, Body),**
>   **prove( Body),**
>   **write( 'Exit: '), write( Goal), nl.**

The cuts are needed here to prevent the display of 'true' and composite goals of the
form ( **Goal1, Goal2**). This tracer has several defects: there is no trace of failed goals and
no indication of backtracking when the same goal is re-done. The tracer in Figure 25.2
is an improvement in these respects. To aid readability, it also indents the displayed
goals proportionally to the depth of inference at which they are called. It is, however,
still restricted to pure Prolog only. An example call of this tracer is:

> **?- trace( ( member( X, [ a, b]), member( X, [ b, c]))).**

> **Call: member( _0085, [ a, b])**
> **Exit: member( a, [ a, b])**
> **Call: member( a, [ b, c])**
>   **Call: member( a, [ c])**
>     **Call: member( a, [ ])**
>     **Fail: member( a, [ ])**
>   **Fail: member( a, [ c])**
> **Fail: member( a, [ b, c])**
> **Redo: member( a, [ a, b])**
>   **Call: member( _0085, [ b])**
>   **Exit: member( b, [ b])**
> **Exit: member( b, [ a, b])**
> **Call: member( b, [ b, c])**
> **Exit: member( b, [ b, c])**

```
% trace( Goal): execute Prolog goal displaying trace information

trace( Goal) :-
        trace( Goal, 0).
trace( true, Depth) :- !.                    % Red cut; Depth = depth of call
trace( ( Goal1, Goal2), Depth) :- !,         % Red cut
        trace( Goal1, Depth),
        trace( Goal2, Depth).
trace( Goal, Depth) :-
        display( 'Call: ', Goal, Depth),
        clause( Goal, Body),
        Depth1 is Depth + 1,
        trace( Body, Depth1),
        display( 'Exit: ', Goal, Depth),
        display_redo( Goal, Depth).
trace( Goal, Depth) :-                        % All alternatives exhausted
        display( 'Fail: ', Goal, Depth),
        fail.
display( Message, Goal, Depth) :-
        tab( Depth), write( Message),
        write( Goal), nl.
display_redo( Goal, Depth) :-
        true                                  % First succeed simply
        ;
        display( 'Redo: ', Goal, Depth),      % Then announce backtracking
        fail.                                 % Force backtracking
```

**Figure 25.2** A Prolog meta-interpreter for tracing programs in pure Prolog.

This tracer outputs the following information for each goal executed:

(1) The goal to be executed (**Call: Goal**).

(2) Trace of the subgoals (indented).

(3) If the goal is satisfied then its final instantiation is displayed (**Exit: InstantiatedGoal**); if the goal is not satisfied then **Fail: Goal** is displayed.

(4) In the case of backtracking to a previously satisfied goal, the message is:

   **Redo: InstantiatedGoal** (instantiation in the previous solution of this goal).

Of course, it is possible to further shape the tracing interpreter according to specific users' requirements.

## 25.2.3 Generating proof trees

Another well-known extension of the basic interpreter of Figure 25.1 is the generation of proof trees. So after a goal is satisfied, its proof tree is available for further processing. In Chapter 15, the generation of proof trees was implemented for rule-based expert systems. Although the syntax of rules there was different from Prolog, the principles of generating a proof tree are the same. These principles are easily introduced into the meta-interpreter of Figure 25.1. For example, we may choose to represent a proof tree depending on the case as follows:

(1) For a goal **true**, the proof tree is **true**.

(2) For a pair of goals ( **Goal1, Goal2**), the proof tree is the pair ( **Proof1, Proof2**) of the proof trees of the two goals.

(3) For a goal **Goal** that matches the head of a clause whose body is **Body**, the proof tree is **Goal** <== **Proof**, where **Proof** is the proof tree of **Body**.

This can be incorporated into the basic meta-interpreter of Figure 25.1 as follows:

```
:- op( 500, xfy, <==).

prove( true, true).

prove( ( Goal1, Goal2), ( Proof1, Proof2)) :-
   prove( Goal1, Proof1),
   prove( Goal2, Proof2).

prove( Goal, Goal <== Proof) :-
   clause( Goal, Body),
   prove( Body, Proof).
```

Such a proof tree can be used in various ways. In Chapter 15 it was used as the basis for generating the 'how' explanation in an expert system. In Section 25.6 we will look at another interesting use of a proof tree, explanation-based generalization.

## 25.3 Top level interpreter for constraint logic programming

It is also easy, in principle, to extend the basic Prolog meta-interpreter to an interpreter for CLP (constraint logic programming, see Chapter 7). The top level of such an interpreter is shown in Figure 25.3 as procedure **solve( Goal)**. **Goal** can be a usual Prolog goal, or a constraint goal, for example $\{ X + 2 < 3 * Y \}$ in CLP(R). So this meta-interpreter proves Prolog goals as in the basic Prolog meta-interpreter. But in addition to this, the meta-interpreter also has to solve

```
solve( Goal) :-
  solve( Goal, [ ], Constr).       % Start with empty constraints, Constr is sufficient condition for Goal

% solve( Goal, InputConstraints, OutputConstraints)

solve( true, Constr0, Constr0).             % "true" is trivially solved, no change in constraints

solve( (G1, G2), Constr0, Constr) :- !,     % Conjunction of goals G1 and G2
  solve( G1, Constr0, Constr1),             % Constr1 is condition for G1 and Constr0
  solve( G2, Constr1, Constr).              % Constr is condition for G2 and Constr1

solve( G, Constr0, Constr) :-
  prolog_goal( G),                          % G is a Prolog goal
  clause( G, Body),                         % A clause about G
  solve( Body, Constr0, Constr).

solve( G, Constr0, Constr) :-
  constraint_goal( G),                      % G is a constraint goal
  merge_constraints( Constr0, G, Constr).   % Add G to Constr0 and check satisfiability
```

**Figure 25.3** Top level of an interpreter for CLP.

constraints when constraint goals appear in the program code. To handle constraints, we need a more general predicate:

> solve( Goal, Constraints0, Constraints)

Here **Constraints0** is a set of 'input' constraints, that is constraints that must be true before **Goal** is called. **Constraints** is a set of 'output' constraints, that is constraints that have to be true for both **Constraints0** and **Goal** to be true. We will assume that sets of constraints are represented as lists, so the empty list, [ ], will mean no constraints. The top level call of a goal has no input constraints, therefore:

> solve( Goal) :-
>     solve( Goal, [ ], Constr).       % Start with empty constraints

The definition of **solve/3** basically follows the definition of the basic Prolog meta-interpreter, with appropriate handling of constraints arguments. There is an additional clause that handles the situation when **Goal** is a constraint goal. In that case, the predicate call

> merge_constraints( Constr0, Goal, Constr)

adds **Goal** to input constraints. The resulting new set of constraints is then simplified and checked for satisfiability. So the burden of solving sets of constraints is delegated to the predicate **merge_constraints**. It is here where the power of the underlying constraint solver lies. A good constraint solver will usually detect whether the constraints are satisfiable at all. If not, then **merge_constraints** will fail and this execution path will be abandoned. For example, a CLP(R) constraint solver should reply:

> ?- merge_constraints( [ { X >= 10}], {X < 0}, Constr).
> no

Of course, in difficult cases **merge_constraints** can just add **Goal** to the list of constraints and do nothing with it. A trivial, but completely impotent, constraint solver may just accumulate constraints and never simplify them or detect the unsatisfiability. Such a vacuous constraint solver will present the user with a 'raw' final result, that is accumulated constraints unprocessed, and it will be up to the user to decide what to do with it.

## 25.4  Abductive reasoning

The best known form of logical reasoning is deduction. Given some logical statements, we may apply rules of deduction to infer other statements that logically follow. One of such deductive rules of inference is called *modus ponens*. Suppose that it is known that $a$ implies $b$ (written as $a \rightarrow b$), and that $a$ is known to be true. Then we may infer by deduction that $b$ is also true. In fact, $b$ logically follows from the formulas: $a \rightarrow b$ and $a$. This inference rule can be written as:

$$a \rightarrow b$$
$$\underline{a}$$
$$b$$

Everything above the line is a precondition for applying the rule, and below the line is the consequence of the inference rule.

As a concrete example, assume that the following statements are known to be true:

(1) For any patient, if the patient has pneumonia then the patient has a high temperature.

(2) John has pneumonia.

Using our inference rule, it follows that John has a high temperature.

This is all logical and correct, but may actually not be very useful. In practice, we normally observe that the patient has a high temperature, and then it may be found through further investigation that he is suffering from pneumonia. To infer, at this point, that the patient has a high temperature is of no interest any more. From the practical medical point of view, a more interesting kind of reasoning in this situation is the other way round. Having observed that the patient has a high temperature, we would like to find a reason for this high temperature. One possible, hypothetical reason is pneumonia. This kind of inference can be formalized by the following, *abductive*, inference rule:

$$a \rightarrow b$$
$$\underline{b}$$
$$a$$

Our medical example can be adjusted to this inference scheme by assuming that the following two statements are true:

(1) For any patient, if the patient has pneumonia then the patient has a high temperature.

(2) John has a high temperature.

Using the abductive inference rule above, we can infer that John has pneumonia. There is, however, something a bit unusual with this inference. Conclusions inferred by deduction are logically necessarily true. However, in contrast to this, in our case the conclusion does *not* logically follow from the two sentences that John necessarily has pneumonia. Instead of pneumonia, John may be suffering from malaria, or some other disease that also causes a high temperature. Therefore we say that abductive inference is not logically sound.

So, how can the above abductive inference nevertheless make sense? The inference is of interest under these circumstances: Given that John has a high temperature, we would like to know the reason for it, to decide on the treatment. Abductive inference produces a *possible* reason for his high temperature. But this reason *may not* in fact be true. Even so it does have some value from the medical point of view. It suggests one among alternative diagnoses that we have to take into account and explore further. Given the undesirable observation – high temperature – pneumonia is a possible cause (or explanation) for the observation. So, abductive inference should be understood not as 'John definitively has pneumonia', but as 'It is not unreasonable to consider that John has pneumonia'.

As suggested by our example, abductive reasoning is a useful tool for medical diagnosis. Even if not logically sound, it may be useful and sometimes even necessary in practice, although possibly risky. Another well-known tricky example from medicine illustrates the possible risk involved. The following statement is true:

If a patient has acute myocardial infarction, then the patient has severe chest pain.

Now consider we have a patient with severe chest pain. Since the situation is critical, there is no time for very thorough analyses and time consuming tests. For a quick decision, the doctor has to make an abductive inference step: acute myocardial infarction would explain the pain. This condition requires a quick decision by the doctor about treatment. So the doctor decides that the patient receives aspirin to prevent blood clotting. In most cases, this is, in fact, the correct decision. Unfortunately, it may be fatal because it is also true that:

If a patient has aortic dissection, then the patient has severe chest pain.

So, aortic dissection is another possible diagnosis, although it is much more rare. However, if this latter diagnosis is in fact true, then aspirin is exactly what this patient should not receive.

Abductive reasoning is also the key to technical diagnosis, and people do it all the time in everyday life. For example, we enter a dark room and switch on the light. We observe no light, so we are interested in diagnosing the problem. By using some knowledge about electrical devices, we can infer through abductive reasoning possible diagnoses that explain the failure. One possibility is that the bulb is blown; another one is that the light is connected to a fuse that has melted, etc.

Abductive reasoning can be implemented by yet another modification of the basic Prolog meta-interpreter. Here we have a goal that cannot be logically derived from the program. Some other assumptions, in addition to what is stated in the program, are needed to prove the goal is true. This will be implemented as the predicate

> **abduce( Goal, Delta)**

which will, for a given goal **Goal**, compute **Delta**. **Delta** is a list of abduced facts that 'explain' **Goal** in the context of the rest of the program. The logical relation is: **Goal** does not follow from the program alone, but **Goal** does follow from the program *and* **Delta**. If the facts in **Delta** are added to the program, then the usual Prolog interpreter would answer the query about **Goal** with 'yes'.

The predicate **abduce** (Figure 25.4) basically follows the basic Prolog meta-interpreter, with the main difference being the abduction of facts which are accumulated in **Delta**. Only facts about the so-called *abducible* predicates can be abduced. In the light diagnosis example, the fact that a fuse has melted is abducible. This is declared in the program by the Prolog fact:

> **abducible( melted( Fuse)).**

An example of using **abduce** to explain why centre light is not working, is:

```
?- abduce(not_working(centre_light), D).
D = [melted(fuse1), connected(centre_light,fuse1)]
```

```
% A Prolog meta-interpreter with abductive reasoning

% abduce( Goal, Delta):
%    Delta is a list of abduced literals when proving Goal
%    Goal logically follows from the program under the assumption that Delta is true

abduce( Goal, Delta) :-
   abduce( Goal, [], Delta, 0, _).

% abduce( Goal, Delta0, Delta, N0, N):
%    Delta0 is "accumulator" variable with Delta as its final value
%    N0 is next "free index" for "numbering variables" in abduced goals, N is final free index

abduce( true, Delta, Delta, N, N) :- !.

abduce( ( Goal1, Goal2), Delta0, Delta, N0, N) :- !,
   abduce( Goal1, Delta0, Delta1, N0, N1),      % Prove Goal1 by extending Delta0 to Delta1
   abduce( Goal2, Delta1, Delta, N1, N).        % Prove Goal2 by extending Delta1 to Delta

abduce( Goal, Delta0, Delta, N0, N) :-
   clause( Goal, Body),
   abduce( Body, Delta0, Delta, N0, N).         % Prove Body by extending Delta0 to Delta

% Abduction reasoning steps

abduce( Goal, Delta, Delta, N, N) :-
   member( Goal, Delta).                        % Goal already abduced

abduce( Goal, Delta, [Goal | Delta], N0, N) :-
   abducible( Goal),                            % Goal is abducible
   numbervars( Goal, N0, N).                    % Replace variables in Goal by Skolem constants

% An example domain: diagnosing faults in lights

:- dynamic not_working/1, no_current/1, switch/1, fuse/1.

not_working( Light) :-
   bulb_in( Light, Bulb),                       % Bulb inside Light
   blown( Bulb).

not_working( Device) :-
   no_current( Device).                         % No electric current in the device

no_current( Device) :-                          % No electric current in Device
   switch( Switch),
   connected( Device, Switch),
   broken( Switch).                             % Switch of Device is broken

no_current( Device) :-
   fuse( Fuse),
   connected( Device, Fuse),
   melted( Fuse).

switch( switch1).       switch( switch2).       fuse( fuse1).

abducible( broken( Switch)).        abducible( melted( Fuse)).
abducible( blown( Bulb)).           abducible( bulb_in( Light, Bulb)).
abducible( connected( Device, SwitchOrFuse)).
```

**Figure 25.4** Abductive reasoning implemented as Prolog meta-interpreter.

A possible explanation of why the centre light is not working is that **fuse1** has melted and the light is connected to this fuse. A somewhat more complicated example is an explanation that the bulb inside the centre light is blown. This answer would appear as:

D = [ blown(A), bulb_in(centre_light, A)]

Now, in this case we do not know the particular bulb, therefore it appears in the answer as variable **A**. This answer is meant to say: there exists some bulb **A** which is blown and is inside the centre light. There is a complication associated with such variables. **A** is actually the program-invented name that denotes some concrete object. **A** may not be matched as normal Prolog variables with any other object. Therefore, from Prolog's point of view **A** is a constant. Such constants are in logic called *Skolem constants*. A Skolem constant is introduced to replace an existentially quantified variable and denotes a concrete object. But since we do not know the name of this object, we invent some unique name to be able to refer to it. Intuitively this can be understood as follows. Consider the logical formula saying: there exists X such that **blown(X)**. We may equivalently replace this by mentioning a concrete object, referring to it as, say, **object123**, such that **blown(object123)**. Here, **object123** is again a Skolem constant. Our program will generate Skolem constants with the built-in predicate

numbvervars( Term, N0, N)

which replaces all the variables in **Term** by atoms (i.e. constants) constructed in such a way that these constant are as if numbered by integer numbers N0, N0 + 1, ..., N−1. So N is the next free number for numbering further variables if needed. For example:

?- T = p( X, g(a,X,Y)), numbervars( T, 0, N), display(T).
p($VAR(0),g(a,$VAR(0),$VAR(1)))
N = 2,
T = p(A,g(a,A,B)),
X = A,
Y = B

This example shows that variables X and Y have been replaced ('numbered') by atoms '$VAR(0)' and '$VAR(1)', and the next 'free' index is N = 2. The atoms like '$VAR(0)', '$VAR(1)' were constructed by Prolog as distinct new atoms, different from any other atom in the program. Such new atoms are written out in a polished form by Prolog as A, B, etc. to look like variables. The built-in predicate **display( Term)** used above writes out a Prolog term in the unpolished form, so that all the details, like the strange atoms '$VAR(0)' etc., are explicitly visible.

To implement **abduce/2**, it is convenient to introduce an auxiliary predicate:

abduce( Goal, Delta0, Delta, N0, N)

The extra arguments serve as accumulator variables for accumulating abduced facts and for counting the introduced Skolem variables. **Delta0** is the initial list of facts before **Goal** is abductively proved, **Delta** is the extended list of abduced facts with those needed to prove **Goal**. **N0** is the initial 'free' index for numbervars, and N is the next free index after proving **Goal**. Figure 25.4 shows a complete abductive prover together with a definition of our diagnosis domain about lights.

Here are some questions that illustrate the use of this interpreter:

?- abduce( not_working( centre_light), D).

D = [blown(A),bulb_in(centre_light,A)] ? ;
D = [broken(switch1),connected(centre_light,switch1)] ? ;
D = [broken(switch2),connected(centre_light,switch2)] ? ;
D = [melted(fuse1),connected(centre_light,fuse1)] ? ;
no

The answers say that a non-working light can be attributed to a blown bulb, a broken switch or a melted fuse. Next, we may switch on both the centre and wall lights, and observe that neither of them is working. Suppose also that we would like to see a 'minimum' diagnosis, that is one that requires the least number of abduced facts (i.e. least number of assumptions):

?- conc( D, _, _),          % Shortest explanations first
abduce( ( not_working( centre_light), not_working( wall_light)), D).

D=[connected(wall_light,switch1),broken(switch1),connected(centre_light,switch1)]? ;
D=[connected(wall_light,switch2),broken(switch2),connected(centre_light,switch2)]? ;
D=[connected(wall_light,fuse1),melted(fuse1),connected(centre_light,fuse1)] ? ;
D=[blown(B),bulb_in(wall_light,B),blown(A),bulb_in(centre_light,A)] ? ;
...

Minimal diagnoses are: Both lights are connected to the same broken switch, or they are both connected to the same melted fuse.

## 25.5 Query-the-user interpreter

Query-the-user interpreter is similar to the interpreter with abduction. However, rather than assuming facts about abducible goals through abductive inference, it asks the user about askable goals. An implementation of such a meta-interpreter is shown in Figure 25.5 as the predicate:

prove_qu( Goal)

Here **Goal** is true if **Goal** follows from the Prolog program and facts interactively provided by the user. The user is prompted by the interpreter to provide such facts when the interpreter encounters a goal that is declared as 'askable'. That means, it is appropriate to ask the user about such a goal. For example, consider the diagnostic domain of Figure 25.4. Let the user ask why the central light is not working. Then, while deriving an answer, the program may find that it is of interest to know what fuse the central light is connected to, and whether that fuse is melted. Having no information about this in the program, it is appropriate at this moment to ask the user about such a fuse. The advantage of querying the user is in that the user does not have to prepare in advance a complete base of facts about the home appliances, switch and fuse connections, their states, etc. Instead, the program prompts the user for relevant facts only at the time when this information is actually needed.

The program in Figure 25.5 basically follows the basic meta-interpreter, with additions similar to those in the abductive interpreter. Instead of assuming some-thing to be true, the program asks the user whether something is true, and then

```
% Prolog interpreter with query-the-user facility

% prove_qu( Goal):
%    Goal logically follows from the program and user's answers

prove_qu( true) :- !.

prove_qu( ( Goal1, Goal2)) :- !,
  prove_qu( Goal1),
  prove_qu( Goal2).

prove_qu( Goal) :-
  prolog( Goal),            % User-declared as 'Prolog goal'
  Goal.                     % Prove this goal by original Prolog interpreter

prove_qu( Goal) :-
  clause( Goal, Body),
  prove_qu( Body).          % Body can be proved if Answers0 is extended to Answers

prove_qu( Goal) :-
  askable( Goal),           % Goal may be asked of the user
  user_answer( 1, Goal).    % Now query the user

% user_answer( N, Goal):
%    retrieve previous user's answers about Goal, indexed N or higher
%    then ask user for further solutions of Goal, assert answers

user_answer( N, Goal) :-    % Retrieve user's answers about Goal indexed N or higher
  last_index( Last), N =< Last,
  ( was_told( N, Goal)      % Answer indexed N
  ;
    N1 is N + 1, user_answer( N1, Goal)
  ).

user_answer( _, Goal) :-
  \+ (numbervars( Goal, 1, _),    % Freeze variables in Goal
      end_answers( Goal)),        % Further solutions of Goal possible
  ask_user( Goal),                % Ask user about Goal
  read( Answer),
  ( Answer = no, !,                          % User says no (further) solution
    asserta( end_answers( Goal)), fail       % Make sure to never ask about Goal again
  ;
    copy_term( Goal, GoalCopy),
    Answer = GoalCopy,
    next_index( I),                % Index for next answer to be asserted
    assertz( was_told( I, Answer)),    % New fact about Goal, assert it
    user_answer( I, Goal)          % More facts about Goal?
  ).

ask_user( Goal) :-
  nl, write( 'Known facts about '), write( Goal), write( :), nl,
  ( \+ was_told( _, Goal), write( '   None so far'), nl, !; true),
    ( was_told( _, Goal), write( '   '), write( Goal), nl, fail; true),    % Display all known solutions
  nl, write( 'Any (other) solution?'), nl,
  write( 'Answer with "no" or instantiated goal '), write( Goal), nl.
```

**Figure 25.5** Prolog meta-interpreter with query-the-user facility.

**Figure 25.5** *contd*

```
next_index( I) :-
    retract( last_index( Last)), !,
    I is Last + 1,
    asserta( last_index( I)).

:- dynamic last_index/1, was_told/2, end_answers/1.

last_index( 0).                    % Initialize index

% Example program to be interpreted by query-the-user interpreter:
% finding chains of supervisors

:- dynamic supervisor_chain/3, chain/3, supervised/2.

askable( supervised( Person1, Person2)).      % Person1 supervised Person2

prolog( conc( L1, L2, L3)).        % conc/3 to be executed by original Prolog interpreter
prolog( length( L, N)).            % length/2 to be executed by original Prolog

supervisor_chain( P1, P2, Chain) :-   % P1 supervised P2 directly, or "indirectly" through P1's student
    length( MaxChain, 10),            % Longest allowed chain length is 10
    conc( Chain, _, MaxChain),        % Generate lists - shortest first
    chain( P1, P2, Chain).

chain( P0, P1, [P0, P1]) :-           % P0 supervised P1 directly
    supervised( P0, P1).

chain( P0, P, [P0, P1 | Chain]) :-    % P0 "supervised" P indirectly
    supervised( P0, P1),              % P0 supervised P1
    chain( P1, P, [P1 | Chain]).
```

remembers the user's answers. This interaction with the user makes this interpreter more complicated than our previous meta-interpreters. First, when asked about a goal, the user not only tells whether the goal is true or not, but also specifies for what values of the arguments the goal is true. For example, the program asks the user whether **connected(Device,switch1)** is true. The user may say that this is true for both the centre light and the wall light. All the answers are recorded, and it is not appropriate for the program to ask the user the same question again. When the user says that there are no further answers to a given question, the program should not repeat the question.

Another complication consists of the sharing of facts between several goals. Suppose some answers have been collected from the user when solving some goal. If these answers are relevant later to the solving of another goal, these answers must be recalled and reused in solving this second goal. So, answers generated at some goal may be consumed at some other goal later. This interaction between goals' producing and consuming answers can become a bit tricky. Suppose the interpreter is solving a list of goals of the form: ..., G1, ..., G2, .... G1 and G2 are goals about the same predicate. At G1, several solutions of G1 may be extracted from the user. When the interpreter has progressed to G2, these solutions applicable to G2 have to be reused ('consumed') at G2. If these solutions do not suffice to solve the remaining goals, the interpreter backtracks to G2 and may ask the user for more solutions of G2. Then, if the program backtracks further back to G1, first the solutions generated at G2 have to be consumed by G1, and then the user may be asked for more solutions of G1, etc.

To enable a reasonable flow of user-program interaction, the answers by the user are indexed so that each answer receives a unique index. Therefore user's answers are asserted as:

was_told( Index, Answer)

The starting index is 1. The user's answers are reused in the order of increasing index, which also reflects the chronological order. When user's answers are collected, they are asserted with indices starting from the last index used. So the program has to keep track of the highest index so far.

Notice that the interaction with the user has to result in a natural interactive *behaviour* so that this behaviour makes sense from the user's point of view. Since time order in a behaviour is important, the program in Figure 25.5 has to pay attention to the procedural aspects. Therefore it is not as elegant and logically clear as our other meta-interpreters.

For illustration, a simple domain definition is added to the interpreter in Figure 25.5. The domain consists of the relations between PhD students and their supervisors. The program also considers 'indirect supervisors'. Suppose John supervised Mary and Mary in turn supervised Patrick. Then we will say that there is a supervisor chain [ john, mary, patrick] between John and Patrick. The program only knows the general definition of the supervisor_chain/3 relation, while the direct supervisor relation is left undefined and declared as askable of the user. Suppose we would like to know whether there is a chain of supervisors between John and Patrick. Here the interaction with the user is carried out by our query-the-user interpreter:

?- prove_qu( supervisor_chain( john, patrick, L)).

Known facts about supervised( john, _780):
  None so far             % Currently nothing known about John's students

Any (other) solution?
Answer with 'no' or instantiated goal supervised( john, _780)
|: supervised( john, mark).     % User tells that John supervised Mark

Known facts about supervised(john,_780):
  supervised(john,mark)

Any (other) solution?

Answer with 'no' or instantiated goal supervised( john, _780)
|: supervised( john, mary).     % User tells John also supervised Mary

Known facts about supervised(john,_780):
  supervised( john, mark)
  supervised( john, mary)

Any (other) solution?
Answer with 'no' or instantiated goal supervised(john,_780)
|: no.             % User says John supervised no other student

Known facts about supervised( mark, _782):
  None so far

Any (other) solution?
Answer with 'no' or instantiated goal supervised( mark, _782)
|: no.                                  % User says Mark did not supervise anybody

Known facts about supervised(mary,_782):
  None so far

Any (other) solution?
Answer with 'no' or instantiated goal supervised( mary, _782)
|: supervised( mary, patrick).      % User says Mary supervised Patrick
L = [ john, mary, patrick]          % Program found supervisor chain John-Mary-Patrick

The following further question shows that the interpreter remembered the user-supplied facts till now about who supervised whom, and only asks for further relevant information:

  ?- prove_qu( supervisor_chain( mary, sarah, L)).

Known facts about supervised( mary, _780):
  supervised( mary, patrick)      % Interpreter already knows Mary supervised Patrick

Any (other) solution?
Answer with 'no' or instantiated goal supervised(mary,_780)
|: no.                                  % User says Mary did not supervise anybody else

Known facts about supervised( patrick, _782):
  None so far

Any (other) solution?
Answer with 'no' or instantiated goal supervised(patrick,_782)
        % Interpreter knows Mary supervised Patrick
        % so it is relevant to know whom Patrick supervised
|: supervised( patrick, sarah).              % User says Patrick supervised Sarah
L = [ mary, patrick, sarah]

## 25.6 Explanation-based generalization

The idea of explanation-based generalization comes from machine learning, where the objective is to generalize given examples into general descriptions of concepts. *Explanation-based generalization* (EBG) is a way of building such descriptions from typically one example only. The lack of examples is compensated for by the system's 'background knowledge', usually called *domain theory*.

EBG rests on the following idea for building generalized descriptions: given an instance of the target concept, use the domain theory to *explain how* this instance in fact satisfies the concept. Then analyse the explanation and try to generalize it so that it applies not only to the given instance, but also to a set of 'similar' instances. This generalized explanation then becomes part of the concept description and can be subsequently used in recognizing instances of this concept. It is also required that the constructed concept description must be 'operational'; that is, it must be stated in terms of concepts declared by the user as operational. Intuitively, a concept description is operational if it is (relatively) easy to use. It is entirely up to the user to specify what is operational.

In an implementation of EBG, these abstract ideas have to be made more concrete. One way of realizing them in the logic of Prolog is:

- A concept is realized as a predicate.
- A concept description is a predicate definition.
- An explanation is a proof tree that demonstrates how the given instance satisfies the target concept.
- A domain theory is represented as a set of available predicates defined as a Prolog program.

The task of explanation-based generalization can then be stated as:

*Given*:

- A *domain theory*: A set of predicates available to the explanation-based generalizer, including the target predicate whose operational definition is to be constructed.
- *Operationality criteria*: These specify the *operational* predicates, that is predicates that may be used in the target predicate definition.
- *Training example*: A set of facts describing a particular situation and an instance of the target concept, so that this instance can be derived from the given set of facts and the domain theory.

*Find*:

- A generalization of the training instance and an operational definition of the target concept; this definition consists of a sufficient condition (in terms of the operational predicates) for this generalized instance to satisfy the target concept.

Thus stated, explanation-based generalization can be viewed as a kind of program compilation from one form into another. The original program defines the target concept in terms of domain theory predicates. The compiled program defines the same target concept (or subconcept) in terms of the 'target language' – that is, operational predicates only. The compilation mechanism provided by EBG is rather unusual. Execute the original program on the given example, which results in a proof tree. Then generalize this proof tree so that the structure of the proof tree is retained, but the constants are replaced by variables whenever possible. In the generalized proof tree thus obtained, some nodes mention operational predicates. The tree is then reduced so that only these 'operational nodes' and the root are retained. The result constitutes an operational definition of the target concept.

All this is best understood by an example of EBG at work. Figure 25.6 defines two domains for EBG. The first domain theory is about giving a gift, while the second is about lift movements. Let us consider the first domain. Let the training instance be:

```
gives( john, john, chocolate)
```

Our proof-generating meta-interpreter finds this proof:

```
gives( john, john, chocolate) <==
   ( feels_sorry_for( john, john) <== sad( john),
      would_comfort( chocolate, john) <== likes( john, chocolate)
   )
```

% A domain theory: about gifts

gives( Person1, Person2, Gift) :-
  likes( Person1, Person2),
  would_please( Gift, Person2).

gives( Person1, Person2, Gift) :-
  feels_sorry_for( Person1, Person2),
  would_comfort( Gift, Person2).

would_please( Gift, Person) :-
  needs( Person, Gift).

would_comfort( Gift, Person) :-
  likes( Person, Gift).

feels_sorry_for( Person1, Person2) :-
  likes( Person1, Person2),
  sad( Person2).

feels_sorry_for( Person, Person) :-
  sad( Person).

% Operational predicates

operational( likes( _, _ )).
operational( needs( _, _ )).
operational( sad( _ )).

% An example situation

likes( john, annie).
likes( annie, john).
likes( john, chocolate).
needs( annie, tennis_racket).
sad( john).

% Another domain theory: about lift movement
% go( Level, GoalLevel, Moves) if
%    list of moves Moves brings lift from Level to GoalLevel

go( Level, GoalLevel, Moves) :-
  move_list( Moves, Distance),            % A move list and distance travelled
  Distance  =:=  GoalLevel − Level.

move_list( [ ], 0).

move_list( [Move1 | Moves], Distance + Distance1) :-
  move_list( Moves, Distance),
  move( Move1, Distance1).

move( up, 1).
move( down, -1).
operational( A  =:=  B).

**Figure 25.6** Two problem-definitions for explanation-based generalization.

This proof can be generalized by replacing constants john and chocolate by variables:

```
gives( Person, Person, Thing) <==
  ( feels_sorry_for( Person, Person) <== sad( Person),
     would_comfort( Thing, Person) <== likes( Person, Thing)
  )
```

Predicates sad and likes are specified as operational in Figure 25.6. An operational definition of the predicate gives is now obtained by eliminating all the nodes from the proof tree, apart from the root node and the 'operational' nodes. This results in:

```
gives( Person, Person, Thing) <==
  ( sad( Person),
    likes( Person, Thing)
  )
```

Thus a sufficient condition Condition for gives( Person, Person, Thing) is:

```
Condition = ( sad( Person), likes( Person, Thing))
```

This new definition can now be added to our original program with:

```
asserta( ( gives( Person, Person, Thing) :- Condition))
```

As a result, we have the following new clause about gives. The new clause only requires the evaluation of operational predicates:

```
gives( Person, Person, Thing) :-
  sad( Person),
  likes( Person, Thing).
```

Through the generalization of the given instance

```
gives( john, john, chocolate)
```

a definition (in operational terms) of giving as self-consolation was derived as one general case of gives. Another case of this concept would result from the example:

```
gives( john, annie, tennis_racket).
```

The explanation-based generalization would in this case produce the clause:

```
gives( Person1, Person2, Thing) :-
  likes( Person1, Person2),
  needs( Person2, Thing).
```

The lift domain in Figure 25.6 is slightly more complicated and we will only experiment with it when we have EBG implemented in Prolog.

EBG can be programmed as a two-stage process: first, generate a proof tree for the given example, and, second, generalize this proof tree and extract the 'operational nodes' from it. Our proof-generating meta-interpreter could be used for this. The two stages are, however, not necessary. A more direct way is to modify the basic meta-interpreter of Figure 25.1 so that the generalization is intertwined with the process of proving the given instance. The so-modified meta-interpreter, which carries out EBG, will be called ebg and will have three arguments:

```
ebg( Goal, GenGoal, Condition)
```

```
%  ebg( Goal, GeneralizedGoal, SufficientCondition):
%     SufficientCondition in terms of operational predicates guarantees that
%     generalization of Goal, GeneralizedGoal, is true.
%     GeneralizedGoal must not be a variable

ebg( true, true, true).

ebg( Goal, GenGoal, GenGoal) :-
  operational( GenGoal),
  call( Goal).

ebg( ( Goal1, Goal2), ( Gen1, Gen2), Cond) :- !,
  ebg( Goal1, Gen1, Cond1),
  ebg( Goal2, Gen2, Cond2),
  and( Cond1, Cond2, Cond).              % Cond  = ( Cond1, Cond2) simplified

ebg( Goal, GenGoal, Cond) :-
  \+ operational( Goal),
  clause( GenGoal, GenBody),
  copy_term( ( GenGoal, GenBody), ( Goal, Body)),     % Fresh copy of ( GenGoal, GenBody)
  ebg( Body, GenBody, Cond).

%  and( Cond1, Cond2, Cond):
%     Cond is (possibly simplified) conjunction of Cond1 and Cond2

and( true, Cond, Cond) :- !.              % (true and Cond) <==> Cond
and( Cond, true, Cond) :- !.              % (Cond and true) <==> Cond
and( Cond1, Cond2, (Cond1, Cond2)).
```

**Figure 25.7** Explanation-based generalization.

where **Goal** is the given example to be proved, **GenGoal** is the generalized goal, and **Condition** is the derived sufficient condition for **GenGoal**. **Condition** is stated in terms of operational predicates only. Figure 25.7 shows such a generalizing meta-interpreter. For our gift domain of Figure 25.6, **ebg** can be called as:

```
?- ebg( gives( john, john, chocolate), gives( X, Y, Z), Condition).
X = Y
Condition =  ( sad( X), likes( X, Z))
```

Let us now try the lift domain. Let the goal to be solved and generalized be to find a move sequence **Moves** that brings the lift from level 3 to level 6:

```
go( 3, 6, Moves)
```

We can invoke **ebg** and cash the resulting generalized goal and its condition by:

```
?- Goal =  go( 3, 6, Moves),
   GenGoal  = go( Level1, Level2, GenMoves),
   ebg( Goal, GenGoal, Condition),
   asserta( ( GenGoal :- Condition)).

Goal  =  go( 3, 6, [ up, up, up])
GenGoal = go( Level1, Level2, [ up, up, up])
Condition  =  ( 0 + 1 + 1 + 1 =:= Level2 – Level1)
Moves = [ up, up, up]
...
```

The resulting new clause about **go** is:

```
go( Level1, Level2, [ up, up, up]) :-
    0 + 1 + 1 + 1 =:= Level2 − Level1.
```

By means of EBG, the straight three-step upward movement has thus been generalized to any two levels at distance three. To solve the goal **go( 3, 6, Moves)**, the original program performs a search among sequences of up/down actions. Using the new derived clause, moving up between any two levels at distance three (for example, **go( 7, 10, Moves)**) is solved immediately, without search.

The **ebg** meta-interpreter in Figure 25.7 is, again, a derivation of the basic meta-interpreter of Figure 25.1. This new meta-interpreter calls the built-in procedure **copy_term**. The call

```
copy_term( Term, Copy)
```

constructs, for a given term **Term**, a copy **Copy** of this term with variables renamed. This is useful when we want to preserve a term as it is together with all its variables, while at the same time processing the term so that its variables may become instantiated. We can use the copy in this processing, so that the variables in the original term remain unaffected.

The last clause of the **ebg** procedure deserves special explanation. The call

```
clause( GenGoal, GenBody)
```

retrieves a clause that can be used to prove the generalized goal. This means that the meta-interpreter is actually trying to prove the generalized goal. The next line, however, imposes a constraint on this:

```
copy_term( ( GenGoal, GenBody), ( Goal, Body))
```

This requires that **GenGoal** and **Goal** match. The matching is done on the copy of **GenGoal**, so that the variables in the general goal remain intact. The point of requiring this match is to limit the execution of the generalized goal to those alternative branches (clauses) that are applicable to the given example (**Goal**). In this way the example guides the execution of the generalized goal. This guidance is the essence of program compilation in the EBG style. Without this guidance, a proof for **GenGoal** could possibly be found that does not work for **Goal**. In such a case the generalization would not correspond to the example at all.

Once an example has been generalized and stated in terms of operational predicates, it can be added as a new clause to the program to answer future similar questions by evaluating operational predicates only. In this way the EBG compilation technique transforms a program into an 'operational' language. The translated program can be executed by an interpreter that only 'knows' the operational language. One possible advantage of this can be a more efficient program. The efficiency may be improved in two ways: first, operational predicates may be easier to evaluate than other predicates; second, the sequence of predicate evaluation indicated by the example may be more suitable than the one in the original program, so that failed branches do not appear in the compiled definition at all. When a program is compiled by the EBG technique, care is needed during compilation so that new clauses do not interfere in an uncontrolled way with the original clauses.

## EXERCISE

**25.3** It may appear that the same compilation effect achieved in EBG can be obtained without an example, simply by substituting goals in the original concept definition by their subgoals, taken from corresponding clauses of the domain theory, until all the goals are reduced to operational subgoals. This procedure is called *unfolding* (a goal 'unfolds' into subgoals). Discuss this idea with respect to EBG and show that the guidance by an example in EBG is essential. Also show that, on the other hand, EBG-generated new concept definitions are only a generalization of given examples and are therefore not necessarily equivalent to the original program (new concept definitions may be incomplete).

 **25.7** Pattern-directed programming and blackboard systems

### 25.7.1 Pattern-directed architecture and blackboard systems

By *pattern-directed systems* we refer to an architecture for program systems. This architecture is better suited for certain types of problems than conventional systems organization. The main difference between conventional systems and pattern-directed systems is in the mechanisms of invocation of program modules. In conventional organization, modules of the system call each other according to a fixed, explicitly predefined scheme. Each program module decides which module will be executed next by *explicitly* calling other modules. The corresponding flow of execution is sequential and deterministic.

In contrast to this, in pattern-directed organization the modules of the system are not directly called by other modules. Instead, they are 'called' by *patterns* that occur in their 'data environment'. Therefore such modules are called *pattern-directed modules*. A *pattern-directed program* is a collection of pattern-directed modules. Each module is defined by:

(1) a precondition pattern, and

(2) an action to be executed if the data environment matches the pattern.

The execution of program modules is triggered by patterns that occur in the system's environment. The data environment is usually called the *database*. We can imagine such a system as shown in Figure 25.8.

There are some notable observations about Figure 25.8. There is no hierarchy among modules, and there is no explicit indication about which module can invoke which other module. Modules communicate with the database rather than with other modules directly. The structure itself, in principle, permits execution of several modules in parallel, since the state of the database may simultaneously satisfy several preconditions and thus, in principle, fire several modules at the same time. Consequently such an organization can also serve as a natural model of parallel computation in which each module would be physically implemented by its own processor.

Pattern-directed architecture has certain advantages. One major advantage is that the design of the system does not require all the connections between

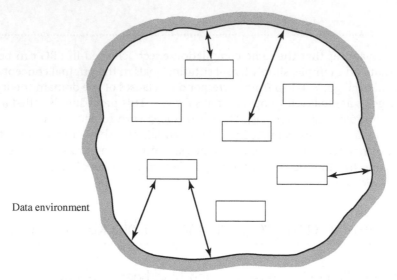

Data environment

**Figure 25.8** A pattern-directed system. Rectangles represent pattern-directed modules. Arrows indicate modules' triggering patterns occurring in data.

modules to be carefully planned and defined in advance. Consequently, each module can be designed and implemented relatively autonomously. This renders a high degree of modularity. The modularity is manifested, for example, in that the removal of some module from the system is not necessarily fatal. After the removal, the system would often still be able to solve problems, only *the way* of solving problems might change. The same is true for the addition of new modules and for modifications of the existing modules. If similar modifications are carried out in systems with conventional organization, at least the calls between modules have to be properly modified.

The high degree of modularity is especially desirable in systems with complex knowledge bases because it is difficult to predict in advance all the interactions between individual pieces of knowledge in the base. The pattern-directed architecture offers a natural solution to this: each piece of knowledge, represented by an if-then rule, can be regarded as a pattern-directed module.

Let us further elaborate the basic scheme of pattern-directed systems with the view on an implementation. Figure 25.8 suggests that the parallel implementation would be most natural. However, let us assume the system is to be implemented on a traditional sequential processor. Then in a case that the triggering patterns of several modules simultaneously occur in the database there is a conflict: which of all these potentially active modules will actually be executed? The set of potentially active modules is called a *conflict set*. In an actual implementation of the scheme of Figure 25.8 on a sequential processor, we need an additional program module, called the *control module*. The control module resolves the conflict by choosing and activating one of the modules in the conflict set. One simple rule of resolving conflicts can be based on a predefined, fixed ordering of modules.

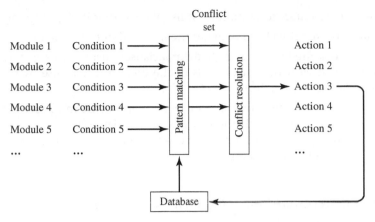

**Figure 25.9** The basic life cycle of pattern-directed systems. In this example the database satisfies the condition pattern of modules 1, 3 and 4; module 3 is chosen for execution.

The basic life cycle of pattern-directed systems, then, consists of three steps:

(1) *Pattern matching*: find in the database all the occurrences of the condition patterns of the program modules. This results in a conflict set.

(2) *Conflict resolution*: choose one of the modules in the conflict set.

(3) *Execution*: execute the module that was chosen in step 2.

This implementation scheme is illustrated in Figure 25.9.

The architecture of pattern-directed systems is very similar to that of *blackboard systems*. The main idea is the same, although the terminology is different, the one in blackboard systems being more imaginative. In blackboard systems, a set of pattern-directed modules are imagined as a committee of experts, all cooperatively solving the same complex problem. The problem specification is displayed on a common blackboard observed by all the experts. Each expert is a specialist in a narrow area of expertise. So different experts are competent for different aspects of the problem, and hopefully they will be able to solve the problem jointly. The collaboration between the experts happens just as in pattern-directed modules. The experts are making their contributions to the solution by modifying the contents on the blackboard. This has the same role as the data environment in pattern-directed systems. The experts may, possibly concurrently, add notes and comments, or rewrite parts of information on the blackboard. This process continues until a solution emerges.

## 25.7.2 Prolog programs as pattern-directed systems

Prolog programs themselves can be viewed as pattern-directed systems. Without much elaboration, the correspondence between Prolog and pattern-directed systems is along the following lines:

- Each Prolog clause in the program can be viewed as a pattern-directed module. The module's condition part is the head of the clause, the action part is specified by the clause's body.

- The system's database is the current list of goals that Prolog is trying to satisfy.
- A clause is fired if its head matches the first goal in the database.
- To execute a module's action (body of a clause) means: replace the first goal in the database with the list of goals in the body of the clause (with the proper instantiation of variables).
- The process of module invocation is non-deterministic in the sense that several clauses' heads may match the first goal in the database, and any one of them can, in principle, be executed. This non-determinism is actually implemented in Prolog through backtracking.

## 25.7.3 Writing pattern-directed programs: an example

Pattern-directed systems can also be viewed as a particular style of writing programs and thinking about problems, called *pattern-directed programming*.

To illustrate this, consider an elementary programming exercise: computing the greatest common divisor $D$ of two integer numbers $A$ and $B$. The classical Euclid's algorithm can be written as follows:

To compute the greatest common divisor, $D$, of $A$ and $B$:
While $A$ and $B$ are not equal, repeat the following:
if $A > B$ then replace $A$ with $A - B$
else replace $B$ with $B - A$.
When this loop is over, $A$ and $B$ are equal; now the greatest common divisor $D$ is $A$ (or $B$).

We can define the same process by two pattern-directed modules:

**Module 1**
*Condition* There are two numbers $X$ and $Y$ in the database such that $X > Y$.
*Action* Replace $X$ in the database with the difference $X - Y$.

**Module 2**
*Condition* There is a number $X$ in the database.
*Action* Output $X$ and stop.

Whenever the condition of Module 1 is satisfied, so is the condition of Module 2 and we have a conflict. This will be resolved by a simple control rule: Module 1 is always preferred to Module 2. Initially the database contains the two numbers $A$ and $B$.

As a pleasant surprise, our pattern-directed program in fact solves a more general problem: computing the greatest common divisor of any number of integers. If several integers are stored in the database the system will output the greatest common divisor of all of them. Figure 25.10 shows a possible sequence of changes in the database before the result is obtained, when the initial database contains four numbers: 25, 10, 15, 30. Notice that a module's precondition can be satisfied at several places in the database.

In this chapter we will implement an interpreter for a simple language for specifying pattern-directed systems, and illustrate the flavour of pattern-directed programming by programming exercises.

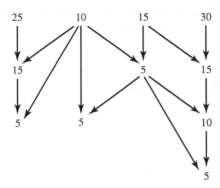

**Figure 25.10** A possible execution of the pattern-directed program for computing the greatest common divisor of a set of numbers. In this example the database initially contains the numbers 25, 10, 15 and 30. Vertical arrows connect numbers with their replacements. The final state of the database is: 5, 5, 5, 5.

## 25.7.4 A simple interpreter for pattern-directed programs

Let us choose the following syntax for specifying pattern-directed modules:

    **ConditionPart** ---> **ActionPart**

The condition part is a list of conditions

    [ Cond1, Cond2, Cond3, . . . ]

where **Cond1, Cond2**, etc. are Prolog goals. The precondition is satisfied if all the goals in the list are satisfied. The action part is a list of actions:

    [ Action1, Action2, . . . ]

Each action is, again, simply a Prolog goal. To execute an action list, all the actions in the list have to be executed. That is, all the corresponding goals have to be satisfied. Among available actions there will be actions that manipulate the database: *add*, *delete* or *replace* objects in the database. The action 'stop' stops further execution.

    Figure 25.11 shows our pattern-directed program for computing the greatest common divisor written in this syntax.

    The simplest way to implement this pattern-directed language is to use Prolog's own built-in database mechanism. Adding an object into the database and deleting an object can be accomplished simply by the built-in procedures:

    **assertz( Object)**    **retract( Object)**

Replacing an object with another object is also easy:

```
replace( Object1, Object2) :-
  retract( Object1), !,
  assertz( Object2).
```

The cut in this clause is used to prevent **retract** from deleting (through backtracking) more than one object from the database.

% Production rules for finding greatest common divisor (Euclid algorithm)

:- op( 300, fx, number).

[ number X, number Y, X > Y ] --->
[ NewX is X – Y, replace( number X, number NewX) ].

[ number X] ---> [ write( X), stop ].

% An initial database

number 25.
number 10.
number 15.
number 30.

**Figure 25.11** A pattern-directed program to find the greatest common divisor of a set of numbers.

A small interpreter for pattern-directed programs along these lines is shown in Figure 25.12. This interpreter is perhaps an oversimplification in some respects. In particular, the conflict resolution rule in the interpreter is extremely simple and rigid: always execute the *first* potentially active pattern-directed module (in

```
% A small interpreter for pattern-directed programs
% The system's database is manipulated through assert/retract

:- op( 800, xfx, --->).

% run: execute pattern-directed modules until action 'stop' is triggered

run :-
    Condition ---> Action,          % A production rule
    test( Condition),               % Precondition satisfied?
    execute( Action).

% test( [ Condition1, Condition2, . . . ]) if all conditions true

test( [ ]).                         % Empty condition

test( [First | Rest]) :-            % Test conjunctive condition
    call( First),
    test( Rest).

% execute( [ Action1, Action2, . . . ]): execute list of actions

execute( [ stop]) :- !.             % Stop execution

execute( [ ]) :-                    % Empty action (execution cycle completed)
    run.                            % Continue with next execution cycle

execute( [First | Rest]) :-
    call( First),
    execute( Rest).

replace( A, B) :-                   % Replace A with B in database
    retract( A), !,                 % Retract once only
    assertz( B).
```

**Figure 25.12** A small interpreter for pattern-directed programs.

the order as they are written). So the programmer's control is reduced just to the ordering of modules. The initial state of the database for this interpreter has to be asserted as Prolog facts, possibly by consulting a file. Then the execution is triggered by the goal:

```
?- run.
```

## 25.7.5  Possible improvements

Our simple interpreter for pattern-directed programs is sufficient for illustrating some ideas of pattern-directed programming. For more complex applications it should be elaborated in several respects. Here are some critical comments and indications for improvements.

In our interpreter, the conflict resolution is reduced to a fixed, predefined order. Much more flexible schemas are often desired. To enable more sophisticated control, all the potentially active modules should be found and fed into a special, user-programmable control module.

When the database is large and there are many pattern-directed modules in the program then pattern matching can become extremely inefficient. The efficiency in this respect can be improved by a more sophisticated organization of the database. This may involve the indexing of the information in the database, or partitioning of the information into sub-bases, or partitioning of the set of pattern-directed modules into subsets. The idea of partitioning is to make only a *subset* of the database or of the modules accessible at any given time, thus reducing the pattern matching to such a subset only. Of course, in such a case we would need a more sophisticated control mechanism that would control the transitions between these subsets in the sense of activating and de-activating a subset. A kind of meta-rule could be used for that.

Unfortunately our interpreter, as programmed, precludes any backtracking due to the way that the database is manipulated through **assertz** and **retract**. So we cannot study alternative execution paths. This can be improved by using a different implementation of the database, avoiding Prolog's **assertz** and **retract**. One way would be to represent the whole state of the database by a Prolog term passed as an argument to the **run** procedure. The simplest possibility is to organize this term as a list of objects in the database. The interpreter's top level could then look like this:

```
run( State) :-
    Condition ---> Action,
    test( Condition, State),
    execute( Action, State).
```

The **execute** procedure would then compute a new state and call **run** with this new state.

## PROJECT

Implement an interpreter for pattern-directed programs that does not maintain its database as Prolog's own internal database (with **assertz** and **retract**), but as a procedure argument according to the foregoing remark. Such a new interpreter would allow for automatic backtracking. Try to design a representation of the database that would facilitate efficient pattern matching.

## 25.8 A simple theorem prover as a pattern-directed program

Let us implement a simple theorem prover as a pattern-directed system. The prover will be based on the *resolution principle*, a popular method for mechanical theorem proving. We will limit our discussion to proving theorems in the simple *propositional logic* just to illustrate the principle, although our resolution mechanism will be easily extendable to handle the first-order predicate calculus (logic formulas that contain variables). Basic Prolog itself is a special case of a resolution-based theorem prover.

The theorem-proving task can be defined as: given a formula, show that the formula is a theorem; that is, the formula is always true regardless of the interpretation of the symbols that occur in the formula. For example, the formula

$$p \vee \sim p$$

read as '*p* or not *p*', is always true regardless of the meaning of *p*.

We will be using the following symbols as logic operators:

~      negation, read as 'not'

&      conjunction, read as 'and'

∨      disjunction, read as 'or'

⇒      implication, read as 'implies'

The precedence of these operators is such that 'not' binds strongest, then 'and', then 'or', and then 'implies'.

In the resolution method we negate the conjectured theorem and then try to show that this negated formula is a contradiction. If the negated formula is in fact a contradiction then the original formula must be a tautology. Thus the idea is: demonstrating that the negated formula is a contradiction is equivalent to proving that the original formula is a theorem (always holds). The process that aims at detecting the contradiction consists of a sequence of *resolution steps*.

Let us illustrate the principle with a simple example. Suppose we want to prove that the following propositional formula is a theorem:

$$(a \Rightarrow b) \ \& \ (b \Rightarrow c) \Rightarrow (a \Rightarrow c)$$

This formula is read as: if *b* follows from *a*, and *c* follows from *b*, then *c* follows from *a*.

Before the resolution process can start we have to get our negated, conjectured theorem into a form that suits the resolution process. The suitable form is the *conjunctive normal form*, which looks like this:

$$(p_1 \vee p_2 \vee \dots) \ \& \ (q_1 \vee q_2 \vee \dots) \ \& \ (r_1 \vee r_2 \vee \dots) \ \& \ \dots$$

Here all *p*'s, *q*'s and *r*'s are literals, that is simple propositions or their negations. This form is also called the *clause form*. Each conjunct is called a *clause*. So $(p_1 \vee p_2 \vee \dots)$ is a clause.

We can transform any propositional formula into this form. For our example theorem, this transformation can proceed as follows. The theorem is:

$$(a \Rightarrow b) \,\&\, (b \Rightarrow c) \Rightarrow (a \Rightarrow c)$$

The negated theorem is:

$$\sim (a \Rightarrow b) \,\&\, (b \Rightarrow c) \Rightarrow (a \Rightarrow c)$$

The following known equivalence rules will be useful when transforming this formula into the normal conjunctive form:

(1)  $x \Rightarrow y$      is equivalent to      $\sim x \,\vee\, y$

(2)  $\sim(x \vee y)$     is equivalent to      $\sim x \,\&\, \sim y$

(3)  $\sim(x \,\&\, y)$     is equivalent to      $\sim x \vee \sim y$

(4)  $\sim(\sim x)$      is equivalent to      $x$

Applying rule 1 to our formula we get:

$$\sim (\, \sim (\, (a \Rightarrow b) \,\&\, (b \Rightarrow c)\,)\, ) \vee (a \Rightarrow c)\, )$$

By rules 2 and 4 we get:

$$(a \Rightarrow b) \,\&\, (b \Rightarrow c) \,\&\, \sim(a \Rightarrow c)$$

Using rule 1 at several places we get:

$$(\sim a \,\vee\, b) \,\&\, (\sim b \vee c) \,\&\, \sim(\sim a \vee c)$$

By rule 2 we finally get the clause form we need:

$$(\sim a \,\vee\, b) \,\&\, (\sim b \vee c) \,\&\, a \,\&\, \sim c$$

This consists of four clauses: $(\sim a \vee b)$, $(\sim b \vee c)$, $a$, $\sim c$. Now the resolution process can start.

The basic resolution step can occur any time that there are two clauses such that some proposition $p$ occurs in one of them, and $\sim p$ occurs in the other. Let two such clauses be

$$p \vee Y \quad \text{and} \quad \sim p \vee Z$$

where $p$ is a proposition, and $Y$ and $Z$ are propositional formulas. Then the resolution step on these two clauses produces a third clause:

$$Y \vee Z$$

It can be shown that this clause logically follows from the two initial clauses. So by adding the clause $(Y \vee Z)$ to our formula we do not alter the validity of the formula. The resolution process thus generates new clauses. If the 'empty clause' (usually denoted by 'nil') occurs then this will signal that a contradiction has been found. The empty clause *nil* is generated from two clauses of the forms:

$$x \quad \text{and} \quad \sim x$$

which is obviously a contradiction.

Figure 25.13 shows the resolution process that starts with our negated conjectured theorem and ends with the empty clause.

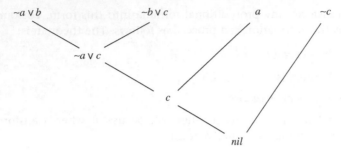

**Figure 25.13** Proving the theorem $(a \Rightarrow b)$ & $(b \Rightarrow c) \Rightarrow (a \Rightarrow c)$ by the resolution method. The top line is the negated theorem in the clause form. The empty clause at the bottom signals that the negated theorem is a contradiction.

Figure 25.14 shows how this resolution process can be formulated as a pattern-directed program. This program operates on clauses asserted into the database. The resolution principle can be formulated as a pattern-driven activity:

*if*

there are two clauses *C1* and *C2*, such that *P* is a (disjunctive) subexpression of *C1*, and $\sim P$ is a subexpression of *C2*

*then*

remove *P* from *C1* (giving *CA*), remove $\sim P$ from *C2* (giving *CB*), and add into the database a new clause: *CA* ∨ *CB*.

Written in our pattern-directed language this becomes:

```
[ clause( C1), delete( P, C1, CA),
  clause( C2), delete( ~P, C2, CB) ] --->
[ assertz( clause( CA ∨ CB) ) ].
```

This rule needs a little elaboration to prevent repeated actions on the same clauses, which would merely produce new copies of already existing clauses. The program in Figure 25.14 records into the database what has already been done, by asserting:

```
done( C1, C2, P)
```

The condition parts of rules will then recognize and prevent such repeated actions. The rules in Figure 25.14 also deal with some special cases that would otherwise require the explicit representation of the empty clause. Also, there are two rules that just simplify clauses when possible. One of these rules recognizes true clauses such as

$a \vee b \vee \sim a$

and removes them from the database since they are useless for detecting a contradiction. The other rule removes redundant sub-expressions. For example, this rule would simplify the clause

$a \vee \ b \vee a$

into $a \vee b$.

```
% Production rules for resolution theorem proving

% Contradicting clauses
[ clause( X), clause( ~X) ] --->
[ write('Contradiction found'), stop].

% Remove a true clause
[ clause( C), in( P, C), in( ~P, C) ] --->
[ retract( C) ].

% Simplify a clause
[ clause( C), delete( P, C, C1), in( P, C1) ] --->
[ replace( clause( C), clause( C1)) ].

% Resolution step, a special case
[ clause( P), clause( C), delete( ~P, C, C1), \+ done( P, C, P) ] --->
[ assertz( clause( C1)), assertz( done( P, C, P)) ].

% Resolution step, a special case
[ clause( ~P), clause( C), delete( P, C, C1), \+ done( ~P, C, P) ] --->
[ assertz( clause( C1)), assertz( done( ~P, C, P)) ].

% Resolution step, general case
[ clause( C1), delete( P, C1, CA),
  clause( C2), delete( ~P, C2, CB), \+ done( C1,C2,P) ] --->
[ assertz( clause( CA v CB)), assertz( done( C1, C2, P)) ].

% Last rule: resolution process stuck
[ ] ---> [ write('Not contradiction'), stop].

% delete( P, E, E1) if deleting a disjunctive sub-expression P from E gives E1

delete( X, X v Y, Y).

delete( X, Y v X, Y).

delete( X, Y v Z, Y v Z1) :-
  delete( X, Z, Z1).

delete( X, Y v Z, Y1 v Z) :-
  delete( X, Y, Y1).

% in( P, E) if P is a disjunctive subexpression in E

in( X, X).
in( X, Y) :-
  delete( X, Y, _ ).
```

**Figure 25.14** A pattern-directed program for simple resolution theorem proving.

A remaining question is how to translate a given propositional formula into the clause form. This is not difficult, and the program of Figure 25.15 does it. The procedure

**translate( Formula)**

translates a formula into a set of clauses C1, C2, etc., and asserts these clauses into the database as:

```
clause( C1).
clause( C2).
...
```

Now the pattern-directed theorem prover can be triggered by the goal **run**. So, to prove a conjectured theorem using these programs, we translate the negated theorem into the clause form and start the resolution process. For our example theorem, this is done by the question:

?- **translate( ~( ( a => b) & (b => c) => (a => c) ) ), run.**

---

% Translating a propositional formula into (asserted) clauses

```
:- op( 100, fy, ~).        % Negation
:- op( 110, xfy, &).       % Conjunction
:- op( 120, xfy, v).       % Disjunction
:- op( 130, xfy, =>).      % Implication
```

% translate( Formula): translate propositional Formula
% into clauses and assert each resulting clause C as clause( C)

```
translate( F & G) :-        % Translate conjunctive formula
   !,                       % Red cut
   translate( F),
   translate( G).

translate( Formula) :-
   transform( Formula, NewFormula),   % Transformation step on Formula
   !,                                 % Red cut
   translate( NewFormula).

translate( Formula) :-             % No more transformation possible
   assert( clause( Formula)).
```

% Transformation rules for propositional formulas

% transform( Formula1, Formula2):
%   Formula2 is equivalent to Formula1, but closer to clause form

```
transform( ~( ~X), X).                        % Eliminate double negation

transform( X => Y, ~X v Y).                    % Eliminate implication

transform( ~ ( X & Y), ~X v ~Y).              % De Morgan's law

transform( ~ ( X v Y), ~X & ~Y).              % De Morgan's law

transform( X & Y v Z, ( X v Z) & ( Y v Z)).   % Distribution

transform( X v Y & Z, (X v Y) & ( X v Z)).    % Distribution

transform( X v Y, X1 v Y) :-
   transform( X, X1).                          % Transform sub-expression

transform( X v Y, X v Y1) :-
   transform( Y, Y1).                          % Transform sub-expression

transform( ~ X, ~ X1) :-
   transform( X, X1).                          % Transform sub-expression
```

---

**Figure 25.15** Translating a propositional calculus formula into a set of (asserted) clauses.

The program will respond with 'Contradiction found', meaning that the original formula is a theorem.

# Summary

• Meta-programs treat other programs as data. A Prolog meta-interpreter is an interpreter for Prolog in Prolog.

• It is easy to write Prolog meta-interpreters that generate execution traces, proof trees and offer other extra features.

• Abduction is a kind of logical inference that aims at finding possible explanations of observations. Results of abductive reasoning do not necessarily follow from the given formulas, so they have the status of *hypothetical* explanations.

• Abductive reasoning can also be implemented as an extension of the basic Prolog meta-interpreter.

• Another extension of the basic meta-interpreter implements the query-the-user facility.

• Explanation-based generalization is a special technique for program compilation. It can be viewed as symbolic execution of a program, guided by a specific example. Explanation-based generalization was invented as an approach to machine learning.

• A pattern-directed program is a collection of pattern-directed modules whose execution is triggered by patterns in the 'database'.

• Prolog programs themselves can be viewed as pattern-directed systems.

• Pattern-directed system architecture is similar to blackboard architecture.

• The parallel implementation of pattern-directed systems would be most natural. The sequential implementation requires conflict resolution among the modules in the conflict set.

• A simple interpreter for pattern-directed programs was implemented in this chapter and applied to resolution-based theorem proving in propositional logic.

• Concepts discussed in this chapter are:
    meta-programs, meta-interpreters
    abduction, abductive reasoning
    query-the-user interpreter
    explanation-based generalization
    pattern-directed systems, pattern-directed architecture
    pattern-directed programming
    pattern-directed module
    blackboard systems, blackboard architecture
    conflict set, conflict resolution
    resolution-based theorem proving, resolution principle

## References

Writing Prolog meta-interpreters is part of the traditional Prolog programming culture. Shoham (1994) and Sterling and Shapiro (1994) give some other examples of Prolog meta-interpreters.

The idea of explanation-based generalization was developed in the area of machine learning. The formulation used in this chapter is as in the paper by Mitchell, Keller and Kedar-Cabelli (1986). Our EBG program is similar to that in Kedar-Cabelli and McCarty (1987). This program is a delightful illustration of how elegantly a complicated symbolic method can be implemented in Prolog. With this program, Kedar-Cabelli and McCarty transformed pages of previous vague descriptions of EBG into a succinct, crystal clear and immediately executable description.

Waterman and Hayes-Roth (1978) is the classical book on pattern-directed systems. Several elaborations of the basic pattern-directed architecture can be found under the name *blackboard systems*. A collection of papers on blackboard systems is Engelmore and Morgan (1988). Our illustrative application of pattern-directed programming is a basic example of mechanical theorem proving. Fundamentals of automated reasoning and mechanical theorem are covered in many general books on artificial intelligence, such as those by Genesereth and Nilsson (1987), Ginsberg (1993), Poole *et al.* (1998) and Russell and Norvig (2010). Robinson and Voronkov (2001) is a comprehensive collection of material on this topic.

Engelmore, R. and Morgan, T. (eds) (1988) *Blackboard Systems*. Reading, MA: Addison-Wesley.

Genesereth, M.R. and Nilsson, N.J. (1987) *Logical Foundation of Artificial Intelligence*. Palo Alto, CA: Morgan Kaufmann.

Ginsberg, M. (1993) *Essentials of Artificial Intelligence*. San Francisco, CA: Morgan Kaufmann.

Kedar-Cabelli, S.T. and McCarty, L.T. (1987) Explanation-based generalization as resolution theorem proving. In: *Proc. 4th Int. Machine Learning Workshop*, Irvine, CA: Morgan Kaufmann.

Mitchell, T.M., Keller, R.M. and Kedar-Cabelli, S.T. (1986) Explanation-based generalization: a unifying view. *Machine Learning* 1: 47–80.

Poole, D., Mackworth, A. and Gaebel, R. (1998) *Computational Intelligence: A Logical Approach*. Oxford University Press.

Robinson, A.J.A. and Voronkov, A. (eds) (2001) *Handbook of Automated Reasoning*. North-Holland.

Russell, S. and Norvig, P. (2010) *Artificial Intelligence: A Modern Approach,* third edn. Prentice Hall.

Shoham, Y. (1994) *Artificial Intelligence Techniques in Prolog*. San Francisco, CA: Morgan Kaufmann.

Sterling, L. and Shapiro, E. (1994) *The Art of Prolog*, second edn. Cambridge, MA: MIT Press.

Waterman, D.A. and Hayes-Roth, F. (eds) (1978) *Pattern-Directed Inference Systems*. London: Academic Press.

# Some Differences Between Prolog Implementations

The syntax for Prolog in this book follows the tradition of the Edinburgh Prolog, which has been adopted by the majority of Prolog implementations and also the ISO standard for Prolog. Typically implementations of Prolog offer many additional features. Generally, the programs in the book use a subset of what is provided in a typical implementation, and is included in the ISO standard. However, there are still some differences between various Prologs that may require small changes when executing the programs in the book with a particular Prolog. This appendix draws attention to some of such more likely differences.

## Dynamic and static predicates

The ISO standard and typical Prolog implementations distinguish between *static* and *dynamic* predicates. Static predicates may be compiled into a more efficient code than dynamic ones. Only dynamic predicates can be manipulated by **assert**, **asserta**, **assertz** and **retract**, and can be retrieved by **clause( Head, Body)**. A predicate is assumed static, unless announced in the program by a declaration of the form:

> :- dynamic PredicateName/ PredicateArity.

For example:

> :- dynamic counter/2.

Predicates introduced through **assert(a/z)** only, are automatically assumed as dynamic.

## Assert and retract

The standard only includes the predicates **asserta** and **assertz**, but not **assert**. Virtually all the implementations also provide **assert**. If **assert** is not available, **assertz** can simply be used instead. To remove all the clauses about a predicate, built-in predicates **retractall( Clause)** or **abolish( PredicateName/Arity)** may be provided.

## Undefined predicates

In some Prologs, a call to a predicate not defined in the program at all, simply fails. Other Prologs in such cases complain with an error message. In such

Prologs, undefined predicates can be made to fail (without error messages) by a built-in predicate like:

**unknown( _, fail).**

## Negation as failure: *not* and ' \+'

In this book we use **not Goal** and \+ **Goal** interchangably for negation as failure. Many Prologs (and the standard) use only the notation

\+ **Goal**

to emphasize that this is not the proper logical negation, but negation defined through failure. For compatibility with these Prologs, only '\+' should be used. Alternatively, the (prettier) notation with **not** can be introduced as a user-defined predicate (see Appendix B) with exactly the same effect as '\+'.

## Predicate *name( Atom, CodeList)*

This predicate is provided by most implementations, but not included in the standard (instead: **atom_codes/2**). There are small differences between Prologs in the behaviour of **name** in special cases, e.g. when the first argument is a number.

## Loading programs with *consult* and *reconsult*

Loading programs with **consult** and **reconsult** varies between implementations. Differences occur when programs are loaded from multiple files and the same predicate is defined in more than one file (the new clauses about the same predicate may simply be added to the old clauses; alternatively, just the clauses in the most recent file are loaded, abandoning the previous clauses about the same predicate).

## Modules

In some Prologs, the program can be divided into *modules* so that predicate names are local to a module unless they are specifically made visible from other modules. This is useful when writing large programs, when predicates with the same name and arity may mean different things in different modules.

## Built-in predicates

Various Prologs provide, in addition to the usual repertoire of built-in predicates, many other built-in predicates. In some Prologs, the frequently used predicates on lists may already be built-in as, for example: **member(X,List)**, **append(List1, List2,List3)** and **length(List,Length)**.

# Some Frequently Used Predicates

............................................................................................................................................

Some basic predicates such as **member/2** and **conc/3** are used in many programs throughout the book. To avoid repetition, the definition of such predicates is usually not included in the program's listing. To run a program, these frequently used predicates also have to be loaded into Prolog. This is done most easily by consulting (or compiling) a file, such as one given in this appendix, that defines these predicates. The listing below includes some predicates that may already be included among the built-in predicates, depending on the implementation of Prolog. For example, negation as failure written as **not Goal** is also included below for compatibility with Prologs that only use the notation \+ **Goal** instead. When loading into Prolog the definition of a predicate that is already built-in, Prolog will typically just issue a warning message and ignore the new definition.

```
% File frequent.pl: Library of frequently used predicates

% Negation as failure
%    This is normally available as a built-in predicate,
%    often written with the prefix operator '\+', e.g. \+ likes( mary, snakes)
%    The definition below is only given for compatibility among Prolog implementations

:- op( 900, fy, not).

not Goal :-
  Goal, !, fail
  ;
  true.

% once( Goal): produce one solution of Goal only (the first solution only)
%    This may already be provided as a built-in predicate

once( Goal) :-
  Goal, !.

% member( X, List): X is a member of List
% This may already be a built-in predicate

member( X, [ X | _ ]).                    % X is head of list

member( X, [ _ | Rest]) :-
  member( X, Rest).                       % X is in body of list
```

% conc( L1, L2, L3): list L3 is the concatenation of lists L1 and L2
% This may already be built-in as append(L1,L2,L3)

**conc( [], L, L).**

**conc( [X | L1], L2, [X | L3]) :-**
  **once( L1, L2, L3).**

% del( X, L0, L): List L is equal to list L0 with X deleted
%    Note: Only one occurrence of X is deleted
%    Fail if X is not in L0

**del( X, [X | Rest], Rest).**                          % Delete the head

**del( X, [Y | Rest0], [Y | Rest]) :-**
  **del( X, Rest0, Rest).**                             % Delete from tail

% subset( Set, Subset): list Set contains all the elements of list Subset
%    Note: The elements of Subset appear in Set in the same order as in Subset

**subset( [], []).**

**subset( [First | Rest], [First | Sub]) :-**           % Retain First in subset
  **subset( Rest, Sub).**

**subset( [First | Rest], Sub) :-**                     % Remove First
  **subset( Rest, Sub).**

% set_difference( Set1, Set2, Set3): Set3 is the list representing
%    the difference of the sets represented by lists Set1 and Set2
%    Normal use: Set1 and Set2 are input arguments, Set3 is output

**set_difference( [], _, []).**

**set_difference( [X | S1], S2, S3) :-**
  **member( X, S2), !,**                                % X in set S2
  **set_difference( S1, S2, S3).**

**set_difference( [X | S1], S2, [X | S3]) :-**          % X not in S2
  **set_difference( S1, S2, S3).**

% length( List, Length): Length is the length of List
%    Note: length/2 may already be included among built-in predicates
%    The definition below is tail-recursive
%    It can also be used to generate efficiently list of given length

**length( L, N) :-**
  **length( L, 0, N).**

**length( [], N, N).**

**length( [_ | L], N0, N) :-**
  **N1 is N0 + 1,**
  **length( L, N1, N).**

% max( X, Y, Max): Max = max(X,Y)

**max( X, Y, Max) :-**
  **X >= Y, !, Max = X**
  **;**
  **Max = Y.**

% min( X, Y, Min): Min = min(X,Y)

```
min( X, Y, Min) :-
  X =< Y, !, Min = X
  ;
  Min = Y.
```

% copy_term( T1, T2): term T2 is equal to T1 with variables renamed
%    This may already be available as a built-in predicate
%    Procedure below assumes that copy_term is called so that T2 matches T1

```
copy_term( Term, Copy) :-
  asserta( term_to_copy( Term)),
  retract( term_to_copy( Copy)), !.
```

% tab( N): write N blanks on current output stream
%    This is usually available as a built-in predicate

```
tab( N) :-
  N < 1.
```

```
tab( N) :-
  N > 0,
  write ( ' '),
  N1 is N−1,
  tab( N1).
```

# Solutions to Selected Exercises

## Chapter 1

1.1    (a) **no**
        (b) **X = pat**
        (c) **X = bob**
        (d) **X = bob, Y = pat**

1.2    (a) **?- parent( X, pat).**
        (b) **?- parent( liz, X).**
        (c) **?- parent( Y, pat), parent( X, Y).**

1.3    (a) **happy( X) :-**
            **parent( X, Y).**
        (b) **hastwochildren( X) :-**
            **parent( X, Y),**
            **sister( Z, Y).**

1.4    **grandchild( X, Z) :-**
        **parent( Y, X),**
        **parent( Z, Y).**

1.5    **aunt( X, Y) :-**
        **parent( Z, Y),**
        **sister( X, Z).**

1.6    Yes it is.

1.7    (a) no backtracking
        (b) no backtracking
        (c) no backtracking
        (d) backtracking

## Chapter 2

2.1    (a) variable
        (b) atom
        (c) atom
        (d) variable
        (e) atom

      (f)  structure

      (g)  number

      (h)  syntactically incorrect

      (i)  structure

      (j)  syntactically incorrect

**2.3**    (a)  $A = 1$, $B = 2$

      (b)  no

      (c)  no

      (d)  $D = 2$, $E = 2$

      (e)  P1 = point(–1,0)
           P2 = point(1,0)
           P3 = point(0,Y)

           This can represent the family of triangles with two vertices on the *x*-axis at 1 and –1 respectively, and the third vertex anywhere on the *y*-axis.

**2.4**    seg( point(5,Y1), point(5,Y2) )

**2.5**    regular( rectangle( point(X1,Y1), point(X2,Y1), point(X2,Y3), point(X1,Y3) ) ).
       % This assumes that the first point is the left bottom vertex.

**2.6**    (a)  **A = two**

      (b)  **no**

      (c)  **C = one**

      (d)  **D = s(s(1));**
          **D = s(s(s(s(s(1)))))**

**2.7**    relatives( X, Y) :-
       ancestor( X, Y)
       ;
       ancestor( Y, X)
       ;
       ancestor( Z, X),
       ancestor( Z, Y)
       ;
       ancestor( X, Z),
       ancestor( Y, Z).

**2.8**    **translate( 1, one).**

       **translate( 2, two).**

       **translate( 3, three).**

**2.9**    In the case of Figure 2.10 Prolog does slightly more work.

**2.11**  According to the definition of matching of Section 2.2, this succeeds. X becomes a sort of circular structure in which X itself occurs as one of the arguments.

# Chapter 3

3.1　(a)　conc( L1, [_, _, _], L)

　　　(b)　conc( [_, _, _ | L2], [_, _, _], L)

3.2　(a)　last( Item, List) :-
　　　　　conc(_, [Item], List).

　　　(b)　last( Item, [Item] ).

　　　　　last( Item, [First | Rest] ) :-
　　　　　last( Item, Rest).

3.3　evenlength( []).

　　　evenlength( [First | Rest] ) :-
　　　　oddlength( Rest).

　　　oddlength( [First | Rest] ) :-
　　　　evenlength( Rest).

3.4　reverse( [], []).

　　　reverse( [First | Rest], Reversed) :-
　　　　reverse( Rest, ReversedRest),
　　　　conc( ReversedRest, [First], Reversed).

3.5　% This is easy using reverse

　　　palindrome( List) :-
　　　　reverse( List, List).

　　　% Alternative solution, not using reverse

　　　palindrome1( [] ).

　　　palindrome1( [_] ).

　　　palindrome1( List) :-
　　　　conc( [First | Middle], [First], List),
　　　　palindrome1( Middle).

3.6　shift( [First | Rest], Shifted) :-
　　　　conc( Rest, [First], Shifted).

3.7　translate( [], [] ).

　　　translate( [Head | Tail], [Head1 | Tail1] :-
　　　　means( Head, Head1),
　　　　translate( Tail, Tail1).

3.8　% The following assumes the order of elements in Subset as in Set

　　　subset( [], []).

　　　subset( [First | Rest], [First | Sub] ) :-　　% Retain First in subset
　　　　subset( Rest, Sub).

　　　subset( [First | Rest], Sub) :-　　% Remove First
　　　　subset( Rest, Sub).

3.9     dividelist( [], [], [] ).                                    % Nothing to divide

        dividelist( [X], [X], [] ).                                  % Divide one-element list

        dividelist( [X, Y | List], [X | List1], [Y | List2] ) :-
            dividelist( List, List1, List2).

3.10    equal_length( [], []).

        equal_length( [_ | L1, [_ | L2) :-
            equal_length( L1, L2).

3.11    flatten( [Head | Tail], FlatList) :-                         % Flatten non-empty list
            flatten( Head, FlatHead),
            flatten( Tail, FlatTail),
            conc( FlatHead, FlatTail, FlatList).

        flatten( [], []).                                            % Flatten empty list

        flatten( X, [ X ] ).                                         % Flatten a non-list

        % Note: On backtracking this program produces rubbish

3.12    Term1 = plays( jimmy, and( football, squash) )

        Term2 = plays( susan, and( tennis, and( basketball, volleyball) ) )

3.13    :- op( 300, xfx, was).

        :- op( 200, xfx, of).

        :- op( 100, fx, the).

3.14    (a)  A = 1 + 0

        (b)  B = 1 + 1 + 0

        (c)  C = 1 + 1 + 1 + 1 + 0

        (d)  D = 1 + 1 + 0 + 1;
             D = 1 + 0 + 1 + 1;
             D = 0 + 1 + 1 + 1                       % Further backtracking causes indefinite cycling

3.15    :- op( 100, xfx, in).
        :- op( 300, fx, concatenating).
        :- op( 200, xfx, gives).
        :- op( 100, xfx, and).
        :- op( 300, fx, deleting).
        :- op( 100, xfx, from).

        % List membership

        Item in [Item | List].

        Item in [First | Rest] :-
            Item in Rest.

        % List concatenation

        concatenating [] and List gives List.

        concatenating [X | L1] and L2 gives [X | L3] :-
            concatenating L1 and L2 gives L3.

% Deleting from a list

**deleting Item from [Item | Rest] gives Rest.**

**deleting Item from [First | Rest] gives [First | NewRest] :-**
  **deleting Item from Rest gives NewRest.**

3.16  **max( X, Y, X) :-**
    **X >= Y.**

   **max( X, Y, Y) :-**
    **X < Y.**

3.17  **maxlist( [ X], X).**                   % Maximum of single-element list

   **maxlist( [X, Y | Rest], Max) :-**         % At least two elements in list
    **maxlist( [Y | Rest], MaxRest),**
    **max( X, MaxRest, Max).**                 % Max is the greater of X and MaxRest

3.18  **sumlist( [], 0).**

   **sumlist( [First | Rest], Sum) :-**
    **sumlist( Rest, SumRest),**
    **Sum is First + SumRest.**

3.19  **ordered( [X] ).**                       % Single-element list is ordered

   **ordered( [X, Y | Rest] ) :-**
    **X =< Y,**
    **ordered( [Y | Rest] ).**

3.20  **subsum( [], 0, []).**

   **subsum( [N | List], Sum, [N | Sub]) :-**   % N is in subset
    **Sum1 is Sum - N,**
    **subsum( List, Sum1, Sub).**

   **subsum( [N | List], Sum, Sub) :-**         % N is not in subset
    **subsum( List, Sum, Sub).**

3.21  **between( N1, N2, N1) :-**
    **N1 =< N2**

   **between( N1, N2, X) :-**
    **N1 < N2,**
    **NewN1 is N1 + 1,**
    **between( NewN1, N2, X).**

3.22  **:- op( 900, fx, if).**
   **:- op( 800, xfx, then).**
   **:- op( 700, xfx, else).**
   **:- op( 600, xfx, : =).**

   **if Val1 > Val2 then Var :=Val3 else Anything :-**
    **Val1 > Val2,**
    **Var = Val3.**

   **if Val1 > Val2 then Anything else Var :=Val4 :-**
    **Val1 =< Val2,**
    **Var = Val4.**

## Chapter 4

**4.5**   The order is defined in the goal **member( Y, [1,2,3,4,5,6,7,8])**.

**4.6**   (a) **jump( X/Y, X1/Y1) :-**              % Knight jump from X/Y to X1/Y1
          **(**
          **dxy( Dx, Dy)**               % Knight distances in x and y directions
          **;**
          **dxy( Dy, Dx),**              % or the other way round]
          **),**
          **X1 is X + Dx,**
          **inboard( X1),**              % X1 is within chessboard
          **Y1 is Y + Dy,**
          **inboard(Y1).**               % Y1 is within chessboard

          **dxy( 2, 1).**                % 2 squares to right, 1 forward
          **dxy( 2, –1).**               % 2 squares to right, 1 backward
          **dxy( –2, 1).**               % 2 to left, 1 forward
          **dxy( –2, –1).**              % 2 to left, 1 backward

          **inboard( Coord) :-**         % Coordinate within chessboard
          **0 < Coord,**
          **Coord < 9.**

          (b) **knightpath( [Square] ).**          % Knight sitting on Square
          **knightpath( [S1, S2 | Rest] ) :-**
          **jump( S1, S2),**
          **knightpath( [S2 | Rest] ).**

          (c) **?- knightpath( [2/1,R,5/4,S,X/8] ).**

## Chapter 5

**5.1**   (a) **X = 1;**
              **X = 2;**

          (b) **X = 1**
              **Y = 1;**
              **X = 1**
              **Y = 2;**
              **X = 2**
              **Y = 1;**
              **X = 2**
              **Y = 2;**

          (c) **X = 1**
              **Y = 1;**
              **X = 1**
              **Y = 2;**

**5.2**   Assume that procedure **class** is called with second argument uninstantiated.

          **class( Number, positive) :-**
          **Number > 0, !.**

          **class( 0, zero) :- !.**

          **class( Number, negative).**

5.3    split( [], [], [] ).

       split( [X | L], [X | L1], L2) :-
         X >= 0, !,
         split( L, L1, L2).

       split( [X | L], L1, [X | L2] ) :-
         split( L, L1, L2).

5.4    member( Item, Candidates), \+ member( Item, RuledOut)

5.5    set_difference( [], _, [] ).

       set_difference( [X | L1], L2, L) :-
         member( X, L2), !,
         set_difference( L1, L2, L).

       set_difference( [X | L1], L2, [X | L] ) :-
         set_difference( L1, L2, L).

5.6    unifiable( [], _, [] ).

       unifiable( [First | Rest], Term, List) :-
         \+ ( First = Term), !,
         unifiable( Rest, Term, List),

       unifiable( [First | Rest], Term, [First | List] ) :-
         unifiable( Rest, Term, List).

# Chapter 6

6.2    add_to_tail( Item, List) :-
       var( List), !,             % List represents empty list
       List = [Item | Tail].

       add_to_tail( Item, [_ | Tail] ) :-
         add_to_tail( Item, Tail).

       member2( X, List) :-
       var( List), !,             % List represents empty list
       fail.                  % so X cannot be a member

       member2( X, [X | Tail] ).

       member2( X, [_ | Tail] ) :-
         member2( X, Tail).

6.5    % subsumes( Term1, Term2):
       %   Term1 subsumes Term2, e.g. subsumes( t(X,a,f(Y)), t(A,a,f(g(B))))
       % Assume Term1 and Term2 do not contain the same variable
       % In the following procedure, subsuming variables get instantiated
       % to terms of the form literally( SubsumedTerm)

       subsumes( Atom1, Atom2) :-
         atomic( Atom1), !,
         Atom1 == Atom2.

       subsumes( Var, Term) :-
         var( Var), !,           % Variable subsumes anything
         Var = literally( Term).     % To handle other occurrences of Var

```
subsumes( literally( Term1), Term2) :- !,    % Another occurrence of Term2
    Term1 = = Term2.
subsumes( Term1, Term2) :-                    % Term1 not a variable
    nonvar( Term2),
    Term1 = .. [Fun | Args1],
    Term2 = .. [Fun | Args2],
    subsumes_list( Args1, Args2).
subsumes_list( [], []).
subsumes_list( [First1 | Rest1], [First2 | Rest2]) :-
    subsumes( First1, First2),
    subsumes_list( Rest1, Rest2).
```

6.6    (a)  ?- retract( product( X, Y, Z)), fail.

      (b)  ?- retract( product( X, Y, 0)), fail.

6.7
```
copy_term( Term, Copy) :-
    asserta( term_to_copy( Term)),
    retract( term_to_copy( Copy)).
```

6.9
```
copy_term( Term, Copy) :-
    bagof( X, X = Term, [Copy]).
```

6.10
```
findterm( Term) :-              % Assuming current input stream is file f
    read( Term), !,             % Current term in F matches Term?
    write( Term)                % If yes, display it
    ;
    findterm( Term).            % Otherwise process the rest of file
```

6.11
```
findallterms( Term) :-
    read( CurrentTerm),         % Assuming CurrentTerm not a variable
    process( CurrentTerm, Term).
process( end_of_file, _) :- !.
process( CurrentTerm, Term) :-
    ( not( CurrentTerm = Term), !     % Terms do not match
    ;
    write( CurrentTerm), nl           % Otherwise output current term
    ),
    findallterms( Term).              % Do the rest of file
```

6.13
```
starts( Atom, Character) :-
    name( Character, [Code] ),
    name( Atom, [Code | _] ).
```

6.14
```
plural( Noun, Nouns) :-
    name( Noun, CodeList),
    name( s, CodeS),
    conc( CodeList, CodeS, NewCodeList),
    name( Nouns, NewCodeList).
```

## Chapter 7

**7.1** We get the same result regardless of the order.

**7.5**

```
% fit( BoxName, [ BlockName1/Rectangle1, BlockName2/Rectangle2, ...])
fit( BoxName, BlocksRects) :-
   box( BoxName, Dim), Box = rect( pos( 0.0, 0.0), Dim),
   fit2( Box, BlocksRects).

fit2( Box, []).                              % No blocks to fit Box

fit2( Box, [ BlockName/Rect | BlocksRects]) :-
   fit2( Box, BlocksRects),                  % Remaining blocks fit into Box
   block_rectangle( BlockName, Rect),
   inside( Rect, Box),
   no_overlaps( Rect, BlocksRects).

no_overlaps( _, []).

no_overlaps( Rect, [_/Rect1 | BlocksRects]) :-
  no_overlap( Rect, Rect1),
  no_overlaps( Rect, BlocksRects).
```

## Chapter 8

**8.2**   `add_at_end( L1 - [Item | Z2], Item, L1 - Z2).`

**8.3**   
```
reverse( A - Z, L - L) :-              % Result is empty list if
   A= = Z, !.                          % A - Z represents empty list

reverse( [X | L] - Z, RL - RZ) :-      % Non-empty list
   reverse( L - Z, RL - [X | RZ] ).
```

**8.6**   
```
% Eight-queens program
sol( Ylist) :-
   functor( Du, u, 15),                % Set of upward diagonals
   functor( Dv, v, 15),                % Set of downward diagonals
   sol ( Ylist,
      [1,2,3,4,5,6,7,8],               % Set of X-coordinates
      [1,2,3,4,5,6,7,8],               % Set of Y-coordinates
      Du, Dv).

sol( [], [], [], _, _).

sol( [Y | Ys], [X | XL], YL0, Du, Dv) :-
   del( Y, YL0, YL),                   % Choose a Y coordinate
   U is X+Y−1,
   arg( U, Du, X),                     % Upward diagonal free
   V is X-Y+8,
   arg( V, Dv, X),                     % Downward diagonal free
   sol( Ys, XL, YL, Du, Dv).

del( X, [X | L], L).

del( X, [Y | L0], [Y | L]) :-
   del( X, L0, L).
```

## Chapter 9

**9.4**   % mergesort( List, SortedList): use the merge-sort algorithm

     **mergesort( [], [] ).**

     **mergesort( [X], [X] ).**

     **mergesort( List, SortedList) :-**
       **divide( List, List1, List2),**         % Divide into approx. equal lists
       **mergesort( List1, Sorted1),**
       **mergesort( List2, Sorted2),**
       **merge( Sorted1, Sorted2, SortedList).**   % Merge sorted lists

     **divide( [], [], [] ).**

     **divide( [X], [X], [] ).**

     **divide( [X, Y | L], [X | L1], [Y | L2] :-**    % Put X, Y into separate lists
       **divide( L, L1, L2).**

     % merge( List1, List2, List3): See Section 8.3.1

**9.5**   (a)  **binarytree( nil).**

        **binarytree( t( Left, Root, Right) ) :-**
          **binarytree( Left),**
          **binarytree( Right).**

**9.6**   **height( nil, 0).**

     **height( t( Left, Root, Right), H) :-**
       **height( Left, LH),**
       **height( Right, RH),**
       **max( LH, RH, MH),**
       **H is 1 + MH.**

     **max( A, B, A) :-**
       **A > = B, !.**

     **max( A, B, B).**

**9.7**   **linearize( nil, [] ).**

     **linearize( t( Left, Root, Right), List) :-**
       **linearize( Left, List1),**
       **linearize( Right, List2),**
       **conc( List1, [Root | List2], List).**

**9.8**   **maxelement( t(_, Root, nil), Root) :- !.**   % Root is right-most element

     **maxelement( t(_, _, Right), Max) :-**     % Right subtree non-empty
       **maxelement( Right, Max).**

**9.9**   **in( Item, t( _, Item, _), [Item] ).**

     **in( Item, t( Left, Root, _), [Root | Path] ) :-**
      **gt( Root, Item),**
      **in( Item, Left, Path).**

     **in( Item, t( _, Root, Right), [Root | Path] ) :-**
      **gt( Item, Root),**
      **in( Item, Right, Path).**

9.10 % Display a binary tree from top to bottom
% This program assumes that each node is just one character

show( Tree) :-
  dolevels( Tree, 0, more).             % Do all levels from top

dolevels( Tree, Level, alldone) :- !.    % No more nodes beyond Level

dolevels( Tree, Level, more) :-      % Do all levels from Level
  traverse( Tree, Level, 0, Continue), nl,  % Output nodes at Level
  NextLevel is Level + 1,
  dolevels( Tree, NextLevel, Continue).  % Do lower levels

traverse( nil, _, _, _).

traverse( t( Left, X, Right), Level, Xdepth, Continue) :-
  NextDepth is Xdepth + 1,
  traverse( Left, Level, NextDepth, Continue),  % Traverse left subtree
  ( Level = Xdepth, !,            % Node X at Level?
    write( X), Continue = more    % Output node, more to do
    ;
    write(' ')              % Otherwise leave space
  ),
  traverse( Right, Level, NextDepth, Continue).  % Traverse right subtree

# Chapter 10

10.1  in( Item, l( Item) ).          % Item found in leaf

    in( Item, n2( T1, M, T2) ) :-     % Node has two subtrees
      gt( M, Item), !,          % Item not in second subtree
      in( Item, T1)           % Search first subtree
      ;
      in( Item, T2).         % Otherwise search the second

    in( Item, n3( T1, M2, T2, M3, T3) ) :-  % Node has three subtrees
      gt( M2, Item), !,       % Item not in second or third
      in( Item, T1)           % Search first subtree
      ;
      gt( M3, Item), !,       % Item not in third subtree
      in( Item, T2)           % Search second subtree
      ;
      in( Item, T3).         % Search third subtree

10.3  avl( Tree) :-
    avl( Tree, Height).         % Tree is AVL-tree with height Height

    avl( nil, 0).               % Empty tree is AVL and has height 0

    avl( t( Left, Root, Right), H) :-
    avl( Left, HL),
    avl( Right, HR),
    ( HL is HR; HL is HR + 1; HL is HR − 1),    % Subtrees heights almost equal
      max1( HL, HR, H).

    max1( U, V, M) :-           % M is 1 + max of U and V
    U > V, !, M is U + 1
    ;
    M is V + 1.

10.4  The item at the root is initially 5, then 8, and finally 5 again.

## Chapter 11

11.1   depthfirst1( [Node | Path], [Node | Path] ) :-
      goal( Node).

  depthfirst1( [Node | Path], Solution) :-
      s(Node, Node1),
      \+ member( Node1, Path),
      depthfirst1( [Node1, Node | Path], Solution).

11.3   % Iterative deepening search that stops increasing depth
     % when there is no path to current depth
     iterative_deepening( Start, Solution) :-
       id_path( Start, Node, [], Solution),
       goal( Node).

     % path( First, Last, Path): Path is a list of nodes between First and Last

     path( First, First, [First]).

     path( First, Last, [First, Second | Rest]) :-
      s( First, Second),
      path( Second, Last, [Second | Rest]).

     % Iterative deepening path generator
     % id_path( First, Last, Template, Path): Path is a path between First and
     %    Last not longer than template list Template. Alternative paths are
     %    generated in the order of increasing length
     id_path( First, Last, Template, Path) :-
     Path = Template,
     path( First, Last, Path)
     ;
     copy_term( Template, P),
     path( First, _, P), !,            % At least one path of Template length
     id_path( First, Last, [_ | Template], Path).   % Longer template

11.6   Breadth-first search: 15 nodes; iterative deepening: 26 nodes

$$N(b, 0) = 1$$
$$N(b, d) = N(b, d - 1) + (b^{d+1} - 1)/(b - 1) \text{ for } d > 0$$

11.8   solve( StartSet, Solution) :-          % StartSet is list of start nodes
      bagof( [Node], member( Node, StartSet), CandidatePaths),
      breadthfirst( CandidatePaths, Solution).

11.9   Backward search is advantageous if the branching in the backward direction is lower than in the forward direction. Backward search is only applicable if a goal node is explicitly known.

     % Let 'origs( Nodel, Node2)' be the original state-space relation
     % Define new s relation:

     s( Node1, Node2) :-
      origs( Node2, Node1).

11.10  % States for bidirectional search are pairs of nodes StartNode-EndNode
     % of the original state space, denoting start and goal of search

     s( Start - End, NewStart - NewEnd) :-
      origs( Start, NewStart),         % A step forward
      origs( NewEnd, End).          % A step backward

% goal( Start - End) for bidirectional search

**goal( Start - Start).**                              % Start equal end

**goal( Start - End) :-**
   **origs( Start, End).**                              % Single step to end

**11.11** **find1**: depth-first search; **find2**: iterative deepening (**conc(Path,_,_)** generates list templates of increasing length forcing **find1** into iterative deepening regime; **find3**: backward search.

**11.12** Bidirectional search with iterative deepening from both ends.

## Chapter 12

**12.2** Not correct. $h \leq h*$ is sufficient for admissibility, but not necessary.

**12.3** $h(n) = \max\{h_1(n), h_2(n), h_3(n)\}$

## Chapter 13

**13.2** % Specification of eight puzzle for IDA*

  **s(Depth:State, NewDepth:NewState) :-**
    **s( State, NewState, _),**
    **NewDepth is Depth + 1.**

  **f( Depth:[Empty | Tiles], F) :-**
    **goal( [Empty0 | Tiles0]),**
    **totdist( Tiles, Tiles0, Dist),**
    **F is Depth + Dist.**                  % Use total dist. as heuristic function

  **goal( _:[2/2,1/3,2/3,3/3,3/2,3/1,2/1,1/1,1/2]).**

% Initial states for IDA* are of the form 0:State, where State
% is a start state for A* (Figure 12.6)

  **showpos( Depth:State) :-**
    **showpos( State).**

For initial state [1/2,3/3,3/1,1/3,3/2,1/1,2/3,2/1,2/2]: A* (using non-admissible heuristic) quickly finds a solution of length 38; IDA* (using total distance heuristic) needs much more time, but finds optimal solution of length 24.

**13.4** Order: *a, b, c, f, g, j, k, d, e, f, g, j, l, k, m, j, l*
Updates of $F(b)$ and $F(c)$: $F(b) = 2$, $F(c) = 1$, $F(c) = 3$, $F(b) = 5$

## Chapter 14

**14.4** There are three solution trees whose costs are: 8, 10 and 11. Intervals: $0 \leq h(c) < 9$, $0 \leq h(f) < 5$.

## Chapter 15

**15.2** No error when $p(A|B) = 1$ or $p(B|A) = 1$. Greatest error (0.5) when $p(A) = p(B) = 0.5$ and $p(A|B) = 0$.

**15.4** A = 6, B = 5, C = 25.

## Chapter 16

**16.1**

(a) $p(a) = p(a \mid c)$

(b) $p(a) < p(a \mid d)$

(c) $p(a \mid d) > p(a \mid cd)$

(d) $p(d \mid bc) = p(d \mid abc)$

**16.2**

(a) $p(\,c \mid \sim a \wedge b \wedge e) = p(\,c \mid \sim a \wedge e)$

(b) $p(\,c \mid \sim a \wedge b \wedge d \wedge e\,) = p(\,c \mid \sim a \wedge d \wedge e\,)$

(c) $p(\,c \mid \sim b \wedge d \wedge e\,) = p(\,c \mid \sim b \wedge d \wedge e\,)$   (Cannot be simplified)

**16.3**  $p(b \mid c) = [\, p(b \mid a)\, p(a)\, p(c \mid a) + p(b \mid \sim a)\, p(\sim a)\, p(c \mid \sim a)] \,/\, [\, p(a)\, p(c \mid a) + p(\sim a)$
$p(c \mid \sim a)\,]$

**16.5**  E = {}, E = {b}, E = {c}, E = {c,e}, E = {b,c}, E = {b,c,e}

## Chapter 17

**17.6**  No. The reason is that one action may achieve more than one goal simultaneously.

## Chapter 19

**19.3**  A diode in series with R5, in direction from left to right, should not affect the voltage at T51. A diode in the opposite direction affects this voltage.

## Chapter 20

**20.1**  Whole example set: I = 2.2925
Ires(size) = 1.5422, Gain(size) = 0.7503
Info(size) = 0.9799, GainRatio(size) = 0.7503/0.9799 = 0.7657
Ires(holes) = 0.9675, Gain(holes) = 1.324
Info(holes) = 1.5546, GainRatio(holes) = 0.8517

**20.2**  Gain = I − Ires
I = − (p(D) log p(D) + p(∼D) log p(∼D))
= − ( 0.25 log 0.25 + 0.75 log 0.75) = 0.8113
To compute Ires we need p(S), p(∼S), p(D | S), p(D | ∼S)
p(S) = p(S | D) p(D) + p(S | ∼D) p(∼D) = 0.75 ∗ 0.25 + 1/6 ∗ 0.75 = 0.3125
Using Bayes formula:
p(D | S) = p(D) p(S | D) / p(S) = 0.25 ∗ 0.75 / 0.3125 = 0.6
p(∼D | S) = 0.4
p(D | ∼S) = p(D)∗p(∼S | D) / p(∼S) = 0.25 ∗ 0.25 / (1–0.3125) = 0.09090
Ires = p(S)∗I(D | S) + p(∼S)∗I(D | ∼S) = 0.6056
Notation I(D | S) means information of disease given symptom present.
Gain = 0.2057
GainRatio = Gain(S) / I(S) = 0.2057/0.8960 = 0.2296

**20.6**  % prunetree( Tree, PrunedTree): PrunedTree is optimally pruned Tree
  %    with respect to estimated classification error
  %    Assume trees are binary:
  %    Tree = leaf( Node, ClassFrequencyList), or
  %    Tree = tree( Root, LeftSubtree, RightSubtree)

```
prunetree( Tree, PrunedTree) :-
  prune( Tree, PrunedTree, Error, FrequencyList).
```

% prune( Tree, PrunedTree, Error, FrequencyList):
%    PrunedTree is optimally pruned Tree with classification Error,
%    FrequencyList is the list of frequencies of classes at root of Tree

```
prune( leaf( Node, FreqList), leaf( Node, FreqList), Error, FreqList) :-
  static_error( FreqList, Error).
```

```
prune( tree( Root, Left, Right), PrunedT, Error, FreqList) :-
  prune( Left, Left1, LeftError, LeftFreq),
  prune( Right, Right1, RightError, RightFreq),
  sumlists( LeftFreq, RightFreq, FreqList),          % Add corresponding elements
  static_error( FreqList, StaticErr),
  sum( LeftFreq, N1),
  sum( RightFreq, N2),
  BackedErr is (N1 * LeftError + N2 * RightError) / (N1 + N2),
  decide( StaticErr, BackedErr, Root, FreqList, Left1, Right1, Error, PrunedT).
```

% Decide to prune or not:

```
decide( StatErr, BackErr, Root, FreqL, _, _, StatErr, leaf( Root, FreqL)) :-
  StatErr =< BackErr, !.          % Static error smaller: prune subtrees
```

% Otherwise do not prune:

```
decide( _, BackErr, Root, _, Left, Right, BackErr, tree( Root, Left, Right)).
```

% static_error( ClassFrequencyList, Error): estimated classification error

```
static_error( FreqList, Error) :-
  max( FreqList, Max),          % Maximum number in FreqList
  sum( FreqList, All),          % Sum of numbers in FreqList
  number_of_classes( NumClasses),
  Error is (All - Max + NumClasses - 1) / (All + NumClasses).
```

```
sum( [], 0).
```

```
sum( [Number | Numbers], Sum) :-
  sum( Numbers, Sum1),
  Sum is Sum1 + Number.
```

```
max( [X], X).
```

```
max( [X,Y | List], Max) :-
  X > Y, !, max( [X | List], Max)
  ;
  max( [Y | List], Max).
```

```
sumlists( [], [], []).
```

```
sumlists( [X1 | L1], [X2 | L2], [X3 | L3]) :-
  X3 is X1 + X2,
  sumlists( L1, L2, L3).
```

```
% A tree
tree1( tree( a,                                    % Root
          tree( b, leaf( e, [3,2]), leaf( f, [1,0])),     % Left subtree
          tree( c, tree( d, leaf( g, [1,1]), leaf( h, [0,1])), leaf( i, [1,0])))).
number_of_classes( 2).
% Test query: ?- tree1( Tree), prunetree( Tree, PrunedTree).
```

## Chapter 21

**21.2**   Seven steps.

**21.3**   The number of hypotheses generated is 373179, the number of hypotheses refined is 66518.

**21.4**   $\{C_0, C_1\}$ is more general than $\{C_0, C_2\}$. $C_1$ does not $\theta$-subsume $C_2$.

## Chapter 22

**22.1**   qmult( pos, pos, pos).

qmult( pos, zero, zero).

qmult( pos, neg, neg).

. . .

**22.2**   resistor( pos, pos).

resistor( zero, zero).

resistor( neg, neg).

diode( zero, pos).

diode( zero, zero).

diode( neg, zero).

**22.3**   (a) First state:      X = zero/inc, y = zero/inc

Second state:   X = zero . . inf/inc, Y = zero . . inf/inc

Third state:    X = zero . . inf/std, Y = zero . . inf/inc, or

X = zero . . inf/std, Y = zero . . inf/std, or

X = zero . . inf/inc, Y = zero . . inf/std

(b) The same as answer (a) except that the third state can only be:

X = zero . . inf/std, Y = zero . . inf/std

**22.4**   At T = t0:   X = zero/inc, Y = zero/inc, Z = zero/inc

At T = t1:   X = zero . . inf/inc, Y = zero . . inf/inc, Z = zero . . landz/inc

At T = t2:   X = zero . . inf/inc, Y = zero . . inf/inc, Z = landz/inc, or

X = zero . . inf/std, Y = zero . . inf/std, Z = zero . . landz/std, or

X = zero . . inf/std, Y = zero . . inf/std, Z = landz/std

Note: These results can also be obtained by the simulator of Figure 22.8 and the following model that corresponds to this exercise:

```
landmarks( x, [minf,zero,inf]).
landmarks( y, [minf,zero,inf]).
landmarks( z, [minf,zero,landz,inf]).

correspond( x:zero, y:zero).

legalstate( [X,Y,Z]) :-
  mplus( X, Y),
  sum( X, Y, Z).

initial( [x:zero/inc, y:Y0, z:Z0]).
```

The query is:

```
?- initial(S), simulate(S,Beh,3).
```

22.5    % Model of U-tube
        % levA0, levB0 are initial levels in containers A and B
        % fAB0 is the initial flow from A to B, fBA0 is the initial flow from B to A

```
landmarks( level, [ zero, levB0, levA0, inf]).
landmarks( leveldiff, [minf, zero, inf]).
landmarks( flow, [minf, fBA0, zero, fAB0, inf]).

correspond( leveldiff:zero, flow:zero).

correspond( flow:fAB0, flow:fBA0, flow:zero).

legalstate( [ LevA, LevB, FlowAB, FlowBA]) :-
  deriv( LevA, FlowBA),
  deriv( LevB, FlowAB),
  sum( FlowAB, FlowBA, flow:zero/std),   % FlowBA = –FlowAB
  DiffAB = leveldiff:_,
  sum( LevB, DiffAB, LevA),              % DiffAB = LevA – LevB
  mplus( DiffAB, FlowAB).

initial ( [ level:levA0/dec, level:levB0/inc, flow:fAB0/dec, flow:fBA0/inc]).
```

22.7
```
legal_trans( State1, State2) :-
  system_trans( State1, State2),
  State1 \ = = State2,              % Qualitatively different next state
  not (point_state( State1),        % Not State1 a time-point state
    point_state( State2)),          % and State2 also a time-point state
  legalstate( State2).              % Legal according to model

point_state( State) :-
  member( _:Qmag/Dir, State),
  not (Qmag = _ .. _),              % Qmag a landmark, not interval
  Dir \ = = std.                    % Not steady
```

# Chapter 23

23.1
```
s( [a | List], Rest) :-
  s( List, [b | Rest]).
```

23.3    The modified definition is less efficient and may lead to indefinite cycling.

## Chapter 25

**25.1**

```
:- dynamic prove/1.
prove( true).
prove( clause( Head, Body)) :-
   clause( Head, Body).              % Prove "clause" by calling built-in clause/2

 prove( A \= B) :-
   A \= B.                           % Prove "\=" by calling built-in "\="
prove( ( Goal1, Goal2)) :- !,
   prove( Goal1),
   prove( Goal2).
prove( Goal) :-
   Goal \= true,                     % Goal must not be "true"
   Goal \= (_ \= _),                 % Goal must not be "\="
   Goal \= clause( _, _),            % Goal must not be "clause"
   clause( Goal, Body),
   prove( Body).
:- dynamic member/2.
member( X, [X | _]).
member( X, [_ | L]) :-
   member( X, L).
```

# Index